VARIATIONS IN VALUE ORIENTATIONS

VARIATIONS IN VALUE ORIENTATIONS

Florence Rockwood Kluckhohn

and

Fred L. Strodtbeck

With the assistance of John M. Roberts, A. Kimball Romney, Clyde Kluckhohn, and Harry A. Scarr

DISCARD

Andrew S. Thomas Memorial Library
MORRIS HARVEY COLLEGE, CHARLESTON, W. VA.

GREENWOOD PRESS, PUBLISHERS
WESTPORT, CONNECTICUT

90417

Library of Congress Cataloging in Publication Data

Kluckhohn, Florence (Rockwood)
  Variations in value orientations.

  1. Worth. 2. Indians of North America--Southwest, New. 3. Mormons and Mormonism in the New Southwest. 4. Spanish-Americans in the New Southwest. I. Strodtbeck, Fred L., joint author. II. Title.
BF778.K58 1973   121'.8   72-12497
ISBN 0-8371-6740-X

1961 Copyright © by Row, Peterson and Company

All rights reserved for all countries including the right of translation

Originally published in 1961 by Row, Peterson and Company, Evanston, Illinois

Reprinted with the permission of the authors

Reprinted by Greenwood Press,
a division of Williamhouse-Regency Inc.

First Greenwood Reprinting 1973
Second Greenwood Reprinting 1975

Library of Congress Catalog Card Number 72-12497

ISBN 0-8371-6740-X

Printed in the United States of America

Homer G. Rockwood
Maxine Vowell Strodtbeck

Contents

Preface viii
Acknowledgments xiii

Chapters

I   Dominant and Variant Value Orientations 1

II   The Five Communities 49

III   The Research Instrument: Development and Administration . 77

IV   Statistical Methods of Analysis 121

V   Variations in Value Orientations Within and Among the Five Rimrock Communities 138

VI   The Spanish-Americans of Atrisco 175

VII   The Mormon and Texan Communities 259

VIII The Zuni 285

IX   The Rimrock Navaho 319

X   Summary and Discussion 340

Appendices

1 Spanish-Language Version of the Value-Orientation Schedule . . 368
2 Further Notes on the Graphic Analysis of Ranked Value Preferences. 379
3 Value Consensus, Observed and Perceived 401
4 Basic Data Elicited from the Respondents of the Five Rimrock Communities. 416

Index 438

Preface

The basic values of peoples and the effects these have upon behavior and thought are matters which have long commanded the attention of philosophers. Increasingly in recent years the interest of social scientists of many kinds—sociologists, anthropologists, psychologists, especially, but also some economists and political scientists—has also been turned to the study of values. The research which this volume reports is one illustration of the combined efforts of a group of social scientists to carry forward the investigation of the nature of value systems and the influences which values have upon behavior.

Primarily the study is concerned with the exposition of a theory of variation in value orientations (a term which is, for reasons which will be explained, preferred to others for the designation of basic value systems) and a method which was devised for the cross-cultural testing of this theory. An historical account of the development of this research program is, we believe, the best way both to state the major aims of the book and to explain the nature and organization of the material presented in it.

The basic theory is stated in Chapter I. It is not a theory which is new to this volume. Florence Kluckhohn, its author, published the first version of it in 1950 and more refined ones at still later dates. (See the footnote at the beginning of Chapter I for these references.) However, as now stated, the theory is considerably elaborated beyond these earlier versions of it, and in part this elaboration is a result of the opportunity provided for the field testing of it. It was a happy circumstance that at approximately the same time the theory was first presented there were funds made available by the Rockefeller Foundation for a fairly large-scale and long-range project in the Harvard University Laboratory of Social Relations for research of several kinds on the subject of values in an area in the American Southwest which in this book we are calling the Rimrock area. This is an area where, within a radius of approximately forty miles, there are five communities which are culturally quite distinctive. The two least different from each other are a Texan homestead community and a Mormon village. The other three—one a Spanish-American village, one a decentralized Navaho Indian band, and the third the highly centralized pueblo of Zuni—are very different from the two English-speaking groups and also different one from another.

John M. Roberts, who was, in 1950, the coordinator of the Values Project (later there was established a codirectorship of Roberts and Evon Z. Vogt), became interested in the theory developed by Florence Kluckhohn and suggested that a program for the testing of it in these five Rimrock cultures be incorporated as a major part of the larger Values Project research program.

A team of three persons started this research program—Florence Kluckhohn, Roberts, and Fred L. Strodtbeck. Although Strodtbeck did not have the knowledge of the Rimrock cultures that F. Kluckhohn and Roberts did, he had conducted one short-term research project on three of the groups. More important, he commanded the knowledge of statistical procedures which was essential for the selection of samples in the communities and methods for the analysis of the data.

A preliminary testing program, which was much too hastily and too informally arranged to be considered a real pilot study, was carried out in the fall and winter of 1950. A few items, somewhat similar to those which were later incorporated into the field schedule which we developed for testing the theory—a type of item which we came to call the "general life situation" item—were evolved. Roberts, who was staying in the Rimrock area in the year 1950-51 for the purpose of conducting research of other kinds, spent countless hours testing on these items in the Zuni and Navaho groups. The results of his testing program were sufficiently interesting to warrant consideration of a fairly large-scale project which would test at least a part of the theory in all five of the communities in the summer of 1951.

Kimball Romney joined the research team in July, 1951. He, too, was skilled in statistical procedures, and, in addition, he was an anthropologist who had, in 1951, an interest in working with a nonliterate group, specifically the Navaho.

Two months were spent on the field program in the summer of 1951 by F. Kluckhohn, Strodtbeck, and Romney. One month was devoted to the development of the testing instrument. Since the kind of instrument which was planned (it is fully explained in Chapter III) required much deduction from the theory, the creation of it was again primarily the task of F. Kluckhohn. But primarily is not solely. The criticisms, suggestions, and additions made by Strodtbeck and Romney were crucial to the development of the research schedule. So also were the ideas for item testing which Samuel A. Stouffer, the director of the Harvard University Laboratory of Social Relations, had communicated to Florence Kluckhohn during her several years of research collaboration with him.

The field administration of the schedule was made by five persons. F. Kluckhohn interviewed all of the Spanish-Americans and some of the Texans of Homestead; Strodtbeck interviewed most of the Homestead Texans and the Rimrock Mormons, and Romney collected all of the Navaho data. In a few instances in the Texan community of Homestead, Evon Z. Vogt, who was carrying on intensive research in this community, did the interviewing. The interviewing of the Zuni was done by Roberts, but not until the fall of 1951.

It is this research which the first half of this volume presents. Chapters I through V set forth the theory, describe the communities in which we tested, explain the nature of the research instrument and describe our use of it, state the statistical methods which were selected and adapted for the analysis of the data, and, finally, present the results we obtained.

But it was not our intent that this "one shot" field research program should constitute the whole of the research design. In the first instance, we did not consider it adequate in and of itself. Because of the limitations of time and research funds which the research team faced, it was not possible either to carry out a satisfactory pre-testing program or to use standard replication procedures.

These deficiencies were not, however, considered to be of great magnitude. Since it was our good fortune to be testing in communities which had been studied, both intensively and extensively, over a long time period by many research investigators who had had widely varying aims, there was at our disposal a large body of data on each group which could be used for checking any results we achieved. We utilized these data and the personal knowledge of several of the members of the research team in two ways. The first of these, reported in Chapter II, was that of venturing informal prior predictions as to the "expected" value preferences in each of the groups. The second, and the more important one, was the incorporation into the research design of chapters on each of the cultures wherein our results would be scrutinized and interpreted by individual members of the team who were specialists on the particular cultures. In this second half of the program we were fortunate in being able to elicit the aid of Clyde Kluckhohn in the interpretation and analysis of the data collected from the sample of the Rimrock Navaho, a group that he had studied intensively in the period 1931–51.

These individual chapters—VI, VII, VIII, and IX—are not uniform in length, nor are they uniform in the kind of analytic treatment given to the data. This, too, was deliberate. The major difference which the reader will note is the much greater detail of the chapter devoted to the Spanish-American group. There were three reasons for this difference in treatment. First, we considered it advisable to have at least one of the cultures treated in sufficient detail to show how pervasive is the effect of value orientations in all aspects of the social life of a group. It was a logical decision that the group to be selected for a fairly detailed analysis would be the one which was the area of speciality of Florence Kluckhohn, who had developed the theory. Second, it is the Spanish-American group on which there is the least published material to which the reader may turn, if he is so interested, for his own independent checking and interpretation of our results against the results and conclusions of other research studies. Finally, it seemed appropriate to present as a kind of monograph within a monograph the results of the research work which Florence Kluckhohn had carried out in the Spanish-American group over a fifteen-year period. There had not been—for a variety of reasons, not the least of which is the "touchiness" of Spanish-Americans to research upon their social and individual characteristics—any detailed presentation of the results of the research which she had started in the year 1936 and continued to pursue up to and beyond the year 1957. We use the word "appropriate" in the first instance because it was the work on this group which was one of the important bases for the evolution of the theory of variation in value orientations. However, it also seemed "appropriate" to add to the general body of ethnological literature by utilizing as our main illustrative material the data from a long-range study of a group which has thus far been much less extensively treated in the literature than most of the other groups in our cross-cultural sample.

The second difference in treatment grew out of our desire to leave each analyst as an independent agent to make the kinds of interpretation which he both deemed necessary and thought important. The Roberts treatment of the Zuni is in large part historical. It reviews and integrates, to the extent that a short statement can, the many different kinds of interpretations of Zuni culture. Clyde Kluckhohn and Romney, knowing that the reader would have much material to refer to on the Rimrock Navaho, confine themselves largely to a critique of the results our schedule yielded against the great backlog of material, much of which actually treats the values of the group. Strodtbeck gives a comparative analysis of the Mormon and Texan groups which is both descriptive and statistical. One aspect of his statistical treatment is a factor analysis.

There were also by-products of the research which are mainly reported in Appendices 2 and 3. These are a result of special interests of Strodtbeck. The first has been mentioned—the use of a factor analysis for the analysis of between-culture differences in the Mormon-Texan comparison. This analysis was developed too late and was also considered to be inappropriate for the limited range of data we had on the region as a whole to be utilized for more than the one comparison, the Mormon-Texan one, at the present time. The illustrative exposition of its use, found in Chapter VII, is supplemented by a fuller explanatory statement in Appendix 2. A second important by-product is presented in Appendix 3. It is an analysis of perceived and actual consensus—an analysis of the first-order value-orientation preferences of the respondents themselves and those they attributed to the majority of the members of their groups.

As is likely to happen in collaborative projects which involve persons whose academic appointments and research interests change through time, there have been delays in the production of this volume because of the scattering across the country of those who originally started the project. It therefore became the responsibility of one person—the one most centrally interested in the project, Florence Kluckhohn—to assemble all the materials of all kinds and to integrate them. In doing this the aid of the sixth of the collaborators, Harry A. Scarr, was elicited. It was he, with the many suggestions and continual interest of Samuel A. Stouffer and Frederick Mosteller, who finally worked out the organization of the combination of statistical techniques which we have used for the analysis of the data, and he, again, who worked closely with Florence Kluckhohn to summarize and integrate the results obtained.

Chapters I (the theory), II (description of the peoples tested), and all of III (exposition of the method of testing), except for the statements the interviewers give of their field experience, were written by Florence Kluckhohn. Chapter VI, treating the Spanish-Americans, and the concluding chapter, Chapter X, she also wrote. But, in the case of Chapter X there was advice and direction by both Strodtbeck and Scarr in the section which summarizes the statistical methods of analysis.

The main statistical analysis presented in Chapter IV and demonstrated in the results given in Chapter V—an analysis which is an adaptation and elaboration of Kendall's method of treating rankings of alternatives—is entirely the work of Strodtbeck. So also are Appendices 2 and 3.

It has already been mentioned that the credit for the exposition in Chapter IV and the presentation in Chapter V of the results of the additional analyses which were utilized for the answering of other questions than those which the graphic analysis treats goes mainly to Scarr.

Each of the chapters on the individual cultures is the work of the author who signs it. Only minor editorial work was done on any one of them. It was, as has been stated, considered important to the total research program that each analyst speak to the results of the testing of the variation theory as he saw fit.

Finally, Appendices 1 and 4. Appendix 1, which gives the Spanish version of the field instrument, is primarily the work of Mrs. Anita Osuna Carr of Albuquerque, New Mexico. Florence Kluckhohn helped to create this translation, but since she did not consider her knowledge of the language adequate to the task of translation she elicited the services of Mrs. Carr, formerly a member of the Romance Language Department of the University of New Mexico. Appendix 4, which presents the raw data, was compiled and organized by Scarr.

Acknowledgments

As has been stated in the Preface, the research which this volume reports was an integral part of the project of the Harvard University Laboratory of Social Relations which was called "The Comparative Study of Values in Five Cultures" but informally came to be known as the Values Project. It is to this project, which was financed by a grant from the Social Science Division of the Rockefeller Foundation, that we are indebted for both the financial support which made possible the field testing of the value-orientation theory and the access to the data of other investigators of which we have made extensive use in the four chapters (Chapters VI through IX) that are devoted to an interpretation of the results of our field research. We acknowledge this indebtedness by stating that we are pleased and proud to have our study listed as one of the products of a research program which was imaginatively conceived and consistently administered in ways that allowed for a great independence of the research interests and research methods of the individual participants (single individuals in some instances, teams of two to five persons in others).

The particular individuals to whom we are indebted for advice, criticism, and aid of many another kind are numerous. First on this list is Samuel A. Stouffer, who provided so many suggestions for both the development of the field method of testing the theory and the selection of the statistical methods for the analysis of the data collected and who also, over a period of ten years, maintained such a sustained interest in the theory and the testing of it that he actually figures as a major contributor to the whole of the research project. It was his wish, not ours, that he have the role of the prompter who remained behind the scenes; he was always ready with the cue when an actor forgot his lines. Our indebtedness to Frederick C. Mosteller is only scarcely less great for he, too, gave invaluable advice and maintained a steady interest in the research from the date the data were collected and ready for analysis to the time of the final reorganization of the monograph. Evon Z. Vogt also gave us help of many kinds which went far beyond any responsibility he had as a codirector of the Values Project. Not only did he take over the task of conducting some of the interviews—a fact which has been mentioned; he also read the chapters of the monograph in their many versions and gave excellent criticism and advice on many details.

The chapters on the theory and the field method reflect the benefit of the criticism and advice of Talcott Parsons, George Homans, Ethel Albert, William Caudill, Barrington Moore, Jr., John Spiegel, Henry A. Murray, Joseph O. Brew, Douglas Oliver, John Pelzel, Joseph Kahl, John Whiting, Beatrice Whiting, and Richard Kluckhohn. To Ethel Albert we are particularly indebted for the painstaking care with which she studied and criticized the statement of the theory which appears in Chapter I.

In the development and elaboration of the graphic method of analysis, which in Chapter IV is presented as the principal method used for the analysis of our data, we wish to acknowledge an indebtedness for advice and suggestions to John Tukey, Richard Solomon, Max Woodbury, Brian Gluss, David L. Wallace, Herman Chernoff, John Gilbert, John Stedman, and Robert Harris. Special appreciation is expressed to Robert Harris for his painstaking plotting of the data which demonstrated that the radius was a function of S. Lee Harmon Hook's contribution was also a large one in a later stage of the statistical analysis. He collaborated with Strodtbeck in making the factor analytic comparison of the Mormon and Texan data which appears in Chapter VII and in preparing the final sections of Appendix 2.

Stuart Cleveland is another person who has figured prominently in the development of the theory and the field method. He did the editing of the first versions of the theory which appeared in articles, and he gave valuable advice and suggestions relative to the method of testing. Finally he took on, at a considerable cost of time to his own personal interests, the arduous task of indexing the volume.

Anita Osuna Carr also made a great sacrifice of time and effort in order to help prepare the Spanish translation of the research instrument. Essentially the translation is her own work. And our indebtedness to Marguerite Cronin who has consistently shown enormous patience and concern as she has carried through with the tasks of typing, retyping, and organizing the many chapters of the book is great indeed.

A tremendous debt is, of course, owed to the many people in the five Rimrock communities, respondents and interpreters, whose willing participation made the research program possible.

Finally, we wish to express great gratitude to the editors of Row, Peterson and Company for the many constructive suggestions they offered and the vast amount of time they spent on the manuscript in 1959–60 when virtually the whole of the volume was reorganized and rewritten.

CHAPTER I

Dominant and Variant Value Orientations*

From philosophy, history, and cultural anthropology the fact has been demonstrated ever more convincingly that there is a definite *variability* in the ways of life human beings build for themselves. Within the past three decades cultural anthropologists especially have gone far in jarring the minds of intellectuals loose from the comfortable but shallow moorings of absolutistic thinking. Indeed, the theory of cultural relativity has at times threatened to override all conceptions of universals and has thus become, when taken too literally, almost as restrictive to an understanding of human behavior as the naive forms of evolutionism or economic determinism. But in spite of the necessary reservations about some of the extreme statements on cultural relativity, no one who concerns himself with the study of either individuals or societies can deny its tremendous significance.

The concepts of relativity which are critically important to the development of the theory presented in this volume are those of the anthropologists who regard a knowledge of the basic assumptions of a people as indispensable to the interpretation of concrete behavior.[1] Of the variety of terms invented to designate the central core of meanings in societies the most familiar are "unconscious system of meanings" (Sapir), "un-

---

* This chapter is a revised and substantially expanded version of two of Florence Kluckhohn's previously published papers. The first of these was "Dominant and Substitute Profiles of Cultural Orientations: Their Significance for the Analysis of Social Stratification," *Social Forces*, Vol. XXVIII, No. 4 (May, 1950), pp. 376–94. The second, a paper entitled "Dominant and Variant Value-Orientations," was read at the Seventy-eighth Annual Meeting of the National Conference of Social Work and later published in part in the *Social Welfare Forum* (1951), pp. 97–113. Two slightly different versions of the complete paper have appeared in Hugh Cabot and Joseph A. Kahl, *Human Relations* (Cambridge, Mass.: Harvard University Press, 1953), Vol. I, pp. 88–98, and in the second edition of *Personality in Nature, Society, and Culture*, ed. Clyde Kluckhohn and Henry A. Murray (New York: Alfred A. Knopf, 1953), pp. 342–57.

The illustrations utilized throughout the chapter for the explanation of the alternatives of the value orientations and types of variation are selections from data collected in research investigations carried out many years prior to the one this volume is reporting. For example, the illustrations of Spanish-American behavior patterns are taken from the continuous research work which Florence Kluckhohn carried on in a Spanish-American village in the years 1936–50. Most of them are recorded in her doctoral dissertation submitted to Radcliffe College in 1941. Because this dissertation is not available for circulation, specific page references to it are not made.

[1] Notably Alfred L. Kroeber, Edward Sapir, Robert Redfield, Ruth Benedict, Margaret Mead, Clyde Kluckhohn, Ralph Linton, Gregory Bateson, Morris Opler, A. Irving Hallowell, and Laura Thompson.

conscious canons of choice" (Benedict), "configurations" (C. Kluckhohn), "culture themes" (Opler), and "core culture" (Thompson). "Basic personality type" (Kardiner and Linton) is an equally familiar concept which has similarities to those just mentioned but differs from them in having a more definitely psychological focus. Still another and more recently formulated concept is that of "world view" (Redfield).[2]

Bateson briefly summarizes one of the major assumptions underlying these variously phrased concepts when he says:

> The human individual is endlessly simplifying, organizing, and generalizing his own view of his own environment; he constantly imposes on this environment his own constructions and meanings; these constructions and meanings [are] characteristic of one culture, as over against another.[3]

A more comprehensive statement is the following one made by C. Kluckhohn:

> There is a philosophy behind the way of life of each individual and of every relatively homogeneous group at any given point in their histories. This gives, with varying degrees of explicitness or implicitness, some sense of coherence or unity both in cognitive and affective dimensions. Each personality gives to this philosophy an idiosyncratic coloring and creative individuals will markedly reshape it. However, the basic outlines of the fundamental values, existential propositions, and basic abstractions have only exceptionally been created out of the stuff of unique biological heredity and peculiar life experience. The underlying principles arise out of, or are limited by, the givens of biological human nature and the universalities of social interaction. The specific formulation is ordinarily a cultural product. In the immediate sense, it is from the life-ways which constitute the designs for living of their community or tribe or region or socio-economic class or nation or civilization that most individuals derive their mental-feeling outlook.[4]

Few persons, we believe, will find much to criticize in either of these two statements, or those made by other anthropologists about the generalized conception of a central core of meanings—basic values. Yet many well justified criticisms have been made of the too facile cultural interpretations which some anthropologists have at times made of both peoples and situations. The admittedly provocative analyses of "national character" seem particularly open to doubt and challenge. Also, some persons question the fruitfulness or the validity, or both, of many of the attempts made thus far to relate and combine the concepts of comparative

---

[2] Redfield distinguishes four concepts—the *culture* of a people, its *ethos*, the *national character* of a people, or its personality type, and *world view*. His distinctions seem in part to be a matter of level of generality, but even more important considerations are the difference of focus of attention upon the evaluative or the existential and the problem of whose point of view is being considered, that of the observer or the observed. For a full discussion of the distinctions, see *The Primitive World and Its Transformations* (Ithaca, N.Y.: Cornell University Press, 1953), especially Chap. IV.

[3] Gregory Bateson, "Cultural Determinants of Personality" in *Personality and the Behavior Disorders*, ed. J. McV. Hunt (New York: Ronald Press, 1944), Vol. II, p. 273.

[4] Clyde Kluckhohn, "Values and Value Orientations in the Theory of Action" in Talcott Parsons, Edward A. Shils, et al., *Toward a General Theory of Action* (Cambridge, Mass.: Harvard University Press, 1951), pp. 409–10.

culture and those of psychiatry or, more particularly, psychoanalysis. Complex problems of conceptual integration are made too simple, and many of the interpretations advanced are far too general and impressionistic to be convincing. Still other persons, notably many sociologists and psychologists, object strongly to the high degree of determining influence often claimed for cultural as opposed to other of the factors which affect social systems and individual personalities. And not the least of the arguments against "cultural determinism" is that it makes small allowance for variability and individual differences.

In large part the difficulties encountered in the understanding and use of the cultural anthropologists' concepts are attributable to the failure to organize these concepts into a systematic and analytic theory of cultural variation. Even the very broad concepts cited above ("unconscious system of meanings," "core culture," "culture themes," and others) are empirical generalizations, not analytical constructs. In both formulation and application they have been too particularized to single cultures to permit systematic comparisons *between* cultures and, at the same time, too grossly generalized to allow for the analysis of the variations *within* cultures. All too frequently, those who have ably demonstrated a uniqueness in the value systems of different societies have ignored the fundamental fact of the universality of some human problems and its correlate that human societies have found for some problems approximately the same answers.[5] Also, in most of the analyses of the common value element in culture patterning, the *dominant* values of peoples have been overstressed and *variant* values largely ignored. These two concomitant tendencies have produced interpretative studies which are, in spite of their great brilliance of insight, oversimplified and static representations of social structures and processes.

Variations in the value orientations of whole societies, of subgroups within societies, and of the individual persons, who are, in the final analysis, the actual carriers of culture, are the subjects of central interest to this monograph. Our most basic assumption is that there is a *systematic variation* in the realm of cultural phenomena which is both as definite and as essential as the demonstrated systematic variation in physical and biological phenomena.

The varying types of life activities which are essential to the functioning of a social system are an obvious source of both a *required* and a *permitted* variation within the system. (These several types of activities, for which we prefer the term *behavior spheres*, and the variation their existence requires or permits will be discussed in a later section of this chapter.) Also, at the individual pole, there are critical differences which make variation in cultural patterning a necessity. The biological differences in the individuals of every society—differences which are so often ignored

---

[5] Clyde Kluckhohn is one of the few anthropologists who have repeatedly stressed the need for more consideration of the universal aspects of culture. See especially his "Universal Categories of Culture" in *Anthropology Today*, ed. Alfred L. Kroeber (Chicago: University of Chicago Press, 1953), pp. 507–24. Robert Redfield also stresses the universals in human experience in his concept of "world view," *op. cit.*, Chap. IV.

by both sociologists and anthropologists—are one of the individual bases of variation. Basic psychological differences, even though they are more difficult to isolate than constitutional differences, are another of the reasons why variation is both permitted and required.

One way to approach the problems of cultural variation is to deal with the variability in the highly generalized elements of culture which in this study are called value orientations. To do this we shall develop a classification of value orientations and subsequently use it as the basis for formulating a first approximation of a theory of variation. But first there is need to define and clarify the concept of value orientation.

THE VALUE-ORIENTATION CONCEPT

Value orientations are complex but definitely patterned (rank-ordered) principles, resulting from the transactional interplay of three analytically distinguishable elements of the evaluative process—the cognitive, the affective, and the directive elements—which give order and direction to the ever-flowing stream of human acts and thoughts as these relate to the solution of "common human" problems. These principles are variable from culture to culture but are, we maintain, variable only in the *ranking patterns* of component parts which are themselves cultural universals. Variation of another kind is variation in degrees of conscious awareness individuals have of the value orientations which influence their behavior. This variation is, as C. Kluckhohn has stated, on the continuum from the completely implicit to the completely explicit.[6]

At first blush this definition of value orientations may not appear, to some readers, to differ greatly from other of the concepts which have been developed to analyze the effects of basic systems of meanings—basic values—upon human behavior. This reaction is to be expected, for, as has been definitely stated, the value-orientation concept both stems from and owes much to the conceptions of basic values, their nature and their effects, which a number of anthropologists have develo[...]d and used. However, a closer scrutiny should reveal several significa[...] differences between our concept and the earlier formulations. These differences are, to be sure, of a greater or a lesser magnitude depending upon which of the previous conceptualizations is used as the basis of comparison.

The most important difference—the one which most clearly sets apart our concept of value orientations from all others which treat of systems of meaning—is the definition of them as complex principles which are variable only in patterning. Some of the reasons for the need to make this distinctive expansion in the conceptualization of value systems have been stated. Further explanation will be presented in the immediately ensuing discussions which are devoted to the classification scheme of the ranges of the universalistic components of value orientations and a discussion of some of the types of intra-cultural variation.

[6] "Values and Value Orientations in the Theory of Action," p. 411.

There are still other respects in which the concept differs from some or all of the previous formulations of basic value systems which require comment as a means of clarifying the conceptual context for these later discussions. We mention first the view that the principles are on an implicit-explicit continuum. Many of the writers who have concerned themselves with basic values have so definitely emphasized the unconscious end of this continuum that the terms they have developed actually include the word "unconscious" (for example, the concepts of "unconscious canons of choice" and "unconscious systems of meanings"). Since the problem of degree of awareness—the degree of implicitness or explicitness—has been well treated by C. Kluckhohn, we shall not dwell longer upon this point.

The question of the elements of the evaluative process—elements which we are calling the cognitive, the affective, and the directive—and the view of these as being aspects of a transactional process are in need of a more extended comment. This is the more the case since it is our contention that it is the *directive* aspect of the total process which is of primary importance in the formulation of the value-orientation concept.

Some of the previously formulated concepts of orienting principles have been concentrated primarily, even solely, upon the cognitive aspect (existential premises) of the evaluative process. Others, notably those found in the works of Hallowell, Whorf, and C. Kluckhohn, treat both the cognitive and the affective elements and consider them as constituting a unity—an amalgam.[7] Two of the statements made by C. Kluckhohn on this issue are:

Since value elements and existential premises are almost inextricably blended in the overall picture of experience that characterizes an individual or a group, it seems well to call this overall view a value orientation, symbolizing the fact that the affective-cognitive (value) and strictly cognitive (orientation) elements are blended.[8]

... a definition of the life situation for the group contains more than normative and aesthetic propositions; it contains also existential propositions about the nature of "what is." The relationship between the existential and normative propositions may be thought of as two-way: on the one hand, the normative judgments must be based upon the group's notion of what in fact exists; on the other hand, the group's conception of the universe (of "what is" and "what is natural or obvious") will presumably be based partly upon prior normative orientations and interests. What must be done is usually closely related to what is believed to be the nature of things; however, beliefs about "what is" are often disguised assumptions of "what ought to be."[9]

---

[7] The publications of A. Irving Hallowell in which one may find material relevant to this problem are too numerous to list. See especially "Culture, Personality, and Society" in *Anthropology Today*, ed. Alfred L. Kroeber (Chicago: University of Chicago Press, 1953), pp. 597–620; and "Handbook of Psychological Leads for Ethnological Field Workers" (mimeographed, 1935). In the case of Benjamin Lee Whorf, reference is mainly to "Science and Linguistics," *Technology Review*, Vol. XLII, No. 6 (1940), pp. 229–48; "Languages and Logic," *Technology Review*, Vol. XLIII, No. 7 (1941), pp. 250–55; "American Indian Model of the Universe," *International Journal of American Linguistics*, Vol. XVI (1950), pp. 67–72.

[8] *Loc. cit.*

[9] *Op. cit.*, p. 410.

Parsons and Shils also express a similar point of view when they state that in the motivational orientation of the actor there are three aspects—the cognitive, the cathectic, and the evaluative.[10]

We accept this structural conceptualization of the evaluative process but do so with full awareness that there remains the knotty problem of its ontological status. This question is one which philosophers must solve, and at present they appear to be divided among themselves in the views they hold concerning the relationships between existential premises and normative standards.[11]

It is relative to the *directive* aspect of the evaluative process that we both go beyond even this conception and also depart most radically from all previously formulated conceptions of value orientation and the nature of the evaluative process. To be sure, in the general idea of directiveness as a characteristic of basic values there is nothing new at all. Everyone who has treated values and value systems has referred to them as principles which "guide," "channel," or "direct" behavior. In most instances this has been stated as either an assumption or an empirical generalization. But in two works, at least—those of C. Kluckhohn and of Parsons and Shils cited above—this general assumption is made a part of the analytic treatment of the total evaluative process and is treated as a "selective" aspect to which is given a consideration equal to that accorded to the cognitive and affective aspects. Clyde Kluckhohn in his discussion of values uses, somewhat interchangeably, the terms "selection," "conation," and "choice" for the analysis of this third element of the process.[12] Parsons and Shils state that there is a third mode in the motivational orientation of the actor—the evaluative one—which "involves the various processes by which an actor allocates his energy among the various actions with respect to various cathected objects in an attempt to optimize gratification."[13] And they, too, in further discussion of this aspect of the process, employ the terms "choice" and "selective mechanism."

This development in conceptualization—a development which made "selectivity" (the "selective mechanism") an analytically distinguishable part *within* the evaluative process rather than leaving it as an empirical generalization *about* the process—was a major step in the clarification of the nature of the process. But there are, we believe, still other improvements to be made.

It is, therefore, here that we turn away from the terms "selective" and "choice"—terms which on the one hand push to the fore the free-will versus determinism controversy and on the other hand focus attention much more upon structural integration than upon process—and adopt, instead, the term "directiveness." This term, as used by Tinbergen and other biologists for the specification of a basic *biological* disposition to react differentially to parts of the receptual field, appears much more ade-

[10] Talcott Parsons, Edward A. Shils, et al., *Toward a General Theory of Action* (Cambridge, Mass.: Harvard University Press, 1951), p. 59.
[11] Cf. *Value: A Cooperative Inquiry*, ed. Ray Lepley (New York: Columbia University Press, 1949).
[12] *Op. cit.*, p. 401.
[13] *Op. cit.*, p. 59.

quate for our conception of the nature and the relationship of the elements of the evaluative process. One statement by Tinbergen is: "It seems to be a property of the innate disposition that it *directs* [italics ours] the conditioning to special parts of the receptual field."[14] A further and more detailed statement is as follows:

... there is a tendency among biologists to regard the study of directiveness as incompatible with that of causation. In the physiologically minded worker this often leads to a certain neglect of the problems of directiveness, while the student of directiveness, as a reaction to this one-sidedness, tends to argue not only that the study of directiveness is just as important as that of underlying causes, but that it should have priority, or even that it should be undertaken *instead* of physiological study.

In my opinion, this is based on a double misunderstanding. First, it is certainly not right to identify 'causal explanation' with 'causal analysis'. Whereas mere analysis does indeed lead to 'a vast intricacy of unrelated detail', a causal explanation is based upon analysis accompanied by continuous re-synthesis; and such an explanation unites the details into a synthetic picture in which the details are not unrelated but arranged in a system.

The demand that directiveness should be studied *instead* of causation seems to me to be another misunderstanding. The two ways of studying life processes are not opposed to each other. The adaptiveness or directiveness of many life processes is a matter of fact and can be revealed by objective study; however, a description of the directiveness of life processes is not a solution of the problem of their causation. Once the survival value of a process has been recognized and clearly described, the biologist's next task is to find out how its mechanisms work; in other words, on what causal systems it is based.[15]

The primary significance which these statements have for the value-orientation concept is found in the argument that *directiveness* in behavior is a biologically determined predisposition. Although it is not possible in the study of the behavior of humans to make either a full or direct application of the concepts and theories which are derived from the investigation of the habits of highly instinct-bound animals, fishes, and birds, this is no reason for ignoring the significance of the biological factors which are to some degree common to all members of the animal kingdom. This is the more true when the biological predisposition under consideration has the high level of generality which directiveness appears to have.

Thus, while we do not in any simple or directly immediate way accept the differentiation which Tinbergen states he and other biologists make between causal mechanisms and directiveness, we do hold to the position that the "causal" influence of the biologically given predisposition toward directiveness has a distinctive nature which both sets it apart from other aspects of the evaluative process and also makes it the most critically important single element for the conceptualization of value orientations.

With our attention ever focused upon evaluation as a *process*, we view the analytically distinguishable elements of the process as a transactional system which is constantly in movement through time. Particular value-

---

[14] N. Tinbergen, *The Study of Instinct* (Oxford: Clarendon Press, 1951), p. 150.
[15] *Ibid.*, pp. 151-52.

orientation orderings are simply the "moment of time" structural formulations of this transactional interplay. It is never easy to investigate process, which in the scientific tradition of thought is the "reality," directly; it must usually be inferred from the structural analyses made of parts of it. And the more analytical the constructs for structural analyses, the greater is the danger of seeming to arrest or freeze process. A frequent criticism of those theorists in the social sciences who devote their main attention to structural or structural-functional analyses is that they provide static representations only—structures well defined, to be sure, but structures for which the antecedent conditions are unknown and the future states are unpredictable. In other words, they so thoroughly rip process apart in order that all aspects of it may be *simultaneously* and *separately* analyzed as structures that it is exceedingly difficult to find the conceptual means of re-creating it.

Many of the analyses which cultural anthropologists have made of basic values and the influences these exert upon behavior, as has been previously noted, are also quite static conceptual representations relating to a particular period of time and a particular location in space. They, too, are more concerned with the question of structural integration than with processual directionality. The major reason for this is, as we have stated, the lack of consideration of variation. The primary aim of the theory and the research to which this monograph is devoted is to fill this critically important theoretical lacuna. But before the variations can be theoretically conceptualized or the variable durability of value systems discussed, it is necessary to make certain distinctions concerning the kind and degree of "causal" influence which each of the three elements in the evaluative process has.

Making full allowance for the fact that human beings are not the instinct-bound creatures which gray geese, herring gulls, or sticklebacks are, there is a general way in which the causal-mechanism–directiveness distinction made by Tinbergen appears to be applicable to the analysis of the evaluative process. The cognitive and the affective elements, each one in itself and both in their relationships one to another, are causal in a way which the directive element is not, and the directive element contains both integrative and guiding influences which the cognitive and affective elements do not possess. It is from the cognitive and the affective elements and the relationships between them that the value system derives its content in the forms of existential premises and normative assumptions. There would be no value system which takes human behavior out of the realm of the purely instinctual were it not for the quite highly developed human capacities for intellection and affectivity. But it also seems apparent that there would be no ordered, no systematic, value system without a directive tendency which both aids in the selection among possible value systems and also serves to give continuity to the total system.

Although it can be argued that such a tendency is also "causal," it seems advisable to differentiate between the kinds of processes which provide content and those which order that content. Simply stating that there are cognitive, affective, and selective elements does not provide an adequate basis for viewing the evaluative process as a *process* through time rather than as a tripartite structure at a given point in time and space.

Directiveness appears to be causally important in at least two senses. First, although the several writers cited above have argued strongly and convincingly that the cognitive and affective elements are inextricably interrelated, they do not go far in indicating the "why" of this relationship other than stating that it appears an irrefutable fact that what a people believe to be true (existential premises) is strongly influenced by their normative judgments and that contrariwise the normative assumptions as to what is right and proper are never truly separable from the existential premises. Selectivity is discussed as an element of the total process, but it is not clearly defined as an element which is distinctive in having relating (integrating) and directive (processual guiding) influences upon the other elements. It is our view that to the extent that the cognitive and affective aspects of the process are a unity it is because of the directive element, which is as much, or perhaps even more, biologically given than are the capacities for either intellection or affectivity.

It is on this basis that we state that in the concept of a value orientation as a guiding principle, it is the directive element which is of primary interest. This is the second way in which the element may be considered as a critically causal one. Any given value system of human beings has both a content and a direction which derive from biologically given capacities and predispositions but are not instinct bound, but it is the directive aspect which is the most crucial for the understanding of both the integration of the total value system and its continuity through time.

In the realm of observed behavior the integration effect is the thematic one. All or almost all aspects of the social life of a people give expression, in varying ways and varying degrees to be sure, to the basic values which are characteristic of one culture as opposed to another. As for continuity through time, it is a fact known to anyone who has become seriously engaged in cross-cultural studies that the ideas and techniques a people either "borrow from" or have "forced upon" them by another culture are far more often adapted to the old ways of thinking and acting than they are disruptive of those ways. It is because of both of these facts that cultural anthropologists, or others who have argued the importance of a study of basic values in the analysis of human behavior, are far less guilty of the charge of an overly "deterministic" conceptualization than are those who view all behavior, no matter what the society or the time period, as being essentially determined by the conditions, the activities, or the ideas in some particular sphere of human life—the economic or the religious sphere, for example.

However, cultures do change in direction—that is, change in their basic values (a change which later we shall distinguish as basic change as contrasted to change which is more of the same thing). Also, the peoples of one culture often do become assimilated, however painfully or slowly, into the ways of another culture. The evaluation process is not, in other words, an ineluctable one either in its content or its direction. But neither is it the randomly varied one which extreme cultural relativists have depicted. If there is, as the most basic assumption of all sciences maintains, a discoverable order in the universe, one must expect to find it in the evaluation processes of human beings as well as in the processes which biologists and natural scientists investigate. The conception of ordered variation in value orientations is essential if we are to steer a safe course between the Scylla of ineluctability and the Charybdis of rampant relativism.

A CLASSIFICATION OF VALUE ORIENTATIONS

That there is an ordered variation in value-orientation systems is the first major assumption of our study. Basic both to the classification of value orientations which is now to be set forth and to the treatment of types of variations and their effects which will follow upon the delineation of the several value orientations there are these three more specifically formulated assumptions.

First, it is assumed that *there is a limited number of common human problems for which all peoples at all times must find some solution.* This is the universal aspect of value orientations because the common human problems to be treated arise inevitably out of the human situation. The second assumption is that *while there is variability in solutions of all the problems, it is neither limitless nor random but is definitely variable within a range of possible solutions.* The third assumption, the one which provides the main key to the later analysis of variation in value orientations, is that *all alternatives of all solutions are present in all societies at all times but are differentially preferred.* Every society has, in addition to its dominant profile of value orientations, numerous *variant* or *substitute profiles.* Moreover, it is postulated that in both the dominant and the variant profiles there is almost always a *rank ordering* of the preferences of the value-orientation alternatives. In societies which are undergoing change the ordering of preferences will not be clear-cut for some or even all the value orientations.

Five problems have been tentatively singled out as the crucial ones common to all human groups.[16] These problems are stated here in the

---

[16] A sixth common human problem which is considered to be necessary to the value-orientation schema is that of man's conception of *space* and his place in it. Unfortunately this problem and the ranges of variability in it have not been worked out sufficiently well to be included at the present time.

Recently Robert Redfield, *op. cit.*, and A. I. Hallowell, "The Self and Its Behavioral Environment," *Explorations: Studies in Culture and Communication*, No. 2 (April, 1954), have also treated the question of the problems universal to all human groups. There are some similarities to the value-orientation concern in each work. Hallowell, for example, stresses the significance of the three *time* orientations, and Redfield treats the variations in the *man-nature* orientation in a way that is strikingly similar to the Mastery-over-Nature, Harmony-with-Nature, and Subjugation-to-Nature positions. But there are also numerous differences noted. Awareness of the self as a universal ground for the development of orientations—a universal ground which is in the main assumed in the value-orientation theory—is discussed at length by Hallowell and also receives considerable attention from Redfield. On the other hand, ordered variation form of questions. After the questions are the titles that will hereafter be used for the total range of variations in the five orientations.

(1) What is the character of innate human nature? (*human nature* orientation)
(2) What is the relation of man to nature (and supernature)? (*man-nature* orientation)
(3) What is the temporal focus of human life? (*time* orientation)
(4) What is the modality of human activity? (*activity* orientation)
(5) What is the modality of man's relationship to other men? (*relational* orientation)

The ranges of variability suggested as a testable conceptualization of the variations in the value orientations are given in Table I:1.[17]

1. *Human Nature* Orientation

To the question of what the innate goodness or badness of *human nature* is, there are the three logical divisions of Evil, Good-and-Evil, and Good. Yet it may be argued that the category of Good-and-Evil is not one but two categories. There certainly is a significant difference between the view that *human nature* is simply neutral and the view that it is a mixture of the good and bad. Moreover, the subprinciples of mutability and immutability increase the basic threefold classification to six possibilities. *Human nature* can, for example, be conceived as Evil and unalterable or Evil and perfectible, as Good and unalterable or Good and corruptible, as an invariant mixture of Good-and-Evil or a mixture subject to influence. Thus, one may rightly question the validity and usefulness of the three-way classification suggested for the range of this orientation. However, the three categories do seem adequate as a first approximation for the analysis of major variations. Furthermore, it may well prove to be the case that some of the finer dis-

---

relative to limits in possible orientations to universal problems is not systematically dealt with in either of the two works.

[17] An explanation of the conventions to be used in differentiating between general type of orientation and the alternatives within types may be helpful. The titles for the types of orientations will be italicized—*human nature, man-nature, time, activity,* and *relational.* The alternatives within the types of orientations will be capitalized but not italicized—for example, Being, Doing, Being-in-Becoming; Future, Past, Present.

Also, in order to minimize confusion between type of value orientation and the variations of orientations within types we shall, wherever possible, use the terms variation, alternative, or position for the designation of the "within-type" orientations. But both because it is often cumbersome to speak always of, for example, the Being alternative of the *activity* orientation and because frequently we will wish to treat only the *dominant* alternatives, we shall sometimes use the term orientation to refer to an alternative as well as to a type. Not only is it a necessary shorthand method to use the terms Future orientation and Future-oriented people; it is an accurate usage according to the theory because each of the alternatives within a general type of orientation is itself an orientation. In the research which this volume reports, our aim was to determine the ordering of the postulated alternatives within each type of orientation. Thus, the alternatives will usually be specified as such. But we feel that the convenience and brevity afforded by being able to use the term orientation to refer to *one* of the variations within a postulated range of orienting principles are a sufficient cause to risk the possible confusion which some may find in our use of the term to refer both to type of orientation and to alternative orientations within a type.

TABLE I:1

THE FIVE VALUE ORIENTATIONS AND THE RANGE OF VARIATIONS POSTULATED FOR EACH[a]

Orientation	Postulated Range of Variations					
human nature	Evil		Neutral	Mixture of Good-and-Evil	Good	
	mutable	immutable	mutable	immutable	mutable	immutable
man-nature	Subjugation-to-Nature		Harmony-with-Nature		Mastery-over-Nature	
time	Past		Present		Future	
activity	Being		Being-in-Becoming		Doing	
relational	Lineality		Collaterality		Individualism	

[a] The arrangement in columns of sets of orientations is only the accidental result of this particular chart. Although statistically it may prove to be the case that some combinations of orientations will be found more often than others, the assumption is that all combinations are possible ones. For example, it may be found that the combination of *first-order* choices is that of Individualism, Future, Doing, Mastery-over-Nature, and Evil-mutable, now changing, as in the case of the dominant middle-class culture of the United States, or that it is, as in the case of the Navaho Indians, a combination of the first-order preferences of Collaterality, Present, Doing, Harmony-with-Nature, and Good-and-Evil (immutable).

tinctions noted in specific values and behavior patterns are derivatives of the interrelationships between the *human nature* and other of the orientations. There is also a possibility that still further desirable distinctions can be achieved by the use of a set of concepts which are the derivatives of the cross-classification of the basic three-way categorization and the twofold subcategorization.

But leaving aside possible derivations at this time, let us illustrate from American culture some of the major variations. Few will disagree that the orientation inherited from Puritan ancestors and still strong among many Americans is that of a basically Evil but perfectible *human nature*. According to this view constant control and discipline of the self are required if any real goodness is to be achieved, and the danger of regression is always present. But some in the United States today, perhaps a growing number, incline to the view that *human nature* is a mixture of Good-and-Evil. These would say that although control and effort are certainly needed, lapses can be understood and need not always be severely condemned. This latter definition of basic *human nature* would appear to be more common among the peoples of the world, both literate and nonliterate, than the one held to in the historical past of this country. Whether there are any total societies committed to the definition of *human nature* as immutably Good is not as yet known and may even be doubted. Yet the position is a logically possible one, and it certainly is found as a variant position *within* societies.

2. Man-Nature (-Supernature) Orientation

The three-point range of variation in the *man-nature* orientation—Subjugation-to-Nature, Harmony-with-Nature, and Mastery-over-Nature—is too well known from the works of philosophers and culture historians to need much explanation. Mere illustration will demonstrate the differences between the conceptions.

Spanish-American culture in the American Southwest gives us an example of a very definite Subjugation-to-Nature orientation. The typical Spanish-American sheepherder, in a time as recent as twenty-five years ago, believed firmly that there was little or nothing a man could do to save or protect either land or flocks when damaging storms descended upon them. He simply accepted the inevitable. In Spanish-American attitudes toward illness and death one finds the same fatalism. "If it is the Lord's will that I die, I shall die" is the way they express it, and many a Spanish-American has been known to refuse the services of a doctor because of the attitude.

If the conceptualization of the *man-nature* relationship is that of Harmony, there is no real separation of man, nature, and supernature. One is simply an extension of the other, and a conception of wholeness derives from their unity. This orientation seems to have been the dominant one in many periods of Chinese history, and it is strongly evident in Japanese culture at the present time as well as historically. It is also the orientation attributed to the Navaho Indians by Clyde Kluckhohn, and the one we have considered dominant in the Mormon group until very recently.

The Mastery-over-Nature position is the first-order (that is, the dominant) orientation of most Americans. Natural forces of all kinds are to be overcome and put to the use of human beings. Rivers everywhere are spanned with bridges; mountains have roads put through and around them; new lakes are built, sometimes in the heart of deserts; old lakes get partially filled in when additional land is needed for building sites, roads, or airports; the belief in man-made medical care for the control of illness and the lengthening of life is strong to an extreme; and all are told early in life that "the Lord helps those who help themselves." The view in general is that it is a part of man's duty to overcome obstacles; hence there is the great emphasis upon technology.

3. *Time* Orientation

The possible cultural interpretations of the temporal focus of human life break easily into the three-point range of Past, Present, and Future. Far too little attention has been given to the full range of major variations in the *time* orientation. Meaningful cultural differences have been lost sight of in the too generalized view that folk peoples have no time sense and no need of one, whereas urbanized and industrial peoples must have one. Whether days are regarded as sunrise-to-sundown wholes or as time units to be split into hours and minutes and whether or not a clock is deemed a useful culture object are not the critically important criteria for a consideration of the orientation to *time*.

Spengler had quite another order of fact in mind when, in his discussion of "time" in *The Decline of the West*, he made this emphatic statement: "It is by the meaning that it intuitively attaches to time that one culture is differentiated from another."[18] The relationship of Destiny to meanings of *time* is the core of Spengler's conception. But for the most part his concern was with the twofold division of orientations into the timeless ahistorical Present and the ultra-historical projection into the Future. Always on the plane of the macroscopic and concerned with directionality as a cyclical unfolding, he apparently did not feel a need to deal with the problems of the traditionalistic or Past *time* orientation which was so important a part of Max Weber's treatment of moral authority. The threefold division proposed for the value-orientation schema has, therefore, a similarity to Spengler's conception in the distinction between a relatively timeless, traditionless, future-ignoring Present and a realizable Future, but it also differentiates from these an orientation which places primary emphasis upon the maintenance, or the restoration, of the traditions of the Past.

Obviously, every society must deal with all three *time* problems; all have their conceptions of the Past, the Present, and the Future. Where they differ is in the preferential ordering of the alternatives (rank-order emphases), and a very great deal can be told about the particular society or part of a society being studied and much can be predicted about the direction of change within it if one knows what the rank-order emphasis is.[19]

Illustrations of the variations in temporal focus are also easily found. Spanish-Americans, who have been described as taking the view that man is a victim of natural forces, are also a people who place the Present *time* alternative in first-order position. They pay little attention to what has happened in the Past and regard the Future as both vague and unpredictable. Planning for the Future or hoping that the Future will be better than either the Present or the Past simply is not their way of life.

Historical China was a society which gave first-order value preference to the Past *time* orientation. Ancestor worship and a strong family tradition were both expressions of this preference. So also was the Chinese attitude that nothing new ever happened in the Present or would happen in the Future; it had all happened before in the far distant Past. The proud American who once thought he was showing some Chinese a steamboat for the first time was quickly put in his place by the remark, "Our ancestors had such a boat two thousand years ago."

Many modern European countries also have strong leanings to a Past orientation. Even England—insofar as it has been dominated by an aristocracy and traditionalism—has shown this preference. Indeed, some of

[18] Oswald Spengler, *The Decline of the West*, tr. Charles F. Atkinson (New York: Alfred A. Knopf, 1926–28), Vol. I, p. 130.
[19] The problem of *time* is certainly not exhausted or fully explained by this range of orientations. Some languages such as the Hopi Indian have no tenses to indicate Past, Present, or Future. It seems best to leave examination of this additional problem until such time as the *space* orientation is better worked out, for there is an aspect of the *time* problem, not now included, which relates to the *space* orientation.

the chief differences between the peoples of the United States and England derive from their somewhat varying attitudes toward *time*. Americans have difficulty in understanding the respect the English have for tradition, and the English do not appreciate the typical American's disregard for it.

Americans, more strongly than most peoples of the world, place an emphasis upon the Future—a Future which is anticipated to be "bigger and better." This does not mean they have no regard for the Past or no thought of the Present. But it certainly is true that no current generation of Americans ever wants to be called "old-fashioned." The ways of the Past are not considered good just because they are Past, and truly dominant (that is, typically middle-class) Americans are seldom content with the Present. This view results in a high evaluation of *change*, providing the change does not threaten the existing value order—the American way of life. This is not to say that Future-oriented Americans are non-conformists or that a more traditionalistic people are rigidly conventional. On the contrary, a good case can be made for stating that the tendencies are in the opposite direction if one examines the conforming process for both type and degree.

The concept of conformity, which is essential in almost every kind of analysis of human behavior, has often been misused. Sometimes the sheer necessity of conformity has been overlooked; more often type and degree of conformity have not been treated as separable problems. And because of these tendencies there is a predisposition on the part of some writers both to give to conformism a negative connotation and to equate it with particular types of value-orientation systems. Although these issues are not of immediate relevance to the presentation and definition of the value-orientation alternatives, they are sufficiently significant for the analysis of the influence of value systems to warrant a brief general discussion. This we shall give once the ranges of the alternatives for all orientations have been discussed.

4. *Activity* Orientation

The modality of human *activity* is the fourth of the common human problems giving rise to a value-orientation system. The range of variation in solutions suggested for it is the threefold one of Being, Being-in-Becoming, and Doing.

In very large part this range of variation has been derived from the distinctions made long ago by philosophers between Being and Becoming. Also, the three-way distinction is to some degree similar to the classification of personality components which Charles Morris has developed. His "Dionysian" component, which is defined as one in which there is a release and indulgence of existing desires, has some degree of approximation to the Being orientation. Also, the component which he calls the "Apollonian" one—a component in which the personality is given to containment and control of desires by means of meditation and detachment—has some similarity to the Being-in-Becoming orientation. Similarities can also be noted between his active, striving "Promethean" component and the Doing alternative of the *activity* orientation.[20]

However, the accordances with these or other philosophical concepts are far from complete. In the conceptual scheme of value orientations the terms Being and Becoming, expanded to a three-point range of Being, Being-in-Becoming, and Doing, are much more narrowly defined than Being and Becoming are in philosophical treatises. Also, we hold to the view that the range of alternatives of the *activity* orientation varies independently from those of the *man-nature, time,* and *human nature* orientations. The tendency of most philosophers has been to treat these several types of orientations as relatively undifferentiated clusters.

The *activity* orientation centers solely on the problem of the nature of man's mode of self-expression in *activity*. And, since each mode is definitely considered to be a type of *activity*, the differences between them are not those which the "active-passive" dichotomy distinguishes.

In the Being orientation the preference is for the kind of *activity* which is a spontaneous expression of what is conceived to be "given" in the human personality. As compared with either the Being-in-Becoming or the Doing orientation, it is a nondevelopmental conception of *activity*. It might even be phrased as a spontaneous expression in *activity* of impulses and desires; yet care must be taken not to make this interpretation a too literal one. In no society, as Clyde Kluckhohn has commented, does one ever find a one-to-one relationship between the desired and the desirable. *The concrete behavior of individuals in complex situations and the moral codes governing that behavior usually reflect all the orientations simultaneously.* A stressing of the "isness" of the personality and a spontaneous expression of that "isness" are not pure license, as we can easily see if we turn our attention to a society or segments of a society in which the Being orientation is the first-order preference. Mexican society illustrates this preference well in its widely ramified patterning of *fiesta* activities. Yet never in the *fiesta*, with its emphasis on spontaneity, is there pure impulse gratification. The value demands of other orientations make for codes which restrain the activities of individuals in very definite ways.

The Being-in-Becoming orientation shares with the Being one a great concern with what the human being is rather than what he can accomplish, but here the similarity ends. The idea of development, so little stressed in the Being orientation, is paramount in the Being-in-Becoming one. Erich Fromm's conception of "the spontaneous activity of the total integrated personality" is close to the Being-in-Becoming mode.[21] He states:

By activity we do not mean doing something but rather the quality of the creative activity which can operate in one's emotional, intellectual and sensuous experiences and in one's will as well. One premise of this spontaneity is the acceptance of the total personality and the elimination of the split between reason and nature.[22]

[20] Charles Morris, *Paths of Life* (New York: Harper & Bros., 1942); see especially Chap. II.
[21] Appreciably closer than Morris' Apollonian type.
[22] *Escape from Freedom* (New York: Rinehart & Co., 1941), pp. 258–59.

A less favorably prejudiced and, for our purposes, a more accurately limited statement would be: The Being-in-Becoming orientation emphasizes that kind of *activity* which has as its goal the development of all aspects of the self as an integrated whole.

The Doing orientation is so characteristically the dominant one in American society that there is little need for an extensive discussion of it. Its most distinctive feature is a demand for the kind of *activity* which results in accomplishments that are measurable by standards conceived to be external to the acting individual. That aspect of self-judgment or judgment of others which relates to the nature of *activity* is based mainly upon a measurable accomplishment achieved by acting upon persons, things, or situations. What does the individual do? What can he or will he accomplish? These are almost always the primary questions in the American's scale of appraisal of persons. "Getting things done" and "let's *do* something about it" are stock American phrases.

Fromm also considers this orientation to be different from the one he defines in his concept of spontaneity, but he does not accord it an equally favored position. Instead he views it as a fertile source of neurotically compulsive behavior. While few would disagree that the Doing orientation of Americans makes for a competition with others which is often extreme and intense, it has yet to be demonstrated that such competition customarily leads to, or reflects, compulsiveness in the technical sense of the term. Here again is an instance in which one must examine, quite objectively and unprejudicially, the relationship of types and degrees of conformity to particular kinds of value systems.

5. *Relational* Orientation

The last of the common human problems to be treated is the definition of man's relation to other men. This orientation has three subdivisions: the Lineal, the Collateral, and the Individualistic.

Sociologists have long used various types of dichotomies to differentiate homogeneous folk societies from the more complex urban societies. *Gemeinschaft-Gesellschaft* (Tönnies), traditional–rational-legal (Weber), mechanical-organic solidarity (Durkheim), and simply rural-urban are the most familiar of the several paired terms. Anthropologists, who have for the most part studied *Gemeinschaft* or folk peoples, have frequently made much of the difference between lineage and a lateral extension of relationships in their analyses of kinship structure or social organization.

The distinctions being made here obviously owe much to the concepts used in both these fields but are not identical with those of either. The Lineal, Collateral, and Individualistic *relational* alternatives are analytical concepts for the purpose of making fine distinctions both *within* and *between* systems rather than generalizing concepts for the specification of the gross differences between systems. It is, we maintain, in the nature of the case that all societies and all subgroups within societies must give heed to all three of the *relational* principles.

Individual autonomy is always found even in the most extreme types of *Gemeinschaft* societies. The like-mindedness and behavioral similarities of individuals in "homogeneous" groups have been overstressed. It is usually, if not always, the case that considerable leeway is permitted for "individuality" within the confines of the definitely fixed customs which *Gemeinschaft* groups require for the ordering of human relationships. Individuality and individualism are both results of attention being given to the autonomy of the individual, but they are vastly different concepts, and significant nuances of meaning are lost when, as is so often the case, they are either confused or equated. Further comment on this distinction is reserved for the discussion of conformism.

Collaterality also is found in all societies. The individual is not a human being except as he is a part of a social order, and one type of inevitable social grouping is that which results from laterally extended relationships. These are the more immediate relationships in time and space. Biologically, sibling relationships are the prototype of the Collateral relationship.

In addition all societies must take into account the fact that individuals are biologically and culturally related to each other through time. There is, in other words, always a Lineal principle in relationships which is derived both from the biological givens of age and generational differences and from the fact of cultural continuity.

Sociologists, who have been the most concerned of all social scientists with the problem of generalized types of *relational* systems, have, as was noted above, consistently made only the two-way distinction between individualistic and collectivist systems. For some kinds of analyses it may be quite unnecessary to make further distinctions. But in most cases it should be of critical importance to know which of the two kinds of collectivist principles is stressed. Also, most of the polar-type classifications so common in sociological theory are too generally descriptive and too static in conception to provide many clues for the study of the dynamics of *relational* orders. With the view of *relational* systems as systems which always contain all three *relational* principles in varying rank-order patterns it becomes possible to treat variability and change much more fully.

There are, for example, important variations within social systems and subsystems, as well as between systems, in the nature and primacy of certain goals which accord with the variable stressing of the three *relational* principles. When the Individualistic principle is dominant, individual goals have primacy over the goals of specific Collateral or Lineal groups. This in no sense means that there is license for the individual to pursue selfishly his own interests and in so doing disregard the interests of others. It means simply that each individual's responsibility to the total society and his place in it are defined in terms of goals (and roles) which are structured as *autonomous*, in the sense of being independent of particular Lineal or Collateral groupings. For example, the man who joins a business firm in the United States is expected, in pursuing his own goals of money-making and prestige, to be cooperative with other similarly oriented fellow workers and, in addition, is expected to have a positive attitude toward the overall goals (purposes) of the organization. Yet it is not expected that this man will remain in cooperation with these particular workers or dedicated to the goals of the particular firm if he receives an offer from another firm which will increase his salary or prestige.

A dominant Collateral orientation calls for a primacy of the goals and welfare of the laterally extended group. The group in this case is always moderately independent of other similar groups, and the problem of a well regulated continuity of group relationships through time is not highly critical. The Navaho extended families and the loosely articulated combination of these which Clyde Kluckhohn calls an "outfit" are illustrations of such groups. Even though the individual Navaho always has some autonomous roles and goals, and also always has some roles and goals which are Lineal in nature, the roles and goals which have primacy for him are those which are *representative* of his Collaterally extended household group or "outfit."

If the Lineal principle is dominant, group goals again have primacy, but there is the additional factor that one of the most important of these group goals is continuity through time. *Continuity* of the group through time and *ordered positional succession* within the group are both crucial issues when Lineality dominates the *relational* system. Though other patterns are possible, it appears to be the case that the most successful means of maintaining a Lineal emphasis are either those based squarely upon hereditary factors such as primogeniture or those which are assimilated to a kinship structure. For example, in England, where there has been a definite Lineality in the aristocracy, there has also been an established pattern of moving successful members of the Individualistically oriented middle class into the peerage. By means of this and other related patterns a fairly dominant Lineality has been maintained in the whole society until fairly recently. And wherever Lineality is dominant, roles are also *representative*, but they differ from the Collaterally defined ones in that they always relate to a definite position in a hierarchy of *ordered* positions.

This discussion of the *relational* value orientation completes the presentation of the classification schema. As has been stated previously, no claim is made that either the problems selected as those most crucially important for all human groups or the ranges of possible solutions of these problems represent more than a tentative formulation. Also, it may prove to be the case that some one or two of the value orientations are more crucially important to the patterning of behavior than others. However, as of the present time there appears to be little evidence for this assumption as opposed to the one that most concrete patterns of behavior give expression, in varying degree, to all of the preferential orderings of all of the value orientations. In some patterns of behavior it is often one orientation which is of critical importance, whereas in other patterns the dominant influence of another orientation can be noted; yet seldom, if ever, is any pattern a pure expression of one and only one value orientation.

Definitive answers to all of these questions—that is, the adequacy of the range of problems and the alternatives of solutions for them, the centrality of the influence of one or another of the orientations, and the degree of the independent variability of the orientations one from another—can only be answered by repeated empirical testings of the total conceptual schema. Meanwhile, the classification schema and the assumptions underlying it provide a solid basis for the development of first approximations to a theory of variation in value orientations. These approximations and their significance for theoretical developments in the analysis of role structure and cultural change are the matters of primary concern in the second half of this theoretical discussion. But, before turning to these issues, we pause to make further comment upon the question of conformism as it is related to varying value-orientation preferences.

CONFORMISM AS RELATED TO THE VALUE ORIENTATIONS

There are, as has been remarked above, many today who seem to wish to lift the concept of conformity out of the context in which it has been customarily used—that is, the socialization of individuals within a cultural tradition of whatever kind—and to equate it with a particular cultural tradition, most especially that of the United States. Fromm, for example, virtually condemns conformism as a disease of modern Western culture generally but most especially a disease of United States culture, which he considers to be primarily a culture of the market place.[23] Whyte has created anxiety in the minds of many who plan a career in business with his picture of the "organization man" whose own individuality, and that of his wife and children as well, is bowed before, or even broken by, the demands for conformism which *The Organization* makes.[24] Erikson, too, although far more relativistic in his ideas about conformity than either Fromm or Whyte, strongly stresses the restrictive aspects of conformity for American culture in his discussion of "The American Identity." He states, for example, that there is a definite restriction of the ego of the American child, especially the male child, which results from a socialization process that places a high premium upon independence (autonomy) while giving few rewards, or opportunities, for the expression of individuality.[25]

We do not dispute what these or other like-minded analysts say about American culture, but we do suggest that a number of the views advanced tend both to give an insufficient emphasis to the requiredness of conformism in every society and also to underplay the problems for personality development which conformity to other kinds of value systems than the American one creates. Conformism (or conformity, as many choose to call it) is not, in other words, a process which is peculiar to one cultural tradition as opposed to others, nor is it one which is inimical to the development

---

[23] See *op. cit.* and also *Man for Himself* (New York: Rinehart & Co., 1947).
[24] William H. Whyte, Jr., *The Organization Man* (New York: Simon and Schuster, 1956).
[25] Erik H. Erikson, *Childhood and Society* (New York: W. W. Norton & Co., 1950), Chap. VIII.

of the human potential for creativity. Riesman voices a similar judgment when he says:

> It will be seen that it is through the concept of conformity that character and society are linked in our analysis, for each type of society is seen as instilling a particular mode of conformity in its members, who then perpetuate the society as they go about its business, including the rearing of the young.[26]

There has been far too much of a tendency in recent years to concentrate attention upon the restrictive rather than the liberating aspects of cultural norms and standards. In the creation of this tendency the ideas and theories of psychoanalysts, beginning with Freud himself, have been most influential.

There is, to be sure, a sense in which the demands of social living—the cultural norms and standards—can be considered as shackles which bind and restrict and make it necessary that there be repression, suppression, and sublimation of basic impulses. But the other side of the coin is that there could be no humanness without these restrictions since the human creature is not instinct bound as are the members of other species of the animal kingdom. Man must learn to be a human being, and in the learning, however slow and painful the process often is, he becomes free in ways that the ant, whose place in an elaborate social organization is instinctively fixed, can never be. This is a truism, of course, but one which is in need of restating lest the restrictive aspects of a culture—a value-orientation system—be grossly exaggerated.

Given the basic fact of the requiredness of conformity if man is to be a *human* social animal, the second question is whether the value systems humankind create are variable in the kind and degree of conformity they demand. Or, to phrase this in another way: Are there some kinds of value systems which restrict the human potential (always to be viewed as basically biological) more than others? This seemingly is the burden of many of the criticisms of American culture. But one wonders whether the serf of the medieval manorial system or the Mexican *peon* on an *hacienda* would agree that the restrictions imposed upon the "organization man" are the equal of those he feels. Is it not a case of the other man's pasture appearing to be greener?

There is, actually, considerable inconsistency in what the currently prominent social scientists are themselves expressing concerning the "virtues" and the "vices" (the freedoms and restrictions) of differing social systems. It is as if we have before us a single social-science concert stage on which there have appeared simultaneously two *major* music bands, each one playing so different a tune that it is only dissonance that the listener hears. One plays a mournful tune decrying the plight of the hampered and frightened "organization man" (the seemingly inevitable product of an industrial society); the other rings forth with a battle tune urging all to help

---

[26] David Riesman, *Faces in the Crowd* (New Haven, Conn.: Yale University Press, 1952), p. 5.

in the liberation of the "backward peoples" of the world in order that they may hastily be brought into that state of industrialization where they, too, can become organization men. And there is even more discord still, for there are a few who have laid claim to a secluded corner of the concert floor for the singing of nostalgic ballads about the virtues of the Middle Ages or some other period of history when men were bound to each other in a more cohesive, a more symbiotic, system than "modern industrialism" permits.

It appears obvious that these varying expressions are largely judgments about variable value systems. Let us, therefore, briefly examine the process of conformism in type and degree relative to the alternatives of three of the value orientations—the *time, activity,* and *relational* orientations—and some of the varying combinations of these alternatives.

It has been a commonplace in sociological studies to draw a distinction between traditionalistic and anti-traditionalistic societies. To some extent this distinction is derived, either explicitly or implicitly, from observations of the varying emphases on the alternatives of the *time* orientation. It has, for example, been repeatedly remarked that the individuals in a traditionalistic society are expected to conform to customary and time-honored norms for behavior which are in and of themselves (as Weber especially has pointed out) a main source of moral authority in the society as a whole. The Past *time* orientation is dominant in societies of this type. In sharp contrast there is the Future-oriented society in which the standards of conformity (*type* of conformity) are the latest, the newest, ideas and modes of acting of the group, a group which often is highly local. "Keeping up with the Joneses" in car purchases, in household furnishings, in the schooling of children, and keeping one's ideas in line with those of others are matters of far greater concern than an adherence to traditional standards.

There are, of course, always some revered traditions in societies of this type, for no society can fail to give attention to all alternatives of the *time* orientation. Future-minded Americans, for example, have a few traditions, some of them remarkably hoary ones. It was once remarked by a member of the British Foreign Office during the period of high feeling against "packing" the Supreme Court: "Americans have so few traditions that they inevitably feel a necessity to prevent change of any kind in those few which do exist." One also notes in many Americans a feeling of need, almost a longing, for fixed traditions. Witness the persons, usually women but not always, who become obsessed with genealogies! Yet, for all of these and all other variations which represent an interest in a Past orientation, it is mainly *sentimentality* rather than traditionalism which characterizes the attitudes of Americans toward yesterday's patterns.

As to degree of conformity—that is, the intensity of the feeling-need to conform in order that one does not become a stranded isolate, a social outcast—there are some grounds for arguing that it is greater in a competitive, Future-oriented society than in either a traditionalistic Past-oriented one or in a Present-oriented one. There is actually more anxiety in the Future-oriented society about what the neighbors or one's peers will think and more general concern about measuring up to current standards of "normalcy." However, there is something illusionary about this argument when it is made the basis of a discussion of conformism. First, it fails to take into account the differing psychological effects which traditionally fixed standards and fluid and ever-changing ones create. Second, it needs correction for the effects of other value orientations than the *time* one alone.

In a society like that of the United States (its dominant middle class, at least) there is a linkage of a first-order Doing *activity* orientation with the Future *time* emphasis. This combination certainly increases the degree of concern about conforming to standards which are momentarily current and largely conceived to be external to the acting individual (see the definition above of the Doing alternative of the *activity* orientation). Let us take, as just one of many illustrations of this kind of conformity, the case of the young Cambridge, Massachusetts, mother who was trying her valiant best to be a "good mother" in accord with the latest books on proper child-rearing practices—the latest in this case being in the direction of "rigid permissiveness" rather than "rigid scheduling." She had read in one of the currently accepted books on child rearing that it was "normal" for a child of two to three years of age to take crayons or pencils and write on the house walls. Imagine her dismay when she realized her own child of this age was not writing on the walls. What other conclusion could there be but that he was abnormal? So, to take care of this discrepancy in "proper" socialization, she bought the crayons and taught him to write on the walls!

But we ask whether this is a more stultifying form of conformity than that required in traditional Chinese culture where a young mother in the training of her children had to follow slavishly the dictates of her mother-in-law, or the expectations produced in the upper classes of Europe (even in America to some extent) that child-rearing practices, and much other behavior as well, must always be in accord with the ideas of mothers, mothers-in-law, and grandmothers.

But it still is not just the variations of the *time* and the *activity* orientations which must be considered. All of the orientations are crucial to the problem of conformity. However, we shall, in this discussion, treat only one more orientation, the *relational* orientation. It was stated above in the definition of this orientation that individua*lism* and individua*lity* were both expressions of this orientation but quite different ones. The difference appears to depend upon the rank ordering of alternatives of the *relational* orientation. When Individualism is given a first-order preference in the total *relational* system the particular individual is given the kind of freedom which makes it unnecessary that he unequivocally bow his head and surrender his autonomy to the demands of either the elders of a Lineally defined hierarchy or to the requirements for unanimous consensus which characterize a Collaterally organized group. Instead, he is "free to be like everyone else." This situation quite obviously makes for a special type of conformism, but whether or not the amount of latitude offered the individual or the intensity of the feeling-need to conform is greater or less in the three types of relationally ordered situations are moot questions. For example, the individual in a Lineally oriented system, especially if it be one in which there is also a dominant Past *time* orientation, may well be allowed numerous fairly idiosyncratic expressions of idea and action which are denied to the conforming members of an Individualistic and Future-oriented society. But usually these somewhat idiosyncratic expressions (we say "somewhat" because there actually is always some cultural patterning to be noted in them) are, for the most part, relative to matters which constitute no serious challenge to the primary demands of the Lineal system. An English duke may go forth with holes in his socks with no thought of what public opinion may be; his duchess may also wear outmoded hats and dresses and express many bizarre ideas which the Individualistically oriented, middle-class woman in the United States, England, France, or other Western countries would seldom venture to do. However, a dominant Individualistic orientation allows far more leeway than either the Lineal or the Collateral ones do for changing one's friends or associates and making preferential relationships among one's relatives.

The Individualistic system gives to the nuclear family a high degree of independence; the Lineal and Collateral ones, in differing ways, envelop and enmesh the nuclear family within the network of relationships of the extended family system. And is it not because of the firm and quite unshakable bonds of the extended family in the Lineal and Collateral systems—bonds which usually keep individuals bound to both a particular locale in space and to a fairly definitely fixed social position—that there can be much permissiveness for an individuality of behavioral expression in many areas of behavior which are not of central importance? The right to be different, eccentric even, is, in other words, actually a reward for the submission to the major restrictive bonds of the system. Of course, this privilege, especially in the case of the Lineal system, is far more frequently granted to the *rulers* than it is to those who are the ruled—be these called serfs, slaves, peons, or simply lower-class minions. This fact, too, is often ignored by many who choose to place a higher evaluation upon the *individuality* which is allowed in a relatively fixed system than upon the *individualistic* adherence to the current norms of a relatively fluid social system.

Since the question of conformism in and of itself is not a central issue of this study, we shall not prolong this discussion of it except to state that the consideration of it points up well the need for a systematic theory for the analysis of variations in value orientations. It is to these variations, both as between and within cultures, that we now turn our attention.

VARIATIONS IN VALUE ORIENTATIONS

The assumptions basic to the classification of the value orientations postulate a variation in emphasis on the orientations of any given range; hence the matter of greatest significance for the development of a theory of variation is the nature of the ordering of choices among possible choices. In the first instance this is a logical problem, because there are logically determined limits to the number and kind of variable patterns of orientation emphases. Figure I:1 gives the logically possible rank orderings for

Pure Rank-Order Types
Individualism over Collaterality over Lineality
Individualism over Lineality over Collaterality
Collaterality over Individualism over Lineality
Collaterality over Lineality over Individualism
Lineality over Collaterality over Individualism
Lineality over Individualism over Collaterality

Linked First-Order Types[a]
Individualism equals Collaterality over Lineality
Individualism equals Lineality over Collaterality
Collaterality equals Lineality over Individualism

Linked Second-Order Types[a]
Individualism over Collaterality equals Lineality
Lineality over Collaterality equals Individualism
Collaterality over Individualism equals Lineality

Nonordered Type[b]
Individualism equals Lineality equals Collaterality

Fig. I:1. Types of Rank-Order Patterns of the Value Orientations (*relational* Orientation as Example).

[a] Although it is to be expected that many individuals will prove to be "linked" cases, it is predicted that for total systems the evidence of a virtually equal stress on two alternative positions, especially in first-order choices, is usually indicative of cultural transition. However, it is also to be expected that there will be some instances of a whole people or a subgroup maintaining a linked value-orientation position over a long period of time.

[b] The thirteenth logical possibility—the "all choices equal" type—should not, according to our theory, be at all common empirically. If it does appear as an overall pattern and can be demonstrated to be realistic and not a result of a fault in the theory or the method of testing, it indicates rapid cultural change—a state of flux.

the *relational* orientation. The logically determined rank orderings for all other orientations, except the *human nature* one, are similar. It is these orderings which provide the ground for both theoretical and methodological developments in the analysis of variation.

Presently we shall attempt to show how a knowledge of these orderings may aid in the analysis of the interrelations of major "institutional" structures and how it also provides a new approach for treating change in social systems. But before dealing with either of these complicated matters, let us briefly examine that more obvious type of variation which results from there being present in every society, but most especially in large and heterogeneous ones, segments or subgroups whose behavior is patterned in accord with either a completely or a partially different ordering of value orientations than that of the dominant group.

The many ethnic groups in the United States are excellent examples of this type of variation. Almost everyone realizes that many of these ethnic groups have patterns of behavior and thought which vary more or less widely from the dominant American patterns. The "melting pot" ideology is based upon a recognition of such variation. But it has not been equally well recognized, either ideologically or behaviorally, that the several groups often vary tremendously one from another. Also it has been for the most part only in such matters as language differences, food habits, and dissimilarities in physical appearance that variation is noted. Even those persons who have worked closely with ethnic groups (social workers, teachers, ministers) have seldom paid much attention to the variation in their ways of life other than the readily observable differences in parental authority, family living patterns, and political and religious affiliations. Because there has been little concern with the variations in deeply rooted value orientations, it has been difficult for many to comprehend why some ethnic groups become Americanized easily while others cling tenaciously to their own ways of life over long time periods.

Since later there is to be a detailed treatment of Spanish-Americans, who represent an extreme example of a minimally assimilated people, it is not necessary to prolong the discussion of this type of variation beyond the stating of this one general hypothesis: *The rate and degree of assimilation of any ethnic group to dominant American culture will depend in large part upon the degree of goodness of fit of the group's own rank ordering of value orientations with that of the dominant culture.*[27]

Social classes are another variety of subgroup which has greatly concerned American social scientists in the last two decades. The best known studies of class structure in the United States are those of Warner and his numerous associates, but there have also been a number of others in which both the points of view and the conclusions have differed somewhat from those of the Warner group. The various studies describe and analyze many aspects of class structuring which, in the past, most Americans have been unwilling to admit or discuss. They bring into the open the great differences between the classes in attitudes toward education and politics, in association memberships, in family life, in occupational interests and opportunities, in reading habits and other recreational interests.

But in spite of all these and the other differences observed and recorded, there has been the tendency in almost all of the studies to assume that all the variation is variation on the same value theme, the so-called American Creed. What is usually remarked is that the behavior and attitudes of some groups, or classes, are harmoniously attuned to this general creed whereas those of other classes are off pitch and limited in range. That the variations may reflect different themes is seldom suggested.

According to the conceptual scheme of dominant and variant value orientations, it is assumed at the outset that there will be a dominant class

[27] An added consideration requiring a carefully worked out qualification of this general hypothesis is the goodness of fit of a group's value orientations one with another. While it is assumed (and evidence collected to date seems to indicate the assumption is in the main a correct one) that any arrangement of the several value orientations is possible, it is not believed that all combinations are equally "good" ones. Some combinations appear to create many more strains for individuals than others; hence the assimilation rate will also be affected by how well or how badly geared to each other a group's original value orientations are. An illustration of one type of "bad fit" is the combination of a Present *time* and a Lineal *relational* orientation which will be discussed in the chapter devoted to Spanish-American culture.

(in the case of the United States, the middle class), in which adherence to dominant values is marked, surrounded by other classes which will hold to variant value orientations in much of what they do and believe. In an earlier paper on value orientations it was suggested that the observed behavior of an upper class in an old and declining community (for example, the community of Yankee City, described by Warner and his associates) shows an adherence to Lineality rather than Individualism, to Past more than Future *time*, and to either the Being or Being-in-Becoming *activity* orientation rather than the Doing orientation.[28] Also in some parts of the lower class, a collection of people so heterogeneous and diffuse that they should be called "classes" and not simply "class," it would appear that the Present and Being orientations are frequently combined with either Individualism or Collaterality.

There has not been sufficient work done to date to know how much the knowledge and appraisal of class differences will be increased by this different kind of approach. In one study of Harvard College students made by McArthur the theory of dominant and variant value orientations was used to make predictions of the differences in certain kinds of responses which would be made by upper and middle-class college students to the pictures in the Murray and Morgan Thematic Apperception Test. Although a separation of the students into these two groups was not an easy task, various kinds of evidence seemed to indicate that for Harvard College students a fairly accurate division could be made on the basis of type of school attended prior to coming to college. Thus, it was assumed that a majority of the public-school students were of the middle class whereas a majority of those who had attended private schools, especially a certain selected group of schools, were upper class. For the former it was postulated that their modal *time* and *activity* orientations would be Future and Doing; for the latter, Past and either Being or Being-in-Becoming. These two predictions were then made as to the variability of response to the first of the pictures of the test (a small boy is seated before a table on which lies a violin; the subject is asked to invent a story about him):

(1) that more public-school boys will tell stories to the violin picture in which the parent demands work from the child.
(2) that more private-school boys will tell violin stories in which the music lesson is seen by the child as a way to create beauty and express and develop himself.

The predictions were borne out by McArthur's data at the .05 level of significance. Twelve similar hypotheses which related to differences in the *time*, *activity*, and *relational* orientations and which were developed for other pictures in the test series were equally well validated by the test data. Three additional ones did not meet the statistical test of significance but were found to be in the same direction as the others. McArthur's summary statement of the results is:

They constituted a neat demonstration that the attitudes of individuals, as meas-

---

[28] "Dominant and Substitute Profiles," p. 387.

ured by one of the psychologist's projective tests of personality, can be predicted from a knowledge of the person's subcultural orientations profile.[29]

Ethnic groups and social classes represent only two of the many possible types of variantly oriented subgroups in a total society. Some societies have many types, others few, but not even the very small nonliterate and folk societies are without any. From the empirical point of view the number and kinds of variant subgroups are matters of great importance. Theoretically the significant fact is that even this type of variation in value orientations contributes greatly to the creation of an intricate *web of variation*. No dominantly oriented group ever escapes being influenced by the variantly oriented ones which surround and constantly impinge upon it, and no variant group survives without numerous relationships to the dominantly oriented ones.

To some extent social scientists have shown an awareness of this interplay of the dominant and variant at the behavioral level, but, as noted previously, little or no attention has been paid to variation in basic value orientations. The view advanced here is that variation in value orientations is the most important type of cultural variation and is, therefore, the central feature of the structure of culture. This is to say that the "system of meanings" of a society, its ethos, is more realistically and adequately derived from an analysis of the dynamic interrelationships of the variations in its value orientations than it is from a study of only the dominant values.

Evidence for this point of view of a different kind than that derived from an analysis of variations in subgroups is found in an analysis of those variations of value orientations which are required by the fact that in every society there are several more or less well differentiated kinds of activities all of which are essential to its successful functioning. Sociologists over the years have classified these activities in varying ways. The now common classification in many sociological writings is that of major *social institutions*—the economic-occupational (with special emphasis upon technology and the occupations of the market place), the religious, the intellectual-aesthetic, the recreational, the political, and the familial. To be sure, not all sociologists make all of these differentiations, and many would insist that the categories as listed do not have a comparable theoretical status. Moreover, even though many anthropologists also use some or all of the categories in their descriptions of nonliterate societies, they do not regard the divisions as empirically meaningful ones for many types of cultures.

---

[29] Charles McArthur, "Cultural Values as Determinants of Imaginal Productions," unpublished Ph.D. thesis, Harvard University, 1952. A short general statement of the plan of this study and the results achieved by it appear in "Personality Differences Between Middle and Upper Classes," *Journal of Abnormal and Social Psychology*, Vol. L, No. 2 (March, 1955), pp. 247–55.

Both McArthur and we realize that the sample in the research program was too small to warrant more than "conservative conclusions." McArthur also stresses the fact that the experiment was a special use of the Thematic Apperception Test. Only certain types of the total range of responses the test elicits were applicable to the testing of the hypotheses of the research.

But in spite of the many difficulties one encounters in a use of the categories either for cross-cultural studies or for sophisticated theoretical analyses of particular social systems, there remains the essential fact that these varying kinds of activities are necessary to the functioning of every society. And, because it seems almost certain that varying value-orientation emphases are related to a stressing of one kind of activity as against others, we intend to make use of four of the categories—the economic-occupational, the religious, the recreational, and the intellectual-aesthetic—without at this point attempting any major theoretical refinements in the categories themselves or in their status relative to each other.[30] The only alteration proposed of any significance is the use of the term *behavior sphere* in place of *institution*. For our purposes, behavior sphere has the advantage of being less connotative of consciously defined and definitely separated spheres of human activity than the term institution.

The relationship between value orientations and behavior spheres, like most relationships, is a reciprocal one. It is possible on the one hand to say that a people who have a particular ordering of value orientations will give a predominant position to a particular behavior sphere (or more probably to a particular combination and ordering of spheres), and on the other hand to state that the predominance of a particular behavior sphere is indicative of a particular ordering of value orientations. But because value orientations are a more generalized and more durable aspect of culture than the specific patterns of the behavior spheres, there is first, a logical, and second, an historical reason for giving priority to the ordering of value orientations. Since variation is intrinsic to the value-orientation system itself, this priority can be granted with no denial of the fact that some kinds of changes in activities and interests in the behavior spheres will eventually produce changes in the ordering of value-orientation emphases. This and other aspects of the relationship of variations in value orientations to cultural change will be discussed later in this chapter.

At the moment let us try, by means of illustrations, to make clear the general proposition that both between cultures and within cultures there is a relationship between value-orientation emphases and the degree of dominance accorded to the behavior spheres which results in an intricately ordered variation in cultural patterning. Starting with the United States as one example of a total culture, we can easily see how its dominant value orientations of Individualism, Future *time*, Mastery-over-Nature, Doing, and an Evil-but-perfectible definition of *human nature* (now changing) make for a high evaluation of the occupational world, conceived as a world of technology, business, and economic affairs in general. One of the many kinds of evidence attesting to this relationship is the general consensus among those who have investigated social classes in the United

[30] Watson Smith and John M. Roberts have recently developed a concept of "value field" which has some similarity to that of behavior sphere as we are using it. However, it appears probable that further development of both concepts will indicate that the "value field" is a concept intermediate between behavior spheres and value orientations. See Watson Smith and John M. Roberts, *Zuni Law: A Field of Values,* Papers of the Peabody Museum, Harvard University, Vol. XLIII, No. 1 (1954).

States that the best *single* index for the determination of class position is occupational status. Other indices have been demonstrated to be important, but no one of them is as individually significant as this one.

In sharp contrast to this ordering of the alternatives of the value orientations stands the Spanish-American system which has been used above to illustrate the alternatives of the orientations and which will be analyzed in detail in a later chapter. In it the dominant orientation emphases have been Lineality (now changing), Present, Subjugation-to-Nature, and Being. And, as anyone with a little thought might guess, with these as the dominant orientations the combination of the recreational and religious spheres is prominent. The ramified patterning of the *fiesta* theme in Spanish-American culture (Mexican also) epitomizes the dominance of these two spheres. Other evidence is not cited here. In Chapter VI the relative evaluation of the several spheres in this culture will be fully discussed.

In instances where emphasis is given to the Being-in-Becoming *activity* orientation, to the Harmony-with-Nature position, to either Lineality or Collaterality, and to a Past or (less probably) a Present *time* orientation, one would predict a focusing of interests upon the intellectual-aesthetic behavior sphere. This relationship of value-orientation emphases and behavior-sphere dominance seems to have been the most prominent one in many of the historical periods of Japan prior to World War II.[31]

These few illustrations do not, of course, do more than suggest the kind of relationship we have ventured to propose as existing between the ordering of value orientations and the ordering of behavior spheres. Since the postulated independent variability of each of the value orientations makes logically possible a very large number of types of orderings among them—even many different profiles of only dominant orientations—the relationship between them and the behavior spheres is obviously enormously complex. And until there has been a reconceptualization of the behavior spheres this complexity cannot be systematically analyzed. Hence we have offered only a few speculative ideas about differences between cultures as a direction to follow in some future work and now wish to present several additional ones on the nature of *intra*-cultural variation which is the more critical kind for the development of a theory of variation.

If it is the case that all the behavior spheres, even as now defined and classified, are found, more or less differentiated, in every society, and if our proposition about their relationships to value orientations has validity, it would appear to be an obvious conclusion that in the patterning of each society there is an ordered variation which stems from—is related to—the variations in the ordering of the alternatives of value orientations.

---

[31] No member of the project group has made a study of Japanese culture. However, this impression was so strong in the mind of Florence Kluckhohn that she discussed it with several Japanese scholars in different parts of Japan in the summer of 1954. There was general agreement among them that aesthetic interests were central in the culture and were a main key to understanding it.
  John Pelzel, who has devoted much time to the study of Japanese culture, states that in his opinion the Doing orientation has been of equal dominance in Japanese culture during and since the Tokagawa period, and political activities have been as prominent, or more prominent, than aesthetic interests. However, he agrees to the great importance of the aesthetic sphere both historically and at the present time.

To function successfully every society must have within it some persons, either individual persons or groups of persons, who will devote themselves to the differing activities of the several behavior spheres. And, if the activities of the differing spheres are to be adequately performed, it is necessary that a majority of the persons choosing each sphere have the rank order of value orientations which provides the motivations proper to the sphere. For example, the American man who elects to be a composer of music or the one who chooses to be an academic intellectual is almost always "variant" in some if not all of his value orientations. In the use of the words "elect" and "choose," attention is being called to *permitted* variation. In the United States, at least, there is much permitted variation of this kind; in other societies less of this type and more of others is permitted. But even in America this variation permitted to individuals is *required* for the social system. Some composers of music and many academic intellectuals are essential to its stability; hence each generation must produce new recruits to each sphere.

In the less differentiated societies variants of this type are less numerous and often they are less clearly demarcated; yet they are never absent from the social scene. If all Spanish-Americans, the representatives of a folk culture, had in the past behaved in accord with the prevailing values of their culture, their social system would never have been created and would not have endured relatively unaltered through many generations. But history shows that most of the successful Spanish-American *patrones* were far more Individualistic in their behavior than average Spanish-Americans, and not infrequently they were also fairly ambitious planners. In both their ambition and their planning they differed, to be sure, from the ambitious Future and Doing-oriented American businessman whose range for planning is a longer one; but still, in some respects, they resembled that businessman much more than they resembled the majority of their own people. And even though one may certainly question the benefits of their kind of variation to the Spanish-American social system because of the numerous strains the *patrón* system imposed upon all those it governed, it still remains a fact that this system was the glue which held the wider social system together for a very long time. Moreover, it was a most firmly set glue, as will be demonstrated later.

But however dominant or variant a particular individual may appear to be when the focus of interest is the whole social system, he is never completely so. No individual, any more than any society, can live wholly or always in accord with the patterns which express a single profile of value orientations. Each one has within himself, *as a part of his personality*, a rank order of value orientations which usually is made apparent by a variable allocation of time and interest in the activities of the several behavior spheres and by variable behavior in the different spheres. For example, not even the most dominantly oriented American businessmen spend all their time on the job; all participate at some times and to some degree in all the other spheres of activity. This fact has been widely observed, but it has not been as frequently remarked that the shifting from sphere to sphere indicates a complex and variable motivational structure.

Still less often has the variability of motivations been seen as a variation in an individual's value orientations. Instead it has frequently been looked upon as a serious conflict within the personality, hence as something to cause concern. One such conflict that has been much discussed is the one many Americans, especially men, seem to have between religious and occupational values. Without denying that there is actual conflict of this and other kinds, we suggest that much of what looks like conflict is often just an expression in behavior of the individual's variation in value orientations. Moreover, if there is a serious internal conflict it is an indication that the value-orientation structure of the individual either is not ordered or is constituted of different orderings which conflict with each other.

Although it far exceeds the aims of the present discussion to deal with these conflicts in ordering and their effects upon both personalities and interpersonal relationships,[32] let us cite one familiar example. It is the child of the immigrant family who within the family structure is socialized in accord with the dominant values of traditionalism (Past *time* and Lineality) and who, outside the family—in schools, play groups, and other associations—comes to know and feel the impact of ways of behaving which express the dominant American values of Individualism and Future *time*. As a type of conflicted personality in the American scene this one has been noted frequently enough to have received a definite name— second generation. Admittedly, no two of these personalities ever exhibit exactly the same symptoms, but they have in common a tremendously important source of conflict which many Individualistically oriented psychologists and psychiatrists either ignore or analyze intuitively.

THE RELEVANCE OF VARIATIONS IN VALUE ORIENTATIONS TO ROLE THEORY

Some readers, especially those with sociological training, will view the variations we have discussed as variations in *social roles*. If one uses the role concept loosely this conversion can easily be made. Even in the illustration of an internal conflict concerning value-orientation preferences just cited—the child of the immigrant family—it may be said that a particular kind of role is being played. But this is only a superficial translation of the ideas of variation which does not capture at all the significance of variation for a further development of role theory.

The importance of the concept of role in studies of social behavior has been well demonstrated. Parsons and Shils state:

The "individual" actor as a concrete system of action is not usually the most important unit of a social system. For most purposes *the conceptual unit of the social system is the role*. The role is a sector of the individual actor's total system of ac-

---

[32] A project under the direction of John Spiegel and Florence Kluckhohn has as one of its specific aims the investigating of these problems. This project, which is devoted to a comparative study of "well" and "emotionally disturbed" families is sponsored by the Harvard University Laboratory of Social Relations and is financed by the National Institute of Mental Health.

tion. It is the point of contact between the system of action of the individual actor and the social system. The individual then becomes a unity in the sense that he is a composite of various action units which in turn are roles in the relationships in which he is involved.[33]

There are many sociologists who hold this view. The role concept is also widely used in the field of social psychology. Some anthropologists, notably Linton, have made significant contributions to the study of role structure.[34] The concept figures prominently in a number of the recent studies of the social organization of hospitals and the doctor-patient relationships in which there has often been a collaboration of clinical psychologists and psychiatrists.

When a single concept is so widely used in so many different disciplines, it is obvious that it has a great potential as a conceptual bridge for crossing over the chasms between these disciplines which differing theoretical interests and differing selections of universes of discourse have created.[35] However, there are still many in all the fields mentioned, most especially psychology and anthropology, who find the concept, as it has thus far been defined and used, still too narrow a concept to serve the purpose. Some psychologists raise the objection that the tendency in the use of it for describing both prescriptions *for* behavior and modalities *of* behavior is to emphasize too much the uniformity of behavior—"shared behavior"— and that hence it is not useful when the focus of attention is directed to individual differences. Many anthropologists consider the definitions of the concept to be too limited in scope for the analysis of the wide range of patterning in cultures. They prefer the broader concept of culture pattern.

We suggest that both of these objections can, in some part at least, be met and the bridging power of the concept increased if, first, it is sufficiently well redefined and expanded to take account of variation in value orientations and, second, if a systematic classification of roles is developed which allows for the distinctions between formal and informal, general and specific, and explicit and implicit roles. Since the research this volume is to report was primarily concerned with variation in value orientations and had no aim of an elaboration of role theory in and of itself, we shall confine our attention, for the most part, to the first of these two requirements. Only brief comment will be made about the second.

Although both the definitions of social role and the classifications of roles are somewhat various, we shall mention here only one central theoretical position on role theory (today best represented by Parsons and the many he has influenced) which is in the tradition of thought that stems, in some large part, from the works of Tönnies, Durkheim, Weber, and other theorists for whom functional *differentiation* was a central issue. From this tradition, no matter whether one utilizes one or another of the

---

[33] *Op. cit.*, p. 190.
[34] Ralph Linton, *The Study of Man* (New York: Appleton-Century, 1936).
[35] Parsons has long emphasized the importance of the concept for the bridging of analyses of social structure and personality. In his recent collaborative work with Shils there are quite explicit statements on this issue.

dichotomies mentioned above—either the *Gemeinschaft-Gesellschaft* distinction of Tönnies, the mechanical-organic solidarity one of Durkheim, Weber's traditional–rational-legal dichotomy, the folk-culture versus civilization one later used by Redfield and others, or the rural-urban distinctions common to many textbooks in sociology—the matter of central concern is *differentiation* relative to *same* values and not *variation* in values. There is in all of these polarized "ideal types" an underlying assumption that the value system in accord with which the differentiation is effected is a unitary one to which the individual conforms or from which he deviates. Thus the *conformity-deviation* dichotomy becomes a second important conceptual tool for the analysis of roles and role systems for these theorists.[36]

Variation in value orientations as we have defined and described it is not easily fitted into this conceptualization of social roles. Since both the role expectations within the system or subsystem in question and the value standards in accord with which they are patterned are seen as invariant, variation can only be treated peripherally and has little meaning other than the differences to be found in the dominant values of the systems or the subsystems. Variation considered as a "built in" feature of roles and role systems, hence a main ordering principle in them, is not a central issue in the approach.

There is, to be sure, some discussion of variation and its significance, but for the most part it is a treatment of the variations *between* systems rather than a consideration of an ordered variation *within* a system. Parsons, for example, treats the kind of variation which derives from the different combinations of the "pattern variables," but as delineated it becomes a factor in the differentiation of either total systems or subsystems. It is, in other words, a use of the concept of variation as a means of making distinctions *between* systems. Within each of the systems (total or partial), it is only the dominant values which are considered.[37] In the essay by Merton and Kitt on reference group theory it is stated that "anticipatory socialization" and "positive orientation to non-membership groups" are ideas which open up to the sociologist a field of inquiry which has heretofore been largely ignored because of a too great concern with the question of in-group cohesion.[38] The statement is certainly very suggestive of the probable importance of "within-system" variation, but these

---

[36] This, obviously, is not to say that these are the only conceptual tools used in the approach. The theory of action as developed by Parsons in particular is concerned with the question of goals, the relation of structure to function, and much else. The concepts of differentiation, conformity, and deviation have been singled out because it is relative to them that there appear to be the greatest problems for articulations with the theory of variation in value orientations.

[37] Talcott Parsons, *The Social System* (Glencoe, Ill.: Free Press, 1951), especially Chap. V. Parsons does, to be sure, recognize that *empirically* the *degree* of agreement on normative standards is problematic, and he states that there is a continuum which ranges from full institutionalization to *anomie*. But this is not at all what we mean by a "built in" and ordered variation.

[38] Robert K. Merton and Alice Kitt, "Contributions to the Theory of Reference Group Behavior" in *Continuities in Social Research*, ed. Robert K. Merton and Paul F. Lazarsfeld (Glencoe, Ill.: Free Press, 1950), pp. 326–32.

authors do not themselves go far in analyzing the positive orientations to nonmembership groups as a problem of ordered variation. In his still more recent discussion of reference group theory Merton comments that papers of Turner, Rosen, and Eisenstadt have opened to consideration for sociological analyses the question of "different reference groups for different norms and values." This statement also can be interpreted as being suggestive of an idea of variation in values, but it is left as suggestion only.[39]

Of all the sociologists who have concerned themselves with the problem of deviation, Stouffer, in his analyses of role conflict, and Gross, Mason, and McEachern, in their study of the role of the school superintendent, have gone the farthest in stressing the need for a consideration of variation in social roles. Stouffer, for example, remarks:

The *range* of approved or permissible behavior as perceived by a given individual is an important datum for the analysis of what constitutes a social norm in any group, and especially for the analysis of conflicting norms.[40]

Then, in the conclusion of the paper from which this statement is taken he poses this argument:

From the theoretical standpoint, the most important implication of this paper may stem from its stress on variability. In essay writing in this field it is common and convenient to think of a social norm as a point, or at least as a very narrow band on either side of a point. This probably is quite unrealistic as to most of our social behavior. And it may be precisely the ranges of permissible behavior which most need examination, if we are to make progress in this realm which is so central in social science. For it may be the very existence of some flexibility or social slippage —but not too much—which makes behavior in groups possible.[41]

But Stouffer himself does not go farther in the conceptualization of the variations than to point out the possible fact of a range of fairly specific norms, and his primary focus of interest in the analysis of the data presented is on the conflicts for individuals created by the discrepancies between the normative expectations of the *different* memberships to which they belonged.

Gross, Mason, and McEachern make this statement in the conclusion of their study:

Most students concerned with role phenomena, assuming consensus on role definition, have tried to account for variability in behavior by invoking such variables as different motivations, attitudes, or personality characteristics. Our research experience suggests that the different expectations held for incumbents' behavior and attributes are crucial for an understanding of their different behaviors and characteristics. Theoretical formulations which attempt to explain different be-

---

[39] *Social Theory and Social Structure*, rev. ed. (Glencoe, Ill.: Free Press, 1957), pp. 330–32.
[40] Samuel A. Stouffer, "An Analysis of Conflicting Social Norms," *American Sociological Review*, Vol. XIV, No. 6 (December, 1949), p. 708.
[41] *Ibid.*, p. 717.

haviors of incumbents of the same position cannot be based on concepts in which the postulate of role consensus is involved.[42]

These writers again stress the importance of variations, but even though they actually cite the theory with which this volume is concerned in their argument,[43] they do not develop a conceptualization of roles in which *ordered* variation is a key principle.

Our conceptualization of ordered variation in value orientations (basic values), and the consequent development of the ideas of the *variant pattern* and *variant personality*, is derived more from the field of cultural anthropology than from the works of the sociologists who have had a primary interest in differentiation and deviation. This is not to say that the cultural anthropologists have gone farther than the sociologists in analyzing the variations in the value systems of *specific* societies. As has been stated, the majority of their analyses of value systems have also been concentrated on only the dominant values.[44] However, because of wide-range differences in the value systems of the numerous societies the anthropologists have studied, the idea of variation in values is clearly emergent in the field as a whole. It has also been these anthropologists, most of whom were mentioned earlier, who have given to social science the clearest conception of the high degree of integration in the patterning of the various activities in a society and the nature of the configurating principles making for that integration. Moreover, because of their "holistic" approach to the study of culture they have been able to show that these thematic principles do not relate just to aspects of the man-man relationships and are not, as Sheldon has remarked, "specifically situational."[45]

Although there is a fairly large area of overlap in the phenomena studied through these two aproaches, and even some conceptual congruity, they have not as yet been well integrated or even articulated. Evidence for this statement is found in the prevalent confusion over what is cultural as opposed to social or vice versa. Still unresolved, this confusion is frequently glossed over by the use of the term socio-cultural with full awareness that the hyphen is no symbol of integration.

Perhaps at this stage of development in the social sciences there is no compelling need that the two traditions be integrated. Some have argued

---

[42] Neal Gross, Ward S. Mason, and Alexander W. McEachern, *Explorations in Role Analysis* (New York: John Wiley & Sons, 1958), p. 321.
[43] *Ibid.*, p. 30 and p. 73.
[44] Variability in the observable patterning of cultures—one type of which would be role patterns—has, of course, been emphasized by a number of anthropologists. Clyde Kluckhohn, for example, has classified patterns as *preferred, alternative,* and *restricted.* All of these types he places at the "ideal level" of patterning; hence he does not regard them as mere alterations or elaborations at the behavioral level. He uses another classification for behavioral patterns. Thus, he clearly sees role patterns as having considerable variability. Moreover, he stresses the importance of biological differences as one of the bases of a necessary variation. See "Patterning as Exemplified in Navaho Culture" in *Language, Culture, and Personality,* ed. Leslie Spier, A. I. Hallowell, and S. S. Newman (Menasha, Wis.: Sapir Memorial Publication Fund, 1941), pp. 109–30.
[45] See "Some Observations on Theory in the Social Sciences" in *Toward a General Theory of Action,* p. 41.

that premature efforts to interrelate them may seriously curtail developments in each.[46] However, partial integration, or articulation at least, is certainly necessary if we are not to fall an easy prey to what Whitehead called the Fallacy of Misplaced Concreteness and are not also to have our studies of human behavior made sterile because of a too exclusive concern with different aspects of it considered discretely and separately, almost as if in a conceptual vacuum. The concept of role offers a means of effecting this articulation, providing it is sufficiently reconceptualized to take account of systematic variation.

It is in accord with the theory of variation in value orientations to view roles as flexibly variable to the extent that they reflect not simply *dominant* values but a *rank order of value orientations*. It will be remembered that when we spoke of the academic intellectual as being variant in some or all of his value orientations we used the qualification of "almost always." Although it is to be expected that most teachers, scholars, scientists, and writers in the United States will have a somewhat variant value system, there still are many who are as strongly oriented to the dominant American rank order of value orientations as the most typical of businessmen. And the reverse is also true; many successful as well as unsuccessful businessmen are as variant as the typical intellectual.

Moreover, it is never the case that the variant patterns are radically different. Constituted of the same components, the differences between them are simply those of a difference in the rank ordering of emphases upon the components. Translated into role theory this means that *roles, to the extent that they are determined by value orientations, are ordered into an interlocking network of the dominant and the variant for which the dominant rank ordering of value orientations is the integrating thread.*

This conceptualization of roles and role relationships makes it evident that there is a hitherto unrecognized complexity in the sociological principle of "strain toward consistency." This principle, which is much better termed as a tendency or trend toward consistency since the concept of strain is so often used to indicate factors which actually hamper integration, focuses attention upon dominant values and does not take into account the variant ones which help to support and sustain the dominant ones.

Our view of variation also calls into question the interpretation of stresses and strains as factors which have mainly a negative effect upon societal integration. Without denying either the existence or the significance of strains in social systems (it has already been pointed out, for example, that there are strains, many of them serious ones, which result from a "bad fit" in the dominant value orientations), it is suggested that the quite negative conception of strain has led to an oversimplification of the processes of integration. If one concerns one's self solely, or even pre-

---

[46] In a recent paper by Kroeber and Parsons—a paper which appeared after this chapter was written—there is an excellent statement of the need for the analytic distinctions between cultural and social systems. See Alfred L. Kroeber and Talcott Parsons, "The Concepts of Culture and of Social System," *American Sociological Review*, Vol. XXII, No. 5 (October, 1958).

dominantly, with the dominant values of a system, it is inevitable that the strains these values generate (and there is no system without strains) and the variant patterns utilized to alleviate them will be viewed as disruptive elements. The *positive* functional values of the variant patterns are not emphasized. The theory of variations in value orientations gives to the variant patterns a quite different status. Although they, and the variant individuals who follow them, are always potential sources of change—a fact which we shall discuss in more detail below—their primary function is seen as that of the maintenance of the system. Both because of the variety of activities needed to keep any society in a state of equilibrium and the fact of differences in the abilities and interests of individuals, there is built into every system a quite wide-range acceptance of variant patterns. These are, to be sure, much less elaborated than the patterns which express dominant values, but they are nonetheless essential; and, as will be shown in the discussion of cultural change, a main indication of basic change, as opposed to change which is simply pattern elaboration of *same* values, is the increase of elaboration of the patterning in one behavior sphere and the concomitant decrease in the elaboration of patterning in another.

This conceptualization, when applied specifically to role patterns, provides the means for extensions in the analysis of the processes of conformity and deviation, especially the latter. As has been stated, the process of deviation and the deviant personality have held a central place in the studies of many sociologists and psychologists. To some extent anthropologists have also concerned themselves with deviation. The most general use of the concept is for the designation of behavior which seriously transgresses the type of moral norms which are essential to the stability of all societies. Deviant persons of this kind are the "social outlaws," and they are both found in all societies and negatively sanctioned in all of them. Certainly some special category is needed for persons of this type, but other highly profitable uses of the term "deviant" make it questionable that this is the right term for the outlaws. Mainly, we refer to the use of the concept of deviant for the classification of all the individuals who show, in varying ways, that they have rejected or altered the patterns of behavior expected of them by the particular groups of which they are members.

This and other more purely psychological conceptions of deviation stress the "going away" aspect of the deviation process. To use Parsons' term, the individual "alienates" himself from the role expectations of the social system or subsystem of which he is a member. Also, there is a fairly general tendency in the classifications of deviant persons to concentrate upon aspects of the psychological motivation for deviation. Often these have a "system reference" in that the motivation is formulated relative to either the goals or means in the role expectations the individual is rejecting. Merton's "rebellion" and "retreatism" as types of deviant behavior are examples. But this kind of system reference is only the *negative* one of a rejection of some or all the values in a system or subsystem.

There are new dimensions to be added to both the analysis of the deviating process and the motivations of deviant persons if these are seen as relative to a value system in which there is *ordered variation*. First, it is to be recognized that the deviating person who has "moved away" from one role or set of roles has "moved toward" others, which are usually recognized to be more or less acceptable alternatives. The concept of variation captures the "going toward" half of the process which the term deviation with its explicit connotation of "away from" cannot include. It becomes necessary, of course, to analyze and classify variant roles for their degree of acceptability or requiredness. But sometimes it is not even a variant but rather a dominant role the deviating individual moves toward. This is the case of the person who deviates from a variantly oriented group to a dominantly oriented one. Many of the socially mobile persons in American culture illustrate well this kind of movement.

Thus, deviation as a process is relative to the interlocking network of dominant and variant roles. This conception of the process makes it possible to study the deviating individual as a part of the system in another sense than the negative one of having rejected, rebelled against, or in any other way withdrawn from roles expressing a given order of values. His behavior can be analyzed relative to the role network into which he has moved as well as the one he has withdrawn from. It is of the utmost importance to have the concepts of variant role and variantly oriented person for the very many deviants who function successfully in acceptable alternative roles which are not at all deviant from the sociological point of view.

Many of the more positive effects of deviation for a society, and its significance for social change as well, are also much more easily analyzed and better understood when both the "going toward" aspect of the deviation process and the variation which is the goal of this movement are taken into account. And, strictly from the individual point of view, it is to be expected that in the motivation for deviation there is a value element which derives from the individual's own rank order of value orientations, or possibly his conflicting rank-order patterns. We suggest that the "anticipatory response" and the "positive orientation to nonmembership groups" cited by Merton and Kitt as important for the understanding of the deviation process are in some large part based upon variations in the individual's rank order of value orientations.

These suggestions are, of course, very general. Before the full implications of the theory of variation for the study of social roles can be shown, there must be, as has already been indicated, some refinement and expansion in the categories for the classification of roles. One suggestion is that the formal role system of a society—both the dominant and variant formal roles—be classified according to the criteria of generality and specificity and that the levels of generality be designated. The general-specific distinction has previously been defined as the distinction between that part of a person's role which is general to many different role relations—one's age, sex, or class role, for example—and the part which is specific to a particular role interaction situation.[47] The question of the level, or degree,

[47] "The Participant-Observer Technique in Small Communities," *American Journal of Sociology*, Vol. XLVI, No. 3 (November, 1940), p. 332.

of generality is one of the pervasiveness of the general referent for role allocation. Age and sex as points of allocative reference are, for example, more general and pervasive than that of class position, and in turn class or caste position is a more general allocative referent than is a behavior sphere.[48]

A classification of informal roles and methods of interrelating them to the formal roles must also be developed if the full implications of the theory of variation are to be realized. In spite of the great interest in informal roles shown by many analysts of small groups of different kinds and of industrial relations, there has not as yet been developed a classification which defines types of informal roles or a theory which relates them systematically to the intra-system variations which arise, in some part at least, because of the strains created by the dominant value orientations.

The suggestions we offer here for such developments derive mainly from the ideas of Spiegel who, through his psychoanalytic therapy, has become intensely interested in the importance to personality development of the roles "assumed" and "assigned" in the interaction process which are not formally defined and frequently are not even explicitly recognized. Many of these roles are, he states, an interactional interpretation of what the psychologists normally call "character traits." A few examples are "the exhibitionist," "the failure," "the hero," "the fool." But there are many other types than these. For example, there is the role of a morally "bad girl" which a child assumes because of having been *implicitly* assigned this role over a long period of time by a mother who *explicitly* preaches the strictest of moral standards. This is not to say that these are not traits or should not be so considered from other points of view. It is only pointing to the facts that the individual, in the process of his socialization, acquires the traits in some large part in his interaction with others and that interaction means the playing of roles by one person vis-à-vis another.[49]

Spiegel, in addition to making the distinction between the implicit and explicit nature of the informal roles, and in pointing to the great significance of the character roles, has developed a still more refined classification. His categories as thus far defined specify two types of informal roles

---

[48] A classification scheme developed by Florence R. Kluckhohn, denoting the kinds and the levels of generality of formal roles, is in a manuscript of the Spiegel-Kluckhohn project of the Harvard University Laboratory of Social Relations which will be published in the near future. The classification owes much to Linton's designation of the invariant points of reference—age, sex, biological relatedness, caste, class—but is an extension to include the general roles of the behavior spheres and an ordering to specify both the levels of generality and the degrees of differentiation in varying types of cultures.

[49] Many interesting ideas about roles of this kind and the interaction process leading to their assumption are found in Norman Cameron, *The Psychology of Behavior Disorders* (Boston: Houghton Mifflin Co., 1947).

Rich material for the analysis of implicitly assigned roles is also found in the following papers even though the concept of role is not explicitly used in the discussions: Adelaide Johnson and S. A. Szurek, "Etiology of Antisocial Behavior in Delinquents and Psychopaths," *Journal of American Medical Association*, Vol. CLIV, (March 6, 1954), pp. 814–17; and Adelaide Johnson, M. E. Giffin, and E. M. Litin, "Specific Factors Determining Antisocial Acting Out," *American Journal of Orthopsychiatry*, Vol. XXIV, No. 4 (October, 1954), pp. 668–84.

—the character roles and the transitional roles—and two types of fictive roles which he calls imaginary and mythological. He also has given attention to the techniques of "role induction" and "role modification" as these relate to the resolutions of role conflict. Still more recent work by Spiegel is concerned both with a classification of the varying methods of allocation of the different kinds of roles and the establishment of the relationships between the formal and informal roles.[50]

With these extensions and refinements in the classification of both formal and informal roles it becomes possible to treat much of the variation in values within a context of role interaction. And while there certainly will still be those who will object to the use of the role concept for the study of both the discrete and always somewhat unique personality of the individual, and also the ramifications of cultural patterning, it would seem apparent that the extensions suggested meet many of the objections raised in the past. Admittedly certain aspects of the individual personality will still be beyond the range of a role analysis and some kinds of culture patterns will continue to be much better formulated when they are abstracted from interaction processes. No single conceptual bridge can completely cover over the chasms which separate intellectual universes of discourse; but increasingly, one which has sound girders, as the role concept has, can be built into a stronger and wider means of communication between those universes. We believe that the theory of variation in value orientations, when it is used for analyses of interaction processes, compels a widening and strengthening of the concept of social role as a bridge concept.

VARIATIONS IN VALUE ORIENTATIONS AS A FACTOR IN CULTURAL CHANGE

The last of the topics to be considered relative to the postulated variations in value orientations is that of cultural change.[51] This subject is one about which many views have been advanced but little agreement reached. Watson, in a paper which is remarkable for its succinctness, states: "The accumulated literature on change is sizable, but there is as yet surprisingly little clarity as to the basic problems and approaches in the field."[52]

---

[50] See "The Social Roles of Doctor and Patient in Psycho-Analysis and Psychotherapy," *Psychiatry*, Vol. XVII, No. 4 (November, 1954), pp. 369–76; "The Resolution of Role Conflict within the Family," *Psychiatry*, Vol. XX, No. 1 (February, 1957), pp. 1–16; "Interpersonal Influences Within the Family," *Group Processes*, ed. Bertram Schaffner (New York: The Josiah Macy, Jr., Foundation, 1956); "Some Cultural Aspects of Transference and Countertransference," *Individual and Familial Dynamics*, ed. Jules H. Masserman (New York: Grune & Stratton, 1959); and "The Structure and Function of Social Roles in the Doctor-Patient Relationship," unpublished lectures delivered at Tulane University, October, 1958, for Annual Lectures in Psychiatry.

[51] A more extensive discussion of this subject may be found in Florence Rockwood Kluckhohn, "Some Reflections on the Nature of Cultural Integration and Cultural Change" in a volume to be published by the Free Press in 1961.

[52] James B. Watson, "Four Approaches to Culture Change: A Systematic Assessment," *Social Forces*, Vol. XXXII, No. 2 (December, 1953), pp. 137–45.

One distinction which Watson makes among the studies is that between Developmental and Causal-Correlational theories of cultural change. Of the former he writes:

> The Developmental interest would include studies which deal with the culture lag cycle or with social movements (revolutions, nativistic movements, etc.) as recurring developmental sequences, and would extend up through large-scale formulations like those of Sorokin, Spengler, or the cultural evolutionists. These examples obviously differ greatly as to scope, but all have a common concern with the "what" of culture change, with regularities of development. They attempt to formulate the repetitive character, whether cyclic or linear, of some class of behavior or culture through time....
> Developmental formulations lack any fundamental concern with causation.... [They] simply formulate a succession of behavioral or cultural events. Whether the criterion is form, function, or content, moreover, does not matter. A biological analogy is the devlopment of the individual, called maturation, and characterized by phases such as infancy, childhood, adolescence, and so on. The relationship among these events is not causal, though the occurrence of each event is necessary for the subsequent phase. Clearly, the Developmental formulation of maturation could scarely be held to consider causality. To put it another way; if one discovers cyclic or linear periodicity in a certain order of events, he need not question that the periodicity has its causes. But the facts sufficient to establish regular sequences of development in this sense do not often establish the nature of their various causes.[53]

Concerning the Causal-Correlational theories he remarks as follows:

> Turning to Causal-Correlational studies, we have a different theoretical interest, fundamentally concerned with causal interdependence and co-variation among events. The difference, moreover, is not only of a theoretical kind but is also operational. In the search for interdependent and co-variant events it is necessary to investigate facts "outside" of the order of data whose occurrence one is attempting to understand.
> Examples of Causal-Correlational problems run in scope all the way from small to large scale, as do Developmental problems. Of limited scope are formulations of the cultural impact of single small changes in environment or the precipitating factors in the occurrence of inventions. Such problems as the effect of revolution upon established religion, the causes of cultural disintegration, or the effects of "crisis" situations are of larger scope. Despite great differences of scope, however, the common problem is the causal nexus among antecedent events and consequent cultural forms, meanings, or functions.[54]

At the end of his article Watson makes this comment of comparison of the two approaches:

> ...although a Causal-Correlational interest is the more explicit and consciously pursued, more results have actually been achieved along the less recognized lines of the Developmental interest in limited possibilities. The ability to predict is no more a product of one than of the other approach.[55]

---

[53] *Ibid.*, p. 139.
[54] *Ibid.*, pp. 139–40.
[55] *Ibid.*, p. 145.

One conclusion to be drawn from this discussion is that while there is a need for, and a validity in, both kinds of theories they have not as yet been well related to each other.

The ideas advanced on the nature of variations in value orientations appear to afford the means of establishing some interrelations between these two kinds of theories. In the first instance the variation theory argues that a clear distinction should be made between changes which are more of the same thing—the pattern elaboration of a dominant value-orientation ordering—and basic changes which are changes in the value-orientation orderings themselves. This argument rests upon the thesis that value-orientation systems are an interlocking network of dominant and variant patterns and are not simply unitary systems of dominant orientations. A second point which is relevant to the study of cultural change concerns the function of the variant pattern and the variant individual. Many of the variant patterns required and permitted in societies arise because of the strains created by the dominant orientations; hence they have as their *primary* function the mitigation of these strains to the extent that the system can be maintained, often over a very long time period, without serious disruptions. But even though this be the primary function of the variant patterns, they and the variant individuals who follow them are always also a potential source of basic change. However, a "potential" is not "cause" in any simple and direct sense, and it is our thesis that only very rarely is a *basic* change in a culture solely the product of either the evolution—the unfolding—of the internal variations or the impact of an external force. On the contrary, we maintain that *basic change is usually, if not always, the result of the interplay of internal variations and external forces which are themselves variable.*

This view clearly offers a basis for some degree of an interrelation of the Developmental theories, all of which rest, in one way or another, upon the doctrine of immanent causation, and the Causal-Correlational theories which are, as the term implies, concerned primarily with the effects of forces which are considered to be external to the system in question. However, it is necessary that there be an elaboration in both kinds of theories to allow for the fact of ordered variation before the significant interrelationships between them can be determined. Briefly we shall state some of the problems which arise on both sides of the argument because of a failure to treat systematically the question of variation.

First, it cannot be denied that the Developmental theories of cultural change have been the more convincing the larger the canvases upon which they are drawn. The systems which the most prominent of these theories treat are so large, both in time and in space, that the question of variations within the system is made quite subsidiary to the unfolding process of the stages of development. Also, in most of these theories there is a definite blurring of the distinction between pattern elaboration (differentiation) and basic change up to the point that a new state of the system either has been or is about to be reached. When a basic change is noted it is usually treated as the inevitable consequence of the system containing within itself "the seeds of its own destruction." This is especially true of the theories which have been called the dialectical, the cyclical, the oscillating, and the undulating theories of change. All these theories enclose the forces of change so tightly within a single system that the only permitted logical argument is that the postulated stages of development—necessary growth—must more or less ineluctably follow one upon another. One may even argue that there is a basic characteristic in these theories which, in the language of Dewey and Bentley, would be called the prescientific theory of "Self-Action"—the view that things act under their own powers and hence neither the concept of interaction (causal interconnection) nor that of transaction is necessary for purposes of explanation.[56]

One fact which is certainly not to be overlooked in the use of the immanent causation idea, a fact which gives rise to real doubts as to its adequacy, is that it has been employed with almost equal success to demonstrate very differently conceived processes of change. There are even differences in the dialectical theories of Hegel and Marx, and these taken together are at variance with cyclical theories such as the one Spengler produced, and the cyclical theories, in turn, differ from the kind of theory of undulation which Sorokin has developed. Linear evolutionary theories provide us with still another variation in the use of the concept of immanent causation. The gamut of these variations in the ideas about internally produced processes of change tempts one to remark that while all may be right in some respects, it would take a mythological character who could be placed at the beginning and end of social time to say which one of them is the more right or the more wrong.

A majority of the Developmental theories also fail to give sufficient heed to the positive—the *maintaining*—functions of variant patterns. They emphasize too much, either implicitly or explicitly, the potential the variations have for the destruction of the system. As a consequence it becomes difficult to explain why certain predicted stages of change did not, or do not, occur. One may, for example, ask—as even Marx himself did before his death—what were the variations which either existed or were developed in bourgeois capitalistic societies, which so relieved the strains in them that the revolution that Marxian theory had so fervently urged and so certainly predicted did not occur.

Causal-Correlational theories err in the opposite direction. Many of them place too much stress upon the power of the external force selected as the main causal element in an *interaction* process and give far too little heed to the nature of the system—its stages of development and its kinds of variation upon which the external forces come to play. There are, for example, many current studies of the effect of Western industrialization upon folk societies which seem to rest upon the two assumptions that the industrial process is itself a universal process (which it is not) and that it will produce more or less universal effects everywhere. The term "underdeveloped country," now so commonly applied to these folk societies, has implicitly imbedded within it both of these assumptions.

[56] John Dewey and A. F. Bentley, *Knowing and the Known* (Boston: Beacon Press, 1949), p. 108.

Since the research of this volume is no more concerned with a detailed study of the vast and complicated subject of cultural change than with a highly refined elaboration of role theory, we shall confine the discussion of the implications of the variation theory for the analysis of the process of change and for the possible articulation of Developmental and Causal-Correlational theories of change to a few general propositions. The first and most fundamental of these have been mentioned—the distinction between pattern elaboration and basic change, the function of the variant pattern, and the definition of basic change as the product of the interplay of internal variation and external forces. Other propositions pertain to the degree of susceptibility to change which a given system, either in whole or in part, may have and to the different effects to be expected in variable types of the interplay of internal variations and external forces.

In the first instance, it is logical to assume that the better integrated a value-orientation system is, the greater will be its power of resistance to the effects of impinging forces. This is most especially true in cases of culture contact (the outside culture being considered as the impinging external force) where the power factor of actual conquest is not a critical issue. As stated above, anthropological studies have amply documented the fact that it is a common tendency of peoples to borrow actively, or accept passively, the ideas, the techniques, the art forms, and many another aspect of other cultures and then remold them in accord with their own basic value system. Our theory would argue that while this is generally true, it is the more likely, as a tendency, the greater is the degree of goodness of fit of the ordering of the several orientations in the total value-orientation system.

But since the evidence collected to date strongly points to the conclusion that it is rare indeed that the orientation orderings of a given value system are *perfectly* geared one to another, this important corollary proposition is suggested: The part or parts of a social system which are most susceptible to the development of a basic change in cultural values will be those in which there has been the greatest proliferation of variant patterns for the relief of strain. This is, of course, only a more specific statement of the general proposition that basic change occurs only, or usually, when the seeds of it, almost always located *outside* the system, fall upon the fertile soil which the variations *within* the system provide. But it points up two additional important facts. The first of these is that the several parts of a value-orientation system seldom change at the same rate. The second is that the persons who are the instigators of basic change—the innovators—are almost always the variants in the system.[57]

Not more than a generation ago the "Great Man" theory of cultural change was still much in evidence, and in the discussion of it there was,

---

[57] Cf. H. G. Barnett, *Innovation* (New York: McGraw-Hill Book Co., 1953). Although Barnett does not explicitly use a concept of variation as a theoretical tool, there is much in his study which fits easily with some of the ideas in our theory of ordered variation. On the point which is of immediate relevance, that is, the persons who most easily yield to the influences of external forces, see especially the discussion of "Acceptors and Rejectors" in Chap. XIV.

implicitly if not explicitly, always some expression of surprise that the man of the hour seemed always to be on the social horizon and ready to appear. It was for this reason that the emphasis was put upon the idiosyncratic character of the Great Man, the man who was so unusual and so different that he was *sui generis*. Little serious attention is given to this theory today, for even though the ideas of internal variation have not been developed to the extent we are urging, they have been well enough recognized to take the spell of mystery off the emergent leaders who so frequently arise to guide a society in different cultural directions in transition periods. Indeed, it can be argued that recently the expectation of the appearance of such leaders has been too much stressed, for there are far too many cases where the role the "affected variant" plays is mainly destructive and not at all creatively oriented to a new synthesis of value-orientation orderings. But whether the variant individual is constructively dedicated to a new synthesis or is, instead, a disruptive influence, he, too, can always be viewed as a product of the interrelationship of variations which are internal to the system and the external forces which come to play upon the system.

These interrelations are, of course, variable. In attempting to make predictions about rates and kinds of basic changes one must give consideration to the degree of goodness of fit between the internal variation and the external force. We have already mentioned this need relative to the question of the rate and degree of assimilation of the ethnic minorities in the United States. Speaking now very generally, the problem is that of distinguishing the differences in both the internal variations and the external forces and then developing hypotheses which will take into account the variable effects which arise between the two situations of *differing* external forces playing upon the *same*, or similar, kinds of internal variations and *same*, or similar, external forces playing upon *different* kinds of internal variations. This is most especially true when the external force which is potentially creative of providing the seeds of a basic change is the impact of another culture—another value system.

When this is the case we need a still greater refinement of the general distinction between *same* and *differing* forces, internal and external, for these terms gloss over the question of the rank orderings of the value orientations in the value systems of both the society which is the encroacher and the one which is encroached upon. It may be, as in the case of the Spanish-American or Italian-American culture, that the orderings of all their value orientations, at the time of their initial contact with dominant middle-class American culture, were so radically different that they were a perfect, or a near perfect, mirror image of it. Or it may be, as will be illustrated in the case of the Navaho group which is discussed in Chapter IX, that while the orderings of some of the orientations are the reverse of those of dominant middle-class American culture (the impinging culture), other preferences are closer together in that the orientation preference which is first in the Navaho value system is second in the Anglo-American one. Finally, there is one orientation in which the ordering is the same in both the Navaho and American systems.

Relative to this problem of the goodness of fit in the orderings of orientation alternatives—a problem which introduces a kind of complexity in the analysis of change which both Developmental and Causal-Correlational theories have tended to bypass—there are these two general propositions. First, it is hypothesized that when put under the dominating pressure of another culture which is not so excessive as to demand sudden change, the impinged-upon societies which have radically different orientation orderings will shift first either their second and third-order value-orientation preferences or their first and second-order ones. Second, we would predict that whenever the pressures are strong enough to prevent this "logical" type of shift and make fairly imperative demands for a shift from a strong first-order preference to a weak third-order one, there will be far more disorganization in the system, both socially and personally, than will occur in the slower, step-wise, kind of change. Both of these hypotheses must, of course, be held within the frame of the hypotheses stated previously concerning the general degree of resistance to change which the whole or the parts of a culture will have because of the way in which their own orientation orderings are geared one to another.

Several still more specific hypotheses can be made, but since these would require a detail of treatment of the differences in the orderings of the orientations of the specific societies which come to influence each other which this discussion does not warrant, we shall give only one illustration. If it is the case that a society which is either Lineally or Collaterally first order on the *relational* orientation and is given also to first-order preferences for the Present, the Being, and the Subjugated-to-Nature alternatives comes strongly under the pressure of a society such as middle-class American culture in which the dominant orientations are Individualism, Future, Doing, and Over-Nature, it should be found that the most serious problems of adjustment in the subordinate culture will arise when there is a too rapid shift on the *relational* orientation. The tremendous problem of cognitively grasping the knowledge of the means for the implementation of the goals which the attempted shift—often little more than lip service—to the Future, the Doing, and the Over-Nature positions makes tantalizingly attractive creates so many potentials for failure that a supportive *relational* structure is badly needed.

As has been stated in the Preface to this study, it was not possible in the field research program which was planned and executed in the summer of 1951 to go far in the testing for the indications of the intra-cultural variations upon which these discussions of variations in roles of cultural integration and culture change depend. Both the field method developed and the statistical methods utilized for the analysis of the data it yielded were necessarily focused primarily upon *cross-cultural* as opposed to *intra-cultural* variations, and, in addition, the instrument used allowed for few conclusions about the changes through time. Except for the one question on the *relational* orientation items posed for the Spanish-Americans (see Chapter III) the field instrument was time bound to the year of testing, the year 1951. Also, because of the limitations on the number of items which could be used in a single interview session, we were not able to test systematically for the intra-cultural variations in the several behavior spheres. The evidence of intra-cultural variations and variations through time which did appear in our data will be set forth in Chapter V, but it will be left mainly to the authors of the chapters on the individual cultures both to interpret these data and to extend the analysis of the significance of intra-cultural variations.

CHAPTER II

The Five Communities

Five communities in the American Southwest were used for the first testing of the value-orientation theory.[1] Although all five communities are within the United States and members of all of them are now voting citizens of the country, the cultural distinctions between four of the groups are marked. Two of the populations are American Indian—one an off-reservation settlement of Navaho Indians whom we shall call the Rimrock Navaho, the other the Pueblo Indian community of Zuni. The third is a Spanish-American village which we have named Atrisco. A Mormon village and a recently established farming village of Texan and Oklahoman homesteaders, for which the names Rimrock and Homestead will be used, are the other two communities. Even though somewhat distinct culturally, these two English-speaking groups are much more similar than any of the others are either to them or to each other.

The pueblo of Zuni with approximately three thousand inhabitants was the largest group; the Spanish-American village, which had declined in population to fifty-odd inhabitants by 1951, was the smallest. All five communities are in the same geographical area, and no one of them is more than fifty miles from any other. Map II:1 was drawn to show both the geographical proximity of the communities and the approximate size and settlement pattern of each of them.[2]

GENERAL CHARACTERISTICS OF THE NATURAL ENVIRONMENT

It was our good fortune to be able to carry out the testing operations in an area where the cultural variations, with the exception of those between the Mormon and Texan groups, are markedly distinct while those of the

---

[1] The five communities are those which for five years were the research ground for the project of the Harvard University Laboratory of Social Relations, called the Comparative Study of Values in Five Cultures (usually referred to as the Values Project). Most of the communities had also been intensively studied by social scientists prior to the investigations of the Values Project. The names used for these communities in this monograph are all fictitious with the exception of the pueblo Zuni. Since there is only one community of Zuni Indians, it is not possible to make a name substitution in this case.

[2] This map and the one which shows the major physiographic features of the area were drawn by Herbert R. Harvey who was a research assistant on the Values Project in the academic year 1952–53.

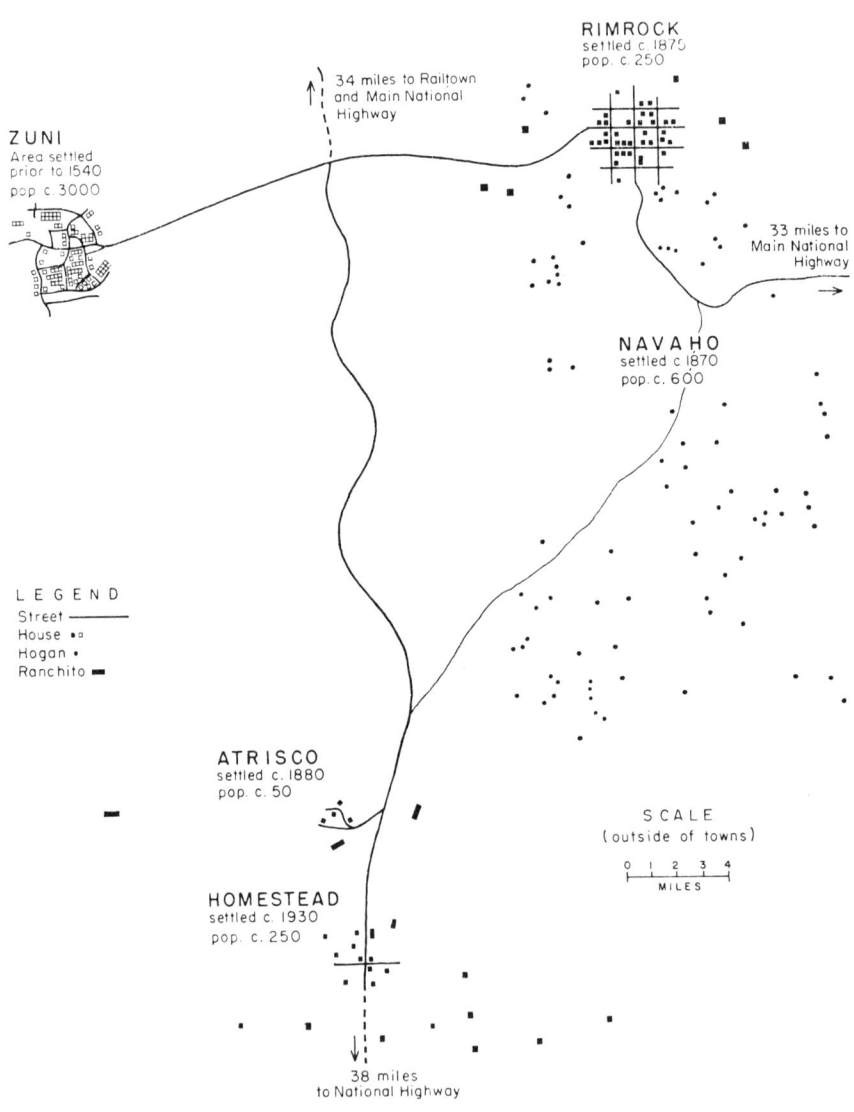

MAP II:1
RIMROCK AREA: PATTERNS OF SETTLEMENT

physical environment from community to community are slight.³ The only difference of great significance in the natural environment of the five communities is the availability of a water supply for home use and for farming and stock raising. The pueblo of Zuni and the Mormon village of Rimrock both have artificial lakes which provide water for some irrigation of fields and gardens except in years of serious drought. Atrisco, the Spanish-American village, once, many years ago, also had small dams to catch water in arroyos (gulches), but these washed away easily, and no effort was made to restore and improve them. The problem of a water supply has always been extremely serious for this community. It has been an equally troublesome one for the Navaho group until very recently when wells were drilled and pit tanks dug with funds provided by the United States government. The people of Homestead must depend almost entirely upon wells for household consumption. For many years a majority of the families of Homestead had to rely upon a single community well which was located in the village center, a center that is several miles distant from many of the individual farms. And the community does not have any stable water supply for agricultural purposes.

The total area in which the five communities are distributed, as if to form a large letter **T**, covers some two thousand square miles in what physiographers describe as the Datil section of the Colorado Plateau province. But while called plateau country, it is not at all a level tableland, and it abounds in diverse features of volcanic origin. Mindeleff partly pictures the area when he states:

> The plateau region is not, as the name might imply, a smooth and level country; on the contrary, it is extremely rugged and broken, and travel is more difficult than in many mountain districts. It is a land of cliffs and canyons, often of great magnitude and often abundant, forming serious obstacles to wagon travel in any direction. The whole surface, apparently smooth and level, is composed of platforms or mesas. There are mesas everywhere; it is mesa country. The flat tops of the plateaus are cut and seamed by gorges and narrow canyons, often impassable to a horse....⁴

To the aesthetically minded this region, the main features of which are shown in Map II:2, has an awesome magnificence. The sandstone mesas, some vast and high and others small, have a chiseled sheerness of line and a vividness of color which have been captured by few if any of the many painters who have felt their challenge. Red is the predominant color of the mesas, but it is of many shades and often is alternated with white streaks which give to particular mesas the look of peppermint candy mountains. The rare atmosphere typical of arid and semiarid lands, but especially

---

³ Many sources have been used for this summary treatment of the environment. Recent publications which deal specifically with the area are John L. Landgraf, *Land-Use in the Ramah Area of New Mexico*, Papers of the Peabody Museum, Harvard University, Vol. XII, No. 1 (1954); and Evon Z. Vogt, *Modern Homesteaders* (Cambridge, Mass.: Harvard University Press, 1955), Chap. I. Among the older sources of information the one most often referred to is Nevin M. Fenneman, *Physiography of the Western United States* (New York: McGraw-Hill Book Co., 1931).

⁴ Cosmos Mindeleff, "The Influence of Geographic Environment," *Bulletin of the American Geographical Society*, Vol. XXIX, No. 1 (1897), p. 2.

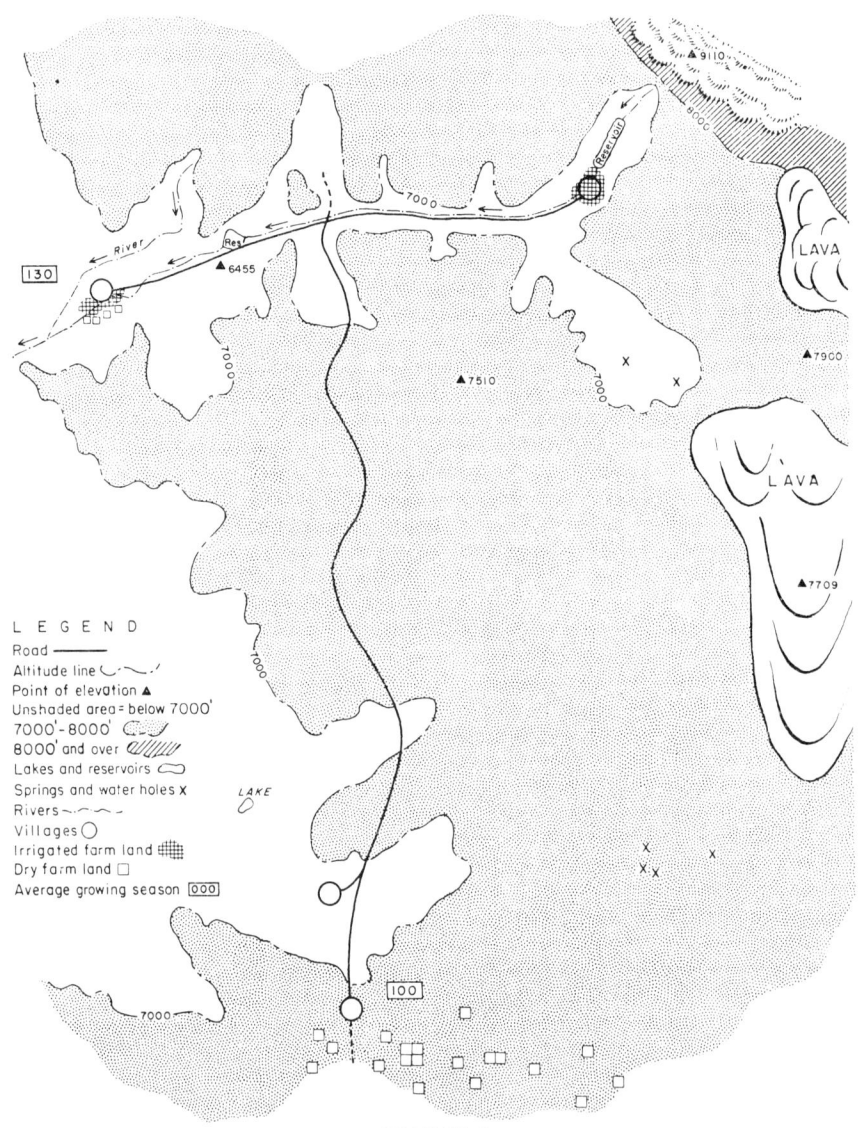

MAP II:2
RIMROCK AREA: PHYSIOGRAPHY

luminous in this country, brings ever-changing lights and shadows which can so quickly change both the scene and the feeling-mood of the observer that what one may think he sees and wishes to portray at one moment is gone in the next. Then, too, there is an intense blueness of sky and a whiteness and magnitude of cumulus clouds which on the size of canvas an artist can use seem unreal, or even garish.

The mountain slopes, the canyon floors, the valleys, and the bottom lands which lie below and between the often bizarrely eroded uplifts, ridges, and canyon walls each has its own type of beauty. Some of the slopes of the mountains, both steep and gradually inclining ones, are forested with ancient ponderosa pines and scrub oaks, which in the autumn have leaves of a deep red. The canyon floors and the larger valleys vary greatly in width and length and vary also in the vegetation they support. Many a long sweeping area has little vegetation on it except sparse desert grasses and exotic desert flowers which dot the already colorful earth with still brighter colors when the summer rains come. Other more rolling expanses are studded with scrub piñon, juniper, and red cedar trees. And here and there throughout the region great patches of sagebrush give the landscape a color tone of frosty green.

Another feature common to some parts of the area is the dark-hued ash of time-forgotten lava flows. The effect of this Fenneman describes in these words: "It [the lava] is scattered about in an irregular way as if the molten stuff had been dashed from a titanic bucket, and lies like inky blots over the brilliantly colored soils and clays."[5]

Magnificence and beauty are almost anywhere one chooses to look, but like many another area of scenic grandeur this one is a harsh environment for those who must obtain their living from it. The rugged terrain makes for great difficulty in travel. Even today, when there have been some marked improvements in two of the main roads of the region, one does not easily move to and fro within the region or in and out of it. Travel is especially hazardous when heavy rains dissolve the earth of many roads into treacherous mud and block off others by filling the innumerable arroyos and washes with water to such depths that they cannot be crossed. Heavy winter snows often create equally bad road conditions. Being stuck in the mud, blocked by snow, or delayed for hours or even a day or more while one waits for the water in canyons or arroyos to recede are the all too common experiences of all persons who try to travel about the Rimrock area in either summer or winter.

But the vicissitudes for travel are minor matters when compared to the problems created for farming activities by the lack of water, the violence of storms, and the shortness of the growing season. The soils of the valleys and bottom lands are fertile for the most part, but a small and highly seasonable rainfall and an altitude which in few places is less than seven thousand feet make the raising of some products impossible and the raising of any products dubious except in areas where irrigation can be practiced.

[5] *Op. cit.*, p. 318.

Although over a twenty-eight year period there have been variations between eight and twenty-three inches of rain annually, the average for the area is slightly less than fourteen inches. Even this figure is misleading, because much of the rainfall in the summer months is in the form of extremely violent storms. The water falls in such torrents over such a short period of time that only a fraction of it can be absorbed by the soil. It runs off either in arroyos which storms of the past have cut into the earth or in new arroyos which its own force creates. It often happens that an entire month's rainfall comes in a single twenty-four hour period. For crops this is infinitely more harmful than beneficial. Also, the localness of the storms is such that not infrequently one field is drenched while a field adjacent to it receives no rain at all. Winter snowstorms, too, are often sudden, heavy, and erratic, and, like the rainstorms, they vary considerably from year to year in the amount of precipitation they provide. Drought occurs at least three years out of every ten.

Add to these uncertainties the wide range of temperature fluctuations, and one can easily understand why both farming and stock raising, the two chief economic enterprises of the region, are always something of a gambler's game. The mean temperature of the region is given as 52.7 degrees Fahrenheit, but the common extremes are a high of 95 degrees summer heat and a low of minus-30 degrees winter cold. Record extremes are 116 degrees and a minus-48 degrees. Moreover, the arrival of killing frosts is almost as unpredictable as the rainfall. Although the average growing season over the years has been 120 days, the variations range between 82 and 169 days.

Dry farming, which the Texans of Homestead have attempted as their basic enterprise, is the most precarious of the agricultural pursuits. Because of the short and uncertain growing season and the small rainfall, dry farming is a venture of high risk taking in any part of the Rimrock area. Other groups than the Texans have attempted it but only as a minor or subsidiary activity. The most consistently successful farming is the limited amount of irrigation farming which the Mormon and Zuni communities have developed. But even these two communities engage extensively in the raising of sheep and cattle. The whole of the Rimrock region is best suited to stock raising. While it is true that the grasses are sparse, so sparse that one must allow at least sixty acres for the grazing of one head of cattle, the land area is sufficiently extensive to support many animals. However, even for this industry, the lack of water and the violence of the storms are constant hazards. There are only two small streams in the whole area, and natural water holes or drainage areas suitable for damming are few and far between. In years of drought even these go dry. Although the recently developed "pit tanks" have improved the general situation, they cannot be depended upon to hold much water in very dry years. Wells are the best solution but also the most expensive since the water table is so very far beneath the earth's surface. Seldom indeed is water found with less than a three-hundred foot drilling, and often the drilling shaft must be sunk eight hundred to one thousand feet. Even when grass and water are both available the livestock may not be safe. Along may come a winter storm approximating the magnitude of the one in 1931, which now has the almost legendary title of the Big Snow, and all possible natural livestock food will be covered to such a depth that herds are badly decimated or totally destroyed within a short time unless supplementary food such as cottonseed cake can be supplied to them. All of these conditions are more or less common to the total area.

BRIEF HISTORICAL SKETCHES OF THE FIVE COMMUNITIES[6]

The Zuni

The oldest of the populations now found in the Rimrock area is that of Zuni. Documentary evidence indicates that when the Spanish conquistadores and missionaries came into the Southwest in 1539 and 1540 they found six large Zuni pueblos, each of them politically independent, in the area. Today there is but the one major Zuni settlement, which consists of a central pueblo of adobe or stone buildings near the banks of the small Zuni River, and several small farming communities in other parts of the reservation allotted to the Zuni by the United States government. This reservation, which contains a total of 442,520 acres, has a high percentage of land suitable for stock raising and several thousand acres which can be farmed. One report states that 387,000 acres are suitable for grazing, some 1300 acres for dry farming, and 2700 acres for irrigation farming.[7]

Farming activities were a part of aboriginal Zuni culture, but stock raising was not known until after the conquest-minded Spaniards brought sheep and horses into the Southwest. At the present time the income derived from both dry and irrigation farming is inconsequential compared to that obtained from the thousands of sheep and the much smaller numbers of cattle, swine, and poultry which Zuni families own. But not even stock raising can be called the main industry at the present time. The income realized from silversmithing and other handicrafts dwarfs that obtained from any other single source. Of the total income of $410,000 estimated for the year 1951 over half was derived from these crafts. Wage work also figures prominently in the income of some families.

---

[6] The immediate sources for these sketches were a summary of the five groups prepared by Herbert R. Harvey and a draft of a chapter prepared by Evon Z. Vogt and John M. Roberts for the forthcoming volume of the Values Project to be called *The Peoples of Rimrock*. The unpublished doctoral dissertation of Florence Kluckhohn and chapters prepared for *The Peoples of Rimrock* by Clyde Kluckhohn, Robert Bellah, and Evon Vogt were also used as references for many details. Other sources are too numerous to cite. Detailed bibliographical references will be given in the discussions of the five communities in the Values Project volume. Many specific references will also be found in the later chapters of the present volume which treat individually the cultures of the five communities.

[7] Marion St. John, "Three Southwestern Non-Anglo Economies," unpublished report on file in the office of the Values Project, Laboratory of Social Relations, Harvard University. Permission to quote from this report was granted by the director of the project.

But even though there have been these changes in the economy and other changes of equal significance, the cycle of life in this tightly knit and quite distinctive subculture is still primarily oriented to agricultural pursuits. The most active periods of work are the spring, when the fields and gardens must be planted and the sheep sheared, and the fall, when there comes first the harvesting of crops and later the marketing of lambs. In the seasons in between, the Zuni devote an enormous amount of their time to the greatly elaborated and magnificent ceremonials which are the most widely known aspect of their culture. And in these ceremonials many, even most, of the basic themes relate to agriculture. There is, for example, a whole priesthood devoted solely to rain making, and the high priest of the total religious hierarchy is the Sun Priest or *pekwin*. Just how long this age-old ritual emphasis will remain is the major question in the analysis of changing Zuni culture. It is becoming more difficult each year to fill ceremonial positions. Very recently it has been reported that no one, at least no qualified person, can be persuaded to assume the duties of the now unoccupied position of *pekwin*. And generally one notes that the elaboration of patterning of ceremonial activities is decreasing and that of the economic sphere of life increasing.

The most important economic and social unit in Zuni is the extended family, which is matrilineal in descent and predominantly matrilocal in its residence pattern. Today there are both patrilocal and neolocal patterns of residence, but typically, still, the household consists of several nuclear families, each often assigned to a separate room, which by lineage are usually dominated by the eldest woman of the matrilineage and in day-to-day affairs often governed by her husband. Matrilineal clan organizations are a further elaboration and extension of this matrilineally oriented social structure.

Prior to the Spanish conquest the Zuni had no governing body separate from the intricately organized ceremonial structure. Today there is a civil government composed of a governor, lieutenant governor, and council. Not the least of the functions of this body is the arbitration and settlement of the many disputes which arise over matters of inheritance, factional decisions, use of land, and more purely personal matters. For while the Zuni have been described by some as a harmonious and group-centered people, there is, beneath the surface of what Benedict has called their Apollonian culture,[8] considerable strife and friction. Cushing years ago described in detail some of the types of arguments and disputes which were common,[9] and recently Smith and Roberts in the study cited in Chapter I, have provided an extensive documentation of them. Even the marriages of the Zuni, theoretically strictly monogamous ones, are so easily and so often dissolved by divorce that many students of the culture describe the marriage system as "brittle monogamy." There would indeed appear to be much variation in Zuni culture, both at the present time and in times past.

[8] Ruth Benedict, *Patterns of Culture* (Boston: Houghton Mifflin Co., 1934).
[9] Frank Hamilton Cushing, *Zuni Breadstuff* (New York: Museum of the American Indian, Heye Foundation, 1920).

One may speculate that the present community, just a single group of what once was several groups, is highly involuted, and hence has contained within itself the variations which in other societies would be found as the minor variations between their various representative populations.

The Rimrock Navaho

Navaho Indians are a more recent population of the Southwest than are the Zuni or other Pueblo Indians. The dates estimated as the time of their arrival range from A.D. 1000 to 1500, the latter being as yet the earliest date ascribable to a Navaho Indian site by the evidence of tree-ring analyses.

In the Rimrock area there was no sizable permanent settlement of Navaho Indians until after the return from what they themselves call "The Long Walk into Captivity" to Fort Sumner. However, the area was not unknown, for in addition to the few families who had lived there prior to the time the Navaho were subdued and sent into exile, there were others who had used it both for hunting and for the planting of small fields. Thus, it is perhaps not surprising that after the return from captivity in 1868 a number of Navaho families chose to settle in the Rimrock region rather than go onto the reservation allotted to them by the United States government.

The small group to make this decision settled first in the well watered valley which we are calling the Rimrock Valley, but they were not allowed to remain there long. The Mormons, who began the building of a permanent community in the eighties, gradually pushed the Navaho back into the less productive lava lands south and east of the Rimrock Valley. The land area the Navaho group now controls amounts to approximately 230 square miles. All of it is either owned or leased, for there has never been any provision of a reservation for Navaho in this region. The southernmost edge of the great Navaho reservation is some fifty miles north of Rimrock.

Very little of the total area the group controls is suitable for agriculture, and none of it is irrigable land. In 1951 approximately 1000 acres were under cultivation, mostly for maize and other cereal products but to some small extent for vegetables and forage. At least 1500 acres of the area are barren and desolate wasteland. Some 125,000 acres are used for the grazing of livestock, mostly sheep, but there is nothing uniform about the livestock business from family to family. Forty-four per cent of the families in 1951 owned no sheep at all, one family owned 9 per cent of the total, and six other families owned from 4 to 6 per cent. In contrast to the Zuni the major source of income for the group as a whole is livestock, but because of this uneven distribution of the herds, it is the wage work, amounting to some $30,000 in 1951, which is the most important source of income for a majority of the families.[10]

---

[10] St. John, *op. cit.* These figures collected by St. John were taken in large part from the detailed data collected by Clyde Kluckhohn and his collaborators.

The Rimrock Navaho Indians do not live in a village-type settlement. Instead they are scattered out over a wide area, as Map II:1 indicates, and the traditional form of dwelling is the one room, six-sided hogan constituted of piñon, juniper, or pine logs, with one door over which usually a blanket hangs, today sometimes a window or two but traditionally none, and a center ceiling smoke hole to carry off the fumes from fires and to provide ventilation. The floor space of these hogans should be round (but today is not always so) as a symbol of the sun, and the fire which is traditionally built in the middle of the floor represents a captured portion of the sun's light and heat.

A single nuclear family usually occupies a particular hogan, and sometimes one finds a nuclear family living alone in isolation from its relatives. The more common pattern is the clustering of a group of two or more hogans which house the members of related nuclear families that form an extended family. Sometimes these are the families of two women, often sisters married to one man, for this is a society where polygyny, and most especially sororal polygyny, is not infrequent. But in other cases, and more typically, the extended family of this group, which like the Zuni reckons its descent matrilineally, is that of "an older woman with her husband and unmarried children, together with her married daughters and their husbands and unmarried children."[11]

A still more inclusive unit of the social organization is that which Clyde Kluckhohn has named "the outfit." This is a group of relatives, characteristically more distantly related than the members of an extended family, who regularly cooperate for certain purposes. The members of an "outfit," in contrast to those of an extended family, are often scattered over an area of many square miles. A matrilineal clan organization crosscuts all these units. Through it ties are maintained with family members still more distantly related than those of either the extended family or the outfit.

At present there is also an overall organization, mainly political, called the "Chapter," in which problems of the group as a whole are discussed. The community also has an elected delegate to represent it in the Navaho Tribal Council which meets on the Navaho reservation.

Ceremonialism, as in the Zuni case, has been the most striking and the most highly elaborated feature of Navaho culture. But there are great differences in the conception and use of ceremony between the two groups. Navaho rituals are predominantly curing ceremonies, and otherwise have to do with the day-to-day problems of living and the warding off of disaster. Unity of the total community, which is so prominent a feature of Zuni ritual, is secondary in Navaho ceremonialism. The greater concern, in most of the ceremonies, is the health and well-being of the members of the ramified family groupings.

Of all the groups in the Rimrock area the Navaho one is the least well off economically and also the one of lowest social prestige. There are many changes occurring in the group. As in the Zuni case, the most important of

[11] Clyde Kluckhohn and Dorothea Leighton, *The Navaho* (Cambridge, Mass.: Harvard University Press, 1946), p. 56.

these are in the ceremonial sphere where pattern elaboration is decreasing. But while there is, as is also true of the Zuni, something of a concomitant increase in the economic and technological areas, one wonders whether the final outcome will be a basic cultural change or the kind of cultural disintegration which will leave the group socially stranded in a truly marginal position.

The Spanish-Americans of Atrisco

Although invading Spaniards saw the Rimrock region as early as 1539 and 1540 and other Spaniards knew it at later dates as well, there was no Spanish settlement in it until after the United States had taken over New Mexico and Arizona and eliminated the dangers of raids from the Navaho and Apache Indians. Even the hostility of the Zuni, whom the Spaniards never really subjugated, except nominally at various times, was a factor militating against their settlement of the area.

The Spanish-speaking people who did finally move in, mainly in the period between 1865 and 1900, to establish village-type communities were not the Spanish conquistadores of the past. They were instead the descendants of the predominantly *mestizo* population which for generations had been struggling for existence in the poorly protected and much neglected northernmost province of Spain's New World empire.

Long accustomed, while Spanish and Mexican colonists, to living in villages under the domination of all-powerful *patrones,* they reproduced this pattern in the Rimrock region. Atrisco, settled in the eighties, was one of several small communities they developed. At first the tiny nuclear settlement of some thirty-odd persons had no definite *patrón* domination. The leader of the group, which was composed almost entirely of the members of two interrelated families, was either not able or not eager to assume the typical *patrón* role. But *patrón* domination was not long in coming, for this early leader soon moved on to other territory, and a young brother whom he left behind, Don Juan Atrisco by name, moved quickly and surely to establish himself as the *patrón*. In Chapter VI the life history of this man—his rise to power and his later loss of it—is treated in detail. It is a story essential to the understanding of both the development and the disintegration of the village.

Once, at the height of its development, the population of Atrisco proper and two tiny adjacent settlements was slightly in excess of two hundred persons. By 1951 the number had dwindled to fifty-odd. Crumbling buildings and piles of rubble from buildings already fully destroyed, now far more numerous than inhabited dwellings, are the material evidence of Atrisco's decay.

The economy of the village was and still is primarily based on the raising of livestock. The *patrón* was a large operator; a few other families had small herds of sheep or cattle, which they either owned or took on a share (*partida*) plan; the heads of other families were wage workers who for the most part were in the employ of the *patrón* as long as he held his power. Few except the *patrón* ever made more than a meager subsistence from either the herds they owned or the herds they operated by the *partida* plan or the wage work they did for others on the range.

The range lands formerly used by the people of Atrisco were extensive in acreage, well over 200,000 acres in all, but virtually all of it was under the control of Don Juan Atrisco. He controlled the political affairs of the village, and dominated the religious activities as well. Indeed, only a very few families were free of this man's control in any aspect of their day-to-day living, and none escaped it in every aspect.

In 1921, a year of economic disaster for stockmen and farmers everywhere in the country, Don Juan, who had borrowed heavily on his holdings for various personal expenditures, had foreclosure proceedings instituted against him. Almost the whole of his business was wiped out, and the control of the land passed into the hands of Anglo-Americans.

Little change came of all this for the village as a whole until late in the twenties and early in the thirties. The era of the twenties was no time to start a livestock business; hence the banker who held the land leases permitted the Atrisco stockmen to continue their use of it. To Don Juan himself he gave a lifetime right for use of enough of it to operate a sizable business, and Don Juan did start anew, although on a much smaller scale than his former operations.

Finally in 1928 the leases were taken up by an Anglo-American company, but not even with the development of its livestock business on the Atrisco range was there a marked change in most aspects of village life. The greatest change in the period from 1921 to 1928 was the seeking out of substitute *patrones* by many of the families. This process and its results are also discussed fully in the chapter devoted to Atrisco.

The years 1936 and 1937, the years during which fences were put up to enclose the Atrisco range, marked the real turning point in Atrisco history. As long as the land had remained unfenced and was still also partly public domain, there was not too much that even an Anglo-American company could do to keep the Spanish-American stockmen off the range. Once the land of the range was consolidated and fenced, everything to keep them off, short of homicide, became possible. Except for the few who had either actually owned some land or had, as did the Atrisco family, a right to some use of it and another small number who were kept in the employ of the new company, all had to go and go hurriedly. The decrease in population and the decay of buildings followed quickly upon this two-year period. By 1951 there were only three families, one of them the family of Don Juan's youngest son, who had herds of any size and the ownership or the right for use of land upon which to graze them. A few other of the nine remaining heads of family units had some livestock but were planning to sell them off. The rest were wage workers.

Obviously, life in Atrisco today is not what it was two to three decades ago. Yet the basic living patterns of the few who remain are not as yet too greatly altered. The primary pattern of community living is still that of a centralized village—a village settlement in which almost all families maintain a residence even though the men who earn the living must go far out on the range, sometimes for long periods, to work with stock or to farm small plots of land. The periods of absence for the men are shorter today than formerly because trucks rather than horses are, for some at least, the new and quicker mode of travel, but the pattern is the same.

Social life is, to be sure, greatly curtailed. Twenty-five years ago there were frequent dances (*bailes*), and life was often made still gayer by wedding *bailes* and several regular *fiestas*. There are no longer enough people for much expression of this type of recreational activity. But not even by 1951 had the annual *fiesta* of the village saint (*santo*) been eliminated. Each year, the former *patrón* would come down from his home in Railtown to see that the *fiesta* was celebrated, and often a sufficient number of other former residents also came to make the celebration successful enough for it to have some semblance of the *fiestas* of former years.

The small houses constructed of mud and stone, the ones still inhabited, have not changed much. Some are now lighted by electricity and one or two have electric refrigerators, but all else in them looks much the same. The single village trading store, long ago owned by Don Juan Atrisco and later operated by the Anglo-American sheep company, is closed, and the schools are empty and crumbling; but there still is a Catholic church, although not the original one, to dominate the village scene.

The greatest change, and it is indeed a great one, has come in the ordering of family relationships. The once definite system of an hierarchical family with the ever-present rule of elders no longer exists. And the effects of such a change are seen in the total relational structure. The second important change, as yet not quite so well marked, is the shift from a deep concern with matters of religion and recreation which the *fiestas* emphasized to a more elaborated emphasis upon the problems of the care of livestock and the methods of farming.

The Mormons of Rimrock

Mormon missionaries also arrived in the Rimrock area in the seventies. One group, following out a program of the Church in Utah, which urged colonization in northern New Mexico and Arizona and proselytization of the Indian populations native to the area, came in 1876 from communities which had already been founded in Arizona. By 1877 a colony had been established at the base of the Zuni Mountains. It was soon abandoned because of a virulent smallpox epidemic which took a heavy toll of lives. It was not until 1882 that another effort was made to establish a new Mormon settlement. This time the site selected was Rimrock in the midst of the Navaho who had themselves only recently settled there after the return from Fort Sumner. This new community endured, but not without great difficulties.

The beginnings were auspicious. It has been reported that by 1884 a school, a meeting house, and a social hall had been built, a post office had been established, and the construction work on a dam which was to provide water for irrigation was far along. Even the crops were good in the first year. The future looked bright.

Then two years later there came a drought which was just the first of many crises which were to threaten the community. A three-year plague of grasshoppers followed on the drought, and before this was over, the railway company which owned the land on which the community had been built served an eviction notice. The only hope for survival was an appeal to the Church in Utah for funds with which to purchase the land. These were given on the condition that work on the dam would continue, because it now seemed certain that an irrigation system was essential for farming activities. It was also expected that the missionary work among the Indians, primarily the Navaho, would continue.

In 1896 and 1897 disaster struck again. First there was serious illness which swept the community in the winter months; a few months later, in the early spring, the dam broke. Once again the Church came to the aid of the community, but this time not without doubts as to the wisdom of maintaining the Rimrock settlement. Three years later a decision was reached, and the people of Rimrock were released from their "call." But only a few left; the majority chose to remain, and now freed from their obligations to convert the Navaho, they turned their full attention to the development of their own community.

Present-day Rimrock is a village of approximately 250 persons. From a distance, as one approaches it in spring, summer, or autumn, it appears as an oasis, for the valley is green and the poplar and cottonwood trees which the Mormons planted long ago are now tall and commanding. It is a regularly laid out village with wide roadways. There have not, even as yet, been many deviations from the original town plan which was the plan Joseph Smith developed for "the City of Zion." Although the houses are variable in size and construction and are of differing values, almost all of them are situated at equal distances from the streets and from each other. Along the widest of the streets there is a large church, a fine new school, a trading store, a garage, and a small cafe. A post office and a few other places of business are found on streets which intersect this main road. The only buildings which lie outside this arranged plan are the homes of the few families who have now moved out on the closely adjacent farm lands.

The economy of the community has always been primarily based upon irrigation agriculture and stock raising. There are 1200 acres of land under cultivation, and the range lands owned or leased are extensive. Within the last ten years an additional vast stretch of land, over 240,000 acres in all, was purchased by a local cooperative known as the Rimrock Land and Cattle Company. The Church in Utah once again helped in providing the funds for this purpose.

But farming and stock raising are not the only economic activities. Although working for gentiles has not been looked upon with favor by the Church, there have always been Rimrock men who have taken wage work outside the community, either on ranches or in Railtown, and today there is an increasing number of families which are either partially or wholly dependent upon this source of income. The owners of the trading stores derive much of their income from trade with the Indians. Other men are working for government agencies, and there are even some of the excellent horsemen of the community who have earned large sums of money as riders in western films.

Nor is one to assume from the existence of the two cooperatives which control the water supply and the recently acquired range lands that there is anything like an equitable distribution of the land resources. Over time the number of farms has been decreasing and their size increasing. The ownership or right to use of range lands is also highly variable. Not all families in the community are shareholders in the cooperatives, and not all shareholders have equal amounts of stock. In both cooperatives there are several large stockholders.

The social organization of Rimrock, as in all strictly Mormon communities, is largely dominated by the Church. Many aspects of family relations, economic affairs, recreational activities, and community government are under the direction of the local church division called the Ward Bishopric and this in turn is under the Stake, a unit consisting of several Wards, which is directly responsible to the General Authorities.

The majority of the men in Rimrock are members of the priesthoods. The two highest of these are the "High Priest" and the "Seventies," and the members selected for them are the men who are considered to have the greatest ability both for religious and political activities. Age and standards of behavior are the two main criteria in accord with which other men are selected for the lower priesthoods. For the women, who are not admitted to priesthoods, there is another type of organization called the Woman's Relief Society. There are still other organizations for young men, young women, and children.

It is mainly through this network of organizations that the affairs of the community are administered. Matters of serious import are, in the first instance, the business of the higher priestly orders; but all adults theoretically have a part in the decisions which, ideally, are always unanimous, and all organizations have some responsibilities which affect the total community.

Although less prominently today than in the past, this cooperative concept of social relations also pervades the relationships of Rimrock families. The nuclear family is an easily recognizable entity, for typically the nuclear family lives alone, but the obligations the related families have to each other are both numerous and time enduring.

The Texans of Homestead

The last of the five populations to establish a community in the Rimrock area were migrants from Texas and Oklahoma who now live in Homestead. There have been individual Texan ranchers in northern New Mexico since 1900, but it was not until the twenties and the thirties that Texan homesteaders came for the purpose of developing farming communities.

The town of Homestead dates from 1930 and 1931 when a few families came in to homestead land in the area south of Atrisco. A majority of the families who arrived between 1930 and 1935 had some capital, some equipment, and some livestock; the rest had barely enough to pay their homestead filing fee. But with or without capital, all who came in those first few years had a difficult time. The winter of 1931, the winter of the Big Snow, was one to try the hardiest of pioneer spirits, and it is doubtful that the community of Homestead would have survived at all had it not been for the interest of a banker in Railtown who admired the courage of the new settlers. He loaned money to some then, and since then has loaned money to many another who has tried to continue with dry farming in an area which "old-timer" cynics say is not, and never will be, suitable for dry farming.

But these individualistic Texans have been optimistic even when bankrupt, and they have been aggressive as well. When first they arrived they were dependent upon the little Spanish-American village of Atrisco for a local store, a post office, and schools. They deplored this situation and were determined to change it. Texans and Spanish-Americans have not got along at all well for generations.

Many changes have come. The town of Homestead, once nothing but a village center notable mainly for the community well which served the homestead farms with water, had become by 1950 a center for activities of various kinds. Schools, churches, a store, two cafes, two machine and repair shops, and a bean warehouse lined the wide road which by the early fifties swept through the farming community from north to south. This road is an "improved" one with a gravel surface.

Radiating out from this center over an area of almost 64,000 acres of land are the individually operated farms of the homesteaders. Most of these farms are owned by the operators, and in the year 1950–51 they averaged some 1200 acres in size. When first the homesteading took place, 160 to 640 acres was the usual range in size, but in a generation the competitive sorting process resulted in the elimination of some land holders and a concomitant increase in the holdings of the more successful. Homestead, which started with a very few persons, swelled in population in 1935 to a total of 374 and then dropped back in the forties and early fifties to a figure which fluctuated between 230 and 250 persons. By 1958 the community had shrunk in size to an estimated total of 180 persons, and not all of these were permanently in residence.[12]

In 1950 approximately 12,000 of the 64,000 acres controlled by the community were under cultivation, and the principal crops, all grown by dryland cultivation techniques, were pinto beans, corn, and wheat. Pinto beans are and always have been the main crop, and it has been the dream of the community from its beginning to develop "the Pinto Bean Capital of the World" in this semiarid and storm-ridden region which so many deem useful only for the grazing of livestock.

Technologically the community is the most advanced of all in the Rimrock region. Almost all farmers owned tractors by 1950, and many had additional machinery as well. The houses had been increasingly well

[12] This figure was obtained from Evon Z. Vogt.

equipped with modern electrical appliances after 1949 when a power line was brought into the area. Gradually on the farms windmills were abandoned as electric pumps were installed to replace them. No family, in 1951, was without an automobile, and many owned trucks. From hand labor to horse power to this degree of mechanization in two decades was no mean achievement.

However, the farming venture as a whole has not been highly successful. Tractors, cultivators, and trucks do not conquer or control drought, torrential storms, and early frosts. The farmers of Homestead have learned to expect that at least one year's crop in three will be a total loss. The remarkable thing is that they clung on to their optimism and kept on trying. Many left after a bad year and took jobs of another kind in Railtown or even at farther distances, but a majority until very recently returned again each year to plant their fields anew.

These Texans are an independent people who have a strong preference for owning their land and running their own business. This is one reason they tried to keep their farms going. Seemingly they also are a people who have always enjoyed the leisure time afforded by the off seasons in their type of farming. There is, as Evon Vogt has stated, a well delineated "loafing pattern" in Homestead.[13]

The independent nuclear family is the basic unit of this community of individualists. Firm ties do exist between some groups of related families and from them there developed a few clan-like groupings. But except for the prevailing spirit of pride in the development of the community, a feeling which has definite overtones of defensiveness, one noted in Homestead even in 1951 little of the community cohesiveness which characterizes most of the other communities. There were several religious denominations represented in the community and much competition between them. Politically the people were divided. There were also the rudiments of the class divisions which have been noted in other small American communities. But according to Vogt the system as a whole was one of factions rather than classes.[14] He states that the kinship divisions, the variations in religious beliefs, and the differentiations in social rank, all of them further complicated by the loyalties many have for particular neighborhood groupings, created a factionalism which became the salient dynamic factor in the social life of Homestead. It certainly was a troublesome deterrent to community unity. One cannot but question, for so many reasons, the permanence of this community, but one also must give credit to the zeal and optimism which made it endure for a quarter century.

THE RELATIONS OF THE COMMUNITIES TO EACH OTHER

There is not a great deal that any of these communities has in common with the others. Even the two English-speaking communities vary suffi-

[13] *Op. cit.*, Chap. V.
[14] *Ibid.*, pp. 164–71.

ciently in religious beliefs and organization, in social habits, and in economic practices for their members to feel small inclination to establish many close relationships. But some interchange between the villages, both social and economic, has been inevitable. Sheer proximity makes for inescapable contacts; a common citizenship creates others; the hazards of the environment put demands of cooperation upon everyone.

Of all the groups the Zuni Indians are the most self-contained and the Navaho Indians the least so. One seldom sees Zuni Indians in any of the other communities except Rimrock, and the only ones to be seen there very often are members of the two outlying farming settlements which are but a few miles from Rimrock. In contrast one can expect to find members of the Navaho group almost anywhere in the area. Zuni Indians seldom if ever work for Spanish-Americans, Mormons, or Texans; but Navaho Indians have often been in the hire of all three, and have worked for the Zuni as well. Moreover, the Navaho, who do not have a centralized settlement, seem more given to an exploring of this small corner of the world than do the other groups.

It is almost as if the Navaho Indians together with their scattered hogans, their horses and sheep, and their wagons are a part of the landscape itself. No one is ever surprised at encountering a Navaho Indian; yet few persons in the non-Indian groups really know the Navaho except for the occasional man or woman who may be hired to haul and chop wood, herd sheep, mend fences, or help with the housework. Some members of the Zuni community are well acquainted with individual Navahos; but there are few close relationships between the two groups.

The Zuni Indians are not better known by the other groups than are the Navaho, but as a total people they are known in a different way. Their picturesque village and their colorful ceremonies are tourist attractions for most of the peoples of New Mexico and for out-of-state visitors as well. Some members of the Navaho, Texan, and Mormon communities of the Rimrock area have all appeared at the great winter solstice ceremony of the Zuni, and many in these groups also drop by the village in the summertime to watch the dances of rain-making ceremonies. Very occasionally a Spanish-American tries to slip into the pueblo to watch the ritual dances, but if seen he is not allowed to stay. The Zuni long ago decreed that no Spanish-American was to be permitted in the village when ceremonies were in progress. For many years there were no contacts at all between the Spanish-Americans of Atrisco and the Zuni in spite of the fact that the mission priest of Zuni is also the *padre* of the Atrisco church. In the thirties a few Atrisco families began to use the trading store in Zuni, and others occasionally went to the doctor in the government hospital located there. Even though the primary contacts the Spanish-Americans made in the pueblo were with the Anglo-American staffs of the store and the hospital, it was inevitable that some contacts would be made with the Zuni themselves. And while the relationships that were established between Zuni and Atrisco families were for the most part casual, they have served to decrease substantially the fears and prejudices the two groups had for each other.

The names of a number of the Spanish-American families of Atrisco are known to all the other groups. Best known, of course, is the name of the former *patrón*. He once had fame throughout the area both because of his livestock enterprise and his political activities. But the relations *los Atrisqueños* have with members of any of the other communities are few. One sees members of the community in Rimrock, the Mormon community, even less often than in Zuni. The greatest number of contacts at the present time are with the Texans of Homestead, but as has been indicated, the relations between these two communities, which are but a few miles apart, have always been tense and are at times even hostile. In years past, when several of the Atrisco families had large herds of livestock, it was not uncommon for Navaho Indians to be hired by them for sheepherding or other jobs on the range. Socially the Spanish-Americans look down upon the Navaho Indians, but there has not been real hostility between the two groups.

It is rare indeed that a Mormon from Rimrock goes into any of the other villages. Business or ceremonials may occasionally take some to Zuni; the job as rural mail carrier has for years taken one Mormon man and his wife to both Atrisco and Homestead twice a week; it also sometimes becomes necessary for business reasons that a Mormon seek out a Navaho family in its hogan. Other relationships are for the most part sporadic and casual. There are only a few families in Homestead and Rimrock who could be said to have interrelationships which are of a social nature.

The Texans of Homestead sometimes come into Rimrock to the store, and very occasionally some matter concerning a government agency brings one or more into the village. A few also attend the Rimrock dances which are the high lights of the Mormon social life. But it is questionable how welcome the Texans are at these affairs. The strict Mormon frowns on drinking and does not like it when some of the visitors from Homestead bring their bottles and make frequent trips from the dance floor to their cars where the liquor is cached.

One prime indicator of the lack of close relationships all of these communities have with each other is the small amount of intermarriage between any of them. There is Navaho blood in Atrisco, but most of it has come from the "marrying off" of persons who were known to have already a large amount of Indian blood. In one additional case the individual was the son, more or less accepted as a family member, whom the *patrón* had by a Navaho woman who was the wife of a sheepherder. Marriage with Indians of any kind is not an approved pattern among the Spanish-Americans. Also, few have married into the Anglo-American groups. One man was forced to marry a Texan girl when her mother maintained that he was responsible for her pregnancy. Two daughters of the *patrón* also married Texans. These girls were more acculturated than other Atrisco girls, and in addition their superior position in the Spanish-American community made it difficult for them to follow the typical pattern of an ingroup marriage.

In recent years there have been only two cases of Navaho-Zuni intermarriage, and in a half century only four cases are known.[15] Between the Texans of Homestead and the Mormons of Rimrock there have been eight marriage alliances. More Mormons than this have married outside their community, but these alliances have been either with members of other Mormon communities or with Anglo-Americans from neighboring cities or from the families of the few prominent ranchers who have long been in the Rimrock area but are not connected with any of the five main settlements in our study. Very occasionally a Zuni marries a member of some other Indian group, but the preferred and still markedly prevalent pattern in this community is that of in-group marriage.

RELATIONS OF THE RIMROCK COMMUNITIES WITH THE OUTSIDE WORLD

The most numerous of the contacts which members of all five communities have with the world beyond the Rimrock region are with the traders, the service people, the bankers and government officials in Railtown, a small but bustling city which is situated approximately thirty miles beyond the northernmost limit of the Rimrock area. On any weekday one sees many members of all the groups in Railtown stores, cafes, and garages. Some can also be found in the post office, the county government offices, and the banks, but there is a difference in the number of persons, community by community, who make use of the latter facilities. The citizens of Rimrock and Homestead make the greatest use of them and the two Indian groups the least. The Spanish-Americans of Atrisco fall between these two extremes.

There are a few other trading centers to which members of the various communities go, sometimes regularly but more often just occasionally, but no one of them is comparable to Railtown as a main trading center. Although Railtown's permanent population is small—approximately 12,000 persons—and is predominantly Anglo-American and Spanish-American, there is daily such a constant flow of transient visitors of many kinds that the town seems much larger than it actually is and, in addition, seems remarkably cosmopolitan for its size.

Its economy is also quite varied, for it is the center for the purchase and sale of Indian craftwork, the pinto beans produced by communities like Homestead, the steers, lambs, and wool which the livestock industry engaged in by many different groups provides, for the piñon nuts which Texans, Mormons, Spanish-Americans, and Indians all gather. The dealers and traders who handle these sales transactions on a large scale are almost all Anglo-Americans, as are also almost all the bankers and government officials. Only very rarely since Railtown was founded has there been a Spanish-American who has been a large-scale trader or a figure of

---

[15] If one includes intermarriages between the Zuni and another small Navaho group which lives north of Rimrock, the total number of intermarriages in this same time period is thirteen according to unpublished vital statistics of Vogt.

real influence in the realms of business and politics which the Anglo-Americans clearly dominate. And very few Indians have ever been incorporated into the economic and political structures of the town.

Yet the influence upon all the peoples we are discussing is a strong one, for when one now finds the wool from the Rimrock area in New England, its beef and lamb in both the East and the Middle West, the pinto beans of Homestead in the Italian markets of New York and Boston and in chain stores throughout the country, the piñon nuts collected by members of all communities in the carts of vendors in New York, it has to be assumed that there is a definite, even though often fairly indirect, linkage of the Rimrock communities to the national economic system.

The political patterns of the nation and the state also affect all the communities. Even the two Indian groups now have the franchise and are beginning to feel strongly the pressures of the two major political parties. Bonds in common are certainly created by the participation of all the groups in the election of national and state officials, but rifts already present have also been accentuated. The most glaring illustration of the latter is the political antagonism between the Anglo-American community of Homestead and the Spanish-American village, Atrisco. Few Homesteaders are Republicans and all *Atrisqueños* are, and have long been, Republicans. Because Verona County, in which the two villages are located, has always been dominated by a Republican county machine in which Spanish-Americans are prominent (the county still in 1950 was largely Spanish-American in population), the Texans of Homestead have felt strongly frustrated politically. They express this frustration by being more aggressive and competitive than usual toward their Spanish-American neighbors when in election years campaigners for the two major parties come into the area to vie for votes. The details of the Texan–Spanish-American feud which arose in the year 1936, the year when Landon was running against Roosevelt for the Presidency, will be reported later.

There have also been other problems which in some large part are political. The two most serious of these concerned the local appointments of a justice of the peace and schoolteachers. Twenty years ago the Texans of Homestead were deeply resentful that the local justice of the peace was a Spanish-American. They were even more bitterly hostile over the fact that their children had to go to Atrisco to high school and that even the teachers sent to them for their own grade school were sometimes Spanish-Americans. By 1950 the Texans, because of their greater numerical strength, had gained the advantage, and it is now the *Atrisqueño* who is troubled that his child must attend school in Homestead and that local affairs in general are much more dominated by his Texan neighbors.

The schools, both the local public schools provided by the state of New Mexico and the day and boarding schools which the federal government developed for the Indian groups, have also served to create some additional ties to the national culture. But here again there are striking differences between the communities both in the number of kind of ties established and also in the understanding of them. As will be shown later, the policy of establishing in the Spanish-American communities the typical

American school, in which all instruction was to be in the English language, did not substantially increase the Spanish-Americans' understanding of the national culture or speed the process of their assimilation into it. As long as most of them remained in tightly knit communities which were either entirely, or almost entirely, composed of Spanish-speaking persons and where the old customs of Spanish-American culture continued to prevail, the education offered by the typical Anglo-American school system had little relevance to their day-to-day life. Much the same can be said of the early programs which were developed for the education of the Indian groups.

At present the situation is different in two important respects. The schools of the Southwest now give some consideration to the study of the non-Anglo-American cultures and the contributions these have made to the total regional culture. Perhaps even more important is the fact that both circumstances and policy changes have now created much more of an actual as opposed to a hypothetical melting-pot situation. In some large part the standardization of the American public school system in the nation as a whole was based upon the fact that any single school might, and often did, have an enrollment of pupils from families with many different ethnic backgrounds, all of whom had, in varying degrees to be sure, a motivation to become assimilated. This has not been the case in the Southwest until very recently. Increasingly, as the Spanish-American rural communities have disintegrated and their citizens have become incorporated into the more urban areas of the region, the Spanish-American school pupil is thrown more into the kind of heterogeneous group common to American cities in general. And very recently the Bureau of Indian Affairs has adopted the policy of gradually abandoning the segregated Indian school and placing Indian pupils in the public schools of the communities near which they live. This plan cannot be fully executed because of the problems of distance and the segregation which reservation life makes inevitable, but it is going forward. For example, there are today many Navaho children in the schools of the town of Rimrock, the predominantly Mormon community of the Rimrock area. Since all of the non-Anglo-American groups have been, for a variety of reasons, steadily moving into a state of cultural transition, there is now every reason to believe that the schools of the Southwest will be a far more effective medium for the development of intergroup understanding than they have been in the past.

Contacts with the wider social system of the state or the country as a whole beyond those provided by these economic, political, and educational channels have not been numerous. To be sure, each of the communities has its share of veterans of the armed services who have been in many distant corners of the world. The Mormon group in Rimrock also has a few members who have done their required missionary service for the Church in such faraway places as Samoa. But normally the distances traveled by members of the several communities are not great, and they are well channeled.

The Mormons, when they can, make trips to Utah, and they also travel into Arizona to see relatives in other Mormon settlements. Many of them have also been in the larger cities of New Mexico. Some of the people of Homestead have made trips back to Oklahoma and Texas to the places whence they came, a few have traveled a bit around New Mexico, and some have even gone as far afield as California. The majority of the Spanish-Americans of Atrisco seldom get farther than Railtown or other equally close places where they have relatives. A number have occasionally gone to Albuquerque, Sante Fe, or other New Mexico cities, but only a few know these cities well. Very few, other than the war veterans, or those who have taken up residence in another state, have been out of New Mexico, and in all cases the states visited by these few have been the nearby ones of Texas, California, Arizona, and Colorado. Members of the Navaho group, when they go farther than Railtown, usually visit other Navaho Indians in small nonreservation communities. Some do go occasionally to the Navaho Agency on the reservation, and a few have also been to Albuquerque, Santa Fe, and other parts of New Mexico or Arizona. The Zuni are traveling greater distances than they have in the past, but they still remain the most community bound of all five groups.

PRIOR PREDICTIONS OF VALUE-ORIENTATION ORDERINGS

Another type of contact with the outside world which all members of all the Rimrock communities have had is that with the many social scientists who have been studying each of them individually and all of them comparatively for many years. Indeed, one may state that in the two Indian groups many individuals have had their main contacts with the wider culture of the nation through their relationships with social scientists. In the Navaho group, for example, Clyde Kluckhohn and a few of his numerous collaborators are better known than are most of the traders, the staffs of hospitals, or the various government officials with whom members of the community have had dealings from time to time. The relations which the Zuni, who are generally fairly hostile to outsiders, have had with social scientists have usually been less amicable than those of the Navaho, but some have been long enduring nonetheless. In the Spanish-American, Texan, and Mormon communities there have also been a number of sustained friendships formed with some of the field investigators who have been coming and going over the years.

Obversely there is the importance of the range and depth of knowledge of the communities which these long-sustained relationships have provided the social scientists. In this study the primary use to be made of this rich body of knowledge is for the purposes of the validation of the general results achieved and a more detailed analysis of *intra*-cultural variations than our field data permit.

But there was still another way in which we decided to take advantage of the quite unusual resources afforded by the many previous studies and the numerous personal contacts. This was the attempt to make "prior predictions" as to what the overall value-orientation orderings would be

72 VARIATIONS IN VALUE ORIENTATIONS

and what some of the specific intra-cultural variations might be. These predictions were made in July of 1951, some weeks before the test schedule was fully developed and administered. In making them the research team had the benefit of the judgments of Evon Vogt, who was at that time studying Homestead intensively, and Clyde Kluckhohn, whose investigations of the life of the Rimrock Navaho have extended over a thirty-year period.

In Appendix 2 of this study it is explained how the efficiency of the statistical analysis of the data obtained from a field schedule such as that developed for the testing of the value-orientation orderings (this schedule is fully discussed in the next chapter) could have been increased had the prior predictions been made with more precision and more formality than we made them. Because of the pressure of time we were not able in the field work of the summer of 1951 to do more than make general predictions about overall outcomes (these not always unequivocal) and a very few specific predictions about intra-cultural variations in the different behavior spheres.[16]

But however informal and incomplete in detail these predictions were, we feel them to be of sufficient interest to report them at this point and later, in the conclusion, to compare them with the actual observed results. In giving these predictions we shall change the listings of the five communities from that of the historical sequence of settlement pattern used in this chapter to the order which will be consistently followed in the rest of the monograph. This order is: Spanish-American, Texan, Mormon, Zuni, and Navaho.

Predictions for the Spanish-Americans of Atrisco

For this group the predictions were primarily the responsibility of Florence Kluckhohn who had, already by 1951, studied the people of this village over a fifteen-year period. The predictions were as follows:

1. RELATIONAL ORIENTATION. The general overall prediction (for the year 1951) was that Individualism would be the first-order emphasis, that the stress on Lineality would still be strong, and the evaluation of Collaterality would be weak. More fully, the prediction was that the Spanish-Americans had only recently (in the past twenty to thirty years) been changing their evaluative emphasis of the *relational* orientation alternatives from a pattern of Lin > Coll > Ind[17] to a dominant emphasis upon the Individualistic position in several spheres of life. It was believed that many men, es-

---

[16] Also, the predictions did not include the *human nature* orientation, and they were limited to two alternatives of the *activity* orientation. Chapter III gives the reasons for these omissions in the research program of 1951.

[17] In stating these predictions we use the symbol ">" to denote "is more than." Later, when we present our research findings, ">" and "≥" mean, respectively, "is significantly more than" and "is nonsignificantly more than," according to the statistical analyses developed in Chapter IV. When we speak of an orientation ordering that is not subjected to statistical tests, we use the convention illustrated by "Lineality over Collaterality over Individualism" instead of "Lin > Coll > Ind."

pecially, would be found to have made this shift in matters having to do with economic affairs and family relations. In other spheres it was expected that the older pattern would be found to be the prevailing one. Thus, the more detailed prediction was that two competing patterns would be found, one in which Individualism was ranked first, the other showing a dominance of Lineality; and of the two the former was expected to be the more frequent.

2. TIME ORIENTATION. The primary prediction on this orientation was for an overwhelming first-order preference for the Present *time* alternative. It was further predicted that in matters having to do with religion the second-order preference would be the Past position, but no prediction was made as to the regular ordering of the Past and Future alternatives of the orientation for second and third-order choices.

3. MAN-NATURE ORIENTATION. Here again, the one prediction about which there was great certainty was the selection of the Subjugated-to-Nature alternative as a first choice. It was further predicted that in matters having to do with farming and stock raising there would be evidence of a switch from the Subjugated-to-Nature to the Over-Nature position. Thus, in general terms the predicted overall pattern was the Subj > Over > With one.

4. ACTIVITY ORIENTATION. On this orientation, for which only the Being and Doing alternatives were posed, it was predicted that the responses would *overwhelmingly* favor the Being position.

Predictions for the Texans of Homestead

For the most part the predictions for this group were those we would have made for generalized Anglo-American culture. They were the following:

1. RELATIONAL ORIENTATION. The pattern predicted was the Ind > Coll > Lin one.

2. TIME ORIENTATION. It was believed the pattern would be the Fut > Pres > Past one with perhaps a somewhat more prominent stressing of the second-order Present *time* alternative than one might find in many Anglo-American communities because of the well defined community pattern which Vogt has called the "loafing pattern."

3. MAN-NATURE ORIENTATION. The pattern expected for this orientation was the Over > Subj > With ordering.

4. ACTIVITY ORIENTATION. As between the Doing and Being alternatives it was expected that Doing choices would predominate. However, the prominence of the "loafing pattern" caused us also to predict a quite strong second-order Being orientation.

Predictions for the Mormons of Rimrock

For this group, which was much less known to the research team and upon which there was much less data than on the Spanish-American and

Texan groups, the predictions were made with considerably less certainty. The following predictions represented our best guesses:

1. RELATIONAL ORIENTATION. We felt unable to predict whether the Collateral or the Individualistic alternative of this orientation would be the dominant value-orientation position. Our reasoning was that the Mormons as a whole have been given to a much greater Collateral conception of man-man relations than more typical Anglo-Americans; hence we expected this emphasis to be strong in many areas of behavior. But it was also known, as evidenced by the increasing number of "Jack Mormons" (see Chapter VII) in the community, that there had been an increasing emphasis upon Individualistic patterns of behavior. As a result of the two lines of reasoning we quite frankly hedged by saying that either Collaterality or Individualism might emerge as the dominant emphasis.

2. TIME ORIENTATION. The prediction on this orientation was the ranking pattern of Fut > Pres > Past. But here, too, we were not at all certain. One member of the research team who was himself a Mormon, Kimball Romney, argued that in the Mormon communities in Utah there was a fairly strong Past *time* orientation. Our final judgment was that this emphasis would not be marked in Rimrock, which is far from the Utah center of Mormonism in which one does find some feeling of traditionalism and in which there is also a prominent elite with great responsibilities to the Church.

3. MAN-NATURE ORIENTATION. The general prediction on this orientation was the pattern of With > Over > Subj. In more detail our judgment was that the Mormons had been in the past predominantly favorable to the Harmony-with-Nature position, but that at the present time there were many signs which pointed to a quite definite preference for the Mastery-over-Nature position. The consensus of the group was that this change had not yet gone far enough for us to expect that the Mastery-over-Nature position would emerge as the dominant orientation.

4. ACTIVITY ORIENTATION. On this orientation we predicted that the Doing alternative would be put into first position.

Predictions for the Zuni

For this group no systematic predictions were made as to the choices among the alternatives of *any* of the four orientations. John Roberts, who was the member of the team actively engaged in research in Zuni in 1950 and 1951, considered the attitudes of the Zuni, especially in that segment of the population in which he was working, to be too equivocal to permit of definite predictions.

Some of the literature on Zuni, of which there is a vast amount all in all, suggests that there had been in the past a highly evaluated dominant profile which had put a first-order emphasis upon the Lineal *relational* orientation, the Past *time* orientation, a Harmony-with-Nature emphasis, and a Being-in-Becoming *activity* orientation, a position which our instrument was not designed to test. But other sources seemed also to indicate that there had been in the group over a long period of time a great deal of variation. Moreover, increased variation as of 1950–51 was quite apparent. For all these reasons we decided to make *no* predictions about the Zuni ranking of orientation alternatives. We did, however, predict (1) that the Zuni preference for the Past alternative of the *time* orientation would be greater than that of any other group and (2) that the Zuni preference for the Lineal alternative of the *relational* orientation would be greater than that of the Navaho.

Predictions for the Rimrock Navaho

The predictions made for the value-orientation preferences of this group were primarily those of Clyde Kluckhohn. There was some feeling on the part of some members of the research team that the Over-Nature alternative would be more prominent than Clyde Kluckhohn indicated. In Chapter IX, C. Kluckhohn and Romney give in detail their reasons for arguing that the Subjugated-to-Nature rather than the Over-Nature position is the second-order one.

The Navaho group in recent years has shown a real confusion in cultural patterning, and it suffers from serious economic deprivation as well. C. Kluckhohn stated that considerable variability was to be expected in the responses we would obtain, but he predicted that there would still be significantly discernible ranking patterns. The total predictions of the overall rankings were as follows:

1. RELATIONAL ORIENTATION. Collaterality was predicted to be the first-order preference, and the expected rank ordering was Coll > Lin > Ind.
2. TIME ORIENTATION. The rank order predicted for the group as a whole was Pres > Past > Fut.
3. MAN-NATURE ORIENTATION. The prediction was that the Harmony-with-Nature alternative would be the first-order choice, but it was doubtful what the ranking of the other two alternatives would be.

TABLE II:1
INFORMAL PRIOR PREDICTIONS ON VALUE-ORIENTATION RANKINGS

CULTURE	ORIENTATION			
	relational	time	man-nature	activity
Spanish-American	Ind>Lin>Coll approximating Ind=Lin>Coll	Pres>Fut=Past[a]	Subj>Over>With	Being>Doing
Texan	Ind>Coll>Lin	Fut>Pres>Past	Over>Subj>With	Doing>Being
Mormon	Ind=Coll>Lin	Fut>Pres>Past approximating Fut>Pres=Past	With>Over>Subj	Doing>Being
Zuni	no prediction	no prediction	no prediction	no prediction
Navaho	Coll>Lin>Ind	Pres>Past>Fut	With>Subj=Over	Doing>Being

[a] The equal sign has been used here when either ordering of two elements was believed equally probable; it is not a prediction of a definite equality of preference.

4. ACTIVITY ORIENTATION. A most *definite* first-order emphasis upon the Doing alternative of this orientation was predicted. Not only was this prediction unequivocal, but it was pointed out that it was on this orientation that the Navaho group most closely resembled dominant American culture.

Table II:1 includes all the predictions on the rank orderings of the value-orientation preferences in the groups which we felt capable of making.

CHAPTER III

The Research Instrument: Development and Administration

The instrument created for the testing of the differences and similarities in the rank ordering of the value-orientation alternatives in the five cultures is a schedule of twenty-two items which are divided among the orientations as follows: *relational* orientation, seven items; *man-nature* and *time* orientations, five items each; *activity* orientation, five items which can be counted as six since one has two parts. The items used for testing the *relational, man-nature,* and *time* orientations test for the ordering of three alternatives. Those which test on the *activity* orientation seek only for the preference between the Doing and Being alternatives. Limitations of time and research funds prevented the development of items which would test all three alternatives of this orientation and also precluded any consideration of the *human nature* orientation.[1]

Each item of the schedule first delineates a type of life situation which we believe to be common to most rural, or folk, societies and then poses alternatives of solution for the problem which derive from and give expression to the theoretically postulated alternatives of the value orientation in question. For example, each of the items developed for testing on the *relational* orientation contains alternatives of solution of a very general problem situation which express the Lineal, Collateral, and Individualistic variations.

In the arrangement of the schedule for presentation to respondents the items of the different series were interlarded but not systematically; it was also thought important to place first and last in the schedule items which

---

[1] Originally there was no intention of testing any part of the *activity* orientation. A late decision to include it in our investigation gave little time for working out the alternatives of the orientation. Because we believed that four of the five groups to be tested would either be first-order Being or first-order Doing, we compromised with time by testing only these two alternatives. Our judgment, based on published material on the Zuni and on the research work of one of the investigators, was that of all the groups the Zuni should have been the most likely, in the past if not at the present time, to have given first-order preference to the Being-in-Becoming alternative of the *activity* orientation. And, as will be reported later, there is some reason to believe that the indecisive results obtained from the Zuni community on their choices between just the two alternatives of Being and Doing can in some part be attributed to our failure to offer the Zuni respondents a choice of the Being-in-Becoming alternative. Even had we not had reason to regret our omission of one of the alternatives of a range in this case, there are theoretical reasons for not omitting any of them. Since the theory assumes that all individuals adhere in some degree to each of the positions, we lack a clear guide for interpretation of responses when only two of the three alternatives are offered.

appeared to be the easiest to comprehend quickly. In presenting the alternatives in the separate series we took the usual precaution of rotating the order of the three, or two, alternatives. This procedure was followed most systematically throughout the schedule.

The two principal questions put to each respondent concerning the alternatives of solution offered in an item are appropriately worded queries which elicit his first choice among all three alternatives (or two in the case of the *activity* orientation) and then his preference between the remaining alternatives. Always, of course, the respondent was permitted the opportunity to give equal weight to two, or even all three, of the alternatives. As has been stated previously, "linked" ranking patterns of several types are possible patterns, both logically and empirically. Moreover, a forcing of choices would have defeated the first purpose of the research, which was to determine whether or not the respondents in the several cultures sensed significant differences between the alternatives and had preferences among them.

The ranking patterns yielded by the use of these two questions were the matter of primary concern to the research program. They constitute the body of data which is the subject matter for analysis in Chapters IV and V.

There were, however, a few other questions put to the respondents which yielded some data additional to that required for answering the four major questions posed by the theory of variations in value orientations. For every choice situation on each of the orientation series of items, every respondent was asked to give his judgment on the first-order choice of the majority of other persons in his community. The purpose of this question was to determine the degree of "perceived consensus" in value choices. The data resulting from this question are analyzed in Appendix 3. Although these data are not systematically integrated with the analyses of the four basic questions which will be formally stated in Chapter IV, some interpretative use is made of them by the authors of the chapters which treat separately the five cultures (Chapters VI through IX).[2]

Another question which was asked about some of the choice situations—primarily those testing for the preference between the Doing and Being alternatives of the *activity* orientation—was what the respondent actually would do in the described situations in contrast to what he considered it would be best to do. The purpose of this question was to see whether respondents could or would differentiate between their actual behavior and their value preference. Since this question was not used consistently throughout the schedule, no detailed analysis of the results it yielded is given. Reference to the answers elicited from particular persons, whose actual behavior was well known from previous studies, also appears in some of the chapters which treat the cultures individually. The most extensive

---

[2] A still more extensive analysis of the results this question yielded appears in a study made by William and Mieko Caudill in Japan in 1957. It is planned that this study, which reports the results of the use of the value-orientation schedule on 614 Japanese respondents, will be published at approximately the same time this volume appears.

use of this material is in Chapter VI, which treats the Spanish-American group.

Still another question was asked of the Spanish-Americans relative to all choice situations used for testing rankings on the *relational* orientation. The phrasing was, "*Which of the three ways do you think most persons in Atrisco would have said was best thirty years ago?*" This query, quite specific to this one group of respondents, was introduced in order to test the validity of our prediction that very recently (within the last twenty to twenty-five years) there has been a significant shift, more in some areas of behavior than others, from a first-order Lineal to a first-order Individualistic *relational* orientation. The results of the question are solely a matter of concern for Chapter VI.

Four major considerations dictated the type of items—the type we are calling "the generalized life situation"—concerning which these several questions were asked. First, there was the problem of constructing items of inquiry which were so predominantly the expression of a single value orientation that the contaminating influence of other orientations could be considered negligible. Second in magnitude was the question of selecting situations which had a relatively equal degree of significance in communities which were culturally quite disparate. The third objective was that of minimizing the distorting effects upon responses which defensiveness, conscious or unconscious, so often produces. The further concern in this main objective was the reduction of the effects of the purely idiosyncratic life experiences of particular individuals. It was primarily because of this twin-headed objective that the method was elaborated beyond the mere statement of a general situation as such and developed as one in which a situation is a hypothetical one where "third persons" are debating and making the choices. The method does not, in other words, request a direct personal judgment among alternatives; it asks that the respondent evaluate the judgments which persons, who are to him figurative and impersonal, are said to have made.

These three objectives were central to the design of our own study, which called for the testing for the variations in the rank orderings of the value orientations in the five cultures by means of the schedule, and the subsequent checking of the statistical analyses of the results achieved against the vast amount of ethnological material which had previously been collected on each of them. The fourth matter we had ever in mind in the construction of the schedule was of quite a different order, for it was, in some sense at least, an end rather than a means. This end was the production of a schedule method, general in nature and limited in length, which could be used as the basis of the development of testable hypotheses about other, more specific, types of behavior patterns.

A fuller discussion of these four objectives as well as the rationale for the limitation of the number of items for the testing of each value-orientation ordering will follow upon the presentation of the English-language version of the schedule. Subsequent to these discussions we shall treat briefly the sampling procedures and then, finally, give the individual interviewers' accounts of their experiences in the administration of the schedule.

THE SCHEDULE: ENGLISH-LANGUAGE VERSION[3]

1. JOB CHOICE   *activity:* Items A1 and A2

A man needed a job and had a chance to work for two men. The two bosses were different. Listen to what they were like and say which you think would be the best one to work for.

    A   One boss was a fair enough man, and he gave somewhat higher
(Doing)   pay than most men, but he was the kind of boss who insisted that men work hard, stick on the job. He did not like it at all when a worker sometimes just knocked off work for a while to go on a trip or to have a day or so of fun, and he thought it was right not to take such a worker back on the job.

    B   The other paid just average wages but he was not so firm. He
(Being)   understood that a worker would sometimes just not turn up —would be off on a trip or having a little fun for a day or two. When his men did this he would take them back without saying too much.

(Part one)

Which of these men do you believe that it would be better to work for in most cases?

Which of these men would most other _____ think it better to work for?

(Part two)

Which kind of boss do you believe that it is better to be in most cases?
Which kind of boss would most other _____ think it better to be?

2. WELL ARRANGEMENTS   *relational:* Item R1

When a community has to make arrangements for water, such as drill a well, there are three different ways they can decide to arrange things like location, and who is going to do the work.

    A   There are some communities where it is mainly the older or
(Lin)   recognized leaders of the important families who decide the plans. Everyone usually accepts what they say without much discussion since they are the ones who are used to deciding such things and are the ones who have had the most experience.

    B   There are some communities where most people in the group
(Coll)   have a part in making the plans. Lots of different people talk, but nothing is done until *almost* everyone comes to agree as to what is best to be done.

---

[3] The Spanish-language version appears in Appendix 1. It was not possible to produce written translations of the Navaho and Zuni-language versions.

THE RESEARCH INSTRUMENT 81

C (Ind)   There are some communities where everyone holds to his own opinion, and they decide the matter by vote. They do what the largest number want even though there are still a very great many people who disagree and object to the action.

Which way do you think is usually best in such cases?
Which of the other two ways do you think is better?
Which way of all three ways do you think most other persons in _____ would usually think is best?

3. CHILD TRAINING   *time:* Item T1

Some people were talking about the way children should be brought up. Here are three different ideas.

A (Past)   Some people say that children should always be taught well the traditions of the past (the ways of the old people). They believe the old ways are best, and that it is when children do not follow them too much that things go wrong.

B (Pres)   Some people say that children should be taught some of the old traditions (ways of the old people), but it is wrong to insist that they stick to these ways. These people believe that it is necessary for children always to learn about and take on whatever of the new ways will best help them get along in the world of today.

C (Fut)   Some people do not believe children should be taught much about past traditions (the ways of the old people) at all except as an interesting story of what has gone before. These people believe that the world goes along best when children are taught the things that will make them want to find out for themselves new ways of doing things to replace the old.

Which of these people had the best idea about how children should be taught?
Which of the other two people had the better idea?
Considering again all three ideas, which would most other persons in _____ say had the better idea?

4. LIVESTOCK DYING   *man-nature:* Item MN1

One time a man had a lot of livestock. Most of them died off in different ways. People talked about this and said different things.

A (Subj)   Some people said you just can't blame a man when things like this happen. There are so many things that can and do happen, and a man can do almost nothing to prevent such losses when they come. We all have to learn to take the bad with the good.

B (Over)   Some people said that it was probably the man's own fault that he lost so many. He probably didn't use his head to

82   VARIATIONS IN VALUE ORIENTATIONS

C (With)	prevent the losses. They said that it is usually the case that men who keep up on new ways of doing things, and really set themselves to it, almost always find a way to keep out of such trouble. Some people said that it was probably because the man had not lived his life right—had not done things in the right way to keep harmony between himself and the forces of nature (i.e., the ways of nature like the rain, winds, snow, etc.).

Which of these reasons do you think is most usually true?

Which of the other two reasons do you think is more true?

Which of all three reasons would most other persons in _____ think is usually true?

5. EXPECTATIONS ABOUT CHANGE   *time:* Item T2

(*a. 20–40 Age Group*)

Three young people were talking about what they thought their families would have one day as compared with their fathers and mothers. They each said different things.

C (Fut)	The first said: I expect my family to be better off in the future than the family of my father and mother or relatives if we work hard and plan right. Things in this country *usually* get better for people who really try.
B (Pres)	The second one said: I don't know whether my family will be better off, the same, or worse off than the family of my father and mother or relatives. Things always go up and down *even if* people do work hard. So one can never really tell how things will be.
A (Past)	The third one said: I expect my family to be about the same as the family of my father and mother or relatives. The best way is to work hard and plan ways to keep up things as they have been in the past.

Which of these people do you think had the best idea?

Which of the other two persons had the better idea?

Which of these three people would most other _____ your age think had the best idea?

(*b. 40-up Age Group*)

Three older people were talking about what they thought their children would have when they were grown. Here is what each one said.

C (Fut)	One said: I really expect my children to have more than I have had if they work hard and plan right. There are always good chances for people who try.
B (Pres)	The second one said: I don't know whether my children will be better off, worse off, or just the same. Things always go up and down even if one works hard, so we can't really tell.

A	The third one said: I expect my children to have just about the
(Past)	same as I have had or bring things back as they once were. It is their job to work hard and find ways to keep things going as they have been in the past.

Which of these people do you think had the best idea?
Which of the other two persons had the better idea?
Which of these three people would most other _____ your age think had the best idea?

6. FACING CONDITIONS   *man-nature:* Item MN2

There are different ways of thinking about how God (the gods) is (are) related to man and to weather and all other natural conditions which make the crops and animals live or die. Here are three possible ways.

C	God (the gods) and people all work together all the time;
(With)	whether the conditions which make the crops and animals grow are good or bad depends upon whether people themselves do all the proper things to keep themselves in harmony with their God (gods) and with the forces of nature.
B	God (the gods) does (do) not directly use his (their) power to
(Over)	control all the conditions which affect the growth of crops or animals. It is up to the people themselves to figure out the ways conditions change and to try hard to find the ways of controlling them.
A	Just how God (the gods) will use his (their) power over all the
(Subj)	conditions which affect the growth of crops and animals cannot be known by man. But it is useless for people to think they can change conditions very much for very long. The best way is to take conditions as they come and do as well as one can.

Which of these ways of looking at things do you think is best?
Which of the other two ways do you think is better?
Which of the three ways of looking at things would most other people in _____ think is best?

7. HELP IN MISFORTUNE   *relational:* Item R2

A man had a crop failure, or, let us say, had lost most of his sheep or cattle. He and his family had to have help from someone if they were going to get through the winter. There are different ways of getting help. Which of these three ways would be best?

B	Would it be best if he depended mostly on his brothers and
(Coll)	sisters or other relatives all to help him out as much as each one could?
C	Would it be best for him to try to raise the money *on his own*
(Ind)	outside the community (his own people) from people who are neither relatives nor employers?

| A | Would it be best for him to go to a boss or to an older important |
| (Lin) | relative who is used to managing things in his group, and ask him to help out until things get better? |

Which way of getting the help do you think would usually be best?
Which way of getting the help do you think is next best?
Which way do you think you yourself would really follow?
Which way do you think most other people in _____ would think best?

8. FAMILY WORK RELATIONS   *relational:* Item R3

I'm going to tell you about three different ways families can arrange work. These families are related and they live close together.

C	In some groups (or communities) it is usually expected that
(Ind)	each of the separate families (by which we mean just husband, wife, and children) will look after its own business separate from all others and not be responsible for the others.
B	In some groups (or communities) it is usually expected that the
(Coll)	close relatives in the families will work together and talk over among themselves the way to take care of whatever problems come up. When a boss is needed they usually choose (get) one person, not necessarily the oldest able person, to manage things.
A	In some groups (or communities) it is usually expected that the
(Lin)	families which are closely related to each other will work together and have the oldest able person (*hermano mayor* or father) be responsible for and take charge of most important things.

Which of these ways do you think is usually best in most cases?
Which of the other two ways do you think is better?
Which of all the ways do you think most other persons in _____ would think is usually best?

9. CHOICE OF DELEGATE   *relational:* Item R4

A group like yours (community like yours) is to send a delegate—a representative—to a meeting away from here (this can be any sort of meeting). How will this delegate be chosen?

B	Is it best that a meeting be called and everyone discuss things
(Coll)	until almost everyone agrees so that when a vote is taken almost all people would be agreed on the same person?
A	Is it best that the older, important, leaders take the main re-
(Lin)	sponsibility for deciding who should represent the people since they are the ones who have had the long experience in such matters?
C	Is it best that a meeting be called, names be put up, a vote be
(Ind)	taken, then send the man who gets the majority of votes

even if there are many people who are still against this man?

Which of these ways of choosing is usually best in cases like this?
Which of the other two ways is usually better?
Which would most other persons in _____ say is usually best?

10. USE OF FIELDS   *man-nature:* Item MN3

There were three men who had fields with crops (were farmers). The three men had quite different ways of planting and taking care of crops.

C
(With)   One man put in his crops, worked hard, and also set himself to living in right and proper ways. He felt that it is the way a man works and tries to keep himself in harmony with the forces of nature that has the most effect on conditions and the way crops turn out.

A
(Subj)   One man put in his crops. Afterwards he worked on them sufficiently but did not do more than was necessary to keep them going along. He felt that it mainly depended on weather conditions how they would turn out, and that nothing extra that people do could change things much.

B
(Over)   One man put in his crops and then worked on them a lot of time and made use of all the new scientific ideas he could find out about. He felt that by doing this he would in most years prevent many of the effects of bad conditions.

Which of these ways do you believe is usually best?
Which of the other two ways do you believe is better?
Which of the three ways would most other persons in _____ think is best?

11. PHILOSOPHY OF LIFE   *time:* Item T3

People often have very different ideas about what has gone before and what we can expect in life. Here are three ways of thinking about these things.

B
(Pres)   Some people believe it best to give most attention to what is happening now in the present. They say that the past has gone and the future is much too uncertain to count on. Things do change, but it is sometimes for the better and sometimes for the worse, so in the long run it is about the same. These people believe the best way to live is to keep those of the old ways that one can—or that one likes—but to be ready to accept the new ways which will help to make life easier and better as we live from year to year.

A
(Past)   Some people think that the ways of the past (ways of the old people or traditional ways) were the most right and the best, and as changes come things get worse. These people think the best way to live is to work hard to keep up the old ways and try to bring them back when they are lost.

C
(Fut)
Some people believe that it is almost always the ways of the future—the ways which are still to come—which will be best, and they say that even though there are sometimes small setbacks, change brings improvements in the long run. These people think the best way to live is to look a long time ahead, work hard, and give up many things now so that the future will be better.

Which of these ways of looking at life do you think is best?
Which of the other two ways do you think is better?
Which of the three ways of looking at life do you think most other persons in _____ would think is best?

12. WAGE WORK *relational:* Item R5

There are three ways in which men who do not themselves hire others may work.

C
(Ind)
One way is working on one's own as an individual. In this case a man is pretty much his own boss. He decides most things himself, and how he gets along is his own business. He only has to take care of himself and he doesn't expect others to look out for him.

B
(Coll)
One way is working in a group of men where all the men work together without there being one main boss. Every man has something to say in the decisions that are made, and all the men can count on each other.

A
(Lin)
One way is working for an owner, a big boss, or a man who has been running things for a long time (a *patrón*). In this case, the men do not take part in deciding how the business will be run, but they know they can depend on the boss to help them out in many ways.

Which of these ways is usually best for a man who does not hire others?
Which of the other two ways is better for a man who does not hire others?
Which of the three ways do you think most other persons in _____ would think is best?

13. BELIEF IN CONTROL *man-nature:* Item MN4

Three men from different areas were talking about the things that control the weather and other conditions. Here is what they each said.

A
(Subj)
One man said: My people have never controlled the rain, wind, and other natural conditions and probably never will. There have always been good years and bad years. That is the way it is, and if you are wise you will take it as it comes and do the best you can.

B
(Over)
The second man said: My people believe that it is man's job to find ways to overcome weather and other conditions just

C	as they have overcome so many things. They believe they will one day succeed in doing this and may even overcome drought and floods.
(With)	The third man said: My people help conditions and keep things going by working to keep in close touch with all the forces which make the rain, the snow, and other conditions. It is when we do the right things—live in the proper way—and keep all that we have—the land, the stock, and the water—in good condition, that all goes along well.

Which of these men do you think had the best idea?
Which of the other two men do you think had the better idea?
Which of the three men do you think most other persons in _____ would think had the best idea?

14. Ceremonial Innovation *time:* Item T4

Some people in a community like your own saw that the religious ceremonies (the church services) were changing from what they used to be.

C (Fut)	Some people were really pleased because of the changes in religious ceremonies. They felt that new ways are usually better than old ones, and they like to keep everything—even ceremonies—moving ahead.
A (Past)	Some people were unhappy because of the change. They felt that religious ceremonies should be kept exactly—in every way—as they had been in the past.
B (Pres)	Some people felt that the old ways for religious ceremonies were best but you just can't hang on to them. It makes life easier just to accept some changes as they come along.

Which of these three said most nearly what you would believe is right?
Which of the other two do you think is more right?
Which of the three would most other _____ say was most right?

15. Ways of Living *activity:* Item A3

There were two people talking about how they liked to live. They had different ideas.

A (Doing)	One said: What I care about most is accomplishing things—getting things done just as well or better than other people do them. I like to see results and think they are worth working for.
B (Being)	The other said: What I care most about is to be left alone to think and act in the ways that best suit the way I really am. If I don't always get much done but can enjoy life as I go along, that is the best way.

Which of these two persons do you think has the better way of thinking?

Which of the two do you think you are more like?

Which do you think most other _____ would say had the better way of living?

16. LIVESTOCK INHERITANCE *relational:* Item R6

Some sons and daughters have been left some livestock (sheep or cattle) by a father or mother who has died. All these sons and daughters are grown up, and they live near each other. There are three different ways they can run the livestock.

> A
> (Lin) In some groups of people it is usually expected that the oldest able person (son or daughter, *hermano mayor*) will take charge of, or manage, all the stock held by himself and the other sons and daughters.
>
> C
> (Ind) In some groups of people it is usually expected that each of the sons and daughters will prefer to take his or her own share of the stock and run his or her own business completely separate from all the others.
>
> B
> (Coll) In some groups of people it is usually expected that all the sons and daughters will keep all their cattle and sheep together and work together and decide among themselves who is best able to take charge of things, not necessarily the oldest, when a boss is needed.

Which way do you think is usually best in most cases?

Which of the other two ways do you think is better?

Which of all three ways do you think most other persons in _____ would think is usually best?

17. LAND INHERITANCE *relational:* Item R7

Now I want to ask a similar question concerning farm and grazing land instead of livestock.

Some sons and daughters have been left some farm and grazing land by a father or mother who has died. All these sons and daughters are grown and live near each other. There are three ways they can handle the property.

> A
> (Lin) In some groups of people it is usually expected that the oldest able person (*hermano mayor*) will take charge of or manage the land for himself and all the other sons and daughters, even if they all share it.
>
> C
> (Ind) In some groups of people it is usually expected that each son and daughter will take his own share of the land and do with it what he wants—separate from all the others.
>
> B
> (Coll) In some groups of people it is usually expected that all the sons and daughters will make use of the land together. When a boss is needed, they all get together and agree to choose someone of the group, not necessarily the oldest, to take charge of things.

Which of these ways do you think is usually best in most cases?
Which of the other two ways do you think is better?
Which of all three ways do you think most other persons in _____ would think is usually best?

18. CARE OF FIELDS *activity:* Item A4

There were two men, both farmers (men with fields). They lived differently.

B (Being) One man kept the crops growing all right but didn't work on them more than he had to. He wanted to have extra time to visit with friends, go on trips, and enjoy life. This was the way he liked best.

A (Doing) One man liked to work with his fields and was always putting in extra time keeping them clean of weeds and in fine condition. Because he did this extra work, he did not have much time left to be with friends, to go on trips, or to enjoy himself in other ways. But this was the way he really liked best.

Which kind of man do you believe it is better to be?
(For men only): Which kind of man are you really most like?
Which kind of man would most other _____ think it better to be?

19. LENGTH OF LIFE *man-nature:* Item MN5

Three men were talking about whether people themselves can do anything to make the lives of men and women longer. Here is what each said.

B (Over) One said: It is already true that people like doctors and others are finding the way to add many years to the lives of most men by discovering (finding) new medicines, by studying foods, and doing other such things as vaccinations. If people will pay attention to all these new things they will almost always live longer.

A (Subj) The second one said: I really do not believe that there is much human beings themselves can do to make the lives of men and women longer. It is my belief that every person has a set time to live, and when that time comes it just comes.

C (With) The third one said: I believe that there is a plan to life which works to keep all living things moving together, and if a man will learn to live his whole life in accord with that plan, he will live longer than other men.

Which of these three said most nearly what you would think is right?
Which of the other two ways is more right?
Which of the three would most other persons in _____ say was most right?

20. WATER ALLOCATION *time:* Item T5

The government is going to help a community like yours to get more water by redrilling and cleaning out a community well. The government officials suggest that the community should have a plan for dividing the extra water, but don't say what kind of plan. Since the amount of extra water that may come in is not known, people feel differently about planning.

 A Some say that whatever water comes in should be divided just
(Past) about like water in the past was always divided.
 C Others want to work out a really good plan ahead of time for
(Fut) dividing whatever water comes in.
 B Still others want to just wait until the water comes in before
(Pres) deciding on how it will be divided.

Which of these ways do you think is usually best in cases like this?
Which of the other two ways do you think is better?
Which of the three ways do you think most other persons in _____ would think best?

21. Housework   *activity:* Item A5

There were two women talking about the way they liked to live.

 B One said that she was willing to work as hard as the average,
(Being) but that she didn't like to spend a lot of time doing the kind of extra things in her house or taking up extra things outside like _____ . Instead she liked to have time free to enjoy visiting with people—to go on trips—or to just talk with whoever was around.
 A The other woman said she liked best of all to find extra things
(Doing) to work on which would interest her—for example, _____ . She said she was happiest when kept busy and was getting lots done.

Which of these ways do you think it is usually better for women to live?
(*For women only*): Which woman are you really more like?
Which way of life would most other _____ think is best?

22. Nonworking Time   *activity:* Item A6

Two men spend their time in different ways when they have no work to do. (This means when they are not actually on the job.)

 A One man spends most of this time learning or trying out things
(Doing) which will help him in his work.
 B One man spends most of this time talking, telling stories, sing-
(Being) ing, and so on with his friends.

Which of these men has the better way of living?
Which of these men do you think you are more like?
Which of these men would most other _____ think had the better way of living?

THE BASES FOR THE TYPE OF ITEM OF INQUIRY

1. Difficulties in the Testing of Single Orientations

The theory of variations in value orientations argues, and the empirical evidence thus far examined tends to support the argument, that most concrete patterns of behavior reflect simultaneously all, or almost all, of the value-orientation orderings. It was this fact which gave rise to the first and most serious problem in the construction of the schedule—namely, that we find items of inquiry which were so heavily slanted toward one orientation that the effects of the others would not be great enough to create ambiguity as to which of the orientations was the most responsible for the response elicited. Our judgment was that the more generalized and the more abstract the item was relative to a class of situations, the greater was the possibility that the referent for it in the mind of the respondent would be the orientation we were aiming to test. For example, while the two items treating of inheritance customs (items 16 and 17) do carry some overtones of the *time* orientation, possibly also the *activity* orientation, they are, in the general problems they pose, sufficiently well geared to the variations of the *relational* orientation to yield quite unambiguous results.

But not all of the items of the schedule are equally good in their testing power of a single orientation. Item 1 of the schedule—the item entitled "Job Choice"—is the least adequate of all the items in this respect. It quite obviously is testing an amalgam of at least the *relational*, the *time*, and the *activity* orientations, and it is listed as an *activity* orientation item only because it seems to be somewhat more an expression of it than the others. Our reason for retaining the item, in spite of this shortcoming, was that the type of situation it depicts is a very important one for most of the Rimrock communities (Zuni excepted—see Chapter VIII). But the reader, in examining the analysis of our data on this item, is requested to keep in mind the fact that it is not generally enough phrased to be an adequate test for the *activity* orientation alone.

Although no other single one of the items is as questionable as this one for the testing of the orientations individually, there were certainly differences in the degree of success achieved in this first attempt to develop a research instrument, both as to the type of item and the phrasing of the alternatives of solution of situations the items depict. The value orientation which created the most difficulties in both these respects was the *time* orientation. In general, we consider the items developed for it to have been the least successful in producing responses which can be considered as fairly clear-cut and accurate indications of the ordering of preferences on a single orientation. There were also some problems encountered in phrasing the With-Nature alternative of the *man-nature* orientation, and had we included the Being-in-Becoming alternative of the *activity* orientation there unquestionably would have been more problems still. To some extent these difficulties, as well as some more minor ones encountered in developing the items on the other orientations, can be attributed to the fact that all of the Rimrock communities are a part of the United States and feel constantly the effects of the dominant American value system. However, they are also suggestive of the problem of culture-boundness which was the second of the major problems we faced in the creating of the schedule.

2. Cross-Cultural Testing

Anyone who has attempted cross-cultural testing, using the medium of language, is well aware of the deep and as yet bridgeless chasms which separate the linguistically ordered thought-ways of the peoples of varying cultural traditions. It is even said that it is not really possible to translate meaningfully from one to another of a group of related languages—Indo-European languages, for example. And the chasms are broader and deeper still when the task is that of translating ideas into the languages of non-literate societies which are extremely varied.

We were aware of this hazard before starting the construction of the schedule and were made the more aware of it as we encountered the mentioned difficulties in selecting the items of the *time* orientation and the phrasing of the With-Nature alternative of the *man-nature* orientation. It was our definite judgment that the use of items which depicted highly generalized life situations was the best possible solution of this problem too. The argument is that the more similarly basic and significant a problem situation is to all societies the less is the likelihood that the translation of it from one language to another will result in a serious alteration of the intended meaning.

The task relative to this judgment, as well as the one made about the first of the problems of schedule construction, was clearly twofold. Initially, it was necessary that there be a selection of types of situations which could be considered to have a *more* rather than a *less* degree of critical significance to all rural or folk peoples. But it was even more important that there also be phrasings of the alternatives of the solution of the problem situations which were generally enough stated that the translation into different languages would not produce serious distortions of meaning.

In some instances both the situation and the theoretically derived alternatives of the solution of it virtually suggested themselves. For example, since it is a fact known to all students of culture that all societies have some form of a family system in which there are incorporated customs and rules that govern the economic rights and obligations of family members, there was no difficulty in deciding that a situation treating of the nature of Family Work Relations (item 8 of the schedule) would be crucially important in most, if not all, societies. And the phrasing of the alternatives of the Lineal, Collateral, and Individualistic variations in these relationships was also not very problematic. All that was required was to find a general and easily translatable phrasing of these questions: (1) Does the nuclear family group operate independently in economic matters or does it function as a collaborative unit of an extended family? (2) If it is an extended family organization which governs work relations, is it the Collateral or the Lineal principle which dominantly dictates the patterning of these relationships?

Judgments about many another kind of situation and the alternative answers to it were also fairly easily made. Specific monographs about particular societies and general sociological and anthropological treatises on the nature of human social life were adequate sources for decisions. But not all the items which finally were used were this easily formulated. Moreover, some which had appeared, upon a first consideration, to be adequate had to be discarded. Since the time we ourselves could spare for pre-testing was limited and the number of cultures being tested was only five, it was necessary to seek other means of checking the items. The most important of these was the Human Relations Area File which had been developed, largely under the direction of G. P. Murdock, at Yale University. In the spring of 1951—several months prior to the creation of the schedule—this file was scrutinized both for the categories utilized in the processing of data on some four hundred cultures and for the amount and kind of data which were filed, category by category, on a fairly large sample of cultures. Several suggestive ideas for items as well as checks on items for their degree of universality resulted from this investigation, brief though it had to be.[4]

A few additional comments are needed to explain more fully the form of the instrument and the use of it as a means of cross-cultural testing. Ideally, it would be best if one were able to test directly at the high level of abstraction at which the value orientations are conceptualized. This is not possible. Since the value orientations are in large part implicit, hence seldom consciously verbalized, no systematic direct testing of them can be made. Not even very many of the persons who are highly sophisticated in their knowledge of cultural differences have the degree of conscious awareness of the total ordering of their own preferences on an orientation to state it abstractly. This ordering must be inferentially derived from the preferences allocated to the theoretically derived alternatives of solution of problem situations which have something of a concrete content. But if the barriers of language differences are to be hurdled in order that a uniform method for cross-cultural testing can be achieved, neither the situations which are described nor the alternatives of solving the problems they pose can be highly specific and particularized.

As several of the comments made above indicate, our attempt to solve this complex problem was to seek out situations which were universal in *type* even though somewhat variable in actual *content*, and then hold constant the alternatives of solution of the problem relative to type rather than content. For example, item 2 of the schedule is general in type in posing a problem demanding community decision, but its content—arrangements for providing a community well—is obviously not universally significant. When this same item was used in the Japanese version of the schedule the situation described was changed to one of bridge building. The

---

[4] The investigation of this file was made in the spring of 1951 by Samuel A. Stouffer, John M. Roberts, and Florence Kluckhohn. This group was aided in its investigation by lists of cultures on which the material was fairly uniform which John W. M. Whiting had developed for his own research programs in the Laboratory of Human Development, School of Education, Harvard University.

Japanese have far too much of a water supply in their land to be faced with many serious problems of bringing in water by means of deeply sunk well shafts, and the peoples of arid New Mexico have all too few streams and rivers for bridge building to be a critical issue for community action.

This kind of variability in items poses no theoretical problem at all, but variation in the phrasing of the alternatives of solutions does. For the method to be used successfully as an instrument for cross-cultural testing the alternatives the respondent is requested to rank-order—alternatives which are always deductively derived from the theory—must have a consistent wording language by language. It is necessary, of course, when questioning in the area of religious activities to speak of *God* when the respondents are a monotheistic people and *the gods* when they are pantheistic, but this kind of alteration, which can be noted in some of the items on the *man-nature* (-supernature) orientation, is too minor to be significant.

We do not consider that all of the alternatives as they are expressed in the schedule we developed in 1951 are equally good. In deriving them there was the problem of the culture-boundness of the investigators themselves which has been mentioned. But ultimately this, too, should not be a very serious issue. It can be overcome to some extent (and in our case actually was) if one or more of the investigators has had a long-time experience of living in societies which are culturally quite variable. And if this kind of experience is still not sufficient, it is possible, in the creation of a more refined instrument than we had time to produce, to utilize the knowledge and reactions of persons who have been reared in quite different cultural traditions.

While no claim is made that the schedule we have presented is adequate for highly detailed cross-cultural research in the medium of language, we consider the results which were achieved from its use in the Rimrock communities, and those obtained from the use of the Japanese translation of it, to be sufficiently impressive to warrant the statement that the method has a great potential for analyzing out major cultural variations. There appear to be two reasons for this potential. The first is the realm of the phenomena being tested—basic values or value orientations—and the level of abstraction at which they are formulated. The second is the use, methodologically, of fairly universal types of life situations for which there are developed, deductively, quite general and comprehensively stated alternatives of solution. Supporting evidence for this argument came from remarks of a number of respondents in all the groups tested which, in sum, voiced the opinion

3. Controlling for Defensive Responses and Other Distortions

that the situations cited and the questions posed in the schedule were really important, really crucial, ones.[5]

The defensiveness of respondents is a road block in the path of virtually all research programs which use either the interview or questionnaire tech-

---

[5] For a more detailed statement of the use of the schedule in cross-cultural studies—a statement which includes the English, Spanish, and Japanese language versions of three of the items—see Florence Rockwood Kluckhohn, "A Method for Eliciting Value Orientations," *Anthropological Linguistics*, February, 1960.

nique. Sometimes it is only particular individuals who are resistive to the answering of certain questions. But it is not at all unusual to encounter defensive evasiveness relative to some types of questions in total groups of respondents. And it is not often possible, in the case of either the individual or the total group, to know which types of questions are going to call forth defensiveness, conscious or unconscious, unless one has a long-time and thorough knowledge of both the culture patterns of the group and the situational exigencies it faces. For example, inquiries about specific religious practices may be easily accepted and fully answered in one community whereas in another, such as Zuni, they are considered so threateningly intrusive that the immediate and direct asking of them can completely disrupt the rapport of the interviewer-interviewee relationship. Or to use another illustration, questions on sexual relations which one people may answer freely will appear to another people to be highly threatening, even insulting. There is even a great difference in the number and kind of specific questions which can be asked about family living patterns in two as closely related cultures as the United States and England.

The highly particularized, often definitely idiosyncratic, life experiences of individuals are also a hazard for research which seeks to delineate cultural uniformities. The accidents of fortune which deprive one of a mother or provide one with a psychotic mother, those which produce psychological traumatization or physical maiming are all experiences which affect an individual's responses to questions about social behavior. If the intent is to study the individual case in all of its particularized detail, effects of this kind are an essential part of the record. But when the aim is that of tapping into the universals of the value systems of individuals which surmount the special incident and the particularized experiences they are not desirable effects.

It is only logical to assume that the highly generalized question which refers to a wide range of similar concrete patterns is a far better means of minimizing these effects than is the particularized question where the referent is narrowly specified. But more precautions still can be taken without reducing in the least the usefulness of the questions as a test for the ordering of the value-orientation alternatives. The first of these is to avoid questioning in areas of behavior where defensiveness might be expected—religious rituals and religious organization, for example, or patterns of sexual relations. The second is the use of the third-person phrasing of the problems used for questioning. There are indications from other research programs that the technique of asking for an evaluation of what others have said or done produces a more accurate statement of the subject's own evaluative attitude than the subject-centered question. The third-person phrasing gives to the instrument some of the projective quality which is featured in such tests as the Murray and Morgan Thematic Apperception Test.

Our experience in the use of the instrument, limited as it thus far is, tends to substantiate these arguments. There were few indications of defensive resistance in any of the groups tested. On the contrary a common response in all groups was some form of the statement, "These are really important questions, questions which everyone should think about."[6] Also it was noted time and again that both the generality of the situations and the third-person phrasing of them permitted the individual respondent to give vent to strong feelings in a third-person phrasing. One illustration of this effect is discussed in some detail in Chapter VI. It was the case of the younger brother in a Spanish-American family giving expression to exceedingly hostile feelings about the domination of eldest brothers but doing so with no mention whatsoever of his own eldest brother and his relationship to him. Still another kind of comment, which was noted more frequently among the Zuni respondents than others, was to the effect that they did not mind answering questions of the kind posed because they were not questions which pried into ritual secrets or personal animosities.

But if we can say that the method seems to have the advantages we have discussed under these first three headings—the testing of the orientations one by one, cross-cultural testing, and the minimization of the distorting effects of both defensiveness and particularized experiences—we are not arguing for more than the fact that it appears to be a method, relative to a particular theory, which is capable of eliciting orderings of value-orientation preferences. Important as this achievement may be in and of itself, there remains the critical question of how and why the knowledge of a value system can be used as the basis of predictions about and explanations of more specific types of behavior patterns.

4. The Use of the Results of Testing on General Life Situations as a Basis for Predictions and Explanations

"Guilty of circular reasoning" is a charge often made against the social scientist who studies basic values and seeks in the analysis of them the explanation of important aspects of human behavior. More specifically, the charge is that the value-system analyst studies a given body of behavioral data for deriving and formulating the value system of a people and then proceeds to utilize the resultant formulation to explain the same body of data.[7] The virtue of being "more scientific" is claimed for other methods which seemingly do not fall so easily a prey to circular reasoning. Statistical methods which place great emphasis upon the isolation of variables, the determination of the independence and dependence of variables, and the generation of the "if A then B" type of hypothesis are among

---

[6] Carl Voegelin in a personal letter reported that he received a similar response when he administered the schedule to one of his main Payute informants.

[7] Barrington Moore, Jr., for example, in a recent memorandum which was distributed to members of the Social Relations Department, Harvard University, makes this statement about the procedure of the investigators of values: "In concluding, it may be appropriate to throw out one general question about values that has bothered me for some time.... Does the whole conception involve a form of circular reasoning? What the researcher does, it seems to me, is observe certain uniformities in social behavior and group them together under certain headings that he then calls 'values,' 'cultural themes,' or something similar. So far this is quite legitimate. But then the investigator turns around and uses these 'values' to *explain* the behavior he has observed. To me this doesn't look like scientific cricket. It is easy enough to make some accurate predictions this way. But do the predictions really confirm any theory?"

those for which this claim is made. So also are some of the historical methods wherein the "causal" effects of varying conditions and varying behavioral events upon each other are ordered in a time sequence relative to a theory of historical process.

There is some truth in the statement that some types of value analyses, most especially those which are focused on a single culture, are more *patently* characterized by a circularity of reasoning than these methods or still others which could be cited. One of the reasons this is so is that their focus of interest is much more upon the underlying "why" of behavior in the many related parts of a society than upon the "how" of the relationship of narrowly specified variables. But this difference is only one of degree, for the questions of why and how in the behavioral sciences are not usually considered to be separable, except by those theorists who cling to an extreme positivistic philosophical position and deny that meanings—values—can ever be a proper subject for scientific inquiry.

This issue, important as it may be in and of itself, should in no way be allowed to obscure the fact that there is an inevitable circularity in all thought processes and most especially in scientific procedures. The first of the reasons this is true is the requiredness of the constant interplay between inductive and deductive processes. An excellent statement of this imperative was uttered long ago by Robert Hooke. It is:

So many are the links, upon which the true Philosophy depends, of which, if any one be *loose*, or *weak*, the whole chain is in danger of being dissolved; it is to begin with the Hands and Eyes, and to *proceed* on through the Memory to be *continued* by the Reason; nor is it to stop there, but to *come about* to the Hands and Eyes again, and so by a *continual passage round* from one Faculty to another, it is to be maintained in life and strength, as much as the body of man is by the circulation of the blood through the several parts of the body, the Arms, the Feet, the Lungs, the Heart, and the Head.[8]

In the short history of the development of the social sciences there have been, to be sure, many futile, even bitter, arguments as to the relative validity of the "constructs of the mind" and the "facts derived from sense perception." But it is our belief that there are few, if any, social scientists today who would argue against Henri Poincaré's statement that the bare facts are not enough, that they must be ordered and organized,[9] or disagree with Alfred Marshall's statement that "the most reckless and treacherous theorist of all is the one who professes to let the facts and figures speak for themselves."[10]

If it is accepted that Laurence J. Henderson was right in his general statement that a fact is a verifiable statement about experience in terms of a conceptual scheme,[11] it logically follows that there is a necessary cir-

[8] Robert Hooke, *Micrographia* (London, 1664), Preface, p. 5.
[9] *The Foundations of Science*, trans. George Bruce Halsted (New York, 1913), p. 129.
[10] This statement is taken from *Memorials of Alfred Marshall*, ed. A. C. Pigou, and is quoted in Talcott Parsons, *The Structure of Social Action* (New York: McGraw-Hill Book Co., 1937), p. 6.
[11] Laurence J. Henderson, unpublished lectures written in the years 1938–42 for a special course in sociology at Harvard University.

cularity of thought processes as one moves back and forth from the concepts which allow for the statement, selection, and organization of facts and the empirical testing which leaves the door ever open for the novel observation to revolutionize theoretical conceptualizations. There is no more dramatic illustration of the impact of the novel observation upon a conceptual frame of reference than the one which altered our view of the planes of the earth's surface from one of flatness to one of roundness.

Another reason that some degree of circularity of reasoning cannot be escaped is the fact that the languages or other symbol systems which make human thought processes communicable are necessarily separated into fairly distinctive universes of discourse. It is not possible to talk about everything at once, even if it is assumed that ultimately all things are interrelated. Lines must be drawn; areas of types of conceptualization must be delimited. This necessity is a handicap of great dimension when the problem is one of integrating the conclusions yielded by one theoretical approach with those resulting from others. Indeed, it is this handicap which is the basis of Whitehead's definition of the "Fallacy of Misplaced Concreteness"—the fallacy which arises from the application of a delimited conceptual scheme to a wider range of the phenomena of ultimate reality than it was designed to treat or explain. It is because of this problem, which has proved to be an especially critical one in the social sciences, that the development of good bridge concepts such as the concept of social role are so badly needed.

But this need for the bridging of the various areas for which delimited conceptual schemes are evolved is not the issue of importance here; instead it is the interrelatedness of the variables within a given universe of discourse. And on this issue, it is not the theorist who seeks to find the interrelatedness of behavior patterns relative to a common value system who is the ostrich with his head in the sand; it is his critic who states that he himself is far less guilty of circular reasoning because he has so isolated his variables that he can study the relationship of one to the other without regard for the common denominators which link them fast one to another.

Admittedly, it is possible to utilize highly sophisticated statistical techniques for the investigation of the degree of correlation between such conceptually unrelated processes as the sale of peanuts in New York City and the death rate in an African tribe, but there are few persons who engage themselves with this kind of statistical nonsense except for pure amusement or, perhaps, as a trial balloon for the testing out of possible extensions of a meaningful universe of discourse.

On the contrary, when one scratches beneath the surface of the various methods—statistical, historical, and others—which are proclaimed to be more free of circular reasoning than those used in value-system analyses, one finds *implicit*—unstated—assumptions which are indicative of considerable circularity. Customarily it is assumed that the variables selected for study should all be contained within a given universe of discourse and should have some degree of intrinsic interrelatedness. It would appear that many of the methods also assume that this intrinsic interrelatedness is dependent upon—derives from—a basic value system. All too often, usually in fact, the value system which is implicitly rather than explicitly acknowledged is the one to which the investigator himself adheres. There is, therefore, ground for arguing that the value-system analyst has every right, first, to deny that he is more culpable on the issue of circular reasoning than most of his critics and, second, to enter the countercharge that these critics are themselves given to the still more hampering fault of "cultural-boundness."

Although our own interest, both in the formulation of theory and in the development of the method of testing, was centered more upon the problem of cultural-boundness than that of circular reasoning, we certainly were not unaware of the need to develop means of controlling and curtailing its effects. Criticisms such as the one of Moore's cited above had been too numerous to be ignored. Actually there are, as is implied in some of the comments made above, some reciprocal relationships between the two problems. Our hope, therefore, was that a theory and a method which were sufficiently trans-cultural to be applicable to many cultures would also offer possibilities for some control of the degree of circularity in procedures in studies which seek to investigate the effects of basic values upon behavior.

First, we point out that the theory of variation, however imperfect and incomplete it may still be, is not a conceptualization derived from the study of the concrete patterns of a single culture which one then utilizes for the "explanation" of these same patterns. To be sure, inductive and deductive processes were both involved in the formulation of it, and some of the materials which were inductively examined were the existent analyses of the value systems of individual cultures; but there is no part of either the classification of the alternatives of the value orientations or the ideas about variation which are generalizations from the observed data in a single culture. The value-system analyses of individual cultures, together with other kinds of materials, were inductively examined and analyzed for the purpose of providing the means of deducing the component parts of value systems in general. Thus the nature of the theory—its transcultural characteristic—destroys the ground of one part of the circularity with which the value-system analyst has been charged—the within-culture type of circularity.

But a large part of the problem still remains. Even if one has a theoretical formulation which is general to many cultures rather than specific to one culture, there should be a fairly systematic separation of the data which are utilized for the testing of the concepts and those to which the conclusions reached are then applied, in the form of either testable predictions or explanations. This separation is primarily, though not solely, a methodological rather than a theoretical question, and as a question it is but one instance of the larger problem of maintaining a distinction between abstractions which are empirical generalizations and those which are analytic constructs and the ordering of both types as to degree, or level, of abstraction. No one has been more forceful in arguing these two points than Parsons, but we believe that he would be the first to agree that the distinctions are not made with care by very many in the behavioral sciences. They are difficult ones to hold to; indeed it sometimes is impossible to draw them with real clarity, but it seems obvious that there should be an increase in the control of circular reasoning which is proportionate to the degree such distinctions can be made and held to.

Consideration of this issue was prominent in the thinking which went into the creation of the schedule for the testing of the value orientations. It appeared probable, at the very least, that the method we were devising in the hope of solving the other problems of testing offered a means of eliminating extreme procedural circularity in the use of value systems for explanatory and predictive purposes. Conceivably, it even suggests a means of controlling for circularity in other kinds of studies than those devoted to the effects of basic values upon human behavior.

If it is granted, and we believe it must be, that there is a relationship between the general and specific aspects of behavior—a relationship between the generalized value and the particularized expressions of it in behavior—it logically follows that a knowledge of a value system which has been gained through a use of general questions provides the ground for the generation of numerous hypotheses about many types of much more specific behavior patterns. Let us assume, for example, that the few general questions posed in the orientation schedule show a dominance of the Lineal, the Present, the Subjugated-to-Nature, and the Being orientations—the fairly typical Spanish-American orientations of a generation ago. It is no problem at all, once these values are known, to make predictions about important aspects of the mother-child relationship, the nature of authority patterns, the patterns relating to the segregation of the activities of the two sexes, the relative importance of the activities of the general behavior spheres, and a host of other similar patterns which are midway between the very general level of abstraction which the value system represents and the variability found in the exceedingly concrete minutiae in specific patterns. A knowledge of values most certainly cannot be used to make predictions about such highly specific matters as styles of dress, particular art forms, or precise linguistic usages, but it can be utilized for predictions as to whether expressiveness in the medium of the arts will or will not be important, or whether or not a mother will be acceptant of her child for what he is rather than what he can accomplish as compared to the performance of his own siblings or the children in other families of a locally circumscribed group.

The results of these predictions, once they are formulated and tested, may then be used in two ways. On the one hand they offer the basis for a fuller "explanation" of the highly concrete pattern of behavior; on the other they can be used as a "play back" testing of the validity of the general question technique and then ultimately the postulates of the theory itself. Very generally the argument is: While one can never eliminate the problem of circularity there are ways of preventing the process from becoming the vicious kind of circularity which the picture of the hungry snake swallowing its own tail depicts. The first, most primary, of these is so sorting out and organizing the relationships between theory and method that the distinction between inductive and deductive process is ever clear and the levels of abstraction in each are clearly defined and rigorously held to.

We cannot, on the basis of the evidence provided in this monograph, offer conclusive evidence that this argument is correct. Our task was the forerunner one of demonstrating that there is a validity in both the theory of variation and the method devised for the testing of it. Moreover, the cultures we were examining were far too well known and too well analyzed for this kind of operation to be of much significance. Hence it was far more important that the great backlog of knowledge on each of the communities be utilized for a checking of the theory and method in and of themselves.

But there is evidence of another kind from another study—the study cited above on the comparison of emotionally disturbed and emotionally well balanced families which is being directed by Spiegel and F. Kluckhohn—which lends some degree of credence to the general argument. While it is true that in this study, as it has thus far been developed, there has been no systematic testing by means of a "general life situation" type of instrument, there was a fairly systematic separation of the material used for the formulation of the value systems of Irish-Americans, Italian-Americans, and Old-Americans from the data which were used for the checking of the predictions made about some of the problems to be expected in each group. Monographs, novels, and historical documents were utilized as the basis of the delineation of the value orientations. Once these were roughly formulated some predictions were made about the types of strains endemic to each system and the kinds of emotional problems to be expected because of particular kinds of strains. More specific predictions still were made both as to the differing types of problems which the Irish-American and the Italian-American face relative to the adjustment to dominant middle-class American culture, and to the problems which would be encountered in a therapy program with members of each group. These predictions have been well substantiated in the very small sample of cases thus far studied in each of the groups.[12]

We therefore conclude that the problem of circularity of reasoning is common to all thought, inclusive of the postulates and procedures of science, and argue that the only question of importance relative to it is that of so ordering one's theoretical concepts and so developing the means of testing these that there is some definite separation in the order of the data one uses for the different purposes. We make no claim to originality in this argument. There actually has never been an analyst of value systems who has used precisely the same data for the delineation of a value system and his later explanation of behavior as expressions of value orientations. The complexity of behavior is such that no inductive and no deductive

---

[12] Two papers which treat some of the material relevant to these expectations are the Spiegel paper entitled "Some Cultural Aspects of Transference and Countertransference," which is cited in footnote 50 of Chapter I, and Florence Rockwood Kluckhohn, "Family Diagnosis: Variations in the Basic Values of Family Systems," *Social Casework*, February–March, 1958.

process encompasses all of it; hence there inevitably is always some difference between the conclusions drawn about the value component in behavior and the specific behavior pattern which is later "explained" by it. All we have suggested is that there be, both theoretically and methodologically, a more rigorous separation than apparently has been customary of the data used for the depicting of a value system and those which are used for either the testing of hypotheses about patterns of behavior or the explanations of behavior. And while, as this discussion has indicated, there are more ways than one of accomplishing this end, we believe that the method of testing on general life situations for the ascertaining of the basic values which may then be used deductively as the basis of both predictions and explanations is a quite clean-cut and fairly unequivocal one. However, we would not wish any reader to conclude that we consider the method to be superior to, or a substitute for, the long-range and detailed studies of the peoples of different cultures. There are, as has been indicated, many detailed aspects of cultures to which the theory and method combined do not apply, at least not directly.

THE QUESTION OF THE NUMBER OF ITEMS NEEDED FOR TESTING

There is as yet no unequivocal answer to this question. Our own decision to create a schedule of not more than twenty-four items for the testing of within-culture regularities and between-culture differences was in large part dictated by circumstance. Time was limited; we had only two months for the two operations of creating the schedule and administering it in the field. The sheer locating of the residence or the sheep camp abode of some of the selected respondents in some of the groups, most especially the Navaho one, required hours of travel over poor roads and dim wagon trails. And since there was no surety that the selected respondent would be found "at home" or willing to talk on a particular day, return journeys had to be contemplated. Given these facts, it clearly was not feasible to plan for more than one interview session with one subject.

Once this decision was reached, the next question was that of estimating the time span of the single interview which would be both endurable for the respondent and optimally productive for the research program. Our judgment—a judgment which proved to be accurate—was that the questioning on six choice situations for each of the four orientations being tested would require one to two hours in time. Two hours was considered the outside limit of time that we could expect to hold the attention of any respondent.

As has been shown, the schedule as finally developed was not precisely a six-item-per-orientation one. The number of items used for testing the *relational* orientation was increased to seven in order to include a second type of inheritance problem, and the number on all the other orientations was reduced to five. These reductions were made because of pre-testing operations which showed that certain items were ambiguous.

The time available for pre-testing was limited; hence not all the dubious items could be weeded out. The one outstanding illustration of a retained item which yielded almost no discriminatory results is the *relational* orientation item labeled Choice of Delegate (item R4 in the schedule). The response pattern to it was virtually the same in all the groups tested. How much this result reflects the general effects in political matters of the dominant American culture upon all the communities is a question which we can pose but cannot answer conclusively. The result in the Spanish-American group—a result which is to be reported upon more fully in Chapter VI—appears mainly to be a reflection of the influence of one strongly variant individual who, in recent years, has had the top-ranking political position.

But even if it is allowed that a more adequate pre-test program than we were able to undertake would have given more certainty of the discriminating powers of the individual items, there still remains a question as to the optimum number of questions for cross-cultural distinctions. We considered that five to seven items for each orientation, distributed to some degree over the different behavior spheres, would be adequate for the main purposes of the research program. These were, we repeat, the testing for within-culture regularities and for between-culture differences in the ranking of the orientation alternatives. Five to seven sets of rankings are sufficient for the demonstration by usual statistical measures that an emergent pattern could not be simply a chance occurrence. One may even argue on statistical grounds that the limitation we placed upon the number of items actually reduced the chances of obtaining significant results for the ranking of preferences among the value-orientation alternatives. On the basis of chance alone there is a greater probability that a discernible pattern will emerge from the testing on fifty rather than five items. This is especially true relative to the summary pattern—the overall pattern—of the value-orientation orderings. If there is the amount of intra-cultural variation in all societies which the variation theory postulates, one should expect the *dominant* ordering of preferences to be the better displayed in proportion to the number of items used for testing.

This statement, both directly and indirectly, points up the most serious deficiency of the research instrument, which is that it does not test either fully or systematically for intra-cultural variations. But there is no apology needed for this deficiency. In any research program one must move forward step by step and use great caution in the stepping. In the case of our own theory and method it was clear that the testing for and demonstration of intra-cultural variations had to wait upon the results of a research program which had the aim of showing that the postulated within-culture regularities and between-culture differences in the rankings of value-orientation preferences do exist.

The later stage of research planning—one which is now in the making—is to so expand the method of testing that there can be a much more extensive testing of the several types of intra-cultural variation. Whether this can be done, or to what extent it can be done, is a question for which, once again, there are no certain answers. There are at least two critical problems to be faced. The first, given the dictates of the method we developed, is that of determining the range of types of general life situations which have a sufficient degree of universality that they are useful for cross-cultural testing. We went a certain distance in this quest but did not make checks adequate to a definite conclusion either as to type or number of items.

The second question relates to the degree of specificity which may be required to test systematically for any such variations as those found in the behavior spheres. Is it possible to hold to the level of abstractness which we tried to use throughout the present schedule in testing on the several kinds of variations? Hopefully and optimistically we say "yes"; honestly and conservatively we say, "we do not yet know."[13] But even if this particular kind of advance and refinement of the instrument proves to be fruitless, it is still possible to test some kinds of variations by using the deductive method discussed in the preceding section.

SAMPLING IN THE FIVE COMMUNITIES

Would it be a better test of the hypotheses about the variations in the value orientations to test intensively in two, possibly three, communities or to sample more thinly in all five of the Rimrock communities? This was the first decision to be made concerning sampling procedures. It was, as has already been made clear, the latter choice that was made. Thus, in the first instance, the total sample was a culturally stratified one of 106 persons.

The two next issues which required decisions were the size of the five samples and the method of sample selection. Here again we faced the circumstantial factors of limited time, limited financial resources, and probable rapport problems in some of the groups. We knew, for example, that it would have demanded all of our time and all of our research funds to contact a sampling fraction of even 10 per cent in the two Indian communities. (Even with the sample size decided upon, the travel and interpreter expenses for these two groups accounted for approximately four fifths of the total field expenses. And the time consumed in interviewing in these two groups was comparably great.) Also in another way the size of the samples within cultures was prejudged. Since the overall sample was by cultures, it was thought wise to have comparably sized samples for each culture. Therefore, the sample size of *twenty-odd* adults in each group was in part dictated by the fact that in the Spanish-American community there were no more than this number of adults available for interviewing.

The method of selecting twenty to twenty-five adult respondents, divided approximately evenly between the two sexes, for the Spanish-American group was the simple one of "total sample." There were thirteen men and

---

[13] The program which has the aim of creating a greatly expanded schedule which will (*a*) test fairly systematically on the behavior sphere variations and (*b*) be appropriate for the testing of urban peoples was started in 1957 by Richard P. R. Kluckhohn. The work he did was jointly sponsored by George Goethals of the Harvard University School of Education and William Caudill of the Harvard University Department and Laboratory of Social Relations.

twelve women over twenty years of age. All except two very young men (see below for comments on these two cases) answered the schedule in full. Thus, the total sample for this group was twenty-three.

Random samples from total populations of persons over twenty years of age were drawn from the Texan, Mormon, and Navaho groups. The postmistresses in the Texan and Mormon communities were the primary sources of the population enumerations necessary for the sampling procedure in these two groups. The only corrections made in their lists were the deletion of the names of three Spanish-Americans who used the Homestead post office and the names of persons on the Rimrock list who were not Mormons. In selecting the sample for the Navaho we had only to turn to the carefully compiled census material which C. Kluckhohn and his assistants have been collecting over a period of many years. In all three of these cases the procedure was, first, to reject the names of all persons under twenty years of age; second, to sort the remaining names into two piles which differentiated by sex; and finally, by use of random numbers to draw the names of ten men and ten women. Alternate names were also drawn in case there had to be substitutions. None had to be made in the Mormon group and only one was made in the Texan group. However, because of an error in interpretation of the sex of one Mormon respondent, the sample for this group was composed of eleven men and nine women rather than ten of each.

For reasons that are explained later we expected that several substitutions would have to be made in the Navaho sample. Therefore, in addition to drawing an original sample of ten men and ten women a full alternate sample of ten men and ten women was drawn. The sample of twenty-two sets of responses which was finally collected and used contained seven substitutes, four male and three female, selected from this alternate sample.

Obtaining a sample of the Zuni was the most difficult of the sampling tasks. The one finally drawn and used was not a random sample representative of the Zuni community as a whole. Instead, it was a selected sample from a particular segment of the population which in 1951 and 1952 was being intensively studied by John Roberts for other purposes. It is better that the difficulties and conditions which prevented us from drawing from this population a sample that was technically the equal of the others be left for Roberts to explain in his discussion of his experience in contacting the respondents of Zuni.

At the time these samples were being selected we believed it preferable to have larger ones for a single culture. Retrospectively the judgment is that the limitation to twenty-odd respondents in five cultures was not only adequate for our stated aims but actually advantageous. By insisting on venturing into five different cultures and thus limiting the number of respondents in any one culture, we were able to carry out the informal validation procedure provided by a comparison of predicted and observed outcomes for the communities. Had we tested in only one or two cultures, this procedure would not have been nearly so useful for validation purposes. Also, because our method was an untried one, we could not be sure that the items in the schedule would produce results as homogeneously representative of the alternatives of the orientations as the analysis of the data will show them to be. To be sure, when later these results are presented, it will be seen that while for some cultures the dominant orderings of the several orientations could have been established with even fewer items than we used, there were other cases—most especially the answers from the Zuni group on all orientations—where both the small size of the sample and its nonrandom character created numerous problems for interpretation.

But it is patently obvious that for a systematic testing on *intra-cultural* variations the sample sizes of respondents is no more adequate than is the number of test items orientation by orientation. Future developments in the method will require an expansion in both directions. This is most especially the case in the testing of peoples where there is not the wealth of extant information which can be utilized for a detailed interpretation of the intra-cultural variations which the data of the schedule suggest.

INTERVIEWER ACCOUNTS OF THEIR FIELD EXPERIENCE IN THE ADMINISTRATION OF THE SCHEDULE

Uniform conditions for administration of the schedule were not possible. Languages were different, the living conditions of the five peoples were different, and the bases for rapport with subjects were also different. In short, we faced all the variations of field conditions which one expects to find in moving from one culture to another. The one uniform requirement which it was agreed that all interviewers should hold to was the method of presenting the questions on the schedule. Whether in one language or another and whether presented directly or through an interpreter, a firm condition was that no explanation could be given of any of the choice situations or the alternatives posed for the solution of them. The question, always presented orally, could be read more than once if necessary, even as many as three or four times, but each reading was to be the same. But, believing that the questions asked by the respondents or the comments they made about particular questions would be of great value both for later interpretation of our results and for future improvement of schedule items, the interviewers were expected to record them in the manner a field anthropologist makes field notes. Each interviewer was requested to submit a summary report of his field experiences and copies of his field notes shortly after completing his interviewing program. The accounts of field experiences, slightly edited and somewhat condensed, are now presented under the name of the individual interviewer.

Experiences with the Spanish-Americans of Atrisco (Florence Kluckhohn)

In some respects the cooperation the Spanish-Americans in the village of Atrisco gave to the research program was better than that of any of the other groups. Primarily the difference was one of degree of motivation. No one of the group displayed any curiosity or concern about the purpose of the schedule of questions, but the will either to help me as an old friend or to comply with the request of my co-workers who were much loved members of the community was strong in almost every member of the community.

I have previously written in some detail[14] and shall later (Chapter VI) give a brief review of my experience as a participant-observer in Atrisco in 1936 and subsequent years. The point to be emphasized here is that over the years both my husband and I had built up enduring relationships with most members of the community. Many we consider close friends.

Yet in all the years I had followed the lives of *los Atrisqueños*, both those who have remained in the village and those who have migrated to other places, I had never used direct research techniques. Hence I was not altogether certain what the response would be to a request for cooperation in a program which required taking a period of time to answer a fixed schedule of questions. I did, however, know that if the cooperation were to be attained it had to be on the basis of friendship rather than any form of a contractual arrangement which offered a specified remuneration. In Spanish-American culture the request of a favor of a close friend (*un amigo*) or a relative is well understood; the contractual relationship, in addition to being an unfamiliar pattern for in-group relations, was actually looked upon with suspicion because of a number of unfortunate experiences members of the community had encountered in contractual relationships with Anglo-Americans.

My first step was to contact a son and daughter of the once powerful *patrón* of the village, both good friends, tell them what I wished to do, and ask for their cooperation in administering the schedule. I needed their help to gain the cooperation of a few persons whom I did not know well because they had not lived in the village proper in the year I worked there most intensively. I also needed it for two other reasons. Because of the strict segregation of the sexes in Spanish-American culture it was not wise that I, a woman, interview alone the men of the village, especially those who had to be sought far out on the sheep range. Indeed the vicissitudes of travel over the range land were such that I could not even have got to them by myself with the car I was driving. A language problem was the other reason. Although I knew the Spanish language and could use it, I did not feel my command of it was adequate for both a careful reading of the questions and a recording of the answers and comments made by respondents.

These two persons, without hesitation and with the graciousness so characteristic of Spanish-Americans, when it is a friendship relationship which is the appeal, offered their service to the extent that they could arrange their daily life work to give it. And the extent was great in both cases. The young man, Fred Atrisco, gave only the very minimum of attention to his herds of sheep all during the interview program. And the woman so arranged her life that we were always free to go in search of

---

[14] My use of the participant-observer technique in Atrisco is treated in "The Participant-Observer Technique in Small Communities," *American Journal of Sociology*, Vol. XLVI (1940), pp. 331–44.

respondents as long as we took her young children along. The children were never a problem, for they stayed where they were told to stay and did not interfere with interview sessions.

Almost all of the arrangements for the interviews were made by one or the other of these two co-workers. Either they made the contacts directly or sent the word via the local grapevine. The dispatch with which the interviews were both arranged and completed tells much about the value orientations of Spanish-Americans and also something about the "culture-boundness" of even moderately sophisticated social scientists. Although I well knew the Present *time* orientation of these people, knew also their strong feelings of obligations to relatives and friends, and knew that Being-oriented behavior would dominate over the Doing type, I was still not quite prepared for what happened. Indeed I had half expected that the interviewing in the community would take a long time. It did not. Not only did the co-workers drop all that they possibly could of their daily routine to expedite the program; so did almost everyone else. Something in the Present had been defined as important, so other things could wait. One respondent, for example, was found at a time when he was supposed to return the laundry his wife had done for a family in the Texan community. "Let it wait," he said, "this is more important; I can take the laundry tomorrow or the next day." One result of this general interpretation of a job important enough that all other work should be severely curtailed or dropped was that I, the interviewer, was required to work night and day and at a rapid pace. And all interviews were completed in the remarkably short time of ten days.

The subjects, many of whom were bilingual, were always given a choice between the Spanish and English versions of the schedule. In the one third of the cases where the English version was selected, I administered the schedule without aid. When the Spanish translation was used, one or the other of the two Spanish-American co-workers read the questions, and I recorded the answers and all comments and questions. In almost all these cases the Spanish-American woman questioned the women and the Spanish-American man questioned the men.

The questioning customarily took place in the respondents' own homes. When it was explained that each person should answer the questions privately, it was usually the case that all other members of the family, including the children, quickly disappeared. In a few of the interviews small children did run in and out, but they said nothing and were no hindrance to the interview situation. The variations from this pattern were the interviewing of two sheepherders out on the range, the interviewing of two other men in the home of the male co-worker, and one interview which was conducted in the car. In this last case the subject was the outstanding deviant of the community, a man, half French-Canadian, who has been a notorious alcoholic and trouble-maker for years. He was the only person who was really diffident about answering the questions, saying that he had not time for them, could spend only a few minutes, and preferred to answer them in the car rather than go into the house. He took only thirty minutes all told, but he seemed to understand the questions easily and was not only firm in his answers but most frank in distinguishing between what he thought best and what he actually did on those questions where this distinction was requested. My co-worker was disturbed by the haste of this interview and doubted the worth of the answers. I myself had no such doubt after checking the answers against the man's case history. His answers, both about what he thought best in contrast to what he did, and about how his views differed from the views of others in the community, were in perfect accord with the many observations of his attitudes and behaviors over a long period of years.

In my contacts with people, many of whom I had not seen for some time, there was first a period of general conversation. When finally the matter of the schedule was brought up, the usual approach was: "We have some questions to ask you," or "Here are some questions Florence would like to ask you." An interesting additional touch was customarily added by the female co-worker. "You are to give your 'confessions' to Florence" was her partly humorous and partly realistic way of phrasing the situation for the subjects. The typical response to this remark was either a smile or outright laughter, but apparently the phrasing also made sense. One elderly woman, of whom I had been somewhat terrified in my earlier visits to Atrisco, laughed most heartily and then said, "You know I don't like to give my confessions even in church; but all right, I will if you want."

A few persons were at first reluctant to answer the questions, saying that they did not know enough for anything they said to be of use. The reticence always vanished when it was explained that we were seeking opinions about matters which concerned everyone and were not testing anyone's knowledge of facts.

The only refusals were the two young men mentioned above, and one of these could scarcely be called a refusal. He is somewhat retarded mentally and members of his family feared the effort would be too much for him. One of his sisters put the matter to me in these words: "He will try if you want him to and if you have to have answers from everyone, but it will be hard on him. We just don't think he can do it." In light of this plea I did not try to question him. In the case of the other young man, the twenty-year-old son of the outstanding deviant referred to above, the trouble apparently was extreme shyness. On the several occasions one of the co-workers and I went to the *ranchito* of his family, he had always vanished. "He is off shooting rabbits," his mother first said, and no doubt he really was. But then she said that he was too shy, too afraid, and it was better not to press him.

Most of the persons who were interviewed seemed much interested in the questions after becoming acquainted with their nature. Several remarked that they were really serious questions and required much thought. On the whole the questions seemed to be well understood, but no one except the man who spent only thirty minutes on them was willing to respond after a single reading of an item. In a number of instances a third reading was requested. One man, a sheepherder who was suffering much pain from arthritis, asked for a fourth reading for some of the items.

The reading technique, although standardized in accord with the requirement that there could be no paraphrasing or explanation of the alternative choices and no replies to questions about the items, did vary somewhat from reader to reader. The man who interviewed the men in Spanish read the questions very deliberately in a monotone which was devoid of any expressive accenting of word or phrase. His sister in her interviewing of the women (and one of the men) spoke more rapidly and had more expression in her voice. The difference between the two was in part a personality difference, but it should also be remarked that the woman had taught school for a number of years and had also had considerable experience interpreting for political meetings. I judge my own reading of the English version of the schedule to have been midway between the modes of the two co-workers. From an analysis of the results for the Spanish-Americans as a whole, it does not appear that either the variable mode of reading or the variation in language made any difference.

One additional fact which has some bearing on the question of interviewer bias is that the woman who read the schedule had, in answering the questions herself, selected alternatives on some of the orientations which were quite different from those chosen by a majority of women. But still another factor was that the subjects themselves, having been asked to give their *own* opinion, did not seem to wish guidance or be assured that they were doing what was expected. In only two cases was anything of this kind noted.

One of these was a young woman whom I interviewed in English. This woman is by far the most conflicted Spanish-American woman I have encountered in twenty-odd years of work with the Spanish-speaking people of New Mexico. While I have neither the knowledge nor the ability to analyze the sources of her great hostility, her profound belief in witchcraft, her extreme bitterness about having to live in isolated Atrisco, and numerous other symptoms, I do know enough about her family background and her personal history to state that one of her problems is being caught between a need to adhere to Spanish-American values and a strong desire to forsake them for Anglo-American ones, as she understands these to be. Her behavior in the interview session was marked by great indecision. Also she had to be reassured several times at the beginning of the session, as no other person was, that there were no "right" answers.

The other case was a man who had long been an especially good friend both of the co-worker who questioned him and myself. He is one of the most jovial and good-natured men in the village. The session with him was gayer than with the other respondents. He was not at all undecided about his answers, but he frequently asked if, in general, he was doing all right. The gaiety came chiefly when, with signs of embarrassment, he consistently selected the Being alternative to the items on the *activity* orientation series.

The question of recompense for time and effort expended was difficult to solve. Even though I knew the cooperation had been granted as a personal favor, I felt that both the co-workers, who spent almost all their time for a ten-day period, and the respondents must be given more than a mere "thank you." And since I was not living in the area continuously, I could not count on the compensation of favors returned. Thus, I insisted that the two persons who assisted me accept a payment in money. Both at first flatly refused even to consider the idea. Finally, after being able to convince them that the payment was not to be from me personally but from research funds allocated for just this purpose, I was able to get both of them to accept some money *for their children*. The decision as to how to compensate the respondents I left to the two co-workers. Their selections were boxes of candy for families where several persons had been interviewed and books in the Spanish language for the two herders who were most of the time alone on the sheep range. And again they insisted that more than this would not be "right," meaning, of course, acceptable. But it was my own decision to do what no one would ask and what really pleased everyone most. I donated a substantial sum of money, partly my own, since I have long felt myself a part of this community, to the fund being raised to convert a vacant schoolhouse into a church. In 1950 the village church had burned to the ground, and the felt need for another church was great, even though the number of people who would use it was growing smaller and smaller each year.

These various reactions give support to the argument that the rewarding of informants and respondents for their help should accord with their own motivations for cooperating. As far as Spanish-Americans are concerned, supportiveness and warm friendly attitudes mean much more than any amount of material goods. And once you are accepted as a friend, which to some extent means being one of their own group, there is almost nothing a Spanish-American will not do to help you, providing he has the means and the ability. Approaching him with any kind of contractual arrangement, whether of money or other kinds, can have, in my opinion, only negative effects.

Field Experience with Texans and Mormons (Fred L. Strodtbeck)

There were few difficulties encountered in the interviewing of either the Texans or the Mormons. A majority of the respondents in both groups had a "built in" readiness to converse with me as an acquaintance, an investigator, or both. Because of a five-month period of residence in the area on research of another kind, I was moderately well acquainted with a number of the respondents in both samples. Also in both communities it was known, and more or less accepted, that project workers were making investigations. Moreover, the field conditions for the interviewing of these two groups were much less arduous than those for any of the other groups. The farms of the Texans were all geographically bound within a fifteen-mile radius, and the distances within the Mormon village were short and those to surrounding ranches not great. A prolonged drought in the summer of 1951, devastating to the farmers and ranchers, was a boon to me in that the roads were dry and moderately passable at all times.

The pattern of approach to the respondents was not entirely uniform. For example, when I located one particularly isolated and impoverished Texan family, I approached the barefooted woman who was making soap in a large black kettle in the yard and called her by name, saying, "I've come

2000 miles to talk to you today." This remark elicited a self-effacing response in which the respondent denied that her views would be important to anyone.

This broad and good-natured approach had been evolved by trial and error in my two previous visits to the Texan community. Because of the embarrassment so many in the community of Homestead showed about the level of convenience of their homes and the degree of development of their community, I had found something of a "joking pattern" the easiest means of establishing rapport. Also this approach seemed, in general, to produce a more relaxed and reflective attitude in the respondents than did a highly cautious and courteous one.

However, there was a difference in response, hence also of approach, which related to variations in social status. The higher-status families of the community had already become much more involved than most of the lower-status families in the intensive research which others were carrying out in Homestead at the time we presented our own schedule of questions. The persons of our sample from these families tended to cooperate much more on the basis of a favor to a friend—or at least a favor to the friend of a friend. Moreover, while they were equally as earnest in answering the questions and making it plain why they chose a particular alternative, they were much more capable than the respondents of lower status of laughing at themselves when they took a long time to explain their position. Judgment cannot here be passed as to whether the laughter meant more rather than less tension.

There were few problems of communication with the Texan subjects. The choice situations seemed to be well understood. Very seldom was it necessary to read a set of alternatives more than once.

The Mormon respondents were equally as cooperative and as interested as the Texans, but there were noteworthy differences in some of their reactions. For most of the Mormon group, once they became familiar with the nature of the questions, the issues involved in the choice situations seemed to have definite moral implications. The men in particular tended to regard the request for their personal convictions (their choices) about the situations as a moral challenge. Thus, in addition to giving their preferences, they almost always set about explaining how and why their own daily life behavior and attitudes either accorded with Church teachings or varied from them. And it seemed to be a most serious matter for them either way. They did not have the Texans' easy and self-effacing grace in dealing with their own over-seriousness.

There were no refusals from the Mormons selected in the sample. This was the more remarkable in that some of the men to be interviewed were hard pressed at the time. A number of them were working all day in an ordnance plant some fifty miles away, and after returning home they still had to tend to irrigation ditches and crops before they could take time for an interview. Obviously in these cases the interview sessions were an encroachment upon the individual's period of rest and sleep. But to a person, the Mormons were unfailingly thorough and cooperative in completing the task of answering the questions.

In both of these groups the sampling lists were inexpensively obtained, there was no problem of refusals, and the respondents were highly cooperative and appeared also to be greatly interested. In short, the combination of conditions was almost all that could be desired.

Interviewing the Zuni (John M. Roberts)

The lot of field workers in Zuni has been variable. Much has depended upon the skill, temperament, resources, and good fortune of the investigator, the nature of his problem, and the changeable temper of the village. Although some short-term field workers have found the way relatively easy and smooth, every anthropologist who has been in the village long enough for opinion to be mobilized and tension to develop has encountered both major and minor obstacles. In this study, problems were met in establishing rapport, selecting the sample, and administering the schedule. The solutions to some of these problems merit discussion.

Rapport was all-important. In the Southwest the comparative difficulty of Pueblo research is an ethnographic commonplace. The Rio Grande Pueblo are more difficult than the Zuni, but the Zuni are more resistant to investigation than the Hopi and substantially more so than the Navaho. In extreme instances investigators have been forced to leave the community, and the near or distant threat of such action is always present.

The ethnologist must be sensitive and always on his guard. He may enter the village when it is relatively open, only to find that as the months pass hostile opinion has been marshaled against him through circumstances quite beyond his control. Again the situation may unaccountably ease. In the course of my overall research program in Zuni, each year from 1949 through 1953 became less difficult than its predecessor. This meant that the research design for testing the value orientations was formulated and the pre-testing of it conducted at a time (1950) when conditions were relatively severe. The administration of the schedule in 1951 was carried out under more relaxed circumstances, although at times the improvement in rapport was not too apparent.

Such a changing, precarious rapport situation cannot be easily analyzed. Unlike the other four communities, this tightly integrated one, which constituted a virtually independent tribe in the recent past, cannot be penetrated easily by any outsider, whether Indian or white. Zuni is too much of an in-group. In addition, a particular antagonism is directed toward whites, and no white man in one of the common white roles in Zuni (trader, missionary, government worker) is fully accepted. Their rejection is masked by a surface friendliness which is the only side of Zuni a casual visitor sees.

Although Zuni has certainly been well studied, "ethnologist" is not a regular role in modern Zuni. In many quarters there is certain to be aggression directed toward the white man who attempts to study Zuni culture. In other quarters there is uncertainty and bewilderment. In the case of the anthropologist, hostility is commonly and recurrently expressed in the charge that he is attempting to buy or steal tribal religious secrets and sacred objects, the loss of which would be a catastrophe in Zuni eyes. The fact that such loss has actually occurred in the past does not mitigate the situation.

In addition to the strong in-group feeling and objection to investigation, factionalism and in-group hostility within Zuni must be considered. No one can truly vouch for the ethnologist to the entire community in the sense that such a person's good opinion would be accepted by all. As a matter of fact, the enemies of an informant will use his aid to the ethnologist as a basis for gossip. Again informant A may not cooperate simply because informant B has already been identified as the ethnologist's friend. Regardless of other factors, every Zuni who cooperates with an anthropologist or sponsors his work accepts some personal risk. Space does not permit the consideration of other facets to this complex situation.

In such circumstances one does what he can. Formal approval by the Indian Service and by the Zuni governor proved useful. Repeated assurances to responsible persons that the religious life of the Zuni would not be studied were very important. This promise was faithfully kept. No attempt was made to establish close connection in Zuni with government employees, missionaries, traders, or other anthropologists for any part of my research. I even decided to live away from the pueblo and visit it for comparatively short periods at a time. This enabled me to adopt the role of "friend," and carry on relationships on a basis of mutual hospitality. Other adjustments I shall refer to below.

The selection of the sample was difficult. As has been stated, the Zuni sample was technically inferior to the others used in the study. Although it was the same size as the others, the village of Zuni is so much larger than the other communities that the sample was proportionately much smaller. Again it was a selected and not, as in the case of three communities, a random sample. Ideally, the sample should have been both larger and random, but this did not seem feasible in view of rapport conditions. The one finally selected was the result of compromise and adjustment to situational factors which could not be altered.

If the research on the value orientations had been the only program under way in Zuni at the time, it is possible that a random sample could have been employed with a very rapid interviewing program which would have allowed the investigators to leave before an ugly situation developed. But other research was being conducted at the time and still more research was planned for the future; hence it was not possible to adopt such a rapid procedure. This particular project had to be fitted into the overall Zuni research program.

Even so, it might have been impractical to use a random sample. When the 1950 pre-test was administered in Zuni, informants were chosen somewhat at random. Tension and suspicion immediately mounted; each individual presented a separate rapport problem; and the entire project was much too "visible." Not only would a random sample in Zuni have been costly (despite the lack of travel and the ease of finding a particular informant), but the factional situation at that time would have made such an approach most onerous. Even under favorable circumstances it took time to win an informant's consent. If factional lines were to be crossed and, more importantly, recrossed, both the time involved and the risks of failure would be multiplied.

It seemed expedient to utilize a sample which had been constructed for another purpose and to draw the twenty informants from it. This sample, which will be described in detail in other publications, can be described as a multiple-role, small-group net.[15] It consisted of a series of interlocking or tangential small groups which had been extended from a central core of five interlocked households to include a representative selection of modern Zuni roles. There was no reason to assume that the persons in this net were atypical or deviant. Particular attention was paid to the individual who was a member of two or more groups in the net since rapport developed with him had a double value. In this instance the goodwill of informant A was a material help in obtaining the cooperation of informant B since the two were usually linked by fairly close ties. This would not have been the case with a random sample.

Despite the fact that the informants were selected, it is thought that they were representative of the small-group net (at least there was variance in age, sex, role, presumed conservatism, etc.). There was an advantage, too, in the fact that the same people were being studied by several scientists with varying problems and viewpoints over a period of time. And it was hoped that current or planned research would eventually enable the small-group net to be placed in the context of the total community. This research unfortunately will not be completed in time to aid the present study. In addition to this collateral research the substantial Zuni literature constitutes a material aid in criticism and interpretation. It must be emphasized, however, that generalizations from the small-group net to the community as a whole can be made only on a most tentative basis.

The administration of the schedule of questions also merits discussion. Here it might be noted that experience in 1950 with a trial set of questions among both the Navaho and Zuni proved invaluable. Pre-testing of the schedule as completed in 1951 also established the fact that the English-language version of it could not be used even for those Zuni who had a working knowledge of English. Dissatisfied with the quality of the Zuni interpretation, I decided to record each question in the Zuni language on a plastic record used in a standard office dictating machine. The records could then be played to the informants so that each would respond to exactly the same stimulus. Under such circumstances it would be impossible for the interpreter to vary his translation with different informants.

A satisfactory set of records was not easily acquired. After lengthy explanation and orientation the questions were read in English to a Zuni interpreter who then dictated his Zuni translation to the machine. I naively assumed that this would be a satisfactory translation, but when the questionnaire was given in Zuni from the records and then later given in Eng-

---

[15] This small-group net is discussed in Watson Smith and John M. Roberts, *op. cit.*, pp. 8–9.

lish by myself to bilingual members of the community, there were differences in the two sets of responses which made it clear that the recorded translation was unacceptable. Next, the entire schedule of questions was reviewed very carefully with the interpreter, and numerous corrections were made. The interpreter then dictated a new set of records, but on this occasion he actually talked to a Zuni informant at the same time. This procedure resulted in an improved translation, but one which on testing still proved unsatisfactory.

It then became necessary to prepare in Zuni a literal translation of the items of the schedule. Careful consideration was given to each word and phrase. I myself, who spoke Zuni most clumsily, dictated the questions in Zuni to the interpreter. He then dictated them in Zuni to the machine. It was necessary to dictate some questions several times before a satisfactory recording was achieved. As an additional check, this new version was given to a bilingual white man who lived in Zuni. He compared the dictated version with the English version and found a number of places where the translation was inadequate. After some discussion the interpreter, the consultant, and I worked together to revise the Zuni version. Finally the complete set of records was finished.

By the time the interviewing was begun, initial rapport and, in some cases, very close rapport had been attained with the informants. But it still was not possible to proceed very rapidly. Both before and after the period of questioning a considerable amount of time was spent in relaxed and casual conversation.

Prior to the questioning, the machine was demonstrated and the informant gained some familiarity with the apparatus. Each question was played twice before the informant answered, and on a few occasions the record was played three times. It seldom took less than two hours to administer the schedule. When an informant chose to think about a matter, he was not hurried, but he was not allowed to consult with anyone. Usually the questions were asked in privacy, in the sense that the interpreter, the informant, and I were alone in a room, but there were always friends and relatives in the background. Sometimes spectators were unavoidably present; fortunately they were always quiet and unobtrusive. In all cases the interviewing took place in Zuni homes where power was not available; hence a converter on a pickup truck was used.

Informants were paid a modest fee, but this was not too important a factor in their motivation. Gifts and services in various connections had previously been extended to members of the small-group net, and there was already some sense of friendship and obligation.

On the whole the reactions of the majority of the respondents to the questions were in line with what was found in the other groups. The level of their understanding of the alternatives appeared to be adequate, and the situations described in the questions were considered to be serious and significant ones. But more important than these reactions was the stated attitude of many that the questions were on the whole innocuous. This is to say, they were not concentrated on religion and did not ask about Zuni "secrets."

Interviewing the Navaho (Kimball Romney)

The settlement patterns of the Navaho Indians created problems of interviewing which were not comparably serious in the contacting of the respondents of the other groups in the cultural sample. Household units were spread thinly over a wide area. And worse still, there were several families who had no fixed place of residence at all during the period of our investigation. Range conditions were especially bad at the time; hence it was more necessary than usual for a family to keep constantly on the move to find the grasslands adequate for the grazing of their sheep. Also a number of the men of the community were periodically away doing various kinds of wage work to supplement family incomes. All of these factors, when added to the extensive visiting which is common among the Navaho, made the interviewing of this group, as has been noted above, comparatively costly both in time and money.

Another serious problem was the language, which I myself did not command. It was necessary, as has usually been the case in doing research work with Navaho Indians (Clyde Kluckhohn and a few others being the exceptions), to make use of an interpreter. First an adequate interpreter had to be found, and then a training period was necessary because the research design called for uniform data from all the cultures. A standardized Navaho version of the schedule had to be developed.

Only two persons in the area were capable of handling the job of interviewing. On advice of others who had worked with the Rimrock Navaho, the one approached was a woman who had had considerable experience over the years interpreting in different kinds of research programs. She was at this time about forty years of age. She had much more schooling than others in the community (some eight years) and was in general much more acculturated. Yet she was definitely of the community. In fact she was viewed by most persons to be an important member of the group. At the time of our research she was the secretary of the local community organization, a Council. Partly because of this official position and partly because of her greater experience with outsiders, she was very often called upon to act as a go-between when members of the community had to have dealings with Anglo-Americans.

Prior to the training period I used the English-language version of the schedule to question the interpreter herself. This was to provide a check upon possible interpreter bias. There was, we believed, some danger that this woman, who was a most forceful personality in addition to being quite acculturated, would tend to influence respondents in the direction of her own value choices. The complete record of her choices was kept and subsequently compared with the results obtained from the whole Navaho sample. Two facts may be stated unequivocally. She did prove to be a variant in her choices; and there was no evidence to indicate that she biased the answers of others. She was most clearly variant in her choices on the *relational* and *time* orientations. Her preference was strongly favorable to the Individualistic *relational* alternative and fairly marked in favor of a Future *time* position. The Navaho group as a whole was found to be dominantly Collateral and Present-oriented. There also was no regular correspondence between her preferences on the *man-nature* orientation and those given by the community. Only on the *activity* orientation was there agreement in that both the interpreter and the community showed a preference for the Doing alternative. But even here there was no item-by-item correspondence. The fact that the Navaho group as a whole responded in accord with our predictions and the fact that there was almost no agreement between the responses of interpreter and group indicate that the precautions taken in the training period were adequate for avoiding an interpreter biasing of the data.

Very briefly, the training procedures were as follows. I first described and explained the general nature of our task. I took great care to emphasize the fact that the schedule was not a test, that there were no "right" answers, and that we wished each person to respond in the way he felt was best. It was further explained that we did not want anyone's answers influenced either by the investigator or the interpreter. Thus if there were misunderstandings or questions it would be necessary to repeat the set of alternatives. I pointed out that it was a policy in administering the schedule in all the groups to repeat questions for the respondents but never to explain or expand upon them.

After these explanations the schedule was then gone over, phrase by phrase. Slowly and painstakingly the interpreter put the questions into Navaho and then explained to me what was implied in the Navaho version as she was giving it. A few slight alterations were necessary in order to retain the same meaning in the Navaho as in the English version. For example, "God (the gods)" came out "holy people" because the use of the former term would have greatly altered the meaning of the question for the Navaho. The few changes made were subjected to a checking by all collaborators on the project before being decided upon definitely.

The next step was a pre-testing of the questions on several Navaho subjects not included in our sample. Again a few very minor changes were made. These were then checked as the others were. Finally the whole procedure was standardized. Had the pressure of time not been so great, it would have been desirable to have used "back-translation" techniques with independent interpreters and to have prepared some such standardized Navaho-language version as was eventually developed for the Zuni. However, I was well satisfied with the kind of standardization we managed to achieve.

Most of the time which the interpreter and I spent together was in our travels to and fro as we sought out our respondents rather than in the actual interview sessions. In these periods the relationship the two of us had was a pleasant and easy one which was further characterized by mild joking. In the interview situations there was rarely anything of the joking relationship. The mood which prevailed there is best characterized as one of "relaxed efficiency."

Probably the interpreter was initially motivated to maintain good relationships because of the pay she received for the job. It is true that in the latter part of the study she developed a personal loyalty to the investigation as a whole and identified me as a nontypical white in my acceptance of her people's ways; but still, the initial motivation sprang from the fact that other interpreters could have been obtained, and the money was important. The work was tiring and exacting for her; yet despite the monotony of repeating exactly the same speeches day after day, she continued throughout the program to perform her task with no apparent change in attitude.

As for my own motivation, I was, of course, concerned about establishing the kind of relations with both the interpreter and the respondents which would yield the desired results. At the same time I had a felt obligation to maintain a level of relations which would not jeopardize the work of others in the field who were contacting some of the same subjects for other types of research. Also I had a personal predisposition to seek acceptance in any group in which I worked.

The average time required to administer the schedule to a subject was between an hour and a half to two hours. One session took less than an hour, and five ran over two hours. Each day the subject to be interviewed was selected from the random sample. Then began the process of locating him or her. Sometimes it took over a half day as we tracked from one abandoned sheep camp to another. After finding the prospective informant, who knew nothing of the reason for our visit, there was a necessary preliminary visiting period during which small gifts of tobacco or food would be offered, and an explanation of our visit made. After a varying interval of time, usually something less than an hour, the respondent would indicate his willingness to be interviewed, and then he or she, the interpreter, and I would retire to privacy. Usually the place this privacy was found was out in the open under a tree which was some distance from the dwelling place (hogan). One interview was conducted in a hogan, and a few took place in the jeep I was driving. In no case during a session did another adult appear. But the notion of privacy did not pertain to children, who were almost always to be found around and about.

The respondents were paid for their time, and in addition small gifts of food and tobacco were sometimes presented. The latter were usually reciprocal gifts for the food which was offered to us. We were also called upon to provide transportation services for several of the families. In almost all cases the favor asked was the transporting of an ill relative to the government hospital. Such trips frequently consumed a half day's time.

Once the Navaho man or woman had been found and had agreed to participate, there were not many problems in administering the questions. The questions seemed to be well understood, and the thoughtful reaction which most respondents had to them indicated that the matters treated in the questions were regarded as "serious matters."

Situational factors were extremely harsh for the Rimrock Navaho in the summer of 1951. Economic conditions were bad, and illnesses were afflicting almost all families. Many families had so far exhausted their resources in providing ceremonial and medical care for their sick members that they were virtually destitute. One wonders how much all these conditions were causing these people to so question their basic values that there was real confusion about some of them. This question is an important one which will be treated in the later analysis of the Navaho data.

The fact that the Navaho are in thought and expression more concrete-minded than are many peoples also has a bearing on this question. The respondents frequently gave quite specific illustrations to back up their answers. The type of question used in the schedule was aimed at getting at a generalization about numerous similar specific situations. Given both the fact of the relatively great concreteness of Navaho thought and the fact that in recent years the group has had to adjust to many specific conditions and demands beyond its own control, it is certainly probable that the issues of what "should be" and what "has to be" were less clear-cut than in other groups. One illustration of this difference was found in the answers of a pre-test subject who is probably the most intellectually sophisticated Navaho in the area. When asked his choice in the matter of the inheritance of livestock he was firm in his selection of the Collateral alternative, but when it was a matter of the inheritance of land his preference was for the Individualistic alternative. When his comments were elicited about the question of land inheritance, his reply was: "Of course it used to be the other way [meaning the Collateral arrangement] and I think *maybe* it should still be that way, but 'Washingtone' tells us it has to be the other way, and that is the way we now do it."[16] In a response like this, one cannot make a clear-cut distinction between the "ought" of the preferred value position and the "is" of the actual behavior. It may well be the more realistic interpretation to say that a change is actually taking place. But this problem, too, must be left for the later interpretation of the Navaho data.

A final comment on my field experience which may have some interpretative significance is that the women were on the whole more difficult to interview than the men. They were much more shy. It was often quite difficult to get them to participate. Two of the substitutions which had to be made in the sample of Navaho women were because of extreme shyness. Moreover, the majority of them who did cooperate were more hurried in their responses than were the men, and they gave many fewer free comments and explanations about their choices.

[16] The term Washington, pronounced *Washingtone*, is the one commonly used to refer to the controls exercised by the United States Indian Service.

CHAPTER IV

Statistical Methods of Analysis

INTRODUCTION

The theory of variation in value orientations has been expounded, and the method developed for a partial testing of it has been explained. We turn now to the problem of the selection and the adaptation of statistical methods appropriate to the analysis of the data obtained in the communities of Atrisco, Rimrock, Homestead, Zuni, and the Rimrock Navaho.

In the selection of these methods the focus of attention was necessarily centered upon the two general questions of the existence or nonexistence of uniformities in the ranking of the orientation alternatives within each of the communities and the existence or nonexistence of differences in these uniformities community by community. As has been previously stated, both the number of items used in the research instrument and the number of persons questioned in each of the communities were too few to permit a statistical treatment of the evidence which was indicative of *intra*-cultural variation. Crucial as this type of variation is, the testing for it by any such method as we were devising had to wait upon the demonstration that there are the within-culture regularities and between-culture differences which the theory postulates.[1] We shall, of course, in presenting our total results give the kinds of variations in patterning which did emerge in the different groups, but it was explicit in our total research design that the discussion of intra-cultural variation was to be left to the specialists who utilize the data collected over many years on each of the communities for a critical examination, culture by culture, of all of the results the value-orientation schedule yielded (Chapters VI, VII, VIII, and IX).

The questions of within-culture regularities and between-culture differences are themselves faceted, and there appears to be no simple or single means of analyzing the data for the finding of the answers to them. The most crucial test is that of ascertaining whether or not there is a significant ordering of the alternatives in the responses given to the individual items in an orientation series of items in a particular culture. But we wish also to know the degree of significance between the choices *within* this ordering, and even more we desire to go *beyond* the item orderings

---

[1] We use the term *within-culture regularities* to refer to *any* statistically significant regularities within a culture. The term *intra-cultural variations* refers to the systematic variation among the items of a single value-orientation series for a particular culture, especially as the differences among the items reflect *behavior-sphere variations* in that culture.

and test for the significance of the overall—the summary—patterns of the orderings of the alternatives for a total series of items. These three types of answers are needed for the assessment of the within-culture regularities, and it is only when we have all of them that we can ask and seek to answer the fourth major question—the question of the degree of between-culture differences.

In presenting the statistical procedures we shall first give the formal statistical phrasing of the four questions. Subsequently, we shall specify, by means of illustrations taken from our own data, the operations which are used for the answering of each of them.

Within-Culture Regularities

The simplest, most straightforward query relative to any one item from the value-orientation schedule is:

(1) *Total Item Patterning.* After members of a culture have ranked the alternatives in a value-orientation item, how likely is it that the resultant pattern of responses could have occurred if, among the members of the culture, there were no preferences for some ranking patterns rather than others?

This is, as we have said, typical of most of the questions directed toward the assessment of within-culture regularity. It has been stated in its formal null form, which is how all of the questions to be asked of the data will be presented. Later on in the chapter, using responses to the Well Arrangements item from the *relational* value-orientation series as an illustration, we shall present a statistical technique for dealing with this part of the problem of within-culture regularity.

Another concern, still utilizing a single item from a single value-orientation series, is the relative popularity of each of the particular alternatives which the respondent is asked to rank-order. To deal with this problem, we analyze in a different way the same responses which are used for question 1.[2] This time each pair of alternatives is considered in turn, and this question is posed:

(2) *Intra-Item Patterning.* After members of a culture have ranked the alternatives in a value-orientation item, how likely is the pattern of responses if they do not prefer one particular alternative to a second particular alternative in their responses to the item?

While question 1 considers a null hypothesis concerned with all three alternatives to an item simultaneously, this question examines three separate null hypotheses designed to increase the information yield of a single item. These are (1) alternatives A and B are equally popular; (2)

---

[2] The *exact* nature of the interdependence of the two techniques is not known in this case. However, it is completely permissible to analyze the same data in a hundred different ways should our interests dictate a hundred different things to be learned from them. As long as the inquiries are kept within separate domains of discourse, the dependency issue is not a problem.

alternatives A and C are equally popular; and (3) alternatives B and C are equally popular. Later on in the chapter a statistical solution for this question will be presented.

In the third and final within-culture inquiry we consider a summary statement utilizing all the items representing a particular value orientation for a selected sample of persons representative of a particular culture. Again, this question addresses itself to pairs of alternatives in turn, this time considering a complete matrix of (persons) × (items) from a value-orientation series:

> (3) *Total Orientation Patterning.* After members of a culture have ranked the alternatives to all the items in a value-orientation series, how likely is the pattern of responses if they do not prefer the alternatives in that series which represent one particular value-orientation position to those which represent a second particular position?

Although the problem of the independence of individual responses to different indicators of one value orientation is raised by this question, we shall leave the treatment of this problem until the time when the statistical technique for handling this question is discussed.

Between-Culture Differences

As the final portion in this conceptual introduction, we shall consider briefly the kinds of between-culture differences for which tests will be made. These are differences in total patterns with respect to the four value orientations. When the statistics for this question are presented, the methodological relation between this question and question 3 will be clear. For the moment we are content with stating that here we wish to answer the query:

> (4) *Between-Culture Differences.* After members of each culture have ranked the alternatives to all of the items in a value-orientation series, how likely are the patterns of responses from each culture if they (the members of the various cultures) do not differentially prefer the alternatives in that series which represent one particular value-orientation position to those which represent a second particular position?

As direct as this question appears conceptually, considerable care is required for its implementation and interpretation. Based upon its outcome, we may say how general tendencies differ between cultures with respect to pairs of value-orientation positions.

Suppose, for example, that we find in culture X a preference for the Lineal as opposed to the Collateral position in the *relational* series, while in culture Y each of these positions is equally preferred. Question 4 allows us to say whether or not the difference between these two *preferences* is statistically significant or not.

Summary

These four questions will be used as reference points to guide the reader through the discussion of the particular techniques we use to implement them. They are not the only questions we might ask of the data. They do, however, address themselves to the focal concerns of this study—within-culture regularity and between-culture difference. With the suggestion to the reader that he keep them in mind as buoys in the sea of detail to follow, we proceed with their further explication and show how they are used in the analysis of the data.

TESTING FOR WITHIN-CULTURE REGULARITIES

1. Within-Culture Regularity on a Single Item from the Value-Orientation Schedule[3]

This concern is the bedrock of our investigation. First, a restatement of the formal question to which we address ourselves:

(1) *Total Item Patterning.* After members of a culture have ranked the alternatives in a value-orientation item, how likely is it that the resultant pattern of responses could have occurred if, among the members of the culture, there were no preferences for some ranking patterns rather than others?

We begin by considering the ranking operation we expect of our informants when they deal with an item from the value-orientation schedule.[4] What a respondent is asked to do is to rank these three alternatives from most preferred (rank = 1) to least preferred (rank = 3). If we designate such alternatives A, B, and C, then (excluding cases in which ties are present) he responds with one of the following patterns (where ">" means "is preferred to"):

$$A > B > C \quad A > C > B \quad B > A > C$$
$$B > C > A \quad C > B > A \quad C > A > B$$

After such ranking is completed, we assign the number 1 (one) to the alternative which he ranks *first*, 2 (two) to the one which is *second*, and 3 (three) to the *third*. When a group of respondents have ranked the alternatives to an item, we sum the numerical assignments to the alternatives across informants to assess the consensus among them. In the most null case each of the six alternate ways of ranking is equally likely to occur.

---

[3] This is the section referred to in the Preface which was written by Fred L. Strodtbeck.

[4] Throughout our discussion of technique, we will deal with the *three-alternative* items (all orientations save the *activity*). Reduction to the *two-alternative* case (the *activity* orientation) is trivial. The reader will at once notice that binomial methods and their elaboration suffice to handle the latter. Only when the two-alternative isomorph to the three-alternative procedure is not obvious will we say anything about it.

We take that case as our null hypothesis. With this null hypothesis, then, except for sampling fluctuations, the sum across respondents for alternative A equals the sum for alternative B equals the sum for alternative C, or cryptically, $A = B = C$. Since, in our case, the sum of the ranking numbers assigned is always 6 for a single individual, if we multiply this by the number (m) of respondents, we have the total sum of ranks for all alternatives. If we divide this total now by 3 (the number of alternatives), we have the expected sum of ranks for each alternative when all ranking patterns are equally likely to occur. The discrepancy of the *actual* sums from these *theoretical null* sums is the "quantity" we deal with in order to determine whether or not the degree of consensus we observe is a chance

TABLE IV:1

RANK BY CULTURES OF THE LINEAL (A), COLLATERAL (B), AND INDIVIDUALISTIC (C) ALTERNATIVES OF ITEM R1, WELL ARRANGEMENTS

Respondent	Spanish-American			Mormon			Texan			Zuni			Navaho		
	Lin A	Coll B	Ind C	Lin A	Coll B	Ind C	Lin A	Coll B	Ind C	Lin A	Coll B	Ind C	Lin A	Coll B	Ind C
1	1	3	2	2	1	3	3	1	2	3	1	2	3	1	2
2	3	1	2	3	2	1	2	3	1	3	2	1	2	1	3
3	1	2	3	2	3	1	2	3	1	3	2	1	2	1	3
4	1	3	2	3	1	2	3	1	2	3	2	1	3	1	2
5	1	2	3	2	3	1	3	2	1	3	2	1	1	2	3
6	1	2	3	3	2	1	2.5	1	2.5	3	1	2	3	1	2
7	1.5	3	1.5	3	2	1	3	1.5	1.5	3	1	2	3	1	2
8	1	2	3	3	1	2	3	1	2	1	3	2	2	1	3
9	3	2	1	3	1	2	3	2	1	1	3	2	3	2	1
10	3	2	1	3	1	2	3	2	1	2	1	3	1	2	3
11	3	1	2	3	2	1	3	1	2	3	2	1	2	3	1
12	1	2	3	2	3	1	2	3	1	1	3	2	2	1	3
13	3	1	2	3	1	2	3	2	1	3	1	2	2	1	3
14	2	3	1	2.5	2.5	1	3	2	1	2	1	3	3	1	2
15	1	3	2	3	2	1	2.5	2.5	1	2	3	1	2	1	3
16	2	1	3	3	1	2	2	1	3	3	2	1	1	2	3
17	1	2	3	3	2	1	3	2	1	3	1	2	3	1	2
18	1	3	2	3	1	2	2	3	1	2	1	3	3	1	2
19	3	2	1	2	1	3	3	1	2	3	1	2	2	1	3
20	3	2	1	3	1	2	3	2	1	1	3	2	3	1	2
21	2	3	1							2	3	1	1	3	2
22	1	2	3										2	3	1
23	3	1	2												
Observed Sum	42.5	48.0	47.5	54.5	33.5	32.0	54.0	37.0	29.0	50.0	39.0	37.0	49.0	32.0	51.0
Expected Sum	46.0	46.0	46.0	40.0	40.0	40.0	40.0	40.0	40.0	42.0	42.0	42.0	44.0	44.0	44.0
Expected Less Observed	3.5	−2.0	−1.5	−14.5	6.5	8.0	−14.0	3.0	11.0	−8.0	3.0	5.0	−5.0	12.0	−7.0
Sum of Squares	18.50			316.50			326.00			98.00			218.00		

TABLE IV:2

KENDALL'S S STATISTIC FOR THE MEASUREMENT OF CONSENSUS

(when n equals 3 and m goes from 8 to 60)[a]

NUMBER OF RANKINGS m	LEVEL OF SIGNIFICANCE			
	.05		.01	
	S	S/m	S	S/m
8	48.1	6.01	66.8	8.35
9	54.0	6.00	75.9	8.43
10	60.0	6.00	85.1	8.51
11*	66.0	6.00	94.3	8.57
12	71.9	5.99	103.5	8.62
13*	77.9	5.99	112.7	8.67
14	83.8	5.99	121.9	8.71
15	89.8	5.99	131.0	8.73
16	95.8	5.99	140.2	8.76
17*	101.8	5.99	149.4	8.79
18	107.7	5.98	158.6	8.81
19*	113.7	5.98	167.8	8.83
20	119.7	5.98	177.0	8.85
21*	125.6	5.98	187.3	8.92
22	131.6	5.98	196.3	8.92
23*	137.7	5.99	205.8	8.95
25**	149.8	5.99	224.8	8.99
30**	179.8	5.99	270.8	9.03
35**	209.9	6.00	317.3	9.07
40**	240.3	6.01	367.4	9.18
45**	270.5	6.01	411.2	9.14
50**	300.5	6.01	457.2	9.14
55**	330.1	6.00	501.3	9.11
60**	359.5	5.99	547.5	9.12

[a] This table is abstracted in part from a table given by Kendall, *op. cit.*, p. 186. (Kendall's values are from M. Friedman, "A Comparison of Alternative Tests of Significance for the Problem of m Rankings," *Annals of Mathematical Statistics*, Vol. II [1940], p. 86.) The single-starred values, computed by the writer, were obtained by interpolation, and the double-starred values by use of the approximation formula given by Kendall, p. 98.

occurrence or not. These discrepancies, squared and summed, are Kendall's S, the statistic whose known probability distribution under the null hypothesis allows us to test our level of consensus.[5]

This reasoning is best illustrated by means of a concrete example. In Table IV:1, the responses of our 106 informants to the Well Arrangements item are presented. To appraise the significance of the difference of an observed column sum from the expected column sum (as described above), one follows these steps. First the "observed" is subtracted from the "expected" in each column. The residuals, thus defined, become a for column A, b for column B, and c for column C. For the Mormon case:

[5] See Maurice G. Kendall, *Rank Correlation Methods*, 2d ed. (New York: Hafner Publishing Co., 1955), pp. 49–52 and *passim*.

	A	B	C
Expected Sum	40.0	40.0	40.0
Observed Sum	54.5	33.5	32.0
	a	b	c
Difference	−14.5	6.5	8.0

The sum of the residuals is always zero. The sum of their squares is denoted S.

$$a + b + c = 0,$$
$$a^2 + b^2 + c^2 = S.$$

For the Mormon case:

$$S_M = (-14.5)^2 + (6.5)^2 + (8.0)^2 = 316.50.$$

It is known that when n, the number of alternatives ranked, is 3, and m, the number of rankings, is not too small, then the probability associated with a given S in the null case may be computed. A brief table of values for the .05 and .01 significance points of S is given in Table IV:2. Under equally likely assumptions, with m equal to 20 as it is in our Mormon sample, an S as large as 316.50 would be attained less than one time in 100, so we may reasonably conclude that preference orders are not equally preferred among our sample of Mormon respondents and that, for this culture, there is consensus on the patterning of responses to this item. The examples for the Spanish-American, Texan, Zuni, and Navaho are included in Table IV:1 as further illustrations of the techniques just discussed.

CHARTING MULTIPLE RANKINGS. With data such as ours, a modification of a technique first used in the social sciences by Lemann[6] gives the reader a visual version of the results attained by this method. We shall first give an example of this charting (by plotting the a, b, and c "points" for the Mormon case just described), and then explain the meaning which may be attached to it. We first compute

$$\frac{a}{\sqrt{m}} = \frac{-14.5}{\sqrt{20}} = -3.24,$$

$$\frac{b}{\sqrt{m}} = \frac{6.5}{\sqrt{20}} = 1.45,$$

$$\frac{c}{\sqrt{m}} = \frac{8.0}{\sqrt{20}} = 1.79.$$

A computing check is that

$$\frac{a}{\sqrt{m}} + \frac{b}{\sqrt{m}} + \frac{c}{\sqrt{m}} = 0.$$

[6] T. B. Lemann, "An Empirical Investigation of Group Characteristics," unpublished A.B. thesis, Harvard University, 1949, especially pp. 39–44.

Graph IV:1 has been constructed with guide lines which are perpendicular to the A, B, and C axes. We plot the summary point for the Mormon rankings as follows: Starting at the center, move a distance -3.24 along the A-axis and draw a line perpendicular to the A-axis. Similarly, move a distance 1.45 along the B-axis and draw a line perpendicular to the B-axis. The point where these two lines meet is the required point, M (for Mormon). If we go a distance 1.79 along the C-axis, the line perpendicular to the C-axis also goes through M, the previously established point. Any two values determine the location of the point. The tracing of the third value constitutes a check on the accuracy of the plotting.

The two circles on Graph IV:1 indicate boundaries for use in connection with a significance test. For example, if the point falls outside the inner circle, the null hypothesis $A = B = C$ may be rejected at the .05 level. If the point falls outside the outer circle, the null hypothesis may be rejected at the .01 level. If we define S' as the value of S associated with a particular significance level, then we may say that the radius associated with this probability level may be found from

$$r = \sqrt{\frac{3S'}{2m}}.$$

The derivation of this relationship is given in Appendix 2. In Table IV:2 it may be noted that the value of S/m changes little and thus it is possible to use a constant radius in determining the significance boundaries.

If one considers the Mormon case in Graph IV:1, it may be seen that the point is well outside both circles, and hence the null hypothesis may be rejected at the .01 level. The coordinates of the Mormon position locate it most distant from the positive Lineal position and almost equidistant from the Collateral and the Individualistic ones. For the Navaho, the point is closest to the Collateral alternative and almost equally distant from the Lineal and the Individualistic ones. The greater the distance from the origin, the greater the S (compare the Mormon and Navaho points on Graph IV:1) and the less the probability of the outcome under the assumption of "equally likely" rankings.

At the other extreme, the point determined from the Spanish-American rankings is very close to the origin; hence, no clear preference is indicated. In statistical language, there are no grounds for rejecting the assumption that Lineality, Collaterality, and Individualism are equally preferred. Since there was no reason to believe that the Spanish-Americans misunderstood the alternatives, and since there were consistent preferences in three of the other cultures, one is inclined to conclude that the statistical nonsignificance arises from a counterbalancing of preference. Far from being displeased with such an outcome, we shall later argue that this is a phenomenon of crucial importance in cultural analysis—particularly when cultures in transition are involved.

SUMMARY. In this section we have done two things. (1) We have presented the answer to the first question we ask of our data. (2) We have described a visual technique for displaying the results of our computations, a technique which facilitates understanding of the results.

GRAPH IV:1
GRAPHIC SIGNIFICANCE TEST FOR m RANKINGS OF THREE ALTERNATIVES

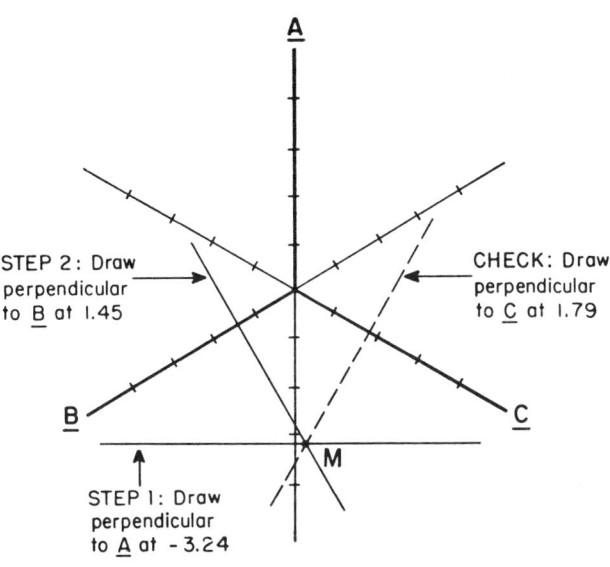

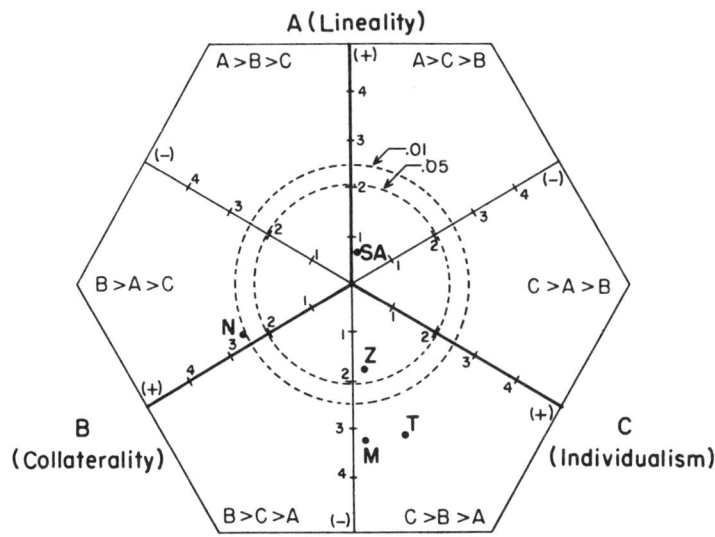

ILLUSTRATIVE DATA: ITEM R1,
WELL ARRANGEMENTS

	A	B	C
Navaho	−1.07	2.56	−1.49
Zuni	−1.75	.66	1.09
Spanish-American	.73	−.42	−.31
Texan	−3.13	.67	2.46
Mormon	−3.24	1.45	1.79

2. A Binomial Analysis of Alternative Preferences Within Cultures

We turn now to an examination of the "reasons" for such consistencies of response which are found among the items which members of a culture respond to. The relative popularity between two alternatives which represent two different value-orientation positions is our focus. We restate now the second formal inquiry:

> (2) *Intra-Item Patterning*. After members of a culture have ranked the alternatives in a value-orientation item, how likely is the pattern of responses if they do not prefer one particular alternative to a second particular alternative in their responses to the item?

Even when we have decided whether or not a non-chance preference patterning of rank orders exists among a group of persons on a particular question, we wish to know more about the differences between alternatives in terms of their individual popularity. For example, we found that the Mormon group had patterned their responses to the Well Arrangements item sufficiently to allow us to reject the null hypothesis $A = B = C$. On inspection their preference ordering seems to be Ind > Coll > Lin. However, examining the numerical sums which suggest this ordering to us, we feel more confidence in their preference of Individualistic over Lineal, and Collateral over Lineal, than we do in their preference of Individualistic over Collateral (see Graph IV:1). We strongly suspect that they may, in reality, be indifferent in their preference between the Individualistic and the Collateral alternatives. The only stable preference they are expressing on this item is that of a preference of either Individualism or Collaterality over Lineality. If this is so, how can we affirm its plausibility or implausibility? In statistical terms, having rejected our general null hypothesis, what new information do our three more specific null hypotheses yield?

By dealing with frequencies expressing the preferential patterning within pairs of alternatives in turn, we can produce most of the information we need. Let us illustrate this method by using, once again, the responses of the subjects in the Mormon sample to the Well Arrangements item. To begin with, we designate three pairs of alternatives and the preferences within them to describe responses to the item. (In this case the three pairs are [Lin, Coll], [Lin, Ind], and [Coll, Ind].) We then count the number of times each is preferred to the other, within each pair, over the entire Mormon sample. We define "preferred to" as follows: For any pair of alternatives A and B, A is preferred to B if (1) A is assigned rank 1, B rank 2; or (2) A is assigned rank 1, B rank 3; or (3) A is assigned rank 2, B rank 3. (In case of tied ranks, we count A's preference to B as $\frac{1}{2}$ and B's preference to A as $\frac{1}{2}$.) For the twenty Mormon respondents, we find the following frequencies of preference on the Well Arrangements item:

> Lin is preferred to Coll 3.5 out of 20 times,
> Lin is preferred to Ind 2.0 out of 20 times, and
> Coll is preferred to Ind 10.0 out of 20 times.

To assess the probability that each of these frequencies would have arisen by chance if the null hypothesis of no preference between alternatives within a single pair is true, we evaluate them against a normal-curve approximation to a binomial distribution. Formally, the null hypothesis is that the observed proportion in any instance of preference between two alternatives does not differ, at the .05 level of significance, from .50. How many persons out of $m = 20$ must prefer one alternative to another for us to reject this hypothesis? To find out, we solve the equation

$$z = \frac{f_{A>B} - E(f_{A>B}) - .50}{\sqrt{m(p_{A>B})(q_{B>A})}}$$

where

$z =$ a unit normal deviate,
$f_{A>B} =$ the observed frequency of persons preferring A to B,
$E(f_{A>B}) =$ the expected frequency of persons preferring A to B,
$.50 =$ a correction for continuity,
$p_{A>B} =$ the expected proportion of persons preferring A to B,
$q_{B>A} =$ the expected proportion of persons preferring B to A,

and

$m =$ the number of persons in the sample,

by setting $z = 1.96$ (for the .05 level of significance, two-tailed test) and filling in the known values. The result for the Mormon case ($m = 20$) is $f_{A>B} = 14.90$ or, rounding, 15.00. Since we are using a two-tailed test of significance, we can reject the null hypothesis of no preference between two alternatives when one is preferred to the other *either* 15 or more times or 5 or fewer times. Thus, in our example, we can say that for the Well Arrangements item, the Mormon group prefers the Collateral to the Lineal alternative at the .05 level, prefers the Individualistic to the Lineal alternative at the .05 level, but prefers equally the Collateral and Individualistic alternatives relative to one another. *Note that as we define it here, we can only talk about preferences within pairs of alternatives.* For example, suppose we find $A > B$ at the .05 level, $A > C$ at the .05 level, and $B > C$ at the .05 level. Though we can conclude that *each* of these preferences holds, we cannot conclude that $A > B > C$ as a *total* pattern holds. To conclude that a total pattern such as $A > B > C$ holds, we would need some means of evaluating the alternate hypothesis $A \neq B \neq C$ as a single expression, and of affirming some variety of it by conventional statistical methods. Such methods of statistical affirmation, to our knowledge, are not yet devised.[7] However, by making three comparisons we exhaust the possibilities for any single ranking; hence little difficulty ensues in drawing conclusions about the internal patterning of responses to the whole item, for certain purposes, if we keep this caution in mind.

SYMBOLIC NOTATION FOR INTERNAL PREFERENCE PATTERNS. Conventions for the use of the connecting symbols ">," "≥," and "*," when we use

---

[7] See Kendall, *op. cit.*, p. 101, for one temporary solution.

them to describe the results of the analysis illustrated in this section, are best defined by example.

$$A > B > C$$

means that all three preferences (A over B, A over C, and B over C) hold at the .05 level or better.

$$A \geqslant B > C$$

means that only A over C and B over C hold at the .05 level; even though A preferred to B is more frequent a response than B preferred to A, the frequency does not reach the required .05 level of significance.

$$A > B \geqslant C$$

means that only A over B and A over C hold at the .05 level—even though B is preferred to C more often than C is preferred to B.

$$A \geqslant B \geqslant C^*$$

means that only the preference of A over C reaches the .05 level of significance. And finally,

$$A \geqslant B \geqslant C$$

means that none of the preference frequencies within the pairs reaches the .05 level of significance. It may happen that frequencies of preferences are exactly equal between two alternatives, in which case the "$=$" sign will be used with its conventional meaning (e.g. $A > B = C$). So, as an illustration, our results for the Mormon Well Arrangements item, analyzed above, would be succinctly yet completely represented as

$$\text{Ind} \geqslant \text{Coll} > \text{Lin.}$$

SUMMARY. If we consider section 1 as dealing with the total null hypothesis which we abbreviated as $A = B = C$, then this section has considered three specified null hypotheses, $A = B$, $A = C$, and $B = C$, to learn more about the internal patterning of the responses to a single item. Since we cannot affirm any one total ordering of three alternatives, our implementation is restricted to dealing with these separate aspects (individual pairs of alternatives of a single item). This procedure is not quite as elegant as we might like, but elegance was not the prime matter of consideration. The fact that we needed the information about specific alternatives for later interpretive purposes was our first concern and made the method satisfactory for our needs.

3. General Preferences Considering a Total Series of Value-Orientation Items

To complete the analysis of within-culture value-orientation regularities, consider this final question:

(3) *Total Orientation Patterning.* After members of a culture have

ranked the alternatives to all the items in a value-orientation series, how likely is the pattern of responses if they do not prefer the alternatives in that series which represent one particular value-orientation position to those which represent a second particular position?

This query stems from a desire to characterize cultures, for certain analytical purposes, as being, for example, "dominantly Lineal," or "dominantly Doing," or "dominantly Future" oriented, regardless of the behavior sphere sampled by the specific items.

Were we sure of the inter-item correlations among the questions tapping a particular value orientation, we could simply summarize the results from our first technique (Kendall's S) across all questions in an area for a particular culture and easily evaluate their general tendencies of ranking. For example, when we ask 20 Mormons seven questions in the *relational* area we can, by knowing the intercorrelations among the items, evaluate the significance of the results directly. If the intercorrelations are not significantly different from zero, we have 140 independent observations to use for our m. If they are of the order of .90, we can use only an m of *20* independent observations. The problem is theoretically distinct but empirically troublesome. It arises in deciding what number of independent observations—which, in our example, we know must lie somewhere between 20 and 140—is the appropriate m. One solution is to determine the a, b, and c values discussed earlier, twice—once assuming complete independence of items, once assuming complete dependence; plot the resulting two points; and assert (correctly) that the true probability of consensus lies somewhere on the straight line connecting the two points. This seems excessive labor, for if it is assumed that the intercorrelations are unstable (given our small m's) and that we know nothing about the relative weighting for each item (that is, how good each is), then should it happen that one point falls within the significance radius of .05 and the other falls outside it, we know no more than when we began our operation. If both points fall either (1) inside the .05 radius or (2) outside it, then, and only then, can we have complete confidence in concluding that there is (1) no general consensus or (2) significant general consensus.

Problems such as this caused us to abandon the elegance which would have accrued from testing the complete null hypothesis $A = B = C$ for general tendency purposes, and led us instead to the consideration of the popularity of single alternatives relative to one another—evaluating such popularity by means of a t-test. Let us again proceed by illustration.

Consider all the responses made by the 23 Spanish-Americans for all the items tapping the *time* orientation (see Appendix 4 for the complete listing of the data). Our formal query is this: If we combine all the information about this value orientation for each of the persons in the group, and if we then average this information across all the persons in the group, are there significant preferences between any two value-orientation positions? Once more we utilize three pairs of alternatives: [Past, Pres], [Past, Fut], and [Pres, Fut]. This time we reason that if there is no general preference within each pair for one alternative over the other, then, calling A

TABLE IV:3

	Observed Mean Frequency	Expected Mean Frequency	S_M	t^*	p
Past is preferred to Present	.48	2.50	.15	−13.47	<.001
Past is preferred to Future	1.72	2.50	.23	−3.40	<.01
Present is preferred to Future	4.20	2.50	.16	+10.62	<.001

* Note that the *sign* of t tells us the alternative which is the more popular; a plus sign means the first alternative listed in the first column is preferred, a minus sign that the second alternative is preferred. In the example, line 1, Present is preferred to Past.

and B any two alternatives, a person should prefer A to B for ½ of the items which he responds to in this value-orientation series, and for the other ½ he should prefer B to A (we define "prefer" as we did in section 2). Thus, when we consider the three pairs of the *time* orientation alternatives for an individual from the Spanish-American sample, we compute three scores for him: (1) the number of times he prefers the Past to the Present alternative; (2) the number of times he prefers the Past to the Future alternative; and (3) the number of times he prefers the Present to the Future alternative. (Note that each of these scores, for a single individual, may vary from 0.0 to 5.0 because there are five *time* orientation items.) We have hypothesized that if he does not prefer one to the other, we would expect 2.50 (½ × 5 items) responses in our "favor" from each individual. We can assess the difference between our observed mean frequency of favorable responses and our expected mean frequency of favorable responses, within each pair of alternatives, via t-tests.

The results for the Spanish-American sample of the *time* orientation are given in Table IV:3.

Using again the notation discussed in section 2, we would characterize this result as

Pres > Fut > Past.

This is the technique which will be used to assess the general tendencies toward consensus within cultures.

4. Summary of Within-Culture Techniques

This completes the discussion of techniques for assessing within-culture regularity. Before we turn to our between-culture technique, a final re-iteration of the three conceptual queries for which statistics have been described will aid the reader in keeping in focus the logical thread of this chapter:

(1) *Total Item Patterning*,
(2) *Intra-Item Patterning*,
(3) *Total Orientation Patterning*.

TESTING FOR BETWEEN-CULTURE DIFFERENCES

We turn now to our second major consideration—the assessment of differences between cultures. The question to be asked is:

(4) *Between-Culture Differences*. After members of each culture have ranked the alternatives to all of the items in a value-orientation series, how likely are the patterns of responses from each culture if they (the members of the various cultures) do not differentially prefer the alternatives in that series which represent one particular value-orientation position to those which represent a second particular position?

Cultures are placed on ten dimensions to carry out this analysis. These dimensions involve two positions from the various value orientations. They are [Ind, Coll], [Ind, Lin], [Coll, Lin], [Past, Pres], [Past, Fut], [Pres, Fut], [Subj, With], [Subj, Over], [With, Over], and [Doing, Being]. Each dimension runs from complete preference of position A over position B (say, Doing over Being) through equal preference for both (say, Doing equals Being) to complete preference of position B over position A (say, Being over Doing). Taking the mean values for cultures on these dimensions (as these means are computed for question 3 above), and testing for between-culture variation of a significant magnitude, gives us the answer to question 4.

Let our example, this time, be the differential preferences of the cultures relative to one another for the Doing and the Being positions of the *activity* orientation. We count the number of "Doing over Being" responses for every member of each culture, over the six items in this series. The scores will vary from 0.0 (no responses of "Doing over Being") to 6.0 (every response "Doing over Being"). A score of 3.0 means equal preference between the two alternatives (generally achieved by preferring "Doing over Being" for ½ of the items and "Being over Doing" for the other ½). Taking the mean values for all cultures, based on the responses of their members, and placing these values along a [Doing, Being] dimension, completes the first step of our procedure. In Figure IV:1 we have done this for the five Rimrock communities.

In method 3, above, each of these means was evaluated, in turn, against

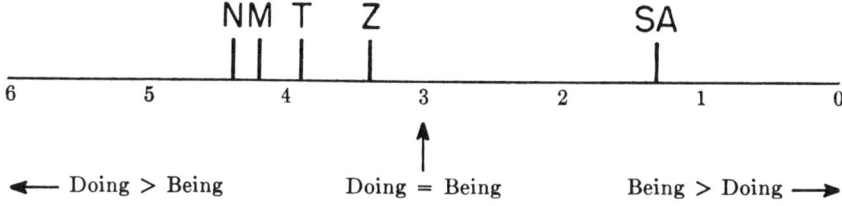

Fig. IV:1. The Five Rimrock Communities on the [Doing, Being] Dimension: Mean Values.

TABLE IV:4
ONE-WAY ANALYSIS OF VARIANCE OF MEAN VALUES
ON THE [DOING, BEING] DIMENSION

Source of Variation	Sum of Squares	df	Mean Square	$F_{b/w}$	p_F
Between	134.35	4	33.59	21.67	< .001
Within	156.71	101	1.55		
Total	291.06	105			

the null mean of 3.00 (that is, equal preference for the two positions) to assess the within-culture consensus for each culture separately. Here, however, we consider all means simultaneously, using a one-way analysis of variance to determine whether or not the variation between cultures is "potent" enough, relative to the variation within the cultures, to allow us to conclude that differences among these means are statistically significant.[8] The results, for this dimension, are presented in Table IV:4.

In this case the differences among the means are highly significant. Again, however, we have more confidence in some differences (because of their relative magnitudes) than others. For example, on this dimension we feel that the Spanish-Americans are certainly different from the Navaho, but we do not think that the Mormons are necessarily so. To turn our hunch into a statistic, Tukey's procedure for testing the gaps among a group of means considered simultaneously proves to be what we need.[9] Applying this technique to the means in Figure IV:1, three groups of mean values occur, between which differences along this dimension of a statistically significant size exist. Figure IV:2 gives the results of these operations.

We can now summarize our information about the cultures on this dimension. First, the cultures fall into three distinct groupings: one group includes the Navaho, Mormons, and Texans, the second includes only the Zuni, and the last only the Spanish-Americans. Second, substantively, the Navaho, Mormons, and Texans are "Doing over Being" in their *activity* orientation; the Zuni equally prefer the two positions; while the Spanish-Americans are "Being over Doing." Third, it is emphasized that these differences are relative to the mean values of the various cultures on this dimension, and the remarks of a substantive nature just cited cannot be construed on the basis of an analysis such as this in any absolute fashion. It is this procedure which will be followed for the statistical testing of the between-culture differences. But prior to this analysis, we shall present graphs of the *kind* used to show the ranking of all items in a single series for one culture, to delineate visually the ranking patterns of *each* of the cultures on the same item.

---

[8] A. L. Edwards, *Statistical Methods for the Behavioral Sciences* (New York: Rinehart & Co., 1955), pp. 315–40.
[9] Edwards, *loc. cit.* Note that in estimating $s_{\bar{x}}$, equal numbers of observations are required. We approximate this by substituting $m = 21$ whenever such a figure is necessary. This results in little bias in our results. The conservative reader may wish to substitute $m = 20$, and recompute our estimates, to doubly insure against *type I* errors.

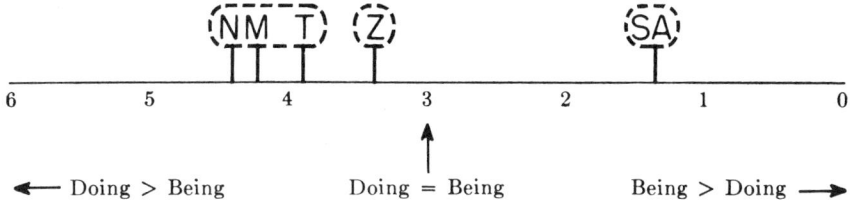

Fig. IV:2. The Five Rimrock Communities on the [Doing, Being] Dimension: Clusters of Communities Differing Significantly from One Another on This Dimension.

SUMMARY AND CONCLUSIONS

Four questions have been asked and four methods for answering them have been described. These methods as a totality represent an integration and something of an expansion of several different methods which are well known and have long been in use. A more aesthetic, or, to use the more common term of statistical parlance, a more elegant, plan of procedure would have been the elaboration of a single technique rather than the integration of several. Steps were actually taken to elaborate the Kendall method. These are set forth in Appendix 2 of our study. Although the method has a degree of elegance which the one just explained lacks, we decided against the use of it in this first study of the uniformities and differences in value-orientation preferences for two reasons. First, it does not permit the use of standard tests for setting confidence limits on the results achieved, except in the case of question 1, the ranking of the preferences item by item. Hypothetical answers for the other questions are suggested by means of both an extension of the graphic analysis and factor analytic techniques.

Since our research was definitely devoted to a first testing of both a theory and a field method which are in many respects new, it seemed wise, in the analysis of our data for the answering of the major questions, to rely upon standard statistics—the probability distributions of which are already well described. In later studies, which conceivably will be expanded to include cross-regional analyses, the elaborative method suggested in Appendix 2 may well prove to have advantages over the variegated one this chapter presents. And there are unquestionably still other methods which can be adapted to the type of data which our theory and method yield. It is because of this possibility that we have included in the study the additional appendix—Appendix 4—in which we record the actual data.

CHAPTER V

Variations in Value Orientations Within and Among the Five Rimrock Communities

Significant within-culture regularities and significant between-culture differences were found in the data as analyzed by the methods which the preceding chapter explains. This, in a sentence, is the outstanding overall result of the research program. Indications of intra-cultural variation were also noted, but, as has been explained, the data collected by means of the schedule were not sufficient to warrant a statistical analysis of this type of variation. In presenting the details of the findings we shall, in general, follow the procedural order set forth in the preceding chapter.

First, we show the kinds of within-culture regularities which were discovered in each of the cultures. Three graphs of the type illustrated in Chapter IV are used to show the preferred rank orders of the alternatives of the items of the three orientations which asked for the ranking of three alternative solutions to a stated problem. It will be recalled that the two circles in the center of these graphs are the means of showing the level of significance or nonsignificance achieved for each of the items of a series. The inner circle measures at the .05 level of significance; the outer one at the .01 level. Accompanying the graphs is a table which records the results of the binomial analysis which was used for the testing for intra-item regularities. This table also gives the summary result—the overall ordering of the total series of the items on each of the *four* orientations. It is this summary which is to be considered the value-orientation profile of each of the groups for the four orientations tested. For the convenience of the reader we repeat the conventions used in the table to describe these results.

$A > B > C$ (A over B, A over C, and B over C—all three are significant at the .05 level of significance or better.)

$A \geqslant B > C$ (Only A over C and B over C hold at the .05 level. The preference for A over B is present but does not appear with sufficient frequency to achieve the .05 level.)

$A > B \geqslant C$ (A over B and A over C both hold at the .05 level. B over C is a more frequent response than C over B but is not a significant result.)

$A \geqslant B \geqslant C^*$ (Only the preference of A over C is a significant result.)

$A > B = C$ (One alternative is significantly preferred as first order; equal preference exists between the other two.)

$A \geqslant B \geqslant C$ (None of the frequencies of preference between the pairs reaches the .05 level of significance.)

In addition to the presentation of the graphs and the summary table we give a *verbal* summary of the data. This summary, which goes somewhat beyond the problems discussed in Chapter IV, serves two purposes. First, it gives a word description of the results we achieved by the two kinds of statistical analyses; second, it sets forth the observed tendencies toward intra-cultural variation which are an important part of the record of findings even though the range of our data was not adequate for a statistical testing of their significance. Judgments as to both the "reality" of these variations and their meanings are, as has been stated, matters of discussion which we most deliberately left to the analysts of the individual cultures who were asked to discuss the totality of our results in the light of data of many other kinds which many investigations over a long time period have collected on the five communities.

The final set of results to be presented are those which show between-culture differences. Here again two methods are used for presenting the results. The first is the graphic method. In the use of graphs for showing within-culture regularities we used one graph to show the ranking preferences of a single sample of respondents for all of the items of an orientation series. Now, for the purpose of giving the reader a visual picture of the variable rankings, culture by culture, we turn this method in the opposite direction and present twenty-three graphs, each of which plots the rankings of all five samples of respondents for each item of each series. Six of these graphs—the six which show the rankings of the Doing and Being alternatives of the *activity* orientation—are simple percentage graphs since only two rather than three alternatives of this orientation were being tested.

In addition to these twenty-three individual-item graphs, we present four graphs which give the summed A and B (and C where necessary) values for all five of the cultures for all of the items of each of the value-orientation series. On these summary graphs there are no circles to indicate the degree of statistical significance of the summary point. In Chapter IV it is explained why it could be misleading to apply standard tests of significance to this particular kind of overall summary.

We then supplement the picture which the summary graphs portray by the results obtained from the one-way analyses of variance of the data used for the between-culture summary tests (see the discussion of question 4 in Chapter IV).

In setting forth the results of these analyses we first present, dimension by dimension, a standard table to describe the source and relative importance of variation along a given dimension. Also, a figure is used both to represent the positions of the five cultures on each dimension and to show where the significant differences between groupings of cultures on each dimension occur.

In the presentation of all of these data the items of the schedule will usually be referred to only by the number each has been given in the orientation series to which it belongs. To save the reader the task of re-

TABLE V:1
The Schedule Items

Relational ORIENTATION ITEMS

Schedule Number	Item Series Number	Short Title of Items
2	R1	Well Arrangements
7	R2	Help in Misfortune
8	R3	Family Work Relations
9	R4	Choice of Delegate
12	R5	Wage Work
16	R6	Livestock Inheritance
17	R7	Land Inheritance

Time ORIENTATION ITEMS

Schedule Number	Item Series Number	Short Title of Items
3	T1	Child Training
5	T2	Expectations about Change
11	T3	Philosophy of Life
14	T4	Ceremonial Innovation
20	T5	Water Allocation

Man-Nature ORIENTATION ITEMS

Schedule Number	Item Series Number	Short Title of Items
4	MN1	Livestock Dying
6	MN2	Facing Conditions
10	MN3	Use of Fields
13	MN4	Belief in Control
19	MN5	Length of Life

Activity ORIENTATION ITEMS

Schedule Number	Item Series Number	Short Title of Items
1	A1	Job Choice (from point of view of employee)
1	A2	Job Choice (from point of view of employer)
15	A3	Ways of Living
18	A4	Care of Fields
21	A5	Housework
22	A6	Nonworking Time

ferring back to the schedule of items in Chapter III we put in Table V:1 the actual schedule number of each item of a series, its series number, and the short title used for it.

WITHIN-CULTURE REGULARITIES AND INDICATIONS OF INTRA-CULTURAL VARIATIONS IN EACH COMMUNITY

Summary of the Results of the Statistical Analyses of the Spanish-American Data

RELATIONAL ORIENTATION. For four of the items of this series of seven items—R2, R4, R5, and R6—the null hypothesis of Lin = Coll = Ind was rejected. The significance level for items R4 and R5 was .01; for items R2 and R6 it was .05. The binomial analyses of these same four items revealed significant preferences *among* the alternatives of choice. Finally,

Analysis of Within-Culture Regularities: Spanish-Americans

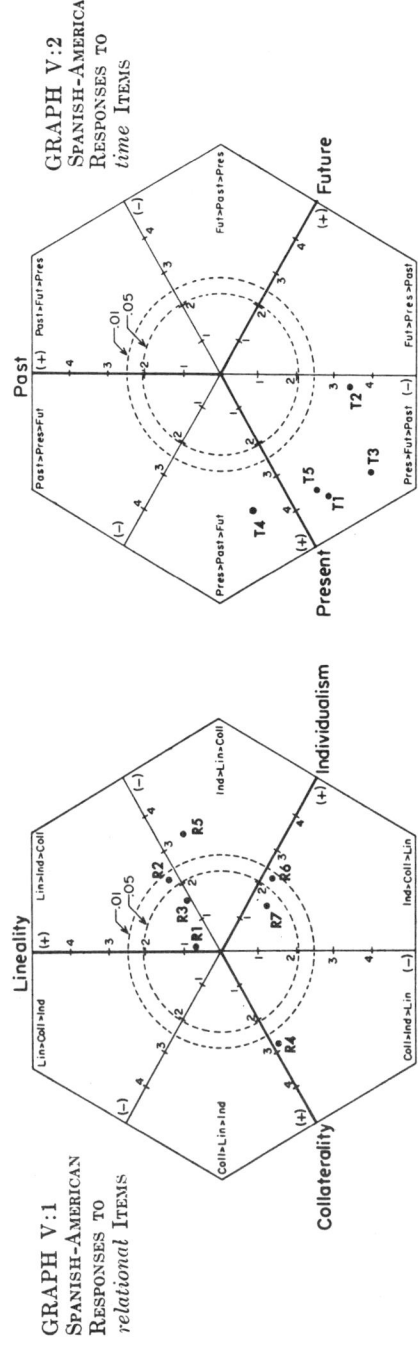

GRAPH V:1
SPANISH-AMERICAN RESPONSES TO *relational* ITEMS

GRAPH V:3
SPANISH-AMERICAN RESPONSES TO *man-nature* ITEMS

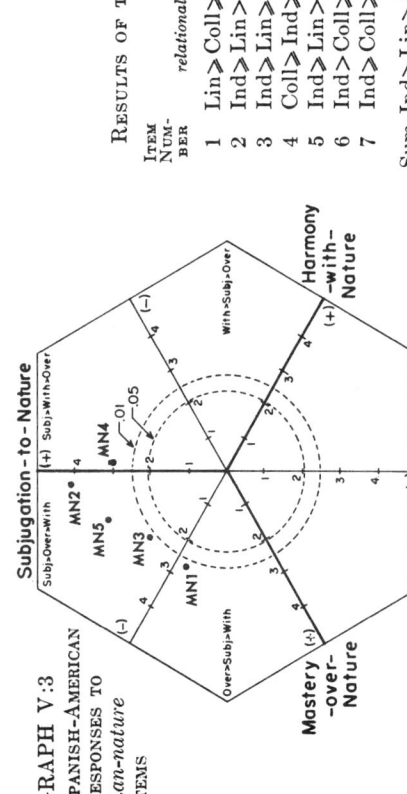

GRAPH V:2
SPANISH-AMERICAN RESPONSES TO *time* ITEMS

TABLE V:2
RESULTS OF THE BINOMIAL ANALYSES OF THE SPANISH-AMERICAN DATA

ITEM NUMBER	ORIENTATION			
	relational	*time*	*man-nature*	*activity*
1	Lin>Coll>Ind	Pres>Fut>Past	Over>Subj>With	Being>Doing
2	Ind>Lin>Coll	Pres>Fut>Past	Subj>Over>With	Being>Doing
3	Ind>Lin>Coll	Pres>Fut>Past	Subj>Over>With*	Being>Doing
4	Coll>Ind>Lin*	Pres>Past>Fut	Subj>With>Over	Being>Doing
5	Ind>Lin>Coll	Pres>Fut>Past	Subj>Over>With	Being>Doing
6	Ind>Coll>Lin			Doing>Being
7	Ind>Coll>Lin			
Sum	Ind>Lin>Coll*	Pres>Fut>Past	Subj>Over>With	Being>Doing

the summary analysis of all the items showed an overall ranking pattern, but the only preference in this ranking which was definite enough to achieve statistical significance was the choice of the Individualistic position over the Collateral one.

TIME ORIENTATION. It was possible to reject the null hypothesis of Pres = Fut = Past for all items used to test this orientation. The .01 level of statistical significance was achieved in all cases. The pair-by-pair analysis showed that the Present alternative was preferred in all instances to at least one of the other alternatives. The summary analysis showed a definite overall ranking pattern of Pres > Fut > Past.

MAN-NATURE ORIENTATION. For the items of this series it was again possible to reject the null hypothesis Over = With = Subj, and all results achieved were also significant at the .01 level. The binomial analysis showed the Subjugated-to-Nature position to be significantly preferred to at least one of the other two alternatives in every item. The summary analysis completely ranked the three alternatives into the pattern of Subj > Over > With.

ACTIVITY ORIENTATION. For all the items in this series except A6 our analysis both rejected the null hypothesis of Being = Doing and affirmed a significant preference for the Being alternative over the Doing one. The summary ordering of Being > Doing was most definite.

Indications of Intra-Cultural Variations in the Spanish-American Data

RELATIONAL ORIENTATION. It was on the *relational* orientation that we had expected to find the most evidence of intra-cultural variation in the Spanish-American group (see the prior predictions in Chapter II). The analysis of the data reveals this to be true. There was no significant patterning disclosed in the responses to three of the seven items, and there were also obvious variations in the patternings on other of the items. Let us look at these items one by one.

For item R1 of the series there was real heterogeneity in the responses. The closest approach to a systematic pattern was the first choice of the Lineal alternative by somewhat more than half of the respondents. In the ranking preferences elicited from item R2 two competing patterns appeared. These were the Lineality over Individualism over Collaterality and the Individualism over Lineality over Collaterality patterns.[1] For item R3 the first choices were again almost equally divided between the Individualistic and Lineal alternatives. In addition there was no clear-cut patterning as between second and third-order choices. However, one finding worth noting in the responses for this item was the variation by sex in first-order preferences. The men were predominantly in favor of the

---

[1] In presenting the material on intra-cultural variations we use the convention of $A > B > C$ when we speak of a pattern which emerged as the result of a statistical analysis. For the intra-cultural variations observed but not statistically tested we use the word "over" rather than the symbol ">" and also give the full spelling of the alternatives—that is, Individualism over Collaterality over Lineality.

Individualistic alternative; a majority of the women selected the Lineal alternative. On item R4 the results show a significant outcome, placing the Collateral alternative in first position relative to the Lineal. The variation found was an almost equal distribution of the two competing patterns, Collaterality over Individualism over Lineality and Collaterality over Lineality over Individualism, which contributed to the ambiguity of the statistical outcome. Two quite definite patterns again emerged in the responses to item R5. In this instance they were the Individualism over Lineality over Collaterality and the Lineality over Collaterality over Individualism patterns. The first of these was only slightly more prevalent than the second. For item R6 the Individualistic position was preferred—was dominant—but the preferences as to the Collateral and Lineal alternatives for second and third choices were ambiguous. Finally, for item R7 there was no consistency in the rank-order responses despite the fact that two thirds of the respondents selected the Individualistic alternative as their first choice. The chief reason that no pattern of significance emerged was the quite consistent tendency of those who did not favor the Individualistic alternative as a first choice to place it in a third-order position.

Taken as a whole these responses show that the people of Atrisco in the year 1951 were only slightly more Individualistically than Lineally oriented in their dominant *relational* value-orientation position. The material also indicates more actual inconsistency of patterning than can be considered normal to any system because of the intra-system demands for variations which have been discussed. There is, in other words, in this instance highly suggestive evidence that there was a transition process occurring.

TIME ORIENTATION. The evidence of intra-cultural variations in the responses to the items in this orientation are less dramatically indicative of a state of cultural transition than those of the *relational* orientation, but they are, nonetheless, highly interesting. On three of the five items there was a quite consistent choice (never completely so, of course) of the Pres > Fut > Past pattern. These items were T1, T3, and T5. For item T2 this pattern also emerged but to a much less significant degree. There was a marked variant pattern of Future over Present over Past which so slanted the results that the final outcome was the Pres $\geqslant$ Fut > Past one. In other words, the Future alternative was definitely preferred to the Past but it was almost equally preferred to the Present, so that no significant result was yielded as between these two alternatives. In contrast to this there was the item on Ceremonial Innovation (item T4) where so many persons selected the Past alternative as either their first or second choice that a pattern of Pres > Past $\geqslant$ Fut emerged. This result, it will be remembered, was a predicted one.

MAN-NATURE ORIENTATION. *Los Atrisqueños* were also remarkably consistent in their responses to the items of the *man-nature* orientation. The important variation to be noted is the significantly consistent rank order of Over $\geqslant$ Subj > With in the responses to item MN1 which was testing in the area of the economic-technological. Also, although the other item used for testing in this area—item MN3—yielded a consistent pattern of Subj ⩾ Over ⩾ With*, the first-order position of the Subjugated alternative was not as marked as it was in the responses to questions that touched on religious attitudes. Some slight and not very significant variation was found in the responses to item MN4. The Subjugated first-order position was markedly dominant here, but second-order choices were much less definite. The With-Nature position was very slightly favored.

ACTIVITY ORIENTATION. In almost all the choices between the Being and Doing alternatives of the *activity* orientation the people of Atrisco were overwhelmingly in favor of the Being position. The one exception to this quite general pattern occurred in the responses to item A6. On this quite economically oriented question a number of men selected the Doing alternative, but it was actually the responses of the women which threw the balance of preference on it to the Doing alternative. Although in the total set of responses to the *activity* orientation questions the women were generally more given to a selection of the Being alternative than the men, they tended to favor the Doing alternative on this one question which tested on attitudes about *men's* work habits. On the preceding item (item A5), which posed alternative conceptions of women's work habits, the women almost unerringly selected the Being alternative.

Findings Compared to Predictions

The results achieved in the analysis of the Spanish-American data are remarkably in accord with the predictions ventured as to the preferences in the group. However, it will be recalled that no general prediction was made as to second and third-order preferences of the *time* orientation; and there was hesitation in predicting the preference between the Over-Nature and the With-Nature positions of the *man-nature* orientation. The only predictions made in both these cases were relative to specific items. It was said that the Past *time* alternative would be second order for the item treating ceremonialism and that the Over-Nature position would be the favored second choice for the items on the *man-nature* orientation which are concerned with economic and technological matters. Thus, the definiteness of the second-order Future *time* and Over-Nature positions are clearly matters for consideration in the later discussion of the Spanish-American community. And, of course, a primary issue for this discussion—which appears in Chapter VI—is the interpretation of the indeterminateness of the preferences on the *relational* orientation.

Summary of the Results of the Statistical Analyses of the Texan Data

RELATIONAL ORIENTATION. For each of the items of this series—R1 through R7—the null hypothesis of Lin = Coll = Ind was rejected. In all instances the Individualistic alternative was significantly preferred to at least one of the other two alternatives. The summary of all the items shows a complete ordering of the alternatives in the Ind > Coll > Lin pattern.

TIME ORIENTATION. The null hypothesis of Past = Pres = Fut was re-

Analysis of Within-Culture Regularities: Texans

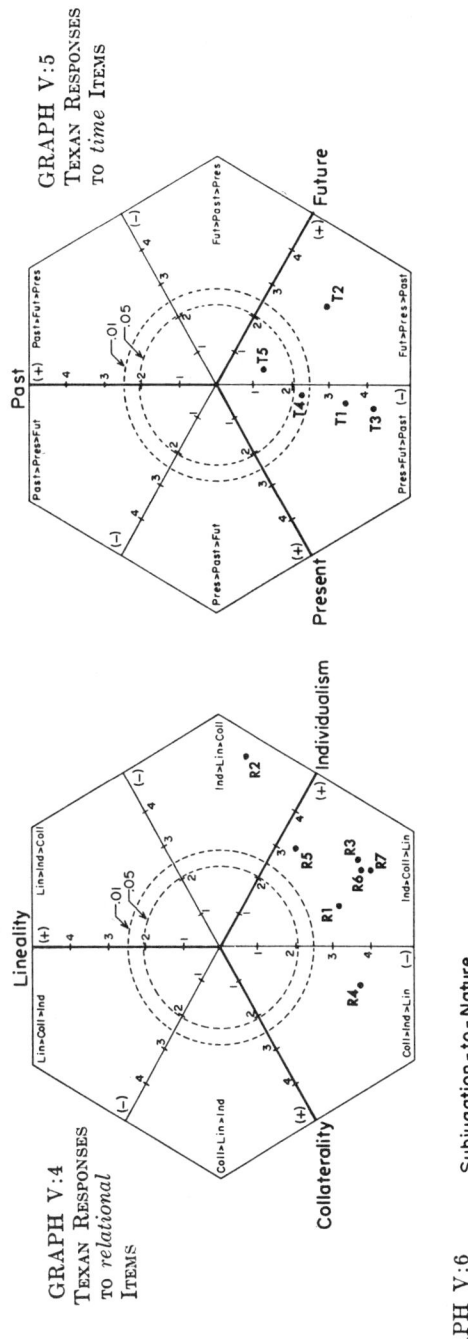

GRAPH V:4
TEXAN RESPONSES TO *relational* ITEMS

GRAPH V:5
TEXAN RESPONSES TO *time* ITEMS

GRAPH V:6
TEXAN RESPONSES TO *man-nature* ITEMS

TABLE V:3

RESULTS OF THE BINOMIAL ANALYSES OF THE TEXAN DATA

ITEM NUMBER	ORIENTATION			
	relational	*time*	*man-nature*	*activity*
1	Ind>Coll>Lin	Pres>Fut>Past	Over>Subj>With	Doing>Being
2	Ind>Lin>Coll	Fut>Pres>Past	Over>Subj>With	Doing>Being
3	Ind>Coll>Lin	Pres>Fut>Past	Over>With>Subj	Doing>Being
4	Coll>Ind>Lin	Pres>Fut>Past	Over>Subj>With	Being>Doing
5	Ind>Coll>Lin	Fut>Pres>Past	Over>With>Subj	Doing>Being
6	Ind>Coll>Lin			Doing>Being
7	Ind>Coll>Lin			
Sum	Ind>Coll>Lin	Fut>Pres>Past	Over>With>Subj	Doing>Being

jected for items T1 through T4 of this series. The Present and Future *time* positions were both significantly preferred to the Past one in each of these items. As between the Present and Future positions the margin of preference for the latter was small; hence the overall outcome was the Fut ≥ Pres > Past pattern.

MAN-NATURE ORIENTATION. We rejected the null hypothesis of Over = With = Subj for three of the items of this series—MN1, MN3, and MN5. The responses to each of these showed at least one significant preference for the Over-Nature alternative. The summary of all the items also shows the Over-Nature position to have been preferred to both the With-Nature and Subjugated-to-Nature positions. There was, however, no significant preference between these two latter alternatives as a second-order position.

ACTIVITY ORIENTATION. Only on item A6 were we able both to reject the null hypothesis of Being = Doing and to affirm a strong preference for the Doing alternative. However, the general trend shown in the summary of the six items of the series was Doing preferred to Being.

Indications of Intra-Cultural Variations in the Texan Data

RELATIONAL ORIENTATION. On four of the items in this series—R3, R5, R6, and R7—there was no appreciable variation from the significant overall ranking pattern of Ind > Coll > Lin. For item R1 the general pattern was the same, but a variant pattern of Collaterality over Individualism over Lineality was so systematically present in the responses that the final outcome was Ind ≥ Coll > Lin. Two items, in differing degrees, revealed a tendency toward a preference of the Lineal alternative in second-order position. On item R2 there was the quite frequent Individualism over Lineality over Collaterality variant pattern which dictated the statistical outcome Ind > Lin > Coll. The responses to item R5 showed the presence of two competing patterns, a somewhat dominant Individualism over Collaterality over Lineality one and a marked variant one of Individualism over Lineality over Collaterality; hence the final outcome was the Ind > Coll ≥ Lin pattern. The responses to item R4 revealed the only variation which markedly deviated from the Individualistic alternative as a first choice. The Collateral alternative was actually somewhat more often chosen as a first choice than the Individualistic one but not often enough to yield a clear-cut Coll > Ind > Lin pattern. The result, instead, was the Coll ≥ Ind > Lin pattern.

TIME ORIENTATION. Item T1 brought forth two strongly competing patterns—the Present over Future over Past and the Future over Present over Past. The difference in frequency was not great but was sufficient to produce an outcome only slightly in the direction of Present *time* dominance. The results for item T2 yielded an unequivocal pattern of Fut > Pres > Past. On items T3 and T4 we again found a sufficient variation in preferences for the Future and Present alternatives as the first choice so that the final outcome, in both cases, was the Pres ≥ Fut > Past pattern. The responses to item T5 contained so much variation in ranking that no significant pattern emerged. All that could be noted was a trend in the direction of Future over Present over Past.

MAN-NATURE ORIENTATION. The variations noted in the Texan responses to the items testing this orientation were fairly marked. The chief of these, as is shown by the overall pattern of Over > With ⩾ Subj, was a variation in choices of the With-Nature and Subjugated-to-Nature positions for the second-order alternative. This variation was clear-cut in items MN1 and MN3 which are primarily technological. But on two items which test primarily in the religious behavior sphere—MN2 and MN4—there really was no statistically consistent pattern at all. All that could be noted was a definite trend in the direction of the dominance of the Over-Nature position. Item MN5 resulted in the consistent patterning Over ⩾ With > Subj.

ACTIVITY ORIENTATION. The summary of the results on this orientation given above states the variation clearly. The Doing orientation was preferred by a majority of the respondents for all save one item (A4), but the leaning of many toward a preference for the Being alternative was marked.

Findings Compared to Predictions

The total analysis of the Texan data shows that there was a high degree of correspondence between the prior predictions and the observed results. We expected to find a great emphasis upon the Individualistic alternative of the *relational* orientation and expected also to find that the Present alternative of the *time* orientation and the Being alternative of the *activity* orientation would be only somewhat less emphasized than the Future and Doing alternatives. However, the strength of the Present *time* preference was somewhat greater than was predicted. The equivocation in second-order preference between the Subjugated-to-Nature and With-Nature alternatives of the *man-nature* orientation was *not* expected.

Summary of the Results of the Statistical Analyses of the Mormon Data

RELATIONAL ORIENTATION. For all items of this series the null hypothesis of Lin = Coll = Ind was rejected. On each the Individualistic alternative was significantly preferred to at least one of the other two. A significant summary outcome which completely orders the alternatives into the Ind > Coll > Lin pattern also emerged; but it should be mentioned that the dominance of the Individualistic alternative over the Collateral one is only very narrowly significant.

TIME ORIENTATION. For items T1, T2, T3, and T5 of this series we were able to reject the null hypothesis of Past = Fut = Pres. On three of these four items (all but T5) either the Future or the Present *time* alternative was significantly preferred to the Past one. The significant summary reflects this tendency. Both the Future and Present *time* positions were preferred to the Past, but the degree of the preference of the Future position over the Present one, while existent, was too slight to achieve statistical significance.

MAN-NATURE ORIENTATION. The null hypothesis of Subj = Over = With

Analysis of Within-Culture Regularities: Mormons

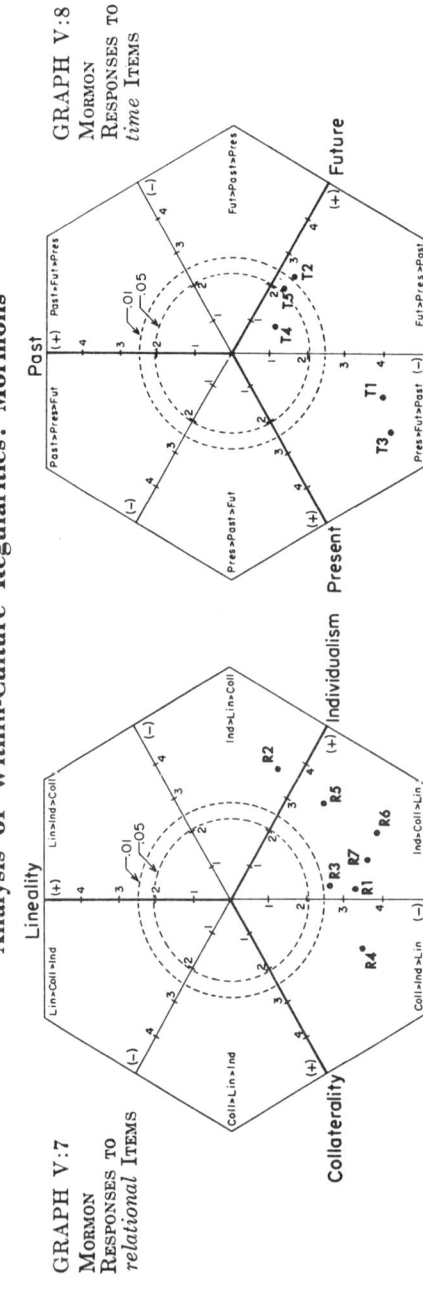

GRAPH V:7 MORMON RESPONSES TO *relational* ITEMS

GRAPH V:8 MORMON RESPONSES TO *time* ITEMS

GRAPH V:9 MORMON REPONSES TO *man-nature* ITEMS

TABLE V:4
RESULTS OF THE BINOMIAL ANALYSES OF THE MORMON DATA

ITEM NUMBER	ORIENTATION			
	relational	*time*	*man-nature*	*activity*
1	Ind≥Coll>Lin	Pres>Fut>Past	Over>Subj>With	Doing>Being
2	Ind>Lin≥Coll	Fut>Pres>Past	With>Subj>Over	Doing>Being
3	Ind≥Coll>Lin	Pres>Fut>Past	Over>With>Subj	Doing>Being
4	Coll>Ind>Lin	Fut>Pres>Past	With>Subj>Over[b]	Being≥Doing
5	Ind≥Coll>Lin	Fut>Pres>Past[a]	Over>With>Subj*	Doing>Being
6	Ind≥Coll>Lin			Doing>Being
7	Ind≥Coll>Lin			
Sum	Ind>Coll>Lin	Fut>Pres>Past	Over>With>Subj	Doing>Being

[a] Fut>Pres only.   [b] With>Subj only.

was rejected for items MN1, MN3, MN4, and MN5. However, the alternative preferences between the Over-Nature and With-Nature positions for first-order ranking were mixed by questions. The summary analysis shows that both the With-Nature and Over-Nature positions were significantly preferred to the Subjugated-to-Nature one, but there was no significant differentiation between the Over-Nature and With-Nature choices. All that can be noted is a trend toward a greater preference for the Over-Nature alternative.

ACTIVITY ORIENTATION. On items A3 and A6 of this series it was possible to reject the null hypothesis of Doing = Being. Although other items do not significantly differentiate between the two alternatives, the trend in the direction of the Doing alternative was sufficiently marked to yield a significant overall Doing > Being pattern.

Indications of Intra-Cultural Variations in the Mormon Data

RELATIONAL ORIENTATION. On item R1 of the *relational* orientation series the Mormon responses like those of the Texans showed the two rank-order patterns of Individualism over Collaterality over Lineality and Collaterality over Individualism over Lineality. But in the Mormon case the prevalence of the second pattern was much greater than in the Texan case. For item R2 the Mormons, like the Texans, dominantly selected the Individualism over Lineality over Collaterality pattern but in addition adhered somewhat to a variant pattern of Lineality over Collaterality over Individualism. The responses to item R3 yielded a dominant pattern of Individualism over Collaterality over Lineality, the pattern from which virtually no Texans departed, but also showed a definite variant pattern of Collaterality over Individualism over Lineality. For item R4 both the dominant pattern of Collaterality over Individualism over Lineality and the variant one of Individualism over Collaterality over Lineality were found as in the Texan responses, but many fewer Mormons than Texans chose the variant pattern. The results obtained from item R5 were very similar to those cited for the Texan group. They showed a clear-cut preference for the Individualistic alternative as first order but varied sufficiently in second-order choices to produce the two rank-order patterns of Individualism over Collaterality over Lineality and Individualism over Lineality over Collaterality. A minor difference between the two groups was the selection by a few Mormons, but no Texans, of a third pattern—the Collaterality over Individualism over Lineality one. On the two questions relating to inheritance customs, items R6 and R7, the Mormon group preferred the Individualism over Collaterality over Lineality pattern but also showed a definite variation of first-order Collaterality which was completely absent in the Texan responses. A most definite variant pattern of Collaterality over Individualism over Lineality was found among the Mormon responses to R7.

TIME ORIENTATION. On item T1 of the *time* orientation series the Mormon responses, like the Texan ones, yielded the two rank-order patterns of Present over Future over Past and Future over Present over Past. Although in both groups the result was in the Present direction, the degree of this emphasis was greater in the Mormon case. In the responses to item T2 there were found the two variant patterns of Future over Past over Present and Past over Future over Present, the compounding of which yielded the Fut > Pres ⩾ Past pattern. This kind of variation in the Past direction never appeared in the Texan responses. The markedly consistent preference of the Mormons on item T3 was the Pres > Fut > Past ranking pattern. There was not, as in the Texan case, a consistent variation in the direction of a first-order Future *time* emphasis. For item T4 there was no consistent pattern in the Mormon responses. Almost one-half the women and a substantial number of men selected the Future alternative as a first preference, but beyond this there was little consistency of any kind. The responses to item T5 yielded a somewhat ambiguous ranking pattern of Future over Present over Past.

The overall results produced by the Mormon responses on this whole series of items are most similar to those yielded by the Texan answers. However, one does note item by item the minor but important difference of a somewhat greater stressing of the Past *time* alternative in the Mormon group.

MAN-NATURE ORIENTATION. For item MN1 of the *man-nature* series the Mormon responses yielded a significantly consistent pattern of Over ⩾ Subj > With. There was a less marked stressing of the Over-Nature position in the Mormon group than in the Texan one. In the answers to item MN2 no consistent pattern was found. The only systematic trend noted was a first-order preference of the With-Nature position. It will be recalled that the Texan responses to this item, also lacking in consistency of pattern, revealed a trend toward the Over-Nature alternative. The Mormons on item MN3 showed an almost equal preference for the two ranking patterns of With over Over over Subjugated and Over over With over Subjugated. The result, very different from the Texan one for this item, was a consistent pattern midway between the With-Nature and Over-Nature positions for first choice. On item MN4 the Mormon result yielded only a significantly consistent pattern of With > Subj. For this same item the Texan responses did not yield a consistent pattern of any kind. For the last item of the series—item MN5—the Mormons once again showed an almost equal preference for the Over over With over Subjugated and the With over Over over Subjugated ranking patterns. And again the final result was a consistent pattern which was almost midway between the Over-Nature and With-Nature positions for first-order preference. The Texan responses for the item showed only one consistent pattern—the Over over With over Subjugated one.

Thus, we see that, while in general the ranking patterns of the Texans and Mormons on this orientation were very similar, there was a meaningfully greater degree of emphasis given by the Mormons to the With-Nature as opposed to the Over-Nature alternative.

ACTIVITY ORIENTATION. On the questions testing for a choice between the Doing and Being alternatives of this orientation the Mormons again were similar to the Texans, preferring the Doing alternative on all items except

A4. The overall difference between the two groups was in the magnitude of the preference for the Doing orientation: 70 per cent of the Mormon responses in contrast to 62 per cent of the Texan responses favored it.

Findings Compared to Predictions

Very generally the prior predictions as to the probable Mormon ranking patterns agree with these results. But there were some discrepancies. The first concerns the *relational* orientation. The prediction was that the Individualistic and the Collateral alternatives were equally likely as first-order preferences. Actually the Individualistic alternative was significantly dominant. However, analysis of the data showed that the Collateral alternative was both a strongly favored second-order choice of most Mormons in a majority of the situations treated in the questions and a first-order preference of some Mormons in several of the situations. The variant pattern of Collaterality over Individualism over Lineality was much more consistently present in the Mormon data than it was in the Texan data. Careful scrutiny of the Mormon data also revealed some variation by sex of respondent. Although in the overall summaries of responses both the Mormon men and women together are shown to have a preference for the Ind > Coll > Lin pattern, the degree to which women favored the pattern was greater than that of the men. The pattern found in the responses of the men very closely approximated the Individualism equals Collaterality over Lineality ranking.

Our prediction on the ranking of alternatives on the *man-nature* orientation is also somewhat discrepant from the observed result. We expected to find the With-Nature position still somewhat more dominant than the Over-Nature one. The data showed the reverse to be true by a narrow margin. The two positions were almost equally well favored. Here again a variation by sex of respondent was noted. The summary of male responses yielded a consistent pattern of With equals Over over Subjugated. Those of the women showed no consistent pattern, but the trend among them toward a first-order Over-Nature preference was strong enough to produce the Over $\geqslant$ With > Subj pattern for the Mormons as a whole.

These variations between the responses of the sexes in the Mormon sample and the differences noted between the Texan and Mormon responses are focal issues for the discussion in Chapter VII which treats comparatively these two English-speaking groups.

Summary of the Results of the Statistical Analyses of the Zuni Data

RELATIONAL ORIENTATION. The null hypothesis of Lin = Coll = Ind was rejected for only two items of this series—R3 and R6. In both of these cases the Collateral and Lineal alternatives were significantly preferred to the Individualistic one, and on item R3 there was also a significant preference of the Collateral over the Lineal alternative. Summarily, the Collateral alternative was a significant first-order choice, but there was

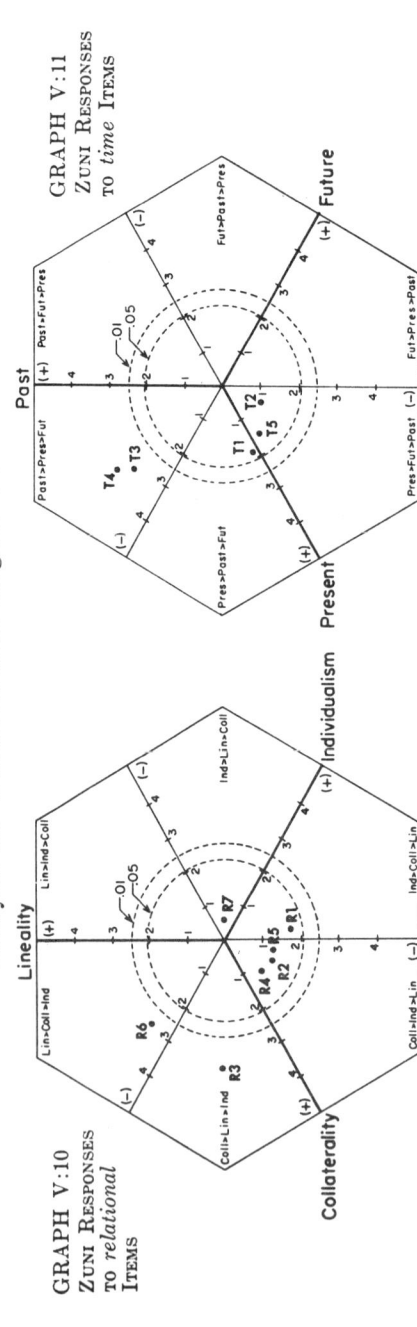

Analysis of Within-Culture Regularities: Zuni

GRAPH V:10 ZUNI RESPONSES TO *relational* ITEMS

GRAPH V:11 ZUNI RESPONSES TO *time* ITEMS

GRAPH V:12 ZUNI RESPONSES TO *man-nature* ITEMS

TABLE V:5
RESULTS OF THE BINOMIAL ANALYSES OF THE ZUNI DATA

ITEM NUMBER	ORIENTATION			
	relational	time	man-nature	activity
1	Ind>Coll>Lin	Pres>Past>Fut	Over>Subj>With	Being>Doing
2	Coll>Ind>Lin	Pres>Fut>Past	Subj>With>Over	Being>Doing
3	Coll>Lin>Ind	Past>Pres>Fut	Over>With>Subj	Doing>Being
4	Coll>Lin>Ind	Past>Pres>Fut	With>Subj>Over	Doing>Being
5	Ind>Coll>Lin	Pres>Fut>Past[a]	Subj>Over>With	Doing>Being
6	Lin>Coll>Ind			Doing>Being
7	Ind>Lin>Coll			
Sum	Coll>Lin>Ind	Pres>Past>Fut	With>Subj>Over	Doing>Being

[a] Pres>Fut only.

no clear-cut differentiation between the other two alternatives as a second-order position.

TIME ORIENTATION. For items T3, T4, and T5 there was a significant preference of the Present over the Future position. The summary of all the items indicated a preference of both the Present and the Past over the Future alternative. As between the Present and Past positions there was no significant difference.

MAN-NATURE ORIENTATION. The null hypothesis of Over = With = Subj was rejected for items MN2 and MN4. On both items the With-Nature position was preferred to at least one of the others a significant number of times. But for the set of items as a whole no significant summary ranking emerged. All that could be noted was a tendency in the direction of a With over Subjugated over Over total pattern.

ACTIVITY ORIENTATION. For items A1, A2, A4, A5, and A6 we rejected the null hypothesis of Being = Doing. On A1 and A2 the Being alternative was preferred to the Doing one; on items A4, A5, and A6 the reverse was true. The summary point was, therefore, indeterminate.

Indications of Intra-Cultural Variations in the Zuni Data

RELATIONAL ORIENTATION. The variations in the Zuni responses to the items of this series, and the other series as well, were marked. A question to be raised is whether or not there were indications of extreme intra-cultural variations which help to account for the inconclusiveness of the ranking patterns, item by item and overall.

We note, first, the difference in the ranking preferences for item R3 which treats of family work relations and items R6 and R7 which question on the subject of inheritance. For the former the Collateral alternative was quite consistently and definitely preferred. In the latter two the trend was more in the Lineal than the Collateral direction, but there was also a difference in the preferences as between the two inheritance items. On the issue of livestock inheritance the Lineal position tended to be the most preferred and the Individualistic position the least preferred. Yet when the question was inheritance of land, a very slight degree of preference was shown for the Individualistic alternative.

It was also noted that in the responses to item R5—an item which treats the question of wage work—there were two fairly clear-cut competing rank-order patterns of preference. These were the Collaterality over Individualism over Lineality and the Individualism over Collaterality over Lineality patterns. Approximately two thirds of the respondents chose one or the other of these patterns. There was, however, little consistency of any kind in the choices of the remaining third of the respondents; hence no significant pattern was achieved. These same two patterns again appeared in the responses to item R1. In this instance the primary reason for the nonsignificant outcome was the choice of the Lineal alternative as a first-order preference by a number of those respondents who did not follow one or the other of these patterns.

On items R2 and R4 there were no observable variations of a consistency worth mentioning.

TIME ORIENTATION. The most significant variation in the responses to the items of this series was that which the summary outcome of Pres ≥ Past > Fut depicts in a general way. It will be recalled that while no prior prediction was ventured as to the Zuni rankings on the *time* orientation (or any other orientation), it was stated that we expected to find them more predisposed to the choice of the Past *time* alternative than any of the other groups. This proved to be true. The preference was clearly evident even on the items for which no significant outcome was achieved. On item T1, one third of all respondents placed Past first. On item T3 the percentage was even higher, and finally on item T4, which tests in the ceremonial sphere, there was an unequivocal Past > Pres > Fut pattern. On the other items for which there was no consistent pattern the Present *time* alternative was sufficiently often preferred as a first choice to give it a slight (but not significant) edge in the final summary outcome for the total series of *time* orientation items.

MAN-NATURE ORIENTATION. The only items in this orientation which yielded consistent results were MN2 and MN4, and the results in the two cases varied between the dominance of the With-Nature and Subjugated-to-Nature positions. The only regular variation in the fairly extreme heterogeneity of responses to these items was the tendency of the men to choose the Subjugated-to-Nature response more frequently than the women.

ACTIVITY ORIENTATION. The major variations in the responses to the items of this orientation are clearly evident in the summing of the results given above. For three items, the choice was clearly the Doing alternative; for the two parts of the double-headed item which we consider the least good for testing on the *activity* orientation—items A1 and A2—the preference went to the Being alternative; on one item the preference was equivocal.

Findings Compared to Predictions

The main statement to be made in this comparison is that it was the Zuni group for which no general predictions were ventured, and it was the Zuni responses which yielded the fewest conclusive results. The specific predictions which were made appear to be corroborated to some extent by the data. The first of these was that the Zuni would be more given to the choice of the Past alternative of the *time* orientation than any other of the peoples tested. The second specific prediction was the statement that the Zuni would show a greater preference for the Lineal alternative of the *relational* orientation than would the Navaho. Generally speaking, this also appears to be the case, but the difference between the two groups in overall ranking patterns is not a significant one.

Relative to the *activity* orientation we considered it likely that the omission of the Being-in-Becoming alternative in the test schedule would have a more serious effect in the Zuni case than any of the others. This point is discussed in Chapter VIII where the totality of the Zuni results is treated.

Summary of the Results of the Statistical Analyses of the Navaho Data

RELATIONAL ORIENTATION. For items R1, R2, and R5 of this series the null hypothesis of Ind = Coll = Lin was rejected. In all of these and in R3 as well, the Collateral alternative was significantly preferred to at least one of the other alternatives. The summary pattern showed clearly that the Collateral position was dominant. There was no significant degree of preference between the other two alternatives.

TIME ORIENTATION. For items T1, T4, and T5 the null hypothesis of Fut = Pres = Past was rejected. In the responses to all three items the Present *time* alternative was significantly preferred to at least one of the other alternatives. The summary of all the items indicates that the Present position was definitely preferred. The Past position was somewhat preferred to the Future one as second order, but the difference in preference between the two was not a significant one.

MAN-NATURE ORIENTATION. On items MN2, MN3, MN4, and MN5 the null hypothesis of Subj = With = Over could be rejected. On each item at least one of the other alternatives was preferred to the Subjugated-to-Nature one. The one significant summary preference found was that of the choice of the With-Nature over the Subjugated-to-Nature position.

ACTIVITY ORIENTATION. The null hypothesis of Being = Doing was definitely rejected on five of the six items in the series of this orientation. On items A3 through A6 the choice was unequivocally the Doing one. On the job-choice item, which has two parts, there was a significant preference for the Being alternative on part 1 and an indeterminate choice between the two alternatives on part 2. The summary outcome for all the items was clearly Doing > Being.

Indications of Intra-Cultural Variations in the Navaho Data

RELATIONAL ORIENTATION. The main variation found in the responses to the total series of the *relational* orientation items was the shifting between the choice of the Lineal and the Individualistic alternatives as a second-order preference. On three items (R1, R3, and R5) it was the Lineal position which was preferred; on items R4, R6, and R7 the Individualistic position was favored; but in no instance was the degree of preference between these two marked enough to be statistically significant. On item R4 there was no significant difference between any of the three alternatives, only a trend in the Collaterality over Individualism over Lineality direction.

There was definite variation of another kind on item R2 which treats of the source of help in case of misfortune. Here the Lineal alternative was significantly accorded the first-order position. Fairly systematic variations showing competing ranking patterns were noted in the responses to two items. For item R3 (Family Work Relations) there emerged two

Analysis of Within-Culture Regularities: Navaho

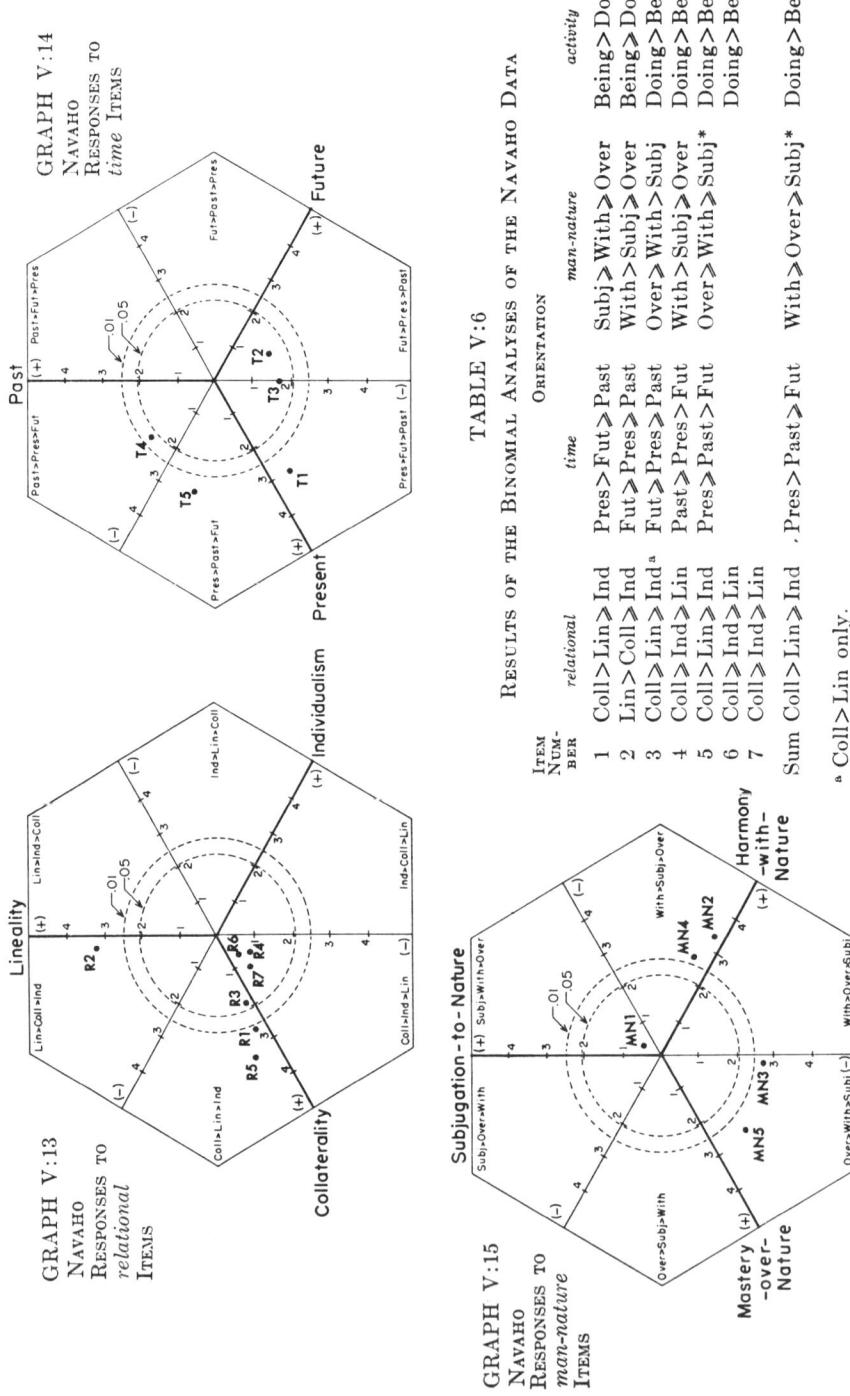

GRAPH V:13
NAVAHO RESPONSES TO *relational* ITEMS

GRAPH V:14
NAVAHO RESPONSES TO *time* ITEMS

GRAPH V:15
NAVAHO RESPONSES TO *man-nature* ITEMS

TABLE V:6

RESULTS OF THE BINOMIAL ANALYSES OF THE NAVAHO DATA

ITEM NUMBER	ORIENTATION			
	relational	time	man-nature	activity
1	Coll>Lin≥Ind	Pres>Fut>Past	Subj>With>Over	Being>Doing
2	Lin>Coll>Ind	Fut>Pres>Past	With>Subj>Over	Being>Doing
3	Coll≥Lin>Ind[a]	Fut>Pres>Past	Over≥With>Subj	Doing>Being
4	Coll>Ind≥Lin	Past>Pres>Fut	With>Subj>Over	Doing>Being
5	Coll>Lin≥Ind	Pres>Past>Fut	Over≥With>Subj*	Doing>Being
6	Coll≥Ind>Lin			Doing>Being
7	Coll≥Ind>Lin			
Sum	Coll>Lin≥Ind	.Pres>Past>Fut	With>Over≥Subj*	Doing>Being

[a] Coll>Lin only.

patterns which were almost equal in strength—the Collaterality over Individualism over Lineality and the Individualism over Collaterality over Lineality patterns. The compounding of these two yielded an outcome in the Collateral direction which was just barely significant. On item R5 (Wage Work) there appeared a minor but nonetheless systematic variant pattern of Individualism over Collaterality over Lineality which competed with the overall result of Coll > Lin ⩾ Ind.

TIME ORIENTATION. On this orientation, too, the main variation noted was the shifting in preference between two alternatives—the Past and Future ones—for a second-order ranking position. And the very interesting aspect of this variation was the division in type of response by sex of respondent. Predominantly the men placed Past in second-order position whereas the women typically selected the Future alternative. Sometimes the women actually placed the Future alternative first.

One also notes from the analysis of separate items of this series that the greatest variation in ranking patterns was found in the responses to the two most abstract and philosophical items, T2 and T3. Since it is well known that the Navaho are a very concrete-minded people who have a highly inflected language, this question is raised for the later interpretation of the Navaho data in Chapter IX: Was the ambiguity of the ranking patterns on these two items a result of a failure in method, or do the responses reflect a real confusion in the minds of the Navaho of today in their *time* orientation preferences?

MAN-NATURE ORIENTATION. Although the With-Nature position was significantly preferred to the Subjugated one in the Navaho responses to the items testing on this orientation, there was, as noted above, considerable variation on items MN3 and MN5 in the Over-Nature direction. As on the *time* orientation there was a fairly marked difference in the responses of the men and women to the items. It was the men who most consistently selected the With-Nature position. While overall the responses of the women showed no significant pattern, there was a definite tendency in them in the Over-Nature direction. It was this difference in the answers given by men and women, together with the definiteness of the choice of the group as a whole for the Over-Nature position on item MN5 (the question which treats of measures to lengthen the life span of human beings), which was mainly responsible for the overall outcome of With ⩾ Over ⩾ Subj*.

ACTIVITY ORIENTATION. On all the items of the series testing this orientation—except items A1 and A2 which we have stated to be questionable items for anything like a "pure" testing of the orientation—the Navaho, both men and women, showed a strong preference for the Doing alternative. The group as a whole gave the greatest percentage of Doing responses of all the groups tested. And in addition to being quite decisive in their choice of this alternative, they also fairly uniformly stated that other members of the group would also make this choice. On other orientations they were much less sure that their own choices would be those of most other Navaho (for a record of this difference in "perceived consensus" see Appendix 3).

Findings Compared to Predictions

On the whole the findings which resulted from the statistical analyses of the schedule data accord well with the prior predictions as to the Navaho ranking patterns. The predominance of the Lineal alternative of the *relational* orientation and that of the Past alternative of the *time* orientation in second-order positions were both somewhat less firm than was predicted, but the ranking patterns observed were the predicted ones. On the *man-nature* orientation no prediction was made as to the ranking of the Subjugated-to-Nature and Over-Nature alternatives in second and third-order positions. Our data show a preference—albeit not a significant one—for the Over-Nature alternative as second order. But this finding is challenged in the later interpretations of the Navaho data. As for the *activity* orientation the congruence between the finding and the prediction was marked.

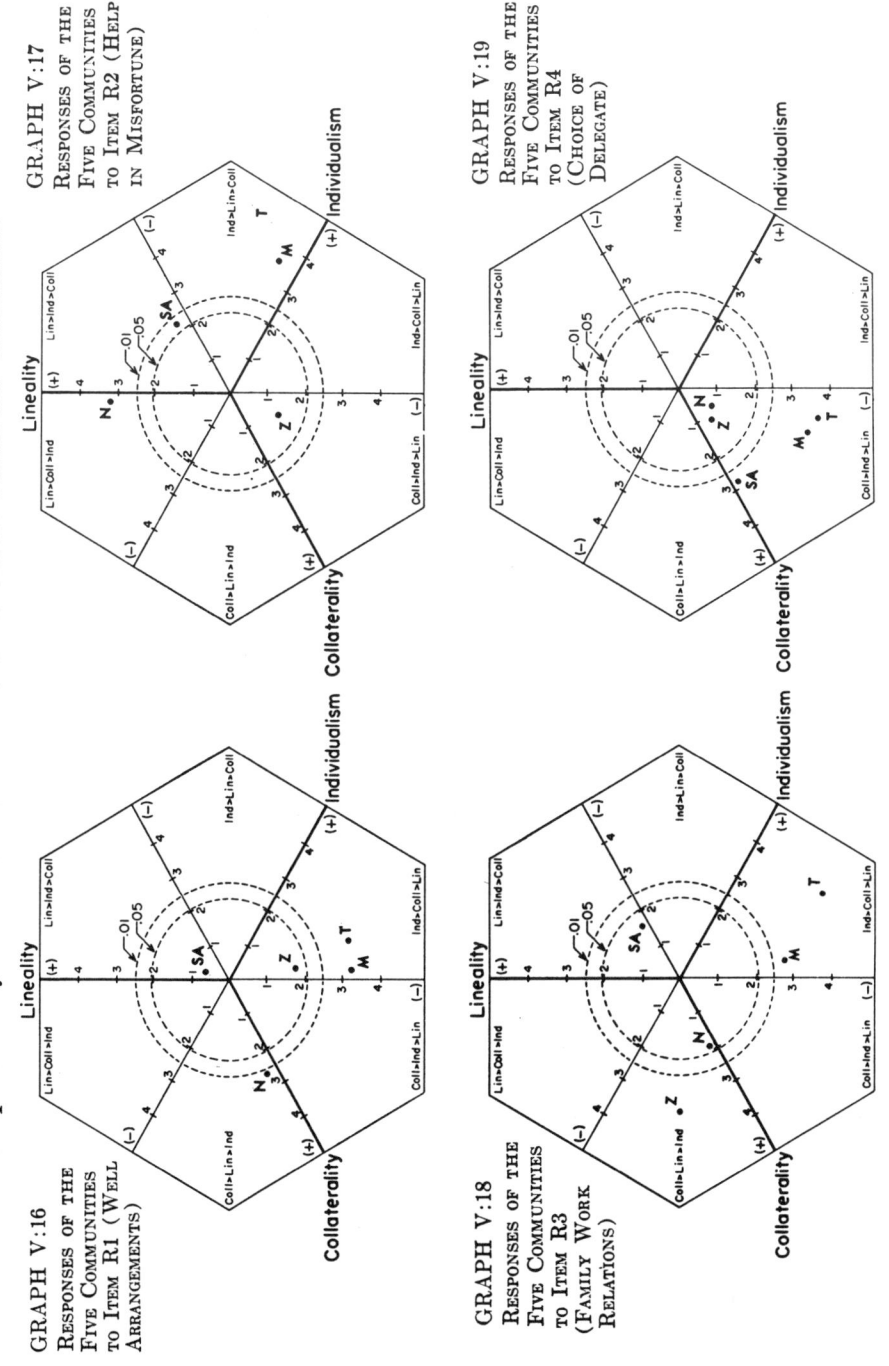

Graphic Analysis of Between-Culture Differences: *relational Orientation*

BETWEEN-CULTURE DIFFERENCES AS ANALYZED BY THE GRAPHIC METHOD

GRAPH V:16 Responses of the Five Communities to Item R1 (Well Arrangements)

GRAPH V:17 Responses of the Five Communities to Item R2 (Help in Misfortune)

GRAPH V:18 Responses of the Five Communities to Item R3 (Family Work Relations)

GRAPH V:19 Responses of the Five Communities to Item R4 (Choice of Delegate)

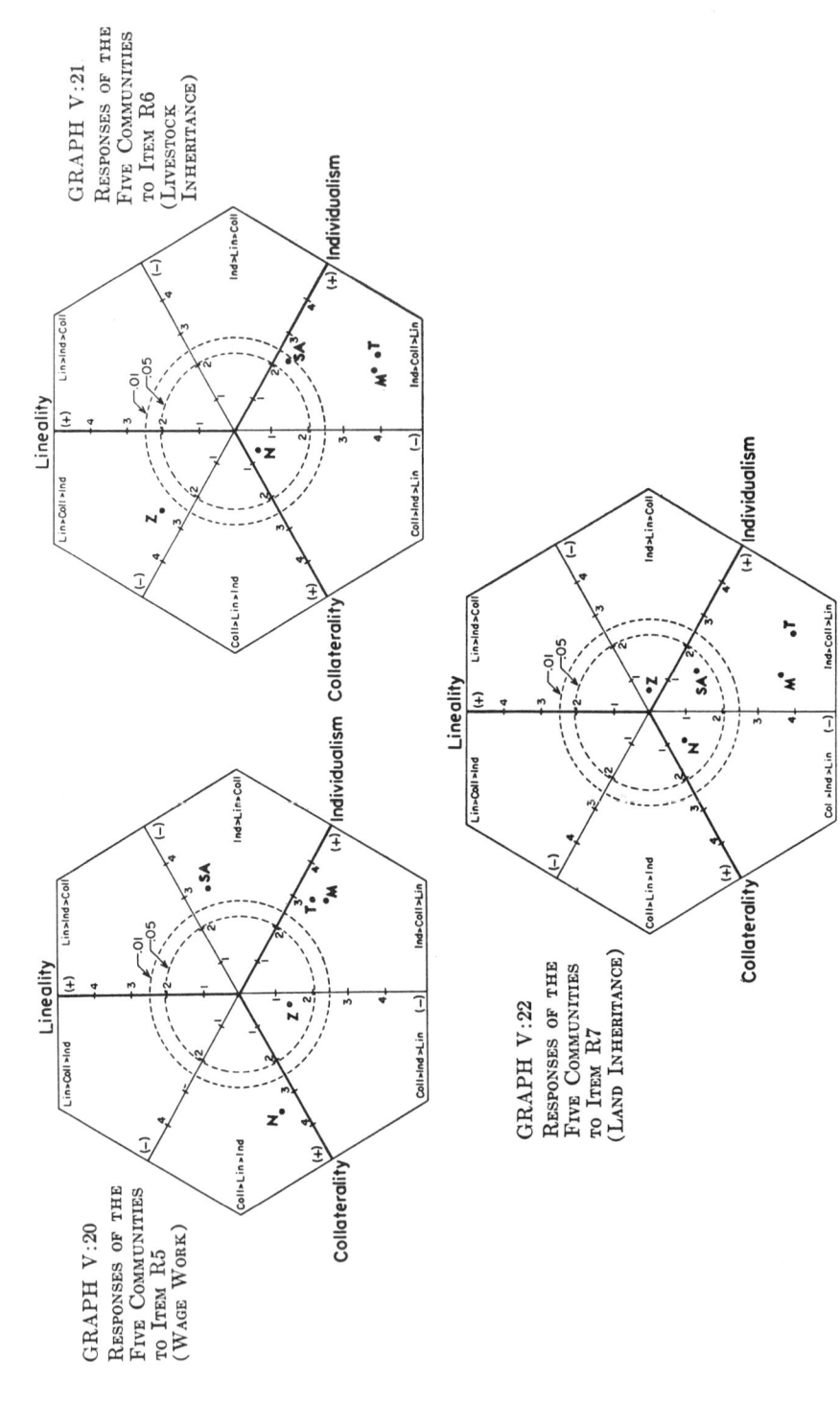

GRAPH V:20
RESPONSES OF THE FIVE COMMUNITIES TO ITEM R5 (WAGE WORK)

GRAPH V:21
RESPONSES OF THE FIVE COMMUNITIES TO ITEM R6 (LIVESTOCK INHERITANCE)

GRAPH V:22
RESPONSES OF THE FIVE COMMUNITIES TO ITEM R7 (LAND INHERITANCE)

Graphic Analysis of Between-Culture Differences: *time* Orientation

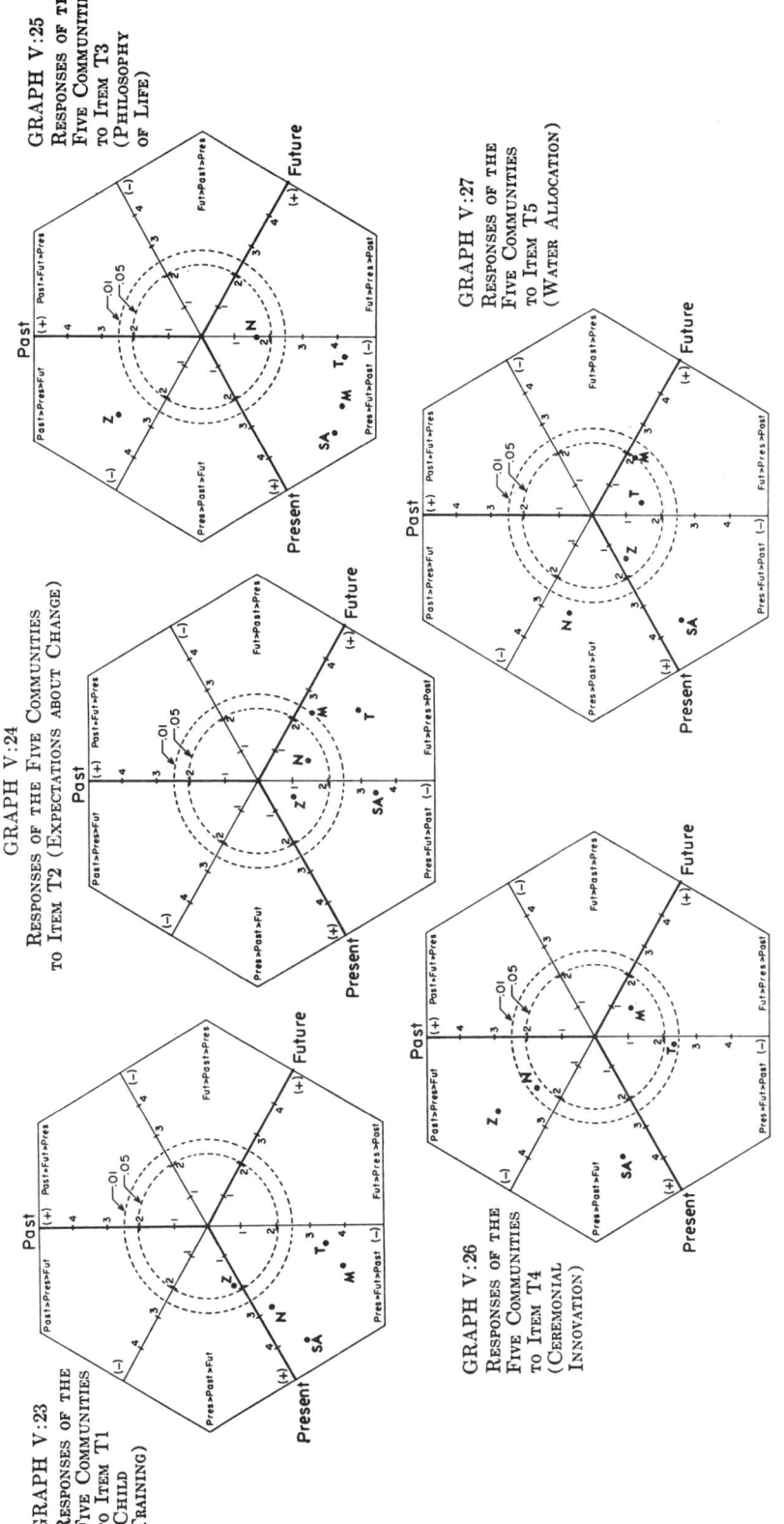

GRAPH V:23
RESPONSES OF THE FIVE COMMUNITIES TO ITEM T1 (CHILD TRAINING)

GRAPH V:24
RESPONSES OF THE FIVE COMMUNITIES TO ITEM T2 (EXPECTATIONS ABOUT CHANGE)

GRAPH V:25
RESPONSES OF THE FIVE COMMUNITIES TO ITEM T3 (PHILOSOPHY OF LIFE)

GRAPH V:26
RESPONSES OF THE FIVE COMMUNITIES TO ITEM T4 (CEREMONIAL INNOVATION)

GRAPH V:27
RESPONSES OF THE FIVE COMMUNITIES TO ITEM T5 (WATER ALLOCATION)

Graphic Analysis of Between-Culture Differences: *man-nature* Orientation

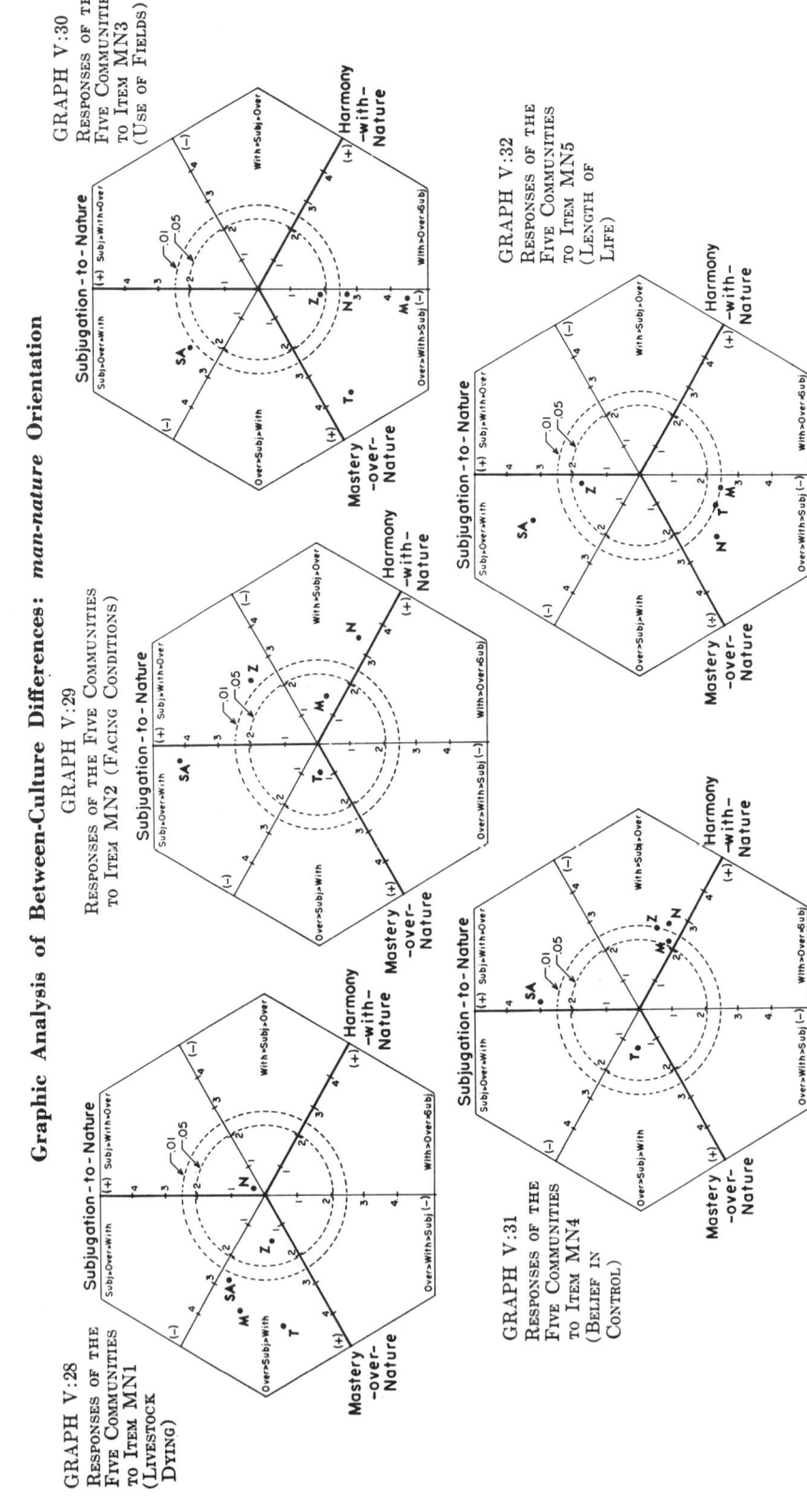

GRAPH V:28
RESPONSES OF THE FIVE COMMUNITIES TO ITEM MN1 (LIVESTOCK DYING)

GRAPH V:29
RESPONSES OF THE FIVE COMMUNITIES TO ITEM MN2 (FACING CONDITIONS)

GRAPH V:30
RESPONSES OF THE FIVE COMMUNITIES TO ITEM MN3 (USE OF FIELDS)

GRAPH V:31
RESPONSES OF THE FIVE COMMUNITIES TO ITEM MN4 (BELIEF IN CONTROL)

GRAPH V:32
RESPONSES OF THE FIVE COMMUNITIES TO ITEM MN5 (LENGTH OF LIFE)

Graphic Analysis of Between-Culture Differences: *activity* Orientation

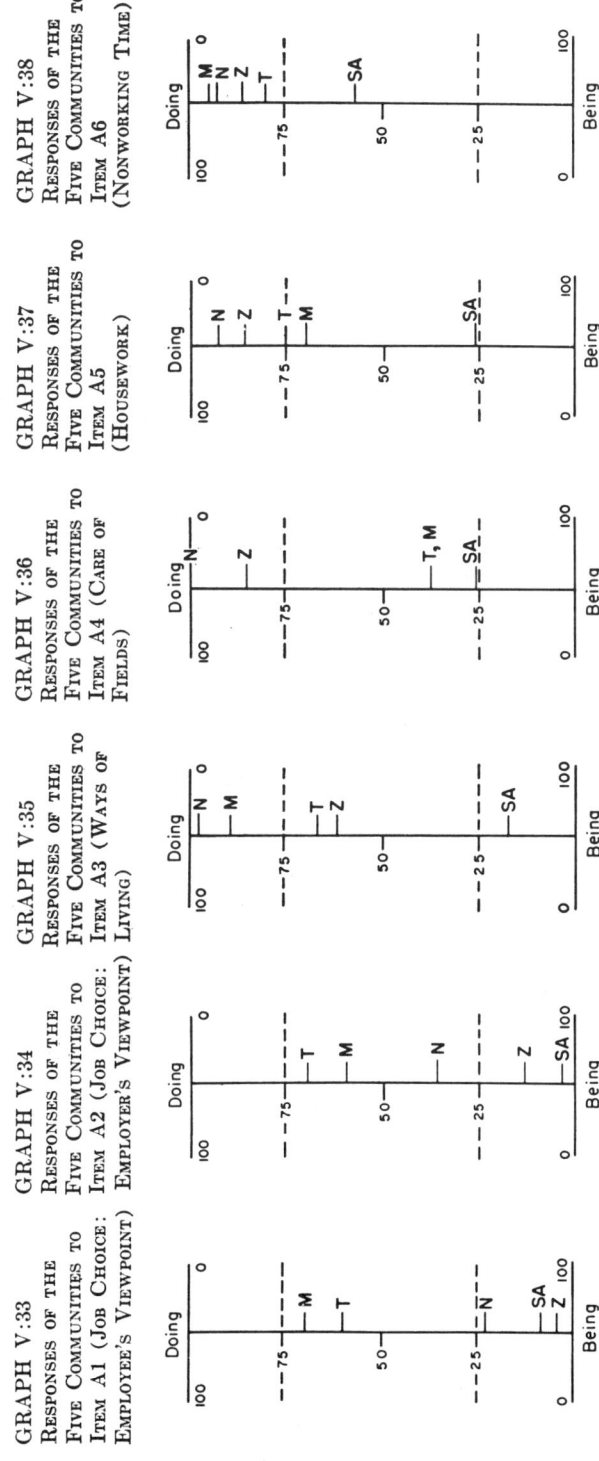

Graphic Analysis of Between-Culture Differences: Composite Graphs

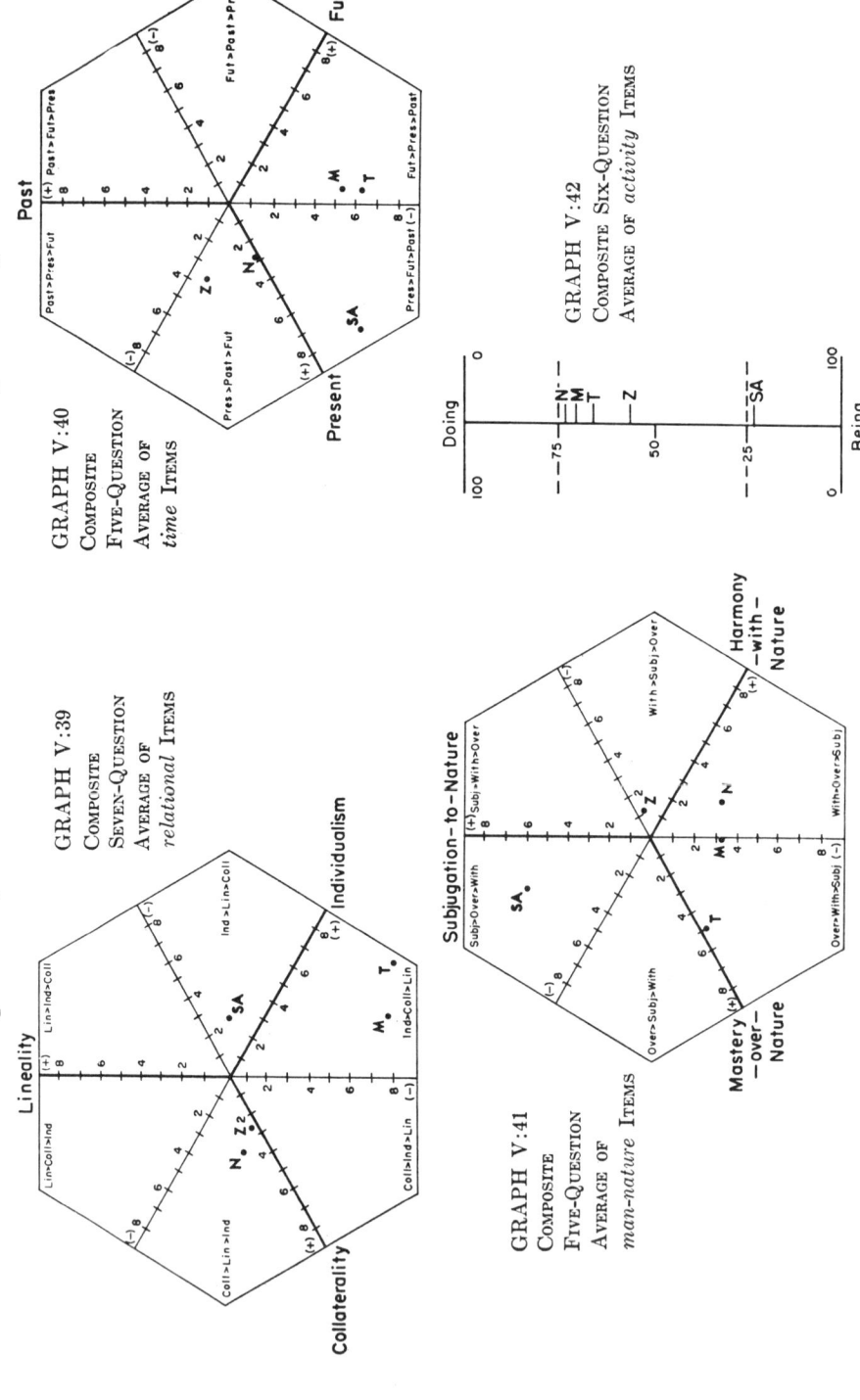

GRAPH V:40
COMPOSITE
FIVE-QUESTION
AVERAGE OF *time* ITEMS

GRAPH V:42
COMPOSITE SIX-QUESTION
AVERAGE OF *activity* ITEMS

GRAPH V:39
COMPOSITE
SEVEN-QUESTION
AVERAGE OF *relational* ITEMS

GRAPH V:41
COMPOSITE
FIVE-QUESTION
AVERAGE OF *man-nature* ITEMS

BETWEEN-CULTURE DIFFERENCES AS ANALYZED BY THE METHOD OF ANALYSES OF VARIANCE

One-way Analyses of Variance of Scores on the Three Dimensions Constructed from Responses to the *relational* Series of Items

1. THE [Ind, Coll] DIMENSION

Source of Variation	Sum of Squares	df	Mean Square	$F_{b/w}$	p_F
Between	121.68	4	30.42	14.21	<.001
Within	216.39	101	2.14		
Total	338.07	105			

2. THE [Ind, Lin] DIMENSION

Source of Variation	Sum of Squares	df	Mean Square	$F_{b/w}$	p_F
Between	236.84	4	59.21	36.78	<.001
Within	162.90	101	1.61		
Total	399.74	105			

3. THE [Coll, Lin] DIMENSION

Source of Variation	Sum of Squares	df	Mean Square	$F_{b/w}$	p_F
Between	66.43	4	16.61	9.28	<.001
Within	180.42	101	1.79		
Total	246.85	105			

Groupings Which Are Significantly Distinct ($p < .05$) on the Three Dimensions Constructed from Responses to the *relational* Series of Items[a]

1. THE [Ind, Coll] DIMENSION

⟵ Ind > Coll   7 {T} 6 {MSA} 5 4 3 {NZ} 2 1 0   Coll > Ind ⟶
                                          Ind = Coll

2. THE [Ind, Lin] DIMENSION

⟵ Ind > Lin   7 {T M} 6 5 {SA Z N} 4 3 2 1 0   Lin > Ind ⟶
                                          Ind = Lin

3. THE [Coll, Lin] DIMENSION

⟵ Coll > Lin   7 {MT NZ} 6 5 4 {SA} 3 2 1 0   Lin > Coll ⟶
                                          Coll = Lin

[a] Boundaries around significantly distinct groupings are indicated by dotted lines.

One-Way Analyses of Variance of Scores on the Three Dimensions Constructed from Responses to the *time* Series of Items

4. THE [Past, Pres] DIMENSION

Source of Variation	Sum of Squares	df	Mean Square	$F_{b/w}$	p_F
Between	46.73	4	11.68	15.57	<.001
Within	75.25	101	.75		
Total	121.98	105			

5. THE [Past, Fut] DIMENSION

Source of Variation	Sum of Squares	df	Mean Square	$F_{b/w}$	p_F
Between	76.84	4	19.21	21.34	<.001
Within	91.37	101	.90		
Total	168.21	105			

6. THE [Pres, Fut] DIMENSION

Source of Variation	Sum of Squares	df	Mean Square	$F_{b/w}$	p_F
Between	56.33	4	14.08	17.60	<.001
Within	80.51	101	.80		
Total	136.84	105			

Groupings Which Are Significantly Distinct ($p < .05$) on the Three Dimensions Constructed from Responses to the *time* Series of Items

4. THE [Past, Pres] DIMENSION

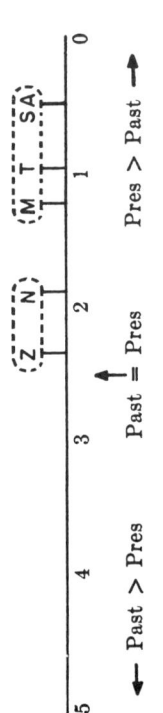

5. THE [Past, Fut] DIMENSION

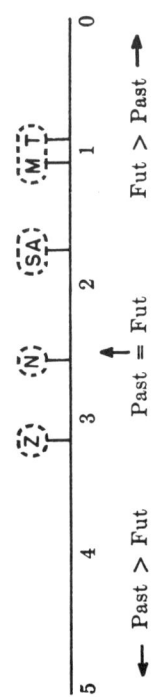

6. THE [Pres, Fut] DIMENSION

One-way Analyses of Variance of Scores on the Three Dimensions Constructed from Responses to the *man-nature* Series of Items

7. The [Subj, With] Dimension

Source of Variation	Sum of Squares	df	Mean Square	$F_{b/w}$	p_F
Between	102.70	4	25.68	17.12	<.001
Within	151.56	101	1.50		
Total	254.26	105			

8. The [Subj, Over] Dimension

Source of Variation	Sum of Squares	df	Mean Square	$F_{b/w}$	p_F
Between	71.99	4	18.00	11.32	<.001
Within	160.17	101	1.59		
Total	232.16	105			

9. The [With, Over] Dimension

Source of Variation	Sum of Squares	df	Mean Square	$F_{b/w}$	p_F
Between	41.34	4	10.34	7.23	<.001
Within	144.70	101	1.43		
Total	186.04	105			

Groupings Which Are Significantly Distinct ($p < .05$) on the Three Dimensions Constructed from Responses to the *man-nature* Series of Items

7. The [Subj, With] Dimension

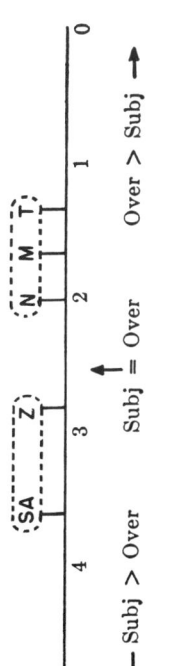

8. The [Subj, Over] Dimension

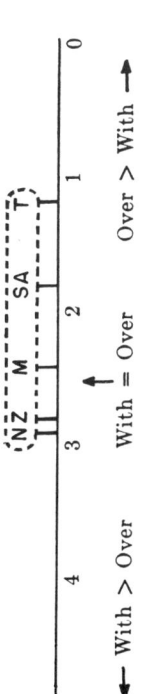

9. The [With, Over] Dimension

One-way Analysis of Variance of Scores on the One Dimension Constructed from Responses to the *activity* **Series of Items**

10. THE [Doing, Being] DIMENSION

Source of Variation	Sum of Squares	df	Mean Square	$F_{b/w}$	p_F
Between	134.35	4	33.59	21.67	<.001
Within	156.71	101	1.55		
Total	291.06	105			

Groupings Which Are Significantly Distinct ($p < .05$) on the One Dimension Constructed from Responses to the *activity* **Series of Items**

10. THE [Doing, Being] DIMENSION

```
     NM  T      Z              SA
      ┬──┬      ┬              ┬
      ┴──┴      ┴              ┴
├─────┼─────┼─────┼─────┼─────┼─────┤
6     5     4     3     2     1     0
←── Doing > Being   Doing = Being   Being > Doing ──→
```

The Analyses of Variance Summarized Orientation by Orientation

RELATIONAL ORIENTATION. Among the three dimensions dealing with the *relational* orientation the [Ind, Coll] is the most efficient in discriminating among the five cultures. Three groupings of cultures result. The Texans stand by themselves in showing extreme Individualism; the Mormons and Spanish-Americans only slightly favor the Individualistic alternative and hence are, as a pair, significantly different from the Texan group; the Navaho and the Zuni form a final grouping which is moderately disposed to a preference for the Collateral alternative. On the [Ind, Lin] dimension both the Texans and the Mormons are extremely Individualistic; the three other peoples constitute a grouping which is relatively indifferent in its choice between the two alternatives. Finally, on the [Coll, Lin] dimension, the Texans, Mormons, Navaho, and Zuni form a grouping which is moderately given to a preference for the Collateral position; the Spanish-Americans are distinctively set apart in being more Lineally and less Collaterally oriented than the respondents of the other four cultures, even though among themselves they are equivocal in their choice between the two positions.

TIME ORIENTATION. The three dimensions generated from the *time* orientation summaries prove to be highly efficient in designating between-culture differences. The [Past, Pres] dimension breaks the five communities into two distinctive groupings. One, composed of the Navaho and Zuni, is more or less indifferent in its preference between the Past and Present. The other (Spanish-Americans, Texans, and Mormons) shows a strong inclination to favor the Present *time* position over the Past one. The [Past, Fut] dimension shows a four-way division of the cultures. The Zuni, who are moderately inclined to the Past position, the Navaho, who are indifferent as between the Past and Future alternatives, and the Spanish-Americans, who moderately favor the Future position, are each a separate grouping. The Texans and Mormons with their strong preference for the Future alternative are coupled in the fourth of the divisions. The third dimension, the [Pres, Fut] one, discriminates only in the degree of strength of preference for the Present *time* position. The Spanish-Americans stand out as strongly favoring this position, the Navaho and Zuni are moderately in favor of it, and the Texans and Mormons constitute a grouping which gives an almost equal emphasis to both the Present and Future *time* alternatives.

MAN-NATURE ORIENTATION. The three dimensions used to test for the between-culture differences on this orientation do not prove to be highly discriminating for the five Rimrock communities except in one particular case, that of the Spanish-Americans. One of the dimensions, the [With, Over] one, does not successfully differentiate between any of the groups. The second, the [Subj, With], is decisive in showing the Spanish-Americans, by their strong inclination to prefer the Subjugated-to-Nature alternative, to be separated off from all the other groups, who are more or less indifferent in their choices between the two positions. The third dimension of [Subj, Over] separates the strongly Subjugated-to-Nature Spanish-Ameri-

170   VARIATIONS IN VALUE ORIENTATIONS

cans and the slightly so inclined Zuni from the other three groups, each of which shows a moderate preference for the Over-Nature position.

ACTIVITY ORIENTATION. The one dimension of this orientation—one, because testing was done with two alternatives only—serves to separate the five cultures into these three groupings: the strongly Being-oriented Spanish-Americans, the Being = Doing oriented Zuni, and the Doing-oriented Navaho, Mormons, and Texans. In this last division the Navaho are the most inclined to the Doing alternative, but they are not sufficiently more consistent in this choice than the other two, especially the Mormons, to warrant designation of them as a distinctive fourth grouping.

The Analyses of Variance Summarized Overall

A scrutiny of the totality of the results of the analysis of the between-culture differences—both those presented on the graphs and those presented in the tables and figures which give the findings yielded by the analyses of variance—shows that the data collected by means of the value-orientation schedule do indicate a number of significant differences which allow a differentiation between the cultures. The degree of differentiation is, of course, variable, according to both orientation and dimension.

The most outstanding of the between-culture differences is the wide separation of the Spanish-Americans from the other groups. This culture was found to be the most distinctively different of the five. This is easily observed from a study of the graphs. It is also most apparent in the results of the analyses of variance. On five of the ten dimensions created for these analyses—the [Coll, Lin], [Past, Fut], [Pres, Fut], [Subj, With], and [Doing, Being] dimensions, which tap into all four of the orientations being tested—the Spanish-Americans stand alone.

The least differentiation found between any single pair of cultures, as was to be expected, was between the Texans and the Mormons, the two English-speaking communities. Although obviously different in more subtle aspects of patterning than our instrument of only twenty-two items was designed to test, these two groups appear in the analyses of our data to be more or less of a unity. They are approximately similar in their ordering of preferences of the value-orientation alternatives on nine of the ten dimensions derived for the analysis-of-variance method of ordering our data. On three of these dimensions—the [Ind, Lin], [Past, Fut], and [Pres, Fut] ones—they appear as a cultural entity which is distinguishable from all the other cultures. However, since these dimensions relate to only two of the four orientations, the conservative conclusion is that the two cultures in combination are a two-headed entity which is *moderately* distinct among the five Rimrock communities. Where the two cultures differ the most one from another as shown by the analyses of variance is on the [Ind, Coll] dimension. The Texans on this dimension were significantly more Individualistically inclined than the Mormons. However, the graphic analysis and another analysis still which is to be reported in Chapter VII both show this difference to be slighter even than that revealed by the analyses of variance, and also indicate that the difference between the Texans and Mormons in the strength of their preferences for the Over-Nature alternative of the *man-nature* orientation is greater than that indicated by the analysis-of-variance method alone. Given the limited number of responses available for analysis and the obvious subtlety of the difference between the groups in each case, it is not surprising that different methods of analysis would produce only these slight differences. The important point is that, small as each of the differences may be, both are important for the understanding of the subtle variations which serve to distinguish these two communities one from the other. Had we had both more items in our schedule and larger samples it is probable that both of these differences would have appeared as more definite and substantial in our data.

The two Indian cultures, the Navaho and Zuni cultures, were found by the analyses of variance to be something of a unity only when contrasted to either the two English-speaking communities or the Spanish-American one. As between themselves they were separated one from another as often as they were found to be a distinct grouping on the ten dimensions. On the [Past, Fut], [Subj, Over], and [Doing, Being] dimensions each falls into a different grouping. On the [Ind, Coll], [Past, Pres], and [Pres, Fut] dimensions they form a distinct pairing. But since the dimensions on which they are separated tap three different orientations while those on which they are a distinct grouping tap only two, their differences seem to loom at least as large, if not larger, than their similarities. The greatest similarity between them is in the *relational* orientation sphere, where they fall into the same grouping on each dimension treating it.

CONCLUSIONS

The results of the several analyses made of the data yielded by the schedule created to test the value-orientation theory permit several firm conclusions.

First, the hypothesized within-culture regularities in the rankings of the alternatives of the orientations did emerge. There were, to be sure, very few significant uniformities in the patterning of the responses of the Zuni; and there was also variability in the degree of significance in patterning from culture to culture and orientation by orientation. But this variability was not uniformly on single orientations. There was not, in other words, any systematic trend in the observed results which would indicate that there was a patent failure of the method in the testing of any particular orientation. Moreover, the fact that there were differences from culture to culture in the degrees of regularity of patterning, orientation by orientation, is in itself an argument for the theoretically postulated variations in within-culture regularities.

This is the more substantiated by the second conclusion, which is that the observed results agree well, although certainly not fully, with the predictions we ventured to make prior to the administration of the schedule to the five samples of respondents. In only a very few instances was there a marked discrepancy between the prediction ventured and the result observed. One of these was the degree of the dominance (not great but nevertheless real) of the Individualistic as opposed to the Collateral alternative of the *relational* orientation in the Mormon responses; another was the lack of a clear-cut dominance of the Subjugated-to-Nature preference as a second-order preference among the Texans; and still another was the second-order choice of the Navaho Indians as between the Future and Past alternatives of the *time* orientation. On balance, a great majority of both the consistencies and inconsistencies of patterning in ranking patterns which were predicted did actually emerge in the analyses of the data obtained from the value-orientation schedule.

The third conclusion which can be confidently stated is that the theoretically postulated between-culture differences in ranking patterns of preferences among the alternatives of the orientations were also an observed result yielded by both the graphic analysis and the analyses of variance. No two of the cultures chose exactly the same patterns of preferences on any of the orientations, and, in addition, the degrees of similarity and difference proved to be, on the whole, the expected ones. The definite two poles of cultural difference were found in the orientation rankings of the two English-speaking groups, which as between themselves do differ but only subtly so, and those of the Spanish-Americans. In between are the two Indian groups, which can scarcely be called a unity since they proved to be different from each other just as frequently as they were in distinct agreement.

The much less firm of our conclusions relative to the actual results are those which indicate evidence of intra-cultural variations. As has been remarked several times, we made no plan of testing systematically for this kind of variation and our instrument was not at all adequate for such a task. However, we have in the verbal discussions of the data which have been presented, culture by culture, incorporated what evidence of it our testing program did provide. This material has been presented solely as suggestive evidence to which the analysts of the several cultures in the four succeeding interpretative chapters will speak as they see fit.

There are also, admittedly, somewhat—perhaps more than somewhat—inconclusive aspects of our study which concern the issues of validity and reliability. The question of validity, we believe, was solved in part by the method of testing items simultaneously in several cultures. For example, had item R3 (Family Work Relations) been used only in the Spanish-American culture, there would have been no basis for judging whether the question was a meaningful one. The Spanish-American responses were most inconsistent, not appreciably better ordered than one would expect had the stimuli been nonsense syllables. Yet this same item yielded quite significant results in all of the other groups we tested. On other items of the schedule it was some other of the groups of respondents which displayed a marked inconsistency of pattern which was in contrast with a consistency in other groups.

From results of this kind one is certainly permitted the assumption that the reason for the lack of pattern in the responses of one or two of the groups of respondents is true cultural inconsistency rather than a faulty question. Or, to state this argument more generally, there appears to be firm ground for maintaining that the statistically nonsignificant outcome in any one culture, when several cultures are being tested simultaneously with the same research instrument, is probably, if not certainly, an indicator of cultural change rather than a response to a meaningless question.

The question of reliability is more troublesome. Concerning that aspect of reliability which means consistency of response over time, we expected the "general question" method to produce more reliable results than a method which depended upon the use of situationally specific questions. But we were not able to put this expectation to the empirical test of repeated questioning.

As for the kind of reliability which looks to consistency of response over a range of questions, there was in our research a theoretical as well as a methodological problem. Since the theory postulates variation of response in different behavior spheres, a consistency of answers to questions designed to test in more than one sphere was *not* expected. Also, since our question battery was not sufficiently extensive to permit the segregation of the spheres within any of the orientations, the usual reliability check of cross-item comparison for the same person was not appropriate. It will be necessary to develop more adequate checking procedures if in later research we wish to show the prevailing influence of a dominant rank ordering of the orientations and at the same time allow for responses which express variant rank orderings.

Thus, in addition to the more general interpretation and explanation of the data which the cultural analysts who have written the next four chapters of this monograph were asked to provide in ways as each saw fit, we look to these interpretative analyses as a means of supplying some measure of the validity and reliability of our data.

TABLE VI:1

SUMMARY OF SPANISH-AMERICAN RANKINGS

Relational Orientation

R1	Lin ⩾ Coll ⩾ Ind
R2	Ind ⩾ Lin > Coll
R3	Ind ⩾ Lin ⩾ Coll
R4	Coll ⩾ Ind ⩾ Lin*
R5	Ind ⩾ Lin > Coll
R6	Ind > Coll ⩾ Lin
R7	Ind ⩾ Coll ⩾ Lin
Sum	Ind ⩾ Lin ⩾ Coll*

Time Orientation

T1	Pres > Fut ⩾ Past
T2	Pres ⩾ Fut > Past
T3	Pres > Fut > Past
T4	Pres > Past ⩾ Fut
T5	Pres > Fut ⩾ Past
Sum	Pres > Fut > Past

Man-Nature Orientation

MN1	Over ⩾ Subj > With
MN2	Subj > Over ⩾ With
MN3	Subj ⩾ Over ⩾ With*
MN4	Subj > With ⩾ Over
MN5	Subj > Over ⩾ With
Sum	Subj > Over > With

Activity Orientation

A1	Being > Doing
A2	Being > Doing
A3	Being > Doing
A4	Being > Doing
A5	Being > Doing
A6	Doing ⩾ Being
Sum	Being > Doing

CHAPTER VI

The Spanish-Americans of Atrisco*

Florence Rockwood Kluckhohn

The decade 1950–60 finds Atrisco, like hundreds of other Spanish-American villages in New Mexico, a shattered and largely deserted community. The once busy store is used as a warehouse for the storage of an Anglo-American rancher's grain. The small building which formerly housed a grade school is empty and locked except for one corner that is walled off and used intermittently as a tiny shop for selling gum, candies, and cigarettes. The church which had always dominated the village scene because of the height of its steeple and cross and its central location is rubble and ash. In 1949 the ancient stove which was always used to heat the building when the *padre* made his infrequent visits to Atrisco told its own tale of decay by breaking apart and creating a fire which was beyond control when discovered. A building more at the edge of the village which many years ago was the high school has now been converted into a church. Many of the houses have fallen apart, and each year more of the adobes or stone pieces which were used in their construction melt or crumble into the earth and lose all markings of the human effort which shaped them into blocks. Other houses, deserted but still standing, are mere shells without roofs, doors, or window frames. All wood and metal have been stripped off for use on other buildings or sometimes, in the case of the wood, merely for firewood. Even the few houses still in use are not, except in a few cases, kept in the state of repair which many of the *Atrisqueños* once strived for.

But the village was not in 1951 (when the research schedule was administered), or even seven years later (when it was last revisited), a real ghost town. Indeed, at night during this period of time it looked more alive than it ever had because the electric lights which the Rural Electrification Administration had provided in 1950 marked off the houses with a brightness which the kerosene lamps of former years, always dull and flickering, could never produce. But the number of families still in the village in 1951 was small, and the total population was only slightly in excess of fifty persons. By 1958 there were only four families which still claimed Atrisco as their permanent residence, and one of these did not reside there all of the time. The decade 1960–70 will, indeed, mark the end of Atrisco.

* The material in this chapter which refers to years previous to 1951 is taken from the writer's unpublished doctoral dissertation which has already been cited in Chapter I. Because of the inaccessibility of this unpublished manuscript to most readers the references to it and quotations from it will not be footnoted.

I first went into the village of Atrisco in 1936. Although it was soon to become apparent to my Anglo-American "Future-oriented" eyes that the village would not for long remain a well integrated community, there were very few *Atrisqueños* who were seeing clearly the handwriting on their wall of history. At that time 142 persons lived in the village proper, and some 50 or more were in two peripheral communities. The annual *fiesta* early in October of that year was as gay an affair as it had ever been. In late October and early November political affairs took precedence over all else, and the scenes enacted lacked little of the color and drama of former years. Indeed they had more, as will be demonstrated later, because of the newly developed and closely neighboring Texan community, Homestead, which was largely peopled with Democrats who were threatening the control of the Republican *Atrisqueños*. The families which had small herds of sheep or cattle were still running them upon a range that was open and unfenced as it had always been in the days of Don Juan Atrisco's great *patrón* power. Family life was well regulated and firmly knit, and few transgressions of the mores were at all obvious. There certainly was not much in the year 1936, in the behavior of the people themselves, to indicate the changes which were to come so soon and make of Atrisco the phantom of former years that it now is.

The history of Atrisco and the patterns I found in it in 1936 are to be used in this chapter as a matrix for the further analysis of the value orientations, dominant and variant, of Spanish-Americans and for the choice of Atrisco as a place to study them.

My first experience with any of the life of the state of New Mexico had come in 1932, and it was a challenging one. There is no other place in the United States, except great urban centers like New York City, where one can find such a wide variety of fundamental differences in cultural patterns and value orientations. The American Indians of New Mexico, two groups of which have been included in this study, are remarkable peoples both for themselves and what they offer to the study of cultural variation. The Spanish-Americans, who still in 1951 constituted approximately one half of the total population of the state, are the only ethnic group other than Indians which has ever been incorporated into the United States by a closing of the country's borders around it.[1] It was mainly in the name of Manifest Destiny, and by means of a war that historians have ceased trying to justify, that the United States in 1846 took the territories of New Mexico and Arizona and all the peoples, Indians and Spanish-Americans, who lived in them.

The Spanish-American group quickly captured my interest. Although I had never known any Spanish-Americans prior to 1932 and had not as yet had the experience of living among Mexicans in Old Mexico, I liked them. This, of course, was a personal and emotional reaction. Intellectually I was challenged by the question of why it was that two peoples—Anglo-Americans and Spanish-Americans—could have lived in such close

[1] Because of the great migration of peoples from other states to New Mexico since 1950, it is certain that the population will be predominantly Anglo-American after 1960.

contact with one another for almost one hundred years and still have so little understanding of one another. Nor was it simply a matter of a lack of understanding. A majority of Anglo-Americans in New Mexico and Arizona expressed and still express, in one way or another, a great intolerance of Spanish-Americans and their patterns of behavior. In the neighboring state of Texas the intolerance is both more extreme and more vicious in its effects.

It was not at all unusual in the thirties, and it is still fairly common today, to hear employers say they hire Spanish-Americans, or "Mexicans" as they frequently call them in tones of contempt, only as a last resort. Many persons then (and some still) declared that almost all Spanish-Americans are irresponsible, shiftless, dishonest, untrustworthy, and sometimes brutal as well as dangerous. Numerous teachers openly expressed their irritation with having to teach Spanish-American pupils whom they regarded as being subnormal in intelligence and generally inferior biologically. A large number of Anglo-American parents have been equally outspoken in their resentment at finding Spanish-American children in the schools their children attend.

Even in political affairs, where concessions had to be made to Spanish-Americans because of their great numerical voting strength, there has been little consideration of the needs of the average Spanish-American. It has been the Spanish-American *jefe politico* (political leader) or *patrón*, usually one and same, who has benefited most in the realm of politics. Both the *patrones* of former years and those ambitious to become *patrones* quickly saw that their best possibility for gaining prestige among Anglo-Americans was in holding government office or party position. To gain and hold these offices and positions a majority of the *jefes* followed the practice, long familiar to them, of "using" the Spanish-American people under their control for their own personal gain.

The average man and woman in the villages voted, but whom he or she voted for was not a matter of individual choice unless the voter wished to suffer the dire consequences of a *patrón's* disfavor. The average villager had no basis upon which to make a choice even had he wanted to assert his rights. Anglo-American politicians, even when they had wider interests than making mutually advantageous deals with the Spanish-American leaders, seemed simply to assume that it was either the business of the *patrón* to educate the people of a village in the ways of democratic government or the business of the people somehow to educate themselves. It was not much to their own interests to labor with the problem. And it certainly was not to the interest of the *patrones* who could see only a threat to their own power in a voting public which was well enough educated in democratic procedures to make independent choices.[2] The result of this situation was the development in New Mexico of a type of machine politics which has often been vicious and sometimes ludicrous.

Only recently has there been any change in the relations of Anglo-

---

[2] Similar conclusions were reached by Ossie Simmons in "Anglo-Americans and Mexican-Americans in South Texas: A Study in Dominant-Subordinate Group Relations," unpublished Ph.D. dissertation, Harvard University, 1952.

Americans and Spanish-Americans in any of the spheres of life, and the changes are not yet great. In 1936 the tensions of one kind or another were still so intense that I was warned not to undertake a study of any Spanish-American community. Serious trouble and few positive results had come from the one or two attempts already made to study aspects of the Spanish-American life and the relationships between Anglo-Americans and Spanish-Americans. Although unwilling to be put off by the various warnings, I was affected by them enough to make the decision to use a true participant-observer technique in whatever study I undertook.

It was partly for this reason that the particular village of Atrisco was selected. Because my husband had a relative in the village and had himself once worked there for a sheep company, I was able to move into it without arousing serious suspicions.[3] And although I feel sure there were some persons who eventually suspected that I was planning to write either a history or "stories," there was never in the total of seven months I first lived in Atrisco, or during the numerous return visits I have made to it since 1936, any discussion of the study. There were never any queries as to why I asked the questions I did, and I seemed to be well accepted as a member of the community. The benefits of this earlier experience for the field work of 1951 have been described in Chapter III.

Other reasons for the selection of Atrisco were its remoteness and its state of integration which was good enough for one to expect to find in it well preserved patterns of Spanish-American life. It has already been remarked that, on the whole, this expectation was accurate, even though certain doom to community integration was just around the corner.

I moved into Atrisco in the summer of 1936 with the aim of trying to find out enough about the behavior and values of Spanish-Americans to provide some of the answers to the questions: Why have Spanish-Americans been so slowly assimilated? Why has there always been so little understanding between Anglo-Americans and Spanish-Americans?

The study was an intensive one and extended to all aspects of village life. Family relations, social organization in general, formal education programs, religious activities, the economic system, and relations with other communities were all studied by means of observation and the kind of indirect interviewing which the participant-observer technique requires. Since I was fortunate enough to gain access to the records of traders, cattle and sheep dealers, county and state agents, and the Dennis Sheep Company which hired a number of village men, the material on the ways of making a living, on income and expenditures, on buying habits, and other matters relating to the economy was extremely detailed. But for all of this concern with a description of village life, the values or value orientations of *los Atrisqueños* were the subject of greatest interest, and the data collected were interpreted within a conceptual framework of basic values.

[3] A detailed account of my entry into the community and my use of the participant-observer technique has been given in "The Participant-Observer Technique in Small Communities," *American Journal of Sociology*, Vol. XLVI (1940), pp. 331–44.

The analysis (Chapter V) of the data collected in Atrisco in 1951 (fifteen years after the original study) by means of the value-orientation schedule has revealed a clear-cut dominance of the Present *time* orientation, the Being alternative of the *activity* orientation, and the Subjugated position of the *man-nature* orientation. A first-order preference on the *relational* orientation was not clearly marked, even though a statistically significant overall rank-order outcome of Ind $\geqslant$ Lin $\geqslant$ Coll* was achieved.

Does this profile in the dominant value-orientation emphases reveal any differences from that which the research of 1936 indicated, and if so what will the earlier material tell us about the reasons for or conditions of change? What also has the earlier and very detailed study to offer by way of validation of the orientation emphases discovered through the use of a standardized schedule of questions?

Not all of the comparisons of the 1936 and the 1951 data can be of a strictly one-to-one variety even were this an advantage, which is doubtful. Not only were the methods employed in 1936 different from those used in 1951; the conceptual scheme used in the analysis of the data was also different in some respects from the one used in this volume. It was primarily the dominant value orientations which were analyzed in the earlier work. The ideas of the rank ordering of value-orientation alternatives within a range of theoretically postulated alternatives and a systematic variation in value orientations had not at that time been worked out. However, I became much interested in the variations I found in 1936, and it was from the study of them that many of the ideas about the variations in value orientations as now presented were developed.

Several of the value orientations which the recent research has shown to be dominant in Spanish-American culture today were discussed at length in the previous study even though the term value orientation was not applied to them. The concepts used in the earlier work were Clyde Kluckhohn's *ideal* and *behavioral* patterns and *configuration*.[4] But "configuration," as it was specifically defined and used for the analysis of the life of Atrisco, is sufficiently similar to the concept of value orientation to permit an equating of the two in this discussion of the community and its people.

The two orientations which were most clearly delineated in the 1936 study were the Present *time* orientation and the Being *activity* type. Moreover, in both these cases the ranges of variation were also suggested. The Subjugation-to-Nature orientation was less well formulated and was generally treated as a pervasive acceptance principle. The range of the *relational* orientation—the Lineal, Collateral, and Individualistic alternatives—was not used, but much was written about both the family structure and the *patrón* system which now lends itself easily to treatment in accordance with these three major *relational* principles.[5] The

---

[4] Clyde Kluckhohn, "Patterning as Exemplified in Navaho Culture" in *Language, Culture, and Personality*, ed. Leslie Spier (Menasha, Wis.: Sapir Memorial Publication Fund, 1941).

[5] I was least satisfied with the analysis of social organization in the 1936 study and felt that the *Gemeinschaft-Gesellschaft* frame of reference was most inadequate for a treatment of the variations in it.

problem of *human nature* was touched on only indirectly. It was also omitted, as has been explained, in the 1951 research.

The descriptions and analyses made in the 1936 study cannot, of course, be given in full. The limitations of both space and interest make it necessary to omit a great deal and give only summary accounts of much of the rest of the material. First, I shall treat the history of the community. Subsequent sections will treat the details of the population, the social organization, the economic life, the religious activities, and the relationship the people of Atrisco had with the outside world.

THE FOUNDING OF ATRISCO AND THE DEVELOPMENT AND DECLINE OF ITS *PATRÓN* SYSTEM

The history of Atrisco as a community goes back only to the early 1880's. As has already been mentioned, the whole of western New Mexico, of which the Rimrock area is but a small part, remained, in spite of claims to the contrary, the territory of Indians until the latter part of the nineteenth century. Extensive settlement of the region was not possible until after a United States army had subdued both the Navaho and Apache Indians. The Spanish-speaking colonists of New Mexico, at first the subjects of Spain and after 1821 the subjects of the newly established government of Mexico, had never been able to bring either the Navaho or Apache under their control. They claimed the land over which these Indians roamed but dared not push far into it with settlements of their own. Both the early Spanish and later Mexican colonizations were largely confined to the valley of the Rio Grande. However, a few settlements were precariously maintained on the periphery of the Navaho and Apache territory. They were from fifty to eighty miles west of Albuquerque, New Mexico, and were always regarded as buffer settlements.

It was from these settlements that the founders of Atrisco, all members of the Atrisco and Lucero families, came. Why the Atrisco family, which was to become Atrisco's *patrón* family, either went voluntarily or was sent by the authorities (it was often the case that colonists in New Mexico were ordered to specific localities) into these western settlements is not known. They were, however, well established in one of them in the seventies, and members of the family state that their ancestors were in another of the frontier communities at the time the United States took over New Mexico in 1846. The Lucero family, which was related by marriage to the Atrisco family, had also lived for some years in the community where the Atriscos lived in the seventies.

Since Spanish-Americans do not have a history of mobility from community to community, it is another question why members of these families decided to leave their home and move into an area which was definitely frontier and little known. The story told by Don Juan Atrisco, who was the head of the Atrisco family from 1898 until his death in 1958, is that his brothers and his mother decided upon their westward move after their father had been killed and most of the family sheep stolen by Geronimo, the famous (or infamous) Apache leader. Although it is more likely that the Indian raider who dealt this heavy blow to the family was a follower of Geronimo rather than the man himself, there seems no doubt that the raid occurred. Don Juan himself was a small boy at the time and the youngest of the family. It was the eldest of the brothers, Don Manuel, who made the decision to move after the raid, and it was he who organized the migration party. This was in accord with Spanish-American custom which until very recently has always made the eldest brother a father's successor in authority.

There were thirty-odd persons in the migrating group, most of whom were members of the Atrisco family. The others were four brothers in the Lucero family, all brothers of Don Manuel's wife, their families, and a small Hopi Indian girl whom the Atrisco family claims to have purchased for a bushel of corn. The entire group went first to a new settlement which had grown up around one of the United States army forts, but they did not remain there long. Don Manuel, who seems to have had much more love of wandering than is usually the case with Spanish-Americans, decided they should all move on into country which at that time had not been explored by either Spanish-Americans or Anglo-Americans. They arrived at the site of the present village of Atrisco in the year 1882.

The first years in the new community were extremely difficult and fearful, too, since the danger of Indian raids was by no means over at that time. Internal dissension also developed because of a bitter quarrel between Don Manuel and one of his Lucero brothers-in-law. This quarrel, reputedly over a woman, led to an actual split in the community, and for a period of several years there were two settlements a few miles apart.

But as new people drifted in and village life became more settled, there came to be little question of Don Manuel's position of leadership. He was successful in building once again a sizable herd of sheep; he opened a small store and thus became that all-important type of Spanish-American *patrón*, the trader; he and his mother organized religious services in their own home and arranged for at least an annual visit of a *padre* from one of the towns to the north. All of these activities were important aspects of a *patrón* position.

But Don Manuel was not very ambitious for a position of power. From the stories one hears about him, he did not seem to have some of those variant characteristics which have gone into the making of New Mexico's powerful *patrones*. Even within his own family, where he was fully recognized as the person of authority, he was not much given to domination. Indeed, one wonders whether the *patrón* position in Atrisco could have been kept in the Atrisco family had Don Manuel remained in the community. There were others coming into the area who were of a kind to challenge his rather mild authority. But Don Manuel, after several years, decided to move on to still another area farther to the south. With him he took his own family of wife and children, one of his brothers, and the families of two of his brothers-in-law—a total of twenty-six persons. All other members of the Atrisco family remained in the village, and it is with the rise to power of Don Manuel's youngest brother, Don Juan, that the history of the community really begins. For Don Juan was determined to be a *patrón*, and he found the ways to weld the little settlement which bore his family name into a typical *patrón*-dominated New Mexican village.

The winning of the position was not for Don Juan either easy or simple. It will be remembered that he was the youngest of all the Atrisco brothers; hence he had no right to assume authority even within his own family. But the situation was a peculiar one because of the fact that Don Juan was the godchild of his brother Don Manuel and looked upon himself as Don Manuel's eldest son. The godparent-godchild relationship in Spanish-American culture is a powerful one and is virtually an equivalent of the parent-child one. In the earlier study I gave this description of the situation:

Manuel left three brothers behind him in Atrisco all older than Juan, and since it is not according to the *costumbres* that a younger brother dominate, it may be expected that there were difficulties. There were. Juan was forced to gain his power by ruse and deception. Yet, in all fairness to him, it must be said that he believed he had the right to that power because of his relationship to Manuel. Juan had been just 10 years old when his father died, and Manuel who was his godfather assumed the role of father to him. Juan looked upon himself as Manuel's son—his eldest son—hence was it not natural for him to assume the leadership role that Manuel relinquished when he left? At least there was a conflict in the ideal patterns in this instance, and Juan was the sort of person to take advantage of the conflict. Moreover, Juan insists that none of the other brothers "knew enough" to take charge of family affairs. Whatever the truth of the situation may have been, it is evident that he was one of those Spanish-Americans who desires power—power over people primarily. In him were the makings of a *jefe politico*. And while it is not to be supposed that he laid careful plans for future action (personal acquaintance with Juan and his recent behavior show him as incapable of planning for the distant future as any other Spanish-American), he did take every advantage of immediate opportunities. Before many years had elapsed he had control over most of the affairs of the Atrisco family and of other village families.

Don Juan's brothers did not concur at all with his interpretation of the situation, but no one of them, and certainly not the eldest of them, came forth at once to challenge him. These brothers, having always been in a younger-brother position, were not accustomed to asserting authority or taking responsibility. Moreover, two of them had become heavy drinkers and gamblers and were much too interested in their own pleasures to take note of the steps Juan was taking to gain control of family affairs. They actually played directly into Juan's hands. One brother took a sum of money which he had made while working on a government project and moved into Railtown (the small town eighty miles to the north of Atrisco), where life was gayer than in the village. He soon spent the money and then began to gamble with the sheep that he had left behind in Atrisco. When finally he returned to the village he found that Juan had taken over what was left of his herd of sheep. Another of the brothers behaved in much the same fashion with similar results. Neither had real grounds for argument since they had both been receiving sums of money from Juan for some time. Thus, even though they protested bitterly against what they termed a younger brother's deception, they had no other choice but to accept his domination if they wished to remain in Atrisco.

Juan also had his brother Manuel's house and the little store he had established. Juan states that he bought both these; others say that Manuel gave them to him. Whichever was the case, there was no contesting the transaction by the other brothers at the time. They themselves had never participated very much in the management of the store and did not seem to realize the strength and degree of authority which went with the position of trader.

By building up his holdings of livestock to the extent that other villagers were frequently in his hire, and by so increasing the volume of business in his store that still more villagers were often in his debt, Juan gradually laid a solid foundation for *patrón* control. He then greatly augmented his control by having the small house which he himself had lived in prior to Manuel's departure rebuilt and enlarged for a village church. The church was, of course, a church for the whole community, but Juan never let anyone forget that it was really his own and had been his gift in the role of leader. He and his wife took over the management of all religious affairs and functions.

Another of Don Juan's master strokes in the winning of a power position came in 1912 when he managed to gain control of most of the range lands used by *los Atrisqueños*. The patterns of land ownership and land use followed by Spanish-Americans in New Mexico have been very different from Anglo-American patterns, and neither of the two groups has understood well the differences. In brief, the older Spanish-American pattern was for whole villages to use the range lands which a *patrón*, or occasionally a community, had received from the Spanish Crown in the form of a land grant. Usually, though certainly not always, the village families would own small plots of land for purposes of irrigation agriculture, but beyond this they were dependent upon the good will of the *patrón* for the use of land for livestock, for firewood, and for any building materials they might need. Where no water was available for irrigation agriculture, the average family frequently owned no land at all except a house site. But because the land grants had never been surveyed during the whole of the Spanish and Mexican colonial periods their boundaries were vague and indefinite. Moreover, only a very few New Mexican *patrones* became agricultural *hacendados* of the type so commonly found in Old Mexico. A majority of the *patrones* ruled over villages by means of a system of debt peonage rather than having *peones* who were bound to the land. The usual result of this system was that the village families who wished to run herds of livestock of their own were permitted to use the *patrón's* land so long as they did not aspire to building herds of a size to threaten the *patrón* economically. Many of the villagers also worked for the *patrón*, of course, and most of them were dependent upon him for more than just land. Only the *patrón*, for example, would have the shearing equipment or the dipping vats necessary for running a sheep business. He also usually had control of the essential but scarce watering places on the range. The system was, in short, one of great land holdings which were operated in accord with quite well defined patterns of limited permissiveness in the use of land and equipment.

When the United States opened up the western part of New Mexico, vast areas of land, including the one in which Atrisco was located, were made into public domain. Public domain was understood by most Spanish-Americans to be much the same as crown land. It was simply a vast expanse of unfenced and open land. In the early days of Atrisco all the families who had livestock simply used the land that was available without thought of acquiring title to any of it. And there was no *patrón* figure who had control of it. Both Manuel and Juan Atrisco up to the year 1912 had held their position of *patrón* on other bases than land control.

After 1912 the situation changed radically. In that year the United States government ceded alternate sections of the land around Atrisco to the Santa Fe Railway in exchange for sections which the railway company had released for an extension of the Navaho Indian reservation. Most of the people in Atrisco paid little or no attention to this transfer, for at that period of time railway land in New Mexico was being used by stockmen much as public domain was used. But the Atrisco family, especially Don Juan who had been having dealings with Anglo-American stockmen, saw a threat to their interests. Don Juan and his brothers knew it was now possible for an Anglo-American to lease the railway land and thus gain control of the whole area. They decided to secure the leases themselves.

But is was Juan alone who undertook negotiations with the railway company. In addition to being the one who was most concerned about the situation, he was also the only one of the brothers who spoke any English. He went to Santa Fe to put through the deal, and it was not until he returned and had obtained the signatures of his brothers that they learned they had not signed the documents as co-lessees but rather as witnesses for Juan in whose name the leases were held.

The third of Juan's brothers, Emilio, who was the only one who still held a sizable herd of sheep in his own name, was infuriated and moved his family and herd twenty miles to the west, just beyond the land area which Juan now controlled. Two other village men, one a French Canadian and the other part German Jew, kept their herds on land which was still open to the south of Atrisco. But all other families in the area and all other Atrisco brothers were now firmly under the domination of Don Juan in the matter of land as in all else.

The tract of land Don Juan controlled was large, for in leasing 77,000 acres of railway land laid out in alternate sections he gained a very real, although not a legal, control over some 70,000 acres of public domain still remaining in the area. The United States practice of ceding alternate sections to railways made it impossible for anyone to gain a legal control of contiguous sections within a railway area. Don Juan could not, therefore, close in and fence his range, and he also could not legally keep others off the land which was still under government control; but the leasing of the railway land gave him a control of the whole area, which was all he wanted. Even though a few families did eventually homestead sections or half sections of public domain within the range and developed upon them small *ranchitos,* their dependence on Don Juan for the use of range land was not decreased. Because New Mexico range land is so sparsely grassed, many sections of land are required for even very small herds of animals.

Don Juan had still another hold on the people of Atrisco in the matter of land. He had purchased outright from the railway company the section of land upon which the village is built. Thus, even though the families could claim ownership of houses, they had no claim to the land upon which the houses stood. Technically every family was a squatter family.

By all these means Don Juan had already made himself into a powerful *patrón* by 1913. From 1913 to 1921—years which saw a boom in the livestock business—he increased his wealth to a reported $250,000; and many in the area, Anglo-Americans as well as Spanish-Americans, called him *el Rey* (the King). It was also during this period that he made his bid for political prestige and authority. Once he had this and was recognized outside the community because of it, his power would be almost absolute.

It was not difficult for Don Juan to become a *jefe politico*. Atrisco is in Verona County which was still in 1951 approximately 75 per cent Spanish-American. Its political machine was definitely Spanish-American in the period 1913–21. All that Don Juan had to do to become a part of that machine was to convince the county political bosses that he was the *patrón* in Atrisco who could and would deliver the votes. There were few in Atrisco at the time who dared to challenge him when it came time to "elect" delegates to the county political conventions. Even had there been resistance to him or the persons of his selection, no one else had the money to pay for the trips to the county seat which was some two hundred miles from Atrisco.

After Don Juan appeared a few times at the conventions as the "selected delegate" of Atrisco, the county officials took his position of *jefe politico* as assured. Then, once having gained a place in county political affairs, he had a stranglehold on Atrisco itself. All appropriations to Atrisco were paid directly to him, and all appeals to county authorities had to be made through him. Few accountings were ever demanded. It did not matter much to the county politicians that the money appropriated for bridges, roads, or other improvements was seldom used for the purposes specified. In time Don Juan even won personal recognition in the county political machine. He held the offices of county commissioner and county treasurer, both of which are prized in New Mexico political life.

In writing of this rise to power in the previous study of Atrisco, I remarked:

Juan Atrisco could never have gained his wide range of power had he not been dealing with people who both understood and accepted the authority of a *patrón* figure. And he could not have held his power had he not been one of those rare

Spanish-Americans who was willing to assume paternalistic responsibility and was fearless in demanding submission.

We have, in other words, in this short story of one man's ambitious bid for power both a clear-cut illustration of a Lineal relationship system and an example of a somewhat variant figure.

But although variant in some respects, Don Juan was very much a Spanish-American in a part of his value orientations. He had, as was remarked earlier, only a little more of a sense of the Future and planning for it than did the average *Atrisqueño*, and his behavior, once he had achieved *patrón* control, became more or less typically Being oriented. Moreover, he never applied to others the rather extreme Individualism which he himself had shown in gaining his position. He did not even allow it to extend to his own children, whom he expected to remain obedient to and unquestioning of Lineal tradition. Like almost all New Mexican *patrones* he could not share responsibility and authority.

Don Juan might have held his position for many years, as did many another similar *patrón*, had it not been that conditions were rapidly changing in New Mexico in the years 1915 to 1925. As has already been noted, Don Juan took full immediate advantage of the strong market in livestock during the war years. He did not, however, consolidate his gains. Having become a man of wealth and something of a political figure as well, he wanted still more power. He became attracted by the political opportunities in Railtown in 1916 and established residence there. For a few years he himself still spent much of his time in Atrisco looking after his affairs, but gradually he began to absent himself for longer and longer periods. The management of both the herds and the store was left in the hands of his two eldest sons. His money began to disappear rapidly. Politics alone cost him large sums because gaining a foothold in Railtown was not the simple matter it had been in Verona County. Railtown itself was fairly large as New Mexico towns go (approximately 10,000) and was in a county much less predominantly Spanish-American than Verona County. To obtain the support of the Republican Party organization, which was largely dominated by Anglo-Americans, Don Juan made many large monetary contributions. Eventually he actually won the election for the position of mayor of the city, but it was a fruitless victory. Since no one else of his party was elected to office that year, he was more or less forced by local custom to resign his own position. He did not again run for office.

He was also gambling heavily during this period. Railtown citizens still tell of the years that Don Juan and another well known Sheep King would while away the hours by betting a thousand head of sheep on the turn of a card. Since sheep were bringing a high price then, thousands of dollars could and did go in an evening. Meanwhile, in Atrisco, Don Juan's sons were drinking up and gambling away the proceeds from the store which their father was no longer watching with care. In 1920, for example, there was a bill of $27,000 from a *single* one of the several wholesale houses supplying the store which was brought into court for settlement.

All in all, the losses were so great that Don Juan negotiated a loan of $50,000 from a Colorado bank in order that he could continue with his business. He might have recouped his fortunes, as other Spanish-American *patrones* in the past had frequently done, had there not quickly come the country-wide collapse of the livestock market. The bank in Colorado went into the hands of receivers, and Don Juan was forced into bankruptcy. A bank in Railtown bought up the whole of the Juan Atrisco business—leases, the land that Juan had actually owned, the store, and all remaining livestock. All that was left to Juan was the fifty-foot strip on which his house stood and some cattle that he managed to hold out as undeclared assets.

This debacle could have brought a definite end to Don Juan's control over Atrisco had it not been that the banker in Railtown was a friend of Don Juan's and was not himself eager to engage in the livestock business. He softened the blow by giving to Don Juan a lifelong right to run fifteen hundred head of sheep on the Atrisco range and by helping him with funds to make another start. Late in 1921 Don Juan went back to Atrisco fully expectant that he could rebuild his herds, but he was full of bitterness, even against the Railtown banker. Like most Spanish-Americans of his time he had little understanding of banks, of interest on money, or of other financial affairs, and he looked upon the foreclosure action as a breach of friendship. By the time I heard the story from Don Juan himself, even the amount of the loan had been altered in his mind. He insisted that the loan was actually for $5,000 and not the $50,000 which the records show, and said he could not understand why a friend—*un amigo*—would take that kind of advantage of him.

Both because everyone in Atrisco who had livestock had been struck by the 1921 depression and because the bank did not see fit to develop a livestock business in the area at that time, there was little change in Don Juan's position for some years. He was still the *patrón* of Atrisco even though economically a sadly depleted one, and life in the village went on much as usual.

The first great change came in 1928. The Railtown bank sold all its rights in the Atrisco property to a newly organized Anglo-American sheep company. Within a few years several thousand head of sheep were again on the range, but this time they were mainly the property of Anglo outsiders. However, the range was still open and unfenced, and in addition the first manager of this new company, Mr. Davis, was a man who had had a long experience with Spanish-Americans, and he made no effort to drive the men of Atrisco off the land. He was willing that the stockmen with small herds should continue to make use of a part of the range, and he also took a number of village men in his employ. Moreover, there was not much that he could do about Don Juan's sheep since the company had accepted Juan's right to run fifteen hundred head on the range when they purchased the property and lease rights.

Mr. Davis did, however, set about to break Don Juan's political control of the village. It was essential to do this if he were to secure funds from the county with which to build roads and bridges and make other improvements in the area. He devoted his own efforts to the county officials since he had no desire to become embroiled in the political life of Atrisco. He prevailed upon other persons to try to undermine Don Juan's position in the village. One of these men, Jose Vidrio, was the Spanish-American husband of Mr. Davis' sister-in-law. He and his Anglo-American wife had moved to Atrisco in 1929 to operate the trading store for the Anglo sheep company. Another was Luis Corona, the eldest son of a man who had come to Atrisco in 1912. Luis Corona needed no urging from Mr. Davis, for he was a domineering and ambitious man who had long resented Don Juan's control and was looking for ways to carve out for himself a *patrón* position. Don Daniel Lucero, a son of one of the first Lucero settlers, was the third. Of the three, Don Daniel was unquestionably the person most people desired for the leadership role, but he was also the most reluctant. He was, and is, as will be shown later, much too variant a person to be an old-style *patrón*.

Through the combined efforts of all these men much of Don Juan's economic and political authority was destroyed within a few years. Since 1929 other men than Don Juan or his relatives or chosen henchmen have often been chosen as the Atrisco delegates to county political conventions. The county appropriations, which were the main concern of Mr. Davis, were no longer paid directly to Don Juan. In almost all activities except the highly important religious ones Don Juan Atrisco's era of firm rule was ended.

But life in the village was still not greatly altered. The Anglo-American sheep company, which was by now legally named the Dennis Sheep Company, was too unsuccessful in its operations in the years 1929 to 1934 to spend money on acquiring title to land or to consolidate the range and fence it. Bad weather conditions and disease had taken such a heavy toll of the company's sheep that it could not even meet current expenses. Ready cash for wages to village men was frequently unavailable, and once more the store, which the Vidrio family by 1932 had leased from the Dennis Sheep Company, became the source of supplies for a number of families on a credit basis. The traders became, after a fashion, *patrón* substitutes in some economic matters. The manager himself was also a *patrón* of sorts. And all those families which had no reason to turn to either the storekeeper or the manager sought elsewhere for a *patrón* figure to replace Don Juan. Some looked to Don Daniel Lucero even though he made it plain that he had no desire for a true *patrón* position. Others—seven families in all—eventually found a fairly satisfactory economic *patrón* figure in the person of an Anglo-American trader in the Indian village of Zuni.

The dominantly Lineal social system which had been, in typical Spanish-American fashion, ruled over by one man was, to be sure, broken up; but the basic patterns were not yet destroyed. Atrisco settled down for several more years of life under a decentralized and piecemeal *patrón* system. The Dennis Sheep Company was vaguely resented by some of the stockmen but no one, with the exception of Don Daniel Lucero, saw it for the destructive force it could and was likely to become.

The first awareness that many had of the company as a disrupting force came in 1934, when a new manager was sent in to direct the company's business. This second manager, Mr. Gray, who was living in the village during the whole of the initial period I spent there, had none of the sympathy or understanding of Spanish-Americans that the first manager had.

He openly admitted to a strong dislike of all Spanish-Americans and frankly stated that he considered them blackguards who would stop at nothing. Moreover, he was actually afraid of them.

The policies which Mr. Gray attempted to put into effect immediately upon his arrival in Atrisco had one aim—that of driving all Atrisco stockmen off the range and of breaking up the village itself. He hoped that by importing laborers instead of hiring village men he would drive out some at once. His greatest effort was put into blocking in and fencing the range. From 1934 through 1936 he carried on continuous negotiations with the Santa Fe Railway for the exchanging of sections in other parts of the state so that the Atrisco range would be one more or less solid unit. If it were made a fairly solid block of land, the range could be fenced and the Atrisco stockmen could be kept off it. By 1937 he had largely accomplished his purpose. The range was fenced, and a number of the village stockmen who had been using the Dennis Sheep Company range either had to sell off stock and go to the cities or had to seek range lands elsewhere.

Although it had been obvious in 1935 and 1936 that the range would soon be fenced, the vast majority of the people in Atrisco had made no preparation whatsoever for what they would do when the fences were finally in place. Some found it necessary to sell many head of livestock hastily and at a loss; others found a temporary solution through urgent last-minute appeals to *patrón* figures to help them find range land in other areas. In all this behavior the Present *time* orientation was vividly apparent as was also the acquiescent acceptance of the inevitable.

But even though a deathblow had been struck, the village was not completely destroyed. Don Daniel Lucero, always atypical or variant, had been over the years acquiring sections of land by having members of his family homestead them or by buying up single sections that others had once homesteaded. By 1937 he had sufficient land to form an eleven-section range within the very heart of the Dennis Sheep Company range. Although this was annoying to the manager, there was nothing he could do about it. Don Daniel would not sell. Mr. Gray also found that he could not invalidate the claim that Don Juan Atrisco had for the right to run sheep on the Atrisco range. Several other families who had their stock on land outside the company range also remained in the area and kept their houses in the village. Moreover, the manager found he was forced to hire some village men. His policy of importing all labor had not been completely successful.

The pressures from the Dennis Sheep Company, many and severe, were not all that the village had to face in these years. In 1931 migrants from Oklahoma and Texas had started to file homestead claims in the region just a few miles to the south of Atrisco. The town of Homestead developed. (A brief description of this small settlement will be given in Chapter VII.)[6]

One effect of this new community upon Atrisco was a further reduction of range land available for livestock. This, however, was not a very serious matter, since most of the land in the Homestead area had formerly been

---

[6] For a detailed study of this community see Evon Z. Vogt, *Modern Homesteaders* (Cambridge, Mass.: Harvard University Press, 1955).

under the control of a Spanish-American *patrón* who had long been Don Juan's rival, and few Atrisco men had dared to poach upon it. The serious blows dealt to Atrisco by the homesteaders were of quite another order.

Almost all the homesteaders had come from regions where prejudice against Spanish-Americans was acute and bitter, and it infuriated them upon their arrival in this new territory to learn that they had to go to Atrisco for their mail and many of their supplies. It enraged them even more that they had to send their children to school in Atrisco to share classrooms with "dirty Mexicans." They soon established a small grade school of their own, but as they were in a Spanish-American county it sometimes happened that the teachers sent to them were Spanish-Americans. The extreme nature of their anti-Spanish-American feeling was shown when members of the community burned their own school rather than have a "black Mexican" teach in it.

Since the Spanish-American teacher at the time of this episode was a member of the Atrisco community, the strain on the relationships between the two villages was great. Neither community has ever forgotten the incident or tried to rationalize it as an accident. The Texans actually seemed to be proud of the feat. Once when I made a remark to a prominent Homesteader that I had heard that a young man from Atrisco was talking of opening a *cantina* (saloon) in their town, he quickly and without a glimmer of humor replied, "It can always burn down."

In the first few years of its existence Homestead was both too poor and too little organized for its citizens to do more than threaten, protest, and grumble about the necessary contacts with *los Atrisqueños*. This they did in abundance, and out of the protesting there eventually crystallized certain lines of action. They began to speak with determination of taking the post office away from Atrisco, they hopefully planned a new road into their growing community which would bypass Atrisco, and they insisted that their growth gave them the right to have the one high school in the region.

By 1937 they had succeeded in convincing the county school authorities that the high school should be moved to Homestead. The issue of the post office was settled by the establishment of a second one in their own community. Atrisco in 1951 still had its post office, but it had so little business that it brought small gain to the local postmistress. Moreover, by 1950 a much improved road had been built into and through Homestead, and it actually was constructed to bypass Atrisco by several miles.

Although resentful and sometimes bitter, the people of Atrisco did almost nothing at any stage of these events to prevent or circumvent the actions of the Texans. It was a one-sided battle between dominantly Individualistic, Doing, and Future-oriented planners and a Present and Being-oriented people, and never at any time was there any doubt as to the outcome.

Relations between the two communities later became somewhat calmer both because the Texans had had their way and because some types of contacts were fewer; but they are still far from good. Real flare-ups in the forms of arguments and fights continued to occur occasionally. Also, Spanish-Americans are not encouraged to trade in the stores and shops of Homestead. One of the two machine shops operating in 1951 refused, by one ruse or another, to service the cars of *los Atrisqueños*. A majority of the Spanish-American children have never been really comfortable in the schools in Homestead to which they all must now go since Atrisco no longer has a school of any type. And to see the ways in which all Homesteaders ignore and snub the few *Atrisqueños* who venture to attend the dances in Homestead is to learn a thorough lesson about the nature of prejudice.

For the most part the people of Atrisco stay away from Homestead. The village, what is left of it, still has bits of life in it, and it continues to function as a separate community to the extent that it can. The old *patrón* system has crumbled, the family system has been badly shaken, and other changes can be noted. Yet, as we shall see in the sections to follow, most of the value orientations of *los Atrisqueños*, whether still in the village or elsewhere, are remarkably similar to those which the 1936 study reported.

THE GENERAL CHARACTERISTICS OF ATRISCO'S 1936 POPULATION AND ITS SOCIAL ORGANIZATION

The 157 persons living in Atrisco in 1936 and early 1937 were easily separated into two groups, which I distinguished by the terms "permanent" and "transient." The permanent members, 142 in number, were those persons who were considered by the villagers themselves to be true *Atrisqueños*. All were related by either blood or marriage to at least one and frequently several or even all Atrisco families. The transients, who numbered only 10 in 1936 and 15 in 1937, were either temporary laborers (most of them single) or teachers. All of them had only recently come into the village and were without relatives in it. It was seldom expected either by the transients themselves or by others that they would remain for long in Atrisco.

The total population of the village, never large, had always been marked by these two separable groups. At the peak of Don Juan Atrisco's power, 1912–20, and again in 1929, there were approximately 75 to 100 more persons than in 1936. The majority of these were transients. There have also always been additional persons in the two peripheral communities. Even with these persons added, the total population figure at no time went far over the 200 mark. But this small size was not at all atypical. Until quite recently most of New Mexico's Spanish-speaking population have lived in tiny villages ranging in size from one or two families to a few hundred persons. Rarely did one reach the 1000 mark.[7]

---

[7] Because of the manner in which census figures have been collected, there is no definite information for the state as a whole on the average size of the villages. The statement on average size is based upon my own observation and upon the information provided by the *Tewa Basin Study*, Vol. II, *The Spanish-American Villages*, released by United States Department of Agriculture, Soil Conservation Service, Albuquerque, N. M., 1939. In this study the population figures given for the thirty-one communities in the Tewa Basin (one of the oldest and most typical Spanish-American areas) range from 26 to 1203 persons. Only two of the villages had total populations over 600 and the average was 240 persons.

For handling of the transients in their midst *los Atrisqueños* had quite definite and well understood patterns. Up to a point all transients were accepted in the easygoing way Spanish-Americans have of accepting most things, yet never were they considered to be well integrated members of the community unless they became bound to one or more of the old and established families through marriage. A frequent comment made about transients was: "They have no relatives here." Moreover, the community as a whole was quick to repudiate and ostracize any transient who transgressed the mores. Members of the permanent community making the same mistakes would be sanctioned, sometimes severely, but would be soon forgiven. The reasons for this demarcation were both obvious and realistically necessary. The only efficacious means of social control in Atrisco were the rules and regulations of a widely ramified family system, and the transients, because they stood outside the system, were not subject to its sanctions. Instead they always represented a possible source of disorganization and trouble. Even as well accepted as I was, after a period of time at least, I was always conscious that a misstep would result in the closing of community ranks against me. And it was interesting to note that family terms were applied to me by some of those I knew best. I was frequently likened to a *tia* (aunt), an *hermana* (sister), or a *prima* (cousin), and it helped greatly that I actually was a relative of sorts of both the first manager of the Dennis Sheep Company and of the family which operated the village store. Although I was not related to one of the old families, I could be placed in a set of family ties which were known and accepted by members of the community.

Still another aspect of the indifferent attitude toward transients was the short memory the villagers had of them once they had departed. All emigrating members of permanent families are kept track of forever, whereas almost all transients have been forgotten completely. This is as true today as it always was, even though a majority of the former permanent residents have now also gone off to the Anglo-dominated outside world, in some cases as far as California.

Atrisco in 1936 had thirty family units of the type a sociologist would call simple or nuclear families (families of just a husband, wife, and children). Twenty-seven of these were in the permanent population; three were transient.[8] In size these units ranged from two to twelve persons who were actually in residence at the time, and their average number was 4.7. But simple family units in Spanish-American villages are frequently not independent in their functioning. In fact, in an earlier period than 1936 it was seldom indeed that such a unit could stand independently apart from the extended family. Even in 1936 nine of the simple families functioned in combination with one or more other such units while carrying on many life activities, especially economic activities. It was necessary, therefore, to designate a second type of family in Atrisco—the extended or, better, the "economic family." There were twenty-one of these divisions which ranged in number

---

[8] I included in the study all transients who were in family units. Itinerant laborers and a single schoolteacher were omitted. Few of the total number of transients were in family units.

from two to twenty resident members and had an average size of 6.7 persons.

All of the families included in these totals actually lived in Atrisco or on ranches close by, with the exception of one which lived in one of the peripheral communities. It was necessary to include this family, composed of the widow and children of one of Don Juan's brothers, because the people of Atrisco themselves considered it to be a part of their closely interrelated permanent population. Other families in the two outlying settlements were not so considered.

Spanish-Americans are a village people even when they have a predominantly pastoral type of economy. Atrisco was no exception. Although the caring for stock required many of the men to be out on the range for periods of many days and often several weeks, it was usually the case, especially in the winter months, that the families made their homes in the village. Only one of the extended families lived more or less continuously on its *ranchito*. This was the family headed by Luis Corona, which in 1936 had in it so many young children that they could demand a school of their own from the county school authorities. But this family, too, had its small village house as a headquarters for *fiestas*, political meetings, or other village affairs.

The houses in Atrisco, all made of adobes or rocks plastered together with mud, were small and were not laid out according to any plan of regular streets or roadways. Winding paths went in several directions through the village, and here and there on both sides of them were either single houses of three or four rooms or a chain of small two-room dwellings which had side walls in common. None of the houses had any conveniences of any kind, not even a well for water. It has never been possible to bring in a well of good water in the vicinity of Atrisco, and even today all water for family use must be hauled from spots many miles distant.

In a dominant position in the middle of the village there was Don Juan's somewhat larger house, one room of which he was using in 1936 for a *cantina* (saloon). Beside it was the store and on beyond a corral and a windmill which pumped a hard water that everyone considered good only for livestock. At one end of the little settlement stood the cluster of community buildings—the church and three schools. One of the schools (all one-room structures) was for the little children, another was the high school which was closed a year later, and the third was a so-called vocational school which the state of New Mexico had provided for a hoped-for program of a revival of Spanish-American crafts. The vocational program had little success in Atrisco (or elsewhere in New Mexico for that matter); hence this building was little used and poorly cared for.

In 1936 family organization was almost the whole of the social organization. Even the *patrón* system was an extension of family organization, and the religious hierarchy, both natural and supernatural, was notable for its familistically defined figures. The families were usually, and certainly by preference, fairly large. There was, in fact, a tacitly understood norm for a family size of four to eight children. A family of two children was considered too small, and a couple without any children at all was an object of great pity. The wife who had no children was never well integrated into community life. There were two such women in Atrisco in 1936, and both led the lives of hermits. They were highly self-conscious about their childless condition and assumed, as did the rest of the community, that the fault was their own. One spent much time and money on mail orders for various patent medicines which she hoped would overcome her sterility. Very large families of ten or more children were also an object of adverse comment. In this case the man was blamed for being "too hard on his wife."

Usually, too, the very small or very large family was brought in line with the notion of an average family by means of adoption. The excessively large family would often give one or more of its children to other relatives to rear, and the couple with no or few children would usually take nieces, nephews, or even more distantly related children into their home. I was utterly baffled during my first few weeks in Atrisco because there were so many children of different surnames living in several of the families. Eventually I learned that over 12 per cent of all Atrisco children were being brought up in families other than those into which they had been born. One of the women whom I knew especially well had two daughters who had surnames different from her own and also different from each other's. One was the daughter of the woman's brother, the other was the daughter of her sister, and both had been taken in infancy after the woman had lost her own twins and learned she could not have more children. Neither of the little girls, then eleven and five years of age, had seen their own parents, who lived over a hundred miles away, more than once or twice.

Bachelors and spinsters were almost unknown in Atrisco. There simply was no place in the community for the unmarried woman, and if any girl ever reached the age of twenty-two or twenty-three without being married or engaged, everyone became concerned. Most especially concerned were the girls themselves, because the number of men that a girl could properly marry were few in Atrisco in 1936. The Church, it was said, forbade marriages between persons of even a fifth-degree biological relationship,[9] and by 1936 there were not many persons in Atrisco who were not related to everyone else to this degree. Moreover, since Atrisco was remote and isolated, there were few opportunities to meet suitable men outside the community. Thus it was not surprising, even though to me it was amusing, that every teen-age girl knew exactly which young men in the village were possible husbands.

One day a very attractive young eighteen year old girl, the daughter of

---

[9] This was what the people of Atrisco insisted the position of the Church to be. Actually the statutes place the limitation only on first and second-degree relatedness. Apparently throughout the state of New Mexico the priests give varying interpretations of the statutes. For example, O. Leonard and C. P. Loomis, "Culture of a Contemporary Rural Community: El Cerrito, New Mexico," *Rural Life Studies*, U.S. Department of Agriculture, Bureau of Agricultural Economics, November, 1941, p. 8, comment as follows: "Existing statutes prohibit marriage between couples related as closely as second cousins. Although the church may sanction and thus bring about such a marriage, these cases are becoming comparatively rare. Many of the rural priests make it a point in their educational program to teach the undesirability, physically and morally, of close intermarriage."

Jose Corona and the niece of Luis Corona, came to me and said, "You know, there are only three boys I can marry here in Atrisco. One is already engaged to Lucia, another is just eight years old, and the other one I don't like." Anxiety that she would not find anyone to marry was very apparent in Rosarita Corona's attitudes. Just a few months after she made this statement, a young man came into Atrisco to work temporarily. He liked Rosarita, and she was determined to marry him even though her parents were against it. Because Rosarita's mother had long been ill, the young girl had been playing the role of housekeeper-mother in her family, and the father especially did not want her to leave until he could find some other way to have the house, his wife, and their five other quite small children cared for. He refused to permit the marriage at the time the young man and his family wrote a formal letter, as was the old Spanish-American custom, for Rosarita's hand in marriage. Rosarita, fearful that her prospective husband might leave and never return, broke with the dominant patterns of Atrisco and eloped. For a time there was great excitement in the village. Jose Corona himself refused to speak or write to Rosarita. But as usually happens among Spanish-Americans, it was only a short while before the fact of the marriage was fairly well accepted even by Jose himself. When I was back in Atrisco in 1937, a few months after the elopement had occurred, I asked several persons if Jose still objected to Rosarita's husband and her marriage to him. The uniform reply was that there was nothing Jose could do about it now that the two were married. One young girl said, "Like him? Why he will have to like him now. She is married with him, isn't she? He is her husband."

There was one bachelor in Atrisco in 1936. This was Pancho Barrida, the eldest son of the Hopi Indian child whom the Atrisco family had brought with them when they established the village. The Atriscos, being family-minded Spanish-Americans, had seen to it that the Indian girl married, but because they were not desirous of having a full-blooded Indian marry a villager they had found for her a husband from the outside. Since he, too, was mostly of Indian blood—Navaho this time—Pancho and his brothers and sisters were always looked upon as being Indians. It was probably partly for this reason that Pancho never married. Pancho's two younger brothers did marry village girls, but there was considerable talk about the marriages, one of which was short-lived since the man died nine months after marrying. Pancho was a herder for the Atrisco family and was out on the range much of the time. But whenever he did come into the village he lived with the family of his younger brother, Jose, and because he never forgot that he was the *hermano mayor* (eldest brother) the strains created by this situation were many. Just how bitter Jose has been all these years I did not fully realize until I interviewed him in the summer of 1951. His comments will be reported later.

There was little question in the Atrisco of 1936 that being married fairly early (the preferred pattern for women was between the ages of seventeen and twenty-four years; for men between the ages of twenty-four and thirty years) and rearing a family of at least four and preferably more children was the ideal pattern, and few failed to follow it. It was also clear at that time that the organization of the family and the familistic superstructures which held all separate families together were dominantly Lineal. The parent-child relationship in which the authority of age and a lifelong obedience to that authority were the main principles was the keystone of the whole *relational* system. And, as is so often the case where these principles are found, there was a clear-cut dominance of the male over the female.

The ideal patterns of the society required parents to be kind and affectionate with children but firm, and the "good child" was the one who remained forever respectful and obedient to his parents. No record of outstanding accomplishment was ever regarded by *los Atrisqueños* as a substitute for a son's or daughter's fully compliant and obedient attitude to parents. A daughter might make a good marriage, a son might become more successful financially than others of his age; but should either fail to adhere to the standards of filial respect, he or she was a *mal hijo* or *mal hija* (bad son or bad daughter). Don Juan Atrisco's second son was an example; he went off on his own and became, for a short time at least, fairly successful in business and politics in Santa Fe. By Anglo-American standards he would have been commended for his initiative and ambition. But the young man had paid too little attention to his father's wishes and authority. Furthermore, he married without consulting his family and later committed the great sin of permitting his wife to divorce him. He was anything but a successful son in Spanish-American terms. I remember well the day I commented favorably to Don Juan on the success of this son. Like a flash came back the bitter remark: *"Es un mal hijo"* ("He is a bad son"). Almost everyone else in Atrisco also branded him a *mal hijo* at that time. When later he failed in his business and came back to Atrisco and showed himself more respectful to his father's wishes, he was forgiven much of his past behavior.

Some fathers in Atrisco were occasionally quite harsh but mothers almost never. The chief criticism that one heard of some of the parents was that they were not firm enough—"did not teach their children well to be nice and have nice ways." But in saying this *los Atrisqueños* were not advocating a really severe discipline. We have already seen that they are a people who accept much from their close relatives and forgive them easily. The Being orientation is strong in Spanish-Americans, and nowhere is it more in evidence than in their rearing of children. Mothers especially, but fathers too, are very permissive in many ways, and they tend usually to give great consideration to the child's needs and even his individuality *providing the child keeps to his proper and respectful role.*

I once expressed some surprise that the eldest son in one family was permitted to leave the village with his grandparents who were moving to another town. The boy's aunt countered my surprise and replied, "Why, of course his father and mother had to let him go. He has always lived more with his grandmother than his mother. He is used to her and it would be bad for the boy to have him change now." In many another way I found frequent concern for what would be "good for the child." The "good" they meant was, of course, the typical *Atrisqueño's* conception of contentment in Present *time*. Only to a very limited degree was there a concern for providing the kind of advantages which would permit a child to become independently successful in the Future. Moreover, it was easy to note that the great love expressed for children did not depend upon their level of performance as compared with others. But the very lack of the competitive element in the socialization process—an element often pointed to as a main source of disturbance in Anglo-American children—required individuals to pay a high price with another kind of emotional currency. Spanish-American children were seldom permitted to show much initiative or express boldly their own ideas. They were as rigorously trained for dependent behavior as the average Anglo-American child is schooled for independence.

Of all the strains for individuals imposed by the dominantly Lineal family organization the most severe were those deriving from the patterning of the eldest-younger brother relationships. The eldest brother, and to a much lesser degree the eldest sister, in the Spanish-American family had a position of authority and responsibility which approximated parental control. As far as the maintenance of family authority was concerned, there was sense in the pattern of training the eldest son, the *hermano mayor*, for this special position of leadership. With families as large as most Spanish-American ones were, it was all too often the case that a father or mother, or both, would either die or become physically incapacitated before all children had reached maturity. Having the eldest brother trained to assume the father's position theoretically insured the family against a disintegration of its Lineally defined authority.

The pattern was considered to be most effective and necessary when there was property to be managed. But even as late as 1936, when a number of the families were economically independent wage-earning families, the typical dominant attitude in Atrisco was that an eldest brother was different and had authority that other brothers could not command. As an example of the way the attitude was expressed, note this remark of a village woman who was in no way dependent economically upon her eldest brother: "I feel toward my brother Juan just like I felt to my father. There are some things I do not feel like saying to him at all as I might to other persons, and I wouldn't ever want him not to approve." In this particular case the woman has kept her attitude unchanged even though the brother made a complete failure of his livestock business and in spite of the still more serious matter of his having been imprisoned recently (1951), at the age of sixty-odd years, for having sexual relations with a thirteen year old village girl. The woman defends her *hermano mayor* and says firmly that he was "framed." Some other *Atrisqueños* share her attitude even though the man himself admits to having intimate relations with the young girl. All he has denied is that he is the father of the girl's illegitimate child, which was the main charge against him.

But even though the authority position of the eldest brother was acknowledged by almost everyone, the resistance to it was strong. The most serious quarrels Atrisco has known have been quarrels between eldest and younger brothers. We have already seen how one of Don Juan's brothers moved his stock off the range and refused for the rest of his life to speak to Don Juan who had dared to assume the eldest-brother role. The quarrels and disputes between legitimate eldest brothers and some of their younger brothers have been even more bitter. Luis Corona, for example, was so autocratic with his two younger brothers that one left the community and moved to another state, and the other, Jose Corona, found ways to sever all social and economic connections with Luis. At the time I first met Jose and Luis Corona, they had not spoken to each other for eight years. Members of the two families remained on friendly terms, but the two men may as well have been on different planets.

The chief problem in the eldest-younger brother relationship was the lack of a grounding of the primogeniture authority in either property inheritance or the strong family traditionalism characteristic of Past-oriented societies. Family property in Atrisco, and in other Spanish-American villages as well, was usually divided among all children. This was the pattern no matter what the type of property—land, livestock, houses, or personal effects. But this division did not extend to the management of income-producing property. It was always thought best, if not actually necessary, that all such property should be held together in a single unit which the *hermano mayor* managed. Younger brothers were seldom allowed to assume any of the direction of family property and related family affairs. Had there been great feeling for the preservation of family traditions and property, the eldest brother would have had a more legitimate basis for his authority, and younger brothers would have been more positively motivated to submit to that authority. Because the strong Present *time* orientation reduced the meaningful time span of the relationship to the current generation, there was an ever-present tendency for eldest brothers to use their positions for self-aggrandizement. This in turn increased the possibilities of rebellion in younger brothers.

The lack of emphasis upon family continuity through time also made for considerable confusion as to the line of authority within individual families and the training for an authoritative role. In a majority of the families eldest brothers who were expected to become *hermanos mayores* within their sibling groups were the sons of men who themselves were subordinate younger brothers. Thus, in their fathers these eldest sons did not have an adequate model for the role they were expected to assume. Although this situation was not carefully studied from a psychological point of view, it seems certain that it was a source of serious difficulties in the father-son relationship. One may even speculate that it is one of the reasons for the hostility and aggression (sadism even) which are noted in the behavior of many Spanish-American (and Mexican) men.

In Atrisco in the thirties, and earlier, there were three generalized variant patterns of behavior which younger brothers resistive to eldest-brother domination followed. Some simply struck out on their own. Frequently they actually left Atrisco and moved to another village or went into one of the larger towns. In the earlier study of Atrisco, family dissension, chiefly that between eldest and younger brothers, was shown to be the main cause of emigration. Almost never did a man leave the village primarily to better himself economically or to take a job which appealed to him more than the one he had at home.

This first kind of reaction was rebellion when analyzed as a type of *deviation*. It was an Individualistic *variation* in the cases where the man either went alone to another place or with just his immediate family. The variation was Collateral in character when two or more brothers, and sometimes other relatives as well, cooperatively separated themselves from the Lineal family system. Another illustration of a Collateral variation was that followed by the Lucero family of Atrisco. According to Don Daniel Lucero, the eldest brother in this family was never a successful leader. When dissension became acute he left the village, partly on his own decision and partly because he was prevailed upon by the others to do so. Don Daniel, the second son, was next in the line of command, but he refused this position of Lineal authority as he has all others. His own words were: "I don't think having one man boss is the best way to get along, so I never took my brother's place. We all just worked things out together."

The third and the most common pattern of resistance was one I have called "acquiescent irresponsibility." In psychological terms it might be called "passive resistance" insofar as it was not open rebellion against eldest-brother domination. But what these brothers did and the effects of their behavior for the social order of Atrisco were not at all passive. Characteristically they did the very minimum required of them in the operation of family economic affairs. They acquiesced completely in their acceptance of the eldest brother's right to make decisions and handle all property and livestock. Having thus greatly increased their own leisure time they took to amusing themselves. Several went often to Railtown on gambling and drinking sprees, and one could always count on a number of them appearing at the dances in the neighboring Texan community. This type of variant pattern had been a familiar one in Spanish-American life for a long time. It will be recalled that two of the younger Atrisco brothers were following it at the time Don Manuel was running the Atrisco family business and later after Don Juan took over. Other examples have been numerous. The difference in the decade of the thirties was that in seeking pleasure outside the community the younger brothers were coming more and more into contact with Anglo-Americans and the patterns of Anglo-American culture. These contacts gave much positive reinforcement to their own variant behavior.

All three of the patterns in different ways have long supported the dominant Lineal *relational* structure by offering an escape when the strains of that structure were felt too keenly. At the same time they were, as was pointed out in Chapter I, always a potential source of change in the *relational* order. When the external forces of Anglo-American economic and political pressures became sufficiently great to threaten seriously the *patrón* system,[10] the variation within the system gradually became linked to them, and a moving force for some kinds of *basic* change was created.

---

[10] Of the many types of pressure probably the most critical were the increasing political control of Anglo-Americans in the state as a whole and the steady absorption by Anglo-Americans of the good range lands and the fencing in of these lands.

The main targets against which this force was aimed were the positions of the *hermano mayor* and the *patrón*. Although still on the horizon, the figures of the autocratic *patrón* and the often domineering *hermano mayor* are now far out and almost lost to sight.

By 1936 it appeared to be inevitable that marked changes were soon to come in Atrisco's social order, and it was equally apparent that the people who were going to be the most instrumental in effecting the changes were the younger brothers and others who were, in one way or another, variants. These predictions made in the earlier study of Atrisco were the reason for adding to the questions asked in 1951 of Spanish-Americans on all *relational* orientation items the query, "What way do you think most people would have said was the right way thirty years ago?" When asked this question, all but two of the respondents said the domination of the eldest in a family or a *patrón* was the proper way. One young woman, who gave first choice to the Lineal alternative on almost all items of the *relational* orientation series, said she simply didn't know enough about the situation a generation ago to make a reply. One man, Jose Barrida, stated that it was necessary to go back fifty years, not thirty, to find a time when Lineal authority was really acceptable.

This man was the younger brother in one of the two sets of eldest and younger brothers that we were fortunate enough to have as respondents in Atrisco. Both brothers, Jose and Pancho, continued to be herders until 1957, and it was they whom Fred Atrisco and I had to search for far out on the sheep range (see Chapter III). Jose was the first we were able to find. He was most cooperative and answered most of the questions with measured solemnness, but whenever a question was put to him on family work relations or property, he grew tense and bitter and gave firmly toned and emphatic Individualistic responses. When Fred would then ask him what would have been considered the right way thirty years ago his reply was: "It should have been just the same, for there is too much fighting among brothers for them ever to get along. You have to go back fifty years to find a time when it was good for an *hermano mayor* to run things. Maybe not even then." He said that most persons thirty years ago would have probably said it was best to have the *hermano mayor* run things, but he knew it wasn't right even then. Jose, fifty-six years of age in 1951, had known well the meaning of an *hermano mayor's* domination for well over the thirty years in question. Although I have no definite evidence, my suspicion is that Pancho, the bachelor *hermano mayor* mentioned above, had in the past asserted his authority to the extent of having, or at least trying to have, sexual relations with Jose's wife.

A few hours after the interview with Jose, Fred and I found Pancho, who was then sixty-six years old. As was mentioned previously (Chapter III), he was crippled from arthritis and was in such pain that it took him a very long time to comprehend and answer our questions. But when he did answer, he was just as firm in his beliefs as Jose had been; yet how different those beliefs were! Certainly, he declared, everyone believed a generation ago that the eldest brother should manage all family business, and he himself believed strongly that it was still the only right and proper way to run things. He knew that other people now felt differently but thought they would incline much more to the Collateral arrangement than to the Individualistic one.

The two other brothers who stood in this relationship were two men from one of the outlying settlements who had moved into Atrisco just prior to 1951. One, in fact, still spent most of his time in the little hamlet some twenty-five miles north of Atrisco. Until 1950 these two brothers and a brother-in-law carried on a small livestock business together. Apparently there were quarrels and disagreements in this case too, for each was, in 1951, intending to go "on his own." The younger of these two brothers, like Jose Barrida, gave clear-cut Individualistic responses to the family work and inheritance questions. The eldest brother made his choice in favor of *hermano mayor* control in family work relations. On the two questions of inheritance he chose the Collateral response and commented that it would be the best way to resolve present-day difficulties in such matters.

When examined carefully and scrutinized for variation between the sexes, the answers of all the Spanish-Americans to the questions on the *relational* orientation reveal much which further substantiates the predictions made about change in Atrisco's *relational* system. For example, it will be remembered that it was in matters of inheritance and the management of family property that the community as a whole showed the most definite shift to an Individualistic position. But if we separate the answers of the men and women, we find that the latter, who had had little or nothing to do with economic affairs and hence had not been subjected to the strains that men—especially those men who were younger brothers—had felt, tended much more than the men to cling to the older patterns. Nine of the twelve men gave Individualistic first-order responses; only six of the eleven women selected this position for a first choice. And it should also be noted that the three men who did not favor the Individualistic mode were the two eldest brothers just discussed and Don Daniel Lucero who has always been a consistently Collateral variant.

The men again were predominantly Individualistic in their responses to the items on family work relations and wage work. Besides the two eldest brothers in the eldest brother–younger brother pairs, the only men who chose the Lineal alternative were two quite young men, one of whom is the eldest brother in his family and the other the eldest brother among those in his family who still live in Atrisco. Only four women thought family work should be organized in accord with the Individualistic *relational* principle, and six held fast to the Lineal position.

In matters of community decision, which the questions on "Well Arrangements" and "Choice of Delegate" referred to, the overall response was much less Individualistic. On the first of these questions there was only one more Individualistic than Lineal first-order choice, and no consistent rank-order pattern was found in the responses. For selecting a delegate all but six of the respondents took the Collateral alternative for their first choice. The discovered rank-order pattern was $\text{Coll} \geqslant \text{Ind} \geqslant \text{Lin}^*$.

Although in general there is considerable doubt about the worth of the delegate-selection item for discriminating the variation between and within the five cultures tested, it did prove to be most illuminating for the analysis of change in the Spanish-American group. The recent emergence of a first-order preference for the Collateral position in community affairs, and most particularly in political matters, was fairly definite and was well recognized by the people themselves. Moreover, the reason for the preference for it in 1951, and into the present time, is a result of the influence of one markedly variant person, Don Daniel Lucero. It has been remarked previously that in spite of the fact that many persons, directly and indirectly, urged Don Daniel to assume the *patrón* role back in the thirties, he always evaded it. In quite recent times he has been more or less forced to become the leader in what remains of the political life in Atrisco because there is no one else who has both the age and the social prestige for the position. But Don Daniel is no *jefe politico* of the kind so long prominent in Spanish-American culture. Just as he would not become a typical *hermano mayor* he has not become a typical *patrón*. His own definite first-order Collateral orientation (on six of the seven *relational* orientation questions he selected the Collateral alternative) has brought changes in the political roles of everyone. This case illustrates well the influence which the variant of a former period can exert in a period of change.

When I was first in Atrisco in 1936, many persons commented on Don Daniel's variation. It was well recognized even then that he was not favorably disposed to Lineally defined authority roles, and many remarks were also made on his patterns of behavior which in the terms of value-orientation theory revealed him to be strongly Doing rather than Being in his position on the *activity* orientation. His behavior at the present time as a leader and the effect it is having are also well understood. One of Don Juan Atrisco's sons who is still living near Atrisco made this remark:

When my dad used to run things he chose the delegates—you remember how it was. But old Daniel just isn't that kind of man. He wants everybody to take a hand in things. He doesn't like running things himself and being a boss. So now when it comes to politics there is lots of discussion, and people say what they think. Of course lots of times they go along with what he thinks anyway.

Fred Atrisco made similar comments to me and further remarked that Don Daniel had been trying to get him to say he would be willing to serve as a delegate. According to him, Don Daniel is willing to play the role of leader if others will work along with him, but he doesn't care for politics and dislikes going to the county seat for political meetings.

An interesting fact about this situation is that almost everyone interviewed expressed great approval of this different way of running the political affairs of the village. There is considerable evidence for the argument that there has always been a powerful Collaterality in Spanish-American culture—and in the culture of Old Mexico as well—which has been throttled by a superimposed Lineality. Neither the authority of the *patrón* (*jefe politico*) nor that of *hermano mayor* has been a legitimate authority by Chester Barnard's definition of authority.[11] Neither has ever been really

[11] See *Functions of the Executive* (Cambridge, Mass.: Harvard University Press, 1938), Chap. XII.

well accepted by those who are "the governed"; hence it has been necessary to use both force and deception to maintain the two positions.

There is not time in this monograph to treat the many aspects of general Mexican history which would have to be considered before the full story of the building of the Mexican Lineal system could be told. I will only remark that the Spanish type of Lineality which was brought to the New World and for which a counterpart was found among some Indian groups of Mexico—most particularly among the powerful though certainly not all-supreme Aztecs—did have two main sources for the legitimation of its authority.[12] These were the Spanish Crown and the Roman Catholic Church. Many groups of people were exploited under Spanish rule, but never to the extent that they have been in many of the political regimes since the 1821 revolution. Both Crown and Church always evidenced some consideration for the welfare of those they controlled. Once the *mestizos*, a half-caste people who had no real stake in either the Spanish or the Indian social system, gained control of the Mexican government, they repudiated both Crown and Church as sources of authority. They kept the dominant Lineal *relational* structure but gave to it a basis of an almost complete personalism and nepotism. The long regime of Porfirio Diaz, which was broken only twice and briefly in thirty-four years, was one of the most extreme examples of nepotistic Lineality known to history. And in spite of the revolutions of 1911 and later, which broke this particular regime, one sees much in recent Mexican history that is reminiscent of the Diaz type of control. Many of the plans and dreams of Mexico's early twentieth century revolutionaries were as of 1951 either still mere dreams on paper or had been realized only partially. A Being, Subjugated-to-Nature, and Present-oriented people do not have many of the behavior patterns and attitudes necessary to the actualizing of their dreams and plans for reform. Certainly in the Mexican case it is easy to see that the tendency is for the people to become again the easy victims of the Diaz-type personalities which their system creates.

In New Mexico the story has been much the same, with the difference that this type of Lineal authority appeared at even an earlier date than it did in Old Mexico. *Mestizo* control came earlier in New Mexico, at least in large parts of it, because the colony was a much too forlorn outpost of the Empire for men of the conquistador type to remain long in it. While it is true that some of the *patrones* of New Mexico inherited land grant properties and thus had a more legitimate right to their authority than persons like Don Juan Atrisco, there has been little difference in the methods all *patrones* have used to maintain their control. Almost all of them (there

---

[12] The conceptions of social organization and land tenure brought to the New World by the Spaniards were not, of course, wholly Lineal in type. The communal village system was well established in Spain by the time of the conquest, and in many parts of Mexico the Spaniards simply legalized the communal-type settlements they found and applied their own terms and legal forms to them. They also actually established some new collective settlements. For an excellent treatment of the two kinds of *relational* principles and reinterpretation of them in the Mexican scene see George McCutchen McBride, *The Land Systems of Mexico* (New York, 1923). See also Lesley Byrd Simpson, *The Ejido: Mexico's Way Out* (Chapel Hill, N. C., 1937).

have been exceptions, of course) have consistently "used" their own people for self-aggrandizement by the triple means of intimidation, deception, and economic indebtedness. Debt peonage was so great in New Mexico at the time the United States took over the territory that the government undertook to outlaw it by a Congressional Act in 1867. In most villages the Act had as few immediate effects as it did in Atrisco where Don Juan kept many people tied to him through indebtedness well into the twenties.

But even with this kind of Lineal control one must take care lest the picture is drawn too black. *Los patrones* of New Mexico always also assumed many responsibilities for the people under their control. Don Juan, for example, seldom allowed any of those who actually worked for him to go without basic food supplies. He also managed, more or less completely, the affairs of many families and gave advice to others; he would occasionally take the ill or dying to doctors or hospitals in Railtown if requested (actually medical attention was seldom sought); and either he or members of his family performed many minor services as well. It was services such as these which many *los Atrisqueños* were seeking from their substitute *patrones* in the year 1936. The habits of dependence which a majority of Spanish-Americans—and Mexicans—are taught early and thoroughly by their family system, by *patrón* control, and by a very paternalistic type of Catholicism are not easily abandoned.

There is no question that Lineality has been until quite recently the dominant *relational* orientation in Spanish-American society; yet it appears equally certain that there was also always a strong second-order Collaterality. In fact, it is doubtful that the village communities could have survived under the kind of *patrón* domination most of them knew had there not been a substantially ramified and well recognized Collaterality. *Los patrones* themselves knew there were many things they could not do because of a unified community resistance. For example, although it was well known and accepted that many *patrones* sought sexual relations with the wives of transient herders, with Indians, or other outsiders, the majority, if not all of them, knew better than to approach a woman within the community. A *patrón's* great neglect of the needs of the persons dependent upon him or his too excessive aggressiveness toward community members also often called forth sufficient passive resistance and concerted criticism to produce an effective brake upon his actions.

Mainly, however, the tightly knit Collateral relations served both as a cushion which softened the strains produced by the Lineal domination and as a channel of actual escape from them. And in both respects the relationships were so well geared to the dominant Lineal system that they actually served as a support for it as long as the total *relational* order was not subjected to powerful external influences for change. That they became well geared and remained so for such a long time was in part, of course, an effect of the other orientations in the culture.

Before concluding this brief sketch of Atrisco's social organization, past and present, some attention must be given to the "class" problem which so concerns social scientists today. It should be obvious that, when viewed in quite general terms, the class system of the Spanish-American villages was a twofold one. One family, the *patrón* family, constituted the top class, and all other families to one degree or another were subject to its control. But in saying to one degree or another, we imply differentiations, and there certainly were some differentiations of which the people themselves had an awareness.

A main distinction was always the degree of interrelatedness the individual or family had. Such a distinction was, of course, just an extension of the one made between permanent and transient members of the population. Transients were separated off because unrelated, and members of the permanent population gained in prestige to the degree they were related to other village families. Other factors sometimes offset the prestige thus awarded, but never was the effect upon general status completely erased.

In discussing the class structure in the earlier study of Atrisco we noted that the people of the village tended usually to have some awareness of differences in economic levels and also of the differences in amounts of known Indian blood. The basis of the economic distinction was the line drawn between those families which had livestock holdings, however small, and those which depended solely upon the wage work of their male members for their income. But it was also noted that this was seldom a firm or a permanent line of differentiation. It was all too frequently the case that a family which was a stock-owning family in one five to ten year period would have fallen to the wage-earning group in the next similar period, or the wage earner would have acquired some stock. Moreover, this kind of occupational distinction did not often break down the prestige based upon degree of relatedness.

Neither did the distinction by blood have much permanent effect upon general status. Partly because of their own past history, but mainly because Anglo-Americans made the Spanish-Indian distinction into a political firebrand, New Mexico Spanish-Americans became self-conscious about the distinction.[13] Although few Spanish-Americans either can or do claim to be pure Spanish in their blood heritage, there is a highly defensive attitude about being part Indian. They frown upon intermarriage with Indians and, when it occurs, express their disapproval by stigmatizing the children of the union with the terms *lobo* and *coyote*. We have seen how the *patrón* family took great care to marry off their Hopi Indian girl to another Indian outside the community. As one woman remarked to me, "A girl like that has to marry who she is told to." Yet in spite of some resistance two of the children of this union married into one of the old and well established village families. In another case, to be discussed below, the resistance was greater still, but the marriage was also finally allowed. The line of distinction by blood is not easily held and seldom remains an issue for very long.

But the case for the difference between the Spanish-American stratification system and one like that found generally in the United States does not

---

[13] Politicians have used the theme of "a splendid Spanish heritage" as a vote-getting device. The aim was to flatter the Spanish-Americans who were given the franchise when New Mexico became a state in 1912 and distinguish them from the Indians who had not been given it. This is one of the reasons that the term Mexican is so disliked and the term Spanish-American preferred by the Spanish-speaking New Mexicans.

rest simply, or even largely, upon the kinship-occupational distinction. In Chapter I it was suggested that variations in value orientations would lead to a variation in emphasis of the several behavior spheres. It was also pointed out that one should expect in the Spanish-American (or Mexican) case a high evaluation of the two spheres of the recreational and religious. One test of whether this really is the case is to look at the importance of prestige and power in this area and its influence upon general status of the social-class type.

It has already been remarked that one of the most important steps taken by Don Juan Atrisco in establishing his *patrón* position was to create a church for the village and make arrangements for services in it. And it was noted that even though he "gave" the church to the community, he never let anyone forget it was his to control. He was, for example, the only citizen of Atrisco who had the liberty to bury deceased members of his family under the earthen floor of the church. Moreover, Don Juan never completely lost his overall *patrón* power; he and his family continued to control most of the church activities and most particularly the annual *fiestas*. Don Juan himself returned with some vestiges of his old glory each year when the *fiesta* was held. And since his death in 1958 members of his family have continued to carry on the *fiesta* celebrations.

Since nothing else compares to *fiestas* as a source of interest for the vast majority of Spanish-Americans or Mexicans, it is logical that those who control them and have the positions of power in arranging them should be the persons of greatest prestige and general power. In New Mexico today this kind of prestige and power is waning rapidly but is still far from gone.

THE MAIN FEATURES OF THE ECONOMY OF ATRISCO AND THE CHANGES OCCURRING IN IT

For analyzing the work habits and spending patterns, the attitudes toward property, and the conceptions of the job world which *los Atrisqueños* had in the thirties—and the changes to be noted here and there in all of these—the rank ordering of each range of orientations has an almost equal significance. But it is well first to recall the answers these people gave to the questions on the *activity* orientation, for these questions more definitely than others tested for the relative evaluation of the work world. Most especially they tested for the comparative evaluation of the economic and recreational behavior spheres. To a degree unmatched by any other group in our sample, the Spanish-Americans selected the Being alternative of the *activity* orientation. This result had been predicted mainly on the basis of the quite extensive analysis made previously of the economic activities in Atrisco. In addition there was corroborative evidence from the few studies made of Spanish-Americans in other parts of New Mexico. The *Tewa Basin Study*, for example, contains many kinds of data on income and expenditures, on jobs and property ownership, which are in agreement with our predictions and findings. Note also this statement made in 1941 by

Leonard and Loomis about the evaluation of work on the part of the people of El Cerrito, a Spanish-American village far removed in space from Atrisco:

Among the native people the values attached to such practices as thrift and hard work as ends in and of themselves have never attained the importance they have with other groups of people. These natives are able to see neither sin nor moral corruption in idleness and leisure time. They neither see virtue nor common sense in keeping busy for the sake of occupying the hands and mind. Work is simply a means of accomplishing that which is valued or desired, and as such these people realize its importance. It is not believed that it adds to the moral fiber of the individual. Furthermore, the mere accumulation of material goods adds little to the popular esteem for an individual. The prestige of the man *depends in no small measure upon his contribution to the fiestas or his activities in the political life and interests of the group* [italics ours].

Contacts with the Anglo-American in recent decades have somewhat affected the attitude of the natives toward hard work and thrift, especially with regard to the latter. Contacts with this new element have convinced them that the emphasis placed upon thrift and hard work by the Anglo has substantially accelerated his progress in New Mexico. It has brought about a general recognition of the need for a greater emphasis upon these practices in order to meet competition successfully.

But these new contacts have failed to alter the social contexture of the village life of these natives. And apparent changes are superficial, scarcely touching the deeper convictions of the people. The real alterations in attitude apparently come from the realization of the need for adaptations in order to compete more successfully in a struggle which to date has been almost disastrous.[14]

Contrary to what many strongly job-oriented Anglo-Americans think, Spanish-Americans are not at all lazy, and they have, by and large, been responsible workers if the definition of responsibility is relative to their own rather than Anglo-American value orientations. Mainly, theirs has been responsibility of dependent behavior which does not require long-range planning or much initiative for the overcoming of obstacles. While Individualism, the Doing *activity* orientation, a Mastery-over-Nature position, and a Future *time* orientation are more apparent in aspects of the economic activities of Spanish-Americans than anywhere else in their day-to-day life, these orientations have been clearly subordinate to the dominant orientations of the culture. Thus, not only has the economic sphere as a whole been less important to Spanish-Americans than the recreational-religious one, but also all patterning in the economic sphere has been such as to maintain the superordinate-subordinate relationship of the two spheres over a long time period.

The quite extensive and detailed data on this patterning collected in 1936 and 1937 and subsequent checkings of them since then cannot here be analyzed in full. Therefore, I shall, after a brief treatment of the type of economy and effect of the land problem upon it, discuss in a summary fashion the topics of property ownership and attitudes toward it, income and expenditures, and family work patterns and their relation to the *patrón* system. In the discussion of each of these, all changes or indications of

[14] *Op. cit.*, p. 17.

208 VARIATIONS IN VALUE ORIENTATIONS

probable change which have been noted in recent years will be analyzed and related to the schedule results recorded in Chapter V.

A Livestock Economy on an Insecure Land Base

Small plot irrigation farming and the raising of livestock were the twin interests in the agricultural economy of New Mexico's Spanish-American villages. Although both pursuits were customarily carried on simultaneously by many of the families in a large number of the villages, it not infrequently happened that only one of them was of much importance to the general economy of a village. A number of the communities reported on in the *Tewa Basin Study* in 1939 had few or no families that owned livestock. The extremely meager living which could be derived from tiny plots of a few acres of irrigable land had to be augmented by other activities, usually wage work. To obtain this work, men of the villages often had to go far afield and become itinerant wage workers in the beet fields of Colorado or on the sheep ranges of Wyoming. In other villages, like Atrisco, the raising of small herds of sheep or cattle or working as herders and rangers for large stockholders were the main sources of family income, and farming activities were negligible in importance. This kind of pattern, still mainly at a mere subsistence level because the majority of families owned only a very few head of stock, became increasingly possible after 1880 when the use of United States currency (there had never been a stable currency of any kind prior to 1846 when the United States took over New Mexico) and the railway constructed by Anglo-Americans facilitated the marketing of livestock.

Los Atrisqueños in the first few years of their community settlement did engage in some irrigation farming. In one canyon, water from a spring was used for a very small amount of it, and more was developed quite near the present site of the village where it was possible to build small dams to catch and hold water in arroyos. But these dams did not hold for long, and no one bothered to build them anew. The livestock business was growing; it was also becoming increasingly possible to buy supplies in the two towns along the railway which were rapidly growing into important trading centers. It was not critically necessary to struggle with a water supply that was always doubtful because it was dependent upon man-made dams and an uncertain rainfall rather than a natural stream. And as for dry farming, it was simply not in the agricultural patterns of Spanish-Americans, at least not until very recently.

Actually, dry farming has not proved to be a reliably successful operation in most parts of New Mexico for anyone. And particularly in the Rimrock region it is a most precarious business, as the Texans in the neighboring community have learned in the thirty-odd years of their efforts to make Homestead the Bean Capital of the World.[15] A few of the families in Atrisco in the thirties did plant small plots with *frijoles* (the New Mexican pinto bean) or with corn, but they did not bother to cultivate these plots to

[15] See Evon Z. Vogt, *op. cit.*

any extent, and they expressed small concern over the outcome of their efforts. As one man remarked to me, "Oh yes, I plant a little each year. If it grows, all right—if it doesn't, all right too." Ideas about crop yields were also extremely vague in the minds of most Atrisco men. For example, one of the owners of a small *ranchito* stopped one day to talk to a Texan farmer about his bean crop. He looked out over the field and said, "How many beans did you plant?" When the Texan replied that he had put in eighty acres, the man from Atrisco said, "No, I don't mean that; how many *beans* did you plant?" The bean farmer then said that he had used sixteen hundred pounds of beans, or roughly sixteen sacks. A puzzled look came to the face of the Spanish-American of Atrisco, and he solemnly said, "Will you get that many back when you pick them?" In the conversation that followed it was revealed that he himself had planted approximately three hundred pounds of beans on three acres of land and was hopefully looking forward to a harvest of another three hundred pounds of fresh beans for his winter larder. The Texan farmer who told me this story was much amused because his farming methods, which were geared to the production of a marketable crop, called for a seeding of twenty pounds of beans to the acre.

A change has come in these views of farming even though there still is little interest in farming and also still a strong belief that the territory in which Atrisco and Homestead are located can never be satisfactorily used for dry farming. Although the answers to the item in the *man-nature* series on Use of Fields (MN3) yielded the characteristic pattern with the Subjugated-to-Nature alternative in first-order position, a marked drift toward the Over-Nature position can be noted. Ten of the twenty-three respondents selected this position as their first choice. The pattern derived from all responses was the Subj $\geqslant$ Over $\geqslant$ With* one.

Statements made to me at the time of the interviewing program and recently collected information on farming activities fully corroborate the results of the schedule. For example, the man who had much trouble in 1936 in understanding the Texan farmer's planting techniques was one of those who most definitely thought that good care and the use of new scientific methods would serve to overcome many of the effects of bad conditions on crops. Moreover, he talked at some length on the subject after stating his choice, and he gave illustrations of some of the new methods being used and the crop rotation programs being followed by two of the Atrisco men. He attributed the change to the influence of the Texans of Homestead.

Crop data collected in 1952 (a year after the administration of the value-orientation schedule) showed that seven men, a number that included almost all of the heads of families remaining in Atrisco, had 160 acres planted in corn, 185 acres in beans, 15 acres in wheat, and 30 acres in oats. No information was obtained as to actual yields, but the investigator gathering the data remarks:

Spanish-American yields are unknown but since this group learned dry farming techniques from Texans, who have had a great deal of experience in this type of agriculture, their yields might be expected normally to run a little higher than those of the Indians. Such superiority is by no means certain, however, as in other parts of the state Indians are sometimes better and more progressive than their Spanish-American neighbors.[16]

Whatever the yields may have been, it is a striking fact that this number of acres was planted by the very few men who then lived in Atrisco. In 1936 the acreage and yields of all twenty-one "economic family" units were completely negligible and accounted for only a tiny fraction of the total estimated "goods in kind" income.

In the year between November, 1935, and November, 1936, ten of the twenty-one units defined as "economic families" either owned livestock or operated a livestock business on a *partida* (share) basis.[17] Three of these I classified as large-herd operators and seven as small-herd operators. Another ten units were classified as wage-earning families. In a majority of these the wage-earning men worked full or part time for either the Anglo-owned Dennis Sheep Company or for one of the large-herd operators. Odd jobs such as work on the vocational school and in a C.C.C. camp were also occasional sources of income for some of them. The remaining unit, the Vidrio family, derived most of its income from the operation of the trading store.

The Vidrio family unit and the three units classified as large-herd operators were categorized as Economic Class I; the seven economic units with small herds constituted Economic Class II; and the ten wage-earning families were grouped together as Economic Class III. These divisions seemed to fit best with the attitudes the people themselves had about economic status, even though in some cases the actual income of the wage-earning families was higher than that of the families operating small herds of sheep or cattle. For, as was mentioned earlier, there has always been some real prestige value in the ownership of livestock even though it has counted less than other factors in evaluating the position of a family.

Thus, we see that the economy of the village in 1936 was almost completely a livestock economy. It was still mainly so in 1951 in spite of some increase of interest in farming. Five of the nine men interviewed who were heads of families actually had livestock holdings; two were herders for the Atrisco family; one worked at various jobs on the range for the Dennis Sheep Company. Pablo Atrisco, who ran a saloon near Homestead, was the only one of the older men who had nothing at all to do with livestock. The three young and unmarried men in the sample of twelve male respondents worked occasionally with livestock, but in the winter months they were usually away from Atrisco on other kinds of jobs.

Early in Atrisco's history sheep, which produce the double crop of lambs and wool, were the preferred animals. By 1936 there was a growing tendency to favor cattle over sheep. Three stock owners in that year had cattle only, and two others ran both sheep and cattle. This preference was stronger still in 1951. All of the stock owners with the exception of the

[16] Marion St. John, "Three Southwestern Non-Anglo Economies," unpublished report on file in the office of the Values Project, p. 12.
[17] The November-to-November year was used because livestock were usually sold in the autumn, and the accounts were balanced by November.

Atrisco family had cattle only. However, because of the size of the Atrisco family holding, the actual number of sheep was three times that of cattle. Fred Atrisco was running a thousand-odd head of sheep and in addition had around eighty head of cattle. Only two of the other four stock owners had herds of any size at all. Daniel Lucero had one hundred head of cattle. Frank Zamorra, one of the men who had sold out in 1936, was back on the range with one hundred head of cattle, but both the land he was using and the animals he had in 1951 were mortgaged so heavily that it is doubtful that he should have been called an owner at all.

One of the reasons sheep used to be preferred over cattle was their greater natural durability, for even as late as 1936 the stockmen of Atrisco had much the same attitude in the handling of livestock that they had about the planting and cultivating of farm crops. The sheep they raised were a scrub type, and as with the crops the attitude was very much the one of "If they live, all right; but if they don't, all right too."

Highly bred stock was not thought a good risk because it could not stand up under adverse environmental conditions or disease over which it was thought man had small control. None of the stock owners, not even those with fairly large holdings, fed stock with cottonseed cake or other feeds in the severe winter months as most Anglo-American stockmen have done. Whenever excessively deep snow made it impossible for the animals to find range fodder, they were just left to die. That was the way life was. Also, although Don Juan Atrisco had dipping vats for sheep by 1936, no others did, and no one of the owners including the Atriscos did very much by way of trying to control the diseases which were always a problem and sometimes struck with real vengeance.

By 1952 there were definite changes in these attitudes. Some of the stockmen had begun to pay much more attention than they did formerly to the quality of their sheep and cattle. According to the St. John report the rams and bulls used in 1952 by the Atrisco family for the breeding of their sheep and cattle were of quite good quality. Also, the report states that in general the sheep of the Spanish-Americans were found to be much superior to those of the Indian groups. About the cattle there was less certainty of a general improvement, since the only herd seen by St. John, other than that of the Atrisco family, was the one owned by Don Daniel Lucero who still "does not believe in herd improvement." Extra feed for livestock was sometimes purchased, and the majority of the men also consulted at times with the county agricultural agent and even with persons in the United States Department of Agriculture office in Albuquerque about matters of livestock breeding and control of disease. In 1936 there had been almost no use of the information or services of either of these agencies.

In addition to these changes in operating procedures there was also a much increased concern about conditions and prices in the lamb, wool, and cattle markets as well as much more information about them. In the thirties most of the families (the Atrisco and Lucero families were an exception) customarily depended upon a trader to market their livestock. Seldom did they have direct contacts with buyers; they even doubted the wisdom of such contacts since two of the men who had attempted to market their stock directly had been very badly cheated.[18]

These changes, some only slight but others more marked, are reflected in the ranking pattern of preferences for the three positions on the *man-nature* orientation for the schedule item (MN1) which definitely referred to the care of livestock—the Over $\geqslant$ Subj $>$ With pattern. But neither the observations of current behavior nor the answers to the items of the schedule give evidence of a strong preference for the Mastery-over-Nature position in any area of behavior. Nine of the twenty-three persons tested still selected the Subjugation-to-Nature position as the preferable one even on this technologically oriented item.

The changes are also in part an expression of the shift in the *relational* orientation. The increasing dominance of the Individualistic over the Lineal conception of family work relations and the management of land and livestock (see items R3, R6, and R7) is clearly corroborated by the observed increase of the individual operator's contacts with buyers, with outside agencies, and even with banks. However, the alterations in operating procedures must still be looked upon more as a trend than a definite and already accomplished shift in patterns. In addition to the fact that the Individualistic *relational* orientation was not found to be as yet markedly dominant and the emphasis upon the Over-Nature alternative of the *man-nature* orientation was clearly only second order except for the one technological item, there is that tenacious clinging to the Being *activity* orientation which makes Spanish-American work habits very different from those of Anglo-Americans.

Although more of the men stated a preference for the Doing alternative on the questions relating to farm work and the use of leisure time than would have been the case in the thirties, there is considerable evidence for stating that a real shift on this orientation will be a long time in coming. For example, Fred Atrisco, who even by dominant Anglo-American standards is quite a conscientious worker, stated a preference for the Being alternative on all the questions asked on the *activity* orientation. He subsequently accurately evaluated what he actually does as expressing much more the Doing alternative but commented that he did not really like the feeling of being compelled to pay so much attention to his business affairs and "thought the other way much better." Then there was the reverse case of Frank Zamorra, the man described earlier (Chapter III) as the only strikingly deviant person in Atrisco, who as his value preference selected consistently the Doing alternative and then stated several times, "but of

---

[18] O. Leonard and C. P. Loomis describe almost identical economic attitudes and practices in El Cerrito in 1939. They comment as follows (*op. cit.*, pp. 12–13):

"This people have little interest in outside trade agreements and the current prices of farm products. No attempt is made to keep abreast of the fluctuations in the outside markets except the one big sheepman whose sole interest is in the current price of wool...."

"The County Agent is a stranger to the local people. It is doubtful if a single villager knows his name. The general opinion is that he exists only for the bigger farmers and stockmen, that he has neither the time nor the interest to help them with their problems."

course I don't act that way myself." This, too, was a most accurate self-appraisal of actual behavior. Three other men—two of them the Barrida brothers, long-time sheepherders—also selected the Doing alternative as "better" in some instances, most particularly in the matter of the better way to spend "nonworking time," but stated that a persistent sticking to work interests was not their way. They felt the need of periodically breaking away from the job and going on prolonged "bats." The eldest of the herders further remarked that he really only thought the Doing alternative "better" because he was now so old there wasn't much left for him but work. A year after interviewing this man I encountered him in the home of his niece in Railtown where he was slowly recovering from the effects of a three-week self-assumed "vacation." All other men in the sample gave answers which indicated they actually behaved in the way they thought the better one. Except for Don Daniel Lucero, who has always been a consistently Doing-oriented person, the majority of the answers favored the Being alternative. Two men were mixed cases, and there is much corroborative data to support their view of themselves. Thus we see that, although variation certainly existed, the Being orientation was still in 1951 quite definitely the dominant one, and indications of a shift in position in the near future were few. It is interesting to note that the answers of the women to the question of how men should spend their "nonworking time" were in large part responsible for the fact that the variation in the Doing direction for this question was much greater than on any of the others. It is the more interesting when one notes that on a question of how women should make use of their own nonworking time (item A5) only one favored the Doing alternative. Off the job the Spanish-American man so often drinks heavily, and many also gamble as well. The women have accepted this behavior but have never liked it when it becomes excessive.

It is evident that although there is a definite elaboration of patterning in the economic behavior sphere of life in Atrisco which indicates that some change has already occurred in the value-orientation system, it is an elaboration that is unevenly distributed over the various aspects of the village livestock economy. It is doubtful that the indicated further elaboration in the economic sphere of Spanish-American life will be very extensive in the livestock industry. Throughout New Mexico fewer and fewer Spanish-Americans each year engage in this business. They have lost their land.

Even before they lost control of vast areas of grazing land, the issue of land control, as has been previously remarked, was critical for most Spanish-American villages. The main facts about the land problem in Atrisco have already been given. But in order to relate better these facts to the livestock economy, I wish at this point to give some of the comparative details of the ownership and control of land for the year 1936, the period immediately following it, and the decade 1950–60.

Although the conceptions of land acreages and range limits had always been extremely vague, there was a general idea in the minds of *los Atrisqueños* in 1936 of an Atrisco area. This total area comprised slightly more than 421 sections of land (approximately 269,500 acres) and extended a number of miles in all directions from the village itself. The center of it was the range which had once been controlled by Don Juan Atrisco and had later passed into the hands of the Dennis Sheep Company. But it also included a range to the west, which members of the community wishing to escape Don Juan's domination had moved onto and which in 1936 was largely controlled by an Arizona sheep company; land to the north, part of which was owned by members of the community and part by a Spanish-American *patrón* of another area; and land to the south, much of which had been homesteaded by Texans in the years 1930–36. But control and ownership even in 1936 were not the same thing. As stated earlier, much of this land was still at that time owned in alternate sections by the Santa Fe Railway and some was still public domain. Specified sections in each township had also been set aside for the state of New Mexico for the purpose of providing income for schools. Tables VI:2 and VI:3 give the complete facts of ownership and control for the year 1936.

At a glance one sees that in 1936 approximately two-thirds of the total area was controlled by but was not yet the property of the two sheep companies—the Dennis Company and the company which had headquarters in Arizona. It had been twelve years (the foreclosure against Don Juan Atrisco was in 1924) since a large part of this area had been under the kind of *patrón* control to which Spanish-Americans were accustomed, but

TABLE VI:2
OWNERSHIP OF LAND IN ATRISCO AREA, 1936

Owner	Number of Sections	Percentage
Santa Fe Railway	227 6/8	54.1
United States	48 3/16	11.4
State of New Mexico	46 5/8	11.0
Texan homesteaders	53 3/8	12.7
Atrisco stockmen	21 15/16	5.2
Other Spanish-Americans	13+	3.2
Dennis Sheep Co.	3 1/2	0.8
All others	6 12/16	1.6
Total	421+	100.0

TABLE VI:3
CONTROL OF LAND IN ATRISCO AREA, 1936

Group or Agency	Number of Sections	Percentage
Dennis Sheep Co.	190	45.1
Arizona sheep company	86	20.4
Texan homesteaders	48 2/8	11.5
Atrisco stockmen	48 1/8	11.4
Other Spanish-Americans	5 6/8	1.4
All others, or not controlled	43 1/8	10.2
Total	421+	100.0

there had been no way of preventing the men of Atrisco from using much of it until the main ranges could be closed in. In 1936 and 1937 both companies achieved this goal. Six of the ten Atrisco stockowners were forced to liquidate their businesses and leave at that time. Three were able to find grazing land elsewhere, and Don Juan Atrisco, the tenth owner, still had his right to use the Dennis Company range.

Within a very few years two of those who had moved elsewhere liquidated their businesses. One became a herder for an Anglo-American stockman, the other moved to Railtown. The third one kept a small herd of cattle up to 1951 on land which he was able to lease under the provisions of the Taylor Grazing Act. However, the main job of this man in the year 1951 was in the ordnance depot in Railtown, and he only very occasionally went out to his small *ranchito*.

In the Atrisco area itself, in 1951, Daniel Lucero and Frank Zamorra were the only Spanish-Americans who owned enough land to graze as many as a hundred head of cattle, and as mentioned, Frank Zamorra did not really own the land. The Atrisco family's use of the range had also been curtailed by the man who had bought the land of the Dennis Sheep Company in the forties. Without at once repudiating the use right, the new owner both placed a ten-year limit on the contract and required that the herds of the Atrisco family be confined to a specified twenty-three sections of land. There was a verbal discussion, but no written commitment, about giving the Atriscos an option to buy these sections.

It seemed virtually certain as of 1951 that within five to ten years there would be no Spanish-American stockmen left in the area. Don Daniel stated he intended to sell his land since he knew none of his children would ever want to come back to use it; Frank Zamorra was on the verge of bankruptcy; and it was becoming more and more unlikely that the Atrisco family would be able to buy the sections they were using or to find other land. Land prices had gone too high, and Fred Atrisco was also having serious family troubles. The prediction appears to have been a correct one. According to information received in 1958, Fred Atrisco had sold his sheep and leased his cattle. He is now in Railtown. Frank Zamorra had also left by 1958, and Don Daniel Lucero had put all his land and livestock up for sale. The land base of another New Mexican village has been completely wiped out.[19]

The Total Property Holdings in Atrisco in 1936 and Attitudes Toward Property

Both in the kinds of property *los Atrisqueños* owned in 1936 and in their attitudes toward property holdings, one sees clearly the expression

---

[19] Additional information is that many of the Texans of Homestead are also leaving. Since they have been permitted to put their land in the soil bank, they will not give it up at once, but the overwhelming odds are that most of them will also be gone within a decade. Meanwhile the new owner of the Dennis Sheep Company and a rancher south of Atrisco are buying up more and more land. Except for a section here and there it is probable that these two ranchers will have control of the entire Atrisco area within a few years.

TABLE VI:4

PROPERTY HOLDINGS OF *los Atrisqueños*, 1936

Type of Property	Estimated Value	Percentage of Total Wealth
Land (and ranches)	$23,900[a]	34.7
Houses in Atrisco	2,600	3.7
Livestock	22,822	33.2
Business equipment, machinery, cars, etc.	5,680[b]	8.3
Personal property	5,810	8.4
Money, credits, etc.	8,026	11.7
Total	$68,838	100.0

[a] Includes two pieces of property outside Atrisco valued at a total of $620, owned by the family which was running the trading store.
[b] Includes equipment and inventory of Atrisco trading store (value of $2,000).

of the Spanish-American value orientations. Land and livestock holdings were, of course, the major types of property. Table VI:4 classifies the types of property, the estimated worth of each, and the percentage of the total wealth each type constituted.

Unimproved range land in the Atrisco area in 1936 was worth only about $1.00 an acre, but the stockmen of Atrisco had little or none of this type of land.[20] All land actually owned was in one way or another "improved land"—land on which there were some buildings, wells, or even, in some instances, windmills. The value of this land in 1936 was between $1.50 and $3.00 an acre. The estimated figure of $23,900 for the total holdings is based on evaluations made by officials in the county agricultural bureau in Railtown and in the United States Land Office in Santa Fe, after they had been given detailed descriptions of all individual holdings.

The livestock holdings included 654 head of cattle, 700 head of sheep, 85 horses, 187 hens, and one pig, all of which were evaluated in accord with prices then current—a total of $22,822.

The total of $5,680 estimated for all business equipment included a sum of $2,000 for the equipment and supplies in the trading store. One can easily imagine both the quantity and quality of ranch and farm equipment when it is noted that all such equipment owned by the ten families which had livestock businesses was worth about $3,000. Bridles, saddles, harness, axes, old and rusty plows, a wagon here and there, and an old and much dilapidated car were the chief items to be evaluated in this category.

The small houses owned by the villagers had a sale value of $75 to $350 for the structure itself (no family other than that of Juan Atrisco owned the land on which its house stood). In all of the houses of more than one room, there was a room set aside for a kitchen–dining room combination, and the other room or rooms were always bedroom–living rooms. Only one house in Atrisco, that of Don Juan Atrisco, had a room which could

---

[20] As of 1958 this land was selling for $5.00 or more an acre.

properly be called a living room in the Anglo-American sense. There were other houses large enough to have such a room, but no one seemed to want one. Household furnishings were also extremely simple. Typically one found one or two beds, pallet mattresses, a few chairs and tables, a cabinet or two, a few rugs (usually Navaho rugs), a stove, and a sufficient number of pans, tubs, dishes, kerosene lamps, and bedding to carry on fairly satisfactory household activities. The average value per family of these items was estimated at $100 to $150. Clothing which was also included in "personal property" varied greatly from family to family, but in no case, not even that of the family of the former *patrón*, was it elaborate or expensive.

The category "money and credits," which totaled $8,026, included money in the bank or otherwise invested by the Vidrios and Daniel Lucero, a cash sum which the Atrisco family had on hand after the sale of lambs, and the credits on trading store books which a few other families had. Over $6,000 of the total belonged to the Vidrios, the Luceros, and the Atriscos. Eight families had no surpluses of any kind; three families had between $400 and $600; three others had credits between $100 and $200; the remaining three had balances from $10 to $100. One other family—that of Luis Corona—showed a book credit of $2,530 at the end of the year which was soon demonstrated to be quite spurious; hence this credit item is omitted from the total. The Corona family had sold off livestock which they were operating on a *partida* basis and had no right to sell. When finally the books were audited, it was discovered that they were actually $5,000 to $6,000 in debt. If this indebtedness were to be included in the over-all balance of money and credits, the total for all families would have been only $2,000 or $3,000.

It is obvious from these facts alone that the typical *Atrisqueño* in 1936 had little inclination to save money or build up property holdings and obvious also that he had no ability for handling his own monetary affairs. With the exception of the Atriscos and Don Daniel Lucero, almost all stockmen of the village depended upon a trader or some other businessman to help them sell their stock and to manage all problems of annual surpluses or deficits. Some, when they had a surplus, buried or otherwise hid it. According to village rumor even the Atrisco family buried the occasional surplus they had. The only man who used a bank in the thirties was Don Daniel Lucero, and it is to be doubted that he put all of the money realized from cattle sales into the bank. Bankers, all of them Anglo-Americans, were not trusted, and neither the use of banks nor any kind of outside investment of money was understood. It takes more of a sense of Future *time* than the Spanish-Americans of New Mexico had in 1936, or even today, to comprehend the concept of interest on invested moneys.

Furthermore, the love of the dramatic and unusual, which has been so characteristic of Spanish-Americans and many Mexicans as well, has yielded many tales of buried treasure, pots of gold, and golden cities to be discovered. Almost all Spanish-American villages, Atrisco included, have their abandoned houses which are pitted throughout with the holes dug by generations of zealous treasure hunters. The Spaniards, centuries ago, came to Mexico and New Mexico in search of gold and hidden treasure, and their descendants have ever continued to seek it.

The mind of the Present-oriented Spanish-American has small comprehension of the notion of preserving and accumulating properties which can be handed down through the generations. In Atrisco the only kind of family property for which there was a sentimental attachment was the houses—houses built on land owned by someone else. In other parts of New Mexico the same feeling of attachment is felt for the tiny plots of irrigable land, but *los Atrisqueños* have no such land. Thus, all property except houses was viewed as temporal—here today and to be used while here, but very probably gone tomorrow. Even Don Daniel Lucero, who was a variant both in his degree of industry and his thriftiness, seemed skeptical that property could be made to last over time. His variant values did not include a Future *time* orientation. Once when I remarked to him that he was apparently going to do better by his children than his own father had by him, his reply was: "Oh, I don't know. I may be broke soon. That is the way it is out here."

The dissipation of estates has been common. The gambling, drinking, and playing of politics which caused the rapid dwindling of the property of the Atrisco family have already been described. In 1936 I saw the Zamorra family estate disappear like water down a drain. These properties, never as large as those of the Atrisco family at the height of its fortunes, were nonetheless considerable in value. They had been accumulated by the maternal grandfather who was French-Canadian—one of the men who escaped Don Juan Atrisco's economic domination by moving his livestock outside the range land which Don Juan controlled. This man's son, a bachelor, managed to keep most of the estate, chiefly livestock, intact for a number of years, and at the same time he endeavored to keep two nephews, the sons of his only sister, under control. When he was about forty, he died suddenly, and the control of the livestock passed to the nephews. The elder of the two is Frank Zamorra. For a few years Frank managed with his younger brother to maintain the family business. And he certainly was the most belligerent of the Atrisco stockmen in resisting the restrictions the manager of the Dennis Sheep Company was putting on the use of range land. But finally, when the fences went into place, he too was forced to leave; and like almost all the other stock owners he had made no plans for the moving of his cattle. Hurriedly he sought out the trader in Zuni who carried his account and asked for help in finding new range land. There was none to be had on such short notice. The only alternative was the selling of the cattle.

If the trader tried to convince the Zamorras to leave some of the money realized from the sale of the family livestock, he did not succeed. The bulk of the money was used by Frank himself in a drinking and gambling spree which went on for several months. Much of the remainder the younger brother quickly dissipated in a similar fashion. Within the short space of ten to twelve months almost the whole of the estate was gone. Frank, as noted above, has in recent years tried without much success to rebuild a livestock business. His brother is now in California where he and his wife both have routine factory jobs. Although this case is somewhat extreme both for the amount of money there was to be spent and the rapidity with which it was used up, it is quite typical of what has happened in many Spanish-American stock-owning families in the Southwest.

Income and Expenditures in 1936 and Family Patterns of Production and Consumption[21]

An economist would describe the Spanish-American standard of living as a "fixed" one. Just as there never was much planning for the accumulation of resources, there was little thought given to the increase of income for the improvement of either a family business or a family mode of living.

INCOME. The incomes of the Atrisco families in the thirties were extremely low even for a period of a national economic depression. The total gross income for the entire community for the year period of November, 1935, to November, 1936, was $36,035. Approximately $9,000 of this amount was used by stockmen for operating costs. However, this figure is misleading because a full half of the $9,000 was spent by Luis Corona who was fast running into numerous difficulties with the livestock company with which he had a *partida* contract. The average amount spent for livestock operations by all other stockmen was $600.

The net income, of which 81 per cent was a cash income and 19 per cent an income "in kind," totaled $26,576. Livestock and wool sales accounted for 54 per cent of the money income and wage work for another 25 per cent. The remaining 21 per cent was realized in the various ways mentioned previously. The two largest sources were the trading store which netted the Vidrio family $1,900 and the *cantina* from which the Atrisco family realized $400. The goods income included the few grain products raised for family consumption, the sheep and cattle slaughtered for home use, the chickens and eggs which some families had, the wood gathered for fuel, the estimated rental value of owned houses, and a few subsidies.

The range of family incomes was $316 to $4,645. The mean average income for the nuclear families which for the time period in question were functioning more or less independently was $1,025, and that of the "economic families" (combined family groups) was $1,746. The medians for the two family types were respectively $548 and $1,233.[22]

If one makes a division of income by the three economic classes which were crudely delineated for the analysis of property holdings, one finds a fairly good correlation of income level and the amount of property owned. Table VI:5 shows the totals of both the money and goods income for the three economic levels.

[21] I am indebted to Carle C. Zimmerman for guidance in the collection of the "family budget" data in the 1936 study.
[22] These averages are very similar to those reported in other studies of New Mexican Spanish-American communities in the period 1934–44. Cf. the *Tewa Basin Study*, Leonard and Loomis, *op. cit.*; and Ernest Maes, "The World and Cundiyo," *Land Policy Review*, U.S. Department of Agriculture, Bureau of Economics, March, 1941.

TABLE VI:5
GOODS AND MONEY INCOME BY CLASS DIVISIONS, 1936

Class	Total Net Income	Money Income	% of Total	Goods Income	% of Total	Average per Family
I (4 Families)	$13,025	$11,604	89.1	$1,421	10.9	$3,256
II (7 Families)	7,431	4,920	66.2	2,511	33.8	1,062
III (10 Families)	6,120	5,046	82.5	1,074	17.5	612

EXPENDITURES. The total amount expended by the village families for the year 1935–36 was $23,059. Approximately $18,000 of this was expenditure of money income, and the remainder was the approximate $5,000 which was the estimate for income in kind. The difference of approximately $3,500 between income and expenditures included the amount of credit or cash on hand which a very few families had at the end of the year, the money placed in the bank that year by Don Daniel Lucero, and a small amount invested by the traders.

In the categorizing of family expenditures for the year 1935–36 this item of surplus was omitted because it was never a stable item. In the year previous to 1935–36 the families as a group had a debit rather than a credit, and over the years the credit-debit balance had always been erratic.

By families the range of total expenditures was $321 to $3,815. The mean average for all families was $1,098; the median was $768. The average expenditure for the combined family units was $1,673 and the median $1,291. The small family units averaged $811 and had a median expenditure of $599.

Table VI:6 summarizes the total expenditures by category of item, and Table VI:7 summarizes them by both item and the three economic class divisions of the family units. Table VI:8 shows the per capita expenditures for the year.

FAMILY PATTERNS OF PRODUCTION AND CONSUMPTION. Both in the earning of a living and in the spending of an income the families of Atrisco in 1936 followed patterns of behavior which clearly showed the dominance of the Lineal *relational* orientation, the Being orientation, the Subjugated-to-Nature orientation, and the Present *time* orientation.

The concept of the independent family—the nuclear family of husband, wife, and children—existed but was so overlaid with patterns of dependent relationships that it was almost totally obscured. The typical pattern for the families owning livestock was that of a business managed by a father or an *hermano mayor* with other male members of the family accepting his guidance and authority. And as has been stated, usually this head of the family was in turn dependent for guidance upon a trader or some other

TABLE VI:6
Total Expenditures, 1936

Type of Expenditure	Money	Goods	Total	Percentage
Food	$7,243	$3,126	$10,369	45.0
Clothing	2,905	50	2,955	12.8
Housing	706	1,811	2,517	10.9
Special purchase	1,111		1,111	4.8
Liquor, tobacco, & gambling	2,352		2,352	10.2
All other	3,736	19	3,755	16.3
Total	$18,053	$5,006	$23,059	100.0

TABLE VI:7
Itemized Expenditures by Class Divisions, 1936

Type of Expenditure	Class I		Class II		Class III	
	Money	Goods	Money	Goods	Money	Goods
Food	$2,313	$946	$2,717	$1,653	$2,213	$527
Clothing	1,385	20	825	20	695	10
Housing	244	447	214	833	248	531
Special purchase	475		177		459	
Liquor, tobacco, & gambling	500		1,260		592	
All other	2,134	8	1,034	5	568	6
Totals	$7,051	$1,421	$6,227	$2,511	$4,775	$1,074
	$8,472		$8,738		$5,849	
Average per family	$2,118		$1,248		$585	

TABLE VI:8
Average Per Capita Expenditures, 1936

Item	Class I	Class II	Class III	Whole Village
Food	$109	$87	$80	$91
Clothing	47	17	21	26
Housing	23	21	23	22
Liquor & tobacco	17	25	17	20
Special purchase	16	3	13	10
All other	71	20	16	33

of the *patrón* substitutes who were sought out after Don Juan Atrisco lost his position of economic power.

The usual procedure in a majority of the families which actually owned stock, instead of operating on a share basis, was to have the trader in Zuni negotiate the sales and handle all money income. The animals and the wool both would be sold in the name of the family head; and the trading store account, also in the name of the family head, would be credited with the amount of cash income realized. Small amounts of money for incidental expenditures would be turned over to the stock owner, but the bulk of the income would be kept in an account against which the family charged their operating business costs and their household living costs. The trader had the various roles of sales representative, banker, advisor, merchant, and general intermediary.

There had been a period of several years just after Don Juan Atrisco had lost his economic control of the village that many of these families had tried to handle their own affairs. The trading store in Zuni at that time was owned by a man who knew little of the ways of Spanish-Americans. He attempted to treat Atrisco families as he would Anglo-American credit customers. The result was that in a few years he had on his books unpaid bills of several thousand dollars which he could not collect. In disgust and anger he shut off the accounts. Fortunately for the Atrisco families, just at the time he did this, he sold his business to a man who intuitively was far more understanding of the needs for control and guidance which Spanish-Americans had. This man, rather than simply charging off the accounts as losses, decided to try to salvage them by assuming at least a partial *patrón* role.

His own story is that within just three years most of the accounts were on the credit rather than the debit side of his ledger. He took over the management of sales, and he trained his clerks to watch the accounts for what they could stand in purchases. And according to what he has said, all the families accepted his direction. He even tells the story of men coming in and asking for items which were in plain view in the store (a large general store) and of being told that these items were not available, because the clerk, or he himself, knew the family account did not have a balance sufficient to permit such purchases.

The stockmen of Atrisco knew that this was his way of keeping them going year after year. They knew also that they were paying for such services. One of them in talking to Mrs. Vidrio one day said:

I really would like to trade here and I know that in Zuni I pay more for what I get than you charge. But it has to be this way because the store there "carries us." If a bad year comes we are carried to the next. Mr. Green keeps things straight for us, and besides he takes care of the selling of lambs and wool.

Whenever a family operated a livestock business on a *partida* contract, much the same pattern was followed, except that it was the owner of the livestock who had to assume a *patrón* role.

The wage-earning families of the village who had men in the hire of the Dennis Sheep Company (six of the eleven such families) were also carried in a similar fashion by the store which the Vidrios ran for the company. Very little actual cash ever went to any of the employees. Even the sums for mail-order purchases from the catalogues were often charged to the store accounts. The wage-earning families who had no *patrón* figure to watch their accounts were constantly in trouble. One, an extended family of a father and two married sons, tried to keep a credit relation in Zuni in 1936 but had it shut off after six months and subsequently had their credit in the Atrisco store shut off after a few weeks.

Interdependent relations within the family units themselves were numerous. It was always expected that closely related families would so share their income that all would be provided for in accord with the accepted standard of living. There could be no question of such a pattern in the cases where stock was owned and a recognized family leader—a father or an eldest brother—was in charge of the family business. But the pattern existed even in those families where the fathers of the separate nuclear families were wage earners in different kinds of jobs.

For example, in the year 1936 there was one extended family which consisted of a father and two married sons, all three of whom were hired as wage workers by different employers. The three nuclear family units maintained separate households, and if at any time all three of the men were working, there was a relatively independent use of the separate incomes. But always it was understood that food supplies, household goods, and even spending money were a common "larder" for the use of all three units. Actually, it seldom happened that all three men were simultaneously employed, and it was not for the lack of opportunity for employment that this was so. Instead there seemed to be a tacit assumption that if any two of the men could make the amount of money required for the maintenance of the three units, the third was free to "lay off" for a while and have a good time. After some weeks he then would again seek employment, and another of the three would take a vacation.

The first obvious fact revealed by the tables showing family expenditures is that the people of Atrisco, like most peoples of the world with low incomes, spent almost half of their incomes for food. Clothing and housing were next in order. But it must be noted that the percentage of expenditures for liquor and gambling almost equaled those for clothing and housing. It also proved necessary in working out the family budgets to incorporate a category of "special purchase" to take care of a highly characteristic spending pattern. Whenever a family did happen to have a small surplus which a trader or *patrón* could not control, or if it received a windfall of some kind, the overwhelming odds were that it would use the money immediately for some highly desired item. Sometimes it was used for a stetson hat or a fine pair of cowboy boots which one of the men particularly wanted; at other times it was spent for a musical instrument which one or more members of the family wanted. There was also in the decade of the thirties a growing tendency to put whatever extra money was available into a secondhand car. All too often these cars were in such a deplorable condition that they were virtually useless to the Spanish-American owners who lacked the experience or the gift for the repairing of machinery. However, they were cars, and they stood in front of houses as symbols of acculturation, just as Montgomery Ward and Sears Roebuck metal beds and kitchen ranges made pronouncements of material progress indoors.

No one of these sporadic and highly spontaneous purchases ever made much difference in the level of family living standards. The houses changed little, if at all; the kind and amount of food remained much the same; and there were only a very few signs of a growing concern about medical care, the education of children, the modernizing of the village, or any other of the countless things which are so characteristic of the Anglo-American.

When one looks at the economic patterns of Atrisco families in the decade of the 1950's (both those which remained in the village and those which have migrated), some changes are to be noted. A few of the changes would seem to be indicative of the slight shifts in the value-orientation emphases which the schedule administered in 1951 revealed; others seem much more to represent an adjustment to situations over which the Spanish-Americans themselves have little control.[23]

In Atrisco itself there are very few major changes to be noted in either the modes of working or the consumption patterns. Family incomes in 1951 and later were higher than in 1936 but so also were prices; hence the standard of living has not been greatly altered. More and better cars and trucks, some fairly good farm machinery, and electricity in the village are the greatest of the changes which have come in a period of almost two decades. But, as noted before, the mechanization of farming activities has not gone far, and the electric power line would never have been put in if it had not been for the Texans in the neighboring community of Homestead. Moreover, *los Atrisqueños*, as compared with the people of Homestead, make small use of this modern facility. Don Daniel Lucero even went so far as to refuse to have his home wired. Others in the village proper now have electric lights, but even as late as 1958 the only family to have any electrical appliances was that of Fred Atrisco, and all it had purchased was a refrigerator and an iron. Just five miles away the Texans who had done the planning for the power line were moving rapidly by 1951 to make electrical appliances an integral part of both farming operations and family living. More and more electric water pumps were appearing, the majority of the families had refrigerators and small appliances, and many also had freezers and washing machines.

The most marked changes in the work patterns of *los Atrisqueños* are to be found in the greater Individualism within the family units and something of a decrease in the dependence upon *patrón* figures. As has been mentioned, one extended family which consisted of the families of two brothers who had always worked together broke apart in 1951. Neither family was managing well. Frank Zamorra was trying to operate without the guidance of a *patrón* figure, and he, too, was failing to manage his affairs. Still another man who was attempting to handle his wages without *patrón* guidance was living a mere hand-to-mouth existence. The two Barrida brothers had become quite openly hostile to each other and no

---

[23] Cf. Leonard and Loomis, *op. cit.*

longer cooperated economically, even though both continued to work as herders for Fred Atrisco until late in the fifties and accepted him, albeit sometimes grudgingly, as a *patrón*.

The families which left Atrisco, both those which had been functioning family units in 1936 and the ones which were later created by the marriages of young people, are now somewhat scattered. Two are near Albuquerque, New Mexico, and a few have migrated to Arizona and California. However, the greatest number are to be found in Railtown and in another New Mexico trading center on the railroad, which like Railtown is less than one hundred miles from Atrisco. Enough details about the fortunes of these families over the years are known to make possible a general description of the variable economic adjustments they have made to a somewhat urban type of life.

The great majority of the men who are the economic supporters of family units are wage earners on jobs which by customary classifications would be categorized as unskilled and semiskilled. Most of the men in Railtown are employed in a government ordnance depot. A few have fairly responsible jobs equivalent to those of foremen, but typically they work at loading, trucking, and maintenance jobs. As of 1951 the average income of these men was between $200 and $300 a month.

According to the norms of the Anglo-Americans who hire the men, the jobs are independently assigned, and all wages are paid directly to the individual worker. The men themselves, when queried, show a tendency to consider the jobs as evidence of an independent and Individualistically oriented work situation. Actually the work patterns are far less Individualistic than they appear to be. In the first instance it is no accident that so many of the Atrisco men in Railtown work in the same place. They have felt the need of the support of the total group of relatives and friends. They have helped each other in getting the jobs, they have filled in for each other whenever the urge to lay off became strong in anyone, and they drive together to work. In general they support and protect each other.

Many of the families of these men live in the same neighborhood in an area of Railtown which is most definitely a segregated Spanish-American settlement. The families as wholes rely upon each other much as the men support each other on the job. Borrowing is almost as common as it was in Atrisco, equipment is passed from house to house, and even food is shared. The children of the closely related families run in and out of houses, eat wherever they happen to be when meals are served, and accept the discipline of whatever adults are present.

Authority and control are no longer dominantly Lineal as they were in Atrisco, but neither are these families behaving as independently and Individualistically organized groups. They have created among themselves a loosely knit Collateral organization which is serving to mitigate the strains created by the discrepancy between the dependent behavior for which they have been trained and the independent behavior which the Anglo-American economic system requires—and which many of them think they actually prefer.

The patterns of day-to-day life are not markedly different from those observed in Atrisco two decades ago. The houses, some owned but more rented, are of approximately the same size—two to four rooms—and some of them are lacking in modern facilities except for electricity. The foods used are also much the same, except that more canned goods are being used and store bread has taken precedence over the wheat-flour *tortilla*. House furnishings and clothing are different mainly in that there is more of both. The possession of electrical equipment such as refrigerators and washing machines is the most obvious change.

For the most part the concept of living is the day-to-day existence— necessary work, and then fun when and where one can find it. In talking to members of many of the families in the past few years, I have caught very little of the feeling that today is but a stone upon which the dreams for a brighter tomorrow are to be built. A few, mainly mothers, talk vaguely of more education for their children, but after following the lives of Atrisco families for some twenty years, I know of only five persons from the village who have had more than a high-school education, and many do not even yet finish high school. All of the five who have gone on for advanced training have come either from the Atrisco family or the Lucero family.

But there have been some who left Atrisco after 1936 who have moved up in the world economically. One son of Luis Corona, for example, was by 1952 the owner of a restaurant in the second of the railroad towns to which many *Atrisqueños* had moved; according to his accounting, it was netting him $7,000 to $8,000 a year. From observation alone it was obvious that his business as of that year was a good one. But he had some brothers who were not doing well. One was recurrently having difficulties with law enforcement officers and another was an alcoholic. Moreover, his father, who had hopefully opened a small grocery store in Railtown, had failed. All of these persons have been in some sense dependent upon this one son. Thus, in spite of his relative success there is not too much that he can count on for the economic mobility of his own immediate famliy.

A grandson of Don Juan Atrisco, a young man who had spent most of his childhood with his grandparents in Atrisco, is the most outstanding example of potential economic success and acculturation. As of 1954, by virtue of the financial help of his uncle, Fred Atrisco, he had completed his training in dentistry in a middle western college and was in search of a location to set up an independent practice. By the year 1958 he was most successfully established in his own office in the state capital.

There are other members of the 1936 Atrisco community who have failed to make what anyone could call an adequate adjustment to Anglo-dominated urban economic life. Several of the young men—some of them born in Atrisco and taken away when very young and others born in Railtown or elsewhere after their families had moved—have never had steady jobs. Some older people also have had serious troubles. The man who was imprisoned for molesting a village girl on one of his visits to Atrisco has been cited. He is now free, but he has no steady work. He is tired and embittered, and his family lives a hand-to-mouth existence. The wife in one of the families I knew best is now a widow and is without income of any kind except what she can make packing carrots in the summer months and working as a domestic at other times. Very recently her troubles have mounted because one of her two daughters has been widowed and left with five small children to support.

It has not been easy for Spanish-Americans to adjust to an economic world which is predicated upon individual initiative and responsibility and at least a modicum of planning for the Future. At the extremes there are the few who are actually succeeding well even by Anglo-American standards and a number who have failed to adjust at all well. In between is the great majority which is managing fairly well at the present time. The "stopgap" Collateral groupings which some of these have formed—groupings which are strongly reminiscent of the Collaterally defined family relationships which always lay close beneath the surface of Atrisco's dominantly Lineal system—are one reason their economic adjustment has been moderately successful. Another is the state of the economy of the nation which all during the late forties and the fifties has been a sufficiently expanding one to make employment possible for almost all who have desired it.

This period has been one in which Spanish-Americans, and many another group which does not really have the basic values upon which the American economy has been built, have been "carried along" and given a vicarious participation in an expanding Future. Even in the responses we received in Atrisco on the questions called Child Training, Expectations about Change, and Philosophy of Life (T1, T2, and T3)—all of which touched on economic expansion in the Future—the responses as a whole showed a definite *second*-order Future orientation. Many in Railtown in 1951 and later have conversationally expressed this same kind of hopeful yet tentative belief that people would continue to have work and perhaps, in time, even better-paying work. They had not had this attitude at all in 1946 and 1947 when it seemed almost certain that the ordnance depot where so many of them worked was to be closed down. Instead they were nostalgically speaking of the "old days" back in Atrisco where, even in bad times, people managed to get along because they helped each other.

One wonders, therefore, what will be the effect upon the Spanish-Americans in the towns should another serious depression strike the country. In the two-year period 1936–38 of the depression decade of the thirties, over 70 per cent of the Spanish-Americans who lived either in the towns or in villages which had already become disorganized were on the relief rolls. Yet in Atrisco in 1936, where there was still community integration in spite of impending economic disaster, there was only one family which was accepting government aid, and it was roundly criticized. A characteristic remark was this one made by an Atrisco woman:

Now take my father. He is *muy pobre* [very poor], but no one has to give him anything. He has almost nothing, just what he gets when he herds. You know herding is hard, but he and my brothers get along.... Frankie [the youngest brother] is there most of the time, but he usually works for himself. And Andres [the eldest brother] isn't there any more except when one of them doesn't have work. Then they all move in together. If my brother Andres has work, and my daddy has work and Frankie doesn't, then they all live together, too. This is the way they get along. It is much better that way, don't you think? Now take that Griego family, it doesn't need help and it shouldn't have it. We all feel that way about them. And what those Texans [referring here to the Texans of Homestead, very many of whom were accepting government relief in 1936] do is really awful.

There are not many of the emigrant Atrisco wage earners in the towns who have become sufficiently successful on their jobs to survive a statewide policy of employers to lay off Spanish-Americans before other employees. Only a very few have made enough of a success of independent businesses or have sufficient professional training to be able to withstand a depression period. And the Collateral supports which have been developed by some in the towns are almost certainly too weak to maintain whole groups of families during a really bad economic period. One questions the ultimate firmness of some of the shifts in value-orientation emphases which appear most prominently in the economic sphere. The strength of the second-order positions of the Future *time* and Over-Nature orientations is most open to question.

RELIGION, RECREATIONAL ACTIVITIES, AND MAGICAL PRACTICES

The most prominent building in Atrisco in 1936, and the most loved one, was the small church with its high steeple and bell tower. It was, of course, a Catholic church, and there was only one family—the Vidrio family, which ran the trading store—which was not Roman Catholic in its religious faith. Indeed, the term *buen Catolico* (good Catholic), so often used in descriptions of people, was virtually synonymous with good Mexican.

But one soon learns when living with Spanish-Americans or the Mexicans of Old Mexico that the Catholicism adhered to is a sufficiently distinctive blend of elements, some Old World and some New World, for one to speak of *Mexican* Catholicism. For example, anyone who has known Mexicans on either side of the border knows that their most revered religious personage is the Virgin and knows, too, that the particular conception of the Virgin which is central to their religion is *la Virgen de Guadalupe*. She is the special Virgin of Mexicans who revealed herself, according to legend, to a simple Indian as he was traveling alone one day. Sometimes she is even called the Black Virgin, and in the symbolic portrayals of her she is often given the dusky skin hue of the Mexican Indian.

The religious sphere of life, until quite recently, has been the dominant one for these people. But their concept of religion is a broad one, and has contained in it much more than the adherents to some faiths in the modern Western world would be willing to call religious belief and practice. The great religious festivals—*fiestas*, they are always called—have long been a main source of release from the workaday world. They are as much recreational in nature as they are religious. Dancing, gambling, drinking, rodeos, races, lotteries, and general conviviality are prominent activities in all large *fiestas*. In Old Mexico great displays of fireworks and native dances give added enjoyment and magnificence to these festive occasions. And while certainly not a part of the teachings of the Church, there are numerous magical practices, many beliefs in and uses of witchcraft, which are also intricately interwoven with the religious beliefs and practices.

In some parts of New Mexico the Catholic religious system is still further complicated by the presence of Penitentism (*Hermanos Penitentes*), which is an autonomous cult movement that developed and flourished in the eighteenth and nineteenth centuries. It has long since been disavowed by the Church, but it continues to persist. Since Atrisco has never had a *Penitente* brotherhood, the history and function of the movement are not critically important to our analysis of religious activities. However, the *Hermanos Penitentes* and certain of their rituals are widely known to Spanish-Americans, and no account of the Spanish-American religion in New Mexico would be complete without some mention of them.

There are some *Penitente* rituals which are distinctively different from those of orthodox Catholicism, and characteristically the rituals are performed in a guarded chapel called a *morada* and on a special ceremonial ground called the *calvario* (Calvary) rather than in a church and in the village plaza and cemetery.[24] The most outstanding and the most widely discussed aspect of the ceremonialism of the cult is that which occurs in the *Semana Santa* (Holy Week). Very briefly, the rituals, which extend over a four-day period, are given over to acts of penance and severe discipline (prayers, fasting, bloodletting, and heavy lashings with whips). They culminate on Good Friday with a re-enactment of the torments administered to Christ and his Crucifixion. Edmonson has given a good summary description of this final day of the ceremony:

The processions of Good Friday begin early in the morning, shortly after midnight. At each procession the whips are freely wielded, and the brothers, who have gone without food or rest for as much as two days, suffer genuine agonies. In the afternoon (or sometimes to avoid publicity, in the evening), the Crucifixion is staged, the chosen "Christ" being tied to the cross in cruel torment. Following this is the dramatic ritual of Tinieblas, held in total darkness amid the clanking of chains and rattling of tin. Special prayers are offered for those who request them. There follows the election of officers for the ensuing year, and the brothers disperse.[25]

For the very many persons in the Southwest who have heard of these rituals, and the not inconsiderable few who have crawled and slinked through corn fields in an effort to witness them, they seem gruesome, and the judgment has often been voiced that Penitentism is but a long-continued and somewhat elaborated and specialized version of medieval flagellantism.

Actually the *Hermanos Penitentes* are much more than this. Back in

---

[24] See Munro S. Edmonson, *Los Manitos: A Study of Institutional Values*, Middle American Research Institute (Tulane University), Pub. 25, 1957, pp. 33-39.
[25] *Ibid.*, p. 37.

time when the harried and struggling colonists of New Mexico were striving to survive against the heavy odds of sorry economic conditions, constant threats from hostile Indian populations, and the neglect and exploitation by mission priests who deemed their own primary obligation to be that of converting the native peoples to Christianity, the cult was developed both as a means of maintaining the Catholic religion and of providing a program of community welfare. The cult has always had psychological and sociological functions which have often been overlooked by those who have limited their descriptions and analyses to certain of the special rituals of the cult.[26] Perhaps in the next few years more of the meaning of the brotherhoods will be better understood, for in some parts of New Mexico there is a revival of them. Seemingly they are developing as a response to the personal anxieties and social disorganization created by the increased pressure of Anglo-American culture.

Although Atrisco had no *Penitentes* it did resemble the old *Penitente* villages (and many non-*Penitente* villages as well) in never having had a resident priest. When the community was first founded, the mother of the Atrisco brothers held religious services in her own home. When later her son Don Juan became, potentially at least, the real *patrón* of the community, she and he, as was mentioned earlier, provided the church for the village and made arrangements for periodic visits of a *padre* to conduct services and administer the sacraments.

It was also Doña Maria Atrisco who selected the patron saint of the community, San Jose. But after she made the choice it was discovered that the birth date of this saint, the day which would be the occasion for the largest of the annual *fiestas*, was a date in the month of March which would all too often be included in the Lenten season of fasting. So an appeal was made by the Atrisco family to the Bishop to have the date of the celebration of the saint's day changed from March to October. The request was granted, and to this day the great *fiesta* of Atrisco occurs at a time in October which is free of restrictions upon dancing, drinking, gambling, and family feasts.

The Catholic ceremonies have been rich in drama. Religious folk-plays, some of them called mystery plays, were numerous. Arthur Campa, who has made intensive studies of the religious folk theater of the Southwest, makes this statement about the origin of the plays:

The dramatization of Bible stories was European custom, but at the time of the conquest, the religious drama was on the decline and most dramatists in Spain were striving to take it out of the church and popularize it. The missionaries, however, revived the religious purpose of the drama in Mexico. Their problem was to convert the Indians to Christianity, not to provide them with a new type of entertainment. When they sought to convert the strange inhabitants of a hitherto unknown world, they found it necessary to employ a vehicle for the transmission of abstruse ideas. In the absence of a common tongue, one of the methods resorted to was that of

---

[26] One of the best interpretations of *los Hermanos Penitentes* is that of Dorothy Woodward in "The Penitentes of New Mexico" (unpublished Ph.D. dissertation, Yale University, 1935).

the drama, and this is the first introduction of the European theater in the New World.[27]

This original function of the plays ceased long ago to be important, but they were retained for a very long time as a part of the body of religious tradition in many areas of New Mexico as well as Old Mexico.

Apparently by the time Atrisco was founded they had really begun to die out entirely, for there is no evidence that very many of the plays were ever performed there. The one set of dramas which is well remembered by the people of Atrisco is the Christmas cycle commonly called *las Pastorelas*. This cycle, Campa states, was always the most popular of all the folk-plays. In its full form the cycle consisted of four dramas, presented in logical sequence, which re-enacted the Biblical stories of the choice of Joseph as the husband for Mary, the journey of Joseph and Mary to Bethlehem, the announcement by the shepherds of the birth of Christ, the arrival of the three kings to bear gifts for the Christ child, and episodes in the life of Christ. In time the several stories had become confused, and parts were dropped out. Certainly as far as Atrisco was concerned the only important part of the cycle was the story of Mary and Joseph going to Bethlehem, the birth of the Christ child, and the coming of the Magi Kings.

As a partial explanation of the popularity of parts of this Christmas cycle Campa writes:

... there is no Santa Claus in Spanish and Mexican tradition, and gifts are not exchanged on Christmas Day. Briefly, nine days before Christmas, groups of children, led by a couple who represent Mary and Joseph, go from house to house asking admittance in song. The first eight days they are denied entrance, but on Christmas Eve they are admitted, and the merrymaking *pinata* broken by the children. Gifts are not exchanged until the seventh of January, when Magi Kings arrived to offer their gifts to the child. It is upon this tradition that the Christmas Cycle is built.[28]

I was told much about performances of these parts of *las Pastorelas* which were usually called *los Pastores*, but I never saw any. Even had I remained in Atrisco in December, 1936, which I did not, I would not have witnessed an enactment of them. The exodus from the village had begun by that time, and those who still remained in the village seemingly had little heart for organizing the nine-day sequence of events. No part of the folk-drama has ever been performed since 1936.

In still other respects there were indications of a diminution of pattern elaboration in the sphere of religious ceremonialism. The number of *fiestas* celebrated annually had been four up to the year 1936. In that year there was only the festival of the saint's day and one minor *fiesta*. Services in the church were also fewer. The *padre*, who had for many years been coming to Atrisco regularly once each month and at other times when needed for marriage, baptism, and funeral services, came less and less fre-

[27] "Religious Spanish Folk-Drama in New Mexico," *New Mexico Quarterly*, Vol. II, No. 1 (February, 1932), pp. 4–5.
[28] *Ibid.*, pp. 8–9.

quently in 1936 and later. More and more, it became the custom for persons to travel to Zuni for the religious part of the marriage ceremony. Only the subsequent wedding *fiesta* was celebrated in the village. As for baptismal services, either they were postponed until such time as the priest did come to the village church, or the children were also taken to the mission church in Zuni. Yet in spite of all these changes, religion and the numerous activities connected with it were still for many years considered the focal point of village life.

In 1936 the annual *fiesta* honoring San Jose was an unusually gay affair. It began on a Saturday. Most of the daylight hours of that day were spent in numerous preparations, because, as usual, these spontaneous and Present-oriented people had made very few plans in advance. Children were sent out to clear the roadways of all clutter and debris and to collect wood for the evening fires. The women were all busy cleaning their houses, cooking special foods, washing and ironing clothes. Almost all of them washed their hair and left it loose to dry as they went about their other chores. Late in the afternoon the men, most of whom had been out on the range all day, began to drift into town. The majority of them went to their homes where they, too, took baths and donned clean clothing. Some, to be sure, went first to the *cantina* and began their celebration early without benefit of a special grooming.

Just at dusk the village became strangely still except for some noisy voices in the *cantina* and the occasional barking of a dog. Few persons were to be seen in the streets or in the store, and the doors of most of the houses remained closed. It was the hushed silence of an expectant people. Suddenly the church bell peeled forth. The time for the evening service in the church —the Rosary, they called it—had arrived. One by one the doors opened, and with solemn slowness the men, women, and children—many in family groups but some with those of their own sex and age—walked to the church. The service was not a long one and lacked the formality of the Mass. Much of it was musical and was led by one of the visiting nuns who played a small organ which had been borrowed for the occasion. The priest spoke briefly, and entirely in English (he did not command the Spanish language), on the importance of family life and the significance of children obeying their parents.

When the service had ended, everyone remained seated or standing in place until the priest, the sisters, and then Don Juan Atrisco had gone outside. It was now the hour for the *fiesta* procession which, as always, was to be organized and led by the officials of the church and Don Juan Atrisco. Gradually the others filed out and fell into two lines, one for women and one for men. A brief period of waiting followed, for the *santo* had not yet been brought out of the church. Finally two altar boys emerged from the church. One carried the church banner; the other the plaster image of the *santo*. As they moved forward to the front of the procession, a sacred chant was started by the priest and his aides. Meanwhile the *luminarios* (festival fires or lights) were lighted. The *luminarios* used in Atrisco were the traditional type—criss-cross piles of small pieces of wood set aflame, rather than the candle set in sand in a paper bag which is the type often used in

New Mexico today. There were many of them lining both sides of all the roadways, for it was the custom that the procession should file past the house of each and every family.

The solemnity of the procession was somewhat marred this year by two unforeseen events. The first of these was the unexpected action of Luis Corona, the man who for several years had been trying to gain the *patrón* position which Don Juan Atrisco once held so firmly. Señor Corona knew full well that Don Juan still held his position as *patrón* in religious matters and if he were seriously to be challenged it would have to be in this sphere. I had noted that Luis had not gone to the church to join the procession but had instead taken up a position in his own doorway. He remained there until the procession approached his house. Then suddenly he dashed out and forced his way into the line in a place just behind the *padre* and just ahead of Don Juan. It was an outright challenge, but outwardly Don Juan took no notice of it. The priest also appeared to ignore the action. But in the days to follow the people of the village devoted much time to the discussion of what might be the result of this blatant affront, which followed so closely on a more or less open feud between Don Juan Atrisco and Luis Corona in a political meeting called for the selection of the Atrisco delegates to the county convention (see below). Actually little came of the episode. Luis Corona's bid for power of any kind had never been a firm one, and within a year his financial affairs were in such a state that he was obliged to leave Atrisco. Don Juan continued on until his death in 1958 as the lay leader in all religious activities.

The second disturbance was caused by some Texans from the neighboring village of Homestead. Always hostile toward the people of Atrisco, some of them had taken this opportunity to visit Atrisco and make themselves obnoxious by means of derisive comments and raucous laughter. It was the woman who ran the trading store who stopped their interfering tactics. She was not a Catholic, hence not in the procession; and when she saw what was happening, she took it upon herself to order the Texan men out of town. They went.

After the procession ended and the *santo* had been returned to the church, there was again a period when all was still and quiet. Most persons had returned to their homes, and there was little of the noise from the play of young boys which one usually heard in Atrisco in the early evening hours. It was perhaps an hour or so later (when one lives with Spanish-Americans the concept of *time* becomes vague) that strains of guitar music were heard throughout the village. The musicians who were to play for the evening *baile* (dance) were announcing to everyone that they had decided it was time for the dance to begin. As one would predict, Spanish-Americans had no scheduled time for a dance which had been announced in advance.

The dance that night was a gay one, and there were times when it seemed not unlikely that some of the men who had been drinking for several hours might become quarrelsome. But nothing truly serious happened except that some of the villagers took umbrage at the attentions a Spanish-American from Railtown was drunkenly trying to shower on me. His behavior was decidedly not "correct" by Atrisco standards, and I myself was too new to those ways to know how to cope with him and also did not have the protection of a family. So certain members of the community took action. He was upbraided, and he so took it to heart that the next evening he fully apologized as he had been instructed to do.

The dance did not last far beyond midnight because the next day was Sunday, and the morning was to be devoted to the Masses—three of them—which were the main religious celebration of the saint's day. Some people, mainly women, attended all three services, many went to two, and very few failed to appear at some one of the three. Following the last of the services in the church there was the *fiesta* breakfast in the homes. The finest of these was that in the Atrisco home where the priest and the sisters were guests. For most of the families the special occasion was celebrated by having plenty of meat in their *chili* and a pie or two. But there were some families in which the day's fare was no different from what it was on other days—beans, *tortillas*, and coffee. For families who owned no livestock, meat was both difficult to find and too expensive to buy even if available.

By the middle of the afternoon the long-anticipated recreational activities were in full swing. A number of men spent long hours over a gambling game in which silver dollars were pitched at a target; the children had their special games; there was time taken out for the spinning of the wheel which would select the winners of the chance holders in a lottery which had been organized to raise money for the church. The *cantina* was being constantly patronized by certain of the men. Other men and almost all the women and children were visiting with friends and relatives when not watching games or the spinning of the lottery wheel.

Then finally evening came, and there was the second of the dances. It was even gayer than the one the night before. The music was more spirited, and there were interludes between dances when several of the men sang the songs, some gay and some sad, which all Spanish-Americans love. Although there were some who left this dance by midnight, the majority carried on their festive activities up to the time that dawn announced the approach of another day. There were very many who stayed in the village that day to rest. Not until Tuesday did the day-to-day work routine become re-established. This fairly detailed description of the *fiesta* has been given because in the *fiestas*, more than any place else in Spanish-American life, one finds an amalgamative expression of all the basic values of the culture.

The saints whom the *fiestas* honor are, with the exception of the Virgin, the most important of the religious figures for the village folk. The patron saint is the supreme father figure of the Lineally organized social structure of the typical Spanish-American village. He is looked upon as both the protector of the people and the all-seeing one who can mete out punishment for sinful behavior. Although I never saw it practiced in Atrisco, it has been a custom of Spanish-American Catholics, in years when crops are failing or livestock dying off rapidly, to place the figure of their *santo* on a litter and carry him about to view the sorry condition of fields, garden plots, and animals. If after this rite there is no improvement in conditions, the interpretation is always that it is they, the people, who have erred in ways for which the *santo* feels a need to punish.

Frequent appeals are made both to the patron saint and to other saints who are believed to have special powers for particular kinds of situations. A prominent part of the appeal is the act of penance which the individual (or a group of individuals) carries out to evidence his own good faith and gratitude. Or the act of penance may be performed to demonstrate one's contrition for supposedly sinful or disrespectful behavior when it appears to the supplicant that the saint is unwilling to grant the favor requested of him.

In Atrisco in 1936 the most frequent form of penance was a long trek, barefooted, to some distant shrine of the saint to whom the appeal had been made. One such case was a journey made by Doña Amelia Lucero, the wife of Don Daniel Lucero and who at the time was an ailing woman and seemingly unfit for such extreme exertion. One of her sons had contracted typhoid fever while off in another part of the state. He had been carried home and lay seriously ill for many days. No medical services were sought. Instead Doña Amelia appealed to a saint and made the vow that if her son were permitted to recover she would travel barefoot to the shrine of this saint, which was some fifty miles south of Atrisco. The son died. Doña Amelia's own interpretation was that the appeal had failed because she or others in her family had been unworthy. She was, therefore, determined to carry out her vow as the means of setting right the relationship between herself and the powers of the supernatural world. Because of her health her family raised strenuous objections to which she finally listened. She did not take the journey. Then within two weeks a daughter who had long been ailing took a turn for the worse and died. This death to Doña Amelia was certain proof that she was being punished for her failure to carry out her vow. No one in the Lucero family even tried this time to dissuade her from performing her act of penance. She took the long trip, alone and barefooted. The only concession she made was to permit members of her family to come to the shrine after her and bring her home by car.

In another case it was a young and newly married couple who walked as penitents to a distant shrine. The young pair had evidently made an appeal to a *santo* to aid them in overriding parental objections to their marriage. By means of a hoax, which is to be described later, they did overcome the opposition of the young woman's parents and other relatives. However, they themselves must have believed that it was the *santo* who was responsible for the success of their plot, for on the morning following their wedding *fiesta* they both set out afoot for a shrine in Zuni.

Dependence upon the *santos* and acceptance of their powers are marked in these and many other beliefs and practices which characterize Spanish-American Catholicism. Toward the entire realm of nature-supernature the attitude of most Spanish-Americans has long been a strongly submissive and accepting one.

The *padre*, who for most Spanish-American village people is the most important of the earthly representatives of supernatural authority, theoretically holds the second position of power in the social structure. Then next in line of authority is the village *patrón*, who also has definite religious responsibilities and prerogatives. Actually this ordering of authority was well delineated only in the villages which had a resident *padre*. Even in a few of these the lines of authority were blurred because the *padre* had assumed the dual position of *padre* and village secular *patrón*. In the many other communities which had never had a resident priest, the role of the *patrón* in religious affairs was often substantially greater in scope than that of the priest, even though it was viewed as a secondary and unofficial role.

In Atrisco in the thirties the position of the *padre*, who was of a different ethnic stock and originally from another part of the country, was not a strong one. He was seldom in the village, and he seemingly did not understand Spanish-Americans very well. Yet the respect for and awe of him was great, and the people tried hard to do as he requested.

One of the most interesting of the failures in communication between the *padre* and the members of the Atrisco church produced by this situation occurred in a matter having to do with the organization of the church. Atrisco had no organizations beyond the family and the secular *patrón* system except the church. This fact in and of itself is another indication of the dominance of the religious sphere of activity. The church was the one single overall organization which knit all families together in a wide variety of social activities as well as the more narrowly religious ones. Also, religious beliefs and the organization supporting them provided social controls for situations in which family controls or the control of the *patrón* were either insufficient or ineffective. But the organization within the church was not organization as Anglo-Americans know organization.

Indeed, it was scarcely an independent organization at all but was instead an extension of the Lineally oriented family system. Since the early days of the community it has been the custom that each year at the time of the big *fiesta* the *padre*, always in consultation with Don Juan Atrisco, would appoint a *mayordoma* for the ensuing year. Actually the appointment was almost always a husband and wife, hence the term *mayordomos* was the one customarily used when church affairs were discussed. For a year the *mayordomos* would be responsible for all church affairs, which would reach their apex at the next annual *fiesta*. Their responsibilities included keeping the church building in good repair, collecting contributions, making the preparations for the services in the church, and, finally, preparing the whole village for the *fiesta*. There were no committees and no regular meetings of any kind. If, in the opinion of the *mayordomos* there was work to be done—a wall to be repaired, inside painting, or a money-collecting campaign—the usual pattern was for the *mayordoma* to call on relatives and friends one evening and tell them that in the morning she would expect them to arrive to help with the work at the time she rang the church bell. Almost always, all of those whose help was solicited appeared. Work with sheep or cattle or on jobs of one sort or another was put aside for a day or so if at all possible, and everyone poured his efforts into getting the work of the church done. And it was not a duty sternly interpreted, because the workers enjoyed being together. The occasion was a convivial social one.

The *padre* had gone along with this method of planning for the first four or five years that he had been the priest assigned to Atrisco. Then in 1935 he made a proposal which indicated that he thought there should be more order and regularity in the management of the church. His proposal was for the organization of a church group of women to be called the Catholic Ladies Society which would meet regularly on Friday of each week. Although I never discussed this proposal with the priest, I assume that he thought such a group would be capable of more careful planning and that not so many things would be left to last-moment and spontaneous action. Perhaps he even thought it would provide a fairer way of eliciting the services of people than the age-old method of asking persons simply to drop their work to participate in the work for the church.

Since it was not the way of *los Atrisqueños* to argue with an authority figure, and since they also revered their *padre* and wanted to please him, the organization was formed. *Its life span was two weeks.* The intentions of the women were excellent, but it takes both more of a Doing orientation and more of a sense of Future *time* than the people of Atrisco had in order to schedule regular weekly meetings and to plan work programs. Moreover, they were much too accustomed to being told what to do and when to do it by someone in authority. Round-table discussions, voting procedures, and committee assignments were not their ways, and they could not easily come to an understanding of them. The priest did not again attempt to create more organization in the church, and to this day the method of handling the work of the church remains much the same as it always has been. Each year at the *fiesta* the priest, as the high authority figure, announces the appointment of a new *mayordoma* (or *mayordomos*). There is, of course, little choice any more in the selection; the permanent population is much too small. For a period of several years in the early fifties the only persons who seemed both available and capable of carrying out the duties were Fred Atrisco and his wife.

Another aspect of Spanish-American (and Mexican) Catholicism which the *fiesta* celebration clearly reveals is the conjoining of religious and recreational activities. *Bailes* (dances) as social occasions have been common in the culture, and music is a part of the very soul of the Mexican both south and north of the border. One also easily notes the love of gambling and drinking which many Spanish-Americans and Mexicans have and the intense sense of the dramatic which almost all of them have. But at no other time is there such a concentration on all these activities and such a sense of release in pursuing them as in the *fiesta* celebrations. And all is combined with a deep religious attitude.

It is from this amalgam of a religious spirit which is bowed before inscrutable and overwhelming supernatural forces and a spirit of joy in the living of the moment that much of the distinctive quality of the Mexican character, as found in the Southwest and Old Mexico, is derived. Anglo-Americans, who characteristically have radically different value orientations, seldom come to comprehend either the deep sense of tragedy or the spontaneous abandonment to momentary pleasures which constitute, when interwoven, the very fabric of life for the typical Mexican. And it is much too simple an explanation to say, as some kinds of economic determinists are wont to do, that economic deprivation and exploitation have made necessary both the spinning of the threads and the fabric which the interweaving of them has produced. The way of life of a people (its system of basic values) is derived from much more than economic factors, and it often persists in the face of many opportunities for economic change.

There are, to be sure, many strains in Spanish-American (and Mexican) culture. No culture is lacking in strains, but the number and kinds vary, and to some extent at least, the variations are related to the variations in the configurations of the value orientations. The most severe strains for Spanish-Americans appear to be those produced by the domination of eldest brothers (*hermanos mayores*) and the general *patrón* domination which were described earlier as types of authority that lack legitimation. But in addition to these strains, there are others in both the social and the natural environment which almost all individuals feel.

The closeness of relationships in the society and the strongly Lineal authority within families as well as in the total community allow for very little real autonomy of the individual and create many restrictions which are productive of frustration and hostility. Additional restrictions then become necessary lest the expressions of hostility become disruptive forces which would endanger the stability of the tightly knit system of relationships. There are also many restrictions in the realm of religious belief and practice which are related to the ingrained attitudes of submission to natural and supernatural forces. Still other strains are created by the culturally distinctive and subordinate position of Spanish-Americans in the state of New Mexico and in the nation as a whole. Patterns of behavior, both approved and disapproved, which would offer releases for the frustrations, the hostility, and the anxiety caused by these restrictions were inevitable. Space does not permit a detailed discussion of these patterns. Some of the more obvious ones I shall mention, and subsequently I shall give more attention to some of the kinds of magical beliefs and practices which have been effective both for the release of individual hostility and as means of social control for the group.

Some patently aggressive behavior can always be observed in Spanish-American communities. Homicides, in the past at least, have not been uncommon; there is often quarreling and fighting among some of the men on social occasions or in the *cantina*; and cruel treatment of animals is often noted. However, in checking the instances in Atrisco of blatantly aggressive behavior toward people, and especially to members of the in-group, I found the aggressors usually to be persons of authority—a *patrón* or his henchmen, a dominating father, or more often still, an eldest brother who was in control of the affairs of an extended family. It appears to be a general expectation that women and subordinate men would exercise great restraint. To be sure, the drinking, the gambling, the "vacations" from work, and other of the patterns which have been described were accepted if not fully approved patterns of release for men of all ages at times. Also the *bailes,* the *fiestas,* and such occasions as the local political meetings (which will be described later) offered outlets of sorts for almost everyone.

However, it would appear that in many individuals, most especially the women, there was a greater store of anxiety and hostility than could be assuaged by any of these activities. Witchcraft beliefs and practices have been one of the ways in which many persons have found an expression for the emotions which could not safely be displayed in overt aggression. But as release was gained, control was also exercised, for there were a number of witchcraft beliefs which worked reciprocally.[29]

In Atrisco in 1936 a majority of the people when asked directly about *brujeria* (witchcraft) either denied having any belief in it or voiced skepticism. This denial was, however, mainly a defense which was evidently engendered in part by a fear of criticism from disapproving Anglo-Americans. There actually were numerous instances of people believing that their illnesses were the result of their having been witched by a hostile relative or friend. There were other cases where it was generally known that an individual threatened a relative or friend fairly openly with witchcraft practice. Also, although there were no *curanderos* (witch doctors) present in the village at any time I was living there, I have reliable information that at least one Spanish-American *curandero* has been in the community frequently during the past twenty years. In 1936 and 1937 the several persons who sought the services of a *curandero* went either to Zuni or to another Spanish-American village.

Some of the witchcraft beliefs and practices found in Spanish-American culture are similar to those of the Indian groups of the region and similar also to many found throughout the world. The belief in the magical production of illness and disaster and the belief in the "evil eye" (*mal ojo*) are, for example, simply particularized versions of fairly universal beliefs. Also, fears that some women were noted to have of eating the food of persons to whom they were hostile, and of serving food to these same persons, are quite common covert expressions of anxieties and hostilities which are denied a more open and direct expression.

But many another of the beliefs, most particularly but not solely those which had to do with social control, were closely related to religious beliefs. The Devil of religious teachings was made to take many malevolent and threatening forms. The most pervasive belief was the one which asserted that evil spirits lurked constantly in the dark to attack the unguarded. Most particularly it was feared that the unprotected woman would be attacked.

I first became aware of this quite general belief when repeatedly I was asked upon coming into the village of a morning after having been alone at night in a small house somewhat removed from the center of the community: *"No tenia miedo anoche?"* ("You were not afraid last night?") At first my reply was "no," and always I received only the most evasive

[29] Cf. Clyde Kluckhohn, *Navaho Witchcraft,* Papers of the Peabody Museum, Harvard University, Vol. XXII, No. 2 (1944).

of answers when I inquired what it was that I was supposed to fear. Later when I simulated the fear (and it was not altogether simulated for I had had one or two scares living in that rather isolated house), I was able to find out that there was ever the danger of some form of the Devil attacking the woman who was alone in the dark. A part of this belief was unquestionably based upon the real possibility of sexual molestation and also the wish for it. But primarily it appeared to be a belief with the purpose of keeping women, most especially young and unmarried women, from having illicit sexual relations. There was a vagueness about the nature of the demons. It would seem that they could have either human or animal forms, but all were in some way representative of the Devil. The most concrete of the stories was the one of a burro, with great horns and nostrils that flamed with fire, which traveled the countryside at nights to attack and punish "bad girls." One woman in telling me this story finally remarked: "But that burro doesn't go around here. He travels up north of here where lots of the girls go loose and don't act right. We don't have girls like that here so he doesn't come here." Other stories were concerned with the strange happenings to people, men or women, who had taken things that did not belong to them, to persons who had been disrespectful to their parents, or to persons who had become lax in religious devotions.

The most interesting of all the tales I learned was that of the *Largo Blanco* (Great White Thing). This is the story of the hoax perpetrated by Carmelita and Guillermo Sanchez to make possible their marriage. I tell it in some detail, first, because it is not often that one can report upon a legend in the making and, second, because in it one sees clearly both the social and the individual uses of witchcraft practices.

Carmelita, the girl of the story, was a member of a family closely related to the *patrón* family, and while this family in 1936 was in the wage-earning group, it had been much better off in the past. This was one reason why the family members did not wish Carmelita to marry Guillermo in whom she had become interested. He had *always* been just a wage worker. But a more important factor in the family opposition was the background of the young man. Many years ago Carmelita's grandfather had reared an Indian girl who, according to village accounts, had been left stranded after some fighting between raiding Yaqui Indians from northern Mexico and the nearby Zuni. This girl was in a sense a slave, but, as with the other Indian child reared by another of the Atrisco families, it was decided that she should marry when she was around sixteen years of age, and a husband was found for her. The husband also was an Indian, or at least predominantly Indian. Guillermo Sanchez was the grandson of this couple; hence it was known to all that he was basically Indian in his (blood) heritage. As was stated earlier, the people of Atrisco frown upon alliances with Indians and stigmatize the offspring resulting from them as *coyotes* or *lobos*. Carmelita's family was especially adamant in its refusal to consent to her marriage to Guillermo, and most certainly the high degree of resistance was a result of the irony of the situation that brought the grandson of their Indian slave girl back to Atrisco as a suitor for their own daughter's hand. Twice Guillermo and his mother went through the typical formal procedure of presenting a letter to Carmelita's family during a visit made especially for this purpose but during which, in accord with custom, the matter was not openly discussed. Twice the letter was simply ignored, which is the Spanish-American way of stating a refusal of a suit.

The situation looked quite hopeless for the young couple, but apparently they were determined. Time went by, and no one that I ever talked to was able to say how they managed—in the face of the customs of the thirties which did not permit unmarried young couples to be alone—to get together and make the plan which was designed to break down the resistance of Carmelita's family.

All that is well known is that one night Carmelita went out of the house alone to the outdoor toilet. This was the first step in the plot, because it was customary for Atrisco women, when they had to go outside at night, to take one or more other women with them. Apparently no one noticed Carmelita leaving. Suddenly the stillness of the night, which is always profound in Atrisco, was rent with screams, and a few moments later Carmelita, scratched and bruised and seemingly frightened half to death, fell in through the door of her home and began telling of the *Largo Blanco* which had attacked her in the dark. The only description she could give of him was that he was a Great White Thing with brimstone burning on his head. He had attacked her by scratching and slaps, but finally she had managed to flee. Once the story was told she virtually collapsed and was put to bed where she lay in a half-dazed state.

The village was in a state of alarm. Carmelita's own family was much frightened and requested that a search be made at once for the white creature. The women in all the homes shut themselves in behind locked or barred doors. The men who happened to be in the village gathered together and organized a search party. Many of them at the time, and many more later, voiced great doubt that the whole affair was anything other than a hoax, but either they were not skeptical enough or their wives and daughters were effectively prodding, for almost all of them set out to see if the *Largo Blanco* could be found and driven away. Although they spent much of the night in the search, no trace of the creature was found.

Carmelita remained in bed seemingly too ill to take up her normal life. This continued for a day or so; then she produced a letter which she stated had appeared mysteriously on the window sill. The note threatened that if she were not permitted to marry Guillermo the *Largo Blanco* would return.

While it seems moderately certain that it was a transient schoolteacher who helped in the plot—at least to the extent of writing the letter and getting it to Carmelita—and more certain still that the whole episode was contrived, no one, and least of all Carmelita's family, could be sure that the *Largo Blanco* did not exist. Consent to the marriage was granted. Just after their marriage the couple performed the act of penance which has been reported.

During the first few years after this episode there were many persons who openly expressed doubt about the other-worldly nature of the *Largo Blanco*. Unquestionably there are many still who regard the whole affair as a successful hoax. Yet it is a fact that the *Largo Blanco* became a legendary figure, and he is referred to as another of the forms of the Devil which hovers in the dark to attack the unguarded woman, or the loose woman. And it is of interest to note that he also seemed to be a legendary symbol of some of the changes which were soon to come in the family patterns of Atrisco. One woman who was the mother of two young girls remarked to me in 1937: "I don't really know whether I believe he was there or not. You know Carmelita's family wasn't sure either, but they didn't dare take any chances. And I know I believe enough so that if one of my girls wanted to marry someone I would say 'yes' right away. I wouldn't want any of that kind of trouble."

There have been some changes and a great loss in elaboration of detail in all of the beliefs and practices having to do with both religion and *brujeria* and changes also in recreational activities which for so long a time were blended with religious practices. It has been noted that in Atrisco itself there have been no religious folk-plays performed since 1936 and also no religious festivals celebrated except the one honoring the patron saint. Also, although as late as 1951 I was still being told tales of persons going to *curanderos* and was able myself to observe one case of a woman who clung to the belief that she should neither accept food from nor give food to those for whom she had deeply hostile feelings, there was, in general, some slight tendency toward a greater rationalization of illnesses and disasters. There was a little less of both the general submissiveness which used to be expressed as the acceptance of "the Lord's will" and the fear of and belief in magically produced illnesses. Just as in the livestock business and farming a few persons by 1951 were beginning to look to technology as a means of controlling some of the effects of the natural environment, so also in the area of human welfare a few were coming to depend more upon medical services and advice of other kinds which trickled in from the outside.

But it would be an error to conclude that in Atrisco itself the supremacy of the religious-recreational sphere had greatly waned by 1951 or even later. On the contrary, one cannot be other than amazed by the efforts which so few persons have exerted to maintain the religious traditionalism. Although it is almost certain that the annual *fiesta* will not be celebrated for many more years now that Don Juan has died, there has been no year as yet (1959) when it has not been an elaborate enough occasion to have great resemblance to the *fiestas* of the past. Somehow the Atrisco family, others who still live in the village, and numerous former residents have managed to gather together crowds of a hundred or more for the occasion. The making of sleeping arrangments for some of the celebrants (many persons in New Mexico habitually carry bedrolls) and the feeding of all of them in a village which is crumbling away and has no store of any kind for even staple goods has been a feat of some magnitude. Fred Atrisco's wife, who is not an Atrisco woman, often spoke to me in 1951 with some bitterness about the exhausting work the *fiesta* celebration required of her and Don Juan's daughters. The daughters apparently did not resent the work.

The rebuilding of the old schoolhouse to make a new church when the old church burned showed again the strength of the religious traditionalism. It is inconceivable that an Anglo-American community which had dwindled to a population of twenty-five adults and some twenty-five children and showed certain signs of a still further decline would seriously concern itself with the rebuilding of a church which, as nearly as possible, would be as large and as well equipped as the former one. In the first year after the destruction of the old church it seemed to me that the people of Atrisco were going to be contented with a makeshift substitute in the one-room schoolhouse. But such was not the case. It was not long before the schoolhouse had been completely refurnished inside. Then the men went to work to build a steeple and bell tower, so that once again the church had the imposing command of height among the village buildings. The difference was that what it commanded was largely rubble rather than the dwellings of numerous devout communicants. Services are not often held in the church, and it is often kept locked, but never has there been any relaxation in the vigilant caring for it. As has often been the case where a profoundly religious people have put their greatest efforts into churches, shrines, and cathedrals, the little church of Atrisco is likely to remain for some time amid the decay which everywhere surrounds it as the more or less intact symbol of the deepest feelings of a people.

Off in the towns and cities where so many *Atrisqueños* now live, the changes have been somewhat greater than in Atrisco. There are no *fiestas* at all for these people unless they make the journey back to the village each year. They also no longer have a patron saint who is their own particularized and personalized protector. While still devout Catholics in most cases (some of the younger people are not notably devout), they are now members of parishes which are fairly large and often somewhat cosmopolitan.

In a number of ways the lives of the urban migrants have been secularized and torn loose from the moorings of both religion and magical practices. Many of the recreational activities now pursued, especially by the younger people, are the commercialized ones common to the typical American small town—movies, dancing and drinking in taverns, and riding about in cars. The older people in general, but most particularly the married women with children, seemed to have few recreational activities at all except family visiting, the radio or television, and an occasional movie, or a trip in the car to visit relatives elsewhere. There has as yet been little development of scheduled parties or other social events which are commonplace in most Anglo-American groups. The *fiestas* and other church-oriented social functions have gone, and no other types of organized activity have taken their place.

One also notes among the families in the towns a still greater reliance upon medical treatment, the use of clinics, and other developments which have to do with the physical welfare of individuals than there is in Atrisco at present. But it is reported that there are some, even among the city dwellers, who still seek out the services of *curanderos*; and I myself have observed in the discussion of the illnesses of both old and young much of the same fatalistic acquiescence that characterized the attitudes of *los Atrisqueños* in 1936.

The responses which the population in Atrisco gave to the questions on the value orientations which touched on the religious-recreational sphere (and indirectly on magical practices as these are related to the religious sphere) indicated that there had been only a slight change in basic values. I have not detected a much greater change, except in a few cases, among the people I have visited with in the two towns. But I do note considerably more social and personal demoralization, which would seem to indicate a great discrepancy between basic values and practice.

I find some people who are simply inuring themselves to a dull and routine existence. Many young persons upon whom there are no longer efficacious social controls are running loose. Quite a few of the young girls who had been brought into Railtown at an early age and reared without either the family surveillance or the sanctions of an integrated community religious system, both of which were strict in Atrisco, have been subjects of much discussion. Several have given birth to illegitimate children who are now being reared by their own mothers. One, in addition to having an illegitimate child, has been twice married and divorced. A number of the young men have been serious problems because of their drinking, fighting, fast driving, and unwillingness to work steadily. Several of them have had one or more encounters with officers of the law and have been jailed for varying periods of time. The case of the old man who was imprisoned for molesting a young girl on one of his return visits to Atrisco has been cited previously. There are some others in the older age groups who seem lost and bowed with a helplessness they cannot understand. A fatalistic acceptance of the inevitable is one thing in a social system where all are trained to support each other in the same kind of acceptance, but it is quite another when one is forced suddenly to cope as an independent individual with a system dominated by a conquering conception of the *man-nature* relationship which one simply does not understand.

The dominance of the religious-recreational sphere of behavior in Spanish-American culture is most certainly on the decrease and that of the economic sphere on the increase, but there is much evidence which indicates that the shift of emphasis will be neither a fast nor a smoothly moving one.

ATRISCO'S RELATIONS WITH THE OUTSIDE WORLD

For generations in New Mexico the small villages in which a majority of the Spanish-Americans lived were isolated, self-contained, and ethnocentric. Few *Atrisqueños* as late even as 1936 had much knowledge of or interest in the peoples beyond their own horizon except for the relatives that some had in the trading centers and in other Spanish-American communities. They also knew very little about the social, economic, and political organization of the state of New Mexico or the nation as a whole. Thus, the most drastic change of all in the lives of many of the Spanish-American village folk occurred when suddenly they were compelled to migrate to towns and cities which were fairly complex and differentiated social orders. In these towns they became an ethnic minority (largely segregated in particular areas) which has had little of the internal cohesiveness so characteristic of the villages except what small groups of related persons could improvise.

With a few exceptions the people of Atrisco were still evading contacts with Anglo-Americans in the trading centers in the 1930–40 decade. It has been shown how they depended upon a *patrón* to negotiate for them with all such persons as cattle and sheep buyers, wool brokers, and county and federal agents. Social contacts with Anglo-Americans in the three towns most often visited (the two railroad towns to the north of the village and a trading center to the south) were virtually nonexistent except in the case of the Vidrio family, where the wife was an Anglo-American. Also only the Atrisco, the Lucero, and the Vidrio families had members who had gone to educational institutions either in the cities of New Mexico or elsewhere in the country.

Contacts with either the Anglo-Americans or the Indian groups in the nearby communities were, for the most part, also either limited or fraught with tension. It was stated earlier (Chapter II) that the people of Atrisco knew few of the Mormons of Rimrock except the mail carrier. Numerous illustrations of the tense relations between the residents of Atrisco and the Texan community of Homestead have also been cited. Only a very few contacts with the Zuni have been made and almost all of these since 1930, at which time some Atrisco families began to trade in Zuni, and others on occasion, usually for childbirth cases, took advantage of the medical services offered in the government hospital in Zuni.[30] The family in Zuni with which some Atrisco families became most friendly is one which is part Yaqui Indian. Several Atrisco women lived with this family for several days while awaiting hospitalization for the delivery of children, and in one case the relations became warm enough for the creating of reciprocal godparent relationships. But all in all, as previously stated, it was the Navaho group which was both the best known to the people of Atrisco and the best liked. In the very early days of the community everyone had a great fear of all Indians, a fear which was not without justification since the Atrisco family had suffered so greatly at the hands of the Apache. However, when it became apparent that the Navaho Indians who settled in the Rimrock region after the return from Fort Sumner were neither marauders nor scalpers, the stock-

---

[30] The infant mortality rate in Atrisco up to 1935 was always high (one third of all the children died prior to two years of age), but maternity mortality was unknown until 1924 when one mother died because of the amateurish midwifery of a neighbor. The concern created by this death caused many of the mothers to seek for the first time the services of the physician in Zuni or one in Railtown.

men of Atrisco, most particularly the Atrisco brothers, began to hire them for herding and for the seasonal work of shearing and lambing. It was a *patrón-peon* form of relationship which was established, and no *Atrisqueño* ever really considered a Navaho Indian to be his social equal. Yet the relationships were always most friendly ones. Those of the Navaho group who used to drop into the trading store from time to time were always greeted in a friendly fashion by the village men. In 1936, when I was living in the village, a few young Navaho men also came to several of the *bailes*. They, too, were treated graciously even to the extent of being accepted as dancing partners by some of the Atrisco girls. It is also known and fully accepted by the community that both Don Juan Atrisco and one of his brothers have had children by Navaho women. Don Juan actually reared the boy a Navaho woman bore him in his own family. The child of the brother remained in the Navaho group.

The seeking out of sustained relationships with Anglo-Americans or others in the outside world was not the way of the average *Atrisqueño*. What, then, of the relationships which were imposed by the outside world by virtue of the fact that the village was a part, however insignificant, of the state of New Mexico and of the United States? There were two types of state-wide, even nationwide, institutions which theoretically had the aim of integrating Atrisco in the wider social order. One of these was the public school system; the other was the political system.

The public school system which was developed in New Mexico in the latter part of the nineteenth and the early part of the twentieth century could well have been a significant means of integrating the Spanish-American communities in the life of a growing state and nation had it been geared to the Spanish-American needs and the Spanish-American way of life. But as has always been the custom of American educators (in large part from necessity, to be sure), the school program provided for an ethnic minority—in this case quite isolated Spanish-American villages—was the standard one used throughout the country and which had as its base line the value system of the average middle-class Anglo-American. In New Mexico the decree was not only that the regulation subjects should be taught but also that the language to be used in their teaching should be English and *only* English. For a number of years no person whose first language was Spanish was accepted for a teaching position. After some years, especially in those counties where Spanish-Americans had a strong political control, this rule was relaxed, but technically all the instruction was still supposed to be in English. The courses to be taught were also those which were standard for the public school system of the nation.

Generally speaking, this kind of an education had little relevance to the lives of pupils in a typical Spanish-American village. Because of it they became rote learners in a language which they seldom used at home or at play, and from it they garnered an odd assortment of esoteric facts which, in Atrisco at least, were mainly useful in a guessing game that an Anglo-American teacher inaugurated in 1934. There was the added fact that a people were being made moderately literate in a language they seldom used while being left quite illiterate in the language they commonly spoke. An important factor in this situation was, of course, the isolation of the villages and their ethnic purity. In other parts of the United States, most especially in the large cities, where the children of various ethnic backgrounds are thrown together in public schools, the common denominator provided by a standard curriculum in the English language has more meaning. Problems between the generations may be created as the new generation tends, ideologically, to present something of a solid front against the varieties of the customs and beliefs of the older generations, but this in itself is not really contrary to the American way of life. In the Spanish-American villages there was neither the need nor the opportunity for putting the melting pot on to boil.

To speak specifically of Atrisco, it had a school of sorts as early as 1908 or 1909, but the memories of this school are so vague that one doubts it amounted to much. The first public school in which English was the language required for teaching was established in 1918. In 1930 the village was granted a high school.

The prevailing attitude toward the school system and the education it aimed to provide was nonunderstanding appreciation. In many of the families the children were sent to school regularly, and there actually developed an ideal norm of an eighth-grade education. But the actual and the ideal behavior were not always the same. There were always some children who went to school for a few years only. A few of these simply wished to stop because they themselves had no interest in the work or could not keep up with it, and their parents acquiesced. Others were removed, either temporarily or permanently, by parents because it was felt their help was needed at home or on the range. Little attention was paid to the state law which required that children be kept in school to the age of fourteen years. This was most particularly true in the case of enrollment in the high school.

Attendance in the high school was always problematic. The people of Atrisco had given no thought to having a high school until word trickled into the village late in the twenties that various Anglo communities were being provided with high schools. The county political officials were then petitioned, and in 1930 the high school of Atrisco was built and staffed with one teacher to handle the three classes—the ninth, tenth, and eleventh grades. Almost immediately the village was faced with the loss of the school because it could not provide the thirty pupils which were required by law for the maintenance of a community high school. Had it not been for the development of the Texan community, Homestead, the school would have been closed after the first year. The Texans, many of them more desirous of a high-school education for their children than Atrisco parents, resentfully accepted the fact that to obtain this education they had to send their children to Atrisco. By 1936 half the high-school enrollment (only twenty-eight persons that year) was Texan; a year later it was predominantly Texan. Atrisco was dwindling and Homestead was growing slightly. It was the turn of the Homesteaders to petition, and as has been stated previously, the high school was moved from Atrisco to Homestead in 1937.

The remarks made about the schools by many *Atrisqueños* indicated that they were believed to be a good thing, but no one knew quite why this was so. There was virtually no expression, other than in the Atrisco, Lucero, and Vidrio families, of the attitude that schooling would enable a person to get a better job or in some other way advance himself or herself. Even in the Atrisco and Lucero families there was some skepticism about the usefulness of an education, especially anything more than an eighth-grade one or possibly a year or so of high-school training. As late as 1951 Don Daniel Lucero was complaining about a son of his who was sporadically trying to make the money for training in a small college in New Mexico. He wanted his son to stop and go to work, preferably in Atrisco in the livestock business with him. Several of the older children in the Atrisco family went to high school in Railtown, and a few had a year or so of college education, but there was no consistency in the pattern. Fred, the youngest son who for many years managed the family livestock business, only finished the eighth grade. In some part this lack of appreciation of the value of education for one's advancement reflects a value system which places a small premium upon individual success. In other part it is a realistic appraisal of the Spanish-American's chances for advancement in the Anglo-dominated economic world. Of course the two—the value system and the reality of the situation—are interrelated.

As for the subject matter taught in the schools, it was poorly comprehended and little used. The high-school courses in general American history, Old World history, geography, and citizenship (American citizenship, of course) left few impressions upon most of the students. The training in English and arithmetic was the most tangible asset of the educational program. However, not even these skills produced much effect. Very few of the people managed any part of their own business or household accounts, and few were given to reading anything other than the mail-order catalogues. Some did occasionally read the Railtown newspaper and a monthly Catholic newspaper which almost all families had subscribed to at the suggestion, or request, of the *padre*, but for the most part the papers were used for shelf lining and fire lighting. Books of any kind were a great rarity, and there were not more than a half-dozen persons who displayed any interest in reading books or magazines.

The verbal knowledge of the English language gained in the schools was, to be sure, of value, since very soon so many of the people were to be uprooted and pushed into towns where almost all work relations demanded a familiarity with it. By 1936 almost all the school children could speak passable English if they had to, and in the older population (over fifteen years) there were twenty-nine of a total of thirty-five men and twenty of a total of thirty women whose command of English would have been rated poor to good. Thirty-three of this total of forty-nine were in the age-grade of fifteen to thirty years. The oldest of this group would have been just twelve years of age when the school was established in

1918. But it should also be noted that nineteen in the fifteen-to-thirty age-grade were rated as having only a poor or fair command of English. And there was only one Spanish-American person in Atrisco who spoke really excellent English. This was the trader, who had had two years of education at the University of New Mexico. Next in proficiency was a daughter of Don Juan Atrisco, who sometimes substituted in the Atrisco school and in addition often acted as the interpreter for the meetings which were held when campaigning politicians came to the village.

An added benefit derived from the high-school program for the few who participated in it in the years 1930–37 was an increased knowledge of their own language. The program included a two-year course in Spanish, and among those who took it there was both a noticeable improvement in their spoken Spanish (the Spanish of the average New Mexico Spanish-American is really a kind of patois in which are many seventeenth century archaisms) and also the achievement to varying degrees of an ability to read and write the language. There had always been a few of the oldest *Atrisqueños*—Don Juan Atrisco, for example—who read Spanish; but virtually none of the persons under fifty had had the opportunity to become literate in the language until the time it was taught in the high school.

The teachers who were sent into Atrisco, with one exception, left few marks of influence on the people or the educational program itself. There were two Spanish-American teachers sent in to teach in the grammar school during the years I knew the community well. The first was a man who came with his family. He remained one year and was succeeded by a young unmarried woman who took up residence with one of the village families. All persons in the male teacher's family and the young female teacher as well were considered as transients and were never integrated into the life of the community. Because the male teacher had let it be known at once that he and his family were Protestants, they were the more ignored. For the most part the teachers ran the school and lived a life apart. Although the people of the village were always both respectful and friendly, the relationships remained quite superficial. For one thing no Atrisco family would have dreamed of interfering with the management of the school or of making any complaints about it. It, like almost everything else, was accepted for what it was.

The one teacher who did become a community figure—virtually a *patrona* in some respects—was an elderly Anglo-American woman who managed the high school and taught all courses in it during almost all of the six-year life span of that school. Although this woman, Mrs. Engels, was both an Anglo-American and a Protestant, it was known that her daughter had married into one of the prominent Spanish-American families of the state. This fact gave some basis for the assumption that she would be more sympathetic to and understanding of Spanish-Americans than the typical Anglo-American was believed to be. But it was chiefly her own behavior in the handling of the constant friction between the Texan and Spanish-American students in the high school and the outright flare-ups created by some of the Texan parents which won for her the loving respect of many *Atrisqueños*. Without ever being unfair in the handling of any of her students, she let it be known to Texan students and parents alike that she would not condone their often aggressive and not infrequently quite intolerant behavior. Once when there had come some really angry protestations from some Texan parents that their children had, together with the Atrisco children, been asked to help clean up Atrisco for the *fiesta*, she walked the six miles to Homestead to reason with the protesters. She had no means of transportation of her own and did not wish to evidence a favoritism by having a member of an Atrisco family take her. People in both communities, but most especially in Atrisco, were greatly impressed by this and other of her methods of maintaining the peace. She was, indeed, remarkably skillful in dealing with a situation which was always tension-ridden.

Gradually, in the years she was in Atrisco, she began to exert a more and more generalized influence on the lives of the people, both young and old. She introduced the idea of evening parties for the high-school-age boys and girls. It was at these parties, of which there were only a few, to be sure, that the knowledge gleaned in school textbooks was used in a guessing game. It was a simple little game of one person thinking about where an X (a girl) went with a Y (a boy). There was much giggling over the pairing of names, which seemed to be the main interest in the game. But it was noted that, in "dreaming up" the places the paired couples were supposed to go, far-off countries such as Egypt, China, and Japan were often cited. Although little was known about these places or their actual location in the world, there had been some stirring of the imagination about them.

Another of Mrs. Engels' enterprises was the establishment and management of a 4-H club for some of the young people. As the club functioned in Atrisco it was really just another social occasion and not at all project-oriented as the 4-H clubs throughout the United States are supposed to be. Actually, it met only a few times, because the date of its organization was only slightly prior to the time many people, including Mrs. Engels, left the village and the high school was shut down.

Mrs. Engels did remain in Atrisco during the troubled 1936–37 period when so many were compelled suddenly to reorient their lives, and all through it she was sought out by young and old alike for advice and support. I doubt that what she had to say to the men about economic matters was significant, but some men found talking to her useful, nonetheless. And she certainly was a source of comfort to many of the mothers who had developed a great anxiety about what might happen to their teen-age daughters now that they were thrown together with Texan boys whose sex mores they did not trust.

Had Atrisco had more teachers like Mrs. Engels, and for longer periods, it is probable that a degree of helpful familiarity with the Anglo-dominated outside world would have been gained, and gained without resentment. But there were few teachers with her kind of understanding. Moreover, even she was hampered in what she could do by a formal educational program which was not designed to meet the adjustive needs of Spanish-Americans.

The political system of New Mexico has not been much more effective than the educational system, either in the integrating of the Spanish-American villages into the social order of the state or the preparing of the people in the villages for what they were to meet when they migrated to towns and cities. The general nature of this system—the county organizations and the autocratic local control by *jefes politicos*—has already been treated. However, there was much which happened in the political sphere of behavior in Atrisco in 1936, a major election year, which will supplement and give life to the general description.

Don Juan Atrisco was trying desperately that year to regain both a firm political control of Atrisco and an official position in Verona county. Helping him was the son, Pablo, who had recently returned from Santa Fe after having failed in his *cantina* business. Pablo had learned something about political strategy while in the state capital, and he was also a most adroit and fairly eloquent speaker. He was more than confident that he and his father together would gain full control of the delegation which Atrisco was to send to the county convention. And he hoped that once the delegation was controlled there could be enough influence brought to bear upon key county officials for his father to be named the Republican candidate for county commissioner.

This confidence was not too well grounded. The total political situation in the Atrisco area in 1936 was a complicated one. One complication was the presence of the newly developed community of Homestead which was predominantly Democratic in its political leanings. This problem was mainly one for the county officials, because Atrisco, even though it had few votes, had always been a Republican stronghold upon which the dominant Republican political organization could count. It is even told—and knowing New Mexico politics in years past, I see no reason to doubt the story—that in years when there were some doubts about election outcomes the ballot boxes of Atrisco and some other quite remote settlements would be delayed for several days because of "muddy and impassable roads." Finally they would arrive with the right number and the right kind of votes. Because New Deal policies and relief funds were giving the Republicans more cause than usual to worry about election outcomes in 1936, the loss of a stronghold like Atrisco had special significance.

However, it was not the Democrats of Homestead who were of great concern to Don Juan and Pablo Atrisco. It was the Republican minority of that community whom they wished to reach and control. Pablo, who had lived among Anglo-Americans for some time and knew their language, thought he would have little difficulty in eliciting the Republicans' support for his father's plans. Again and again he went to Homestead to urge and promise, and almost always he took with him the bottles of liquor which have always been a medium of exchange in Spanish-American politics. Many of those contacted seemed amenable enough, on the surface at least, but Pablo did not really know Texans of the type who built Homestead.

In the long run a number of them proved to be unaccountable in their support of the Atriscos.

A greater obstacle still for Don Juan and Pablo was the stubborn and artful competition of Luis Corona. This was the man who was later to fling the gauntlet at Don Juan by pushing his way to the head of the *fiesta* procession. That he dared to do so was in large part the result of a temporary triumph in the political arena.

One of the main political events for the village in an election year was always the meeting at which its delegates to the county political convention were chosen. Theoretically this was supposed to be a democratic meeting with nominations from the floor for a chairman, a secretary, and finally the delegates, and subsequent elections by majority vote. Actually it never was, and this year everyone was keyed to a high pitch to see how the feud between the dethroned *patrón* who was attempting a comeback and his unseasoned but guileful contender would come out.

Luis Corona had let it be known that he was the person whom the county officials considered to be the *jefe politico* of Atrisco, and he had further announced that he and one of his sons should be the two delegates to the county convention, or, if the two votes were to be halved (this was allowable), he and his son should certainly constitute half the total delegation. Don Juan and Pablo Atrisco were equally determined to control the meeting and the delegation to be selected in it. In addition, they desired a commitment on the part of the delegates, whether two or four, to support Don Juan's candidacy for county office.

Because the procedures and events of the meeting held on October 9 in the grammar school illustrate so well the kind of political tactics common to Atrisco and similar villages, I shall quote in full the description of it written shortly after it occurred.

This meeting, to which almost everyone in the village went except very small children, was opened by Luis Corona, who claimed support of the county officials. Hardly had he opened the meeting, however, before young Pablo Atrisco hastily addressed the chair and rushed to the front of the room to make a speech. This speech, fiery and even eloquent, was given in English largely for the benefit of the homesteaders in the audience. It was rapidly translated by the male schoolteacher. In context it was a general diatribe upon the Democratic administration as a whole. Following young Pablo one or two other villagers and a few of the Texans made short speeches of a similar nature. Luis Corona finally interrupted the speeches and asked that the meeting attend to the business of the day which was the selection of delegates. He proposed that anyone interested in being a delegate make that interest known and then a choice would be made among such persons. In making such a suggestion he was following a custom inaugurated in the days of Don Juan's supremacy. Moreover, from his own point of view it was a safe suggestion because practically none of the villagers had the money to make the journey to the county seat, and both he and his sons in voicing their willingness to go were virtually certain of election. But on this occasion he had no sooner made his proposal when Don Juan Atrisco rose and said quite firmly that such procedure was improper. Delegates, he insisted, must be nominated and elected from the floor. He made a motion incorporating his proposal which was quickly seconded by his son. Then without even waiting for word from the chairman he called for a vote and pronounced the motion carried on the strength of a few loud "ayes" from several of the already intoxicated young men in the rear of the room. When questioned afterwards these men admitted they did not even know what the question under consideration was. One young man even went so far as to say: "I only come to these meetings to hear them argue and for the dances which come afterwards."

The chairman tried to protest but the rapid-fire arguments of the Atriscos were too much for him and he finally assented to letting the motion stand as carried. He asked that the meeting proceed with the election of a president and secretary. Again there was quick action, this time on the part of the schoolteacher whom the Atriscos had under their control. He nominated Don Juan for president of the meeting. Not even the chairman of the meeting contested the legality of the nomination made by a man who was not a legal resident of the village. And no one protested when young Pablo Atrisco leapt to the floor and called for a vote on his father's name without waiting for further nominations. The Atriscos, so long in control of the village, knew the methods to employ, and the villagers, so long accustomed to their domination, would probably have hesitated to name anyone else even had they been interested. Don Juan took charge of the meeting as president, and the next act was to have his daughter elected secretary. This election was, however, almost necessary because Cecelia Atrisco was the best equipped of the village women, by virtue of her quite good command of the two languages, to keep the minutes of the meeting. The secretary is often selected from among the women because they are not supposed to take an active part in the meetings.

The next issue to be attacked was the number of delegates to be sent. The village is permitted two delegates, but it was possible to select four, to each of whom would be accorded a half vote. After some bickering between the Atriscos and the Coronas it was decided to send four instead of two. The delegates, quickly selected by a procedure as lacking in the elements of accepted democratic method as other procedures of the meeting, were Don Juan, Luis Corona, a son of Luis, and a member of one other village family. In only the case of the fourth delegate did the villagers have any voice at all in the selection, and one could scarcely call it a choice since the man was a close relative of the Atriscos and under their instruction.

Once the delegates were decided upon, Pablo Atrisco made another long speech in which he disclosed the goal he and his father had in mind—namely, the nomination at the county convention of Don Juan for county commissioner. In the course of the speech he stated that he wished to *suggest* that all the Atrisco delegates be instructed—or "tied" as he worded it (from the Spanish verb *amarrar*)—to vote for his father. At the end of the speech he put his suggestion in the form of a motion and called for an immediate vote himself. He was well aware that he could get an immediate response from the audience which, while not deeply concerned with the matter at stake, liked to give verbal expression to their excitement in the form of yelling "aye." He received the expected response and declared the motion carried.

Up to this point Luis Corona had permitted the Atriscos to dominate the meeting, but this last move was too much for him. At first and in relatively calm tones he stated that he did not approve of delegates being "tied," being careful to add each time: "Not, of course, that we do not approve of this candidate." Luis Corona apparently had had no desire to antagonize the Atriscos openly in light of the power they once had over the people and might still regain, but his plan to outwit them at the county convention might be endangered were it known that all delegates were even theoretically bound to the support of Don Juan for a county office. When, therefore, each of his protests was answered by the glib Pablo Atrisco, he began to speak his mind more strongly. An extremely heated and futile discussion lasting for more than an hour ensued. Pablo Atrisco had the floor much of the time, and on several occasions he offered to put the matter to the vote "of the people of Atrisco." But no sooner would he make this remark when his politically wise father as president of the meeting would say in firm tones: "That motion has already been carried." Don Daniel Lucero—who never liked arguments—finally intervened and suggested that delegates give their support to Don Juan. Since the argument had obviously reached an *impasse*, the Coronas agreed for the moment and the meeting was adjourned in favor of a *baile* in the schoolhouse. Atrisco had been given a full measure of excitement for one evening, and conversation at the dance was centered on the fight between the two families. Few discussing the matter had an opinion to voice, however. The main theme of the talk was the speculative one of which side would win out at the county convention.

As many of the villagers seemed to suspect, the Coronas did not regard themselves as bound to Don Juan at all. Immediately upon arriving in the county seat they sought out Don Juan's enemies in the county and made plans for his defeat, and since Don Juan had several enemies in positions of power who did not wish him prominent again in county politics, their task was not a difficult one. When the nominations for county commissioner were made, Don Juan received only two votes, his own and that of his relative.

Defeated in their plans, the Atriscos withdrew from Atrisco's political activities for the year of 1936. Pablo, in a conversation with the writer, threatened to call a meeting and expose the Coronas for what he termed treachery, but he never called it. His father probably would not have permitted it, for no one knows so well as a *Mejicano jefe politico* himself the completeness of defeat that can be dealt a village political leader. Don Juan was well aware that the county officials had, for the moment at least, recognized Luis Corona as the *jefe politico* and that into his hands would be placed all the money and the liquor with which they intended to control the election.

For just one year Luis Corona was actually the *jefe politico* of Atrisco, at least to the extent that the county officials worked through him at election time. A number of the people in the village quietly voiced doubts that he would remain long in power, but the doubts did not lead them to defy him or prevent them from enjoying the election benefits he had to dispense.

All in all, Atrisco had the most dramatic and exciting political bill of fare of its existence in the months of October and November of 1936. In addition to the excitement of its own local feud, it was treated to several meetings and celebrations by groups of candidates on the state and county tickets of both parties. A few Republican candidates, mainly those running for minor offices, had for many years made it a point to visit the village in election years, and there had usually been at least one politically sponsored dance. But these visits were on the whole courtesy visits, for there had been little cause to worry about the election outcome in Atrisco as long as Don Juan reigned supreme and the village stood alone in the voting district. The year 1936 was different both because of the many Democrats in Homestead who were now voters in the Atrisco district and because of the sweeping power of the Democratic Party everywhere in the nation.

The Democrats of Verona County, always in the minority prior to 1936, seized upon the double advantage the total situation offered them and made a concerted effort both to consolidate and placate the Texans of Homestead and to woo the Spanish-Americans of Atrisco. Luis Corona, who had the funds and the authority to plan the meetings of the Republican Party candidates, was hard put to it to compete with the show staged by some of the visiting Democratic candidates. In the first instance some of the Democratic candidates were far more eloquent speakers than members of the Republican delegations, and, in 1936 with Roosevelt at the helm of the party, they had more to talk about. It was obvious that many in Atrisco were impressed by the eloquence. The drama and fire of one particular Democrat's speech was meat for conversation for days. In other ways, too, the Democrats outshone the Republicans. Accompanying their delegations were regular dance bands—small, to be sure, but good—and there was no stinting on the supply of liquor. The rally *bailes* they sponsored were gay indeed and much more novel than those sponsored by the Coronas, where the music was provided by three of Luis Corona's sons.

Señor Corona, none too secure in his newly acquired political chieftainship, apparently did not dare refuse the Democrats the right to speak or to provide entertainment for the village. He did, however, insist upon opening the meetings (there were two of them), and he went to great pains to welcome the delegates as *guests* of Republicans and to remind them, and *los Atrisqueños* as well, that they were being given the privilege of speaking in a building (the village grammar school) which had been built by "Republican labor."

The formal rallies held for the presenting of the Republican candidates and their cause were much less colorful on the whole, but they did not differ greatly in their general platitudinous nature except in one particular. This was in the use of the racial issue by means of the propaganda appeal of the "great Spanish heritage." This appeal, which New Mexico politicians have used ever since 1912, was eschewed by the Democrats who no doubt feared the effect it would have upon the Texan voters whose intolerant attitude toward Spanish-Americans was well known.

Informally, the Republicans had the advantage, of course, for they were the guests of Luis Corona and were taken about by members of the Corona family for personal introductions. There was a personalized paternalism in their approach to the people of Atrisco which was lacking in that of the Democratic delegation. It was an approach which fitted well with the age-old custom of voting as the *jefe politico* dictated, and when election day came the Spanish-American vote of Atrisco was solidly Republican as usual.

One of the most intelligent of the village women, who had herself been tempted to vote for the Democrats but did not, made the following comment in somewhat bitter tones: "These people, they do not know what they are doing. They have never understood politics and no one ever comes out here to teach them. For years they have been voting just as they are told to without knowing what they are doing."

By 1937—the year which also marked the beginning of the withering away of the Atrisco school system—this kind of political regime received its deathblow. Luis Corona after one short year of triumph had to leave Atrisco because of his financial problems; many of the voters had also moved; and Don Juan Atrisco, probably because he saw that there would soon be little left to dominate, showed no inclination to try again to win back his old role of *jefe politico*.

The small amount of political activity still to be found in the village is now, it will be recalled, under the leadership of Don Daniel Lucero, who has given to its organization a decidedly Collateral *relational* character. A majority of those who have moved to the towns and cities of New Mexico are still lacking in an understanding of a majority-rule democratic government, but they are learning. Moreover, now that they are out from under the tight control of a *jefe politico*, they have become sufficiently independent in their voting behavior to have been an important factor in the breakdown of much of the personalistic political organization which had great control in the government of New Mexico for a very long time.

SUMMARY STATEMENT

From the comparisons of the data collected in 1936 and later years with data yielded by the value-orientation schedule used in 1951 and by subsequent investigations, certain definite conclusions can be reached and other suggestive interpretations made. It is to be noted in the first instance that no change has come in the first-order (the dominant) orientations of the Spanish-Americans except the predicted one of a shift from a dominant Lineal to a dominant Individualistic position. Not even here is the change as yet a radical one, because the older pattern in which Lineality was ranked first prevails as a strong competitor of the new pattern which gives a first preference to the Individualistic alternative. The summary pattern found in our data was Ind $\geqslant$ Lin $\geqslant$ Coll*.

As for the other orientations, what can be noted is either a slight decrease in the strength of the first-order positions or a shifting in the ordering of the second and third-order choices. Although the material gathered in the earlier study of Atrisco was not greatly concerned with total rank orders, it gave indications that the orderings on the *man-nature* and the *time* orientations were Subjugated over With over Over and Present over Past over Future. The 1951 data revealed these patterns of these two orientations: Subj > Over > With and Pres > Fut > Past. How definite and firm these shifts are is a question, as has been indicated. Should the economy of the United States as a whole continue to expand without serious recessions, it is to be predicted that the new second-order positions will become more firm and will in time be accorded a first-order position for many Spanish-Americans. The acculturation process among these people is progressing at a speed hitherto unknown, but it could be seriously deterred were there to be a recession which resulted in the laying off of countless Spanish-American workers.

The as yet quite slight shift away from the Being to the Doing alternative of the *activity* orientation is probably the most significant of the reasons for the prediction that the internalization of American middle-class values will be a slow process and one which will be highly subject to conditions which are relatively external to the Spanish-American group. Even Joe Atrisco, admittedly more Doing-oriented than most *Atrisqueños* and more so than he himself wanted to be ideally, said to me after he had sold off his livestock and left Atrisco (1958): "I had to put the money in houses in Railtown because I knew that otherwise I would quickly spend it on having a good time." Others, who now have high-paying jobs by Spanish-American standards, are living better than they ever have, but few are saving against a future when work may be hard to find.

All in all, the study over the years of *los Atrisqueños* indicates, as was predicted, that few firmly significant changes have as yet come to the basic value system except for the uprooting of the long-resented control of the Lineally defined autocratic figures of the *patrón* and the *hermano mayor*. The serious strains created by this kind of control have always been the greatest potential source of social change; and when finally those who suffered most from the strains came sufficiently under the influence of middle-class Anglo-Americans to have their rebelliousness supported, they attempted an outright overthrow of the old-type Spanish-American *relational* authority system. But few of the rebels have been up to the demands of their rebellion. The shift from a strong first-order Lineal *relational* position to the formerly weak third-order Individualistic one has not been easy for a majority of them. We have seen how "stopgap" Collateral groupings have been created by some of the Railtown *émigrés*, and seen also that many another has become personally disoriented.

At the present time the changes to be noted are, as Leonard and Loomis stated, the superficial ones made necessary by the demands of adaptation, and they have as yet scarcely touched the deeper convictions of the people.[31] But however superficial these changes may now appear to be relative to Spanish-American *dominant* value orientations, they nonetheless indicate that basic changes in the total value system are to be expected. There can be no turning back by these people, given the facts that they are firmly held within the borders of the United States and are increasingly subjected to dominant Anglo-American culture as one by one the small villages like Atrisco decay and the inhabitants of them move off to urban centers. Even though erratic and uneven in pace, there is a continuous increase in the pattern elaboration of Spanish-American economic activities and a concomitant decrease of pattern elaboration in the recreational and religious spheres. A majority of the people we tested in 1951 were still firm in their value choices of the Subjugated-to-Nature, the Present, and the Being orientations in matters having to do with recreation and religion, but year by year the patterns which support these values wither away.

Two alternative end results appear possible. One is that of a greater acculturation of a majority of the group, *providing* the conditions in the wider United States culture are propitious for a slow assimilation process. Even so, some have been lost and others will become lost. The other prospect is a fairly thoroughgoing disorganization both for the group as a whole and for personalities within the group. At the moment the first of the two prospects seems the more likely.

[31] See the statement quoted on p. 207.

TABLE VII:1	TABLE VII:2
SUMMARY OF TEXAN RANKINGS	SUMMARY OF MORMON RANKINGS

	Relational Orientation		*Relational* Orientation
R1	Ind ⩾ Coll > Lin	R1	Ind ⩾ Coll > Lin
R2	Ind > Lin > Coll	R2	Ind > Lin ⩾ Coll
R3	Ind > Coll > Lin	R3	Ind ⩾ Coll > Lin
R4	Coll ⩾ Ind > Lin	R4	Coll ⩾ Ind > Lin
R5	Ind > Coll ⩾ Lin	R5	Ind > Coll ⩾ Lin
R6	Ind > Coll > Lin	R6	Ind > Coll > Lin
R7	Ind > Coll > Lin	R7	Ind ⩾ Coll > Lin
Sum	Ind > Coll > Lin	Sum	Ind > Coll > Lin

	Time Orientation		*Time* Orientation
T1	Pres ⩾ Fut > Past	T1	Pres ⩾ Fut > Past
T2	Fut > Pres > Past	T2	Fut > Pres ⩾ Past
T3	Pres ⩾ Fut > Past	T3	Pres > Fut > Past
T4	Pres ⩾ Fut > Past	T4	Fut ⩾ Pres ⩾ Past
T5	Fut ⩾ Pres ⩾ Past	T5	Fut ⩾ Pres > Past[a]
Sum	Fut ⩾ Pres > Past	Sum	Fut ⩾ Pres > Past

	Man-Nature Orientation		*Man-Nature* Orientation
MN1	Over > Subj ⩾ With	MN1	Over ⩾ Subj > With
MN2	Over ⩾ Subj ⩾ With	MN2	With ⩾ Subj ⩾ Over
MN3	Over > With ⩾ Subj	MN3	Over ⩾ With > Subj
MN4	Over ⩾ Subj ⩾ With	MN4	With ⩾ Subj ⩾ Over[b]
MN5	Over ⩾ With > Subj	MN5	Over ⩾ With ⩾ Subj*
Sum	Over > With ⩾ Subj	Sum	Over ⩾ With > Subj

	Activity Orientation		*Activity* Orientation
A1	Doing ⩾ Being	A1	Doing ⩾ Being
A2	Doing ⩾ Being	A2	Doing ⩾ Being
A3	Doing ⩾ Being	A3	Doing > Being
A4	Being ⩾ Doing	A4	Being ⩾ Doing
A5	Doing ⩾ Being	A5	Doing ⩾ Being
A6	Doing > Being	A6	Doing > Being
Sum	Doing > Being	Sum	Doing > Being

[a] Fut > Pres only.
[b] With > Subj only.

CHAPTER VII

The Mormon and Texan Communities

Fred L. Strodtbeck

Although rural America is much studied, our dependence upon formal reports for knowledge of it is not great. A people who have been but one full generation in the city have little need to be told again what, for most, is a part of family culture. So it is with Rimrock and Homestead, the Mormon and Texan communities of the study; they are rural villages whose daily routines will surprise few. They were founded during the last eighty years by migrants from the western plains and inter-mountain states. The older men in these communities have known the Great Depression and both World Wars. However, it has only been since 1950 that these communities have firmly linked fingers with the rest of rural America by installing electric lines and paving the roads to their trading center.

In order to come more quickly to grips with the value-orientation materials, it will be assumed that the brief description in Chapter II, Vogt's monograph on Homestead,[1] O'Dea's papers on Rimrock,[2] and, in time, chapters in the forthcoming values report on both cultures[3] may be consulted by readers who wish a more detailed view of the communities. It is, however, particularly essential that the reader have in mind the general way in which the communities differ in their organization.

Rimrock is clearly a planned village. In the central square of the village is the Mormon church. The towering poplar trees, now more than fifty years old, rise in regular patterns from near the banks of the village irrigation system. They contrast dramatically with the piñon and juniper growth of the nearby hills. The thriving irrigated trees are the most accessible clue to the casual visitor of an underlying and continuously functioning social organization. The trees depend on the dam; the continued existence of the dam depends upon decisions and guidance of groups organized in the church. It was the teaching of the Mormon Church which caused Rimrock to be laid out in the plat of the City of Zion, and it is the sectarian sense of uniqueness coming from the identity as Mormon which reinforces the integration of the community.

---

[1] Evon Z. Vogt, *Modern Homesteaders* (Cambridge, Mass.: Harvard University Press, 1955).
[2] Thomas F. O'Dea, "The Effects of Geographical Position on Belief and Behavior in a Rural Mormon Village" and (with Evon Z. Vogt) "A Comparative Study of the Role of Values in Social Action in Two Southwestern Communities" from *The Sociology of Mormonism*, Publications in the Humanities Number 14, from the Department of Humanities, Massachusetts Institute of Technology, 1955.
[3] To be published by Row, Peterson & Co.

The water economy of Homestead is also a singular symbol of its social organization. The tower at the main crossroads dispenses water for ten cents a barrel, and each man hauls his own water in his own barrels in the back of his own pickup truck. The pattern of house location requires no consensus—each man builds upon his own section. Vogt describes in detail the adversities under which the community was formed and the precarious lottery with frost and drought which was ever present in its development. It has more recently been saved from a total decline by the soil-bank provisions, which in turn are now being withdrawn. From founding to the present near-decline a stubborn Individualism based on the nuclear family as a social unit has characterized the community.

The reader is thus put on notice that even though both our groups speak English, wear jeans, and drive pickup trucks, there are conspicuous behavioral differences. It is clear that if the value-orientation responses showed no differences whatsoever when the behavioral differences are as large as these alluded to, then surely we would be forced to conclude that the instrument is less sensitive than might be desired. At the same time both communities are now in contact with the current culture of the United States, and both were developed by persons who were of the main stream of north European, Protestant migrants to America. They necessarily carry many common values. Hence, if the similarities between the groups were found to be very small, might one not be disappointed that there was so little continuity of cultural values? Thus our task does not involve exotic contrasts; it is rather a matter of careful search for variation around familiar themes.

Our comparisons will be facilitated by the relative homogeneity of each community. Stratification is, however, not absent. And curiously, in Homestead, where the status differences are really smaller, they appear the greater. The upper, Presbyterian, status extreme in Homestead is strongly motivated to achieve dominant middle-class values and life styles. They would like to be closer to where something is going on—like big-league baseball or restaurants serving sea food, for instance. But most of all they strive for the middle-class conveniences, first in their cars, then in their kitchens, next in their living rooms, and finally—only one instance by 1953—in the exterior appearance of their homes.

That the Homesteaders have not won the margin above subsistence to move very far, a visitor like myself, an urban person from the East, is never permitted to forget. They turn the gracious usage of apologizing to one's guest about his accommodations into a masochistic game. Even the modern bathrooms, or the new fluorescent fixtures which might be displayed with pride, are in fact an occasion for self-conscious tension and shame. It is almost as if the steps toward their middle-class ideal which they had taken were so slight that they emphasize the great distance of their goal rather than the magnitude of their advance.

For the lower, Baptist, status extreme in Homestead, the felt deprivation at not having achieved middle-class comforts is not so great. It is almost as if there were a quantum of energy which, if required for subsistence alone, is not available for mobility and status concerns. Psychologically, being lower status simply means that one is less ashamed of the outhouse, oil lamps, and wood stove which remain from the early pioneering period. It is important to stress that being at the lower status extreme in Homestead does not imply a symbiotic interdependence with higher-status families such that the lower work for and are protected by the higher. Wage work is interchanged, but broader Collateral responsibilities are sharply limited. An individual loan from the bank is sought by both the upper and lower status extremes in response to a crisis. The rare situations in which work is exchanged between two families are frequently sources of tension without regard to the relative status of the families involved.

In Rimrock the status system appears to be modified by the facts that there is only one church and that the emergent economic elite are foreclosed by their identity as Mormons from elaborating their social contacts with non-Mormons. Thus the elite turn to the church community for their social satisfactions and, in turn, it is in their relative position in the church hierarchy that one sees the reflection of their achievements. This has the net effect of creating a force toward the homogenizing rather than differentiating of life styles.

In contrast to the Texans, Mormons seem to have very little shame about the level of convenience in their homes. While it is true that Mormon homes are generally more convenient and durable than Texan homes, one senses a social organizational element in the difference of attitude. When a Mormon wishes to extend a gracious invitation, he invites a person to come to the next community dance or bake-sale. The Mormons are accustomed to having others present in their homes to eat or sleep, but they tend to look to community facilities for all important social occasions. Perhaps because of this, or because of his possible participation in their building, a Mormon takes particular pride in speaking of the community facilities. In short, entertaining and being entertained are to a much lesser degree competitive activities of nuclear families; hence the furnishings and level of convenience of one's home have less status significance.

O'Dea[4] reports that in 1950, a relatively prosperous year, seven of the families in Rimrock received church relief. The existence of this marginal economic group was not immediately evident to me during my first residence in the village. Without the benefit of prior observation, I erroneously perceived the calm ongoing situations as being static. In successive years it was apparent that the balance between the more prosperous families had been seriously disturbed. The creation of a supermarket in the trading center and the greater accessibility of the trading center due to new roads reduced trading in Rimrock to the point that only the best-established family could keep their trading post in operation. They have subsequently been able to take over trading outlets which were relinquished by former owners, and during this same period they have purchased the competing

---

[4] See *The Sociology of Mormonism*, cited in footnote 2.

gasoline station, closed their own pump which was in need of repair, and now have the station operated on a lease arrangement.

One comes to feel that there is one class of property which is subject to economic concentration through competition and another class which is managed so as to maximize its contribution to the community. Land close to the village which can be irrigated is, thus far, not under the sharpest possible competition. Study of the land-exchange patterns suggests that the latent norm is for every family to have some irrigable land and it should in general be in the direct control of the person physically able to do the work on it. Detailed study of ownership in the Rimrock Dam Company, ownership of land, and the allocation of water in times of scarcity is not available, but the functioning of this system is clearly a matter of symbolic importance to the community—even after a period in which its economic importance has decreased.

The building sites within the village are also handled with a view to the further development of the community. Any young Mormon man who wishes to marry and build a home seems to find a place. The mechanism by which this works differs from family to family, but certainly there is no evidence that any of the more wealthy families have purchased village tracts to hold or to resell at a profit. Shortly after World War II the joint purchase of twenty-seven sections of land for the Rimrock pasture was expressly conceived as a device for enabling a larger number of young men to find it economically possible to continue living within the community. A part of the financing of this transaction was arranged through the Mormon Church in Salt Lake City.

The mobilization of a desire to maintain the village for good Mormon families to the exclusion of others has never arisen, simply because few non-Mormons have sought residence in Rimrock. The community has refused the offer of the state to stock the lake behind the dam for commercial fishing for the stated reason that they would have to agree in time of drought to hold the dam at a minimum depth to protect the fish. They have quite pointedly not built up conveniences around the dam to encourage fishing by outsiders, and the beer cans and debris which outsiders leave around the dam draw negative comment. It is of course not clear that the dam could become an important economic asset as a recreation spot unless a lodge were built. This in turn would probably require that the drinking of alcoholic beverages be tolerated, and so the line of possible negative consequences might be elaborated. Whatever line of analysis different members of the community follow leads them to conclude that there are difficulties which would more than offset the possible financial gain involved in developing Rimrock as a recreation center.

The collective desire to keep the village going and the strong individual desire for each family to expand into ranching come into opposition in the competition for the same lands. The large rancher, whose holdings are contiguous, is more disposed to buy land than to sell. Many of the sections held by the Navaho are held under the limitation of reservation lands—they may not be sold to non-Navaho. Other lands held by the Navaho can be sold, and within the past fifteen years they have been sold in great quantities to the family which is becoming economically predominant in the village. Since it is this family which now has a trading monopoly and since it is in the course of settling trading bills that most transfers of Indian lands take place, this one family stands in a very good position to further its holdings.

It is difficult to see the ultimate implications for community functioning of this economic concentration. At the present time there is a general awareness that many of the sons from the poorer families have been forced to move elsewhere to make a living; but those from poorer families who do remain are never far from a social and economic interdependence with the wealthier families. In recent years it has been the wealthier families which almost exclusively have taken the leadership in church affairs and community projects. They work on such matters as if they were carrying out a personal business venture; and if one takes a slightly detached view of the importance of the community to their way of life, one may easily see personal salience in what at the same time is manifestly community activity. The trend of economic concentration and the attendant narrowing base for community life will be difficult to break. The leaders of the community can scarcely be expected to join in a collective plan which is to the detriment of their long-term economic well-being.

Forecasting future social organization is difficult because it is hard to predict when community consensus will fall below the critical level required to get things done. There is little evidence at this time that consensus is declining—quite the opposite. The families recently vied with one another to contribute to the road-paving fund. It is true that a road contractor working in the area was hired to oil and fill the streets. At an earlier time a local work group would have done the job. But it is also true that the job could be done more efficiently with the contractor's equipment. There is a clear consensus for pragmatic results in community activities. The best available machinery and the most competent men are called to do the jobs. In the local missionary work there is a tendency for church members to put in their time without regard to whether they do any good, but in more salient community projects local gossip discourages ritualistic participation.

The two conspicuous areas in which local resources fall shortest of community requirements are health and technical religious scholarship. For Rimrock, as for Homestead, the improved roads have increased the accessibility of medical services in the trading center; hence the problems of disease are now less important. But with regard to religious doctrine, the scholarship of the lay leadership in Rimrock does not compare favorably with the scholarship of comparable lay leaders in Salt Lake City and nearby communities. As a result, an official visit from a state officer or higher official of the Church provokes a real status challenge. The prestige of such visiting officials is built upon the legitimated Church doctrine no less than the community itself. The official visits are important to all members of the community even if it is the more prosperous families who feel the challenge most strongly.

Comment upon the marginality of religious competence in Rimrock serves to emphasize that Rimrock is not a representative Mormon community. It is a "fringe" community, a poor relation of the proud and progressive Utah Mormon communities. The implication of this fringe status upon religious belief is not clear beyond the fact that many church meetings are less challenging and less expertly handled than they might be. There is certainly no evidence of heretical local beliefs. The sons from the poorer families who might have become a mildly dissident force have left the community and, in most cases, the Church as well. If the local leaders recognized any gaps between local beliefs and new or technical Church doctrine, they would quietly move to bring local doctrine in line with Salt Lake City.[5]

Thus, in summary, the Texans of this study are not representative of Texans in Texas; they are sampled from one community in New Mexico. In addition, the Mormons are not representative of the Mormons in Utah. However, in the area under study the Mormons and Texans are similar to one another to a degree that would make it hard for a casual visitor to distinguish between them. But even a casual visitor could read the shibboleths of speech, color, and dress well enough to distinguish them from the Zuni, Navaho, and Spanish-Americans considered in this book. The geographical fact of their residence in the study area, the contrasts in their social organization, and their relatively greater similarity to rural Americans in the Southwest are the factors which guide our more detailed inquiry into the value orientations of Rimrock and Homestead.

RELATIONAL ORIENTATION

The belief that Texans strongly favor Individualism and are quite negative toward Lineality was the basis for the Ind > Coll > Lin *relational* prediction given in Chapter II. For the Mormons, however, the picture was not so clear. It was not known to what extent the sense of rank associated with the Church hierarchy would be matched by Lineal preferences. In addition, Jack Mormonism seemed in essence to be a rejection of religious constraints on smoking and drinking accompanied by an intensification of the energy directed toward Individualistic business success. Against these possibilities was the conspicuous frequency of Collateral arrangements in the business and social life of the community. As the data in Chapter V have already shown, this hesitancy in the prediction was unnecessary. Both Mormons and Texans were significantly Ind > Coll > Lin. And even though the Mormons proved to be more strongly oriented to the Collateral position than the Texans, the prediction that Collaterality would be roughly as strong as Individualism for Mormons was not sustained.

To illustrate both the outcome by questions and the between-culture differences, Graph VII:1 presents a line between the Texan point and

---

[5] One or two families recently adopted Navaho children into their families in response to a suggestion from Church authorities.

the Mormon point for each of the seven *relational* questions. Two questions, R4 (Choice of Delegate) and R2 (Help in Misfortune), are inconsistent with the summary outcome[6] in that they fall outside the Ind > Coll > Lin sector. In the first of these, R4, Mormons and Texans are close together, but in the second it is the Texans who pull away toward the Lineal alternative of the greater dependence upon the patron-like banker in the nearby trading center. The greatest difference between Mormons and Texans occurs within the Ind > Coll > Lin sector on R3 (Family Work Relations) where the Mormons are strongly toward the Ind = Coll fringe of the sector and the Texans are exactly on the Ind > Coll > Lin line bisecting the sector. For the remaining questions the differences are not great. In terms of the direction of the difference, six of the seven differences are consistent in showing that the Mormons of Rimrock show a stronger preference for the Collateral alternative than do the Texans. For one item, R5 (Wage Work), there is no difference.

With our sample the answers to the different questions are not independent because in each culture the same twenty persons are involved. One might suspect therefore that the differences between the two cultures might be wholly attributable to one or two individuals. To satisfy our curiosity on this matter we have plotted the location of the twenty individuals in each culture on Graphs VII:2 and VII:3. For convenience of reference a line has been drawn in the same place on each of the graphs which divides the two populations as follows:

	Left of Line	Right of Line
Texans	2	18
Mormons	9	11

Since the plottings had been inspected before the lines were drawn, it is not appropriate to utilize a statistical test. We do, however, take the distribution which results as tangible evidence that a substantial number, rather than just one or two, of our Mormon respondents are more given to Collaterality in their preferences.

Using the same reference lines it may be shown that Mormon men are more Collaterally oriented than Mormon women:

	Left of Line	Right of Line
Mormon Men	9	2
Mormon Women	0	9

There is no comparable trend among the Texans; hence one is led to conclude that the emphasis on Collaterality which differentiates the Mormons from the Texans arises almost wholly from the greater disposition toward Collaterality of the Mormon men.

Certain ethnographic details come to mind which are consistent with this finding. First, it is to be noted that the major cooperative activities

---

[6] The summary points are not shown on the graph. They would extend far outside the boundary of the graph, in the Ind > Coll > Lin direction.

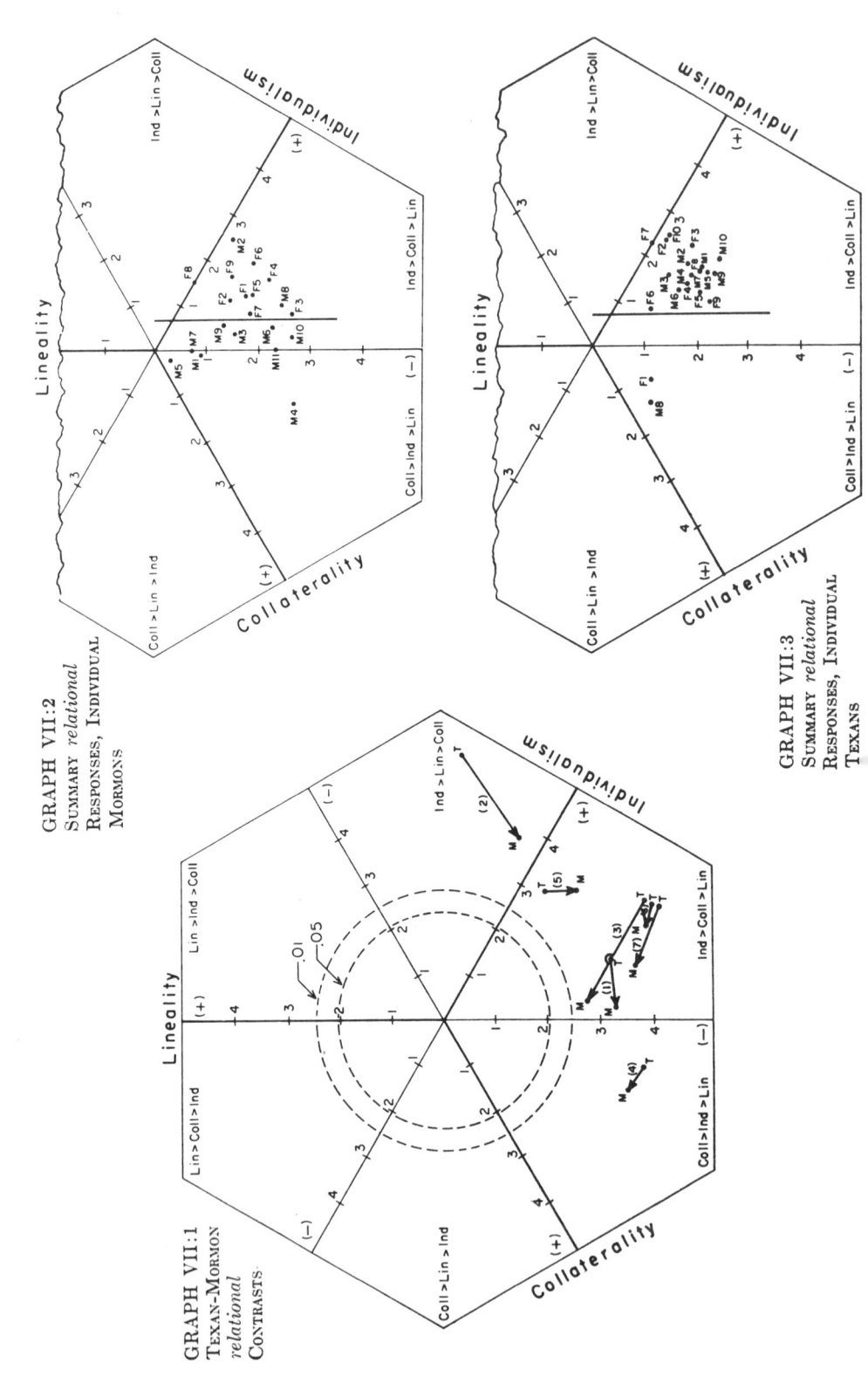

GRAPH VII:2
SUMMARY *relational* RESPONSES, INDIVIDUAL MORMONS

GRAPH VII:3
SUMMARY *relational* RESPONSES, INDIVIDUAL TEXANS

GRAPH VII:1
TEXAN-MORMON *relational* CONTRASTS

in the communities which are facilitated by the Mormon Church involve men who are simultaneously members of the priesthood as well as participants in the activity in question—land in the Rimrock pasture, the local water company, and the Rimrock dam. One wife expressed her fears with respect to the jointly held Rimrock pasture by observing that if something were to happen to her husband, she would not know how she would cope with decisions which would be made by the "men at the church."

In addition, ownership of land in Rimrock, particularly in the irrigable areas, has moved from older men to younger men who are physically able to do the work. From the larger families it is the boys who stayed behind in Rimrock who were given the preference. In these matters also, the wives talk of the transaction as having taken place between their husbands and their sons as if they themselves were not members. Transactions between brothers are also believed to be generally out of the wife's direct control. It is possible that if the questions had turned more specifically on modes of organization for welfare and related work, the Mormon women would have responded in a manner more supportive of Collaterality. For the given questions, women strongly favored Individualistic responses.

In summary it may be said that while the clarity of the Ind > Coll > Lin pattern was marked in *both* groups, there were subtle differences in our results which indicated that the Texans are more extremely Individualistically and less Collaterally oriented than are the Mormons, especially the Mormon men. When we turn to the literature on the two groups, this difference is substantiated and looms larger than our results indicate.

For example, Vogt stresses the strength of Individualism in Homestead as a major thesis. He argues that the highly developed independence of others was adaptive during the original hardships of settlement and that it subsequently impeded the development of Homestead as a community. In collaboration with O'Dea, he documents a striking differentiation between Homestead and Rimrock in the organization of state assistance for the construction of a school.

Concerning Rimrock—

In 1951 a plan for the construction of a high school gymnasium was presented to the villagers. Funds for materials and for certain skilled labor would be provided from state school appropriations, providing that the local residents would contribute the labor for construction. The plan was discussed in a Sunday priesthood meeting in the church, and later meetings were held both in the church and in the schoolhouse. Under the leadership of the principal of the school (who is also a member of the higher priesthood), arrangements were made whereby each ablebodied man in the community would either contribute at least 50 hours of labor or 50 dollars (the latter to be used to hire outside laborers) toward the construction. The original blueprint was extended to include a row of classrooms for the high school around the large central gymnasium.

Work on the new building began in late 1951, continued through 1952, and is now [in 1953] nearing completion. The enterprise was not carried through without difficulties. A few families were sympathetic at first but failed to contribute full amounts of either labor or cash, and some were unsympathetic toward the operation from the start. The high school principal had to keep reminding the villagers about their pledges to support the enterprise. But in the end the project was successful, and it represented an important cooperative effort on the part of the majority.[7]

The parallel account for Homestead is as follows:

The same plan for the construction of a new gymnasium was presented to the homesteaders as was presented to the Mormon village of Rimrock. As noted above, this plan was accepted by the community of Rimrock, and the new building is now nearing completion. But the plan was rejected by the residents of Homestead at a meeting in the summer of 1950, and there were long speeches to the effect that "I've got to look after my own farm and my own family first; I can't be up here in town building a gymnasium." Later in the summer additional funds were provided for labor; and with these funds adobe bricks were made, the foundation was dug, and construction was started—the homesteaders being willing to work on the gymnasium on a purely business basis at a dollar an hour. But as soon as the funds were exhausted, construction stopped. Today a partially completed gymnasium, and stacks of some 10,000 adobe bricks disintegrating slowly with the rains, stand as monuments to individualism of the homesteaders.[8]

The difference in responses to a potential development is, in part, a result of the sounder economic base of the Rimrock community, but a good measure of this current soundness is based upon successful community projects. On the evidence, one must wonder why the observed Individualism-Collaterality differences between the two cultures are not greater than they have proven to be, or alternatively, one may view with deepening appreciation the contribution to community organization of an institution like the Mormon Church, when its doctrine of progress through cooperation is superimposed on a typically Individualistic *relational* orientation.

TIME ORIENTATION

An essential tenet of Mormonism deals with *time* quite simply: "Things can be better in the future—if man keeps working to improve them." It is assumed that man will keep working, and through his energies and intelligence will transform the universe. Here in America, and at this time, each man may increase his own Godliness by his work. Later, in Heaven, the Godliness attained on earth will be retained and can be added to by further good deeds. By such a process each man can become progressively more like God, who Himself, by a similar process, has worked hard toward perfection and is, presumably, by activities appropriate to the level attained, still working toward greater perfection in the future.

Some may view with surprise the possible further development of Godliness in Heaven. This Mormon conception of the relevance of one's actions through *time* differs from the Calvinist conception in two important respects. First, Mormonism views the attainment of the Church in America

---

[7] Evon Z. Vogt and Thomas O'Dea, "A Comparative Study of the Role of Values in Social Action in Two Southwestern Communities," *American Sociological Review*, Vol. XVIII, No. 6 (December, 1953), p. 644.
[8] *Ibid.*, p. 650.

as being a sufficiently tangible sign of progress toward perfection to warrant a view of the attainment of perfection as a continuous process. Consistent with this, it is believed appropriate to have the same models of conduct on this earth as in Heaven. Mormons do not view the process of working toward perfection as culminating with death. One is not taken from earth to Heaven; it is rather that Heaven is being extended in a way which avoids the discontinuity recognized by Calvinism.

If this interpretation is correct, does it follow that Mormonism is more, or less, Future-oriented than Calvinism? The temptation to see a continuity which stretches into Eternity as being more Future-oriented is great. But insofar as this implies both working toward and enjoying the fruits of greater perfection now, it need not imply the foregoing of the pleasures of life at this time and the attendant depreciation of the Present.[9] In this sense Mormonism may be viewed as being clearly Future-oriented even though distinguished from Calvinism.

Turning to Homestead, the sources of Future *time* emphasis do not appear to be so definitely related to religious beliefs and practices. The formal theology of the Presbyterian and Baptist churches in Homestead can, of course, be differentiated in terms of the Presbyterians' relatively greater emphasis on work on this earth, in addition to faith, for the attainment of grace. But there is an ever-present pressure in the thinking of the community which takes priority over doctrinal considerations. They need to justify why they left west Texas or Oklahoma to come to Homestead and why they are staying in Homestead in lieu of going elsewhere. To remove the possible doubt that they have made a poor decision, they indulge in Texan boosterism. Boosterism is going to make the community flower, "the Pan-American highway will come through Homestead," "I'm goin' to have ten motel cabins right there in that section of beans by the road." Some measure of this boosterism may be discounted, but the essential point that the Texans are not working to re-create anything that has existed in the Past cannot be doubted. More than this, the Texans cannot face the prospect of letting things go as they are at Present. They fiercely want to use the technology available to them to increase productive capacity and, through this, the level of convenience they enjoy. The energy they have to work for short-run improvement in the lot of their individual families is great. But whether or not that energy would continue to be available after their more pressing needs are satisfied is quite another matter.

In Chapter V the reader learned that the summary points for the Mormons and Texans were remarkably close together in the Fut > Pres > Past sector of the graphic summary chart. Both points are near the Fut = Pres division line, and the outcome is very close to Fut = Pres > Past. It may be seen in Graph VII:4 that the Mormon point is higher than the Texan one in showing a differential preference for the third choice, the

---

[9] This distinction is not unrelated to the postulated orientation which was not checked in the field, namely innate *human nature*. Calvinism would hold that *human nature* was essentially mutable and Evil; Mormonism, mutable and Good. Such a basic assumption would give further weight to the necessity of foregoing pleasure to attain grace.

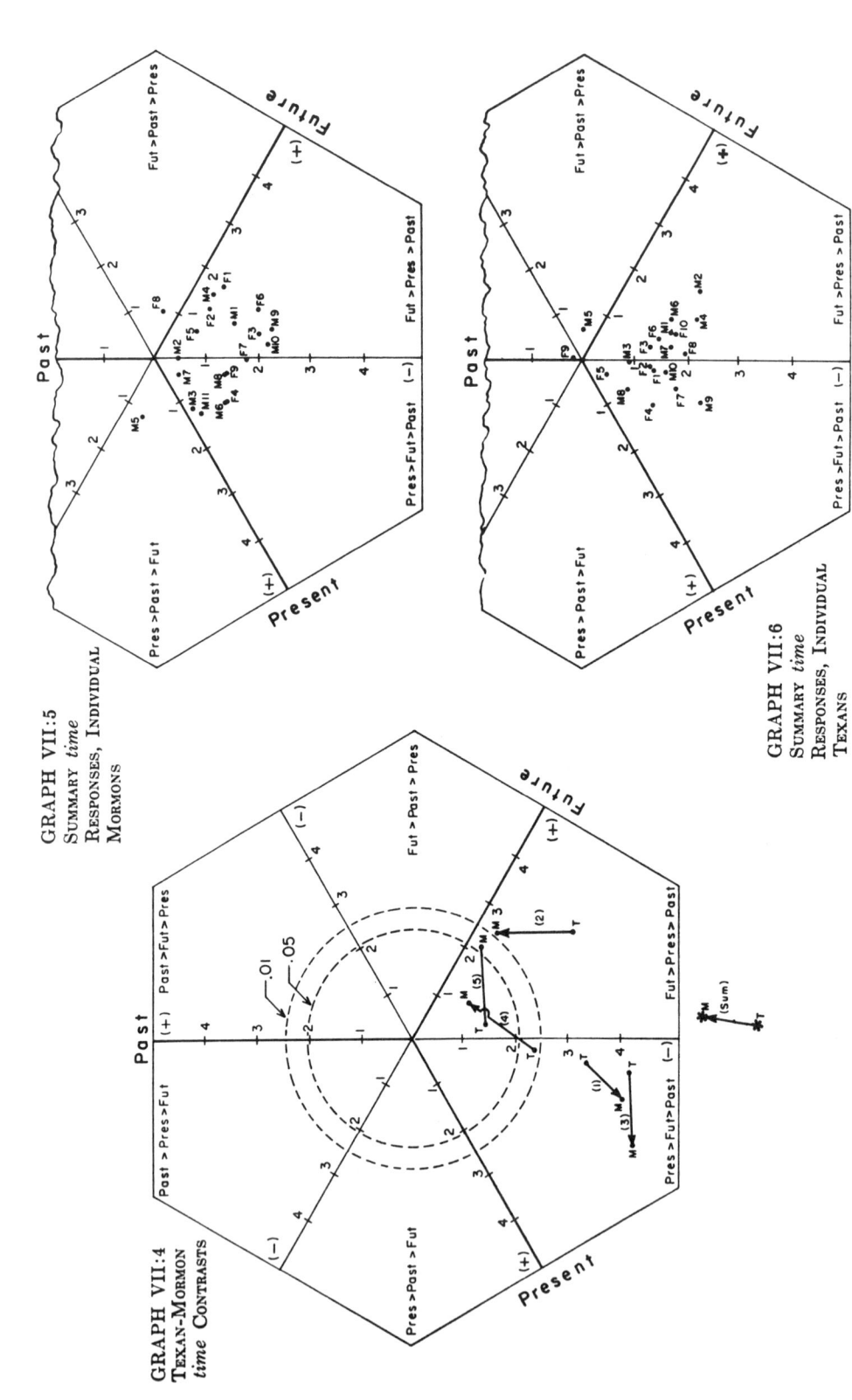

GRAPH VII:5
SUMMARY *time*
RESPONSES, INDIVIDUAL
MORMONS

GRAPH VII:6
SUMMARY *time*
RESPONSES, INDIVIDUAL
TEXANS

GRAPH VII:4
TEXAN-MORMON
time CONTRASTS

Past alternative, but it is a very slight difference. It is also to be noted in Graph VII:4 that the summary points represent a statistical reconciliation of highly heterogeneous individual question outcomes.

Looking to the individual questions for further detail, it may be noted that for T3 (Philosophy of Life), the Mormon outcome is Pres > Fut > Past and the consistency of the responses is reflected by the relatively great distance from the origin. When one rereads the Present alternative, which reaffirms the importance of what is happening now, it may be inferred that this phrasing would be completely in harmony with the sense of continuity between the Present and the Future to which the Mormons subscribe. On the other hand, one would assume from the earlier analysis that Mormons would reject the second sentence of the Present alternative which implies that the Future is unpredictable. From the evidence at hand, it is impossible to explain with certainty this one instance in which the Mormons were sharply more Present-oriented than Texans.

For T4, treating of Ceremonial Innovation, the Mormon support for each alternative was almost equal and the desire to maintain things as they had been in the Past was notably strong. It was the more frequent church attenders in Homestead who were most Future-oriented, and the less active parishioners were satisfied to maintain church practices as they were at Present.

One wishes that there might have been more *time* questions, for with a set of only five it is quite difficult to make an assessment of the relative strength of the Future in contrast with the Present alternative. Graph VII:5 shows a somewhat greater dispersion for individual Mormons than does Graph VII:6 for Texans, but further study reveals no unusual pattern in the distribution. If in fact there is a mixture of Future and Present emphases for Texans and a fusion of the Present with the Future for Mormons, then substantial increase in both subjects and questions and perhaps even a differently designed set of alternatives might be required to corroborate the difference. Within the range of precision possible in the present inquiry, there is no basis for distinguishing between Texans and Mormons, because the considerable question-to-question differences between the cultures are not uniform in direction. Hence, despite the success of this orientation in differentiating Mormon and Texan cultures from the other three cultures, it does not discriminate between them. It is clear that further information on the admittedly slight between-culture differences would be required before it could be reliably used to guide a theoretical extension or revision.

MAN-NATURE ORIENTATION

Before the research team reached the field, the view of the Texans as the ideal embodiment of a Mastery-over-Nature people had not been questioned. But in the community of Homestead the sight of arid fields and spirals of dust moving before the winds weakened the confidence of some members of the team. Could any Texan answer our questions with the bright optimism of a Mastery-over-Nature conviction in the face of the unyielding harshness of a two-year drought and the personal failure that it implied? It was not believed that this current hardship would bring Texans to a Harmony-with-Nature sense of coparticipation—there was no basis for this; but it was certainly plausible that the Subjugation-to-Nature emphasis would be augmented by current ruinous circumstances. Thus, the prediction was little more than an uneasy guess of Over > Subj = With, for there was little basis for assessing the relative strength of the disposition toward the Subjugated-to-Nature in contrast to the With-Nature position. Both would clearly be subordinated to Over-Nature.

The Mormon community did not suffer so severely from the drought, so the ambiguity attending the prediction was not based upon an immediate local circumstance. The With-Nature and Over-Nature themes, both in what we saw and in what we read, were nearly in balance. There was no evidence of a Subjugated-to-Nature orientation, but there was little to guide a choice between the other two possibilities. The prediction of With > Over > Subj represented a vote of confidence in the emergence of religious themes of coparticipation with God in the management of fields and resources.

The plot of the Mormon and Texan outcomes for particular questions in Graph VII:7 provides a point of entry into the more detailed discussion. The Texan outcome point is for all practical purposes Over > With = Subj, although technically it is Over > With $\geqslant$ Subj. This clarifies our prediction. Subjugated is less favored than With, despite the drought, and the gap between these two and Over is sizable. The distance of the Texan outcome point from the origin is considerably greater than would be required to establish significant consistency.

For the Mormons, significance is scarcely attained, and for practical purposes the pattern is Over = With > Subj although, again by a small margin, the pattern is technically Over $\geqslant$ With > Subj. Contrary to our predictions, Over exceeded With, but this failure is as much attributable to our feeling of necessity of resolving what seemed to be equally likely outcomes as to a misappraisal of the cultures. It may be noted that the Mormons were significantly closer to the With-Nature responses on three of five questions, MN2, 3, and 4. To re-create something of the flavor of the perception of this orientation, it is appropriate to comment upon one of the Mormon interviews—one which took place on the one Sunday in the month in which services are not held in the afternoon. It was a proper time to talk about serious matters. For each of the two preceding *man-nature* questions a rather liberal addition of commentary on the Mormon view had been added to the responses. This respondent had lived in Mormon communities closer to Salt Lake City and still had modest commercial interests outside of Rimrock. He was a man near sixty, and in recent years he had shifted from farming to church work and his commercial business interests. The chance to talk about the MN3, Use of Fields, was therefore an opportunity to reminisce and casually proselytize. He had stressed time and again that he kept busy, that when he turned from a private task he would undertake a community task. It

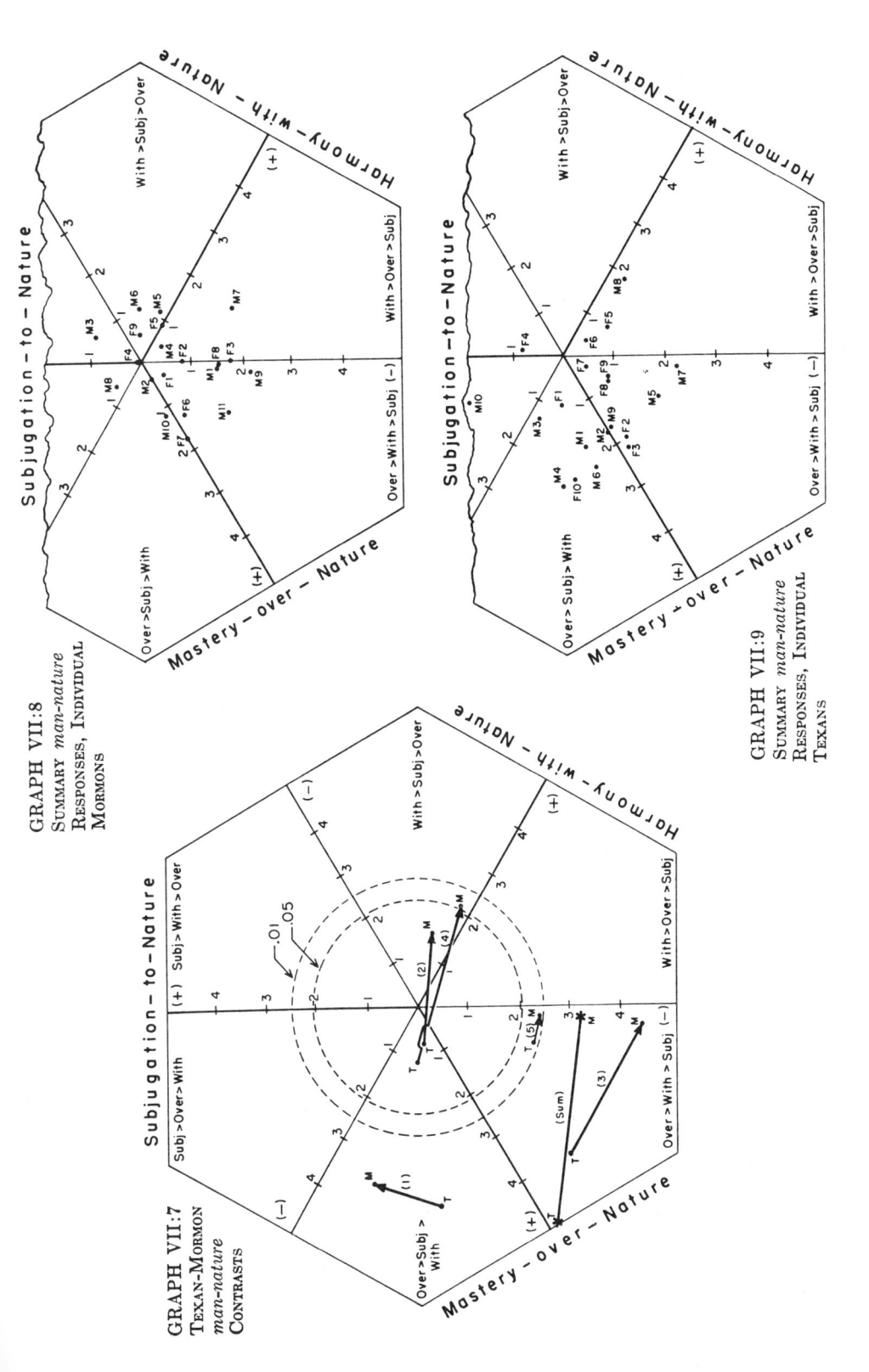

GRAPH VII:8
SUMMARY *man-nature* RESPONSES, INDIVIDUAL MORMONS

GRAPH VII:9
SUMMARY *man-nature* RESPONSES, INDIVIDUAL TEXANS

GRAPH VII:7
TEXAN-MORMON *man-nature* CONTRASTS

was easy for him to continue this theme in discussing use of fields. He could never understand why it was that some men did not get their furrows straight. For him, cultivating and hoeing weeds was not solely to give the crops a chance; it was a man's responsibility to keep his place up, to keep it looking nice, to keep after it all the time. In tending to select the Over-Nature alternative on this question, it seemed that he in no way wanted to minimize the role of God and a good life, nor did he wish to take a specific stand for or against the use of scientific methods. What he appeared to want to emphasize was the propriety of the "worked on (the fields) a lot of the time" theme in the Over-Nature alternative. The tension of choosing the Over-Nature in lieu of the With-Nature emphasis on this question is reflected further by the fact that only on this question did this respondent report that he had no opinion on what most other Mormons would think, and this was the only *man-nature* question for which he did not give a With-Nature first choice. His answer was in this sense the eloquent exception which proves the rule. He clearly thought of the partnership with God in the transformation of the earth as a serious business, but not one in which God has maliciously placed frustration in the way to harass one. The world is like a garden: it can be tended and it will prosper, or it can be neglected and it will go to weeds. God's interest in the garden gives meaning to the activity, but the hoeing is up to you!

Our Mormon respondent may be contrasted with one of the lower status, more isolated Texans. It had been difficult for us to find his place, and in the process of the search we took note of a nearby section which had not been grazed for years. We asked him whether the short grass increased when a field was not grazed, and it was his opinion that it did not. This was an invitation to go beyond the questions and reflect further. For him it was a simple matter: if there were rains, the crops grew; if there weren't, they didn't. He went ahead to explain how he felt about his farming. It was his job to cause his machine, his tractor, to do as much of the work as possible. It was his ideal to work an entire field without getting off his tractor. He had headlights on it, and when the knife sled was working right and the beans needed it, he didn't mind running the tractor nights and Sundays if it looked like it would do any good. In a small field across from his place he had been putting in corn in recent years. There had not been enough rain for the corn to do any good, so he had not wanted to waste any time on harvesting it. He bought some pigs and turned them out to eat the dwarf stocks in the field. It was a messy farming operation but he took particular pride in the fact that the pigs got fat, they dropped their manure in the field, and he personally didn't have to do a thing about it.

This Texan's position is not that of a trickster-trader who wins at the expense of another person; he essentially does battle with an impersonal system. He sees the question as one of either winning or losing, and he is not disposed to compromise his chances by assuming that any force relating to nature has his interest at heart. While this Texan's view is more extreme than most, it is consistent with the general picture that religion pertains to marriages and baptisms and funerals but not to work. There were some operations like grazing, where one needs to be in Harmony-with-Nature—you can't really do much about the rain and it's a bad long-term policy to overgraze—but in general, man should and can subordinate nature to his purpose.

The distinctions in Graph VII:7 between Mormon and Texan responses are clear when management of land is concerned, but in the very human concern with MN5 (Length of Life), Texans join Mormons in manifesting a With-Nature emphasis. Similarly, when livestock is concerned, Mormons drop substantially the characteristic With-Nature emphasis and become more Subjugated than the Texans for MN1 (Livestock Dying). For the three behavior spheres, man-land-stock, With-Nature extends to the first two for the Mormons and only to the first one for the Texans. In this sense, the With-Nature emphasis in use of fields is a critical point of distinction between the Mormons and Texans.

With regard to MN2 (Facing Conditions) and MN4 (Belief in Control), it is difficult to understand why there is so little consistency in the patterns. The previous explanation accounts well enough for the Mormon outcomes being closer to the With-Nature extreme; but why is there so little consensus among Mormons, and what is to be inferred from the fact that there is even less consensus among the Texans? The answer is not clear. It appears that members of both cultures believe in God, but they are less clear on whether he is inscrutable, indifferent, or known to be involved in their activities. It may be guessed that some of the respondents most disposed to believe God either inscrutable (the Calvinistic themes in Presbyterianism) or involved (the devout Mormons) also were disposed to believe that man's own contribution was of paramount importance. Fortunately, even within the range of low consensus, there were typical Mormon-Texan differences which contributed to the differential outcomes for the *man-nature* set.

It is notable in Graph VII:8 that the two Mormons who gave the most Subjugated responses were devout, old, and very poor; the two who gave the most With-Nature emphases were devout, young, and privileged, one economically, and the other by virtue of his superior education. There seems to be no marked difference in the responses of men and women for the Mormons in Graph VII:8 or for the Texans in Graph VII:9. The conspicuously Subjugated Texan is a physically disabled laborer who lives as a bachelor in a squatter's cabin near the escarpment to the west of the community. While there is a poetic congruence between his view of life and his plight, too much should not be made of it, for there are others in the community who suffer under almost equal duress and whose value dispositions seem little affected.

ACTIVITY ORIENTATION

One bright, sunny afternoon in August I had occasion to overhear some early-adolescent Mormon girls plotting a minor delinquency. They were going to put on their bathing suits and go to a nearby yard which was fringed by a tall stand of wheat—so they would not be observed—and go sunbathing. There were two main components to the taboo being broken. First, devout Mormons wear ritually prescribed undergarments after marriage and are admonished to avoid nudity at all times. It is a matter of comment and criticism if a man chooses to work with his shirt off; so sunbathing, even in conservatively cut bathing suits is a risqué affair. But it is to be noted that the girls did have bathing suits so the exposure alone did not account for the conspiratorial hush.

The other consideration involved deals directly with *activity*—Mormons are supposed to be busy. This is not to say that men do not stop to gossip with one another; it is just that they always have a piece of harness in their hands, or they are just going out to the field, or they are on their way to the post office. You don't come to loaf, you never really give up the pose that you are working; both tacitly and overtly the norm holds that a man should be active. If his own work is done, there is always something to be done for the church. As for the women, their best opportunities to visit each other occur when they stop at the trading post and while they are doing church work.[10] One scarcely ever sees adolescents in Rimrock sprawling in the near-prone positions so popular in middle-class urban culture.

For Homestead it is a different matter. The following excellent quotation, taken from Vogt's chapter on Working and Loafing, captures the sense with great economy.

I guess the people in Homestead expect to work hard in the working season and then loaf hard in the loafing season. In the farming season, they get up early and work twelve or fourteen hours a day and enjoy it. But when that work gets done, it's hard to do more than cut wood and do the chores.[11]

There is the further theme that when you work on a farm you can keep your freedom to loaf, freedom which you would only lose in the city—particularly if you were working for someone else. The Texans take pride in the fact that they are not lazy like the Spanish-Americans, but they would hold no envy for a group like the Mormons who felt uncomfortable when they were not working. There is a social elaboration of roles such that a greater measure of status can be gained among Texans than Mormons by being a good storyteller.

It has recently been noted in studies of lower-class boys in our larger cities that there is a real resistance to doing anything more than just standing around together. In a schoolyard they shoot baskets but generally do not choose up teams. When they do form teams to play boys from another area, it is a very explosive matter for the team that loses. The accumulated tension of having worked out a chain of authority is released by defeat. After a few interpersonal explosions of this type, it comes to be recognized that it's better just to hang around together, letting each

---

[10] For an account of some of the interpersonal relations of a Mormon wife alleged to be lazy because she read while her husband did chores she might have done, see the author's "The Interaction of a Henpecked Husband and His Wife," *Marriage and Family Living*, Vol. XIV, No. 4 (November, 1952), p. 305.

[11] *Op. cit.*, p. 109.

fellow shoot some fancy shots, or not, as he likes. It's too complicated to get a whole group involved.

Texans' loafing may be very similar. One has the feeling that each man's sensitivity to invidious comparisons in rank is so great that organization of any sort would not be attractive to them. Their sense of identity as they loaf seems to come from the pleasure of escaping the scrutiny of their wives, for whom they typically use the term of address, "mother." If the men had anything to do at which they could make money, it is almost certain that they would not be loafing. The thing that they are not disposed to do is to make work just to keep busy.

The Texan homes are generally so small that they provide few opportunities for privacy. One wife, whose husband is typically both a good worker and a good loafer, described how she cherished their 5:30 A.M. breakfast together. She stressed that this was before the kids were up, and it was then she enjoyed the privacy with her husband. This same lack of opportunity for privacy at home provides a goad for the husband to get out of the way during the day. It must be assumed that in most cases the chores are done and that all the money available for supplies for home repairs has been spent. Under these conditions some people might turn to reading or to giving special training to their children or to expressive painting or weaving. But that is not a part of the Texan pattern. They can be ingenious engineers in the design of tools to operate from atop their powerful tractors, but the expressive arts are feminine for them. Even the humanism of the Rimrock male, who speaks of his sporadic study of Mormon theology as the study of history, is absent. And, so they say, if you're not working hard, you might as well loaf hard.

It was distinctly our original impression that both cultures were Doing-oriented. We were dependent upon Vogt's more detailed study for our knowledge both of the extensity of loafing in Homestead and the degree to which it seems to be induced by the failure of other institutions to provide a respite from nuclear-family isolation or off-season productive work. These further considerations provided a basis for the later expectation that while both cultures are Doing-oriented, Texans may be less so than Mormons.

Our prediction is sustained in two ways in Graph VII:10. Both Mormon and Texan outcomes are in the Doing range, and the Mormon outcome is slightly, though not significantly, more so. In terms of individual-question responses, Texans are more Doing-oriented than Mormons on only one question, but the average difference is only about 8 per cent.

Items A1 and A2 involved in the reversal deserve a brief comment. In A1 the question is whether you would rather work for a demanding or lax boss, and on this the Mormons preferred the demanding boss slightly more than the Texans. In A2 the question is whether it is better to be a demanding or a lax boss, and on this the Texans exceeded the Mormons in choosing the demanding boss. For such a case, one is tempted to wish the difference were statistically significant, for this indication of a lesser concern for experiencing authority by Mormons and a lesser concern for

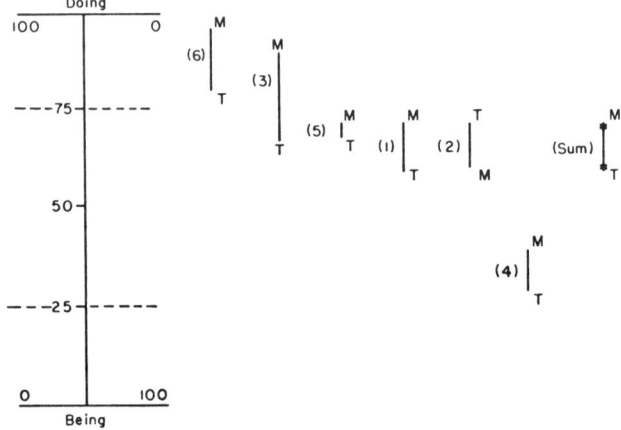

GRAPH VII:10
Texan-Mormon *activity* Contrasts

expressing authority by Texans is consistent with the differential success of cooperative work in the two cultures.

A4 (Care of Fields) drew few Doing responses from either Mormons or Texans because it clearly pitted care of fields against contact with friends. On a question like this it is believed that more acceptance of the Doing alternative could have been won from the Mormons if there were an alternative stressing both a high level of church-related activities *and* concern about fields.

COMBINED ORIENTATIONS

In search of a perspective from which to view the forty Mormons and Texans on the four orientations simultaneously, it is possible to use a type of direct factor analysis. This process views each set of responses from one individual as coordinates of a point in space. Since there are two *independent* dimensions from the *relational* ranking, two from *time*, two from *man-nature*, and one from *activity*, the points under consideration have seven coordinates.

Seven coordinates and the underlying seven dimensions greatly exceed the conventional two or three with which we can easily work. However, this step of visualizing points in n-dimensional space in itself suggests that we might look for two or three artificial dimensions which could be inserted through the cluster of forty points so as to define their locations with reasonable practical precision. The process for doing this involves the insertion of successive dimensions at right angles to each other. In each case, the sum of the squares of the deviations of the points from the dimension is minimized and the dimension which is extracted first makes the largest contribution to the location of the points, and the remaining dimensions are convergently less important until with seven artificial dimensions the original locations are again fully and completely specified.

In the present problem, when the process described above is used, the first dimension "takes out" 74.4 per cent of the sum of squares, the second and the first combined take out 83.7 per cent, and the first three factors combined take out 90.5 per cent. Thus, the less than 10 per cent of the sum of squares which remains has been shifted to the remaining four dimensions, which, in turn, we propose to disregard.

The three dimensions which result necessarily constitute new combinations of the original orientations. These new combinations are not viewed as having intrinsic significance in themselves; they are viewed as being tailored for the particular purpose of displaying simultaneously the points for these two cultures. If other cultures had been under consideration, differently placed artificial dimensions would have been produced. Despite their *ad hoc* character, rough definitions of the dimensions are desirable for interpretative purposes. These definitions are given below in two ways. First, the relative weight of the two major components is given; and second, the interpretation of a positive value is indicated. In all cases, a negative value represents an emphasis on the alternatives in an order which reverses that specified in the positive description. Thus, the negative of Ind > Coll > Lin is Lin > Coll > Ind.

Weights	Factor I
.67	Ind > Coll > Lin
.22	Fut = Pres > Past
	Factor II
.62	With > Over = Subj
.37	Coll > Ind = Lin
	Factor III
.73	Subj > With > Over
.15	Pres > Past > Fut

It is to be noted that the *activity* orientation did not make an appreciable contribution to the first three factors. This is in part due to the great similarity of the forty respondents on these questions, but, in addition, the decision simply to use the percentage of Being responses as the *activity* score resulted in a measure which was smaller in magnitude and less variable than the other scores and hence less important in the calculation. In the absence of information on Being-in-Becoming, the third *activity* alternative, this lesser emphasis was believed desirable.

Turning next to the new dimensions, we may plot the location of individual Mormons and Texans on dimensions I and II in Graph VII:11.[12] In this graph we distinguish the culture and sex of each respondent. To facilitate comparisons we draw an area banded by Mormons with extreme

---

[12] For a more complete statement of the material, see section 7 of Appendix 2 and references cited there.

280   VARIATIONS IN VALUE ORIENTATIONS

GRAPH VII:11
DISTRIBUTION OF MORMONS AND TEXANS ON ARTIFICIAL DIMENSIONS I AND II

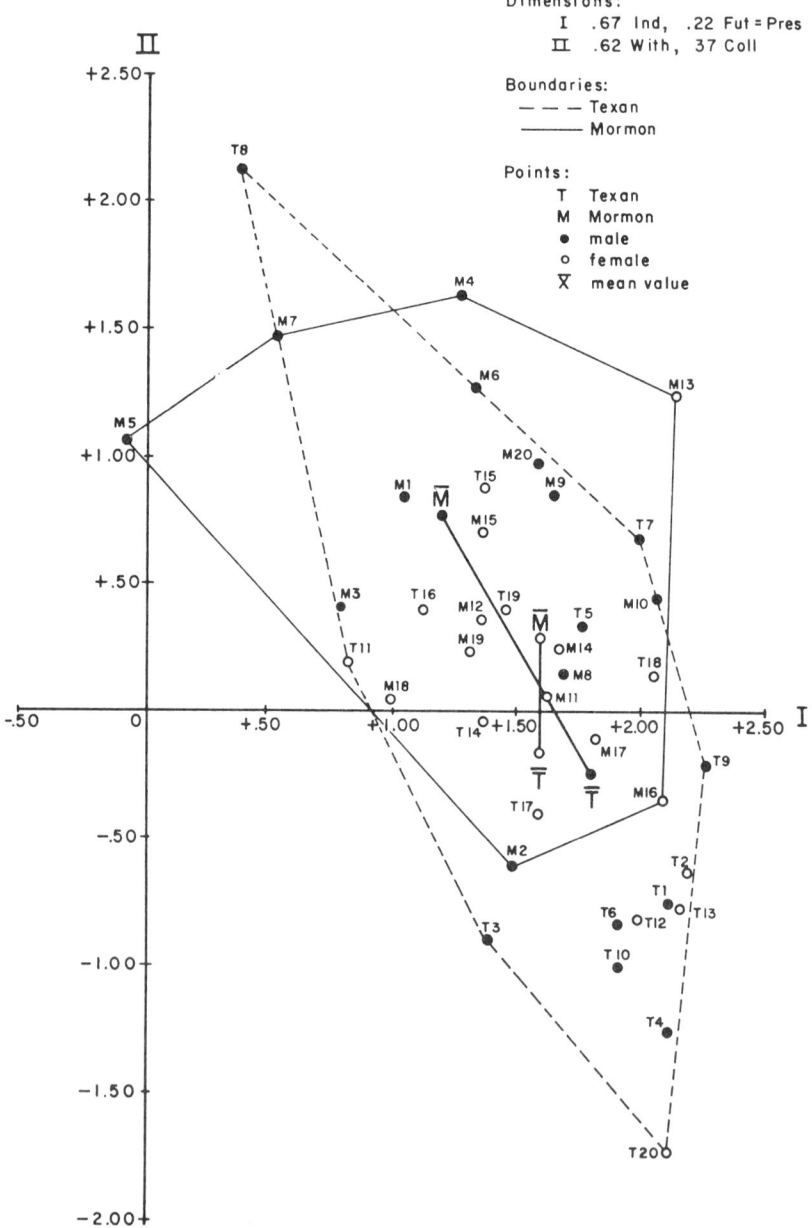

GRAPH VII:12
Distribution of Mormons and Texans on Artificial Dimensions I and III

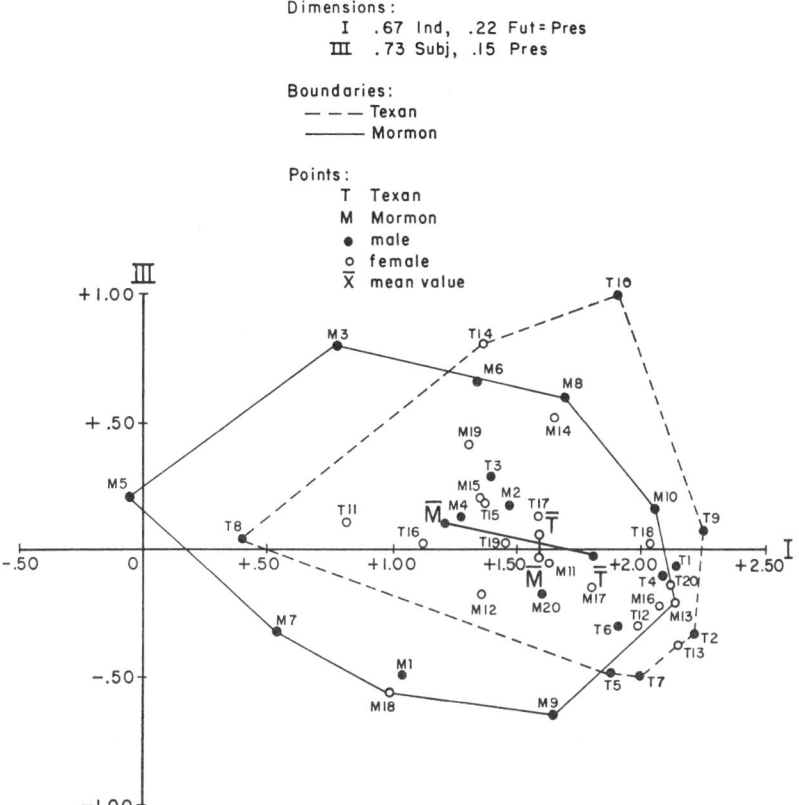

positions and another one for corresponding Texans. These two areas define a common region by their intersection and two unique regions, which we may take as a working designation of those Mormons and Texans who are similar in location and those who are different.

It may be seen that the two regions are approximately the same distance out on dimension I, but the Mormon one moves toward the left at the top. There is a slight Texan-Mormon difference on the degree to which they emphasize Individualism and Future-Present (i.e. non-Past) *time*. On the other hand, there seems to be a clearer difference between the location of the two regions on dimension II: Mormons are higher on this With-Nature and Collaterality dimension.

Graph VII:12 gives the location of our forty respondents on dimensions I and III. It appears that dimension III, Subjugation-to-Nature and Present *time*, does not differentiate the groups but does show some further distinctions between individuals. By use of the same convention as previously employed, regions can again be drawn. There is a third charting of dimensions II and III which is not shown but which has been prepared and handled in a parallel manner. The simultaneous consideration of these three operations enables us to rank respondents according to the number of times they are included within the common locus of Mormon-Texan values. Some respondents have remained within the intersecting areas in all three instances, others in two, one, or none. The distribution of respondents by cultures is as follows:

Times in Inter-secting Area	Mormon M	Mormon F	Texan M	Texan F
Three	4	7	1	6
Two	1	1	1	0
One	5	1	6	2
None	1	0	2	2

It may be seen that 18 of the 40 respondents are consistently in the space common to the two cultures. Of these 18, 13 are women, 7 Mormon and 6 Texan. This is a very powerful indication of similarity between Mormon and Texan women. Correspondingly, the fact that 5 Mormon men and 6 Texan men are in only one intersecting area is again a clear indicator that the differences between Rimrock and Homestead are to be found in the differences between the men of these cultures.

The most extreme Mormon is the same respondent whose views were presented in the discussion of MN3 (Use of Fields). It appears that in Mormonism, as in other organized religions, there are some of the older and more devout members whose insistence on the letter of the doctrine becomes as deviant from the perspective of the community as that of a disbeliever. His responses set him off as the "noblest Mormon of them all," but in fact, he was somewhat peripheral in the community because of his brief periods of residence outside the community and the color his doctrinal strictness gave to his personality.

The two extreme Texan women were engaged in trade. One operated the most prosperous grocery in the community, and the other was the attendant at the only gasoline pump being operated in 1953. These occupations brought them frequently into contact with the men of the community—particularly in the loafing discussions. Whether their choice of occupation was a selective factor or whether they were influenced by their occupational contacts cannot be clearly separated, but their value responses were distinctive in that they were close to the Individualism and Future *time* extreme of dimension I. Their extreme, near-caricature pattern of the Texan themes was shared only by the man regarded as a founder of the community. He was one of the earliest arrivals, and he subsequently relocated his father, mother, brother, and two sisters in the community. In 1953 he continued to serve as a political leader and social initiator in the community.

The other Texan identified by his consistent avoidance of the Mormon-Texan overlap areas differed from other Texans by being much more Present-oriented and Subjugated-to-Nature. He is the physically handicapped laborer who was previously commented upon. This respondent typified a southern "poor white" person, and the uniqueness of his pattern is notable because one might have been disposed to believe that many of the other marginal Baptist families would have had similar patterns. On the contrary, the Baptist and Presbyterian cliques in the community were not distinguishable in terms of their responses. This supports Vogt's interpretation of a single status continuum in the community.

Returning again to the several indications of difference between Mormon and Texan men, it is suggested that the reader refer back to Graph VII:11 where the average outcome by culture and sex is shown. It may be seen that Texan men and women have average locations which are very close together. Mormon women differ from Texan women by being more oriented to the With-Nature position and less Individualistic. The Mormon male is more With-Nature and Collaterally oriented that the Mormon female. Compared with the Texans, particularly the Texan males, Mormons are markedly more With-Nature and Collaterally oriented. Thus it becomes clear that the slight differences in the reported value orientations between the Mormon and Texan samples can be most accurately attributed to the With-Nature and Collateral emphases of the Mormon men. And if this is true, is not the difference between the cultures uniquely in the sphere of influence associated with the priesthood of the Mormon Church? One doubts that the slight differences observed could be maintained if the Church were not present in Rimrock. The Mormon who relinquishes his active commitment to the Mormon priesthood—the so-called Jack Mormon—is very much like a Texan. Do not the discriminating With-Nature and Collateral emphases rest precariously in the sectarian culture of the Mormon Church? Hence one can expect that when the Church loses its hold, the drift in values will inevitably be toward the patterns of the dominant American culture. But, so long as the Church retains its prominence, the Mormons and Texans are not one. And this difference, however slight in the individual instance, makes an important collective difference between the two communities.

TABLE VIII:1
SUMMARY OF ZUNI RANKINGS

	Relational Orientation
R1	Ind ⩾ Coll ⩾ Lin
R2	Coll ⩾ Ind ⩾ Lin
R3	Coll > Lin > Ind
R4	Coll ⩾ Lin ⩾ Ind
R5	Ind ⩾ Coll ⩾ Lin
R6	Lin ⩾ Coll > Ind
R7	Ind ⩾ Lin ⩾ Coll
Sum	Coll > Lin ⩾ Ind

	Time Orientation
T1	Pres ⩾ Past ⩾ Fut
T2	Pres ⩾ Fut ⩾ Past
T3	Past ⩾ Pres > Fut
T4	Past > Pres > Fut
T5	Pres ⩾ Fut ⩾ Past[a]
Sum	Pres ⩾ Past > Fut

	Man-Nature Orientation
MN1	Over ⩾ Subj ⩾ With
MN2	Subj ⩾ With > Over
MN3	Over ⩾ With ⩾ Subj
MN4	With > Subj ⩾ Over
MN5	Subj ⩾ Over ⩾ With
Sum	With ⩾ Subj ⩾ Over

	Activity Orientation
A1	Being > Doing
A2	Being > Doing
A3	Doing ⩾ Being
A4	Doing > Being
A5	Doing > Being
A6	Doing > Being
Sum	Doing ⩾ Being

[a] Pres > Fut only.

CHAPTER VIII

The Zuni

John M. Roberts

It will be recalled that the answers given by the Zuni respondents yielded few instances in which the consensus was statistically significant; hence the assessment of the Zuni findings constitutes an intriguing problem. The summaries of the responses to questions on the *man-nature* and the *activity* orientations were definitely nonsignificant. The summary outcome for the responses on the items of the *relational* orientation was also less significant, statistically, than that of any other of the groups tested. It was only on the *time* orientation series that the Zuni responses produced an outcome which was at least more firm for the Zuni than the Navaho if not the other three groups. The total results for the Zuni are given in Table VIII:1. The concern of this chapter will be the search for the meaning of these responses in the light of both the historical accounts of the culture and current observations of it.

If responses to the value-orientation schedule had been obtained only from the Zuni sample, it most certainly would not be known whether the absence of pattern reflected the actual state of the Zuni value-orientation structure or arose, instead, from defects in the method of testing or, perhaps, in the theory itself. But four other cultures were tested, and each yielded significantly consistent results. Thus it is a strong possibility that the Zuni responses mirror the reality of present-day Zuni culture.

In the assessment of this possibility, consideration will be given to the numerous studies which have treated the question of Zuni values and Zuni social organization. These include substantive accounts of many kinds, which range from analyses of prehistoric Zuni and ethnographic materials over a fairly long time period down to contemporary ethnographic observations and personality testing data.

However, before we review this material, some further discussion of the method of the translation of the value-orientation schedule and the characteristics of the sample of persons tested is necessary to give the reader an opportunity to assess our own conviction that the inconsistent results obtained were not simply a matter of faulty testing procedures.

THE FIELD METHODS

The recent works of Newman and his associates emphasize the difficulties which inevitably confront one in efforts to translate Zuni into English or English into Zuni.¹ Knowing the magnitude of the problem, I took special precautions. Although I had not detected any greater difficulty in communicating with the Zuni than with the Navaho when I administered the 1950 version of the value-orientation schedule (the pilot study instrument) to samples of equal size in each group, I had concluded that there were some disadvantages in working *directly* with an interpreter. Consequently, for the testing of the Zuni with the 1951 version of the schedule, time was taken to develop a machine recording of the linguistic text. In doing this I had the advantage of several checkings by persons who spoke both English and Zuni.

Each question of the schedule as thus recorded was played twice to informants with whom rapport had already been established. The interpreter was present, almost solely for the purpose of translating the responses. The interpreter's main contribution had been in the initial stage of the development of the recorded text. Thus, given the problems of field administration, considerable care was employed both in the translation and in the method of questioning. Control in the administration of the schedule to the Zuni was greater than that used for the Navaho, and since consistent results were obtained for the Navaho, we seriously doubt that faults of administration explain the low consistency.

The sample in Zuni, unlike the sample for the other four cultures, was specially selected. Since Zuni was much larger than the combined populations of all the other groups, the size of the sample relative to the size of the community was unquestionably very small. It undoubtedly would have been desirable to have it larger; but in Chapter II we have discussed the factors which prevented our drawing a larger and more representative sample.

Concerning the question at issue, the bias in the sample, if any, should have favored homogeneity and a lack of variation instead of the contrary.

Each of the respondents was a full-time resident of the pueblo and a full participant in Zuni culture. All, with one possible exception, were parents and nearly half of the respondents had reared children to adulthood. In one way or another, fifteen of the Zuni respondents appear in the records of daily activities published in *Zuni Daily Life*,² and these records document normal participation in the life of the pueblo. With the possible exception of one young man, who, incidentally, held high ceremonial office, no respondent appeared to be sociologically or psychologically atypical. There were no marriages to non-Zunis, nor are there alternative hypotheses about bias which would lead to expectations of non-uniformity in values.

The eleven men and ten women interviewed were residents in ten Zuni households. Seventeen of the twenty-one lived in six households, and three of these six households have been described in detail in the published daily life sequences.³ In that source they are designated as households A, B, and

---

[1] The unpublished materials on the Zuni psycholinguistics project are most suggestive and exciting.
[2] John M. Roberts, *Zuni Daily Life*, Monograph II, Note Book No. 3, Laboratory of Anthropology, University of Nebraska, 1956.
[3] *Ibid.*, pp. 9–91.

D.[4] The selected sample, then, involves fewer households than the samples in the other communities. Since each household is a social group with its own pattern of integration, the reduction in the number of households represented should increase rather than decrease consistency.

The Zuni sample as a whole was selected from a net of persons who were linked through a complex set of interpersonal relationships among which kin relationships were most important. The three households and the sheep camp group were part of a multiple-role, small-group net which also included the households from which the remaining respondents were drawn and which has been under study for some time.[5] Many of the groups intersected with household A, and in all cases the linkage could be made through kinsmen although alternative linkages also existed. Even though no respondent was related to every other respondent, each respondent could be connected to every other respondent through a short chain of relationships. It is to be stressed that Zuni respondents were drawn from a small interaction system and were not chosen at random from the larger community. If close kin ties, frequent face-to-face interaction, and easy communication contribute to any bias, it should be one of consistency rather than difference.

It should be noted that the eleven male respondents (ages 73, 68, 58, 53, 47, 39, 37, 32, 29, 26, and 20) with a mean age of 43.8 years and the ten female respondents (ages 70, 65, 53, 51, 51, 38, 28, 26, 26, and 20) with a mean age of 42.8 years might be biased toward conservatism because they are older than the average Zuni adult. The values of these respondents should be closer than the average to those reported by Benedict since many of them were adults at the time of her study. The oldest male, for example, professed to have seen Frank Hamilton Cushing in the late nineteenth century (the respondent's *exact* age was never determined). Since Zuni acculturation appears to be accelerating, it might be argued that more variation would be expected in a sample more representative of the age distribution in the pueblo. A number of the respondents from highly respected families had priestly or other religious affiliations of importance and several had held political offices. The higher status of such respondents should also favor a conservative and consistent bias.

The respondents did differ somewhat in their formal educations. Although the data are not altogether accurate, the following years of school-

[4] Of the individuals cited in household A's daily life sequence, FaElBr73, Fa58, FaYoBr53, Mo51, FaSiSo47, and AdYoSo26 were used as respondents while AdElSo27 was used as the interpreter; in household B, Fa58 and Mo51 were respondents; and in household D, FaSiSo37, ElDaHu33, ElDa28, YoDaHu22, and YoDa20 were used as respondents. Another respondent, Fa68ASo39, a son of Fa68, household A, together with others mentioned above, appears in the two sheep camp lambing and shearing sequences.

[5] Watson Smith and John M. Roberts, *Zuni Law: A Field of Values,* Papers of the Peabody Museum, Harvard University, Vol. XLIII, No. 1 (1954), p. 8.

Eric H. Lenneberg and John M. Roberts, *The Language of Experience: A Study in Methodology,* Indiana University Publications in Anthropology and Linguistics, Memoir 13 of the *International Journal of American Linguistics,* 1956, p. 23.

David M. Schneider and John M. Roberts, *Zuni Kin Terms,* Monograph 1, Note Book No. 3, Laboratory of Anthropology, University of Nebraska, 1956, p. 1.

John M. Roberts, *op. cit.,* pp. 4–5.

ing were reported for the men: none, 3; fourth grade, 1; fifth grade, 2; eighth grade, 1; ninth grade, 1; tenth grade, 2; and eleventh grade, 1. The following years of schooling were reported for the women: none, 4; seventh grade, 1; ninth grade, 1; tenth grade, 3; and eleventh grade, 1. Seven respondents professed to know no English, and some of the remaining respondents had little facility with the language. Some of the men, but none of the women, had had school, travel, or job experience outside the pueblo. While differences in education and experience would be expected to contribute to variation, there are no reasons to believe that such differences are more present in this sample than in the pueblo at large.

In general, the presence of close kin ties, the grouping into a few households, and the weighting in favor of age and prestige should favor consistency of responses rather than variation. In spite of the indicated biases toward consensus, great variation was present. If it is not simply to be assumed, prima facie, that the limitations in translation and sampling were responsible for the recorded differences, then explanation of the variation must be sought.

BACKGROUND FACTORS

If the variation discovered does mirror the reality of Zuni today, then should it not be assumed that there are important historical antecedents for this variation? I wish, therefore, to discuss a series of features of Zuni culture in the past as well as present—features which are not likely to be disputed by most students of the culture—which have a bearing on the general argument.

Zuni Cultural Isolation

In a recent article Murdock has given the world position of the Zuni Indians in terms of a series of important ethnographic coordinates.[6] In none of these features is the Zuni tribe unique; such tribes as the Hopi and Acoma present virtually the same constellation of ratings. The Acoma, for example, differ only in possessing matrilineal succession rather than councils. Even such remote tribes as the Chiriguano of the Gran Chaco share many ratings with the Zuni. Within North America, in contrast to the world, Kroeber has placed Zuni in the Pueblo division of the Pueblo sphere of the Southwest culture area.[7] More recently, Driver and Massey have placed Zuni in the Oasis culture area:

This area includes a continuous stretch of farming peoples from the American Southwest down the west coast of Mexico. The term "Oasis" refers to those farm-

---

[6] George Peter Murdock, "World Ethnographic Sample," *American Anthropologist*, Vol. LIX (1957), pp. 664–87.
[7] A. L. Kroeber, *Cultural and Natural Areas of Native North America*, University of California Publications in American Archaeology and Ethnology, Vol. XXXVIII (1939), pp. 32–35.

ing peoples in a predominantly desert environment. The Pueblan section of this large area was formerly separated and called "Southwest"; but the term proved ambiguous as more came to be known about the tribes of northwest Mexico, and it became necessary to group the latter culturally and historically with the old Southwest. Generally these Oasis peoples are culturally more complex than their Desert neighbors. At the same time they are culturally less sophisticated than most tribes of Meso-America. In the text to follow, we sometimes divide the Oasis area into the Pueblan, Athapaskan, and Yuman-Uto-Aztecan sub-areas. The sharpest break among these sub-divisions is between the Pueblos and Athapaskans, although even here the amount of shared culture is sizable.[8]

More specifically within the Pueblo area, the Zuni have been classed as "western Pueblo" by Eggan:

The Pueblos form a cultural unit for comparison with other groups, but closer examination makes it possible to establish various divisions based upon differences in location, language, or institutions. The basic cultural division which is recognized is that between the eastern Pueblos of the Upper Rio Grande drainage and the western Pueblos of the mesa and canyon country to the west.... For our purposes, the western Pueblos consist of the Hopi villages, Hano, Zuni, Acoma, and Laguna.[9]

Reed has also placed Zuni in a western Pueblo class.[10]

When viewed in terms of the scale of Murdock's world ethnographic sample, it is clear that Zuni shares features with many of the world's societies. Indeed, it becomes apparent that, while cultural differences between the Zuni, Navaho, Spanish-American, Mormon, and Texan cultures are significant, the five cultures encompass only a fraction of the possible cultural variation in the world. When the scale is reduced to the range of the western Pueblos, the similarities between Zuni and the other pueblos are striking. Yet, a case can well be made for the cultural isolation of the aboriginal Zuni tribe and the modern pueblo as well.

Nowhere is this isolation more apparent than in the area of language. Although Swadesh has classified Zuni as a Penutoid language with Tarasco as its nearest relative,[11] the full demonstration of this relationship has yet to appear. Suffice it to say for the present that Zuni has no close affiliation with any other known language. When the Rimrock Navaho visit their cultural kin, the Chiricahua Apache, they can communicate after a fashion. In contrast, the nearby Zuni have no close linguistic cousins. Moreover, the population of the modern Zuni pueblo and its satellite farming villages defines the entire Zuni speech community. Once a Zuni leaves the reservation, he must always deal with alien languages—whereas the Navaho and Spanish-American can speak their languages in communities

---

[8] Harold E. Driver and Wm. C. Massey, *Comparative Studies of North American Indians*, Transactions of the American Philosophical Society, n.s., Vol. XLVII, Part 2 (1957), p. 174.

[9] Fred Eggan, *Social Organization of the Western Pueblos* (Chicago: University of Chicago Press, 1950), p. 2. Extracts reprinted by permission of University of Chicago Press.

[10] Erik K. Reed, "Eastern-Central Arizona Archaeology in Relation to the Western Pueblos," *Southwestern Journal of Anthropology*, Vol. VI (1950), p. 132.

[11] Morris Swadesh, "Problems of Long-Range Comparison in Penutian," *Language*, Vol. XXXII, No. 1 (1956), pp. 17–41.

other than their own. This strong linguistic isolation must be an ever-present factor in all considerations of Zuni.

The Zuni culture is also unique in more features than language. The whole of the social and religious organization is unique. The individual who becomes dissatisfied with life in Zuni and leaves the community goes into exile. True, the farming villages provide temporary refuge for those who wish to withdraw from active community life for a time, but since these villages are not continually occupied and do not duplicate, even in miniature, the central pueblo, no permanent resident of such a village could at the same time be fully participant in Zuni tribal culture. The man who leaves the reservation voluntarily or even involuntarily must always adjust to a new culture, whether it be Hopi, Spanish-American, Anglo, or whatever. This is not true of any of the four cultures represented in the other communities. A Mormon, Texan, Spanish-American, or Navaho has a wide choice of alternative communities. Since for many a Zuni the task of becoming naturalized in another culture would be long, difficult, and unpleasant, many individuals who might otherwise seek adjustment elsewhere elect to remain in the pueblo. The cultural isolation of Zuni has made for the *containment* of variant individuals. Away from the reservation, every Zuni is alone.

Zuni Cultural Complexity

Despite its small population the modern Zuni community is surprisingly complex. It is not possible within the brief compass of this chapter to present a full description of the complexity of modern Zuni culture, but it is pertinent to consider some illustrative materials.

The Zuni language is rich in words relating to interpersonal relations, personal states, and activities, as the following examples taken from Newman's *Zuni Dictionary*[12] and, in a few instances, from the author's field notes show (dashes indicate alternative definitions):

be satisfactory, behave well, be capable, be daring—be successful without effort, be or become lazy, play, be or become angry, be married, be like, be saying things to—gossip, feel cold, become fat, be hungry, disappear—become lost, make weeping sounds—mourn, be brave—have endurance, be an intermediary—be entrusted with a duty—hold office, run away, be painful—be mean, be rough—be coarse, sweat—feel hot, be reckless—be careless—behave crazily—lose self-control temporarily, be drunk, be lucky in achievement, have many lovers, be courting, initiate (a person), consent, permit a person to do something, answer, call—demand, laugh—smile, observe (i.e., watch and listen), watch, hit a person, ceremonial relationship, plant—have sex relations with a woman, grasp—hold back—receive, ask, old age, be attractive—be nice, be weak—be lazy, be annoying—be aggressive, dirty—nasty, be fortunate—be lucky, be hardy—be healthy—be heavily built, be dead—act thoughtlessly—act without restraint, fear—become afraid of, be taboo—be dangerous, be noisy—be overactive, smile at—sneer at, bewitch, love—feel affection for, act as interpreter—teach ritual to, tease—joke with, like, make a mar-

---

[12] Stanley Newman, *Zuni Dictionary,* Publication Six of the Indiana University Research Center in Anthropology, Folklore, and Linguistics, 1958.

riage proposal too aggressively, say, say to, say things to each other—argue, ask for permission or information, come, causative, show it to, bet—expose a person, request—petition, elope with a woman, elope with a man (applied only to a married woman), admire, meet—assemble, spread the news, busy oneself—become aware, indeterminate dislike—hate, inhibit—reside, cry—make weeping sounds, be the leader—be boss, talk—speak, have a meeting, injure—be satisfied with food, be boiled—be angry, become angry—exert oneself, be very lazy— be inactive, become infected, become feeble—behave irresponsibly, be alike—be a person, be attracted to— imitate, be frisky—behave happily, be good—be obedient—be attractive.

The Zuni language, of course, has its vocabulary for kin relationships and for various stages of maturation, but there are also expressions for children:

disobedient girl, one who is young, monkey—overactive child, goat—flighty young person—overactive child, donkey—stubborn person—disobedient child, child—young of animals.

For women:

wife (mildly derogatory—"the old woman"), loose woman, beautiful woman, wife-mistress.

And for men:

fellow (familiar), male, husband—lover, loose man, handsome man, rich man.

While other terms may be applied to anyone:

bastard, empty-headed person, generous person—kind person, moth—giddy person, gossiper, coyote—sly person, stingy person, stupid person—ignorant person, irresponsible person—nervous animal, braggart, mimic, queer person—person lacking motor control, trembling person, person who wheezes and coughs, corpse, carcasses—bodies, animal carcass—living human body, chubby person—bulging sack, scarred person—splotched object, grey—dawn color—sickly-looking person, skeleton—skinny person—spirit, one who is weak, stocky person, poor, rich, one who has information—witness, many, someone, friend, visitor, important, unimportant, tall, short, gossip, braggart, popular, stubborn, brave, cowardly, witch, joker, serious, happy, nagger, handsome, old, generous, stingy, honest, dishonest, fat, thin, mimic, crazy, stupid, crippled, intelligent, respected.

The foregoing entries simply indicate that interpersonal relations and states of personality in Zuni can be rich, colorful, and varied, but even the formal structure has its complexities. The following groups are mentioned in Eggan's chapter "The Social Organization of Zuni":[13]

Residential: Household, Farming Village (Ojo Caliente, Pescado, Nutria, and Hill Ranch), Village (Zuni), Reservation.
Clans: Crane, Grouse, Yellowwood, Bear, Coyote, Redtop plant, Sun, Sky (extinct), Eagle, Frog, Water (extinct), Rattlesnake, Parrot-Macaw.
Cults: 1. Cult of the Sun—Sun Priest or *pekwin*.
    2. Cult of the Uwanami, or "rain-makers"—twelve priesthoods.
    3. Cult of the Katcinas—six *kivas*.
    4. Cult of the Katcina Priests.

[13] *Op. cit.*, pp. **176–222**.

5. Cult of the War Gods—Bow Priesthood.
6. Cult of the Beast Gods—twelve curing societies.
Political: 1. Caciques—council of priests.
2. Tribal Council.

In addition to the above, other groups are either found in modern Zuni or known to have existed in recent years:

cattle growers' association, 4-H club, home economics club, sheep growers' association, Zuni band, Zuni veterans' organization, the Great Council, Zuni basketball team, Zuni PTA, garage, nominating committee, public meeting, etc.

Some mixed Zuni and white groups should be noted:

Christian Reformed Mission School, St. Anthony's Mission School, Zuni Day School, the four trading stores (counting employees and customers as part of the group), the Kiva Cafe.

Other relevant groups include the hospital at Black Rock (Zuni employees and patients), the agency at Black Rock, and many groups in Railtown and other points outside the reservation such as trading posts, curio stores, service stations, banks, theaters, hotels, drug stores, and ten-cent stores.

Each of the Zuni groups has its own internal system of status positions; they are too complex to be described in detail here. In Zuni of today there is the additional complexity of the varied full- or part-time occupations pursued. Some of these are:

auctioneer, carpenter, farmer, herder, laborer (off the reservation), sheriff (deputy), silversmith (ordinary, inlay, and casting), stock raiser, government employee, blacksmith, fire fighter, powerhouse engineer, general mechanic, service station attendant, ward attendant, maintenance man, assistant engineer, coal mine worker, road grader, interpreter, soldier, sailor, trucker, policeman, cook, maid, stonemason, weaver, potter, trader, carpenter, painter, day curer, midwife, tourist guide, adobe brick maker, electrician.

Although these illustrations are only an indication rather than a full documentation of the complexity of the Zuni social order, they are sufficient to demonstrate that its role system (particularly in the ceremonial or ritual behavior sphere) is highly differentiated relative to the size of the total population of the pueblo. Eggan has said, "The social organization of Zuni is perhaps the most complex to be found in the western Pueblos...."[14] In a recent publication Edmonson has reviewed the status terminologies and social structures of nine North American Indian tribes, including Zuni, as of A.D. 1600. The nine tribes were Chipewyan, Eskimo, Shoshone, Sioux, Algonkin, Choctaw, Kwakiutl, Zuni, and Yokuts. In discussing one of his hypotheses, Edmonson states the following:

It is likely in this connection that our data are not altogether typical, since it happens that our most "complex" cultures (Kwakiutl and Zuni) happen to have the smallest populations. It is unlikely that a larger sample would continue to display this negative relationship between population size and cultural complexity....[15]

[14] *Ibid.,* p. 210.
[15] Munro S. Edmonson, *Status Terminology and the Social Structure of North American Indians* (University of Washington Press, 1958), p. 50.

It must be remembered that the complexity of Zuni culture in relationship to the size of the community must have increased since 1600. Zuni culture *is* complex, and it has *long been* complex.

Zuni Cultural Integration

Zuni has also been remarkably well integrated. Although many of the students of Zuni culture, most notably Cushing, have concerned themselves with the degree of integration found in it, the most explicit formulation of it has been made by Kroeber:

It is impossible to proceed far into the complexities of the social and religious organization of the Zuni without being impressed with the perception that this community is as solidly welded and cross tied as it is intricately ramified. However far one form of division be followed, it branches off by innumerable contacts into others, without ever absorbing these. Four or five different planes of systematization cross cut each other and thus preserve for the whole society an integrity that would be speedily lost if the planes merged and thereby inclined to encourage segregation and fission. The clans, the fraternities, the priesthoods, the kivas, in a measure the gaming parties, are all dividing agencies. If they coincided, the rifts in the social structure would be deep; by countering each other, they cause segmentations which produce an almost marvelous complexity, but can never break the national entity apart.

Let us take an individual in this society. First to him as to us, in time and probably ultimately in importance, are the ties of blood and of household association. But, basic as these are, they are scarcely organized into a definite pattern: the personal element still outweighs the institutions. But beyond is the clan, into which the Zuni is born. It includes half his kin, indeed, but only half; and it includes a large group of persons outside the lines of blood. The clan, in turn, is more or less associated, directly or through certain fetishes and the houses that hold them, with certain priestly offices. Our Zuni may become a priest of a fetish connected with his clan; or, through kinship running counter to the clan scheme, or through mere personal selection, he can be made a member of a priesthood not connected with his clan. If, as is still more likely, he is not a priest himself, he is almost certain to possess a relation to certain priests through the medium of clan and to others through kinship. His kiva is one of six that perform the outward ritual of which the priests hold the more sacred keys; but there is no connection of personnel between kiva and priests. Our individual is a member of the kiva to which the husband of the woman belonged who first touched him on his entrance into the world. Thus father and son, mother's brother and nephew, the several associates of one priesthood, co-members of a fraternity, are likely to pertain to different and more or less rivalizing kivas. The fraternity is entered occasionally by choice; usually by the affiliation and consequent predilection of the near relatives who summon its medical assistance in case of the individual's sickness. The racing and gaming parties are little known; but everything points to their being in the main independent of every other mode of organization.[16]

Eggan has also acknowledged the strength of Zuni integration:

We will be interested in why the Zuni have been able to maintain a greater degree

---

[16] A. L. Kroeber, *Zuni Kin and Clan*, Anthropological Papers of the American Museum of Natural History, Vol. XVIII, Part II (1917), pp. 183–84.

of village integration in the face of stronger acculturative factors than have the Hopi.[17]

And again:

The social organization of Zuni is perhaps the most complex to be found in the western Pueblos; the social integration here achieved is both strong and successful. The consolidation into one village, following the events of the Pueblo Rebellion of 1680–96, has been maintained down to the present. And while an adequate water supply and sufficient land were essential conditions, the key to this integration lies in the social structure.[18]

Eggan also stresses the importance of integration through time and says, "This integration is carried out through the lineage principle, in large measure." Finally, Bunzel states:

Despite modern expansion the main village still remains a unit whose physical compactness is reflected in an intricate and closely knit social organization.[19]

Other views of Zuni, such as the descriptions of daily life, show how households and sheep camp groups, for example, can be linked with one another in complex ways.[20] Thus, it can be firmly asserted that the extraordinarily varied group and individual roles found in Zuni society are contained and interrelated through an intricate social organization.

Zuni Culture History

Obviously, the cultural isolation of the Zuni, the varied role structure, and the tight cultural integration are the products of a complex culture history. This history displays several persistent and leading themes which have a bearing on the arguments to follow: (1) the Zuni have long lived in a threatening natural and social environment; (2) the Zuni tribe has had a history of steady contraction and concentration; (3) the Zuni culture has steadily been augmented by diverse cultural elements through the operation of amalgamation, diffusion, and acculturation; and (4) at no time has this tribe lost its cultural identity even though the pressures on the tribe have been continuous and extreme.

Since it is not possible to discuss these factors either at length or separately, I shall cite some of the evidence which concerns all of them.

Woodbury, in discussing a prehistoric "Zuni" site, the Atsinna Ruin on the El Morro National Monument, has reviewed the archaeological evidence relating to several of these sites as follows:

There were scattered one-family settlements at the foot of the mesa and out into the valley in the Pueblo I and II periods (approximately A.D. 700 to 1100), and possibly on top of the mesa also. It was during Pueblo III times, about 1100 to 1300, however, that the population of the Zuni region began to concentrate in large pueblos, most of them on mesa tops. This movement took place in many other parts

[17] Eggan, *op. cit.*, p. 176.
[18] *Ibid.*, p. 210.
[19] Ruth L. Bunzel, *Introduction to Zuni Ceremonialism*, Forty-seventh Annual Report of the Bureau of American Ethnology, 1932, p. 476.
[20] Roberts, *op. cit.*

of the Southwest at about the same time, and has been variously explained. It was a gradual trend, and not a sudden shift, just as there has been a trend in the past century for pueblos to expand into a more scattered type of settlement, with movement down from mesa tops and out into small, summertime farming colonies. The change in settlement patterns in the 12th and 13th centuries appears to have had a variety of causes, with the incursion of Athabascan or other nomads playing at the most a minor role. Hostility and outright warfare between neighboring pueblos may have been a factor, and it seems especially probable that the increasing complexity of the social and ritual organization of an expanding population made such a village pattern desirable and that, at the same time, an increasingly productive economy with a surplus to be diverted to the support of various specialists made it possible....

In the Zuni area, round kivas occurred in a Pueblo III village about 20 miles northwest of Atsinna in Nutria Canyon (Roberts, 1932) and in a small site near Hawikuh (Hodge, 1923). In both instances kiva details in the associated pottery showed strong similarities to the Chaco Canyon area, about 75 miles to the north. The Zuni drainage, at the time of these Chacoan Pueblo III kivas, was near the southern periphery of a large region of San Juan Anasazi culture, of which Chaco Canyon was a major center of population concentration and cultural elaboration. When most of that area was abandoned in the 12th and 13th centuries the Zuni region remained continuously occupied and probably received some minor population accretions from the deserted area. At that time, however, the Zuni drainage came increasingly under Western Pueblo influence, from eastern and central Arizona, an influence that extended through the Zuni towns to the Acoma area and eventually to the Rio Grande. The round kiva at Atsinna, which sherd analysis can probably date in the 14th century, would thus represent one of the last expressions in the Zuni area of a northern tradition in religious architecture that can be traced back in the San Juan drainage through the earliest round kivas to their pit house prototypes of the fifth and sixth centuries (Brew, 1946)....

A reason for this contraction is not immediately apparent. It parallels the withdrawal of the ancestral Acomas to the eastward at about the same time.... It is possible that a decline in population, the reason for which we have yet to discover, was the impetus for abandoning outlying settlements and withdrawing into fewer but larger towns....

Second, Zuni burial practices deserve careful study and may provide important clues to historical origins. The Spanish chroniclers report cremation as a Zuni practice, and Hodge found cremations in the late prehistoric period. Since this is an unusual burial practice for the Pueblo area, and is characteristic of the Hohokam of southern Arizona, influence from the south appears to have taken place. Recently excavated cremations from the Point of Pines area of Arizona will also need to be considered for their bearing on the problem of Zuni antecedents.

In conclusion, there seems little doubt that Zuni civilization has been subjected to a great variety of contacts and influences through the past six or seven centuries, particularly from the Chaco area in Pueblo III times, and probably, subsequently, from the south and east. The Zuni contacts with both the Hopi and Acoma groups have been close, and through the latter it has influenced the Rio Grande. That Zuni has preserved its distinctiveness and independence testifies to the vigor of its conservative tradition.[21]

A few entries from the brief chronology published by Stevenson document the same points of continued acculturation and contraction.

[21] Richard B. Woodbury, "The Antecedents of Zuni Culture," *Transactions of the New York Academy of Sciences,* Ser. II, Vol. XVIII, No. 6 (1956), pp. 558–62.

1539, May.	Fray Marcos of Niza visited Cibola in this month and viewed Hawikuh ... from a neighboring height. This pueblo was the scene of the death of his negro companion Estevan at the hands of the Zunis about May 20.
1540, July 7.	Francisco Vasquez Coronado, after a conflict in which he was wounded, captured Hawikuh and applied to it the name Granada.
1542, spring.	Coronado and his army passed through Cibola on their way back to Mexico, leaving some natives of Mexico among the Zunis.
1581, summer.	Francisco Sanchez Chamuscado, with a small force, visited the province of Zuni (misprinted Cami in the records) which comprised six pueblos....
1670, October 7.	The Apaches (or Navahos) raided Hawikuh, killing the Zuni missionary, Fray Pedro de Avila y Ayala, by beating out his brains with a bell while he was clinging to a cross. The priest at Halona, Fray Juan Galdo, recovered Fray Pedro's remains and interred them at Halona. The mission of La Concepcion de Hawikuh was henceforth abandoned, but the pueblo was occupied by the Indians for a few years.
1680, August 10.	A general revolt of the Pueblos against Spanish authority took place.... At the time of this rebellion the Zunis, who numbered 2,500, occupied, in addition to Halona, the villages of Kiakima, Matsaki, and Hawikuh. Two villages (Canabi and Aquinsa) had therefore been abandoned between Onate's time (1598) and the Pueblo revolt (1680).
1699, July 12.	The pueblo of La Purisima de Zuni (evidently the present Zuni village, which meanwhile had been built on the ruins of Halona) was visited by the governor, Pedro Rodriguez Cubero, to whom the inhabitants renewed their allegiance.
1798–99.	The population of Zuni is reported at 2,716 (In 1820–21 it had apparently dwindled to 1,597.)[22]

Subsequently new acculturative influences appeared, and the independence of Zuni was often threatened. Finally, Zuni entered the reservation or modern period with its steadily increasing acculturative changes. In sum, the theme in Zuni life of significant acculturation and contraction combined with the preservation of Zuni cultural identity is known to have persisted over a period of some centuries.

ZUNI VARIATION

Each of the points mentioned in the discussion of Zuni's cultural background (isolation, complexity, integration, amalgamation, contraction, and acculturation) is pertinent to a discussion of Zuni variation. It is somewhat

---

[22] Abstracted from Matilda Coxe Stevenson, *The Zuni Indians: Their Mythology, Exoteric Fraternities, and Ceremonies*, Twenty-third Annual Report of the Bureau of American Ethnology, 1904, pp. 283–86.

unusual, however, to consider this particular problem, for despite the fact that many writers on Zuni culture have attested to its diversity and complexity, other scholars attempting to analyze the basic values of the culture (its integrative themes) have tended to regard them as a system of all-pervading dominant principles.

The best-known formulation of this sort appears in Benedict's *Patterns of Culture,* one of the most widely known volumes in the entire anthropological literature. It was Benedict who said:

> Apollonian institutions have been carried much further in the pueblos than in Greece. Greece was by no means as single-minded. In particular, Greece did not carry out as the Pueblos have the distrust of individualism that the Apollonian way of life implies, but which in Greece was scanted because of forces with which it came in conflict. Zuni ideals and institutions on the other hand are rigorous on this point. The known map, the middle of the road, to any Apollonian is embodied in the common tradition of his people. To stay always within it is to commit himself to precedent, to tradition. Therefore those influences that are powerful against tradition are uncongenial and minimized in their institutions, and the greatest of these is individualism. It is disruptive, according to Apollonian philosophy in the Southwest, even when it refines upon and enlarges the tradition itself. That is not to say that the Pueblos prevent this. No culture can protect itself from additions and changes. But the process by which these come is suspect and cloaked, and institutions that would give individuals a free hand are outlawed.[23]

And again:

> The ideal man of the Pueblos is another order of being. Personal authority is perhaps the most vigorously disparaged trait in Zuni. 'A man who thirsts for power or knowledge, who wishes to be as they scornfully phrase it "a leader of his people," receives nothing but censure and will very likely be persecuted for sorcery,' and he often has been.[24]

And:

> Membership in a clan with numerous ceremonial prerogatives outweighs wealth, and a poor man may be sought repeatedly for ritual offices because he is of the required lineage. Most ceremonial participation, in addition, is the responsibility of a group of people. An individual acts in assuming ritual posts as he does in all other affairs of life, as a member of a group.[25]

And finally:

> It is difficult for us to lay aside our picture of the universe as a struggle between good and evil and see it as the Pueblos see it. They do not see the seasons, nor man's life, as a race run by life and death. Life is always present, death is always present. Death is no denial of life. The seasons unroll themselves before us, and man's life also. Their attitude involves 'no resignation, no subordination of desire to a stronger force, but the sense of man's oneness with the universe.' When they pray they say to their gods,
>
> We shall be one person.[26]

---

[23] Ruth Benedict, *Patterns of Culture* (Boston: Houghton Mifflin Co., 1934), p. 80.
[24] *Ibid.,* pp. 98–99.
[25] *Ibid.,* p. 78.
[26] *Ibid.,* p. 128.

Again, space does not permit a full discussion of the Benedict synthesis. It is possible, however, that her discussion can be viewed as treating the following dominant value emphases: a Lineal position on the *relational* orientation, a Past *time* orientation, a Being-in-Becoming orientation, and a Harmony-with-Nature preference. Certainly, the Benedict view is centered on *dominant* values.

Although the Benedict view has been pervasive, it has not been undisputed. Some years ago Bennett discussed the interpretation of Pueblo culture in an extraordinarily interesting way:

A controversy over somewhat different issues and having a more direct importance for broader problems will be discussed in this paper. In a series of publications appearing during the past few years two principal interpretations of the basic dynamics of Pueblo society and culture have gradually emerged. These two interpretations have appeared not entirely as explicit formal, theoretical positions, but more as implicit viewpoints within the matrix of methodological and empirical research on Pueblo communities....

In the background of the controversy lie the criticisms of Benedict's and others' interpretation of Pueblo culture as "Apollonian," which often were not explicit denials of the truth of her characterization, but rather pointed out that there was another side to the story and that her method contained unexpressed value-orientations. In a sense this older phase of the difference in perspective goes to the heart of the problem; namely, if interpretations of the same fact differ, must this not in part be a consequence of differing values?

I wish now to describe, by paraphrasing, the two viewpoints:

1. Pueblo culture and society are integrated to an unusual degree, all sectors being bound together by a consistent, harmonious set of values, which pervade and homogenize the categories of world view, ritual, art, social organization, economic activity, and social control. Man is believed to have the ability to act freely and voluntarily in ordering his own affairs and fitting them into an harmonious universe. The outcome tends to be virtually a fulfillment of the ideal-typical folk-preliterate homogeneous, "sacred" society and culture. Associated with this integrated configuration is an ideal personality type which features the virtues of gentleness, non-aggression, cooperation, modesty, tranquillity, and so on.

In some analyses, this generalized ideal pattern is presented as the "real," that is, it is presented as lived up to more often than it is not. In other writings the correct estimation of the ideal patterning is acknowledged, but qualifying materials from "real" patterns are added. In still others, the ideal pattern is described as an ideal without *explicit* information as to its "real" manifestations or its consequences in other contexts of the society and culture.

2. Pueblo society and culture are marked by considerable *covert* tension, suspicion, anxiety, hostility, fear, and ambition. Children, despite a relatively permissive, gentle, and frictionless early training, are later coerced subtly and (from our viewpoint) brutally into behaving according to Pueblo norms. The ideals of free democratic election and expression are conspicuously lacking in Pueblo society, with authority in the hands of the group and chiefs, the latter formerly holding the power of life and death over his "subjects." The individual is suppressed and repressed. Witchcraft is covert, but highly developed.

Like the first, this view is qualified in analysis in many ways, and as I have noted, is not necessarily in conflict at all points with the first....[27]

[27] John W. Bennett, "The Interpretation of Pueblo Culture: A Question of Values," *Southwestern Journal of Anthropology*, Vol. II (1946), pp. 361–63.

Bennett's explanation of the difference is challenging:

> I believe, therefore, that the differences in interpretation, plus the relative avoidance by each of the views of the other, are evidence of a genuine difference in outlook and are not simply the result of conscious, objective choice of problem. I mean here that the social scientific research may have been directed and influenced in part by personal-cultural differences between the respective workers, and not merely by the division of scientific labor.[28]

Bennett makes a convincing case for the differences in the interpretations of Pueblo culture.

While these differences in interpretation may have been partially a function of the values of the investigators themselves, it can also be argued that there is now, and has long been, more variation in the Zuni value system than is to be typically expected in a majority of societies. Since the theory presented in this volume states that variation, both permitted and required, will be found in all societies, it will be necessary here to show why variation of both kinds is so great in Zuni and why, indeed, so much is seemingly necessary. The explanation should have a bearing both on the responses to the value-orientation schedule and on the various interpretations of Zuni culture which have been offered in the literature.

Sources of Zuni Cultural Variation

It has long been suggested that the contraction of the Zuni tribe may have contributed to its cultural complexity. This view has been stated somewhat obliquely by Cushing:

> Although the early Spaniards doubtless exaggerated the population of Cibola (more through imperfect means of getting data than from willfulness) in stating it as great as "eleven thousand souls," we may safely conclude from a computation of the rooms in the six ruins above named, that altogether they and ancient Zuni contained more than six thousand inhabitants. This seems only reasonable when we study the immense stock of lore, ritual, and ceremonial of the tribe, and, more than all else, the elaborate and highly differentiated organizations above mentioned. All these point not to a vast or dense population, but still to a very numerous and quite highly yet naturally developed ancestry.[29]

Kroeber has expressed the same idea more succinctly:

> The size of the Zuni community, and its reduction to a single pueblo, may have caused its social fabric to be more intricately knit than usual.[30]

It is indeed easy to think that the steady contraction of the Zuni towns must have added to the complexity of the ceremonial and other structures. Successful curing societies, for example, were not likely to be abandoned simply because their members ceased to live in an isolated village and, instead, joined forces with the inhabitants of another village. Moreover,

---

[28] *Ibid.*, p. 364.
[29] Frank Hamilton Cushing, *Zuni Breadstuff,* Indian Notes and Monographs, Vol. VIII (1920), p. 130.
[30] Kroeber, *op. cit.*, p. 188.

these alliances must have resulted in many compromises which in turn contributed to cultural complexity.

Although Zuni has long maintained a distinctive cultural identity, it is likely that the absorption of folk with quite alien cultures, which may have happened in prehistoric times and which is known to have occurred in historic times (Coronado's Mexican Indians, the modern Navaho, etc.), also enriched the community's role structure. Certainly, the close proximity of Anglo-American traders, missionaries, and government employees must be considered if one is to understand the dynamics of the modern pueblo.

In addition to contraction and amalgamation, diffusion and acculturation must have played their parts. The addition of such new elements to Zuni aboriginal culture as sheep, cattle, horses, peaches, wheat, silversmithing, and pickup trucks has been accompanied by consequent changes in the role structure, i.e., the addition of the roles of sheepherder, silversmith, truck driver, etc. The nominating committee, Zuni-held U.S. government positions, and other recent innovations in Zuni roles are again clear responses to modern acculturation. Since at the same time much of the aboriginal culture was maintained—at least on an intermittent or stand-by basis—there was, in sum, a substantial increase in the total content of the tribal culture through a long period of time.

The cultural isolation of Zuni may also have been a factor. Variant persons, even real deviants, could not escape to another community. They had either to remain in the tribe or to go into exile. At the same time, the threatened community stood to gain as human resources were conserved. This complex set of circumstances may also have favored adjustments contributing to internal variation.

Undoubtedly there are other sources of variation, but enough evidence has been submitted in the cultural background section to substantiate the presence of wide-range cultural variation. However, it must be remembered that this variation exists within the framework of a strong cultural identity and a tight integration.

The Variation Hypotheses

The data cited, as well as many more which could be cited were the space available, strongly suggest that had the Zuni *not* developed patterns of a wide-range "contained variation" they would long ago have been either absorbed or destroyed.

Without here trying to resolve the question of why one culture faced with the problem of adjustment to numerous external forces finds the means to survive as a more or less distinct entity whereas another one does not (a problem which in some sense is almost certainly related to basic values), it appears to be a fact that the Zuni have long recognized the survival value of extensive intra-cultural variation. In dealing with both their hostile natural environment (scanty rainfall, early frosts, floods, and the like) and an equally menacing human environment which included the overt threats from Apache, Navaho, and Spaniards and the somewhat more covert ones from Anglo-Americans, they have seemingly chosen the path of garnering and storing "cultural information" of widely variant kinds.

This complex "informational economy"[31] had its preservative functions but was at the same time always a potential threat to cultural identity, which in turn had to be contained by means of intricate integrative patterns. The containment process can be seen as the product of a massive commitment to preservation in the face of strong external pressures which on the one hand barred movement and increased isolation and on the other hand threatened active penetration or annihilation.

The result for the social structure—a result attested to by all who have dwelt upon the degree of complexity in Zuni culture—was the development of a social role network which over a long period of time has been extraordinarily ramified for a community of so small a size. For a very long time the complexity of pattern elaboration was mainly discernible in religious and ceremonial activities. This was to be expected according to our theory, if it is assumed that the traditional *dominant* Zuni values were those analyzed by Benedict and others (value orientations which favored the religious behavior sphere). However, as has been indicated, there has long been considerable variation in other areas as well. Currently the evidence is strong that there is actually a *decrease* in the pattern elaboration in the ceremonial sphere and a fairly rapid *increase* in the elaboration of economic interests and activities. Some illustrations of this process have been mentioned; others will be cited below.

In sum, our thesis is that Zuni tribal culture is a fairly extreme example of contained cultural variation. Although this hypothesis cannot at this time be fully tested, it is possible to cite evidence from the literature which is even more specifically in support of it than the general statements made thus far about the complexity and integration of the culture.

In presenting some of this evidence I shall treat first a few of the results of investigations which had the aim of testing for personality differences among the Zuni. Subsequently I shall briefly discuss statements and conclusions which bear more directly on variations in the value orientations.

Personality Variations

Relative to the hypothesis of variation the primary question to be asked of the personality-testing data is whether or not the high degree of variability in the role structuring of Zuni social organization is reflected in a somewhat greater degree of individual variation than is found in societies which are less isolated and less involuted. This question is not, however, as simple as it sounds. It can well be argued that the tight integration of the society is conducive to the development of a definite modal personality. Yet opposing this argument is the equally tenable one that such a wide variety of roles (and the interests relating to them) contained within a

---

[31] I have profited greatly from hearing Dr. Gene Weltfish discuss this concept.

single community rather than being distributed over several should mean that the Zuni individual receives his socialization at the hands of persons who are themselves various and is therefore likely to show considerable variation within himself.

It may well be that there is some degree of validity in both of these arguments. Moreover, the two tendencies are almost certainly interrelated. If this be the case, it is possible to reason that the high degree of variation in a culture such as Zuni makes it the more imperative that there be great firmness to what may be called a "core" modal personality. This is only speculation at this time, but should it prove to be more than speculation we may have part of the answer as to why some students of Zuni culture have been so deeply impressed by the modal patterns whereas others have been equally insistent upon the great variability of the Zuni.

The variability of personality in Zuni may not be greater than in the other four cultures. Kaplan, who in 1947 administered Rorschach tests to 157 individuals in four of the same communities in which the value-orientation schedule was used, states:

One of the conclusions we feel most confident about is that very great heterogeneity of personality occurs in all the groups studied.[32]

Kaplan also asks:[33]

Do the cultures differ as to the degree of individual variability within them? A very rough index of the overall variability is the sum of the eight coefficients of variation. Comparing the sums for each culture, we find the following:

Navaho	546
Zuni	616
Mormon	575
Spanish-American	603

It is apparent that although Zuni is variable, it is not significantly more variable than the other cultures by this measure. However, Kaplan does report that judges had greater difficulty separating Zuni projective materials from Navaho, Mormon, and Spanish-American protocols than was true for any one of these other three cultures.[34] From this and related evidence Kaplan concluded that it was more difficult to substantiate the hypothesis of a modal personality for Zuni than for the other cultures.

Hollenberg found that variations in child-training practices were greater among the Zuni, both for the community as a whole and for individual extended family groups, than among Mormons or Texans. The variation was particularly evident in the case of weaning practices:

... the range of weaning ages are as follows: from 4 to 12 months for the Texans; from 9 to 18 months for the Mormons; and from 9 months to 6 years for the Zuni. The distribution for the 20 Zuni mothers of our sample is as follows:

---

[32] Bert Kaplan, *A Study of Rorschach Responses in Four Cultures,* Papers of the Peabody Museum, Harvard University, Vol. XLII, No. 2 (1954), p. 32.
[33] *Ibid.,* p. 16.
[34] *Ibid.,* p. 27.

Age of Weaning	Number of Cases
9 months	1
12 months	7
18 months	1
24 months	7
36 months	1
48 months	1
60 months	2

Although I have no specific evidence on this point, I presume that the reason for this variation is because the Zuni pattern is to wean at the time of the next pregnancy rather than at a specific age. If this is true, presumably five years is the upper limit for nursing even the youngest child.[35]

The proper weighing of such variation as an antecedent condition to adult variation must be left to the psychologists.

The weaning data, however, lead to a consideration of other data on Zuni children. Hollenberg[36] examined the principal techniques of discipline in the three societies:

It can be seen from the above table that Zuni mothers have a relatively low rating with respect to denial of love. Both Zuni and Texans have ratings of 3 on denial of love whereas Mormon mothers not only use denial of love more extensively, but they use it as their main technique of discipline....
It has already been shown in Table II that the main technique of discipline used in Mormon is denial of love; the main technique used in the Texan community is physical punishment, and the main technique of Zuni is use of supernatural threats.[37]

Thus the Zuni achieve displacement to the gods or to the society as a whole. This point is relevant to the problem of Zuni identification.

Hollenberg collected some interesting data on Zuni identification which are sufficiently pertinent to the present argument to justify some extensive treatment:

Two measures of identification were used to test this hypothesis. The identification (a) measure attempted to get at the child's preference for adult status, and is a measure of desired *age in years*. The identification (m) measure consists of the number of matching choices which the children made between statements describing the interests and traits of *their same sex parent* and statements which described *their* interests and traits....
The mean identification scores for Zuni children are considerably lower than the mean scores for Texan and Mormon children. On the identification (a) measure, the mean score for Zuni children is 12.1 years whereas the mean scores for Mormon and Texan children are 17.3 years and 17.6 years, respectively. This difference is significant beyond the 1% level of confidence ($t=5.0$). On the identification (m) measure, the mean score for Zuni children is 0.6 number of matching choices out of a possible six matches whereas the mean number of matching choices for Mormon and Texan is 2.1 and 2.6 respectively. This difference is sig-

---
[35] John W. M. Whiting, personal communication, 1958.
[36] Eleanor Hollenberg, "Child Training Among the Zeepi," unpublished Ph.D. dissertation, Harvard University, 1952.
[37] *Ibid.*, p. 90.

nificant well beyond the 1% level of confidence ($t=9.00$). These results tend to suggest that Zuni children as measured by the number of matches have a relatively low amount of identification, both with the parent of the same sex and adult status, as measured by the scores of desired age.

With respect to identification with the same sex parent, it has already been pointed out in the descriptive chapter of Zuni that the Zuni child grows up with a generalized relationship to a group of parents rather than with a fixed relationship toward one parent. Mothers and mothers' sisters are designated by the same term, and women within a household will nurse one another's children. The child grows up in an atmosphere surrounded by many adults; aunts, uncles, grandparents and other relatives are usually present to help him gratify his needs. Thus, it would seem that the Zuni child has a more diffuse type of identification than the Texan or Mormon child. Rather than identifying strongly with any one particular adult, the Zuni child may identify with many adults. This argument might account for the relatively low scores on the identification (m) measure, since it was a measure of identification with a particular adult.[38]

Although a presentation of the data in detail is not warranted, it is to be noted that Hollenberg found internal differences in child socialization in Zuni, and also discovered that her first identification measure showed Zuni children to be far more variable than those of any other group. There was actually a bimodal distribution. Some Zuni children actually wanted to be younger than their chronological ages while others wanted to be older. In the other cultures the children invariably wanted to be older.[39]

Hollenberg is undoubtedly correct in thinking that life in the typical matrilocal Zuni extended family has a direct bearing on identification with parents by Zuni children and on the internalization of values. One has only to compare the daily life sequences of the two extended families reported in *Zuni Daily Life* (households B and D) with similar sequences of typical American nuclear families to see the great contrasts. Not only is the interaction of each member distributed among many other members with the resultant possibilities for variation in identification, but such a life situation gives training in relating to a larger and more diverse group of people. This training, in turn, may generalize to life in the community and tribe.

It is submitted that to some degree the variation in responses to the Rorschach tests, and to even a higher degree the differences found in child-training practices, the low degree of internalized control, the use of supernatural beings in child socialization, the low amount of identification with particular adults, the wide variation in responses to the identification tests, and complexities of life in an extended family are consistent with the general argument of this chapter. Unfortunately, the data are not conclusively convincing; they are only suggestive.

Variations in Value Orientations

In discussing what the literature on Zuni has to tell us more directly about the variations in the value orientations, I shall treat the orienta-

[38] *Ibid.*, p. 94.
[39] *Ibid.*, p. 104.

tions in this order: *activity, man-nature, time,* and *relational.* Because some of the orientations, called by other names to be sure, have been far more extensively treated than others, the discussion will necessarily be uneven.

ACTIVITY ORIENTATION. Considerable attention has been devoted to aspects of Zuni life which in some sense are expressions of the *activity* orientation. Usually, of course, the discussions of the Zuni value system have not attempted to separate out analytically the different value orientations or at least not in the way the theory being used here defines them. But consider this quotation from Benedict's *Patterns of Culture* which certainly in part refers to what we are calling the *activity* orientation.

The problem of social value is intimately involved in the fact of the different patternings of cultures. Discussions of social value have usually been content to characterize certain human traits as desirable and to indicate a social goal that would involve these virtues. Certainly, it is said, exploitation of others in personal relations and overweening claims of the ego are bad whereas absorption in group activities is good; a temper is good that seeks satisfaction neither in sadism nor in masochism and is willing to live and let live. A social order, however, which like Zuni standardizes this 'good' is far from Utopian. It manifests likewise the defects of its virtues. It has no place, for instance, for dispositions we are accustomed to value highly, such as force of will or personal initiative or the disposition to take up arms against a sea of troubles. It is incorrigibly mild. The group activity that fills existence in Zuni is out of touch with human life—with birth, love, death, success, failure, and prestige. A ritual pageant serves their purpose and minimizes more human interests. The freedom from any forms of social exploitation or of social sadism appears on the other side of the coin as endless ceremonialism not designed to serve major ends of human existence. It is the old inescapable fact that every upper has its lower, every right side its left.[40]

Many parts of Benedict's total interpretation, not simply the above quotation, were challenged more than twenty years ago by Li An-che who in relation to the specific point in question said:

A healthy amount of ambition is in existence in any living society. Only the means of acquiring prestige and realizing ambitions are different, being culturally conditioned. Once agree to play the game, it must be played according to the rules of the game. The rules are different in different societies, but their existence is universal. With reference to Zuni in particular, not only do ordinary forms of struggle for individual supremacy exist, but violent forms also occur once in a while.[41]

Other authors have also challenged the Benedict position in analogous ways.

More discussion of the *activity* orientation is not warranted because the present inquiry does not provide the essential data. A free interpretation of the differences of opinion in the literature concerning this basic value, as well as others, is that all protagonists have given little weight explicitly to the existence of variant orientations. Instead, the argument has been centered on dominant orientations. Benedict held, perhaps, that the domi-

---

[40] *Op. cit.,* p. 246.
[41] Li An-che, "Zuni," *American Anthropologist,* n.s., Vol. XXXIX (1937), p. 69.

nant *activity* orientation was Being-in-Becoming while the others—citing, in the main, Doing evidence—said that this could not be the case. The compatibilities and interrelationships of the several *activity* orientations were not considered.

Because of the importance of the *activity* orientation in many of the controversies about Zuni, it is most regrettable that the Being-in-Becoming possibility was not tested by the schedule. As things stand, there is little point in discussing this orientation further, other than to say that the literature supports the presence of Being and Doing orientations as well as the dominant Being-in-Becoming orientation.

Despite the ambiguity of results which almost certainly stems in part from the omission of the Being-in-Becoming alternative, it is my opinion that the Doing orientation is either first or second order in the Zuni system at the present time. True, the response to the two questions dealing with the employer-employee relationships were unequivocally Being, but these questions involved a relationship which is not typically Zuni and may have carried overtones of white-Indian relations. Also these items were avowedly much less purely related to the testing of the orientation than others in the schedule (see Chapter III).

MAN-NATURE ORIENTATION. On the *man-nature* orientation, which was tested in its full range, the Zuni results were inconclusive. Statistically speaking, the results were close to With = Subj = Over—no pattern at all. Does this virtual equivalence of positions mirror the cultural reality? I think a case can certainly be made for such a view.

The traditional view of the Zuni, of course, is that the dominant orientation is Harmony-with-Nature. Supporting statements for this conclusion can be found in the works of Cushing, Benedict, and others, but the best is that of Bunzel, who wrote:

> Man is not lord of the universe. The forests and fields have not been given him to despoil. He is equal in the world with the rabbit and the deer and the young corn plant. They must be approached circumspectly if they are to be persuaded to lay down their lives for man's pleasure or necessity. Therefore the deer is stalked ritualistically; he is enticed with sacred esoteric songs, he is killed in a prescribed manner, and when brought to the house is received as an honored guest and sent away with rich gifts to tell others of his tribe that he was well treated in his father's house.
>
> So, too, the great divinity, the sun, and all the lesser divinities, the katcinas, the rain makers, the beast gods, the war gods, and the ancients, must be reminded that man is dependent upon their generosity; and that they, in turn, derive sustenance and joy from man's companionship.[42]

The position of the Subjugation-to-Nature orientation is less easily documented from the literature and field notes. An important underlying Zuni theme, however, is that life can be hard; hence it can be argued that the Harmony-with-Nature and the Subjugation-to-Nature orientations have long been balanced and integrated in Zuni culture.

The changing orientation which is most likely to account for uncertainty

---

[42] Ruth L. Bunzel, *Introduction to Zuni Ceremonialism*, Forty-seventh Annual Report of the Bureau of American Ethnology, 1932, pp. 488–89.

and variation in present-day Zuni is the Mastery-over-Nature orientation. There is clear evidence that this orientation is growing in strength as Zuni acculturation progresses.

At one level, of course, the Zuni have long displayed a cultural competence. Cushing, for example, after an elaborate description of the preparation of a Zuni corn field—a task, by the way, which was accompanied by ritual and prayer—said:

> The effect of the network of barriers is what the Indian prayed for (attributes, furthermore, as much to his prayer as to his labors), namely, that with every shower, although the stream go dry three hours afterward, water has been carried to every portion of the field, has deposited a fine loam over it all, and moistened from one end to the other, the substratum. Not only this, but also, all rainfall on the actual space is retained and absorbed within the system of minor embankments.[43]

Moreover, less competent tribes were regarded with contempt:

> So, too, a Zuni will say of the wandering Hua-la-pai [Walapai]: "Why have they teeth, since they eat their food, like dogs, with little waiting and less chewing? Unlike dogs, they have fingers, and need not fangs for the catching! Why, then, have they teeth?" This to a Zuni understanding is an exceedingly cogent allusion to the perpetually half-famished condition of the non-farming Hua-la-pai, to their dependence from day to day on chance for their food supply, and to their consequent habit of eating with avidity and dispatch whatever they can lay hands on.[44]

Whether or not the Over-Nature orientation was strongly visible in the older culture, it has unquestionably been strengthened by recent acculturation. These acculturative changes have worked in many directions. The intimate association of the Zuni with the natural environment, for example, has become modulated. Not only have hunting and collecting ceased to be major economic activities, but many Zuni are more dependent by far on silver work and wage labor (their own or that of close relatives) than they are upon agriculture or stock raising. In the time of Cushing, the Zuni subsistence economy was entirely self-sufficient, but today, weaving, basket making, pottery making, and other crafts have virtually disappeared and the houses are filled with the products of our modern industrial economy. The Zuni household inventories to be published fully document this point. Today there are some Zuni who, for all practical purposes, do not farm, herd, hunt, or collect.

The Zuni is no longer dependent upon man or animal power. Even remote sheep camps are supplied by truck, not burro. Travel is commonly in automobile or truck, and in 1951 the numerous horses on the reservation were more liabilities than assets. At the time of the study, electric lights and appliances were becoming increasingly important. Today, electric power is a commonplace. The Zuni, in short, exploit sources of power which were unknown in the last century and which have yet to figure in the elaborate religious symbolism.

Changes, too, have occurred in the management of water. The large dam

[43] Cushing, *op. cit.*, pp. 164–65.
[44] *Ibid.*, pp. 520–21.

at Black Rock has long supplied water for irrigation, and it is not certain that today's young men still know how to make the skillful use of floodwaters known to Cushing's Zuni. The community which was once dependent upon shallow wells now has a public water supply utilizing deep artesian wells. There has even been an interest in scientific weather control.

Stock raising has, in some instances, become marked by changes compatible with the new orientation. One Zuni informant said:

We don't save our own lambs for bucks. If we did, we would ruin the whole herd—it would become too inbred. We have to get bucks raised from some other herd so that there will be no inbreeding. This is better than using the same old bucks every year.[45]

The same informant displayed other relevant behaviors.

On September 17, 1951, FaSiSo47A was observed preparing a Lysol solution to be sprayed in the nostrils of sheep to eradicate worms....

On September 22, 1951, FaSiSo47A was observed setting up a trough where he was going to feed the sheep salt to which phosphorus had been added. At this time FaSiSo47A was treating sick sheep with penicillin, which he had purchased on the recommendation of the county agent. A few days later he was enthusiastic about the cures he was apparently obtaining from penicillin, but he was scornful about a preparation for "screw worms" which another sheep man had obtained from a trader for his sheep. Incidentally, FaSiSo47A kept his penicillin, the needles, and other equipment in the sheep camp house where it was cool.[46]

These examples could be compounded.

Changes are occurring in the area of curing. A single Zuni house contained evidences of the following "white" medicines: Alka Seltzer, argyrol, aspirin, boric acid, calamine and denadryl-hydrochloride lotion, colic remedy, cough syrup, Cuticura ointment, Ex-lax, eye salve, haliver malt with Viosterol, Kaopectate, lactated pepsin, Mentholatum, Murine, hydrogen peroxide, Sal Hepatica, potassium permanganate tablets, methylate tincture, Vaseline, Vick's Vapo-Rub, and more. Almost all Zuni households at some time have seen the hospitalization of one or more of their members, and exposure to white medical care is a commonplace. This is not to say that ancient curing practices have disappeared, for they continue. Nevertheless, most of the Zuni have some familiarity with modern medicine.

Today the Zuni listen to radios, attend movies, send young men to the military services, and educate their children in modern schools. Surely, all of these influences, particularly in instances where dominant American orientations conflict with orientations in the old culture, must make for ambivalence and confusion.

Considering both the literature on Zuni of past generations and the mounting evidence of current technological (economic) elaborations, it would seem to be the case that on the *man-nature* orientation the traditional Zuni ranking which was almost certainly With over Subjugated over Over is in a state of flux with the Over-Nature position gaining constantly.

[45] Roberts, *op. cit.*, p. 97.
[46] *Ibid.*

TIME ORIENTATION. As far as the *time* orientation is concerned, there is considerable evidence to support the view that the Zuni ranking order is Present over Past over Future. The lengthy quotation from Kroeber is confirmatory, for it describes a Present over Past combination:

I have talked casually with many Zuni about ruins and excavations, and the above seems typical of their point of view. Remains that are post-Spanish and others that are obviously very ancient are thrown together into one blurred past, the *innote* or "long ago," which seems to begin very nearly where the experience of living individuals ends. I have never heard from a Zuni the least reference to a historic event. They may possess a stream of semi-historical tradition, distinct from their mythology and schematized conceptualizing of the past; but if so, it drains but a minute fraction of their minds. I have waited two summers for a spontaneous manifestation of something of the kind. Direct inquiry probably would reveal certain traditions; but they would not be the kind that the natives habitually tell each other. The Zuni are intensely interested in the scheme of structure of their society, and in its divine institution; but their invariable assumption is that since its institution this society has remained a constant unit, unchanged except for little irregularities that come with the wear of time. Such minor variability they seem to regard as obvious, trivial, and not particularly worthy of attention; and such are the conquest of Coronado, the establishment of a mission in the heart of their town, and other actions of the Spaniard with reference to themselves. As a matter of fact, any change imposed on the social scheme is very quickly absorbed into it; a generation or two suffices, the alteration has become fixed, and is reckoned as perpetual as the structure, though perhaps obviously incongruous.

An example. The Zuni are professedly anti-Catholic and anti-Christian. During the summer of 1916, the proposed establishment of a Catholic mission incurred the displeasure of the whole tribe except a small minority of individuals standing in special relations to Mexicans. In the meeting at which the affair was brought up, the sentiment of the overwhelming majority was so vehement that the negative decision was unanimous; and the result was received not only with general satisfaction but open rejoicings. Yet every Zuni that has died within the past two centuries lies buried in the unkempt little graveyard that was first consecrated by Catholic fathers, and in the center of which a constantly renewed cross rears its beam. The mission church in the heart of the town is to us the ever impressive reminder of the Christian influence imposed on the nation for many long generations; to the Zuni it is anything but a symbol of the alien religion which they struggle to ward from themselves. They make attempts, mostly ineffectual, it is true, to roof and preserve the crumbling structure of adobe. Some years ago, a wider passage was wanted between its altar end and the nearby houses. The western wall was therefore torn down. But it was re-erected in its entirety, a few feet farther in! The northern face gives evidence of having been similarly shifted. This by a people that resent the coming of the priests, that will not tolerate a Catholic Mexican within view of their religious observances, and from among whom only playing boys, hens, and hogs trouble to enter the edifice which they toil to preserve. We face here a strange conservatism indeed: but it is a conservatism of the present, with no feeling for the past. The church, the graveyard, the cross are not Catholic; they are Zuni; therefore they are clung to and treated as things integrally and inherently Zuni.

The habitual attitude of the Zuni, then, is unhistorical. He derives satisfaction from recognizing his national system, and from thinking of it as fixed since its first establishment. In everything else his interest is but intermittent and perfunctory. That now and then he may preserve fragments of a knowledge of the past that approximate what we consider history, is not to be doubted. But it is equally certain that such recollection is casual and contrary to the usual temper of his mind. From these conditions we must conclude that the shape of these recollections, and even the very selection of their content, is likely to be randomly fortuitous in our sight, whenever it is not wholly determined by the Zuni's prevailing and sufficient systematization of his narrowly encompassed world.[47]

Other authors have seen the importance of the Past orientation. Adair and Vogt, for example, wrote:

> The problem thus arises: why have the Zuni responded with a "nativistic reaction," going to great great lengths to reabsorb their veterans into the traditional social and cultural forms, while the neighboring ... Navaho have tended to regard their veterans as potential forces for change in the direction of white patterns of culture?[48]

No one has made a case for the strength of a Future orientation.

Once again, then, a complex situation emerges from the data. It can be argued that the Present *time* orientation has been pervasively, but unobtrusively, dominant while the variant Past *time* orientation has been visibly and dramatically evident. The latter orientation is particularly noticeable in the religious behavior sphere where it has caught the eye of many writers. Benedict, for example, wrote:

> The Zuni priest holds his position because of relationship claims, or because he has bought his way up through various orders of a society, or because he has been chosen by the chief priests to serve for the year as impersonator of the kachina priests. In any case he has qualified by learning vast quantity of ritual, both of act and of word. All of his authority is derived from the office he holds, from the ritual he administers. It must be word-perfect, and he is responsible for the traditional correctness of each complicated ceremony he performs. The Zuni phrase for a person with power is 'one who knows how.' There are persons who 'know how' in the most sacred cults, in racing, in gambling, and in healing. In other words, they have learned their power verbatim from traditional sources. There is no point at which they are licensed to claim the power of their religion as the sanction for any act of their own initiative. They may not even approach the supernatural except with group warrant at stated intervals. Every prayer, every cult act, is performed at an authorized and universally known season, and in the traditional fashion.[49]

Bunzel stated:

> All more important prayers are fixed in content and form, and great importance is attached to their correct rendition. The rigidity increases in proportion to the importance of the occasion.... That the desired undeviating repetition claimed for prayers is not always achieved is illustrated by a study of variants ... which shows also the very narrow margin of variability. That a long prayer should have changed [very] little in the 50 agitated years since Cushing's time is really remarkable.[50]

The Past *time* orientation is manifested in religious activities other than the exact repetition of prayers, but this concern with detail serves to sym-

---

[47] Kroeber, *op. cit.*, pp. 203–4.
[48] John Adair and Evon Z. Vogt, "Navaho and Zuni Veterans: A Study of Contrasting Modes of Culture Change," *American Anthropologist*, Vol. LI (1949), pp. 554–55.
[49] Benedict, *op. cit.*, pp. 96–97.
[50] Bunzel, *op. cit.*, p. 493.

bolize the overall concern. It is altogether pervasive in religious thinking, and this, in turn, affects much that would ordinarily be called secular. The strength of the orientation to the Past is manifested in other ways. A religious organization which may appear defunct may be revived at the last minute as recently happened in the case of the Bow Priest Society. Other examples could be cited.

This orientation, however, is not so evident in other behavior spheres. The Present, or even the Future orientation, seems to prevail in the realms of economics and technology. Even in religion, dramatic changes can be found. Bunzel was able to describe the *pekwin* in the following way:

> The pekwin is the most revered and the most holy man in Zuni. Even in this society which diffuses power and responsibility until both become so tenuous as to be almost indiscernible, the pekwin is ultimately held responsible for the welfare of the community.[51]

Yet this all-important office is now vacant. Some curing societies have become extinct. The *kivas*, to be sure, are flourishing, and masked dances, if anything, are growing in importance, but this is a congregational development, not a priestly one. Zuni religion is steadily becoming more secularized. The influence of long-continued missionary activity, too, has yet to be assessed. True, few converts have appeared, but some changes have undoubtedly occurred.

In summary, then, the Pres $\geqslant$ Past $>$ Fut ordering of the *time* orientation alternatives appears to be old in the culture. A formerly weak third-order Future *time* orientation is gaining in strength as acculturation progresses, and it is probable that it is the Past *time* orientation which is being dislocated in this change of balances. Or in other words, it would appear that on the *time* orientation the fairly rapid acculturation process of today is effecting a change in second and third-order rankings. If the process continues, and if the impinging culture—Anglo-American culture—does not itself change, it can be predicted that the shifting will continue in the direction of a greater emphasis upon the Future *time* position.

RELATIONAL ORIENTATION. The responses to the items testing on the *relational* orientation showed a moderately consistent pattern of Coll $>$ Lin $\geqslant$ Ind. It is the Lineal and Collateral distinctions I wish to focus upon, since they are the positions which have been the basis of much discussion by the various investigators of the culture.

This is not to deny the importance of the Individualistic position, which certainly appears to be gaining in strength. For example, many roles, particularly those representing adjustments to the dominant American culture, such as motor mechanic, blacksmith, maintenance man, seem to depend on the attainment of individual technical competence in a way which is not to be found in the older individual and group roles. But even though this emergent Individualism is becoming increasingly an important factor, the deeper problems in Zuni social structure even today appear to be linked with the interplay of the Collateral and Lineal emphases.

No better case for the significance of Lineal relationships in Zuni society

[51] *Ibid.*, p. 512.

could be made than that formulated by Eggan in his chapter on Zuni social organization. Speaking of all of the western Pueblos, Eggan said:

> The lineage group is probably the basic unit for segmentary or formal organization in all the western Pueblos. There is no special name for this unit anywhere—any more than there is for the household—so that it has not had the attention it deserves. The clan is the major grouping in western Pueblo thinking. It has a name, frequently a central residence known as *the* clanhouse, relations with sacred symbols, often control of ceremonies or status positions, and sometimes control of agricultural lands or other territories.[52]

Turning to Zuni specifically, Eggan, in commenting on Kroeber's widely quoted statement on the integrative pattern of Zuni, said:

> This is a brilliant cross-sectional summary of Zuni social integration, but there is also an integration through time. This integration is carried out through the lineage principle, in large measure. We have noted that the lineage principle, which underlies the kinship system and furnishes the core for the clan organization, also provides a mechanism for the inheritance of ceremonial duties and obligations and the transmission and preservation of fetishes and other ceremonial paraphernalia. In Zuni this inheritance is phrased in terms of the household, but it is clear that it is the lineage segment born into the household that is important. This lineage segment, or at least the female line thereof, also owns land and holds it in trust for succeeding generations, to be worked by the men who marry into the household. In Zuni the clan is a weaker institution than among the Hopi. With regard to maintaining the socio-ceremonial system the clan provides an added safety factor against lineage extinction, and the phratry grouping may have operated similarly at one time, but clan control of ownership of ceremonies is not stressed. Likewise, the clan does not have an economic base. In Cushing's time control of land was phrased in terms of clan, but there were already processes at work modifying this relationship. Today land is controlled by households or by individuals.
>
> While the clan is weaker among the Zuni in comparison with the Hopi, tribal organization seems much stronger....[53]

And again:

> On the contrary, I believe the evidence shows that kinship is organized on a lineage basis and that even in the "bilateral" recognition of the mother's and father's lineages there is not equality but a complementary relationship. The ritual activities are primarily in the hands of the father's household; 'during the crises of individual life as well as upon public occasions it is the father's people or clan which is charged with performing the requisite rites.' The economic activities on the other hand, are primarily in the hands of the mother's household and lineage, aided perhaps by her clanspeople.[54]

And finally:

> The clan, through the lineage principle, provides a mechanism for both stability and continuity in the group serving as trustee for the fetish; alternative mechanisms, such as 'child' of the clan, are subordinate to the lineage principle of descent. Where extinction of the clan takes place, the fetish may be sealed in the house....

[52] Eggan, *op. cit.*, p. 299.
[53] *Ibid.*, p. 217.
[54] *Ibid.*, p. 196.

The association between the clan system and the different ceremonial groupings varies in each case. The chief Rain priesthoods are associated with the directions; if there were ever an association with the directional phratries, as implied in Cushing's scheme, it has long since been lost, since three of the priesthoods are now associated with households in the Pikchikwe clan, and one each with the Badger and Eagle clans. The Katcina society is likewise organized on the basis of six kiva groups associated with the directions. While there is no relation between the kiva groups and clans, the director of the society and his deputy should belong to the Deer and Badger clans, respectively. The individual masks belonging to the Katcina gods are kept in particular households and impersonated by particular clansmen in many cases; they are frequently associated with kivas as well. The Medicine societies have both a directional and a clan association....[55]

It is regrettable that the entire chapter cannot be quoted. In sum it might be said that Eggan, while admitting the evident Collaterality in Zuni, would favor the dominance of the Lineal orientation.

The evidence, however, can be interpreted another way. Admittedly, Lineal principles are important. Not only are the authority and recruitment of the key priesthoods Lineally organized, but even within the curing societies there are conditions that officers must be drawn from a specific clan or matrisib. In the recent past, the Zuni priesthoods were at the apex of Zuni social structure and ultimately all decisions were reviewed by the senior priests. At the same time, there have always been in Zuni many Collaterally organized groups such as the *kivas*, curing societies, and the Bow Priesthood. An individual could become a member of a curing society by becoming cured of an illness, a member of a *kiva* by participating in the general initiation, and a member of the war society by fighting. This underlying Collaterality merits further discussion.

Lineality is not as important in Zuni kinship as one might conclude at first glance. Schneider and Roberts concluded their monograph on Zuni kinship with the following paragraphs:

Data collected in 1953 on Zuni kinship terms and their usages are presented. The terminological system shows three particularly interesting characteristics: first, it is neither pure lineage in type nor pure generation, but can best be described as 'modified' Crow. Second, alternate terms occur for significant kinsmen. Third, a high incidence of apparent irregularities or 'wrong' usages occurs. These three characteristics of the Zuni terminological system are closely interrelated.

Zuni terminology is modified lineage, rather than 'pure lineage,' in type. The modified lineage type is a reflection of the relatively weak corporate character of the matrilineage. The presence of alternates and the high occurrence of irregularities are correlated with the fact that genealogical position is not the sole determinant of role but is only one from a group of determinants. This derives from the fact that the lineage is, as compared with Hopi for instance, but weakly corporate. This permits, but does not require, that kinship terms be valued primarily as role designating symbols and only secondarily as classification mechanisms. The integration of Zuni social structure is bilateral in type, that is, the structure is not organized in terms of the relations between groups but in terms of the relations among individuals, so that the maintenance of the particular pattern of relations

---

[55] *Ibid.*, pp. 215–16.

is valued above the concern with whom these relations are maintained. Since this pattern of relations is configured around the central values of kinship, these valued relations are best symbolized by kinship terms. Kinship terms thus symbolize the important roles but do not stress, though they imply, genealogical positions since groupings are not the central units of Zuni social structure.[56]

Romney and Metzger, conducting a further analysis of the Zuni data, concluded with Schneider and Roberts that the terminological system is basically bilateral. Romney and Metzger thought that the Lineal features may have represented a more recent addition.

Perhaps the balance between Lineality and Collaterality in present-day Zuni is best demonstrated by the conflict over political authority. In the recent past, the situation described by Eggan obtained:

> 'Political' authority is in the hands of a council of priests composed of three members of the chief priesthood and the heads of three other priesthoods. The head of this hierarchy is the 'house chief', who is head of the chief priesthood (that of the north), assisted by the *pekwin* or Sun Priest, who acts as a talking chief for the priesthood. The two Bow Priests act as an executive arm; the heads of the Katcina society serve as advisers. The principal matters which come before the council relate to the appointment of secular officers, impersonations of the gods, the time of tribal initiations, changes in the ceremonial calendar, and questions of tribal policy. They have the welfare of the pueblo in their hands and are too sacred to be concerned with secular quarrels and problems. Internal crimes such as witchcraft are the concern of the Bow Priests; formerly they tortured suspects to induce confession.
>
> The council appoints a set of secular officials: a governor, lieutenant-governor, and some eight assistants to carry out relations with outsiders and to deal with civil suits, quarrels over property, co-operative work on roads and irrigation ditches, etc. These officials hold office at the pleasure of the priests and may be removed at any time. The governor and lieutenant-governor should not be from the same clan, and their assistants are generally chosen from different clans. Whether or not this civil government is "in substance a native institution," as Kroeber believes, its activities were expanded to deal with the new problems brought about by Spanish contacts.[57]

Within the last few decades, this pattern has been changed. During the period of the study, officers were nominated by a nominating committee and then elected by the adult males in a public meeting. Several times since the institution of this procedure the pueblo has had two sets of officers, one sponsored by the priests working from a Lineal over Collateral base described by Eggan and the other elected by the men of the tribe working, perhaps, from a heavily Collateral over Lineal base. Thus far the conflict has always been resolved in favor of the elected officials. In one case, to quote Smith and Roberts:

> This episode was cited by one informant as evidence of the decay of priestly authority in Zuni today. He said that "in the old days" there would have been no thought of overriding the authority of the head cacique.[58]

[56] Schneider and Roberts, *op. cit.*, p. 22.
[57] Eggan, *op. cit.*, p. 210.
[58] Smith and Roberts, *op. cit.*, p. 25.

These political conflicts, which are much too complicated to be detailed here, reinforce the hypothesis that the Lineal orientation is losing strength and that the Collateral-Individualistic combination is becoming more prominent.

In general, it is my own opinion that the responses to the items on the *relational* orientation schedule are quite congruent with the situation in present-day Zuni. The relative strengths of orientations are changing, but it would seem that the first change to occur has been the strengthening of the Collateral orientation at the expense of the Lineal one. While the Individualistic orientation is certainly gaining in strength, it seems unlikely that it will be pushed into a dominant position in the near future.

SUMMARY STATEMENTS

Incomplete and impressionistic as this review has necessarily been, the evidence examined and discussed does indicate that Zuni culture has long been a fairly extreme example of "contained variation." While the theory of variation in value orientations argues that variation, both permitted and required, is to be found in all cultures, the important aspect of the Zuni case is that Zuni, relative to its size, has seemingly had more intra-cultural variation than would normally be expected. It is for this reason that the term "contained variation" has been adopted to describe a highly evolved network of variant patterns which in one way or another and to a greater or lesser degree has served to maintain the dominant patterns and augment the feeling of tribal identity.

Groups may interact with other groups of diverse culture patterns in a variety of ways. Some place a premium upon expansion and the extension of their own cultures. Others seem to yield more or less easily to the impact of encroaching cultures. In another category still are those which struggle to maintain their own cultures, showing little desire either to expand and conquer or yield and be conquered. The Zuni fall in the last category. They have not been eager to convert others to the Zuni "way of life," but neither have they been willing—thus far, anyway—to so yield to outside influences that their strong sense of cultural identity and uniqueness would be seriously impaired. The result has been a great tolerance for intra-cultural variation providing it did not produce so intricate a pattern background that the dominant motifs of the culture were obscured.

It has been shown that some investigators of Zuni culture have been deeply impressed by these dominant motifs whereas others have been equally firm in their insistence that a wide-range variation exists in the culture. In a consideration of why both points of view may be correct, several factors have been discussed within an historical context. The isolation and contraction of the culture are two of these. It is also almost certainly true, as the theory of variation in value orientations contends, that the degree of strain created for many individuals by the dominant values has been such as to demand variant patterns for the channeling of frustrations and hostilities.

The important question concerning Zuni culture today is whether or not the situation described for the past can be maintained. Although it has not been an aim of this discussion to treat any part of culture change as it may be considered to be a product of the effect of the pressure of varying types of external forces upon the existent intra-cultural variation,[59] one is tempted to speculate that the ever-increasing strength of the pressures of Anglo-American culture will be such as to bring about some truly basic changes in the Zuni value system. This is not to say that there will be a wholesale taking over of Anglo-American values. On the contrary, as has been noted, relative to the *relational* orientation the shift appears to be a strengthening of the Collateral relations at the expense of the Lineal ones whereas there is little evidence for predicting a dominant Individualistic *relational* orientation in the near future.[60] And while the results of the value-orientation schedule show something of a definite increase of both the Mastery-over-Nature position of the *man-nature* orientation and the Doing *activity* orientation, there is no comparable shift as yet to a Future *time* orientation.

However, in general, the decrease in the pattern elaboration of the ceremonials and rituals and the increase of technological activities—both to be noted from other sources than the value-orientation schedule—are indications of the type of change which in the value-orientation theory is called basic change.

To answer any question as to why the changes are of one degree in one area and of other degrees in other areas would require a far more intricate analysis of the kind and degree of intra-cultural variation in Zuni and its similarity or dissimilarity to the nature of Anglo-American value orientations than could be attempted in this paper. Our concern has been only with showing that the degree of variation in Zuni culture both in the past and the present has been sufficiently great to lend considerable support to the view that the great variability in the Zuni responses to the value-orientation schedule is, for the most part, actually the cultural reality.

---

[59] For a discussion of these effects see Chapter I of this volume and the more detailed account given in Florence Kluckhohn, "Some Reflections on the Nature of Cultural Integration and Cultural Change" (see Chap. I, footnote 51).

[60] This is a result similar to that which Caudill has found in the case of Japanese culture. This material, as yet unpublished, should appear in 1961.

TABLE IX:1
SUMMARY OF NAVAHO RANKINGS

	Relational Orientation
R1	Coll > Lin ⩾ Ind
R2	Lin > Coll ⩾ Ind
R3	Coll ⩾ Lin ⩾ Ind[a]
R4	Coll ⩾ Ind ⩾ Lin
R5	Coll > Lin ⩾ Ind
R6	Coll ⩾ Ind ⩾ Lin
R7	Coll ⩾ Ind ⩾ Lin
Sum	Coll > Lin ⩾ Ind

	Time Orientation
T1	Pres > Fut ⩾ Past
T2	Fut ⩾ Pres ⩾ Past
T3	Fut ⩾ Pres ⩾ Past
T4	Past ⩾ Pres > Fut
T5	Pres ⩾ Past > Fut
Sum	Pres > Past ⩾ Fut

	Man-Nature Orientation
MN1	Subj ⩾ With ⩾ Over
MN2	With > Subj ⩾ Over
MN3	Over ⩾ With > Subj
MN4	With > Subj ⩾ Over
MN5	Over ⩾ With ⩾ Subj*
Sum	With ⩾ Over ⩾ Subj*

	Activity Orientation
A1	Being > Doing
A2	Being ⩾ Doing
A3	Doing > Being
A4	Doing > Being
A5	Doing > Being
A6	Doing > Being
Sum	Doing > Being

[a] Coll > Lin only.

CHAPTER IX

The Rimrock Navaho

A. Kimball Romney and Clyde Kluckhohn

The aim of this chapter is to take a close look at the data summarized in Chapter V, both in the light of materials available from other sources on Navaho values and on the Navaho situation[1] and in the context of free comments made by the subjects and of other notes recorded by Romney in administering the value-orientation schedule. Our procedure will follow these steps:

(1) A rather bald summary of the dominant and variant profiles.
(2) A somewhat microscopic examination of the responses and volunteered remarks, question by question.
(3) Summaries on perceived consensus and on age and sex differences.
(4) A final overall interpretation.

FIRST (CRUDE) SUMMARY

The predictions on the Navaho (see Chapter II) were borne out satisfactorily with the exception of the responses from the female sample on the *time* orientation which yielded a Present over Future over Past rank order instead of the predicted Pres > Past > Fut. However, the results from the male sample and from the sample as a whole which was Pres > Past ⩾ Fut did closely approximate the predicted ordering.

The overall dominant profile has been summarized as Collateral, Present, With-Nature, Doing. On other evidence (see below) one may add with some confidence that the conception of *human nature* is that of an invariant (immutable) mixture of Good-and-Evil. The Navaho data fully validate Florence Kluckhohn's theory that all orientations are expressed to some degree in every culture. Indeed, in this case the variation is so considerable that it is not possible to state without inference and interpretation a second-order variant profile applicable to the whole group. Straining and giving equal weight to each question, one could say that the total sample gives second-order preference to Lineality and to Past *time*. But this problem requires more intensive examination. One can say that the female second-order preference is the Future alternative and the male one the Past alternative. This is all that is immediately clear.

[1] A brief description of Navaho culture and its ecological setting has been given in Chapter II.

ITEM-BY-ITEM SUMMARY OF RESPONSES

Relational Orientation

ITEM R1 (WELL ARRANGEMENTS). About the most unfavorable moral judgment that one Navaho can pass on another is to say, "He acts as if he didn't have any relatives." Navaho social structure is focused upon an extended series of patterned kin reciprocities. Even today Navaho workers are "undependable" from the point of view of Anglo-Americans primarily because Navaho thought and behavior give easy priority to the Collateral framework. A Navaho will in all honesty agree with a government employee or missionary or trader about something but will fail to carry out his "promise" because discussion in the extended kin group has taken a negative turn. Taking or leaving a job is not a matter for purely individual decision but rather must be considered with the family.

The definite choice of the Collateral alternative on the Well Arrangements question is decisively supported by the free comments. Consider the following remarks[2] of six men and four women:

You can't just have one leader or one family. This wouldn't be fair to the rest. You should get together and discuss.

It is easy to vote, but it doesn't turn out. The only way for the people would be discussing.

The community gets together in a group to decide.

And another thing is for the group to work it through together.

The ones in a group make a choice.

They could decide the matter by themselves and by discussing it so it would work all right with everyone.

The best thing is to get together in a group and make an agreement.

By watching ... by making plans in a group.

By groups making plans.

The one that talks and has the most discussing. This is the way.

In this and in other cases (which will not be examined at as great length) the spontaneous comments make it evident in most instances that the point was grasped and that the choices do reflect the orientation held in fact. In this case the comments of even those who chose first the Lineal or Individualistic alternative have a Collateral flavor. For example, one man who plumped for "the leaders of important families" adds immediately, "They can discuss." None of the Lineal comments suggest thoroughgoing emphasis upon the ordered positional succession exhibited in the true Lineal orientation. There is a fairly often remarked general respect for the experience of older people, but this is sometimes qualified by "old men with good ideas" (i.e., not just old men as such) or by a skepticism as to the wisdom of the old. And one of the most prestigeful old leaders makes explicit his conception that the whole group must finally

---

[2] Unless otherwise specified, quotations come from Romney's field notes.

decide whether the elders have made a good decision. The voting (Individualistic) choice is also qualified. One man, who says that in voting "everyone gets a fair chance," adds, "Another way is in the group making plans.... If the community wants to work it out in the group, good...." A different individual noted, "... a vote doesn't turn out good, we fight it, so the ... thing is for the older leaders to discuss it that way." Indeed one may plausibly speculate from the total context of the field notes that almost no Navaho is wholeheartedly enthusiastic about voting. They recognize it as "the white man's way" and hence as a factual reality to be faced, and some of them (a little grudgingly?) admit that it is "fair."

Taking the answers and the free remarks together, one can be quite sure of the picture. The Navaho are overwhelmingly oriented to the Collateral position. There is a fairly frequent recognition of the necessity for leadership; but the leaders must be "good," and this attribute is not unfailingly attached to age or any other specific position. Competence is stressed in various contexts. The young should "maybe" have a voice, but only if the younger person has experience or education. In other words, the Lineality is to some degree a "fake" Lineality. The elders and other leaders (such as ceremonial practitioners) are deferred to within the Collateral group less because of their position as such than because of their special experience and competence. The kind of Individualism implicit in voting (as opposed to participation in group discussion) is definitely foreign to Navaho thinking, but somewhat accepted as part of reality.

ITEM R2 (HELP IN MISFORTUNE). The responses to this question have probably been affected more than those to any other question by the economic problems of the Rimrock Navaho and by their experience with government agents and other Anglo-Americans in this century. Bad droughts and general poverty marked the period when the schedule of questions was administered. A considerable number of the Navaho were on relief; many others had been forced to leave for varying periods of wage work on the railroad and other poorly paid jobs. Relatives were seldom able to give much help. Typical of the spontaneous comments is the following:

Getting help from boss, like agency [government], that's all you can depend on. You can always get help there if you really need it, it has been told by our agency. Next, from the brothers, sisters, and relatives. But you can't be sure. That's why it's second. They may have only a little. That's the only thing we can think of [the agency]. It isn't easy for brothers and sisters.

That this is a change is indicated by an old man who was talking about conditions before the turn of the century:

If there were many brothers and sisters, they could go there first. If they didn't [help], they could go [to] close relatives and discuss in a little meeting and decide what to do.

Another man said, "Go to important man or boss" and explained this as "Washingtone" (that is, the Indian Service).

Again, we must be careful not to overemphasize the apparently Lineal elements in the responses to this question. They reflect much more of situation and experience than of fundamental value orientations. The Rimrock Navaho in these difficult times have learned that government, traders, and well-off ranchers can help them where their relatives cannot. That they would still prefer to depend upon their families is evidenced by the remarks of several: "If they [brothers and sisters] had something, I would depend on them." This comes out equally in the explicit statement above to the effect that relatives are mentioned second only because of reality factors. Another subject, after saying, "from the boss or leader, then from the outside," adds, "For my people, it is brothers and sisters." The note of competence is struck again in referring both to outside "bosses" and to wealthy or leading relatives. The Collateral emphasis stands out once more in the phrase "they could discuss in a little meeting and decide what to do." Individualism enters only once into the volunteered remarks, and this remark is susceptible of more than one interpretation.

ITEM R3 (FAMILY WORK RELATIONS). Total responses on this question yield a result that is on the borderline of statistical significance. Most of the individuals, however, fall into one of two competing patterns: Collaterality over Lineality over Individualism (nine) and Individualism over Collaterality over Lineality (seven).

The following are comments characteristic of the first pattern: "Working with brothers and sisters and family" is best. "You can depend on oldest one; he has experience, especially in important problems." Another said he would take brothers and sisters "because the relatives and family would work together, even as in olden times. Next is the one the family could work with oldest boss if it could be done too." Another said, "Usually it is best to work in groups, that is the one, and then you can depend on the oldest."

The most common reason given for working alone was the possibility of fighting. As one man put it, "I'm most in favor of taking my own by myself... some don't go by a group because they don't get along." This comment was made by one of the younger and most highly acculturated men in the sample. He also indicated that most other Navaho would prefer the Collateral alternative. Another man who chose the Individualistic response added, "... but if you don't have the equipment, you get it done within the group. This is faster... and if all the relatives want to run it together, that is okay." In general, the free remarks raise some doubts as to whether there is evidence for more than an incipient orientation of Individualism. It is in the economic behavior sphere, of course, that increasing dependence on working for non-Navahos and other experiential and situational pressures tend almost to force an Individualistic orientation. And, while this is not explicitly mentioned in the comments, one may speculate that keeping the business of the nuclear family segregated may lead to weakening of all ties to the extended family and the wider circle of relatives. Remember always, however, that this question is still placed in a *family* context—not that of individual members of a family making their own separate decisions without consultation.

In the spontaneous comments on this question there are some indications of genuine Lineality. The *experience* of the eldest is still frequently mentioned, and one acculturated man says, "I'm not in favor of the oldest because you can't tell what kind of person he might be." But two informants in response to a probe made it clear that they meant the oldest person, regardless of his qualifications. And another specified the "respect" due to the eldest.

ITEM R4 (CHOICE OF DELEGATE). There is no statistically significant result to this question. This may be because the ideas of agreement reached by discussion and agreement by voting do not seem mutually exclusive to the Navaho. Certainly the volunteered comments often merge these two ideas in the same sentence. For example:

Call a meeting and put up men with experience and talk it over, and then vote. They would discuss it before you put up names so it would be fair to everyone. They could all agree on one leader.

The themes of leadership, competence, and age emerge frequently again in the remarks on this question as in these:

The older ones know a lot more than the young, and they can do much good for the people. I know that the people would suggest that the old leaders decide. They do the most for us.

Once more it is plain that voting is an alien idea but accepted as a reality factor. One conservative old man remarked: "We're taking on white ways and are setting up vote for a man. Now there are a lot of people, and voting is all right for me."

On a qualitative basis one has little hesitation in saying that this question comes out Collaterality first, Lineality second, and Individualism a very weak third.

ITEM R5 (WAGE WORK). The dominant Collateral orientation is generally followed by the Lineal. The following are representative comments:

The working with the group is it. It is easy for men to overcome what they are working on. They can choose those that get along easy. Also, you can have a boss deciding for the people, for they lack experience. My people would say it is the group. They always get someone to help.

In favor of the second one. About the first one, he makes the men work too hard, and the workers are his slaves, and this isn't the way.... The one giving the less wages but the easy one who is understanding in order not to lay off and to keep good men.

Notes frequently struck are: steadiness of work versus high wages for a short time, an "understanding" and fair boss, and (again) competence and experience.

A few individuals gave a rank order of Individualism over Collaterality over Lineality. These were younger and more acculturated persons.

A number of the comments suggest that this question was misinterpreted at least as regards its focus. To a Navaho, working (other than on one's own place or with one's "outfit") implies predominantly a "boss" in Anglo-American fashion. Hence many of the respondents concentrated their remarks on the question of what kind of a "boss" is preferable. But these comments are also revealing of a Collateral over Lineal over Individualistic rank order.

ITEM R6 (LIVESTOCK INHERITANCE). There is a trend in the Collateral direction as a first-order choice, but the consistency is not statistically significant. As in the case of item R3 both items R6 and R7 reveal two competing value profiles: Collaterality over Lineality over Individualism and Individualism over Collaterality over Lineality. There can be little doubt that we have here the results of acculturation, even though the variations do not strictly follow age differences and differences in personal and acculturative experience. The factor of family friction was mentioned several times by those who took the Individualistic alternative as first choice:

It's best to run them separately. If you can get along, it's okay to run them in a group.

I don't believe that it should be in a family because you can't get along that way.

Sometimes brothers and sisters don't think alike. Some might want to sell, others to improve the herd.

Family tension among the Navaho at this period often follows lines of value conflict. Those who have spent more time among Anglo-Americans often want to introduce new ideas or to claim privileges of individual inheritance and autonomy that they have discovered prevail among Anglo-Americans.

ITEM R7 (LAND INHERITANCE). There is again an extreme heterogeneity in rank-order choice but with a statistically nonsignificant tendency to favor the Collateral position:

Get some kind of agreement among brothers and sisters, and then that works. It is usually the oldest, but you can't tell if he is the good one or bad. Maybe next one is better. If you can't agree at all, take it alone.

... they could do it better together and then it will be better.

Because if the brothers and sisters work together, they won't have any trouble....

Individualistic responses, as with the preceding question, often are justified on the ground of family friction or the selfishness of some members. Comments stress the inevitable question of competence, refusing to accept categorically the eldest or qualifying an assertion with "usually." Yet there is a bit of Lineal overtone to some of the remarks.

SUMMARY. The general statistical finding of a dominant Collateral orientation with a somewhat weak emphasis on Lineality as a second-order position is fully substantiated by an analysis of the field notes. There are also indications of an emerging Individualistic leaning, though this is seldom as yet expressed in terms that would be recognized as Individualistic in Anglo-American culture. Three significant factors somewhat weaken the dominant Collateral orientation:

(1) In the political behavior sphere the feeling about choosing individuals is influenced by recognition that voting is "here to stay."

(2) Economic problems and the experience of getting help from Lineal figures like government agents and traders has lessened reliance upon the extended kin group.
(3) Answers about inheritance and family work relations are colored by the high level of friction now prevalent in most Navaho families—partly because of value conflict, partly because of general poverty and uncertainty.

Time Orientation

As mentioned in Chapter II, the *time* orientation appeared to be the most difficult of the orientations to test. This is certainly true with the Navaho. The aim of the items of the schedule was to elicit a generalized orientation response by means of a somewhat specifically phrased question. The Navaho—and this trait may be linguistically conditioned—are a concrete-minded people. In a majority of the interviews the subject would ask for more concrete specifications in the questions. It seemed very difficult for some to answer the questions in an "as if" fashion. The answers to some questions would be answered first in the form of a concrete personal experience. One could argue, on the basis of projective theory, that an individual's report of his behavior could be validly interpreted for generalized orientations. This is probably a fairly valid argument but one which may be negated under severe environmental difficulties. Unfortunately, the group of Navaho being studied were under severe environmental pressures. Within the past few decades they had been pushed onto the poorest land in the area, and in the three years prior to 1951 they had been experiencing very harsh drought conditions. Thus, regardless of what general orientations they may hold, they have been forced to make realistic adaptations to changed environmental conditions. For example, traditionally the Navaho has turned to his extended family group in times of trouble. This has been the proper behavior in terms of traditional Navaho values and has been sound realistic behavior, since under previous circumstances the extended family was usually able to help members in need. In the last few years the Rimrock Navaho have been under so much economic pressure that this assistance has greatly diminished. Thus, in times of trouble, more and more Navaho individuals have been forced to seek help from outside sources.

At present the dominant *time* orientation among the Rimrock Navaho is clearly the Present one. This is borne out by both the results of the value-orientation schedule and extensive field data on file in the Values Project. The problem of the variant and second-order orientations is a more difficult one. The present environmental and acculturative factors apply pressure in the direction of a Future *time* orientation. Traders, government representatives, and other carriers of the dominant American culture are all Future-oriented and try to require behavior on the part of the Navaho which conforms to this Future orientation. On the other hand, there is some material indicative of a Past *time* orientation. In the volunteered elaborations of responses to questions on various orientations there is often a nostalgic glorification of "the good old days." And the Past is frequently revered in Navaho myths, prayers, and ceremonials. But the matter is complicated. Navaho ceremonials are for curing individual patients, and hence every chant is in one quite explicit way oriented to the Future, as well as to the restoration of Past harmony. Also, the reverence expressed for the Past in the ceremonial sphere is perhaps less worship of the Past as such than another expression of the high evaluation of knowledge so often manifested by the Navaho. On the other hand, it can be repeatedly observed that ceremonial objects of antiquity acquire added power and sanctity just because they are old. Finally, it should be noted that much of the ceremonial attitude toward *time* would appear to be more intimately related to the *man-nature* than to the *time* orientation in the strict sense. The Navaho looks back, not because he values the Past for itself, but because the Past is the source of important knowledge and because only by looking back can one maintain continuity, keeping the Present stable and the Future predictable by making them conform to the Past in an orderly way.

ITEM T1 (CHILD TRAINING). Three males and one female respondent chose the Past alternative as their first choice. They were all older people. One man said that the old days were best and recalled such practices as having the children run barefoot in the snow, using the whip on them if they were cranky, letting them go to sleep without their meals. "All this was good for them." He recognized that nowadays children are taught new ways. A ceremonial practitioner said:

I'm more in favor of the old ways. They were taught in the old way, and I can imagine how well they were taught in those days. Now everything is going in the future, and the reason is the white people teaching them in school, and someday they will be like white people. The second choice is because we have to adapt to the white people's schools. Now it is mostly between the whites and the children.

Another old ceremonialist tried to combine in a constructive way:

The first choice is all right with me. That sounds right; they should be taught old ways as children, then when they grow up, they can learn new ways. Learn the old ways and then learn the new.

An old woman who chose Present as first alternative nevertheless wished to combine:

The first thing is to teach them for the present, then you teach them about the old ways.

Another woman said that she thought "the ways of the old were good," but that children didn't care about them any more and needed to learn the new ways. A man justified his choice of the Present on the explicit ground that "the Past was good, but we don't know much about it any more."

The Present *time* position, held by the majority of the respondents, is further illustrated in these excerpts:

... because it will be all right if they try to teach their children in the olden way, but now they want them to learn the right ways and learn new things, but they don't go by old ways any more. Suppose you have a family. You don't teach them old ways. They look forward for themselves.

They ought to be taught some of the old, but they need some school ... to help their own ... people. Those that don't teach [the new] at all get into trouble.

Only one woman took the Future alternative as first choice. She said, "They didn't have schools [in the old days] and couldn't learn new ways, but now this is best." However, at least three individuals used Future-oriented phrases ("look forward," "ought to look forward") in their free comments.

Not all of these materials are clear-cut on the *time* orientation. For the issue is confounded somewhat by the choice between two ways of life. The Navaho way happens to be "old" in this context yet it is also *their* way as opposed to the Anglo-American way. Navaho culture is on the defensive, but there remains some pride in it and, moreover, active hostility and still greater ambivalence toward Anglo-Americans and their way of life. Hence the Navaho were not choosing entirely between Past and Present (or Future); they were expressing some identification with and some allegiance to their customary habits. The number of respondents who grudgingly conceded that instruction in the "new" was needful were, first and foremost, making decisions in terms of reality.

Even though more individuals took the Past rather than the Future alternative as their first choice, the Future position came out as the overall second-order response. This is because those that took either the Present or Past as a first choice then took the Future as the second choice. Hence the Past alternative came third in the great majority of cases. However, older males at least are revealed by the comments as tending to hold a nostalgic Past orientation. The basic second-order position is Future because of the realistic perception of the need to adapt to the white man's world—more particularly, the school. Although the school is not mentioned in the question, nearly half the subjects introduced the school in their free remarks.

ITEM T2 (EXPECTATIONS ABOUT CHANGE). No statistically consistent pattern emerged in the responses to this item. It did, however, elicit some very interesting and revealing comments. The Navaho view of the universe is essentially one in which everything is interrelated. Thoughts and events are not to be completely separated. This conception of experience apparently led many of the subjects to take the Future response. The following remarks are samples of this attitude:

If you know special things and live right, you live longer.

If the children work hard and know what they do, they will be better off.

If they have mother and father who plan out right way for children, then that is best, and they will know how to get more improvement.

You can work hard to make things go smoothly and can get along that way. I think that people are looking to the future.

One can look toward the future, and the children can get all those good chances.

Thus good thoughts, planning, and hard work will make for a good Future.

We recur here once more to the inescapable "competence" theme. There is likewise an obvious link to the Doing alternative of the *activity* orientation. It is impossible to say exactly how much of the forward-looking thinking and explicit reference to "planning" comes from Anglo-American culture. In any case such ideas are by no means completely absent from the myths, though the phrasing is less manifest.

A competing theme in the responses, and one which is actually stressed to a greater extent in the comments, is a "can't tell" attitude:

You just can't tell how things will work out. You just can't tell.

You can't tell what comes up. Just take it. You can't tell about a child either. If you keep your nose out of other people's business and work hard, this is best.

The last notion, that of "mind your own business," is a standard Navaho value norm. The idea that people are at the mercy of events has implications of a Subjugated-to-Nature orientation. The two themes of "can't tell" and Future sometimes appear together:

The first one [Future] because you notice that is the only chance to go forward. If you work hard and the children work hard, they will get ahead. The second [Present] is my second choice because they might be worse off tomorrow than today. For example, we just had a nice meal, but it might be our last. The same way with our children.

ITEM T3 (PHILOSOPHY OF LIFE). As with the preceding question, no statistically significant response emerged. This question exceeded all others in length, and there may have been a certain loss in reliability in oral presentation. That the question nevertheless struck home is indicated by the length of many spontaneous comments.

A recurrent theme again is the nostalgia for old ways and a resigned acceptance of the need to change and to plan for the Future:

Can't depend on the old. New things are showing up. This is what I think. Most of them living now don't think of oldest days. New people are here, and the old ones are gone. Now they [other people] look to the future.

In the old days it might have been the past, but work for new ways is the only thing now.

Invocation of experience and of current reality occurs in almost every observation:

The first is the present. This is true about us. If we try to think back to olden days, it's no use. Now things are changing and we are right in the middle. In the olden days they knew the kind of lives they live. Now we can't even say. Next, I take the future.

Olden ways and traditions is best. If we had that, I'd like it.... Everyone is now going to the future so I just go along on this because the old ways are gone....

I think the old ways were true. They didn't have many new ways, but they always knew how to do it. For example, if they go on a trip, they went on horses. The olden times were more better. The people are living up to today. Things have been changed a whole lot from tradition.... One thing is the olden way. Now it is past.

The people look toward the future because even the language is changing fast, and they will be way ahead in the future. Old ways don't do any good, and old people are way behind, and it is going faster and faster.

Note, however, that the nostalgia is not altogether for the Past as such but rather for a stable time when people knew what to do and what to expect. And those who "just go along" (on the Future) "because the old ways are gone" are perhaps better interpreted as Present rather than Future-oriented since they introduce the Future primarily because they recognize the rapidity of (inevitable) change.

ITEM T4 (CEREMONIAL INNOVATION). It is in the ceremonial behavior sphere that one would expect the greatest conservation of values. This expectation was borne out. There is a significant and consistent pattern which rejects the Future position, and affirms usually the Past, and sometimes the Present one, as the dominant value orientation. The majority of the volunteered comments run along the following lines:

We are using a ceremonial now, but it is changed, and people don't get well. But if it was the same as in the old days when they were kept sacred, then they would cure.

I am a medicine man, and if you make any changes, it is very hard to cure anyone. You shouldn't make any changes. If you try to change sings, you get in accidents like falling off the horses.

It is more better to keep the sings the same. You have to keep them right or they don't do any good.

Again, however, one must not refer the content of these remarks too easily and exclusively to the *time* orientation. Change must be avoided not altogether because the Past was good but, even more, because this is the nature of things. The universe works along somewhat mechanical lines. Any violation of the rules threatens disaster. To be sure, the rules are usually validated by reference to the Past *time* orientation.

Two men (one of them a "progressive" considerably influenced by Homestead) openly advocated ceremonial change:

It is good for things like this to change. The changes are good. The people who look forward.

Two women struck the "can't tell" attitude:

What I have on my mind is the future, and you can't tell how it will be. Things are changing.

We are using a sing now, but it is changed, and people don't get well. The people, some of them, believe in sings, and some don't. But they have to take what comes.

For the men there was generally a longer comment on questions in which there was doubt in their minds as to the proper choice, as if they were trying to talk out their decision. Among the women doubt showed itself in silence and embarrassment which may have been overcome by making a choice in the dark, as it were.

ITEM T5 (WATER ALLOCATION). The responses reveal a consistent pattern with a dominant and a variant Past *time* orientation. This question evoked fewer and briefer comments:

You shouldn't make plans beforehand. Then you won't disappoint anyone if you wait until it is in. This is the fairest way.

To wait and see.

Just one well. Have to go by the past.

Better to wait until it is in. Once it is done, do it the same way.

As soon as it comes in, then you divide it.

Wait till it is in to divide, then the one that does it the old way.

Wait until the water comes up. It has been done already, and then no one will come up and make trouble.

These remarks merely repeat the notes of prudence and preference for stability.

SUMMARY. On the total series of items of the *time* orientation the Navaho first-order preference was the Present alternative. There was, however, a difference between the men and the women in second-order choices. The men chose the Past position; the women the Future one. The resultant pattern for all respondents was the Pres > Past ⩾ Fut one. Analysis of elaborations and volunteered statements supports these results but also makes possible some interpretations and qualifications. In the Navaho case what appears at first glance as allegiance to the Past is in part a reaction to the almost unbearable confusion of the Present. The nostalgia is more for stability than for a golden age. Antagonistic acculturation is also involved.

On the other hand, the variation among different behavior spheres is significant. The tendency toward the Past alternative of the *time* orientation is most prominent in the religious and moral areas. And the tendency is much more marked among the men than among the women. This must be related to Rapaport's finding that Rimrock Navaho women are much more prone to abandon the old religion for one or another form of Christianity.[3] The clearest evidence for affiliation with the Past orientation is definitely associated with the ceremonial sphere.

Although on the basis of the total literature, one may conjecture that traditional Navaho society lived primarily in the Present, today a resigned acceptance of the Present, rather than a genuinely spontaneous and timeless Present orientation, characterizes the Navaho. In the educational behavior sphere, where the Present orientation is strongly dominant, one senses practical realism rather than enthusiasm. Though not statistically significant, in the generalized questions on Expectations about Change (T2) and Philosophy of Life (T3), there was hope expressed that the Future would be better. Yet these gropings toward the Future likewise fail to indicate confidence. Both the responses to the items of the schedule and the free comments must be read in the light of the history of the Rimrock Navaho in this century and the current situation. Reality makes it impossible to place wholehearted emphasis upon the maintenance of Past customs or to trust a realizable Future. One must live from day to

---

[3] Robert Rapaport, *Changing Navaho Religious Values*, Papers of the Peabody Museum, Harvard University, Vol. XLI, No. 2 (1954).

day as best one can. The conception of *time* as a "thing" or "commodity" which can be divided by a clock and "saved" is foreign to the traditional Navaho view and indeed to most Rimrock Navaho at present. In arranging interviews, for example, it was never possible to make an appointment by "clock time." *Time* is reckoned only crudely in terms of gross natural phenomena. "Tomorrow" or "in three tomorrows" is about as precise an appointment as can be made except vague (from the Anglo-American viewpoint) intervals such as "toward sunset." Actually, interviews were ordinarily given when the informant was found.

Man-Nature Orientation

Minimizing friction in human relations and maintaining harmony between man and supernaturals, between man and nature, and in the universe generally, are the basic goals toward which the Navaho is oriented. The aim is to maintain "balance" or "harmony" among the various aspects of the universe. Disequilibrium may bring trouble such as human illness, drought, or social disruption. In Navaho thought disequilibrium may be brought about by human action since the universe is to a great extent personalized. Probably one of the most general anxieties present among the Navaho is the fear of bringing about "disharmony" or "disequilibrium" in the universe. This anxiety may be characterized in its positive aspect as a drive for security and stability. The Harmony-with-Nature orientation fits the Navaho view of the relationship between man and nature remarkably well. We shall see from an analysis of the responses to the questions that this correspondence is supported.

ITEM MN1 (LIVESTOCK DYING). This is the only *man-nature* orientation item which did not give statistically reliable results. An analysis of the comments on this question, and they were quite extensive, seems to indicate the following juxtaposition of ideas. One's thoughts and actions, both with respect to the livestock and in life generally, can affect the losses (With position). However, these thoughts and actions may be committed either deliberately or unwittingly. Therefore, the man may be blamed (Over position) or he may not be to blame (Subjugated position). Thus the three alternatives are not necessarily mutually exclusive in the Navaho way of conceptualizing things. Almost every comment contained the premise of harmony, i.e., the idea that thoughts and actions affect the losses. It seemed, however, to be an idiosyncratic factor that determined whether the individual attributed blame for the losses.

Consider the following remarks:

You have to use your thinking and you can prevent it [livestock loss] by doing things. I have heard about people who lost sheep because they were bad. I don't know how it works, it is a secret, but I know it works that way.

A person has to live right to keep harmony, the right natural ways, and this is what my people would say.

If a fellow takes good care and saves feed for winter, and isn't careless, things like this don't happen. If you lead a better life, this never happens, but this happens if you are bad.

It is true that you can't blame anybody for something like that, and then another thing, if a person doesn't live right, you can't expect to have protection for your horse or sheep; if you don't, it will save up and you get it later on.

ITEM MN2 (FACING CONDITIONS). This item elicited a large majority of first choices for the With-Nature alternative. The answers were almost entirely favorable to this one alternative and rejected both other alternatives.

Representative comments are:

It is true that if they live the right way, there will be harmony. You can't tell what the holy people will give you for harmony. We believe that if we don't live right way, we will get from the holy people to destroy our crops.

It's true that if you live right, that this is best. For my people it seems that they don't think there is the right harmony, and this is why there is no rain.

[With-Nature alternative] because holy people and us people, if we try to do our own best to live the right way and we will have harmony for crops.

ITEM MN3 (USE OF FIELDS). It is in the area of farming that the Navaho have been hardest hit by the drought. This factor, coupled with the idea that actions and thoughts are closely interrelated, seems to have resulted in a pattern of responses which gives about equal weight to the Over-Nature and the With-Nature positions. The juxtaposition of ideas is represented in the following comment:

I'm in favor of [Over-Nature position] if you have equipment and new ideas we know you could do some work. If you depend on rain you have to live the right way to get along. I'm not in favor of only keeping them going, you have to live right even if it doesn't rain.

Another man phrased it as follows:

Everyone notices we are not living in the right ways; if we still lived the right way, we wouldn't have no harm, maybe we're not acting right and maybe that's why the holy people don't send no rain; if we were living right, we would have good crops, even if we don't have rain, you can get a crop with new ways and equipment.

Another said:

Work real hard on the fields, the lazy ones won't get along. If you think the wrong things, it is true that they won't grow.

ITEM MN4 (BELIEF IN CONTROL). This item, like item MN2, elicited clear-cut With-Nature responses from the Navaho respondents. The general feelings of the Navaho on the subject are revealed in the following responses:

It's true that when you live in the right way, if you do good, then later on something will come along and make it up.

It is best when you get to thinking about what is best for you.

The way I think about rain and snow is the people live right, it is best; also it isn't true about [its being] a man's job, that isn't true.

Anyone can live that way if they do the right thing, they will get it fair enough. The people know about that and live the right way is the only way to control those things. Nobody can control wind and rain, it is just natural; people get bad luck if they joke about this.

ITEM MN5 (LENGTH OF LIFE). The statistics show a rank-order pattern of Over ≥ With ≥ Subj* for the Navaho on this question. This modal position is illustrated in the following remark:

It's true about doctors and vaccinations, because I've had experience that way, and also if you do something bad, it affects your life, and if you are good, you don't worry.

SUMMARY. Except in the behavior sphere of medical care, all the responses of the Navaho were fairly consistently oriented to the With-Nature position. On the whole, the Rimrock Navaho are by now convinced that vaccinations and other aspects of Anglo-American medicine "work." Individuals who have exhausted their own and their families' resources in the native ceremonials have often benefited when they went to the hospital. The items on Livestock Dying (MN1) and Use of Fields (MN3) provide insight into the interrelatedness of thought and action in Navaho conception.

In only one respect does further analysis suggest a modification of the statistical findings. It has already been pointed out that the free comments on certain other questions indicated an implicit premise of Subjugated-to-Nature. Others could be added:

Lots of cases you just can't help. Sickness just comes.

It's true that sometimes you just can't tell how things will turn out.

A close look at the elaborations and remarks made about the items of the *time* orientation reveals a common second-order position of the Subjugated-to-Nature alternative which does not show in the statistical summary on the *man-nature* orientation itself. Consider the following:

We don't know how long our life is going to be. Only holy people know and they don't tell. We might live today and die tomorrow. We can't tell. Another thing is vaccination, but I don't think so. If you live longer, your time just isn't up. I don't believe it.

We don't know how long we're going to live. If the time is up the holy people won't give you an extra day of life. A man can't plan his life, but the holy people are planning our lives for us.

This belief that men are at the mercy of their destinies is ancient, for it appears frequently in the myths. Ordinary Navaho will often remark that "The holy people have a law like white people's law, and we must obey it." In considerable part this notion is an exemplification of Navaho "determinism" and "mechanism." Things work out in a lawful and orderly and somewhat inevitable way. This view is tempered by conviction in the efficacy of the ceremonials and competent effort (the Doing orientation). Nevertheless, as a second-order position, the Subjugated emphasis must be acknowledged as part of the orientation system. It is plausible that this accent may be stronger at present because the recent experience of the Rimrock Navaho has not been conducive to confident optimism.

Activity Orientation

It will be recalled from Chapter V that *activity* orientation items presented only the Being and Doing alternatives. The *activity* orientation is the only one in which the Navaho and the generalized American orientations correspond. The Navaho choice of the Doing orientation is reinforced by tradition, by current economic circumstances, and by increased influence from the wider American culture. A combination of these factors results in the Navaho putting a stronger emphasis upon the Doing alternative than any of the other groups tested. The Being alternative was stressed only on the two items having to do with employer-employee relations which, as was pointed out in Chapter III, were not testing the *activity* orientation in a satisfactorily pure form. It is also important to remember that activities other than wage work—ceremonial participation, for example—loom important in the lives of the Navaho. Very few of them work for an employer full time. Thus the emphasis upon regular attendance at work does not have the same meaning for them as it may to other groups where wage work is a more crucial aspect of life.

It will be unnecessary to analyze each individual question as we have done for the other orientations, since there is no question as to the almost unanimous choice of the Doing alternative of the *activity* orientation. We will simply give here some representative remarks drawn more or less at random to illustrate the flavor of the Navaho Doing orientation.

The ones that are doing something, if you think about good results and work for it, that is it.

If you do the right things and work hard, then you are happy.

It is perfectly plain, right before me, that the man who runs around is the wrong one.

You can't depend on the ones that go out and talk all over. The thing that is important is to really work and do your work like washing.

The one that learns how to do the work, you can't get nothing out of the man that just runs around.

The distinctively Navaho flavor here comes mainly from the union of thought and action previously noted.

Human Nature Orientation

Although this was not part of the testing program, it may be useful to say a few words about it. A classic statement occurs in a myth of the Shooting Way.

Those you subdued were great ones. You killed them because your father approved, but these are not definitely bad although they are not entirely good either. They meet somewhere between that which causes satisfaction and that which causes pain.[4]

[4] Franc Newcomb and Gladys Reichard, *Sandpaintings of the Navajo Shooting Chant* (New York: J. J. Augustin, 1937), p. 32.

"Not definitely bad although not entirely good either" is a view reiterated time and again in the whole corpus of Navaho texts. As McNair says after a careful examination of the mythology:

> The supernaturals on the one hand steal, lie, become angry with one another, curse, behave evilly, have wicked intentions; on the other hand they are on occasion, generous, kind, polite, friendly, proper.[5]

The Navaho conception is not Neutral toward *human nature*. It is definitely a mixture of Good-and-Evil, and this mixture is immutable (invariant). Nature in general is as unchangeable as it is lawful. One respondent made this spontaneous comment:

> I never heard of anything that changed nature. Just lived through anything that comes up. Even old people said this.

There are other remarks made in the course of the field research that are congruent with the conceptualization of this orientation on grounds of other evidence:

> The way natural things come out, then things show up nicely for you. But if people are not living right, it won't work. There is nothing true about doing something. I go by the same ones. If you do the right things, you will be okay. For my people, I know that they are mostly like that [the Being response], but some children don't know better.

> Nobody can control wind and rain. It is just natural. People get bad luck if they joke about this.

In short, this orientation is tinged by the second-order Subjugated response of the *man-nature* orientation. Nature, as well as experience, is orderly and determined. One of the properties of nature is that human beings have invariably a Good and an Evil side. This is reflected in the Navaho belief that the ghost of even the best human being is dangerous because of the "bad side." Conversely, while witchcraft is Evil, a ceremonial practitioner must have some of it—"else he will go dry." In sum, as Wyman remarks, "Good and Evil are not... abstract ethical concepts but complementary components of the universe or any part of it."[6]

PERCEIVED CONSENSUS AND SEX AND AGE DIFFERENCES

Perceived Consensus

In every value orientation except the *activity* one the Navaho were consistently low in perceived consensus. The facts that the Navaho and Zuni were lowest in perceived consensus but that the Navaho were next

---

[5] Robert McNair, "The Ideas of the Good in the Mythology of the Navaho Indians" (unpublished Ph.D. dissertation, Harvard University, 1948), p. 24.
[6] Leland C. Wyman, "The Religion of the Navaho Indians" in *Forgotten Religions*, ed. Vergilius Ferm (New York: Philosophical Library, 1950), p. 344. See also Leland C. Wyman, W. W. Hill, and Iva Osanai, "Navaho Eschatology," *University of New Mexico Bulletin*, No. 377, 1942.

to Spanish-Americans in actual consensus are not surprising. While the Navaho provided plenty of variant material, their culture and that of Atrisco have been most isolated from outside influences that have had a chance to spread their widely divergent ideas in depth. On the other hand, the Navaho and the Zuni are most conscious of their cultures, being on the defensive and given the confusion within these groups.

For the Navaho males the comments on *activity* orientation items were uniformly short except for the first question on employer-employee relations which touches on a subject of immediate experience and concern. If we take perceived consensus as an index of certainty along with the length of comment (short comments indicating certainty), then we have two lines of evidence which reinforce each other. Both lines indicate that only the *activity* orientation is not under pressure. On all the other orientations both lines suggest that there is great doubt and uncertainty among the Navaho. To state it another way: The Navaho are in a period of forced transition. On the *time* orientation they are under pressure to change to the Future. On the *relational* orientation they are being instigated in an Individualistic direction. On the *man-nature* orientation the With-Nature attitude is already being altered in the technological and medical spheres to the Over-Nature position.

The Navaho are themselves aware of the impossibility of perceived consensus:

I can't say for the people because some are one way and some another. They are all mixed up.

You can't tell what will happen. Things are changing, and we don't know how people will act.

Only one old man denied this:

I have told you for me, and there is no other way. It is the same way they think.

Sex Differences

So far as statistical results are concerned, the females differed from the males only on the *time* orientation and the *man-nature* orientation. On the *time* orientation the females showed no consistent results. The difference in the *time* orientation can probably be accounted for by the fact that the women had little formal place in the ceremonialism of traditional Navaho culture—and it is in the ceremonial behavior sphere that the Past *time* orientation shows up the strongest.

More important and consistent than the statistical summaries were two other general features of the sex differences among the Navaho. First, the women were far more shy with the male investigator than were the men. It seems likely that they resorted to a passive response more frequently than the men and would be less likely to indicate by action or word that they did not understand a question. This would make for greater unreliability among the answers of the females. The fact that the female responses were far less consistent than the male responses may well be due primarily to lack of reliability from this source. Second, the women's spontaneous comments were short as compared to the men's. They most frequently answered by number and would not elaborate or discuss their choice. For the men there was generally a longer comment on questions in which there was doubt in their mind as to the proper choice, as if they were trying to talk out their decision. Among the women doubt showed itself in silence and embarrassment which may have been overcome by making a choice in the dark, as it were.

If we took the statistical results at face value, we would be prone to say that the men are generally more conservative and consistent. But because of the two factors mentioned above which emerged consistently in the field situation, it would be safer not to assume that the men are more conservative and consistent in actual values held. On the other hand, it should be remarked that in the traditional culture men were much more the repositories of values and expected to be more articulate about them. The lack of consistency in the female responses seems partly attributable to this factor which would heighten confusion and also to the fact that women have less participation in the Anglo-American world except in connection with Christian activities.

Age Differences

There is less consistency here, less indeed than might have been anticipated. Some younger men show the effects of schooling and experience in the outside world. Yet other younger men evidence less explicit acceptance of the need for change than do some of the oldest men. Among the women there is almost no difference save that it is only three older women who make comments of any length. This is traditional; only women of some age were expected to express themselves in extended family or local group discussions.

Almost the only generalization that would not require strong qualification is that older men exhibit more active nostalgia for "the old days," though they themselves recognize that this is not realism but feeling. Perhaps the explanation of the lack of clear age lines in the responses is the fact that everyone, regardless of age, is directly or indirectly cognizant of the main features of the present picture. All are concerned with the existent confusion, but no one fails to manifest some ambivalence to Anglo-American culture. No one (not even the Christians in the sample) is prepared to say flatly: "Let's start with a clean slate, adopting without reservation the values of the more powerful group."

FINAL SUMMARY

That all first-order orientations were correctly predicted corresponds to the fact that the basic values of Navaho culture remained, as of 1951, on the whole, dominant. There is abundant evidence of variant positions, both in forms that may be presumed to have been present for a considerable time and in other forms resultant upon Anglo-American pressure and the total recent and contemporary situation of the Rimrock Navaho. From the perspective of studies of Navaho culture and Navaho values, the most striking findings of the present research are these:

(1) The evidence that the dominant values have stood up this long and to this degree under attack.
(2) The lack of clear-cut generational patterns.
(3) Documentation of the range of variation in a random sample and inability to correlate this unmistakably with age, sex, position in the society, and acculturative experiences. A good deal of the variation reflects constitutional temperament plus the vicissitudes of purely idiosyncratic life experience—the total precipitate rather than such isolable factors as role, attendance at an Anglo-American school, and the like. Some of the variance, of course, is simply that which the theory postulates as inherent in all value systems.
(4) Data indicating that Navaho women in some respects are more labile than men as regards their value orientations.
(5) Clues as to the manner in which different orientations are interrelated.
(6) Clear manifestations of the directional dynamisms of the present Anglo-American system—that is, toward Individualism, Future *time*, Mastery-over-Nature.

In a way, the most impressive demonstration made by this study of the Rimrock Navaho is the economy of this instrument of field work. A single investigator, working upon the Navaho for the first time, not only accomplished in one brief field season a great deal of what it had taken many other field workers years to achieve, but also added to and clarified the picture drawn by them. Nothing brought out by this investigation is contradicted or brought into serious question by the substantial body of earlier work. Rather, the earlier work is in general confirmed by this more systematic and economic approach, but with useful additions and implications.[7] This is not to suggest that this study could have been carried out so easily and quickly without the basis of previous research. We do suspect, however, that a research design of this sort could have materially shortened the time required to explore Navaho values and value orientations by more diffuse, unsystematic, and leisurely efforts.

Taking into account *both* the statistical analyses and the contextual evidence, we would summarize the Rimrock Navaho value-orientation profile in 1951 as follows:

> *relational:* Collaterality over Lineality over Individualism;
> *time:* Present over Past over Future;
> *man-nature:* With-Nature over Subjugated over Over-Nature;
> *activity:* Doing over Being.

---

[7] Even where (see above) there is evidence that a question was not fully understood or was distorted a bit by the peculiarities of the Navaho language, material was still produced that provided highly appropriate grist for the values mill. Often the very off-center nature of the responses was more illuminating in a qualitative and contextual fashion than a bull's-eye would have been.

Although there is some question in some instances about the clarity of the second and third-order choices, as the statistical analyses indicate, the "total feel" of all the data makes us confident that the ordering as given is for the most part an accurate representation.

How stable this profile is can be argued. As the Navaho data in this book show, Navaho values are in a transitional state, though possibly a temporary equilibrium has been achieved. Navaho morals as described in Kluckhohn[8] are gone as a system, but Navaho values as described by Albert[9] may persist in recognizable form much longer. There is no doubt, however, that events in the last thirty years (stock reduction, economic crises, etc.) have represented a tremendous shock to the total Navaho value system. The deeper aspects of this shock go far beyond the economic threats and consequences. The fundamental existential postulate of the Navaho system (that of a balance in nature, of a harmony which can be redressed) was challenged. This may be the tacit basis for the shift from immanent to transcendent deity which Rapaport has documented for many Rimrock Navaho women and some Rimrock Navaho men.[10] It may well be that Navaho women, in spite of their relatively favorable position in some obvious respects, have less stake in the old system, and they may be key figures in the value shift in progress. Some of the findings of Bruner and Rotter also seem to point in this direction.[11] In any event, external pressure combines with intra-cultural variation, and the trends are also, of course, influenced by the varying ways in which old Navaho value orientations fit or fail to fit those of dominant Anglo-American culture. Thus, for example, the primacy of the Doing orientation in both cases means less ambiguity in many alterations in Navaho economic activities. On the other hand, the dominant Collateral *relational* orientation among the Navaho is strong enough and contrasting enough with Anglo-American culture so that as yet the Navaho manifest almost no Individualism, understood as autonomous decision and behavior.

[8] Clyde Kluckhohn, "Navaho Morals" in *Encyclopedia of Morals,* ed. Vergilius Ferm (New York: Philosophical Library, 1956), pp. 383–90.
[9] Ethel Albert, "The Classification of Values: A Method and Illustration," *American Anthropologist,* Vol. LVIII (1956), pp. 221–48.
[10] Robert Rapaport, *Changing Navaho Religious Values,* Papers of the Peabody Museum, Harvard University, Vol. XLI, No. 2 (1954).
[11] E. M. Bruner and J. B. Rotter, "A Level of Aspiration Study Among the Ramah Navaho," *Journal of Personality,* Vol. XXI (1953), pp. 375–85.

CHAPTER X

Summary and Discussion

In the introduction to this volume we stated the main objective of the research program to be the exposition of a theory of variations in value orientations and the development of a method for a cross-cultural testing of it. The second objective stated was one of almost equal importance—that of having the results yielded by our research instrument examined and interpreted within the context of the large body of data which many others over a long period of years have collected on the cultures we selected for the testing of our theory. And although statistical methodology was not a primary concern in and of itself, the selection, adaptation, and integration of statistical methods for the analysis of the data collected in the five Rimrock communities were issues of considerable magnitude in the total research design.

We now, in this conclusion to our study, wish to draw together the results of the two central parts of the research. We do this by means of a summary and discussion which is divided into three sections. The first reviews and summarizes the theory, the method created for the testing of the theory, and the statistical methods used in the analysis of the data. The second section first summarizes the findings yielded by the statistical analyses of the field data. Subsequently, it briefly reviews the results of the examination of these findings against the evidence contained in prior predictions as to the ranking preferences (really expectations since they were not formal predictions) and the culture-by-culture interpretative discussions to which the second half of this book (Chapters VI through IX) is devoted. Finally, in the third section, we pose and speak to the question of the place and significance of a theory of variations in value orientations in studies of human behavior.

THEORY, METHOD, AND STATISTICAL ANALYSES

The Theory

The title used for the monograph—*Variations in Value Orientations*—contains, by implication at least, the two main ideas which together constitute the theoretical cornerstone of our study. The first of these is the conceptualization of that order of cultural phenomena which has been variously defined by others as "systems of meanings," "unconscious canons of choice," "integrative themes," "ethos," or "configurations." The second is the idea that there is normally an ordered variation in the value-orientation systems of all societies.

Very broadly a value orientation may be defined as a generalized and organized principle concerning basic human problems which pervasively and profoundly influences man's behavior. But this very comprehensive definition leaves open the question of the nature of the principle—the elements which are found in it and the relationships between those elements. Our own more specifically delineated definition is:

Value orientations are complex but definitely patterned (rank-ordered) principles, resulting from the transactional interplay of three analytically distinguishable elements of the evaluative process—the cognitive, the affective, and the directive elements—which give order and direction to the ever-flowing stream of human acts and thoughts as these relate to the solution of "common human problems."

The conceptual scheme used for the classification of the value orientations and the ranges of variation postulated for them rests upon these three further major assumptions: (1) There is a limited number of common human problems for which all peoples at all times must find formulae. (2) While variations in these formulae certainly exist, they are neither limitless nor random but are, instead, variations within a limited range of possible solutions. (3) All variants of recurring solutions are present in all cultures at all times but receive, from one society to another, or one subculture to another, varying degrees of emphasis.

The five common human problems for which, thus far, ranges of solutions are postulated concern the nature of man himself, his relation to nature and supernature, his place in the flow of time, the modality of human activity, and the relationship man has to his fellow human beings. The names given to the evaluative principles relating to each of these are *human nature* orientation, *man-nature* orientation, *time* orientation, *activity* orientation, and *relational* orientation. For all orientations except the *human nature* one, the postulated range of variation is threefold. On the *man-nature* orientation there are the Mastery-over-Nature, the Subjugation-to-Nature, and the Harmony-with-Nature positions. The *time* orientation has the range of Past, Present, and Future. The varying emphases of the *activity* orientation are called Being, Being-in-Becoming, and Doing. Lineality, Individualism, and Collaterality specify the varying modalities of the *relational* orientation. In the case of the *human nature* orientation the primary classification designates the four positions of Good, Good-and-Evil, Neutral, and Evil; and because it appeared necessary to elaborate this orientation with the secondary principles of mutability and immutability, the complete classification for the orientation is more complex than the threefold ones developed for the others.

Two major theoretical formulations flow directly from the basic assumptions and the classification schema developed to accord with their conceptual demands. First, and most important, is conceptualization of the variation in value orientations of a culture as an interlocking network of *dominant* (most preferred) value orientations and *variant* value orientations which are both required and permitted. This is to say that the value-orientation systems of societies are not to be thought of as unitary systems of dominant values only. Persistently they contain *permitted* and *required* variant value orientations (more in some cultures than others, to be sure) which differ from the dominant value orientations even though they are, to varying degrees, always controlled and ordered by the dominant ones. The "strain toward consistency"—better termed a tendency toward consistency—which has long been accepted as a basic principle in sociological analyses is not, according to this conceptualization, simply a pull in the direction of *dominant* values but is instead a prevailing influence of one type of rank ordering upon variant orderings which have the same component parts.

Many of the studies made of the value systems of societies have been primarily, if not solely, concerned with dominant values. The result has been a quite static conception of the system into which life and dynamism are frequently injected by means of the concept of individual idiosyncratic behavior. That there is behavior which is more or less idiosyncratic relative to any given value system is a certainty, but the argument of the variation theory is that much of what has been described as idiosyncratic departures from *dominant* values is really well-ordered variant behavior.

The second major deductive proposition is: The differences between the value-orientation systems of seemingly quite distinctive cultures, as well as those between the varying segments within a given culture, are not absolute. Instead they are the representatives of varying rank orderings of the same value-orientation components which are common to all cultures at all times.

The theory also postulates, as do other of the theories which treat of basic values, that most of the observable patterns of action and thought give simultaneous expression to all of the value elements. The degree of influence of one or another of the value orientations upon a particular concrete behavior pattern may be appreciably greater than that of others, but it is not often that any one of them has no effect at all. Therefore, it follows that systems of value orientations must be examined for the degree of congruence each of the value components has with the others. This is obviously a task of great complexity when it is rank orders of value orientations and not just single dominant values which must be considered. But however complex the analysis may be, it is essential to the evaluation of the type and degree of cultural integration a social system has and its distinctive resistances and susceptibilities to change.

The next step in the development of the theory of variations was the singling out of two of the major types of *societal differentiation* common to all societies. The first of these is subgroup differentiation of the kind one encounters in regional, ethnic, class, or other fairly well marked social units. The second we have called "behavior sphere" differentiation, and mean by it the differentiation of the broad categories of activities which are essential to the functioning of any society. In treating these, attention was centered primarily upon the economic-technological, the religious, the intellectual-aesthetic, and the recreational behavior spheres. As yet little consideration has been given to the political sphere of activities and its relationships to the other spheres.

In cross-cultural comparisons it is certainly to be expected that subgroup differentiations will differ in types and numbers, but there is no society, no matter how homogeneous it may appear to be, which is completely lacking in them. The degree of differentiation of the behavior spheres will also vary widely from society to society. In some the extent of the differentiation is so great that the interrelations between the behavior spheres appear to be tenuous; in others—many nonliterate societies, for example—there is such a fusion of the patterns of two or more spheres that distinctions are seemingly obliterated. But however extreme one or the other of these tendencies may be, the clues for an *analytic* determination of behavior-sphere distinctions and interrelationships are always present. More important still, it is always possible to distinguish the sphere, or combination of spheres, of greatest prominence. The extent of pattern elaboration in one sphere as opposed to others is a main clue for making this distinction.

A knowledge of the behavior-sphere differentiation—both the degree of it and the relative stressing of one sphere in contrast to others—is essential in the use of the variation theory because it appears to have an association with variations in types of value-orientation profiles. In American middle-class society there is, for example, the association of the dominant orientations of Individualism, Future *time*, Mastery-over-Nature, Doing, and Evil (or Good-and-Evil) mutable *human nature*, with a most extensive elaboration of patterning in the economic-technological behavior sphere. In traditional Spanish-American society, in contrast, one notes the association of the dominant orientations of Lineality, Present *time*, Subjugation-to-Nature, Being, and Good-and-Evil mutable *human nature*, with a strong stressing of a fusion of the religious and recreational behavior spheres.

These ideas when extended to the study of *intra*-cultural variation give the basis for a systematic analysis of both the interrelationships of the more or less definite subsystems in a society and the interlocking of behavior-sphere activities and interests. Still further, it becomes possible to establish certain relationships between these two different types of intra-system differentiation.

An example of the latter interrelation is to be seen in the use of the recreational sphere as a road to occupational success by many Italian-Americans whose first-order value orientations stress this sphere. While the recreational sphere certainly has great importance to middle-class Americans, it is clearly secondary to the economic-technological one. Few truly dominant middle-class parents will give willing approval to their child's choice of the role of entertainer as a major occupational pursuit. There have always been, to be sure, some members of the American middle class performing in the legitimate theater, and recently one finds an increasing number appearing both in the movies and on television programs. But it is mainly from other groups such as the Italian-Americans that the movie actors and actresses, the big-league ballplayers, the prize fighters, night club entertainers, and musicians in dance bands are drawn. In this instance of variable behavior we have an illustration of one type of variation which is "permitted" to individuals or groups of individuals and at the same time "required" for the social system as a whole. It is difficult to imagine what the current American scene would be like without its highly developed world of recreation in which masses of dominantly oriented Americans are daily the passive "spectators" of a wide variety of entertainments which are provided, to a very large extent, by variants within the system.

All variant patterns, those permitted as well as those required, are seen as having the maintenance of the ongoing system as their primary function. But at the same time they contain the seeds of potential change which often spring into growth when nurtured by external influences. Further comment upon the significance of variant patterns to the analysis of cultural change is reserved for the final section of this discussion.

The Method of Testing and the Peoples Tested

The peoples used as the subjects of the research program were the five communities in the Rimrock region of the American Southwest which various investigators in the Values Project of the Harvard University Laboratory of Social Relations were studying from other points of view than ours. Two of these communities are American Indian (Navaho and Pueblo), one is Spanish-American, another is a fairly tightly knit Mormon village, and the last is a community of homesteaders who came into the Rimrock region from Texas and Oklahoma in the early 1930's. To varying degrees each of these groups had been studied intensively prior even to the general Values Project investigations.

Random samples of twenty to twenty-five individuals were selected in three of these groups—the Navaho, the Mormon, and the Texan communities. In the Spanish-American village, a community which has declined markedly in recent years, a total enumeration of the twenty-three adults over the age of twenty years was used. In the Zuni group, where the drawing of a random sample was precluded because of rapport considerations, it was necessary to make use of a group of related individuals.

The method created for the testing of the variation theory in these five quite distinctive communities was a schedule of twenty-two items which were distributed approximately evenly over the four orientations we decided to test. Seven items were used to assess the ranking of the alternatives of the *relational* orientation, five items tested for the ranking of the alternatives of the *time* and *man-nature* orientations, and five items (really six, since one item had two separate parts) asked for a choice between just two alternatives of the *activity* orientation—the Being and Doing alternatives. Because of limitations of time and financial resources it was not possible to test this orientation fully or to give any consideration to the testing of the *human nature* orientation.

The schedule has several distinctive qualities which were developed because of a concern for four different, but not unrelated, problems. These problems in a logical order of importance for our research were: (1) the need to find items which would—moderately well, at least—test the different orientations one by one; (2) the search for both the items and the phrasings of them which would have a more or less equal degree of significance and meaning in each of the cultures; (3) the control of the distorting effects of defensive reactions and particularized—even idiosyncratic—kinds of individual life experiences; (4) the creation of a means of providing conclusions about the nature of basic values which would allow for the generation of testable hypotheses about patterns of behavior other than those which are used for the formulation of the value systems themselves.

All four are problems of real magnitude. Since the observed facts support the postulate of the theory which states that usually the behavior patterns of peoples are expressions of several or even all of the value orientations, it was questionable that items could be found which would test for the preferential rankings of the alternatives of *single* orientations. The difficulties in the second problem are familiar to all investigators who have attempted cross-cultural studies in the medium of language. Indeed there are many who argue that "meanings" are always somewhat altered as one translates them from one language to another. The third problem, too, is a familiar one. There is always some defensiveness to be expected both in the individual respondent and in whole groups of respondents and always some distortion to be expected because of the particularized experiences of the individual respondent. These are an important part of the record if the research aim is the full study of the individual case, but they are productive of undesirable effects when it is a knowledge of cultural uniformities (dominant or variant) that is sought. The fourth problem, stated in a phrase, is the problem of circular reasoning. Although this problem is necessarily one of concern for all types of investigations, the analyst of value systems is more often accused of circularity in his procedures than are other kinds of analysts.

It was our belief—or let us say, hope—that a method could be created which would provide some measure of solution for all of these problems. The judgment was in favor of what we have labeled the "highly generalized life situation" type of item. Ideally one would prefer to test directly at the high level of abstraction at which the value orientations themselves are formulated. This is not possible, for not even those few persons who are highly sophisticated in the matter of cultural variation are sufficiently well aware of their own implicit value orientations to give clear distinctions on all orientations at this level of *analytical* abstraction. The solution seemed to be that of finding items for questioning which were at a sufficiently high level of *empirical* generalization to offer some certainty that what was being elicited was a response to the effects of a single orientation in a very wide range of generally similar situations rather than a response to the effects of the interrelations of several, or all, of the orientations in more specifically delineated types of situations.

This method seemed also to offer a great potential for the crossing of cultural lines. All that was required in addition to the delineation of very general situations which cover many particulars was a selection among such general situations on a basis of their universality of significance from one culture to another. It was this criterion which caused us to search for the types of situations which investigators of many kinds and the comprehensive coverage of cultures in the Human Relations Area File indicate to be life situations which rural peoples—folk peoples—of all kinds typically face.

And it took nothing more than a logical deduction to assume that if items could be phrased to help in the solving of these first two problems, we would also be going a long way in eliminating the distorting effects of defensive reactions and idiosyncratic experiences. But to be sure that these effects would be further minimized, we took the added precautionary measure of giving to all the generalized life situation items a "third person" phrasing. The effect of this measure was that of making the instrument something of a projective technique.

Finally, it also seemed probable that the method offered the means of controlling to a significant degree the problem of circularity in procedures as one moves back and forth between inductive and deductive processes. If a very few general types of life situations can be used for the formulation of the value-orientation system, the ground is then laid for developing predictions about many types of relatively specific behavior patterns. One also escapes from extreme circularity in using the value system which is derived from a limited number of general questions for "explanations" of many of the details of cultural patterns and relationships between patterns. Only to a minor extent should there be in this method the need to utilize the same data for both the formulation of the value system and the explanation of its effect on concrete patterns of behavior.

We do not, of course, consider that this type of method offers the means for a *full* solution of any one of these problems. Nor do we consider it to be a substitute for the greatly detailed analyses of cultures which anthropologists have now provided in some abundance. It is simply an adjunct—but, we believe, a very important adjunct—which can serve to economize on the time required to ascertain the value systems of peoples, the differences between value systems, and the nature and significance of intra-cultural variations. But it must be understood that these are arguments for the method as a method, not for our own quite limited and imperfect version of it. And certainly it remains to be seen whether it will prove possible to so elaborate and develop a "general life situation" schedule of items that there can be a fairly systematic testing for intra-cultural variations.

Statistical Methods

As has been indicated above, the conscious intent throughout the research program was to subordinate all considerations of sampling and statistical methods of analysis to the requirements of the theory, the practical realities of the field situation, and the emergent demands which the collected data might themselves impose. And it was a rewarding surprise that it proved possible to elaborate known methods or to create minor inventions which met, with some real degree of satisfaction to us at least, these various demands. Thus, we may state that in some respects the totality of the statistical methodology finally used represents a growth process whereas in other respects it represents our best effort to effect an integration of methods for the answering of the several different kinds of questions we wished to ask of the data our field instrument yielded. There were also some interesting emergent problems which led to the utilization and elaboration of still other kinds of methods than those used for the answering of the four primary questions of the basic research program. These developments, which in the Preface we have referred to as "by-products" of the research program, are for the most part given an independent reporting in Appendices 2 and 3.

In the program of research which was central to the testing of the theory, sample selection was, of course, the first of our problems. The major decision it required—given the limited amount of time and funds available for the research program—was the choice between using small samples of respondents in all five of the cultures or larger samples in only two or three of them. The first alternative definitely posed the calculated risk that there would be so little consensus in responses that no analyzable product would result. Nonetheless, it was this alternative—the thin coverage of all five cultures—upon which we gambled. It both offered more possibilities for the future development of the theory and represented a better use of the research opportunities afforded us.

Fortunately, the discovered "within-culture" regularities and the "between-culture" differences were marked enough to state that "the gamble paid off" for our main research objectives. For the analysis of *intra*-cultural as opposed to *cross*-cultural variation the results were only suggestive. It was not expected that they would be more than this. The decision to have competent analysts discuss the intra-system variations in the cultures, one by one, was deliberate for two reasons. First, our limited coverage of the cultures most certainly could not yield the data for a systematic assessment of the internal variations; second, not all of the ideas concerning intra-cultural variation as now presented in Chapter I of this volume had been worked out at the time the field project was undertaken. Some of them are actually a result of the playback of empirical testing upon the theoretical construction. For all those who believe, as we do, that theory is best evolved when there is considerable interplay between concept construction and empirical testing, the theoretical advantage afforded by the full coverage of the cultures is obvious.

The major statistical method used in our study—the graphic method (see Chapter IV) which was primarily developed for the analysis of the within-culture regularities in value-orientation rankings—was itself the result of a fairly long growth process. Given the nature of the field schedule created to elicit ranking preferences among the orientation alternatives, it did not at first appear necessary to develop a method which went beyond that elaborated by Kendall in *Rank Correlation Methods*. Since respondents were asked only to state their first and second preferences among the three alternatives posed (only two alternatives for the *activity* orientation), the results obtained could be expected to be a ranking order which, in form, did not differ appreciably from paired comparisons.

It was not until the work sheets containing all of the data collected in the field were assembled and before us that there came a recognition of a need for some graphic method of analysis. It was not long before the value of such a technique for the demonstration of the three-way ranking of preferences asserted itself. It became apparent in the specific technique used that the distance of the plotted point from the origin was a measure of consistency in ranking preferences—the greater the distance, the more consistent the ranking preference. This insight, gained almost a full year after the field data had been collected, provided the basis for an elaboration of method which offered the promise of a more detailed and precise analysis of the data than that offered by the rank-correlation method.

A major concern in this elaboration was establishment of the relationship between the distance of the plotted point from the origin and conventional .05 and .01 significance limits. In the first attempts to achieve this aim no change was made in the plotting of the points. The actual a, b, and c deviations from the mean were plotted without dividing by the differing number of respondents. For showing the relationship of the number of respondents to the distance from origin a separate reference grid was developed. From it could be learned the appropriate distance relative to any given number of respondents, and the significance circles were then drawn on the graphs by means of a compass. This development in turn paved the way for the suggestion made by John Tukey that the deviations should be divided by the square root of the number of rankings. Once this requirement was met, the use of the reference grid could be eliminated, and a single chart was developed to contain all the relevant information.

Such, in brief, is the history of the evolution of the graphic method which we used, first, to show the rank ordering of the orientation alternatives which each of the culturally diverse samples of respondents chose for each item of a total value-orientation series of items (fifteen graphs in all) and, second, to give the results of the differences found in the preferential orderings of all five samples of respondents on each item of each orientation series (twenty-three graphs in all). Seventeen of the latter are for the orientation series with three choices; six are simple percentage graphs for the two alternatives posed for the *activity* orientation. On the assumption that scrutiny of the numerous graphs showing these variations has given the reader a thorough familiarity with the basic procedures followed in creating them, we shall not here recapitulate them.

Although this graphic method was the major statistical development of our study and served well, we believe, to show the ranking of the alternatives of the value orientations item by item and culture by culture, it was not the only technique we used. There were more demands made upon the data than it alone could meet. In the first instance, it was troublesome that the method offered no means for affirming an alternative hypothesis once the chosen null hypothesis of $A = B = C$ had been rejected. If, for example, a point fell outside the .01 significance circle in the $A > B > C$ sector, only a least-squares "guess" could be made, in the context of the S technique, that the real rank ordering among the observations was $A > B > C$.[1]

There were also other questions posed by the theory which the graphic method did not answer to our full satisfaction. These are listed in Chapter IV as questions (2) *Intra-Item Patterning*, (3) *Total Orientation Patterning*, and (4) *Between-Culture Differences*. It was Samuel A. Stouffer who suggested the methods for the additional analyses which would answer these questions, and it was he, together with Frederick Mosteller, who guided us in the use of them. The first to be used was a standard binomial technique. Although this technique did not permit us to treat the three alternatives of one orientation simultaneously as did the statistically more elegant graphic analysis, it did allow us to say considerably more about the patterns of responses than the mere *fact* of their patterning (which is basically what the rejection of the $A = B = C$ null hypothesis implies). Moreover, the results this analysis yielded gave us the material needed for the application of the additional analyses which speak to questions 3 and 4.

While certainly the graphic analysis can be, and was, used to *picture* both the summary—the overall—ranking outcomes in the individual cultures on total series of orientation items and also the comparative between-culture differences in these summary outcomes on total series of items, there has as yet been no development of the method which permits standard tests of the significance of the summary outcomes.

To overcome this shortcoming of our principal method—and to supplement it also in the case of summary results—we first used scores which summarized the preferences of each individual over all items in a single series. These scores were treated as observations conforming to t-distributions, and the determination of their significance was a test for the summary preference orderings within the various cultures.

Once these summary results were obtained, it was possible to move forward in a quite simple and straightforward manner with one-way analyses of variance for a statistical determination of the kinds and degrees of between-culture differences. The ten "arbitrary dimensions" constructed for this purpose were simply the ten variates constructed for question 3; only this time a comparison was made across the five cultures for each dimension, rather than dealing with all dimensions for each culture separately.

Although the dependency problem between dimensions remained a troublesome one, we consider that both the caution used in reporting the results in Chapter V and the freedom allowed the authors of the interpretative chapters on the individual cultures are means of fully acknowledging the problem while, at the same time, not affording to it a dictatorial license in a work which in no way was intended to be a treatise on statistical methods.

---

[1] See Maurice G. Kendall, *Rank Correlation Methods*, 2d ed. (New York: Hafner Publishing Co., 1955), pp. 101-2 and Chap. VII, *passim*.

In sum our task, statistically speaking, was one of a selection, adaptation, elaboration where needed, and integration of already established methods which would, overall, best serve our purpose of answering, in whole or in part, the rather complicated set of questions which our theory and our method of investigation posed. If, in this process, we have been able either to elaborate some methods or to effect an integration of others in ways which will be useful to persons engaged in different kinds of research from ours, we shall consider the effort expended both worthwhile and rewarding.

THE OBSERVED RESULTS VIEWED IN LIGHT OF PRIOR PREDICTIONS AND THE INTERPRETATIVE ANALYSES OF THE FIVE CULTURES

Within-Culture Regularities Compared to Prior Predictions

The "prior predictions" we ventured to make concerning the rankings of the value-orientation alternatives of the five cultures in which we tested were, as was clearly stated (see Chapter II), most informal and were intended only as an impressionistic means of validating, or invalidating, the results of our research program. As the research design was set up, we counted much more upon the interpretative discussions devoted to each of the cultures as a measure of checking on validity and reliability then we did these prior predictions. But having made the predictions, we wish to report in full the degree of goodness of fit between them and the actual observed results. Not only are the overall results of this informal experiment interesting in and of themselves; they also, in some of the discrepancies noted, but more especially in some of our hesitancies in predictions, pointed up special interpretative problems which were posed for the analysts who examined and interpreted our results culture by culture.

The most efficient means of showing goodness of fit of the predictions and the observed results is a table in which the predictions and the results of the binomial analysis of the data are systematically juxtaposed. For purposes of review there is no reason to recapitulate also the graphs which plot the results. All that the reader is asked to keep in mind as he examines this table—Table X:1—is that in the binomial analysis any result which was *not* statistically significant is symbolized by the $A \geqslant B$ convention whereas in the predictions our doubts about the significant preference of one alternative over another (either because we felt they actually were likely to be found almost equally preferred, or because we did not believe we had the bases for judging which of two alternatives would be preferred) are symbolized by the convention of $A = B$. The discrepancies between the predictions ventured and the results observed were not many, but those which did appear should be noted since they were a part of the problem of interpretation.

TABLE X: 1

A Comparison of the Results from the *Total Orientation Patterning* Analyses with the Prior Predictions About Value-Orientation Preferences for the Five Rimrock Communities

Culture	relational		time		man-nature		activity	
	Predicted	Observed	Predicted	Observed	Predicted	Observed	Predicted	Observed
Spanish-American	Ind>Lin>Coll approximating Ind=Lin>Coll	Ind≫Lin≫Coll*	Pres>Fut=Past Pres>Past>Fut on religious items	Pres>Fut>Past Past second-order preference on religious items	Subj>Over>With	Subj>Over>With	Being>Doing	Being>Doing
Texan	Ind>Coll>Lin	Ind>Coll>Lin first-order Ind very strong	Fut>Pres>Past	Fut≫Pres>Past	Over>Subj>With	Over>With≫Subj	Doing>Being	Doing>Being
Mormon	Ind=Coll>Lin	Ind>Coll>Lin Coll more emphasized than in Texan case	Fut>Pres>Past approximating Fut>Pres=Past	Fut≫Pres>Past	With>Over>Subj	Over≫With>Subj With almost as preferred as Over	Doing>Being	Doing>Being
Zuni	no prediction	Coll>Lin≧Ind	no prediction	Pres>Past>Fut	no prediction	With≫Subj≧Over	no prediction	Doing≧Being
Navaho	Coll>Lin>Ind	Coll>Lin≧Ind	Pres>Past>Fut	Pres>Past≧Fut	With>Subj=Over	With≧Over≧Subj*	Doing>Being	Doing>Being

In the Spanish-American case there were no discrepancies of any significance between the predictions made and the ranking patterns the analyses of the data revealed. However, no prediction had been made as to the second-order preference on the *time* orientation except for the question on religion where a preference for the Past alternative was predicted. This specific prediction was substantiated, but the strength of the Future alternative generally as a second-order preference was something of a surprise.

The Texan results differ from the predictions in two respects. One difference is of degree only; the other is in actual ordering. We expected this group to be given to a quite strong second-order preference of both the Present *time* orientation and the Being alternative of the *activity* orientation; we found them, in the responses to the schedule items, somewhat more inclined to these alternatives than was expected. On the *man-nature* orientation we predicted a second-order Subjugated-to-Nature preference. The result, statistically, was indeterminate as between the two, but it was the With-Nature alternative, not the Subjugated-to-Nature one, which was slightly more preferred.

The most discrepancies were found in the Mormon material. Both the Individualistic alternative of the *relational* orientation and the Over-Nature one of the *man-nature* orientation were given a greater emphasis than we had expected. There also was more of a stressing of the Present alternative and less of a stressing of the Past than was expected.

No general predictions for any of the orientations were made for the Zuni except one of great variation, and it was certainly great variation which was found. The specific prediction that they would be more disposed to emphasize the Past alternative of the *time* orientation than the other four cultures was borne out in the data.

In the case of the Navaho there proved to be a quite good fit between the predictions and the findings which is the more impressive since C. Kluckhohn, who was, for the most part, responsible for the predictions, stated that considerable variation would be found because of the state of flux the Navaho are in at the present time. There was, however, somewhat less of a preference of the Lineal alternative over the Individualistic alternative on the *relational* orientation in second-order position and also a less definite second-order preference for the Past over the Future *time* orientation alternative than was expected. The data also indicated a somewhat more marked preference (not great, as the With $\geqslant$ Over $\geqslant$ Subj* pattern shows) for the Over-Nature position of the *man-nature* orientation as the second-order choice.

Between-Culture Differences

Both methods of analysis used for comparing the summary rankings of the five cultures on each of the orientation series revealed that there were both important differences in the rankings of the orientation alternatives as between all five cultures and important similarities in the rankings of two pairings of the five cultures. The outstanding results were (1) the highly distinctive position of the Spanish-American group as a culture which stands apart from all of the others; (2) the great, but certainly not absolute, similarity of the two English-speaking communities which as a unity stand at the opposite pole from the Spanish-Americans; and (3) the in-between position of the two Indian groups which were, when compared to each other, distinctively different one from another on approximately half of the comparisons made.

More specifically the results of the analyses were as follows. The strength of the preference of the Spanish-Americans for the Present *time* orientation, the Being alternative of the *activity* orientation, and the Subjugated-to-Nature position on the *man-nature* orientation made it possible to separate the group off and call it the most unique of the five cultures.

The Texans and Mormons, who in gross—overall—terms gave virtually the same response patterns, were found to differ in three respects. The Mormons, although they significantly preferred the Individualistic alternative of the *relational* orientation as their first-order orientation, did not give the degree of emphasis to it that the Texans did. They also were less favorably disposed to the dominance of the Over-Nature as opposed to the With-Nature alternative of the *man-nature* orientation. Finally they showed a slightly greater tendency than the Texans to choose the Past alternative of the *time* orientation over the Present alternative.

The two Indian groups, alike in some respects—most especially in their responses to the items which tested the *relational* orientation—were found to be so different in other respects that a two-way distinction between them was necessary. In these differences the Navaho—in large part because of their strong preference for the Doing alternative of the *activity* orientation—were moved out toward the pole on the scale of differences which the two English-speaking communities occupy, and the Zuni were moved somewhat in the other direction toward the pole of the uniquely different Spanish-Americans.

These results, like those which show the within-culture regularities, coincide well with our expectations as to what the between-culture differences would be.[2]

The Results as Interpreted by the Analysts of the Individual Cultures

In the four chapters devoted to the examination of our results against a considerable body of data of other kinds than ours which has been

---

[2] Although, certainly, the two Indian groups, whether considered separately or together, are in the minutiae of cultural patterning (dress style, languages, food habits, ceremonial rituals, and a host of other specific patterns) greatly different from the three other cultures, which are in two instances (Texan and Mormon) definitely western European and in one (Spanish-American) partially western European, it has long been a contention of F. Kluckhohn that the Spanish-Americans are the most distinctively different of the five groups in their basic value system. Ethel Albert in a comparative analysis of the values of the five cultures of the Rimrock area which is to appear in the first of the general publications of the Values Project also reaches this conclusion.

accumulating over a period of many years, each of the analysts was urged to choose what he or she thought were the important issues to be discussed and urged also to choose the method of presenting his or her interpretations and criticisms. In summarizing the results yielded by these interpretative analyses we can only point out the most salient of the conclusions reached. This we shall do, culture by culture, in the ordering of the cultures which has been used consistently subsequent to Chapter II (where the description of the cultures was ordered by the criterion of time of entrance of the various peoples into the Rimrock region).

SPANISH-AMERICANS. The treatment of this group was designedly made the longest both because the heretofore published information on it was the least and because we wished, as has been stated in the Preface, to have at least one of the cultures treated in sufficient detail to show the ways in which the value orientations of a people are reflected in all aspects of their lives. And, as was also remarked in the Preface, we wished to present—in a condensed form, to be sure—the results of the study of these people which had extended over a fifteen-year period as of 1951 (and has been continued since 1951) because it was this study which played so large a part in the development of the theory of variations in value orientations.

First, we refer back to the statement that it was in the ranking preference of the Spanish-Americans that we found the greatest congruence between predictions and observed results as far as the within-culture regularities are concerned. It was also an expectation that the value-orientation profile of rankings of the Spanish-Americans would be the most distinctively different of all the groups. This expectation was also substantiated by the results we achieved.

The discussion given by F. Kluckhohn in Chapter VI goes into considerable ethnological detail to show how the value-orientation system which our investigation reveals them to have is expressed in patterns of family organization, economic activities, religious beliefs and rituals, political behavior, attitudes toward education, and intellectual-aesthetic interests in general.

The discussion also treats of the kinds of strains noted in the social system, the variant patterns which have long existed in the society as means of mitigating these strains, and the processes of change which occurred when some of the "strain-induced" variant patterns and variantly oriented individuals (most particularly younger brothers) came under a strong and consistent influence of dominant Anglo-American culture.

Relative to these issues—the variations in the system and the changes they helped to effect—it had been predicted that there would be the greatest inconsistency of response pattern in the group as a whole on the items which tested on the *relational* orientation. Because it was expected that the traditionally dominant Lineal orientation was being supplanted by the Individualistic one—formerly the third-order preference—an additional question, asking what the preference would have been a generation back (thirty years ago), was put to all Spanish-Americans on all of the *relational* orientation items.

The most interesting addition to the body of data on the Spanish-Americans which our field investigation provided was the evidence of the strength of the Future over the Past alternative of the *time* orientation in second-order position. Although it was suspected that this shift in second-order and third-order positions was occurring, there was not enough certainty of its definiteness to warrant a prediction as to whether the Future or the Past alternative would receive a second-order emphasis. All that was predicted on the basis of a long-time knowledge of the group was that the Past position would still be chosen as second-order in matters concerning the religious behavior sphere. This specific expectation also proved to be correct, but the strength of the Future alternative as a second-order choice in other areas of behavior was an indication of change which the previously collected data gave hints of but did not clearly substantiate. The question raised in the interpretation in Chapter VI is whether this finding represents a firm shift in the direction of a second-order Future orientation or is simply a result of the better conditions the Spanish-Americans have experienced in a period of fairly general prosperity in the whole of the United States.

The judgment rendered was that the degree of the increase in the emphasis upon the Future *time* alternative (still not at all great) will be maintained as a quite firm choice only if the economy of the United States continues to expand without serious recessions. This judgment—"prediction," if one wishes to give it scientific dignity—was only one of several which aimed to show how the value-orientation system of the Spanish-Americans, a system which has been and still is in most respects virtually a mirror image of the dominant American culture, has been a key factor in the extremely low rate of assimilation of Spanish-Americans into dominant American culture.

TEXANS AND MORMONS. Strodtbeck in Chapter VII makes a comparison of the two English-speaking groups, and in making it he uses, in addition to the analyses used on all of the cultures, a factor analysis of the rankings of the orientation alternatives which the graphic analysis showed each of the cultures to have.

The outstanding fact about these two groups revealed in our data was their great similarity. Taking the two groups as a fairly distinctive cultural unity relative to the other three cultures, there are these important points which Strodtbeck stresses. First, the two groups are English-speaking ones and are both, in some sense, in the main stream of American culture as the other three Rimrock peoples are not. Second, the common characteristics the two communities have in dress, manners, and in many a type of interest in technology and in regional and national political affairs might well lead the casual observer—who sees members of both communities on the streets of Railtown, in trading stores, in banks, or in the offices of county agencies—to conclude that all were from the same or highly similar Anglo-American communities.

But underneath these obvious similarities there are a host of differences which mark off the communities one from another fairly distinctly. Unfortunately the number of items we used to test for cultural differences was not large enough to give us evidence of the subtle differences between two such similar groups as the Mormons and Texans which would be as conclusive as the evidence for the more gross differences between these two cultures and the three others. But the evidence of difference was not entirely lacking, and that which was revealed is well substantiated by the results of previous studies of Homestead and Rimrock.

We had predicted that there would be significant differences between the two cultures on only two of the value orientations we were testing—the *relational* and the *man-nature* orientations. We predicted (1) a strong preference for the Individualistic alternative on the *relational* orientation items in the Texan case and an equivocal choice between the Individualistic and Collateral alternatives among the Mormons; and (2) a first-order preference among the Texans for the Over-Nature position of the *man-nature* orientation in contrast to a first-order With-Nature preference in the Mormon sample.

These predictions were borne out by our results but not to a degree that one might have much confidence in them without the supporting evidence of other data on the two groups. Strodtbeck's factor analysis showed little difference between the two cultures on the *relational* orientation but did reveal the predicted difference on the *man-nature* orientation. The analyses of variance which were used to give between-culture discriminations pointed up the greater emphasis upon Collaterality among the Mormons but did not mark them off as being substantially more prone to the With-Nature as opposed to the Over-Nature alternative of the *man-nature* orientation. The results of the binomial analysis did, of course, show the Mormon pattern of responses to be the Over $\geqslant$ With $>$ Subj one in contrast to the Texan Over $>$ With $\geqslant$ Subj one. Hence we may state, on the basis of the total analyses made, that the results show the predicted difference of a greater preference of the Mormons in contrast to the Texans for the Collateral and With-Nature alternatives as opposed to the Individualistic and Over-Nature ones.

These differences were, however, slight, and we ourselves would not argue strongly for their significance unless there were data of other kinds to support them. These there were. Indeed, both the material which Strodtbeck himself gathered in free comments and the publications of Vogt and O'Dea give ample evidence that on both the *relational* and the *man-nature* orientations the preference rankings of the alternatives are significantly, if not markedly, different as between these two groups.

One of the most interesting of the findings relative to these differences was a variation by sex of respondent in the Mormon sample. It was the women in the Mormon group, not the men, who were the more Individualistic and the more Over-Nature in their responses. Had only men been tested, the predicted gap between the two cultures on these two orientations would almost certainly have loomed much larger. But as Strodtbeck warns us, we must, in coming to this conclusion, take into account the fact that the items we used to test on the *relational* and *man-nature* orientations, especially the former, were primarily centered on interests which can be considered as more masculinely than femininely oriented. But offsetting this argument is the one that the data cited to substantiate the greater preference of the Mormons for the Collateral *relational* orientation also refer to types of situations and problems which typically are decided by the men—not the women—of Mormon Rimrock (school construction and road building).

Two additional minor variations between the two groups deserve mention. First, it was the Texans who on item R2 (Help in Misfortune) pulled farther away than did the Mormons toward a second-order Lineal as opposed to the Collateral alternative. There also was noted a slight difference between the groups in their degree of preference for the Past alternative of the *time* orientation, the Mormon leaning in this direction being the stronger. When we looked at all the groups for the purpose of making the prior predictions, there was actually considerable discussion as to whether the Mormons might not be given to a second-order preference of the Past alternative. The basis for this speculative conclusion was a consideration of the Utah Mormons about which none of the research team knew much except Romney who himself was a Utah-reared Mormon. It was finally concluded that the fringe status of the Rimrock group was too marked for it to be greatly concerned with the traditionalism of the Utah communities. However, there was some feeling that the leanings of the Mormons of Rimrock in contrast to those of the Texans of Homestead would be toward a Past *time* orientation. Ever so slightly this hunch was borne out in our data, and it may conceivably be a larger difference than our data show. It was relative to this question that Strodtbeck stated the great desirability of having more items, most especially on the *time* orientation, for the testing of the differences between these two groups which are so very similar in many respects.

THE ZUNI. Roberts in his interpretation of the Zuni results in Chapter VIII poses the argument that while the great variation found in the Zuni responses may be a result of a failure of our method in this one group, it is more probably the reality of Zuni society of today. And even more than this, he suggests that the highly "involuted" Zuni culture has long contained within itself more variations than one might normally expect in a majority of societies. Since Zuni has been studied fairly intensively over a longer time period and by more numerous investigators than is the case with any of the other four Rimrock peoples, Roberts had a wealth of published source material upon which to draw in the discussion of his hypothesis that the society is a quite extreme illustration of "contained variation."

Any reader who has himself some familiarity with the literature on the Zuni is well aware that there has long been an argument as to whether the picture Benedict paints of them in *Patterns of Culture*—a picture of a profoundly serene and well integrated culture which she calls Apollonian—or the picture others have drawn of a fairly quarrelsome people who are divided into many factions is the more correct one. It is a part of Roberts' general argument that both pictures are partially correct, but neither one wholly correct. His overall picture of the culture is one which portrays extensive variations which are so self-contained within the confines of a single community that the culture appears to be, vis-à-vis all outsiders, both tightly knit and highly ethnocentric. In this judgment he is voicing, as he himself states, a view similar to that Kroeber presented when he said, "It [Zuni] is as solidly welded as it is intricately ramified."

Thus, while our own research can provide no proof (the kind of proof, for example, that replications of our procedures might have offered) that the inconsistencies in our Zuni data reflect reality much more than a failure of method, there appears to be substantiation of this view when one compares the varying views and conclusions of the many others who have studied Zuni culture. Moreover, and this is one of the chief virtues of a cross-cultural testing instrument, it seems unlikely—though not impossible, of course—that a method which yielded significantly consistent results in four other cultures could be the "reason" for many statistically nonsignificant results in a fifth culture. This argument is made the stronger by the fact that one of the four cultures in which significant results were obtained is another American Indian group (the Navaho) which we considered would be even more difficult to test in the medium of language than the Zuni.

Roberts' second general thesis is that the increased strength of the impact of dominant American culture upon the Zuni in recent years has resulted in a still further development of variant patterns. But again it is to be noted that the hypothesized capacity of the Zuni to "contain" variation has seemingly allowed them to absorb these additional variations without some of the shattering effects one notes in the case of the Rimrock Navaho.

Quite specifically, it was noted in the Zuni responses that the Collateral alternative of the *relational* orientation was the most preferred and that the Lineal one was second order but was not significantly preferred over the Individualistic one. Although the Benedict analysis of the Zuni would seem to indicate the dominance of the Lineal alternative of this orientation, there also is much evidence in other analyses—those on social organization, kinship, economic arrangements—that the Collateral alternative has long been strongly in evidence in many spheres of Zuni life. If it is true that this was the ordering of the alternatives in traditional Zuni culture, it would appear that there are changes now occurring of a kind that our theory calls a "logical" shifting between first and second-order preferences. We have labeled as logical both a shifting between first and second-order positions and one between second and third-order positions. The more difficult type of attempted shift, hence the more illogical one, is the shifting between first and third-order preferences. It was this kind of shift which many Spanish-Americans have tried with results that have been most disruptive, even disastrous.

In their responses to the items which tested the *time* orientation the Zuni did prove to be more disposed to select the Past alternative than any other group. The actual pattern, however, was the Pres $\geq$ Past $>$ Fut one, and according to the analysis Roberts has made of the literature on the culture it appears that this is the patterning the Zuni have held to for a long period of years. The emphasis upon the Past alternative was, according to the former studies, strong in all matters which touched on ceremonialism. This accords with our findings of a clear-cut Past > Pres > Fut pattern on item T4 (Ceremonial Innovation) and the Past ⩾ Pres > Fut pattern on T3 (Philosophy of Life). But it is also pointed out in Chapter VIII that the emphasis upon the Future alternative is gaining, and Roberts' conclusion is that a shift is taking place in the second and third-order positions on this orientation. The Past alternative is losing ground and the Future one gaining in strength as a second-order preference.

The variability of response pattern on the items testing on the *man-nature* orientation was indeed great. But once again there is evidence which gives some support to the view that the variations found do, in fact, exist. Very briefly, it would appear that there has long been a highly traditional Harmony-with-Nature preference which was not, however, markedly stronger than a Subjugated-to-Nature preference. Recently, in Roberts' view, the impact of general American culture has so increased the preference for the once weak third-order Mastery-over-Nature position that there is actually a highly indeterminate pattern as of the present time. A wide variety of American technological developments are now well accepted and much used by the Zuni.

One of the great problems in the Zuni case in interpreting the results of the responses to the items which tested the *activity* orientation was the omission of the Being-in-Becoming alternative. As was stated in Chapters II and III, we regretted this omission most particularly relative to the Zuni, since all that has been written about them indicates them to be the most inclined to this alternative of all the groups we tested. The interpretation of the results had, therefore, to be confined to the interesting split which was found in the selection of the Doing and Being alternatives. On the two items which we realized did not in any sense of the word test purely on the *activity* orientation we found a consistent Being > Doing response. On the other four the response was almost equally a consistent Doing > Being pattern. Roberts makes only two general comments concerning the response patterns on this orientation. He first states that although the literature tends generally to support the view that the missing Being-in-Becoming alternative of the *activity* orientation was dominant in Zuni in the past, he considers that the evidence as of the 1950's shows the Doing orientation to be dominant. Second, he states that the first two items—the ones we knew were really testing on an amalgam of orientation preferences —posed a situation which was not typically a part of Zuni experience, and to the extent that they did understand the situation it depicts they imparted to it overtones of Indian-white relationships. There is, therefore, little that can be said about the inconclusive results on the *activity* orientation except to state that on the four relatively pure items used for testing on it, the choice was a quite unequivocal Doing over Being one.

If the analysis and the interpretation of the variations in Zuni society which Chapter VIII sets forth as having been demonstrated by others in varying ways and in varying degrees are accepted, it does then, indeed, appear to be true that much, if not most, of the variation revealed by the Zuni responses to the value-orientation schedule is real. And to the extent this is the case, we can cite the Zuni results as one instance of cases wherein cultural inconsistencies (wide-range variation) and the inconsistencies revealed by statistical techniques are not at all the same thing.

THE RIMROCK NAVAHO. One of the concluding statements made by Romney and C. Kluckhohn in their analysis of the Navaho data was "Nothing brought out by this investigation is contradicted or called into serious question by the substantial body of earlier work." The predicted profile of dominant orientations—the profile of Collaterality, Present, With-Nature, and Doing—did clearly emerge; the expected wide-range variation was also found.

C. Kluckhohn warned us that we should expect considerable inconsistency in responses, even assuming that the schedule of test items could be meaningfully translated into the Navaho language. In the interpretative discussion (Chapter IX) it is stated that the economic crises of the past thirty years and the increased pressures imposed by various groups in the dominant Anglo-American culture have caused much shattering of the traditional Navaho way of life. Economic deprivation is marked in the group, and its low social status—the lowest among the five peoples—makes it an easy prey for discriminatory practices of persons in other groups, including some in other Rimrock communities. In addition there has been a confusion created as to the "right way" to behave when there arises a conflict between the typical, old, Navaho patterns and the patterns which powerful government agencies seem to expect. However well intentioned, however rational or, at least, seemingly rational, the policies of the Indian Service or other government agencies may have been, it is a fact that they have been, for the most part, based on the value tenets of dominant American culture which are at odds with Navaho basic values in all instances except the *activity* orientation. The equilibrium of the economy of the Rimrock Navaho was, for example, so seriously upset by the stock-reduction program of the United States government that repercussions were felt, still are felt, through the whole social system. Many Navaho men were forced to move out of the Collaterally organized and family-contained economic activities and move into the general labor market as wage workers. And almost all who made this move were clearly placed in the unskilled-labor category at the very bottom of the scale of occupations. Moreover, the jobs they could find have often required that the men leave their families and go off for fairly long periods of time to other areas, sometimes even as far away as Montana. Most of them remain away for awhile, then return, and later leave again. In almost no cases have families or even parts of families moved out with these men and established a permanent residence elsewhere. It is one thing to move a fairly self-contained middle-class American family from New York to California when the father of it wishes to change his job; it is quite another to sever the ties of a small family unit which has only a small degree of independence from ramified ties to many other units.

The effects upon the Navaho value system of all these conditions are easily seen in some of the fairly consistent variations our data revealed. Note, first, that on item R2 (Help in Misfortune) the Lineal alternative was significantly preferred to the otherwise dominant Collateral one. The Romney-Kluckhohn statement on this finding is that it fits the recorded facts on recent developments in the Navaho group and reflects the growing feeling of the need to depend upon United States government agencies, outside employers, and traders. Second, we note that there is no clear-cut (significant) dominance of the Collateral over the Lineal alternative on the Family Work Relations item, R3. Finally, we see the reflection of the conflict between the Anglo-American and the Navaho conceptions of property ownership in the Coll $\geqslant$ Ind $\geqslant$ Lin patterns which items R6 (Livestock Inheritance) and R7 (Land Inheritance) evoked. Some Navaho, at least, are quite consciously aware of this conflict. As was reported in Chapter II one person who was questioned in our pre-testing program gave an equivocal answer as between the Individualistic and Collateral alternatives on these items but then volunteered the comment that the Individualistic way was not really the right one or the one his people would have selected in the past, but it was the way *Washingtone* (the term these Navaho use to refer to the Bureau of Indian Affairs) demanded, so it must be accepted.

On the *time* orientation items the predicted Present over Past over Future was actually observed, but the margin of preference of the Past over the Future alternative was not a significant finding. Relative to these results as a whole, Romney and Kluckhohn first comment that the Present *time* orientation of the Rimrock Navaho of today is more of a resigned acceptance of conditions than it is the kind of genuinely spontaneous "timeless" Present orientation which characterized traditional Navaho culture. It is, they state, much more realism than enthusiasm. They also remark that, in general, the signs of a growing emphasis upon the Future alternative (the alternative that formerly was definitely a third-order preference) which comes forth most clearly on the most general of the items—T2 (Expectations about Change) and T3 (Philosophy of Life)—represent a hopeful groping more than a real confidence. It may also be suggested, as was done in the case of the Spanish-American responses, that the response pattern to these two items reflects an attitude that it is possible, no matter how low one's status may currently be, to participate, vicariously, in the overall American "wave of the future." If this be true, we would predict that for the Navaho as well as the Spanish-American this value-orientation bubble would burst were there to be a serious and prolonged economic recession in the United States. It has been said that if economic conditions in the country as a whole were to worsen to a state of depression the Spanish-Americans would be the first to be fired from jobs and the last to be rehired. The statement describes the Navaho occupational status even more accurately than the Spanish-American one.

There is, however, one other highly interesting variation in the Navaho data relative to the increase of the emphasis upon the Future *time* orientation (and the increased emphasis upon the Over-Nature one as well) which deserves special comment. This is the variation by sex of respondent. It was the women who most strongly favored the Future position. Indeed there was a real split in the patterns by sex; the men came forth quite consistently with the pattern which we assumed was the traditional one—the Present over Past over Future; but the responses of the women yielded a pattern which directionally (not really significant, to be sure) was the Present over Future over Past one.

This result, too, is given corroboration by two studies (see citations in Chapter IX on the investigations of Rapaport and of Bruner and Rotter) which show that the women of the Navaho group were actually somewhat less "conservative" in their views than were the Navaho men, even though in dress, in outside contacts, and other quite specific patterns they have appeared to be more conservative.

Romney and Kluckhohn warn against making too much of this finding since the Rimrock Navaho women were generally more difficult to interview than the men and their responses were more obviously inconsistent, but they do state that the responses yielded accord well with the Rapaport and the Bruner and Rotter data and give real indications that in basic values the women are less averse to change than the men. And while they state it would be safer not to assume that the men are actually more conservatively attached to the traditional Navaho values, they do suggest that the data (both kinds) lend support to the view that the women are reacting to a general situation wherein they have held a position less favorable to that of the men in the dominant behavior sphere of Navaho culture (ceremonialism and ritual). This difference may have been felt to be the greater because of the fact that the society is matrilineal in its inheritance patterns and is also predominantly (not totally) matrilocal in its residence patterns.

In the data on the *man-nature* orientation there was something of a discrepancy between the results achieved from the value-orientation schedule, the predictions, and the interpretation. The schedule results show the overall pattern to be the With $\geqslant$ Over $\geqslant$ Subj* one—the With-Nature position first order as predicted but not significantly more predominant as a choice than the Over-Nature alternative, and both the With-Nature and Over-Nature positions preferred to the Subjugated-to-Nature one. The interpretative analysis in Chapter IX presents the argument that the "real" pattern as displayed by other data is With over Subjugated over Over. But Romney and Kluckhohn also state that the ever-increasing conviction among these Navaho that Anglo-American medicine does work makes the results of the Over $\geqslant$ With $\geqslant$ Subj* pattern on item MN5 entirely convincing. Since this item and item MN3, which treats of technology in farming activities, were the ones to throw the balance in our data in favor of a second-order Over-Nature position as opposed to a second-order Subjugated-to-Nature one, it may be said that here again we have an indication of some acceptance and belief in a value position which an encompassing culture expresses. The Navaho do not themselves as a people produce the medicines or the techniques found in the hospitals to which many of them now go nor do they produce the techniques related to farming and stockraising which some now use, but they have been impressed by both and to some extent have accepted both. But here again it should be noted that our data showed the women of the group were more given to an acceptance of the dominant Anglo-American Over-Nature position than were the men.

On the *activity* orientation items it was both predicted and found that the Rimrock Navaho were strongly given to a preference of the Doing as opposed to the Being alternative—more strongly than any other of the groups tested. Moreover, it was on the items which tested for preferences on this orientation that there were found both the most decisiveness in responses and the highest degree of congruence between the perceived and observed consensus, as between the preferences the individual respondent made and those he attributed to other members of his group (see Appendix 3). Since it is on this one orientation that the Navaho value system is strongly in accord with the dominant American one, these observations are extremely interesting for the analysis of cultural change. Stress and strain, confusion even, were strongly evidenced in the responses to the items of the orientations which vary from the dominant and controlling American middle-class culture, but little confusion or indecisiveness was noted in the preferential rankings of this one orientation where there is such a high degree of congruence that no change is required of the Navaho in their efforts to adapt their ways to generalized American culture.

The outstanding summary fact about the Navaho—a fact which both the results of the value-orientation research program and much other data support—is that they have managed in the face of tremendous odds to cling to their dominant value-orientation system for such a long period. But as Romney and C. Kluckhohn suggest, the present equilibrium is probably only a temporary one. The society is obviously in a critical state of transition, and the question to be raised is whether it will survive at all in any other condition than as a truly marginal and suppressed group out on the fringe of the total United States society. The prognosis for the survival of the Zuni culture is seemingly better, and it would appear to be the case that the argument which Roberts advances about the degree of tolerance the Zuni have long shown for variations is one very important factor in the difference of prediction to be made about the future of the two groups.

DISCUSSION: THE PLACE OF THE VARIATION THEORY IN STUDIES OF HUMAN BEHAVIOR

The results of the investigation of the cultures of the Rimrock region, and still others achieved in research programs of a later date,[3] have been sufficiently conclusive to warrant according the value-orientation theory an independent status in studies of human behavior. And in this status the

---

[3] These programs, previously cited, are William and Mieko Caudill's use of the value-orientation schedule for the testing of 614 Japanese respondents and the Spiegel–F. Kluckhohn comparative study of mental health and illness in Italian-American, Irish-American, and Old-American families in a metropolitan area.

theory is not to be regarded as one which is applicable only to the analysis of cultural phenomena. While, in the first instance, the aim of the theory is that of ordering the dominant and variant values of cultures and subcultures, its analytic value reaches far beyond a study of cultural factors in and for themselves.

Although it is both appropriate and necessary for many kinds of studies to treat cultural forms and symbols as a distinctive phenomenological system, there is actually, as opposed to conceptually, no part of a culture which is clearly separable from the social structure of groups, large and small, and the psychological systems of individuals. Culture exists, and is observable, only in the behavior, attitudes, motives, and perceptions of "reality" which individuals show, in the interaction systems individuals develop, and in the products which individuals, singly or collectively, create. Conversely, there is no aspect of human behavior which is not influenced to some degree, either directly or indirectly, by culture. Basic values are a particularly pervasive cultural factor of influence.

But this is not to argue that considerations of social structure and individual behavior are to be subsumed and made subsidiary to cultural interpretations. Nor is it to say that societal and cultural factors are one and the same. As has been stated, we agree, for the most part, with the recent statement of Kroeber and Parsons which argues that there is a definite analytic distinction between cultural and social systems (between these and personality systems, too, as Parsons elsewhere argues) which must consistently be recognized lest there be real confusion in our conceptualizations of human behavior.[4] As we ourselves have stated in Chapter I (a statement which was written prior to the appearance of the Kroeber-Parsons paper), there has long been an unresolved confusion as to what is cultural and what is social—a confusion which "is frequently glossed over by the use of the term socio-cultural with full awareness that the hyphen is no symbol of integration."

Our argument, and seemingly that of Kroeber and Parsons as well, is that the possibility of understanding the interrelations between the systems increases in accord with the degree to which the analytic distinctions between them are recognized. Thus, when speaking of the use of the value-orientation theory as a tool in the analysis of social and personality systems, the only claim we make is that value orientations strongly influence aspects of both. However, we do contend that for an analysis of the degree and kind of influence exerted by basic values the theory of variation we have elaborated and put to a fairly severe cross-cultural test is a far better tool than theories which treat only of the dominant value orientations of a culture.

Differentiation, a key concept in many societal analyses, is much more fully understood when the value system to which it is related and by which it is strongly influenced is seen as an interlocking network of dominant and variant values rather than a unitary system of dominant values only. The conformity-deviation dichotomy, which is extensively used in socio-

---

[4] A. L. Kroeber and Talcott Parsons, "The Concepts of Culture and of Social System," *American Sociological Review*, Vol. XXIII, No. 5 (October, 1958).

logical studies, is also augmented in strength by the theory of variation. Even though the fact of variation has frequently been recognized by those who use the concepts of conformity and deviation, little consideration has been given to the theoretical, as opposed to the empirical, significance of variation in values. As a result the concepts of the deviation process and the deviant personality are used somewhat indiscriminately to treat both the cases of deviants who defy any socially acceptable codes and the many others whose deviations lead to the adoption, or attempted adoption, of values which are either fully accepted or at least tolerated in the wider society. Deviation, as a concept, captures only the "going away" aspect of the total social process, and unless it is recognized that variation is always present in the total culture, and in subcultures as well, there is no way, other than an empirically *ad hoc* one, of analyzing the "going toward" half of the process. In some instances, many indeed in a mobile society like the United States, the deviations from a variant subculture represent a going toward the patterns of the dominant culture. The group which Whyte calls the "College Boys" in his study, *Street Corner Society*, illustrates well this kind of movement.[5] But as can be deduced from our earlier contrast of Italian-American and dominant middle-class American values, these young men, in making the shift in value preferences that they did, were not moving toward a value system which was *absolutely* different from the Italian-American one. Nor were they as deviants within the Italian-American subculture ever completely alienated from it. Most of the analyses of deviation, even the very sophisticated ones contained in the studies of reference groups, leave much unexplained because of a lack of a theory which delineates the ordered relatedness of the various subsystems within a total society.

These statements lead directly to the use of the theory in studies of variations in individual personalities. Value-orientation preferences which the child, in being socialized in one cultural tradition as opposed to another, has subtly built into his total apperceptive mass through the role expectations imposed upon him are an extremely important aspect of his total personality. The Spanish-American younger brother, socialized consistently for dependent behavior and greatly frustrated because of training which requires much submission without adequate rewards to make him feel that he is significantly contributing to the welfare of the family unit, is obviously a different personality from the middle-class American who is trained quite systematically—though sometimes conflictingly—for fairly independent behavior from a very early age. There are again differences to be expected in the Navaho Indian male who is socialized in a Collaterally oriented system which has a unilateral, matrilineal stress and the Mormon male who grows up in a Collateral system that has a unilateral, patriarchal emphasis. Irish-American culture with its conflicting value demands created by the juxtaposition of a Lineal *relational* orientation and a view of *human nature* as being basically Evil creates different personalities than Italian-American culture which characteristically is

[5] See William F. Whyte, *Street Corner Society* (Chicago: University of Chicago Press, 1943).

Collaterally oriented and given to a view of *human nature* as a mixture of Good-and-Evil. All such differences as these and many others have been found to be profoundly important in the current research program which is devoted to a comparative study of mental health and illness in samples of Irish-American, Italian-American, and Old American lower-class groups in a metropolitan area. Indeed the importance of the value-orientation factor has loomed so large in this research that a serious question has been raised as to the magnitude of the therapy problem which is created because the patients of these groups and their middle-class American therapists are so disparate in their value-orientation preferences.[6]

Behind these specialized uses of the theory there is the central issue of the study of the integration of cultures and the changes which occur in them. Unless we know the nature of the integration and know also the areas of strain within the system which bring about the development of much of the variation within the system, there is not much which can be predicted about the influence of the value-orientation system upon either the social structure or the personalities of individuals.

Since this whole study has been devoted primarily to this type of analysis, there is little needed by way of recapitulation. Relative to the question of integration the theory argues that the value systems of cultures are not systems of single dominant values but are, instead, interlocking networks of dominant and variant value positions which differ only in that there is a variable ordering of the same value-orientation alternatives. For a number of reasons, not the least of which is the strain imposed upon categories of individuals by the patterned demands expressive of the dominant orientation ordering, variation in value-orientation preferences is both required and permitted. These variations, while seldom a main source of cultural change in and of themselves, are nonetheless always partial potentials for change. Variant individuals playing variant roles are far more susceptible to external influences than are dominantly oriented individuals who play dominant roles. Thus, the thesis developed relative to cultural change is that basic change (meaning change in the value orientations themselves and not simply elaborations of the same values) seldom occurs until such time as there is a fairly sustained impact of one or more external forces upon the system which leads to an interplay between them and the internal variation.

The question of analyzing and appraising the degrees of influence of one kind of external force as opposed to another is a large and difficult one—much too large and difficult to be treated in this study. But even raising the issue focuses attention upon the place of the value-orientation theory in the whole field of study devoted to human behavior. It has, we feel sure, been made abundantly clear that no claim is made that value orientations are a more deterministic factor than many another except to the extent that they are highly perduring. Very generally, our view is that there is no one of the behavioral sciences, or any other branch of the now wide-

---

[6] See John Spiegel, "Some Cultural Aspects of Transference and Countertransference" in *Individual and Familial Dynamics*, ed. Jules H. Masserman (New York: Grune & Stratton, 1959).

spread tree of human knowledge, which has the potential for a total explanation of human behavior. Empirically the terrain in need of exploration is too vast and the powers of man too limited for the development of any single body of thought which could even attempt to answer all questions. But this fact should in no way be a deterrent to the effort to find the means of systematically interrelating the theories of the many different disciplines.

There are some today who seek the means of solving these problems in the evolution of a "general-systems theory." Parsons, Bertalanffy, and others assume the theoretical position that there are discoverable laws which apply so universally to systems of all kinds that many of the relationships between systems become virtually axiomatic. While there is no question of the great possibilities this approach offers for a part of the solution of the problems, it is by no means the only one. Nor is it likely to be adequate to the task of a full analysis of the interrelationships. Indeed, it is very doubtful that there are a sufficient number of properties common to all the variable systems for such theories to provide more than a partial explanation of either the nature of the systems themselves, the relationships between them, or the dynamics of the changes in the relationships.

If this be true, it may prove highly beneficial even to the theory of general systems that other means be found to establish system relationships at other levels than the highly general one with which that theory is concerned. These other means, especially since they are more commensurate with our present technical level of empirical measurement and testing, could well provide the proving ground for what should or should not be incorporated in a general-systems type of analysis.

One of these different ways of seeking a part of the solution to the problem of the interrelatedness of systems is to view them all as component parts of a "transactional field."[7] While there is no denying in this approach that the different systems may have, almost certainly do have, properties in common, it is also recognized that each has particularistic ones which require serious consideration of it as an independent and distinctive system. Reconceptualization in search of "common denominators" is certainly required in this approach, but the degree required is far less general and less enveloping than that which the general-systems approach demands.

The theory of variations in value orientations is a theory which fits easily into this approach. Indeed, a major concern in the development of the theory was that of so reconceptualizing the theories of basic values, cultural themes, unconscious canons of choice, that they could be made more amenable to an articulation with theories concerned with the many other factors which influence human behavior. We hope that the effort has been sufficiently effective to provide a challenge to others in different fields to seek for both the reconceptualizations of their own theories and also the evolution of bridging concepts between theories which will make truly systematic transactional analyses possible.

[7] For a published statement of this approach see John P. Spiegel, "A Model for Relationships Among Systems" in *Toward a Unified Theory of Human Behavior*, ed. Roy R. Grinker (New York: Basic Books, 1956), Vol. I, Chap. 2.

APPENDIX 1

Spanish-Language Version of the Value-Orientation Schedule

Escogiendo trabajo   Pregunta No. 1

   Un hombre necesita trabajo, y dos hombres muy diferentes le ofrecen trabajo. Escuche como eran ellos y diga para cual de ellos usted piensa que sería mejor trabajar.

(1) Uno es bastante justo, y paga algo más que los otros patrones pero es un patrón duro. Insiste que sus empleados trabajen duro y siempre estén a sus horas. Se disgusta mucho cuando un empleado toma tiempo para salir de viaje o a divertirse. Casi siempre desocupa al empleado que hace esto.
(2) El otro paga solo sueldos regulares, pero no es un patrón tan duro. Entiende porque a veces un empleado no viene a trabajar, ha salido de viaje o a divertirse por un día o dos. Cuando vuelve, casi siempre lo sigue ocupando sin decirle mucho.

(1)

¿Para cuál de estos hombres cree usted que sería mejor trabajar?
Por lo general, ¿cuál de estos dos hombres diría la gente de aquí, sería el mejor patrón?

(2)

¿Cuál de estos dos patrones preferiría usted ser?
¿Cuál preferiría ser la mayoría de la gente de aquí?

Arreglos sobre las norias de agua   Pregunta No. 2

   Si es necesario que la gente en una placita haga arreglos para conseguir más agua —por ejemplo, hacer una noria—hay tres diferentes métodos de hacer los arreglos, tal como, el lugar donde se va a poner, y quién va a hacer el trabajo.

(1) Alguna gente cree que es mejor cuando una persona de importancia como un jefe, un mayordomo o quizás un patrón hace los arreglos. Todos los demás generalmente aceptan lo que él decida sin argumento porque él está acostumbrado a decidir tales cosas y tiene más experiencia.

(2) Otra gente cree que todos deben tomar parte en hacer los arreglos. Muchas personas tienen opiniones y discuten el asunto por mucho tiempo pero no se hace nada hasta que *casi todos* están de acuerdo en lo que es mejor.
(3) Otra gente cree que es mejor que cada persona tenga su propia opinión y la sostenga. El asunto se decide con el voto. Lo que quiere la mayoría se hace aunque haya todavía mucha gente que se opone fuertemente y sigue peleando el resultado del voto.

¿Qué método le parece mejor en estos casos?
¿Cuál escogería usted como el segundo?
¿Qué método cree usted que escogería la mayoría de la gente aquí como el mejor modo?

La ensenanza de ninos   Pregunta No. 3

Aquí hay tres diferentes opiniones sobre la manera de enseñar a los niños.

(1) Algunas personas creen que a los niños se les debe enseñar las costumbres del pasado con mucho cuidado. Esta gente cree que las viejas costumbres son siempre las mejores, y dicen que cuando los niños no siguen estas costumbres viejas, vienen dificultades.
(2) Otras personas creen que los niños deben conocer las costumbres del pasado, pero no se debe insistir en que se sigan estas costumbres al pie de la letra. Dicen que los hijos *necesitan* aprender y aceptar muchas cosas nuevas para vivir mejor, hoy en día.
(3) Hay todavía otras personas que no dan casi nada de atención a todas las costumbres viejas. Enseñan las costumbres viejas *solo* como un cuento interesante. Estas personas dicen que la vida es mejor para todos cuando los hijos aprenden a querer buscar por sí mismos nuevos modos de hacer las cosas, e ir en direcciones nuevas aparte de sus padres.

¿Cuál de estos métodos de enseñar a los niños le parece mejor?
¿Cuál escogería como el segundo?
¿Cuál de estos métodos cree usted que la mayoría de la otra gente escogería como el mejor?

Perdida de ganado   Pregunta No. 4

Una vez un hombre tenía mucho ganado. Con el tiempo la mayor parte murió por diferentes razones. La gente al hablar de esta pérdida pensaba de diferentes modos.

(1) Alguna gente decía, "Uno no puede culpar a un hombre cuando pasan estas cosas. Tales cosas pasan todo el tiempo, y no hay mucho que se puede hacer cuando viene pérdidas como éstas. Tenemos que aprender a aceptar lo bueno con lo malo. ¡Así es la vida!"
(2) Otra gente decía, "Probablemente las pérdidas sucedieron porque el hombre no ha hecho las cosas buenas que debía hacer en su vida. No

ha vivido en la manera propia para estar en armonía con las fuerzas de la naturaleza, eso es decir, las fuerzas que hacen el viento, la lluvia, y la nieve, y tienen que ver con todo lo que vive."

(3) Otra gente decía, "Seguramente era la culpa del hombre mismo que él perdió tanto ganado. Por lo visto, no hizo suficiente fuerza para aprender los modos mejores de mirar por el ganado." Esta gente cree que casi siempre puede uno encontrar algún modo de evitar los apuros, si se empeña en conocer y usar varios modos conocidos de atender a su ganado.

¿Cuál de esta gente, en su opinión, tiene más razón?
¿Cuál opinión escogería en segundo lugar?
¿Qué razón escogería la mayor parte de la gente de aquí?

ESPERANZA   Pregunta No. 5

(*a. Años 20 a 40*)

Tres jóvenes estaban hablando de lo que creían que sus familias—eso es decir, ellos mismos y sus hijos—tendrían algún día, comparado con lo que sus padres tuvieron. Cada uno pensaba de distinto modo.

(1) Uno dijo, "Yo creo que mi familia tendrá más en el futuro que la familia de mis padres o mis parientes, si trabajamos duro y hacemos nuestros planes con cuidado. La vida en este país *casi siempre* mejora para la gente que de veras trabaja duro."

(2) Otro dijo, "Yo no sé de seguro si mi familia vivirá mejor, lo mismo, o peor, que la familia de mis padres o mis parientes. La vida sube y baja aún cuando la gente trabaja duro. ¡Así es la vida!"

(3) Todavía otro dijo, "Yo creo que *mi* familia, vivirá más o menos como vivieron las familias de mis padres y de mis parientes. Lo mejor es trabajar duro para guardar todo lo del pasado."

¿Cuál de estos jóvenes cree usted pensaba mejor?
¿Cuál opinión escogería en segundo lugar?
La mayoría de la gente de aquí, ¿con cuál de estos jóvenes estaría de acuerdo?

(*b. Años de 40 arriba*)

Tres personas mayores hablaban de lo que esperaban que sus hijos tuvieran cuando fueran grandes. Aquí está lo que dijo cada uno.

(1) Una persona dijo, "Realmente yo creo que mis hijos tengan más de lo que yo he tenido, eso es, si trabajan duro y hacen sus planes con cuidado. Siempre hay buenas oportunidades para los que trabajan duro."

(2) Otra dijo, "Yo no sé si mis hijos vivirán mejor o peor, o lo mismo, que yo he vivido. La vida sube y baja, aún cuando la gente trabaja duro. ¡Así es la vida!"

(3) La tercera dijo, "Yo espero que mis hijos vivan más o menos como yo

he vivido, y que hagan volver la vida como era antes. Es la responsabilidad de los hijos mantener la manera de vivir del pasado."

¿Cuál de estos tres hombres cree usted que tenía el mejor modo de pensar?
¿Cuál opinion escogería en segundo lugar?
La mayor parte de la gente de su edad, ¿con cuál de estos hombres estaría de acuerdo?

ACTITUDES HACIA CONDICIONES   Pregunta No. 6

Hay diferentes modos de pensar sobre las relaciones entre Dios, la naturaleza, y el hombre. Aquí tenemos tres maneras diferentes de pensar.

(1) Alguna gente dice, "Dios, la naturaleza, y el hombre, todos son uno, y deben obrar siempre en conjunto. Solo cuando el hombre vive como se debe para sostener bien esta armonía del conjunto, están buenas las condiciones y el tiempo para las cosechas, los animales, y todo lo que vive."

(2) Otra gente dice, "Los cambios en el tiempo, que traen los años buenos y los años malos, *no* vienen directamente del poder de Dios. Eso es decir, que Dios no usa su poder directamente en estas cosas. Es el hombre mismo, de por sí, que tiene que resolver como obra de la naturaleza. Es *el hombre* quien tiene que buscar modos de vencer los problemas que vienen con el mal tiempo y otras condiciones naturales."

(3) Todavía otra gente dice, "No es el lugar del hombre saber como usa Dios su poder para mandarnos años buenos y años malos. El hombre no debe creer que, con su voluntad, puede él cambiar mucho las cosas de la naturaleza que Dios manda. Tiene que aceptar lo que venga y hacer lo mejor que se pueda."

¿Cuál de estos modos le parece a usted el mejor?
¿Cuál le parece debe ser el segundo?
¿Cuál de estos modos de pensar cree usted que la mayoría de la gente de aquí escogería?

AYUDA EN CASO DE PERDIDA   Pregunta No. 7

Un hombre ha perdido su cosecha, o su ganado. El y su familia van a necesitar ayuda para el invierno. Hay tres diferentes modos en que este hombre puede conseguir ayuda. ¿Cuál debe escoger?

(1) ¿Debe ir a sus hermanos o sus hermanas, ú otros parientes, y de esta manera conseguir la ayuda que necesita de varios parientes?

(2) ¿Debe ir fuera de su placita y conseguir la ayuda, de por sí, de gente que no son ni parientes ni patrones?

(3) ¿O, debe de ir al jefe de la familia o a su patrón, esto es decir, a una persona que está acostumbrada a ver por muchos asuntos de la gente, y pedirle la ayuda que necesita?

¿Qué modo le parece mejor?

De los otros dos modos, ¿cuál le parece mejor?
¿Qué modo escogería la mayor parte de la gente de aquí como el mejor?

ARREGLOS ENTRE FAMILIAS   Pregunta No. 8

Cuando las familias son parientes y viven cerca las unas a las otras, hay tres diferentes modos de hacer la vida y llevarse bien.

(1) Algunas veces, y en algunos lugares es la costumbre de cada familia entre sí (eso es decir, solamente un esposo, su esposa y sus hijos) manejar sus propios negocios enteramente aparte de las familias de los otros hermanos.
(2) Otras veces y en otros lugares hay otra costumbre. En este caso, las familias de todos los hermanos o la mayor parte de éstas, trabajan juntas, y deciden entre sí mismas la mejor manera de arreglar los problemas. Cuando es necesario tener una persona especial para hacerse cargo del trabajo, todos se juntan y deciden entre ellos quién ha de ser.
(3) Todavía en otros lugares hay otra costumbre. Las familias de los hermanos también trabajan juntas, pero en este caso, el hombre mayor—eso es decir el padre o el hermano mayor—si todavía es capaz, es el que decide como se han de hacer los trabajos.

¿Cuál de estos modos de dividir el trabajo le parece mejor?
¿Cuál escogería como el segundo modo?
¿Cuál cree usted que la mayoría de la gente de aquí escogería como el mejor modo?

PARA ESCOGER UN REPRESENTANTE   Pregunta No. 9

Si una placita como ésta, tiene que mandar un delegado o representante a una junta lejos de aquí, como a una junta política o una Convención de Ganaderos, ¿cómo se escoge este delegado?

(1) Algunas veces y en algunos lugares toda la gente se junta para discutir el asunto. Discuten y discuten hasta que casi todo el mundo está de acuerdo. Entonces cuando votan casi todos están conformes con el delegado escogido.
(2) Otras veces y en otros lugares son los jefes o patrones los que toman la mayor parte de la responsabilidad de escoger el delegado, puesto que ellos son los que han tenido más experiencia en estos asuntos.
(3) Todavía en otros lugares la gente se junta, los nombres se proponen, y entonces la gente vota. La persona que recibe la mayoría de los votos es la que representa la placita, aunque haya todavía mucha gente, alguna de importancia, que esté muy disgustada con el delegado escogido.

¿Cuál de estas maneras de escoger un delegado es mejor en casos como este?
¿Cuál manera escogería como la segunda?
¿Cuál escogería, por lo general, la mayoría de la gente como la mejor?

Maneras de sembrar   Pregunta No. 10

Hay tres hombres que siembran cosechas. Cada uno tiene un modo diferente de cuidar su siembra y un modo diferente de vivir.

(1) Uno siembra y trabaja duro, pero él cree que lo más importante para hacer crecer la cosecha (una cosecha buena), es vivir buenamente y en armonía con la naturaleza, eso es decir, vivir completamente unidos con las fuerzas que hacen el calor, el frío, la lluvia, etc., y tienen que ver con todo lo que vive.
(2) El segundo siembra, y después él trabaja lo suficiente para hacer crecer bien su cosecha. Pero este hombre cree que no vale la pena trabajar más de lo necesario; cree que lo que le sucede a la cosecha tiene mucho que ver con el tiempo y el tiempo cambia mucho. Es inútil trabajar más de lo necesario porque uno no puede con el tiempo.
(3) El tercero siembra su cosecha y después trabaja mucho, haciendo uso de los nuevos modos científicos. Este hombre cree de veras, que si uno busca y estudia métodos nuevos se pueden vencer muchos de los males que trae el mal tiempo.

Por lo general, ¿cuál de estos modos de cuidar la siembra cree usted el mejor?
¿Cuál modo escogería como el segundo?
Por lo general, ¿cuál cree usted que la mayoría de la gente creería el mejor?

Filosofia de la vida   Pregunta No. 11

La gente tiene muy diferentes ideas sobre lo pasado y sobre lo que se puede esperar en el futuro en esta vida. Tenemos aquí tres diferentes maneras de pensar sobre esto.

(1) Algunas personas creen que el tiempo hoy en día es el que más necesita nuestra atención. Dicen que el pasado, ya ha pasado y el futuro es demasiado incierto para darle mucha atención. La vida va cambiando pero nadie sabe como va a cambiar—a veces mejora, a veces empeora. Esta gente es la que quiere guardar las costumbres que más les gustan del pasado, cuando es posible. Pero también quiere aceptar lo nuevo que mejora la vida hoy en día.
(2) Otras personas creen que la vida del pasado era mucho mejor. Dicen que los cambios siempre empeoran la vida. Son estas personas las que quieren guardar con cuidado las costumbres viejas y hacerlas volver cuando están perdidas.
(3) Otras personas creen que lo que venga en el futuro tiene que ser, casi siempre, mejor. Dicen que los cambios siempre traen mejoras aunque uno no vea las mejoras inmediatamente. Estas son las personas que hacen planes lejos en el futuro y se sacrifican muchísimo ahora para que el futuro sea mejor.

¿Cuál de estos modos de ver la vida le parece mejor?
¿Cuál de estos modos escogería usted en segundo lugar?

¿Cuál de estos modos cree usted que la mayoría de la gente de aquí escogería?

Modos de trabajar   Pregunta No. 12

Hay tres modos de trabajar para personas que no emplean trabajadores ellos mismos.

(1) Un modo es trabajar por sí mismo. En este caso el hombre es su propio amo. El decide casi todos los asuntos él mismo y su éxito depende en sí mismo. El solo tiene que ver por sí y no espera ayuda de otros.
(2) El segundo modo es trabajar con otros hombres donde todos trabajan juntos sin tener algún jefe especial. Cada hombre tiene algo que decir sobre los asuntos del negocio y todos los hombres pueden contar uno con el otro.
(3) El tercer modo es trabajar por un patrón o un jefe. En este caso los empleados no toman parte en los asuntos del negocio, pero tienen la confianza que el patrón les ayudará en muchos diferentes modos.

¿Cuál de estos modos es el mejor para un hombre que no emplea trabajadores?
¿Cuál modo escogería usted en segundo lugar?
¿Cuál de estos modos le parece que la mayoría de los otros escogerían?

Se puede vencer el tiempo, etc.   Pregunta No. 13

Tres hombres de diferentes lugares estaban hablando de lo que puede' o no puede, cambiar el mal tiempo y otras condiciones de la naturaleza. Cada uno dijo algo diferente.

(1) Uno dijo, "La gente mía no cree que el hombre tiene el poder de cambiar o vencer la lluvia, el viento, o las otras condiciones naturales. Estas condiciones son las que hacen las sequías y las inundaciones—los años buenos, y los años malos. Creen que estas cosas son como son, y es mucho mejor cuando todos aceptan lo que viene y hacen lo mejor que se puede."
(2) Otro dijo, "La gente mía, de veras cree que la obligación de la gente es buscar modos para vencer el tiempo y otras condiciones naturales como han vencido otras cosas. Ellos aún creen que algún día van a hallar modos para vencer las secas y las inundaciones."
(3) El otro dijo, "La gente mía cree que si uno se va a llevar bien en la vida, es necesario vivir en armonía con la naturaleza. Esto es decir, se tiene que vivir buenamente en todo lo de la vida. También se tiene que vigilar con mucho cuidado todo lo que nos da la naturaleza—por ejemplo, la tierra, el agua, y todo lo que crece."

¿Cuál de estos tres hombres cree usted tiene el mejor modo de pensar?
¿Cuál opinión escogería en segundo lugar?
¿Cuál de estos modos de pensar cree usted que la mayoría de la otra gente de aqui pensaría el mejor?

Cambios religiosos   Pregunta No. 14

La gente en una placita como ésta, notaron que las costumbres religiosas y las fiestas religiosas iban cambiando de como eran. Diferentes personas tenían diferentes opiniones sobre estos cambios.

(1) A algunas personas le gustaron mucho estos cambios. Esta gente cree que las nuevas costumbres, por lo general, son mejores que las costumbres viejas, y quieren seguir lo nuevo en todas las cosas, aún en las costumbres religiosas.
(2) Otra gente estaba muy perturbada con los cambios de las costumbres religiosas y las fiestas religiosas. Esta gente quiere guardar las costumbres exactamente como eran en al pasado.
(3) Todavía a otra gente le gustan las costumbres religiosas y las fiestas religiosas del pasado, pero saben que no es posible guardarlas exactamente. Esta gente cree que la vida es mucho más facil cuando se aceptan los cambios que vienen con el tiempo.

¿Cuál de estos modos de pensar es más como usted piensa?
¿Cuál modo escogería el segundo?
¿Cuál de estos modos de pensar le parece que la mayoría de la gente de aquí piensa?

Maneras de vivir   Pregunta No. 15

Dos personas están hablando de como les gustaría vivir, y cada una tiene diferentes ideas.

(1) Una dijo, "Lo que más me importa a mí, es acabar muchas cosas y hacerlas tán bien o mejor que los demás. Me gusta ver resultados y creo que vale la pena trabajar para conseguirlos."
(2) La otra persona dijo, "Lo que más me importa a mí, es que me dejen solo, para pensar y hacer las cosas de la manera que mejor me cae a mí. Sí no siempre tengo resultados, pero puedo gozar de la vida de día en día esto me parece el mejor modo de vivir."

¿Cuál de estas dos personas, cree usted tiene la mejor manera de pensar?
¿Cuál de estas dos personas es más como usted?
¿Cuál de estas maneras de pensar cree usted que la mayoría de la gente escogería?

Herencia de ganado   Pregunta No. 16

Cuando una persona anciana, que tiene ganado (vacas y ovejas) se muere, las familias manejan el ganado de distintos modos. Si los hijos ya son grandes y viven cerca uno al otro, hay tres maneras de manejar el negocio.

(1) Algunas veces y en algunos lugares es la costumbre que el hombre mayor—eso es decir el hijo mayor—si todavía es capaz, maneja el negocio para todos, lo que es de él, y de todos los demás hermanos.
(2) Otras veces y en otros lugares hay otra costumbre. Cada uno de los

hijos y de las hijas, toma lo que le toca y lo maneja como un negocio completamente separado de los hermanos.
(3) Todavía en otros lugares, hay todavía otra costumbre. Todos los hijos y las hijas tienen el ganado juntos y manejan el negocio juntos. Cuando se necesita a alguien para hacer decisiones o tomar cargo del negocio, se reúnen todos y escogen entre ellos a esta persona. Esta persona puede ser cualquiera.

¿Qué costumbre le parece a usted la mejor?
De las otras dos costumbres, ¿cuál le parece a usted mejor?
¿Qué costumbre cree usted que la mayoría de la gente escogería como la mejor?

Propiedades   Pregunta No. 17

Cuando muere un padre o una madre dejando propiedades a hijos que ya son mayores de edad y viven cerca unos a otros, hay tres modos de manejar los terrenos.

Ahora tengo la misma pregunta que hacerle sobre los terrenos en vez del ganado.

(1) Algunas veces y en algunos lugares es la costumbre que el hombre mayor—eso es decir, el hijo mayor—si todavía es capaz, tome cargo del terreno que le toca a él y el terreno que les toca a todos los hermanos.
(2) Otras veces y en otros lugares hay otra costumbre. Cada uno de los hijos y las hijas recibe su parte de los terrenos y hace lo que quiere con lo que le toca, sin consultar con los otros.
(3) Todavía en otros lugares hay otra costumbre. En este caso, todos los hijos y las hijas usan el terreno juntos, sin que ninguno sea jefe. Cuando se necesita a alguien para hacer decisiones o tomar cargo del negocio, se reunen todos y escogen a la persona. Esta persona puede ser cualquiera de los hermanos.

¿Cuál le parece a usted la mejor costumbre?
De las otras costumbres, ¿cuál le parece a usted mejor?
¿Qué costumbre cree usted que la mayoría de la gente escogería como la mejor?

Sembradores   Pregunta No. 18

Dos hombres que tienen siembra, viven muy diferentemente, uno al otro.

(1) Uno da a su siembra el cuidado que es necesario pero no cree que debe darle a la siembra más tiempo de lo necesario. Prefiere tener horas libres para andar de visita con sus amigos, andar de paseo, y hacer otras cosas que le divierten. Esta manera de vivir es la que le gusta más a él.
(2) El otro trabaja con su siembra casi todo el tiempo. Siempre está sacando hierbas, escarbando y trabajando, porque al trabajar de esta manera no tiene mucho tiempo de andar de visita o de viaje, o di-

vertirse de otros modos. Esta manera de vivir es la que le gusta más a este hombre.

¿Cuál de estos hombres es mejor ser?
¿Cuál de estos hombres se parece más a usted?
¿Cuál de estos modos de vivir escogería la mayoría de la otra gente de aquí como mejor?

SE PODRA VIVIR MAS ANOS   Pregunta No. 19

Tres hombres hablaban sobre la cuestión de si se podía hacer la vida del hombre más larga.

(1) Uno dijo, "Es verdad que el hombre de por sí, ya está aprendiendo modos de hacer la vida más larga. Hay medicinas de los doctores, también el estudio de alimentos propios, y otras cosas como las vacunas. Si los hombres dan buena atención a estas cosas, la vida, seguramente, va a ser más larga."
(2) Otro dijo, "Realmente, yo no creo que el hombre, de por sí, pueda hacer mucho para hacer la vida de la gente más larga. Yo creo que todo el mundo tiene ciertos años de vida, y, cuando llega su hora, llega."
(3) El tercero dijo, "Pues *yo* creo que hay un gran plan de la vida entera, que obra para adelantar todo el conjunto. Los hombres que comprenden este plan y aprenden a vivir en acuerdo con este plan, tendrán una vida más larga que los hombres que no lo siguen."

¿Con cuál de estas tres opiniones esta usted más en acuerdo?
¿Cuál escogería usted como la segunda?
¿Cuál escogería la mayor parte de la gente de aquí?

ARREGLOS DEL AGUA   Pregunta No. 20

Digamos (vamos a decir) que una placita como esta tiene una noria que se necesita limpiar y arreglar para conseguir más agua. El gobierno va a ayudar a la placita, y quiere que la placita haga un plan para dividir el agua que venga. Pero, puesto que nadie sabe cuanta agua va a haber, la gente tiene diferentes opiniones sobre el plan. Aquí hay tres opiniones.

(1) Algunos dicen que el plan para dividir el agua debe ser el mismo que han tenido siempre en el pasado.
(2) Otros quieren hacer un plan nuevo de antemano, de veras bueno, para dividir cualquier cantidad de agua que venga.
(3) Todavía otros dicen que es mucho mejor esperar, y ver cuanta agua llega antes de hacer el plan.

¿Cuál de estos modos cree usted que es el mejor en estos casos?
¿Cuál de estos modos escogería usted en segundo lugar?
¿Cuál de estos modos cree usted que a la mayoría de la otra gente de aquí le gustaría más?

Trabajo de casa   Pregunta No. 21

Había dos mujeres que hablaban de la manera en que les gustaría vivir.

(1) Una dijo, "No me importa a mí trabajar en mi casa tanto como la mayoría de las otras mujeres, pero no me gustaría pasar mucho tiempo haciendo cosas que no son necesarias, como bordar, coser, lavar, o limpiar lo de la casa demasiado seguido. En vez de pasar tanto tiempo haciendo estas cosas, prefiero tener tiempo libre para platicar con mis amigas, salir de paseo, y gozar de la vida."

(2) La otra dijo, "Pues lo que a mi me gusta más, es estar ocupada casi siempre, haciendo muchas cosas que no son de veras necesarias, como bordar, coser, lavar, o limpiar o pintar la casa. Estoy más contenta trabajando."

¿Cuál de estos modos de vivir le parece mejor para las mujeres?
¿A cuál se parece usted más?
¿Qué modo de vivir escogerían las otras mujeres de aquí como el mejor?

Horas libres   Pregunta No. 22

Dos hombres pasan sus horas libres, eso es decir, las horas cuando no están trabajando, en diferentes modos.

(1) Un hombre usa la mayor parte de sus horas libres aprendiendo o probando cosas nuevas que le puedan ayudar en su trabajo.

(2) El otro prefiere pasar sus horas libres divirtiéndose, platicando, contando cuentos, o, quizás, cantando.

¿Cuál de estos hombres tiene el mejor modo de vivir?
¿Cuál de estos dos modos de vivir escogería la mayoría de la otra gente de aquí como el mejor?

APPENDIX 2

Further Notes on the Graphic Analysis of Ranked Value Preferences

The present appendix consists largely of an expansion of selected algebraic details relating to the graphic analysis. While these materials are not essential to the substantive argument of the book, they will nevertheless be of value to persons who contemplate making an independent use of these ranking methods.

In sections 1 and 2 the step in the development of the graphic method which consists of the derivation of the transformation used to set a radius equal to a given significance level in two-dimensional space is given in detail. In section 3 an empirical instance of an underlying frequency surface is shown to indicate what is involved if a directional hypothesis like $C > B > A$ is to be tested. In addition, the frequency diagram indicates the roughness of the grain of the underlying frequencies. This latter point is built upon in section 4 where it is shown that there are slight biases in the correspondence between the radius at which the .05 circle falls and the actual frequencies due to the step character of frequency intervals. Fortunately, when one has twenty or more respondents this bias is negligible. These first four sections constitute the part of this appendix which is an addendum to the first part of Chapter IV.

The remaining sections go beyond Chapter IV to establish the basis for the direct factor analysis used in Chapter VII. In section 5 an algebraic simplification for the computation of the average rank-order correlation between two sets of respondents is presented. In the simple case of the responses by different cultures to the same question, it is empirically demonstrated that a factor analysis of the between-culture average rank-order correlations reproduces, after a slight rotation and change of scale, the original plottings. Then, in section 6, it is demonstrated that a direct factor analysis of the original a, b, c vectors offers a way of working with composite data on several orientations. We conclude the appendix with the details of the use of this technique to identify persons who were in differing degrees central to the core of common Mormon-Texan values.

1. THE TRANSFORMATION OF RANK DEVIATION TO CARTESIAN COORDINATES

Given three axes, a, b, and c, which with reference to the x-axis are defined as

a with positive direction of 90°,

b with positive direction of 210°,

c with positive direction of 330°,

then the Cartesian coordinates (x, y) are given by

$$x = a \cos 90° + b \cos 210° + c \cos 330°,$$
$$y = a \sin 90° + b \sin 210° + c \cos 330°.$$

Since $\cos 90° = 0$, $\sin 90° = 1$, $\cos 30° = -\cos 210° = \cos 330°$, and $\sin 30° = -\sin 210° = -\sin 330°$, we have

$$x = (c - b) \cos 30°,$$
$$y = a - (b + c) \sin 30°,$$

or, since $\cos 30° = \sqrt{3}/2$ and $\sin 30° = \tfrac{1}{2}$,

$$x = \frac{\sqrt{3}(c - b)}{2},$$
$$y = a - \frac{b + c}{2}.$$

If we identify our axes a, b, and c with the $(2m - A)$, $(2m - B)$, and $(2m - C)$ rank deviations defined in Chapter IV, the points in which we are interested satisfy the added condition, $a + b + c = 0$ or $b + c = -a$. Under this condition the Cartesian coordinates of such points simplify to

$$x = \frac{\sqrt{3}(c - b)}{2},$$
$$y = \frac{3a}{2}.$$

2. THE RELATIONSHIP BETWEEN S AND r

Our objective is to employ our two basic identities,

$$a + b + c = 0, \tag{1}$$
$$a^2 + b^2 + c^2 = S, \tag{2}$$

and the transformations to Cartesian coordinates,

$$x = \frac{\sqrt{3}(c - b)}{2}, \tag{3}$$
$$y = \frac{3a}{2}, \tag{4}$$

to express the relationship of r, the radius of a circle centered at the origin, to S. Note first:

$$r = \sqrt{x^2 + y^2}. \tag{5}$$

It is desirable to find the coordinates of a point relative to the axes a, b, and c when we know its Cartesian coordinates, i.e., to find (a, b, c) when (x, y) is known, subject to the condition (1).

From (4),

$$a = \frac{2y}{3}. \tag{6}$$

From (1),

$$c - b = -2b - a.$$

And substituting into (3),

$$a + 2b = \frac{-2x}{\sqrt{3}}.$$

Using (6),

$$2b = -\frac{2x}{\sqrt{3}} - \frac{2y}{3}$$

or

$$b = -\frac{y}{3} - \frac{x}{\sqrt{3}}. \tag{7}$$

Again using (1),

$$c = -a - b,$$

and from (6) and (7),

$$c = -\frac{2y}{3} + \frac{y}{3} + \frac{x}{\sqrt{3}}$$

$$= \frac{x}{\sqrt{3}} - \frac{y}{3}.$$

Thus,

$$a = \frac{2y}{3},$$

$$b = -\frac{x}{\sqrt{3}} - \frac{y}{3},$$

$$c = \frac{x}{\sqrt{3}} - \frac{y}{3}.$$

Consequently,
$$S = a^2 + b^2 + c^2$$
$$= \frac{4y^2}{9} + \left(-\frac{x}{\sqrt{3}} - \frac{y}{3}\right)^2 + \left(\frac{x}{\sqrt{3}} - \frac{y}{3}\right)^2$$
$$= \frac{4y^2}{9} + \frac{2x^2}{3} + \frac{2y^2}{9}$$
$$= \frac{2(x^2 + y^2)}{3}.$$

From (5),
$$S = \frac{2r^2}{3}$$
or
$$r = \sqrt{\frac{3S}{2}}.$$

The more general result
$$r = \sqrt{\frac{nS}{n-1}}$$
has been demonstrated by Mr. Brian Gluss.

To show the effects of dividing through by m, the number of rankings, let $a' = a/\sqrt{m}$, $b' = b/\sqrt{m}$, and $c' = c/\sqrt{m}$ designate coordinates with respect to a', b', and c', and use the same arguments as above. This gives
$$S' = (a')^2 + (b')^2 + (c')^2$$
$$= \frac{a^2}{m} + \frac{b^2}{m} + \frac{c^2}{m}$$
$$= \frac{S}{m},$$
and
$$(r')^2 = \frac{3S'}{2} = \frac{3S}{2m}$$
or
$$r' = \sqrt{\frac{3S}{2m}}.$$

It may be noted from Table IV:2 that for a given level of significance $\sqrt{3S/2m}$ is approximately constant.

3. THE DIRECTIONAL HYPOTHESIS

Let us assume that an investigator were able to state in advance of his data collection that he was interested in evaluating the null hypothesis against a particular ordering, say $C > B > A$.

To illustrate the problem, the 6^8 rankings of eight sets of three alternatives have been computed, transformed to (x, y) coordinates, and plotted with their observed frequency on Graph A2:1. It may be demonstrated that as m, the number of rankings, increases, the center frequencies become heavier, and the margins expand to cover greater area. The top left dot represents the situation where all eight rankings favor $A > B > C$; five similar dots with similar frequencies occur elsewhere. The greatest density occurs at the origin, for there are many different ways in which the sums of the columns for A, B, and C ranks can be even. Study of this distribution suggests an interesting modification of the usual "equally likely" null hypothesis for the investigator who is willing to predict a particular ordering in advance.

GRAPH A2:1
THE FREQUENCY DISTRIBUTION OF EIGHT THREE-ALTERNATIVE RANKINGS

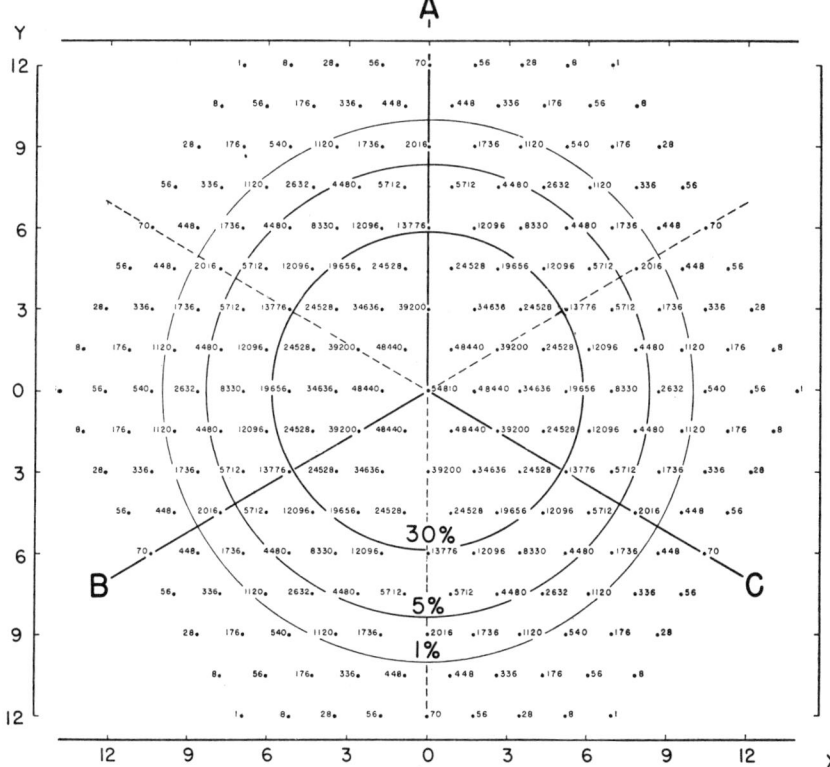

384 VARIATIONS IN VALUE ORIENTATIONS

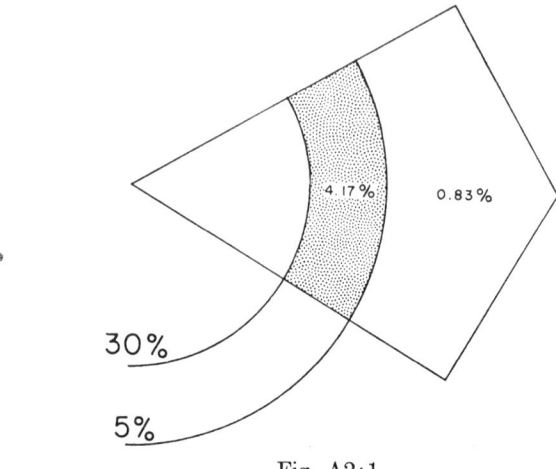

Fig. A2:1

Note, after distributing the frequencies of the points exactly on the dividing lines, one-sixth of the total frequency is to be found in each sector. Therefore, if one predicts in advance a particular ordering, he will have a chance of being correct one time in six. The one-in-six relationship represents a probability level of 0.167. To accept a directed, or directional, hypothesis at the conventional .05 level it is necessary to use a criterion which goes beyond the requirement of having the outcome be located in a particular sector. The required further criterion is easily supplied. If one determines a circle such that 30 per cent of all observations fall beyond it, then the area in a sector outside the circle will contain one-sixth of 30 per cent, or .05 of the total frequency.

To illustrate the relative shape of the "acceptance" area, the reader may inspect the area beyond the 30 per cent circle and within a specific sector on Graph A2:1. As shown in Figure A2:1, this total area is 5 per cent of the total frequencies. Five-sixths of this 5 per cent of the frequencies are found within the 5 per cent circle. If the path of successive trials were in the given sector, then an experimenter might reject his null hypothesis in the intermediate range, and effect a general economy in the number of trials. The "gain" is not further formalized here because it is not clear that the sector boundaries would necessarily be the best way to define acceptance limits.

4. PROBABILITY-LEVEL APPROXIMATIONS AND TIED RANKS

Due to the fact that frequencies are not continuous, a division of the frequency surface cannot in all cases be made so that it will divide the frequencies exactly in accordance with the desired probability level. For the $m = 8$, $n = 3$ surface given in Graph A2:1, one has difficulty in hitting exactly on the .01 and .05 levels. When one determines the radius by the technique specified, the frequencies obtained are best approximations, which slightly underestimate the frequency in the target area. If bias is to be present, this is a conservative way for it to operate. The dangers of a systematic error decrease as m increases and even when $m = 8$ the discrepancy is not great at the .01 level for the data in Graph A2:1.

Target Level	Actual Level	Per Cent in Next Increment
.01	.0098986	.009
.05	.0469071	.016
.30	.2851104	.072

It should be quite apparent that our heuristic computation did not involve the possibility of ties; if it had, the points would have been denser and their relative frequency less. When ties are obtained in the respondent's report, this offers no complication in plotting, for, as was previously indicated, the sum of the ranks occupied by the tied alternatives is simply distributed evenly between them. Kendall[1] has shown that the effect of ties is quite small in comparable situations, and in the present study only 6 per cent of all responses were tied.

5. AVERAGE CORRELATION BETWEEN SETS OF RANKINGS

The correlation between two rankings may be described by Spearman's coefficient, denoted by the Greek letter ρ (rho), which is defined as

$$\rho = 1 - \frac{6d^2}{n^3 - n},$$

where d is the difference of paired ranks. The computation may be illustrated with two arbitrary rankings:

	#1	#2	d	d^2
A	1	2	−1	1
B	2	3	−1	1
C	3	1	2	4
			0	6

$$\rho = 1 - \frac{6(6)}{27 - 3} = -0.5$$

The coefficient is 1 when the correspondence is perfect, 0 when there is no relation, and −1 when the two series are ordered in opposite directions. Kendall has previously shown that if more than two sets of values are in-

---

[1] Maurice G. Kendall, *Rank Correlation Methods*, 2d ed. (New York: Hafner Publishing Co., 1955), p. 100.

volved, the average rho (ave ρ) for all pairs can be determined from S. The required formulae are

$$\text{ave } \rho = \frac{mW - 1}{m - 1},$$

where W, the coefficient of concordance, is defined

$$W = \frac{12S}{m^2(n^3 - n)},$$

where S is the sum of squares of the actual deviations. The ave ρ for all pairs of Mormon respondents for item R1 may be determined from the values of Table IV:1 in this manner:

$$S = 316.50, \quad m = 20, \quad n = 3,$$

$$W = \frac{12(316.50)}{20 \cdot 20(27 - 3)} = \frac{316.50}{800} = 0.396,$$

$$\text{ave } \rho_M = \frac{20(0.396) - 1}{20 - 1} = \frac{6.92}{19} = 0.364.$$

The comparable value for the Texans is

$$\text{ave } \rho_T = \frac{20(0.41) - 1}{20 - 1} = 0.376.$$

It is not surprising to find that both groups have high and apparently significant within-group average rank correlations. It is possible to compute the between-group correlations by obtaining the ave ρ for Mormons and Texans taken together, then subtract the weighted within-group correlations among Mormons and the weighted within-group correlations among Texans from the average correlation between all pairs. To illustrate this computation, ave ρ for Mormons and Texans combined is first computed:

	a	b	c
Mormon	−14.5	6.5	8.0
Texan	−14.0	3.0	11.0
Combined	−28.5	9.5	19.0

$$S = (-28.5)^2 + (9.5)^2 + (19.0)^2 = 1263.50,$$

$$W = \frac{12(1263.50)}{40 \cdot 40(27 - 3)} = \frac{1263.50}{3200} = 0.395,$$

$$\text{ave } \rho_{M+T} = \frac{40(0.395) - 1}{40 - 1} = \frac{14.8}{39} = 0.379.$$

In the present case the combined ave ρ_{M+T} may be assumed to be based upon the correlations between $m_1 + m_2$ rankings taken two at a time. For Texans alone, and Mormons alone, the number of correlations is $20(20 - 1)/2$.

To substitute a more compact general notation, we use the binomial coefficient notation $\binom{m_1}{2}$ and $\binom{m_2}{2}$ for m_1 or m_2 items taken two at a time.

$$\binom{m_1+m_2}{2} \text{ ave } \rho_{1+2} - \left[\binom{m_1}{2} \text{ ave } \rho_1 + \binom{m_2}{2} \text{ ave } \rho_2\right] = m_1 m_2 \text{ ave } \rho_{1:2}.$$

The 1:2 subscript is introduced to describe the correlations, taken two at a time, *between* (not *within*) groups. To illustrate:

$$\text{ave } \rho_{M+T} = 0.379, \quad \text{ave } \rho_M = 0.364, \quad \text{ave } \rho_T = 0.376,$$

and

$$\binom{40}{2} = 780, \quad \binom{20}{2} = 190, \quad m_1 m_2 = 400.$$

So

$$780\,(0.379) - [190\,(0.364) + 190\,(0.376)] = 400 \text{ ave } \rho_{M:T}$$

$$\text{ave } \rho_{M:T} = \frac{155.0}{400} = 0.388.$$

Though it is not clear how one might appraise the significance of such correlation between sets of rankings, it is apparent that Mormons and Texans agree with one another to about the same degree that they do with members of their own group.

6. VECTOR ANALYSIS OF RANKINGS COMPARED WITH FACTOR ANALYSIS OF AVERAGE RHO

Proceeding by the method outlined in section 5, it is possible to compute the between-culture correlation for all ten pairs of the five cultures. For the Well Arrangements item (R1) given in detail in Chapter IV, the matrix of between-culture average rank correlations is as follows:

	N	Z	SA	T
Mormon	.107	.209	−.082	.388
Navaho		.044	−.065	.032
Zuni			−.043	.210
Spanish-American				−.078

With the data arranged in this form, one might well be tempted to factor the matrix to determine the relative position of the cultures on the principal dimensions obtained. In the context of the present discussion, one objective of factoring the matrix would be to determine what similarity, if any, there would be between the factor plot and the original plotting of the rankings developed in Chapter IV. To illustrate, factoring by the principal-components method produces the following unrotated loadings.

Culture	Factor	
	I	II
Mormon	.617	−.019
Navaho	.152	−.413
Zuni	.323	.015
Spanish-American	−.131	.079
Texan	.613	.130

With a slight rotation and an appropriate choice of scale values, it may be shown that factoring the between-culture correlation essentially reproduces the original ranking chart in Chapter IV.

It thus becomes apparent that instead of the factor analysis, one might more economically work on the vectors associated with a, b, and c. To illustrate this, the earlier formulae for ave ρ and ave $\rho_{1:2}$ may be simplified.

Let

$$k = \frac{12}{n^3 - n}.$$

Then

$$W = \frac{12S}{(n^3 - n)m^2} = \frac{kS}{m^2}$$

and

$$\text{ave } \rho = \frac{mW - 1}{m - 1} = \frac{\frac{kS}{m} - 1}{m - 1}$$

$$= \frac{kS - m}{2\binom{m}{2}}.$$

Hence, rewriting the formula given at the end of section 5,

$$m_1 m_2 \text{ ave } \rho_{1:2} = \binom{m_1 + m_2}{2} \frac{kS_{1+2} - (m_1 + m_2)}{2\binom{m_1 + m_2}{2}} - \binom{m_1}{2} \frac{kS_1 - m_1}{2\binom{m_1}{2}}$$

$$- \binom{m_1}{2} \frac{kS_2 - m_2}{2\binom{m_2}{2}}$$

or

$$\text{ave } \rho_{1:2} = \frac{k}{2m_1 m_2} (S_{1+2} - S_1 - S_2 - m_1 - m_2 + m_1 + m_2)$$

$$= \frac{k}{2m_1 m_2} (S_{1+2} - S_1 - S_2).$$

Since $n = 3$, $k = \frac{1}{2}$, and we have
$$\text{ave } \rho_{1:2} = \frac{S_{1+2} - S_1 - S_2}{4m_1 m_2}.$$

Employing vector notation,
$$S_1 = a_1^2 + b_1^2 + c_1^2 = \mathbf{u} \cdot \mathbf{u},$$
$$S_2 = a_2^2 + b_2^2 + c_2^2 = \mathbf{v} \cdot \mathbf{v},$$

where
$$\mathbf{u} = (a_1, b_1, c_1),$$
$$\mathbf{v} = (a_2, b_2, c_2).$$

Then
$$\begin{aligned} S_{1+2} &= (a_1 + a_2)^2 + (b_1 + b_2)^2 + (c_1 + c_2)^2 \\ &= (a_1^2 + b_1^2 + c_1^2) + (a_2^2 + b_2^2 + c_2^2) + 2(a_1 a_2 + b_1 b_2 + c_1 c_2) \\ &= \mathbf{u} \cdot \mathbf{u} + \mathbf{v} \cdot \mathbf{v} + 2\mathbf{u} \cdot \mathbf{v} \\ &= (\mathbf{u} + \mathbf{v}) \cdot (\mathbf{u} + \mathbf{v}), \end{aligned}$$

where
$$\mathbf{u} + \mathbf{v} = (a_1 + a_2, b_1 + b_2, c_1 + c_2).$$

Thus
$$\begin{aligned} \text{ave } \rho_{1:2} &= \frac{1}{4m_1 m_2} [(\mathbf{u} + \mathbf{v}) \cdot (\mathbf{u} + \mathbf{v}) - (\mathbf{u} \cdot \mathbf{u}) - (\mathbf{v} \cdot \mathbf{v})] \\ &= \frac{2\mathbf{u} \cdot \mathbf{v}}{4m_1 m_2} \\ &= \frac{\mathbf{u}}{\sqrt{2m_1}} \cdot \frac{\mathbf{v}}{\sqrt{2m_2}}, \end{aligned}$$

which explicitly gives the factoring for the matrix of average between-culture correlations.[2]

The mapping of ranking results onto a vector system has the general utility of opening the use of various methods of analysis suitable for linear spaces. In the present context we are primarily interested in the factor analytic application which will be discussed in the next section.[3]

---

[2] John Tukey and John Gilbert both gave helpful suggestions in connection with this proof.

[3] One is reminded by this result of L. L. Thurstone's suggestion in the introduction to *Multiple Factor Analysis* (Chicago: University of Chicago Press, 1947) that nonmetric factor analyses deserve further investigation.

7. DEFINING PERSONS WITH COMMON MORMON-TEXAN VALUES BY DIRECT FACTOR ANALYSIS

In Chapter VII we encountered the problem of identifying the segment of the Mormon-Texan population which accounted for the observed value-orientation differences. We identified selected individuals as being less central and noted that Mormon males, as a class, seemed to be differentiated by their greater emphasis on the With-Nature alternative of the *man-nature* orientation and the Collaterality alternative of the *relational* orientation. To carry out this computation we built upon the vector approach of the previous section in the following way.

First we took from Appendix 4 the composite individual value scores for the twenty Mormons and twenty Texans on each of the four orientations and, using the (x, y) transformation described in section 1 of Appendix 2, formed the data matrix on the next page.

We consider the data as an m by n matrix X. Such a matrix can be shown to be the product of two vectors, u and v^t, where u and v are column and row vectors respectively and v^t is the transpose of v; i.e., $X = uv^t$. The u and v^t used minimize

$$\sum_{ij}(X_{ij} - u_i v_j)^2$$

and

$$u = \frac{Xv^t}{N^2 v}, \quad v = \frac{u^t X}{N^2 u}.$$

The vectors u and v^t are determinate to a scalar constant; that is, multiplying one by a constant and dividing the other by the same constant leaves the solution unchanged. The notation N^2 above is an abbreviation for "norm-squared," the constant formed by squaring and adding the components of the vector.

If we alternately premultiply X by u^t and postmultiply by v^t, we initiate a procedure which is to a degree analogous to the extraction of principal components (axes which successively minimize the sum of squares) by Hotelling's iterative method.[4] The steps in the procedure are as follows:[5]

$$u_i = X v_i^t, \quad (1)$$

$$v_{i+1} = u_i^t X. \quad (2)$$

Substituting (2) in (1), after taking the transpose ($v_{i+1}{}^t = X^t u_i$) and raising i by unity in (1),

$$u_{i+1} = XX^t u_i. \quad (3)$$

---

[4] Harold Hotelling, "Analysis of a Complex Statistical Variable into Principal Components," *Journal of Educational Psychology*, Vol. XXIV (1933), pp. 417–41, 498–520.

[5] Adapted from Duncan MacRae, Jr., "Direct Factor Analysis of Sociometric Data," *Sociometry*, Vol. XXIII (1960), pp. 360–71.

Composite Orientation Coordinates by Mormon and Texan Individuals

(a) Data Matrix, X_0 Sum of Squares = 5359.7036

Individual		relational		Orientation time		man-nature		activity
		x	y	x	y	x	y	x
Male	M1	−0.4	−3.8	2.2	−5.3	−0.4	−5.3	0.33
	M2	8.7	−6.0	0	−1.5	−1.3	−0.8	0.33
	M3	1.7	−6.0	−3.0	−2.3	1.7	3.0	0.67
	M4	−4.3	−10.5	3.9	−3.8	0.9	−1.5	0
	M5	−0.9	−1.5	−3.9	0.8	3.5	−1.5	0.50
	M6	1.7	−9.0	−2.6	−4.5	3.5	0	0.50
	M7	0	−3.0	−0.9	−1.5	3.5	−6.0	0.17
	M8	3.0	−9.8	−0.9	−4.5	−1.7	1.5	0.50
	M9	2.2	−5.3	1.7	−7.5	−0.9	−7.5	0
	M10	0.9	−10.5	0.9	−7.5	−3.5	−1.5	0.33
	M20	0	−9.0	−3.5	−3.0	−3.5	−6.0	0.50
Female	M11	4.3	−7.5	4.3	−4.5	−0.9	−1.5	0.17
	M12	3.5	−6.0	3.0	3.8	0	−3.0	0.67
	M13	2.6	−10.5	1.3	−6.8	0	−6.0	0
	M14	5.6	−8.3	−2.6	−4.5	0	0	0.33
	M15	4.3	−7.5	1.7	−3.0	2.6	−1.5	0.17
	M16	6.1	−7.5	3.0	−6.8	−3.5	−3.0	0.33
	M17	2.6	−7.5	0	−6.0	−5.2	−3.0	0.33
	M18	5.2	−3.0	3.0	−0.8	−0.4	−5.3	0.08
	M19	5.2	−6.0	−0.9	−4.5	1.7	0	0
Male	T1	5.6	−8.3	1.7	−6.0	−6.1	−1.5	0.17
	T2	6.1	−7.5	4.3	−7.5	−5.2	−3.0	0.25
	T3	5.2	−6.0	0	−3.0	−4.3	1.5	0.17
	T4	4.3	−7.5	2.6	−7.5	−8.7	0	0.17
	T5	5.2	−9.0	1.7	0	−3.0	−6.8	0.08
	T6	3.9	−6.8	2.6	−6.0	−7.4	−2.3	0.25
	T7	5.2	−7.5	0.9	−6.0	−0.9	−7.5	0.33
	T8	−4.3	−4.5	−1.7	−3.0	4.8	−3.8	0.67
	T9	5.2	−9.0	−2.6	−7.5	5.2	−3.0	0.67
	T10	6.5	−9.8	−0.4	−5.3	−3.5	6.0	0.92
Female	T11	−2.6	−4.5	−0.9	−4.5	−3.5	0	0.50
	T12	8.7	−6.0	−0.9	−4.5	−5.2	−4.5	0.25
	T13	7.8	−7.5	0.9	−4.5	−6.1	−4.5	0
	T14	4.3	−7.5	−2.6	−4.5	0	3.0	0.58
	T15	3.9	−8.3	−0.9	−1.5	1.7	−3.0	0.33
	T16	2.6	−4.5	1.3	−5.3	0.9	−1.5	0.50
	T17	7.8	−4.5	−1.7	−6.0	−0.9	−1.5	0.67
	T18	5.6	−8.3	0.4	−6.8	−1.7	−3.0	0.33
	T19	3.5	−9.0	0	0	−1.7	−3.0	0.25
	T20	8.7	−6.0	1.7	−6.0	−8.2	−0.8	0

This iterative procedure converges when u_{i+1} equals u_i, within a constant multiplicative factor λ, to a desired degree of tolerance. Similarly,

$$v_i X^t X = v_{i+1} \qquad (4)$$

also converges as (3) converges. If λ is considered the multiplicative constant applied to the right-hand side of (3) or (4), then at convergence the index i can be substituted for $i + 1$, u and v are conjugate eigenvectors of XX^t and X^tX respectively, and λ is the eigenvalue associated with both. The value of the eigenvalue is

$$\lambda = N^2 u N^2 v,$$

where

$$N^2 u = \sum_{j=1}^{N} u_j^2$$

and

$$N^2 v = \sum_{j=1}^{N} v_j^2.$$

In ordinary (R-type) factor analysis, no attention is paid to v because the correlation matrix is standardized by rows. But when the rows and columns of the data matrix are standardized to the same mean and Σ, the R and Q techniques yield the same factors. In the present case we are concerned with orientation dimensions and individual locations; hence it is not helpful to think of a dimension made of certain clusters of individuals, even though such factors could be meaningfully extracted.[6] The first step in the analysis is to determine the two vectors u_i and $v_i{}^t$ such that they will minimize $N^2(X_0 - u_1 v_1{}^t)$—the sum of squares indicated above. The values in the present case are given on the next page.

[6] See Madow in R. B. Cattell, *Factor Analysis* (New York: Harper & Bros., 1952), p. 98.

$$u_1 = \begin{matrix}
1046 \\
1477 \\
0790 \\
1278 \\
-0066 \\
1345 \\
0530 \\
1694 \\
1654 \\
2057 \\
1596 \\
1635 \\
1361 \\
2140 \\
1662 \\
1357 \\
2076 \\
1819 \\
0990 \\
1315 \\
2111 \\
2208 \\
1394 \\
2103 \\
1770 \\
1911 \\
1991 \\
0397 \\
2260 \\
1908 \\
0826 \\
1982 \\
2148 \\
1377 \\
1374 \\
1135 \\
1581 \\
2040 \\
1456 \\
2108
\end{matrix}
\qquad v_1{}^t = \begin{matrix}
0670 \\
-1163 \\
0094 \\
-0765 \\
-0395 \\
-0353 \\
0047
\end{matrix}$$

394   VARIATIONS IN VALUE ORIENTATIONS

When we subtract from X_0 the product of $u_1v_1{}^t$, the extraction continues as follows:

(b) First Residual Matrix, $X_1 = X_0 - u_1v_1{}^t$ Sum of Squares = 1369.9255

Male	M1	−3.02	0.74	1.83	−2.31	1.14	−3.92	0.15
	M2	5.01	0.41	−0.52	2.72	0.88	1.15	0.07
	M3	−0.28	−2.57	−3.28	−0.04	2.86	4.04	0.53
	M4	−7.50	−4.95	3.45	−0.15	2.78	0.18	−0.23
	M5	−0.73	−1.79	−3.88	0.61	3.40	−1.59	0.51
	M6	−1.66	−3.16	−3.07	−0.66	5.48	1.77	0.26
	M7	−1.33	−0.70	−1.09	0.01	4.28	−5.30	0.08
	M8	−1.24	−2.45	−1.49	0.34	0.79	3.73	0.20
	M9	−1.94	1.88	1.12	−2.77	1.54	−5.32	−0.29
	M10	−4.24	−1.57	0.18	−1.63	−0.47	1.21	−0.03
	M20	−3.99	−2.07	−4.06	1.56	−1.15	−3.90	0.22
Female	M11	0.21	−0.40	3.73	0.17	1.51	0.66	−0.12
	M12	0.10	−0.09	2.52	0.09	2.00	−1.21	0.43
	M13	−2.75	−1.21	0.55	−0.69	3.15	−3.18	−0.38
	M14	1.44	−1.08	−3.18	0.25	2.45	2.19	0.04
	M15	0.91	−1.61	1.22	0.88	4.60	0.29	−0.07
	M16	0.91	1.51	2.27	−0.87	−0.44	−0.26	−0.04
	M17	−1.95	0.39	−0.64	−0.81	−2.52	−0.60	0.01
	M18	2.72	1.30	2.65	2.03	1.06	−3.99	−0.09
	M19	1.91	−0.29	−1.36	−0.74	3.64	1.73	−0.23
Male	T1	0.32	0.86	0.96	0.03	−2.99	1.28	−0.20
	T2	0.58	2.08	3.53	−1.19	−1.95	−0.09	−0.14
	T3	1.71	0.05	−0.49	0.98	−2.25	3.34	−0.08
	T4	−0.96	1.63	1.86	−1.49	−5.60	2.77	−0.20
	T5	0.77	−1.31	1.08	5.06	−0.39	−4.47	−0.23
	T6	−0.87	1.49	1.93	−0.54	−4.59	0.22	−0.09
	T7	0.22	1.14	0.20	−0.31	2.03	−4.88	−0.02
	T8	−5.29	−2.78	−1.84	−1.87	5.38	−3.28	0.60
	T9	−0.45	0.81	−3.39	−1.05	−1.87	−0.02	0.27
	T10	1.73	−1.52	−1.07	0.15	−0.69	8.52	0.58
Female	T11	−4.67	−0.92	−1.19	−2.14	−2.28	1.09	0.35
	T12	3.74	2.61	−1.59	1.16	−2.28	−1.89	−0.10
	T13	2.43	1.82	0.15	1.63	−2.94	−1.67	−0.38
	T14	0.86	−1.52	−3.08	−0.57	2.03	4.82	0.33
	T15	0.46	−2.34	−1.38	2.42	3.72	−1.19	0.09
	T16	−0.24	0.43	0.90	−2.06	2.57	0	0.30
	T17	3.85	2.36	−2.25	−1.48	1.43	0.58	−0.39
	T18	0.50	0.55	−0.31	−0.97	1.30	−0.31	−0.03
	T19	−0.14	−2.68	−0.51	4.16	0.44	−1.08	−0.01
	T20	3.43	3.15	0.96	0.02	−5.09	1.98	−0.37

$$u_2 = \begin{matrix} -0843 \\ 0612 \\ -0410 \\ -1649 \\ -1064 \\ -1277 \\ -1479 \\ -0152 \\ -0845 \\ -0450 \\ -0964 \\ -0078 \\ -0372 \\ -1251 \\ -0189 \\ -0705 \\ 0342 \\ 0125 \\ -0044 \\ -0259 \\ 0757 \\ 0648 \\ 0904 \\ 1258 \\ -0330 \\ 0843 \\ -0694 \\ -2146 \\ 0208 \\ 1012 \\ -0208 \\ 0813 \\ 0775 \\ 0030 \\ -0890 \\ -0403 \\ 0406 \\ -0154 \\ -0406 \\ 1735 \end{matrix}$$

$$v_2{}^t = \begin{matrix} 1178 \\ 0876 \\ 0290 \\ 0099 \\ -1618 \\ 1013 \\ -0056 \end{matrix}$$

(c) Second Residual Matrix, $X_2 = X_1 - u_2 v_2^t$ Sum of Squares = 874.5211

Male	M1	−1.33	1.99	2.24	−2.17	−1.17	−2.47	0.06
	M2	3.78	−0.50	−0.82	2.62	2.55	0.10	0.13
	M3	0.54	−1.96	−3.08	0.02	1.74	4.75	0.49
	M4	−4.20	−2.50	4.26	0.13	−1.74	3.02	−0.38
	M5	1.39	−0.21	−3.35	0.79	0.48	0.24	0.41
	M6	0.89	−1.26	−2.44	−0.44	1.98	3.97	0.14
	M7	1.63	1.50	−0.36	0.26	0.22	−2.76	−0.06
	M8	−0.93	−2.22	−1.42	0.36	0.38	3.99	0.19
	M9	−0.25	3.14	1.54	−2.63	−0.78	−3.87	−0.37
	M10	−3.35	−0.90	0.40	−1.55	−1.70	1.98	−0.08
	M20	−2.07	−0.64	−3.59	1.72	−3.79	−2.24	0.13
Female	M11	0.37	−0.29	3.77	0.18	1.29	0.79	−0.13
	M12	0.84	0.46	2.71	0.15	0.98	−0.57	0.39
	M13	−0.25	0.65	1.17	−0.48	−0.28	−1.03	−0.50
	M14	1.82	−0.80	−3.09	0.28	1.93	2.52	0.02
	M15	2.31	−0.56	1.57	1.00	2.67	1.50	−0.14
	M16	0.23	1.00	2.11	−0.93	0.50	−0.85	0
	M17	−2.20	0.21	−0.70	−0.83	−2.18	−0.82	0.02
	M18	2.81	1.36	2.67	2.04	0.94	−3.92	−0.10
	M19	2.43	0.09	−1.23	−0.70	2.93	2.18	−0.26
Male	T1	−1.19	−0.26	0.59	−0.10	−0.92	−0.02	−0.13
	T2	−0.72	1.12	3.21	−1.30	−0.17	−1.20	−0.08
	T3	−0.09	−1.29	−0.93	0.83	0.23	1.78	0.01
	T4	−3.47	−0.24	1.25	−1.70	−2.15	0.61	−0.08
	T5	1.43	−0.82	1.24	5.11	−1.30	−3.90	−0.26
	T6	−2.56	0.24	1.52	−0.68	−2.27	−1.23	−0.01
	T7	1.61	2.17	0.54	−0.20	0.13	−3.68	−0.09
	T8	−1.01	0.41	−0.79	−1.51	−0.50	0.41	0.40
	T9	−0.87	0.50	−3.49	−1.08	−1.30	−0.38	0.29
	T10	−0.29	−3.02	−1.57	−0.02	2.09	6.78	0.68
Female	T11	−4.25	−0.61	−1.09	−2.11	−2.85	1.45	0.33
	T12	2.12	1.40	−1.99	1.03	−0.05	−3.28	−0.02
	T13	0.88	0.67	−0.23	1.50	−0.81	−3.00	−0.31
	T14	0.79	−1.57	−3.10	−0.57	2.11	4.76	0.34
	T15	2.24	−1.02	−0.94	2.57	1.28	0.34	0
	T16	0.57	1.03	1.10	−1.99	1.47	0.69	0.26
	T17	3.03	1.76	−2.45	−1.55	2.54	−0.11	0.43
	T18	0.81	0.78	−0.24	−0.95	0.88	−0.05	−0.05
	T19	0.67	−2.08	−0.31	4.23	−0.67	−0.38	−0.05
	T20	−0.04	0.57	0.11	−0.27	−0.33	−1.00	−0.21

$$
u_2 = \begin{matrix} -0507 \\ 0178 \\ 0811 \\ 0128 \\ 0230 \\ 0674 \\ -0324 \\ 0601 \\ -0651 \\ 0155 \\ -0170 \\ -0050 \\ -0177 \\ -0210 \\ 0535 \\ 0205 \\ -0221 \\ -0145 \\ -0568 \\ 0403 \\ -0059 \\ -0348 \\ 0299 \\ -0078 \\ -0487 \\ -0309 \\ -0500 \\ 0048 \\ 0070 \\ 1004 \\ 0120 \\ -0300 \\ -0363 \\ 0811 \\ 0180 \\ 0030 \\ 0145 \\ 0009 \\ 0039 \\ -0149 \end{matrix}
\qquad
v_2{}^t = \begin{matrix} 0044 \\ -0443 \\ -0511 \\ -0016 \\ 0356 \\ 1052 \\ 0064 \end{matrix}
$$

(d) Third Residual Matrix, $X_3 = X_2 - u_3v_3^t$ Sum of Squares = 511.4069

Male	M1	−1.20	0.67	0.72	−2.22	−0.11	0.67	0.26
	M2	3.74	−0.03	−0.28	2.63	2.18	−1.01	0.06
	M3	0.33	0.15	−0.64	0.10	0.04	−0.28	0.19
	M4	−4.24	−2.17	4.65	0.14	−2.01	2.23	−0.43
	M5	1.33	0.39	−2.66	0.81	0	−1.19	0.32
	M6	0.71	0.50	−0.42	−0.38	0.56	−0.21	−0.11
	M7	1.71	0.65	−1.33	0.23	0.90	−0.75	0.06
	M8	−1.09	−0.65	0.39	0.42	−0.88	0.27	−0.04
	M9	−0.08	1.44	−0.42	−2.70	0.59	0.17	−0.13
	M10	−3.39	−0.50	0.87	−1.53	−2.03	1.02	−0.13
	M20	−2.02	−1.08	−4.10	1.70	−3.44	−1.18	0.19
Female	M11	0.38	−0.42	3.61	0.18	1.40	1.10	−0.11
	M12	0.89	0	2.17	0.13	1.36	0.53	0.46
	M13	−0.20	0.10	0.53	−0.50	0.16	0.27	−0.42
	M14	1.68	0.59	−1.48	0.33	0.81	−0.80	−0.18
	M15	2.26	−0.03	2.19	1.01	2.24	0.23	−0.21
	M16	0.28	0.42	1.44	−0.95	0.96	0.52	0.08
	M17	−2.16	−0.17	−1.14	−0.84	−1.87	0.08	0.08
	M18	2.96	−0.12	0.97	1.98	2.13	−0.40	0.11
	M19	2.32	1.14	−0.02	−0.66	2.08	−0.32	−0.41
Male	T1	−1.17	−0.42	0.41	−0.10	−0.79	0.35	−0.11
	T2	−0.63	0.22	2.16	−1.34	0.56	0.95	0.05
	T3	−0.17	−0.51	−0.03	0.86	−0.39	−0.07	−0.10
	T4	−3.45	−0.44	1.01	−1.71	−1.99	1.10	−0.05
	T5	1.56	−2.10	−0.22	5.07	−0.28	−0.88	−0.08
	T6	−2.48	−0.56	0.59	−0.71	−1.63	0.68	0.11
	T7	1.74	0.87	−0.96	−0.25	1.18	−0.58	0.10
	T8	−1.02	0.53	−0.64	−1.50	−0.60	0.11	0.38
	T9	−0.88	0.68	−3.28	−1.07	−1.45	−0.81	0.26
	T10	−0.55	−0.40	1.46	0.08	−0.02	0.55	0.30
Female	T11	−4.28	−0.29	−0.73	−2.10	−3.10	0.70	0.29
	T12	2.20	0.62	−2.90	1.00	0.58	−1.42	0.09
	T13	0.97	−0.27	−1.32	1.47	−0.05	−0.75	−0.17
	T14	0.59	0.55	−0.66	−0.49	0.41	−0.26	0.03
	T15	2.20	−0.55	−0.40	2.59	0.90	−0.78	−0.07
	T16	0.56	1.11	1.19	−1.99	1.40	0.50	0.25
	T17	3.00	2.14	−2.02	−1.54	2.24	−1.01	0.37
	T18	0.80	0.81	−0.21	−0.95	0.86	−0.10	−0.05
	T19	0.66	−1.97	−0.19	4.23	−0.75	−0.63	−0.06
	T20	0	0.18	−0.34	−0.29	−0.02	−0.08	−0.15

FURTHER NOTES ON THE GRAPHIC ANALYSIS 399

By these steps we have extracted three factors which account for 90.5 per cent of the original sum of squares. The reduction proceeded as follows:

	Sum of Squares	Cumulative Percentage
Original	5360	—
After 1st factor	1370	74.4
After 1st and 2nd factors	875	83.7
After 1st, 2nd, and 3rd factors	511	90.5

TABLE A2:1

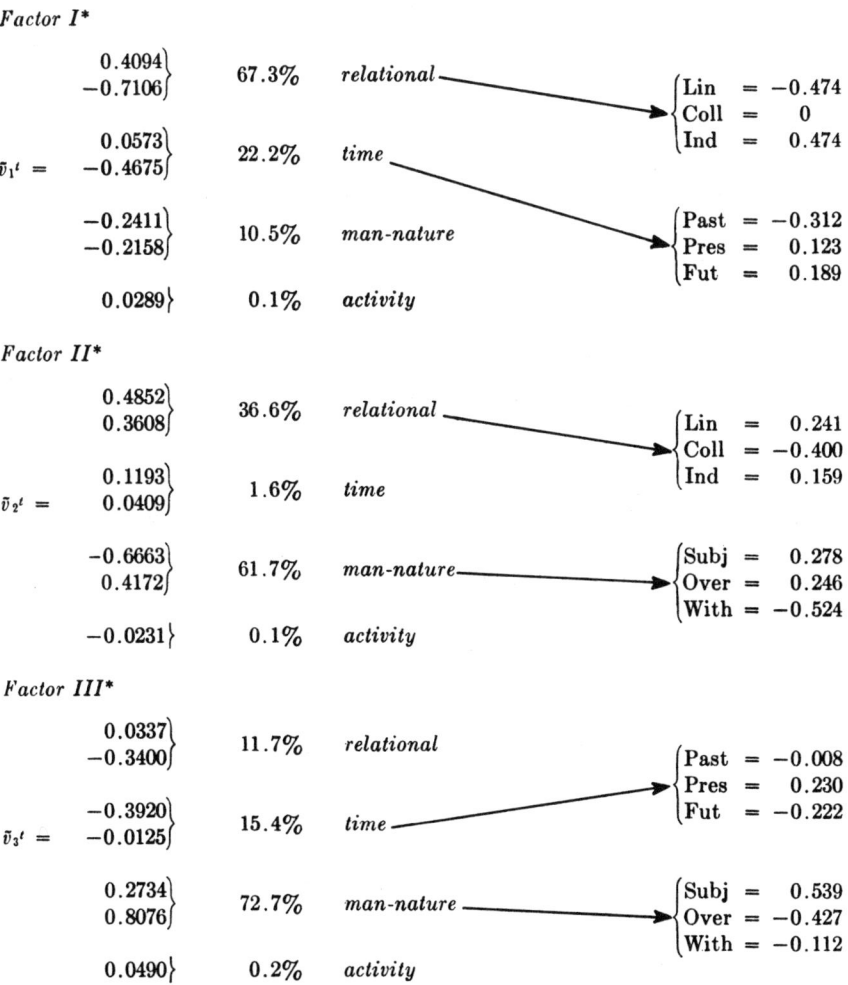

* These are the normalized forms of $v_1{}^t$, $v_2{}^t$, and $v_3{}^t$ respectively.

The fourth factor would have accounted for 95.3 per cent, if we had proceeded to utilize it.

Perhaps the most difficult step to visualize in the interpretation is the characterization of dimensions which are made up of the differential emphases on the alternatives within the orientation. In Chapter VII we characterized the dimensions as I, II, and III, and simply indicated the order relations among alternatives. In the present more detailed tabulation we indicate over on the right-hand side how the x, y vectors provided by the analysis can be translated into a, b, and c vectors for interpretation (see Table A2:1).

For example, it may be seen that the *relational* component which accounts for 67.3 per cent of dimension I is clearly centered in the Ind > Coll > Lin sector. This conclusion is reached by translating $x = 0.4094$ and $y = -0.7106$ into the a, b, and c components shown for the Lineal, Collateral, and Individualistic alternatives. On dimension II, by extension of the same logic, it may be shown that *relational* contributes to Lin = Ind > Coll. For interpretative purposes it is more convenient to talk in terms of the single outstanding dimension; so this factor was reflected by changing signs and reported as Coll > Ind = Lin in Chapter VII. This means, of course, that *man-nature*, the heavy component of dimension II, is reflected also and is, therefore, presented as With > Over = Subj. The reader may wish to look back to the last section of Chapter VII to study again the scatter of individuals in order to fix more clearly the meaning of the composite dimensions in the context we used them—namely, to characterize differentially central Mormons and Texans.

It should be clear that if extensive data were available for a representative set of cultures, this technique would provide a powerful tool for the assessment of the orthogonality of postulated value dimensions when the relevant data have been obtained by the present forced-choice ranking technique. It is also possible that an analysis of this type would provide important guidance for decisions relating to the inclusion or exclusion of questions in an orientation battery of a value schedule.

APPENDIX 3

Value Consensus, Observed and Perceived

After our respondents had completed an answer to a value-orientation question, they were always asked, "Which of the above alternatives would most others in your community say was the best?" The degree of consensus which was actually present in the communities was previously described in the text. In this appendix consideration will be given the relationship between the consensus which is apparent from the values instrument and the consensus which is reported to prevail by the members of the communities.[1]

It has long been assumed that as the normative maxims decline in the degree to which they are clear to, and held in common by, all members of a group, many other aspects of the social functioning of the group are impaired. In the present volume the conception of uniform values is challenged by an emphasis upon permitted, even required, variation in value orientations. This new emphasis does not categorically deny the probable negative social effects which attend low normative consensus; it simply cautions the investigator that greater care must be used in the assessment of consensus. In some instances adequate social functioning may continue with low consensus, in others it may not. In particular, the new emphasis suggests that the social consequences may be less easily read from the actual consensus present in the group than from the disposition of group members to over- or underestimate whatever consensus is present.

The unique characteristic of the present data is the availability of samples from five cultures. In the body of the text we have previously described the pains that were exercised to insure that the questions were understood. In the presentation which follows we shall want to assume that the respondents have not been prevented by particular cultural perspectives from understanding the information we required and that hence the observed between-culture differences are meaningful and deserving of careful attention. In the discussion of findings this assumption can be re-ex-

---

[1] The decision to report these materials in an appendix represents an uneasy editing assessment. Since this social psychological consideration was not central to the value-orientation theory, it would be cumbersome to intrude observations on perceived consensus in the main data chapters of the book. This argued for exclusion from the book and publication as a separate paper. On the other hand, the low perceived consensus for one of the cultures becomes quite central to the interpretation, and although it was not commented upon save in the concluding chapter, the higher perceived consensus in the other cultures took on further importance by virtue of the contrast. This degree of relevance argued for inclusion in the volume. When this consideration was coupled with the additional advantages arising from the fact that the instrument and sample characteristics would not need to be described again, the use of an appendix was decided upon.

amined, for cultures may well maintain consensus in different ways, and the implications of a change in consensus may differ according to the prevailing social organization.

This inquiry may be viewed by some readers as introducing still another difficulty in the somewhat confused literature of person-perception studies.[2] Into an area already fraught with ambiguities at the person-to-person level, this technique brings the further ambiguity attendant upon the investigator's not knowing exactly whom the respondent has in mind as the referent of "most others in your community." It is equally true that despite the advantage of questions which generally motivate the respondents to be responsive, even expansive, on their own views, we have no certain knowledge that these same questions have ever been explicitly discussed with a representative sample of other persons in the community. On the other hand, inferences at the level of generality of the value-orientation questions can quite probably be made from observation of daily life routines, even in the absence of opportunities for discussion.

It is to be noted that these data were on hand and substantially analyzed before 1953 when the Cronbach papers[3] ushered in the new criticism of empathy studies. For this reason readers familiar with more recent studies will find differences in nomenclature like the use of "perceived consensus" in lieu of "assumed similarity" and "actual consensus" in lieu of connotations of accuracy or visibility. These differences are attributable to the independent origin of this inquiry and, after some consideration, are here permitted to persist in order to signal the somewhat different interpretations involved.[4] Contemporary criticism has more frequently informed us how to examine rather than how to eliminate completely some of the interpretative and statistical artifacts encountered in the manipulation of person-perception scores. Since some of the issues are so recently resolved, it is desirable to present details which might well be suppressed if the conventions of analysis were better established. We shall therefore start directly with a definition of terms.

DEFINITION OF TERMS

If there were just two alternatives to each question, as in the case of the *activity* orientation, the respondent would be able to report that he be-

---

[2] For a convenient summary see R. Tagiuri and L. Petrullo (eds.), *Person Perception and Interpersonal Behavior* (Stanford, Calif.: Stanford University Press, 1958).
[3] See *ibid.*, p. 378, for citation.
[4] To acknowledge an earlier debt, I should like to report spending several rewarding days with Ron Tagiuri, a fellow graduate student at Harvard in 1949, working on possible typologies for sociometric choices and guesses. Somewhat later, I worked briefly as a fellow committee member with Urie Bronfenbrenner as he developed the chapter which appeared in *Talent and Society*, by McClelland, Baldwin, Bronfenbrenner, and Strodtbeck (Princeton, N.J.: Van Nostrand, 1958). During the writing up of these materials, William Caudill at Harvard has collected comparable perceived-consensus materials in Japan and, in addition, shares with this inquiry an interest in the comparative assessment of consensus between communities. All of these earlier contacts have been personally rewarding and have sustained my interest in this topic.

lieved that "most others" were either *similar* to or *different* from himself. By comparison with the community rankings, one could determine whether the designation of community choice was *correct* or *incorrect*. Since we are primarily concerned with three-alternative situations, our classification must be slightly expanded.

Let us use the letters MC for the *most chosen* alternative and O_1 and O_2 for the *other* two possible alternatives. When these symbols are arranged in tabular form with the self-reports at the left and the guesses about "most others" at the top, Figure A3:1 results.

The response types which constitute instances of perceived consensus are the following:

1. Respondent makes a self-report which is *the same as* the most chosen alternative and *perceives correctly* the alternative which is most chosen by other members of the community.

4. Respondent reports on own choice which is *different from* the most chosen alternative and *fails to perceive correctly* the most chosen alternative. In addition, the error in assessment of the most chosen alternative is made by assuming the most chosen alternative *corresponds* to the self-report. This response may arise in the two ways indicated by 4a and 4b.

By combining the number of respondents whose answers result in type 1 with those of the two type 4 responses, we obtain the totality of respondents who believe that "most other persons" in their community think as they do. This number, expressed as a percentage of the total number in the com-

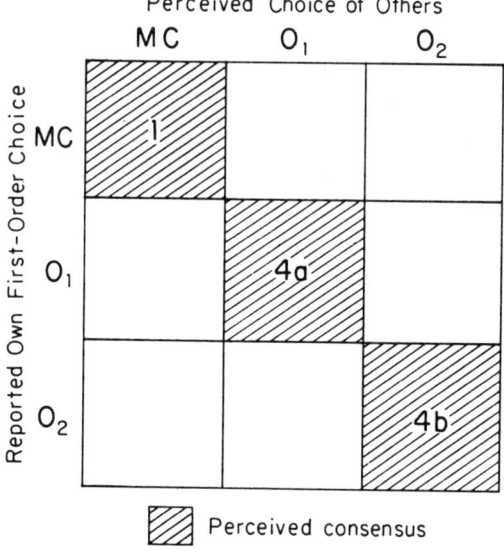

Fig. A3:1

munity, is the measure of *perceived consensus*. It is important to stress that although perceived consensus may be positively correlated with the consistency of own choices, or actual consensus in the community, there is no necessary relation between the two. The respondent who has reported his own choice may select any of the three alternatives as his perception of the most favored alternative in the community as a whole. Our measure of perceived consensus does not reflect whether the respondent is, or is not, correct. It is solely a measure of whether he believes "most others" in the community think as he does.

For purposes of the present discussion *actual consensus* is the percentage of respondents whose own first-order choices correspond to the alternative most chosen by the total group. See Figure A3:2.

Since we have defined response type 1 above, we need here only define the second type of actual consensus:

2. Respondent himself makes a choice which is the *same* as the most chosen alternative but *errs* in assessment of the most chosen alternative in that he *believes it to be different* from his own choice when it is in fact similar. This response may arise in the two ways indicated by 2a and 2b.

Type 2 responses suggest a wry failure in human communication: the individuals are in fact like the group but think of themselves as different. They have their counterpart in type 4, the individuals who are in this instance different from the group but think of themselves as similar. To index the tendency of a community to over- or underestimate consensus, it is possible to inspect the observed level of type 2 and type 4 responses and

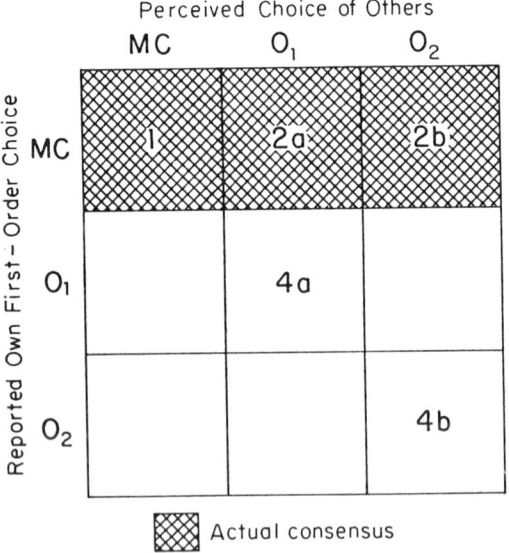

Fig. A3:2

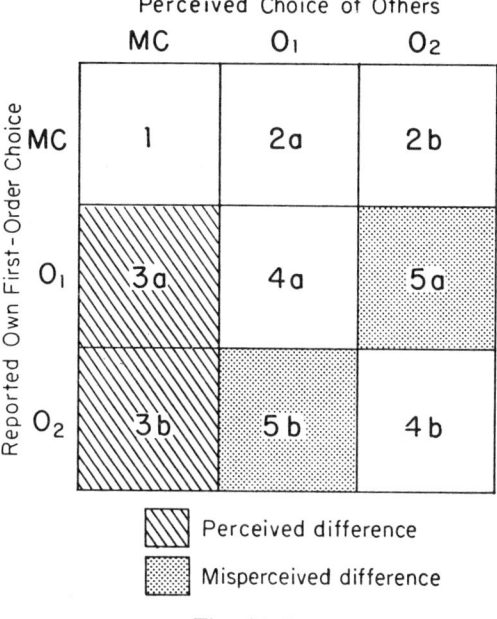

Fig. A3:3

consider the difference between them. Perceived and actual consensus may be regarded as producing our definition of an overestimate of consensus by the following subtraction:

perceived consensus	(Type 1) + (Type 4)
less, actual consensus	−[(Type 1) + (Type 2)]
equals, overestimate of consensus	(Type 4) − (Type 2)

So long as members of a community are equally likely to err in the type 2 or type 4 manner, the overestimate of consensus will be approximately zero; when type 4 exceeds type 2, an overestimate is present; when type 2 exceeds type 4, a negative overestimate, that is, an *underestimate* of consensus is present.[5]

To complete the development of the possible types, attention may be directed to two other logical possibilities (Fig. A3:3).

3. Respondent does not make a choice which corresponds with the most chosen alternative even though he correctly assesses the most chosen alternative of the community. This response, described as an instance of *perceived* difference, may arise in the two ways indicated by 3a and 3b.

---

[5] The result of the subtraction has the disadvantage that it assumes the observed levels of 32−30 have the same meaning as 4−2. When highly variable observed levels of prediction to a criterion are involved, an investigator is better advised to work with the component scores in lieu of the differences.

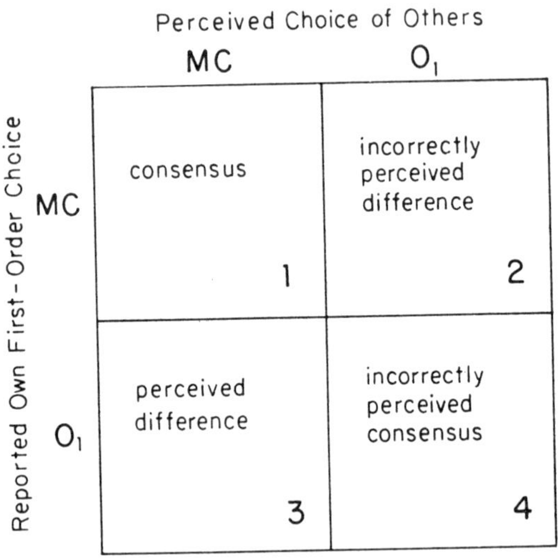

```
                    Perceived Choice of Others
                     MC              O₁
                 ┌─────────────┬─────────────┐
                 │             │ incorrectly │
                 │  consensus  │  perceived  │
              MC │             │  difference │
                 │             │             │
                 │      1      │      2      │
                 ├─────────────┼─────────────┤
                 │  perceived  │ incorrectly │
                 │  difference │  perceived  │
              O₁ │             │  consensus  │
                 │             │             │
                 │      3      │      4      │
                 └─────────────┴─────────────┘
```

Fig. A3:4

5. Respondent does not make a choice corresponding to the most chosen alternative; he assesses the most chosen alternative of the community as different from his own choice; and he assesses the most chosen alternative incorrectly. This response, described as an instance of misperceived difference, may arise in the two ways indicated by 5a and 5b. The residual type 5 response could not arise in a two-choice situation.

Type 3 plus type 1 responses represent those responses in which the first choice of the community is *correctly* perceived. All other responses represent inaccurate perception of the community's first choice. To anticipate the two-choice situation, the prior distinctions can be recapitulated in a four-cell figure (Fig. A3:4).

In the present application it is possible to prepare an array of scores in the three-by-three matrix for each person, each question, and each culture on the *relational, man-nature,* and *time* orientations. It is of course necessary to make a modification for *activity* questions (with only two alternatives) of the type illustrated in Figure A3:4, but this is not troublesome since the type numbers are consistent save for the fact that type 5 is absent in this instance.

SUMMARY OF FINDINGS

In the absence of alternative norms, the base line for the culture-by-culture comparisons is provided by a composite tabulation of all the responses collected. It may be noted in Figure A3:5 that in 48 per cent of the cases the respondents chose and perceived others as choosing the most chosen

Perceived Choice of Others
(Percentage Distribution)[a]

	MC	O₁	O₂
MC	48 (1)	9 (2a)	8 (2b)
O₁	4 (3a)	9 (4a)	2 (5a)
O₂	5 (3b)	2 (5b)	9 (4b)

Reported Own First-Order Choice (Percentage Distribution)[a]

Total = 2438

Fig. A3:5

[a] For types 2, 3, 4, and 5 the percentage observed has arbitrarily been divided equally between the a and b possibilities except when the percentage in question was odd; then one alternative exceeds the other by one.

The total is 96 per cent because 4 per cent gave no answer.

alternative. Knowledge that this value is exactly 48 per cent does not provide the background required for interpretation. What was to be expected? One can begin to reason about the observed magnitude by thinking of extreme possibilities. For example, if more than 95 per cent of the total responses had been type 1, little latitude would have remained for inquiry into differences between over- and underestimates of consensus. In this sense, the observed result of 48 per cent does not foreclose interesting differences.

From a different perspective, it may be said that the observed 48 per cent is about 11 per cent higher than would have been expected if guesses for most others' choices had been determined by a random process which was completely independent of own choices.[6] Or, if every response had been determined by an arbitrary strategy to say that most others' choices are the same as own choices, then 65 per cent would have been type 1.

It is probably wrong to make any assumption about which came first—"own" or "most other" choices. For while the question was always asked in an "own"–then–"most other" order, it is to be expected that the respondent was quickly able to anticipate the "most other" inquiry. The basic Heider formulation, insofar as it is applicable in this situation, would lead one to expect that type 4 responses, incorrectly perceived consensus, would be

[6] The chance estimate of 37 per cent arises from the weighted average of three (orientations) times ⅓ plus one times ½.

relatively high in contrast to type 2 and type 3, which do not involve mutuality. This does not appear to be the case, for while type 4 is 18 per cent, type 2 is 17 per cent, and type 3, 9 per cent. Type 1, of course, involves mutuality, but the interpretation is clouded, for it is both an accurate and a mutual response. It could arise from the correct reading of the visible signs in the community; it could also arise from the disposition to assume

TABLE A3:1

PERCEIVED CONSENSUS BY QUESTION AND CULTURE

(Per Cent)

Questions	Cultures					Mean
	SA	T	M	Z	N	
relational						
1	74	85	85	48	50	68
2	52	85	85	52	64	68
3	61	90	50	57	36	59
4	35	80	85	71	41	62
5	52	85	55	57	36	57
6	70	100	75	48	55	70
7	61	90	80	62	45	68
Mean	58	88	74	56	47	65
time						
1	70	70	70	52	45	61
2	65	75	85	43	45	63
3	65	85	80	57	23	62
4	78	60	80	67	36	64
5	78	75	75	38	41	61
Mean	71	73	78	51	38	62
man-nature						
1	65	80	70	62	18	59
2	65	75	95	62	55	68
3	78	70	70	38	41	59
4	65	70	80	57	41	62
5	65	75	80	57	41	64
Mean	68	74	79	55	39	63
activity						
1	91	65	55	86	82	76
2	96	55	60	86	82	76
3	74	60	55	62	77	66
4	87	60	70	76	91	77
5	83	70	75	71	82	76
6	61	90	85	67	73	75
Mean	82	67	67	75	81	74

others similar; or it could be a false positive which arises when a respondent who perceives the community's position as different makes a faulty assessment. Type 5, the misperceived difference, is only 4 per cent, and there were also 4 per cent "no answer" responses on either "own choice" or reported perception of "most others." Therefore, types 1 through 4, which are centrally involved in the analysis, constitute 92 per cent of the total responses.

In the composite data, overestimates and underestimates are approximately balanced: type 4 less type 2, 18 minus 17, is plus 1 per cent. This indicates that the disposition to assume most others similar is counterbalanced by the disposition to assume most others different when an erroneous assessment of most others is being made. The composite result for the Rimrock region does not, however, establish that important biases may not be present for individual cultures. To assess this possibility one must consider first the perceived-consensus scores (type 1 and type 4 responses) for the five cultures on the four orientations (Table A3:1). It is permissible to make the comparison of the data in Table A3:1 to scores by culture and orientation (Table A3:2) because analyses of variance (which are not shown) have indicated that the individual questions do not differ significantly with regard to the perceived consensus they elicit. In the tabulation, the values for "percentage perceived consensus" are used to determine the ordering, and the significant gaps between adjacent values are indicated by vertical lines.

On the right-hand side of Table A3:2 is shown the probability associated with the null hypothesis that there is no difference between cultures. There are significant differences for the first three orientations. For the three orientations in which there are significant differences, it is quite striking that Mormon and Texan cultures are high on perceived consensus and Navaho is low. This tendency is somewhat reversed for *activity*, but since these values appear to be homogeneous, it does not strongly offset the first impression.

The question-by-question relation between perceived consensus and actual consensus is generally uneven, and since only the twenty respond-

TABLE A3:2

CULTURES RANKED BY ORIENTATION AND PERCEIVED-CONSENSUS SCORES

Orientation	Percentage Perceived Consensus					Probability
relational	Texan 88	Mormon 74	Sp.-Amer. 58	Zuni 56	Navaho 47	< .001
time	Mormon 78	Texan 73	Sp.-Amer. 71	Zuni 51	Navaho 38	< .001
man-nature	Mormon 79	Texan 74	Sp.-Amer. 68	Zuni 55	Navaho 39	< .001
activity	Sp.-Amer. 82	Navaho 81	Zuni 75	Mormon 67	Texan 67	N. S.

ents are involved it is difficult to establish an instance of marked disparity for one culture. Among the Texan responses MN4, Belief in Control, represents one relatively clear exception. The actual consensus on this question is low, but the tendency to perceive most others as similar is high. If our evidence were firmer, we might be inclined to take this as an indirect commentary on the degree to which the Individualistic organization of labor, augmented by exchange relationships among cliques, permits individuals, or subgroups, to hold to their own farming philosophy without the need to expose and reconcile possible differences. For Mormons there is a disposition to markedly overestimate consensus on the same question MN4, and also on T4, Ceremonial Innovation. In this last instance a slightly different process is suggested. It is true that most of our Mormon respondents are involved in the church activities and probably talk quite a bit about them. What appears to be lacking is an element of conflict to create identifiable subgroups. They want to be as much like the Salt Lake church as possible, even though some believe this involves change and others believe it involves the maintenance of the *status quo*.

At the other extreme, an excess of consensus over perceived consensus arises in the Mormon responses to R5, Wage Work. Respondents clearly favored Individualism, but they frequently imputed Collateral choices to "most others." As our earlier analysis has suggested, the Mormon ideology requires a strong Individualism to be reconciled with Collateral church requirements. The disposition, in Rimrock, to impute the Collateral position to others may be interpreted in one of two ways. On the one hand, it might forecast an early modification of the system at that moment when the pluralistic ignorance is dispelled. On the other hand, this result may be taken to indicate the stability of the community organization and church ideology, for the relation between Individualistic personal persuasions and the Collateral position may have been persistent over a long period. These comments upon the individual questions must be regarded solely as an illustration of how departures between observed and perceived consensus might be interpreted if hypotheses had been formulated in advance. Without the advanced hypothesis, there is great danger of being influenced by chance variations.

Moving from individual questions to a consideration of the estimation of consensus for cultures as wholes, it is helpful to turn to the tabulation by orientation and culture which also shows the previously defined response types. See Table A3:3.

(1) Consider first the relative ability of persons in the five cultures to say *accurately* what "most others" preferred. The composite figures are surprisingly consistent.

	Types 1 and 3
Spanish-American	57
Mormon	60
Texan	56
Zuni	53
Navaho	57

TABLE A3:3

TYPOLOGY OF RESPONSE BY ORIENTATION AND CULTURE[a]

Culture and Orientation			Type (in per cent)					Total Respondents Times Questions
			1	2	3	4	5	
Mormon	relational		55	12	10	18	2	140
	time		56	8	7	20	4	100
	man-nature		43	9	7	35	2	100
	activity		52	12	9	14	—	120
		Mean	52	11	8	21	2	460
Navaho	relational		32	24	21	14	8	154
	time		27	31	17	11	12	110
	man-nature		27	34	15	12	11	110
	activity		75	11	5	6	—	132
		Mean	41	24	15	11	7	506
Zuni	relational		33	19	16	24	8	147
	time		33	23	17	18	9	105
	man-nature		30	21	13	26	10	105
	activity		63	21	5	12	—	126
		Mean	40	21	13	20	7	483
Spanish-American	relational		34	24	10	24	7	161
	time		61	17	6	12	3	115
	man-nature		52	15	17	15	0	115
	activity		70	9	9	12	—	138
		Mean	53	17	4	16	3	529
Texan	relational		71	4	1	17	1	140
	time		44	7	2	29	4	100
	man-nature		48	9	3	26	4	100
	activity		45	19	5	20	—	120
		Mean	53	10	3	22	2	460

[a]Differences between the sum of per cents and 100 per cent is due to cases in which there was no response. For the *activity* orientation only two alternatives were offered; therefore, type 5 is not possible.

(2) Consider next the levels of *actual consensus* in the five cultures. Here again, the observed values are quite homogeneous.

	Types 1 and 2
Spanish-American	70
Mormon	63
Texan	63
Zuni	61
Navaho	65

(3) It is only when levels of *perceived consensus* are considered that the greater differentiation represented by two values in the 70's, two in the 60's, and one in the low 50's becomes apparent.

	Types 1 and 4
Spanish-American	69
Mormon	73
Texan	75
Zuni	60
Navaho	52

To show exactly the way in which this differentiation occurs, it will be advantageous to look carefully at Graph A3:1 which shows separately three types of information. Inset in the circle is the per cent of type 1 responses, that is, those instances in which the respondent selects the most chosen alternative and assumes others do likewise. On the vertical axis incorrectly perceived consensus is shown—that is, the choice combination which designates "most others" as similar when in fact they are different. And the horizontal axis shows incorrectly perceived difference, the choice

GRAPH A3:1
THREE COMPONENTS OF THE ESTIMATE OF CONSENSUS
(In Percentages)

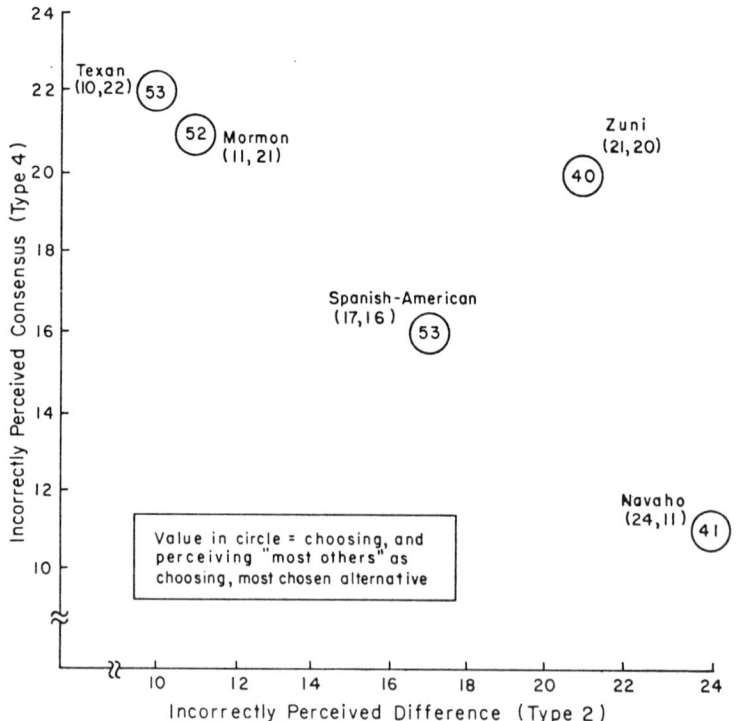

TABLE A3:4
Type of Response Pattern

Culture	Correctly Perceived Consensus (Type 1)	Incorrectly Perceived Consensus (Type 4)	Incorrectly Perceived Difference (Type 2)
Class I			
Mormon	high	high	low
Texan	high	high	low
Class IIa			
Spanish-American	high	rel. high	rel. high
Class IIb			
Zuni	low	high	high
Class III			
Navaho	low	low	high

combination which designates "most others" as different when in fact they are similar. When these three values are considered simultaneously, they define four analytic classes, three of which contain one culture and one of which contains two. Consider Table A3:4.

As a first approximation one might conclude after looking at the Mormon and Texan pattern that the following holds:

(1) When type 1 is high, type 4 will be high and type 2 will be low.

Inspection of the Spanish-American pattern demonstrates that type 1 and type 4 can be high and type 2 high also. In light of this, (1) could be restated:

(1') When type 1 is high, type 4 will be high.

But in this case the Zuni instance contradicts the complement of (1'), for it demonstrates that type 1 need not necessarily be high when type 4 is high.

Or taking another beginning, one might reason that in four of the five cases type 1 and type 2 are negatively correlated. From this perspective the concern is not to enumerate possible patterns, as it was in the paragraph above; but alternately the concern is for the dependence which, on the basis of the experience in four of the five cultures, one could estimate would be observed in a large set of cases. From this perspective it is indeed quite likely that correctly perceived consensus and incorrectly perceived differences will be negatively correlated in general, notwithstanding the Spanish-American exception. And it is also possible that correctly perceived consensus and incorrectly perceived consensus will be positively correlated notwithstanding the Zuni exception. Or to state the matter in another way, it appears that there can be no hypothetical set of relations between types 1, 2, and 4 for this data which would explain the observed results as arising solely from patently tautological part-whole artifacts of correlation.

TABLE A3:5
OVERESTIMATE OF CONSENSUS BY CULTURE
(Negative Value Indicates Underestimate)

Culture	Orientation				Total
	relational	time	man-nature	activity	
Class I					
Texan	13	22	17	1	12
Mormon	6	10	26	2	10
Class II					
Zuni	5	−5	5	−9	−1
Spanish-American	0	−5	0	3	−1
Class III					
Navaho	−10	−20	−24	−5	−13

A slightly simpler classification of the cultures is possible if the level of correctly perceived consensus is disregarded and the overestimate of consensus is computed by subtracting type 2 from type 4. This is shown in Table A3:5.

CONCLUDING REMARKS

In the present discussion, the problem of determining whether or not a difference in consensus exists has taken priority over consideration of the possible meaning of differences in consensus for at least two reasons. First, the assessment of consensus is not in itself an inconsiderable task; and second, the meaning of consensus comes to be so closely dependent upon the mode of implementation used to assess it that less surplus meaning is encountered if one works from the implementation to the construct than the reverse.

More particularly, the assessment of consensus requires samples from two universes. First, there must be a sample of questions from a representative set of normative areas. One can reread the questions presented in Chapter III and then consider whether these questions map the salient areas of culture. It is at least clear that neither the Yale Cross Cultural Index nor any similar source constitutes a frame of constructs of cultural relevance from which, by random methods, a representative set of questions might be drawn. While the present questions were designed to implement the value-orientation theory, they were not intended to be as exhaustive as might ideally be desired, but they have the great virtue of being concretely implemented in terms of the day-to-day life experiences of these peoples.

Second, the assessment of consensus requires a sample of respondents from the given cultures. In four of the five cultures (Zuni excepted) it was possible to follow the prescribed routine of enumeration and, after stratification by sex, random sampling. The shortcoming for present purposes is not in the selection of the population sample so much as it is the size of the sample. When we report 80 per cent for a culture, we really are saying 16 out of 20. The limitation of the sample size is not fundamentally mitigated by the fact that twenty-three questions distributed into four orientation areas have been asked of each respondent because of the probable correlation between responses by the same subject.

Coupled with the problem of sample size is the analytic problem of the interdependence of scores within the three-by-three paradigm. There are at best only four degrees of freedom and internal correlations may reduce these. In many instances, when one has interpreted one measure, he has probably used a high proportion of the independent information. Therefore, with the joint problem of statistical significance and analytic interdependence in mind, it is best to consider the substantive accomplishment of the perceived-consensus analysis as being essentially limited to having established the following rank ordering of the five cultures by their tendency to overestimate consensus:

Class I, Overestimating Consensus: Texan and Mormon,
Class II, Unbiased: Zuni and Spanish-American,
Class III, Underestimating Consensus: Navaho.

APPENDIX 4

Basic Data Elicited from the Respondents of the Five Rimrock Communities

Tables A4:1 through A4:20 present the rank ordering, for each respondent, of each item from the value-orientation schedule. Respondents are arrayed along the horizontal axis; items along the vertical. Each table contains the complete response patterns for all respondents from one culture in one value-orientation series.

Table A4:21 contains the ages of the respondents from the five communities where these are either known or can be reasonably estimated. The ages are ages at the time of interviewing.

The respondent numbers, though arbitrary, are constant across all tables, so that a reconstruction of a single respondent's complete schedule can be achieved, if desired.

TABLE A4:1

RESPONSES OF THE SPANISH-AMERICANS TO ITEMS FROM THE *relational* VALUE-ORIENTATION SERIES

Item and Alternatives		Men												Women										
		1	2	3	4	5	6	7	8	9	10	11	12	1	2	3	4	5	6	7	8	9	10	11
R1	Ind	2	2	3	2	3	3	1.5	3	1	1	2	3	2	1	3	2	3	3	2	1	1	2	1
	Coll	3	1	2	3	2	2	3	2	2	2	1	2	1	3	2	3	1	2	3	2	2	1	3
	Lin	1	3	1	1	1	1	1.5	1	3	3	3	1	3	2	1	1	2	1	1	3	3	3	2
R2	Ind	1	3	3	2	2	1	1	1	3	1	1	3	1	2	2	3	3	2	2	1	1	2	1
	Coll	3	1	2	3	3	2	3	3	1	2	3	2	3	3	3	1	1	3	3	3	3	3	3
	Lin	2	2	1	1	1	3	2	2	2	3	2	1	2	1	1	2	2	1	1	2	2	1	2
R3	Ind	1	1	1	1	2	1	3	1	1	1	1	3	1	3	1	3	1	2	2	2	1	3	1
	Coll	3	2	2	3	3	3	2	3	2	2	3	2	2	2	3	2	2	3	3	3	3	2	3
	Lin	2	3	3	2	1	2	1	2	3	3	2	1	3	1	2	1	3	1	1	1	2	1	2
R4	Ind	2	2	1	1	3	3	2	2	2	1	2	3	2	1	3	3	3	3	3	1	2	2.5	1
	Coll	1	1	2	3	1	1	1	3	1	2	1	1	1	3	1	1	2	1	1	2	1	1	3
	Lin	3	3	3	2	2	2	3	1	3	3	3	2	3	2	2	2	1	2	2	3	3	2.5	2
R5	Ind	1	1	3	1	3	1	2	2	1	1	2	1	2	1	1	2	2	2	2	1	2	2	1
	Coll	3	3	1	3	2	3	1	3	3	2	1	3	1	3	3	3	3	3	3	3	1	3	3
	Lin	2	2	2	2	1	2	3	1	2	3	3	2	3	2	2	1	1	1	1	2	3	1	2
R6	Ind	1	3	3	1	3	1	3	1	1	1	1	1	2	1	1	3	1	2	3	2	1	1	1
	Coll	3	1	2	3	2	3	1	3	2	2	2	3	3	3	2	1	2	1	2	3	2	2	2
	Lin	2	2	1	2	1	2	2	2	3	3	3	2	1	2	3	2	3	3	1	1	3	3	3
R7	Ind	1	3	1	1	3	1	3	1	1	1	1	1	2	2	1	3	1	2	3	3	1	3	1
	Coll	3	1	2	3	2	3	2	3	2	2	2	3	3	3	2	1	2	1	2	2	2	2	2
	Lin	2	2	3	2	1	2	1	2	3	3	3	2	1	1	3	2	3	3	1	1	3	1	3

TABLE A4:2

RESPONSES OF THE SPANISH-AMERICANS TO ITEMS FROM THE *time* VALUE-ORIENTATION SERIES

Item and Alternatives		Men												Women										
		1	2	3	4	5	6	7	8	9	10	11	12	1	2	3	4	5	6	7	8	9	10	11
T1	Past	2	2	2	2	3	3	3	2	2	3	3	3	3	3	3	3	3	3	1	3	3	3	2
	Pres	1	1	1	1	1	1	1	1	1	1	2	1	1	1	1	1	1	1	2	1	1	2	1
	Fut	3	3	3	3	2	2	2	3	3	2	1	2	2	2	2	2	2	2	3	2	2	1	3
T2	Past	2	3	3	3	3	3	2	2.5	2	3	3	2	3	3	3	3	3	2	3	2	2	3	3
	Pres	1	2	1	2	2	2	3	1	3	2	1	1	1	2	1	1	2	3	1	1	3	2	1
	Fut	3	1	2	1	1	1	1	2.5	1	1	2	3	2	1	2	2	1	1	2	3	1	1	2
T3	Past	3	3	2	3	3	3	3	3	3	2	3	2	3	3	3	3	3	3	3	3	3	3	2
	Pres	1	1	1	2	2	1	1.5	1	1	1	1	1	1	1	1	1	1	1	1	1	1	1	1
	Fut	2	2	3	1	1	2	1.5	2	2	3	2	3	2	2	2	2	2	2	2	2	2	2	3
T4	Past	1	1	2	3	2	3	3	3	2	1	3	3	2	2	2	2	3	2	1	1	3	1	2
	Pres	2	2	1	1	1	1	1	1	1	2	1	1	1	1	1	1	1	1	2	2	1	2	1
	Fut	3	3	3	2	3	2	2	2	3	3	2	2	3	3	3	3	2	3	3	3	2	3	3
T5	Past	3	3	3	2	2	3	3	2	3	3	3	3	2	2	3	2	3	2	2	2	3	3	2
	Pres	1	1	1	1	1	1	1	1	2	2	1	1	1	1	1	1	1	1	3	1	1	1	1
	Fut	2	2	2	3	3	2	2	3	1	1	2	2	3	3	2	3	2	3	1	3	2	2	3

TABLE A4:3

Responses of the Spanish-Americans to Items from the *man-nature* Value-Orientation Series

Item and Alternatives		Men												Women										
		1	2	3	4	5	6	7	8	9	10	11	12	1	2	3	4	5	6	7	8	9	10	11
MN1	Subj	1	3	3	2	1	2	1	1	3	3	2	2	1	1	3	2	2	2	3	1	2	1	1
	With	3	2	2	3	3	3	2	2.5	2	1	3	3	3	3	2	3	3	1	2	3	3	2	3
	Over	2	1	1	1	2	1	3	2.5	1	2	1	1	2	2	1	1	1	3	1	2	1	3	2
MN2	Subj	1	2	1	1	1	1	1	1	2	2	1	1	1	1	1	1	1	1	1	1	1	1	1
	With	3	1	2	3	3	3	2	3	3	1	2.5	2	2.5	3	3	3	3	3	2.5	2	3	2	2
	Over	2	3	3	2	2	2	3	2	1	3	2.5	3	2.5	2	2	2	2	2	2.5	3	2	3	3
MN3	Subj	1	2	1	1	1	2	1	1	2	2	1	1	2	1	2	2	2	3	1	3	1	1	2
	With	2	1	3	2	2	3	2	2	3	3	2.5	2	3	3	3	3	3	2	3	2	2	3	3
	Over	3	3	2	3	3	1	3	3	1	1	2.5	3	1	2	1	1	1	1	1.5	1	3	2	1
MN4	Subj	1	2	1	1	2	1	1.5	1	2	3	1	1	1	1	1	1	1	1	1	1	3	1	2
	With	3	1	2	2	1	2.5	1.5	2.5	3	2	3	2	2.5	2.5	2	3	3	2	2.5	3	2	2	3
	Over	2	3	3	3	3	2.5	3	2.5	1	1	2	3	2.5	2.5	3	2	2	3	2.5	2	1	3	1
MN5	Subj	3	2	1	1	1	1	1	1	3	1	1	1	1	1	1	1	1	1	1	2	2	1	3
	With	1	3	2	1	3	2.5	2	2.5	2	3	2.5	2.5	2.5	3	2.5	3	3	3	2.5	3	2.5	3	2
	Over	2	1	3	2	2	2.5	3	2.5	1	2	2.5	2.5	2.5	2	2.5	2	2	2	2.5	1	2.5	2	1

TABLE A4:4

Responses of the Spanish-Americans to Items from the *activity* Value-Orientation Series

Item and Alternatives		Men												Women										
		1	2	3	4	5	6	7	8	9	10	11	12	1	2	3	4	5	6	7	8	9	10	11
A1	Doing	2	1	2	2	2	2	2	2	2	1	2	2	2	2	2	2	2	2	2	2	2	2	2
	Being	1	2	1	1	1	1	1	1	1	2	1	1	1	1	1	1	1	1	1	1	1	1	1
A2	Doing	2	2	2	2	2	2	2	2	2	1	2	2	2	2	2	2	2	2	2	2	2	2	2
	Being	1	1	1	1	1	1	1	1	1	2	1	1	1	1	1	1	1	1	1	1	1	1	1
A3	Doing	2	1	1	2	2	2	1	2	1	2	2	2	2	2	2	2	2	2	2	2	2	2	2
	Being	1	2	2	1	1	1	2	1	2	1	1	1	1	1	1	1	1	1	1	1	1	1	1
A4	Doing	2	1	2	1	1	2	2	2	1	2	2	2	2	2	2	2	2	2	1	2	2	2	2
	Being	1	2	1	2	2	1	1	1	2	1	1	1	1	1	1	1	1	1	2	1	1	1	1
A5	Doing	2	1	2	1	1	2	1	2	2	2	2	1	2	2	2	2	2	2	2	2	2	2	2
	Being	1	2	1	2	2	1	2	1	1	1	1	2	1	1	1	1	1	1	1	1	1	1	1
A6	Doing	2	1	1	1	1	2	1	2	1	2	2	1	2	1	2	1	2	1	1	2	1	1.5	2
	Being	1	2	2	2	2	1	2	1	2	1	1	2	1	2	1	2	1	2	2	1	2	1.5	1

BASIC DATA ELICITED FROM THE RESPONDENTS 421

TABLE A4:5

RESPONSES OF THE TEXANS TO ITEMS FROM THE *relational* VALUE-ORIENTATION SERIES

Item and Alternatives		Men										Women									
		1	2	3	4	5	6	7	8	9	10	1	2	3	4	5	6	7	8	9	10
R1	Ind	2	1	1	2	1	2.5	1.5	2	1	1	2	1	1	1	1	3	1	1	2	1
	Coll	1	3	3	1	2	1	1.5	1	2	2	1	3	2	2	2.5	1	2	3	1	2
	Lin	3	2	2	3	3	2.5	3	3	3	3	3	2	3	3	2.5	2	3	2	3	3
R2	Ind	1	1	1	1	1	1	1	1	1	1	1	1	1	1	1	1	1	1	1	1
	Coll	3	3	3	3	2	3	3	3	3	2.5	3	3	3	3	3	3	3	2.5	3	3
	Lin	2	2	2	2	3	2	2	2	2	2.5	2	2	2	2	2	2	2	2.5	2	2
R3	Ind	1	2	2	1	1	1	1	1	1	1	2	1	1	1	1	1	1	1	1	1
	Coll	2.5	1	1	2	2	2	2	2	2	2	1	2	2	3	2	2	2.5	2	2	3
	Lin	2.5	3	3	3	3	3	3	3	3	3	3	3	3	2	3	3	2.5	3	3	2
R4	Ind	1	1	2	2	2	2	2	2	1	1	3	1	1	2	2	3	2	2	2	1
	Coll	2	2	1	1	2	1	1	1	2	2	1	2	2	1	1	1	1	1	1	2
	Lin	3	3	3	3	2	3	3	3	3	3	2	3	3	3	3	2	3	3	3	3
R5	Ind	1	1	1	1	1	1	1	3	2	1	2	1	1	2	2	1	1	1	1	1
	Coll	2	2	3	3	2	2.5	3	1	1	2	3	2	2	1	1	3	2.5	2	2	2
	Lin	3	3	2	2	3	2.5	2	2	3	3	1	3	3	3	3	2	2.5	3	3	3
R6	Ind	1	1	1	1	1	1	1	3	1	1	2	1	1	1	1	1	1	1	1	1
	Coll	2	2	2	2	2	2.5	2	1	2	2	1	2	2	2	2	2	3	2	2	2
	Lin	3	3	3	3	3	2.5	3	2	3	3	3	3	3	3	3	3	2	3	3	3
R7	Ind	1	1	1	1	1	1	1	3	1	1	2	1	1	1	1	1	1	1	1	1
	Coll	2	2	2	2	2	2	2	1	2	2	1	2	2	2	2	2	3	2	2	2
	Lin	3	3	3	3	3	3	3	2	3	3	3	3	3	3	3	3	2	3	3	3

TABLE A4:6

RESPONSES OF THE TEXANS TO ITEMS FROM THE *time* VALUE-ORIENTATION SERIES

ITEM AND ALTERNATIVES		MEN										WOMEN									
		1	2	3	4	5	6	7	8	9	10	1	2	3	4	5	6	7	8	9	10
T1	Past	3	3	3	3	1	3	3	2	3	3	3	3	3	3	3	3	3	3	1	3
	Pres	2	2	1	2	2	1.5	1	1	1	2	1	2	2	1	2	1	1	2	2	1
	Fut	1	1	2	1	3	1.5	2	3	2	1	2	1	1	2	1	2	2	1	3	2
T2	Past	3	3	2	3	3	2	3	2	3	3	3	3	3	3	1	2	3	3	3	2
	Pres	2	2	3	2	2	3	2	1	1	2	2	2	2	2	2	3	2	2	1	3
	Fut	1	1	1	1	1	1	1	3	2	1	1	1	1	1	3	1	1	1	2	1
T3	Past	3	3	3	3	2	3	3	3	3	3	3	3	3	3	3	2.5	3	3	3	3
	Pres	1	2	1	2	3	1	1.5	2	1	2	2	1	1	1	1	1	1	1	2	1
	Fut	2	1	2	1	1	2	1.5	1	2	1	1	2	2	2	2	2.5	2	2	1	2
T4	Past	2	3	3	3	1	3	3	3	3	2.5	3	1	1	3	3	3	3	3	1	3
	Pres	2	2	2	2	2	2	2	1	1	1	1	2	2	1	1	2	2	2	2	2
	Fut	2	1	1	1	3	1	1	2	2	2.5	2	3	3	2	2	1	1	1	3	1
T5	Past	3	3	1	3	3	3	2	2	3	2	1	3	3	1	1	3	2	2.5	2	3
	Pres	2	2	2	1	2	2	2	3	2	1	2	1	2	2	3	2	1	1	3	2
	Fut	1	1	3	2	1	1	2	1	1	3	3	2	1	3	2	1	3	2.5	1	1

BASIC DATA ELICITED FROM THE RESPONDENTS 423

TABLE A4:7

Responses of the Texans to Items from the *man-nature* Value-Orientation Series

Item and Alternatives	Men										Women									
	1	2	3	4	5	6	7	8	9	10	1	2	3	4	5	6	7	8	9	10
MN1 Subj	2	2	2	2	2.5	2.5	3	3	3	1	2	2	2	1	3	1	3	2.5	1	2
With	3	3	3	3	2.5	2.5	2	2	2	3	3	3	3	3	2	3	2	2.5	3	3
Over	1	1	1	1	1	1	1	1	1	2	1	1	1	2	1	2	1	1	2	1
MN2 Subj	2	3	1	2	3	2	3	2	2	1	2	3	2	1	1	2	1	2.5	3	2
With	3	2	3	3	2	3	1	1	3	2	1	2	3	3	2	1	2	1	2	3
Over	1	1	2	1	1	1	2	3	1	3	3	1	1	2	3	3	3	2.5	1	1
MN3 Subj	3	2	2	2	3	2	3	3	3	1.5	2	3	3	3	3	3	3	3	3	2
With	2	3	3	3	2	3	1.5	1	2	3	3	2	2	2	2	2	2	2	2	3
Over	1	1	1	1	1	1	1.5	2	1	1.5	1	1	1	1	1	1	1	1	1	1
MN4 Subj	1	2	3	2	3	2	3	2	1	1	1	2	3	1	3	2	1	3	2	2
With	3	3	2	3	2	3	1.5	1	3	3	3	3	2	2	1	1	2	2	1	3
Over	2	1	1	1	1	1	1.5	3	2	2	2	1	1	3	2	3	3	1	3	1
MN5 Subj	3	3	1	2	3	3	3	2.5	3	1.5	3	3	3	2	2	3	3	1	3	2.5
With	2	1	2	3	1	2	2	1	2	3	2	1.5	2	1	1	2	2	2.5	2	2.5
Over	1	2	3	1	2	1	1	2.5	1	1.5	1	1.5	1	3	3	1	1	2.5	1	1

TABLE A4:8
Responses of the Texans to Items from the *activity* Value-Orientation Series

Item and Alternatives		Men										Women									
		1	2	3	4	5	6	7	8	9	10	1	2	3	4	5	6	7	8	9	10
A1	Doing	1	1	1	1	1	1	1	1	2	2	2	1	1	2	2	2	2	2	1	1
	Being	2	2	2	2	2	2	2	2	1	1	1	2	2	1	1	1	1	1	2	2
A2	Doing	1	1	1	2	1	1	1	1	1	2	2	1	1	2	1	2	1	2	1	1
	Being	2	2	2	1	2	2	2	2	2	1	1	2	2	1	2	1	2	1	2	2
A3	Doing	1	1	1	1	1	1.5	1	2	2	1.5	1	2	1	2	1	1	2	1	2	1
	Being	2	2	2	2	2	1.5	2	1	1	1.5	2	1	2	1	2	2	1	2	1	2
A4	Doing	2	1.5	2	1	1	1.5	2	2	2	2	2	1.5	1	1.5	2	2	2	1	1	1
	Being	1	1.5	1	2	2	1.5	1	1	1	1	1	1.5	2	1.5	1	1	1	2	2	2
A5	Doing	1	1	1	1	1.5	1.5	1	2	2	2	1	1	1	1	1	1	2	1	1.5	1
	Being	2	2	2	2	1.5	1.5	2	1	1	1	2	2	2	2	2	2	1	2	1.5	2
A6	Doing	1	2	1	1	1	1	2	2	1	2	1	1	1	1	1	1	1	1	1	1
	Being	2	1	2	2	2	2	1	1	2	1	2	2	2	2	2	2	2	2	2	2

TABLE A4:9
Responses of the Mormons to Items from the *relational* Value-Orientation Series

Item and Alternatives		Men											Women								
		1	2	3	4	5	6	7	8	9	10	11	1	2	3	4	5	6	7	8	9
R1	Ind	3	1	1	2	1	1	1	2	2	2	2	1	1	2	1	1	2	1	2	3
	Coll	1	2	3	1	3	2	2	1	1	1	1	2	3	1	2.5	2	1	2	1	1
	Lin	2	3	2	3	2	3	3	3	3	3	3	3	2	3	2.5	3	3	3	3	2
R2	Ind	1	1	1	1	3	1	1	1	1	1	3	1	1	1	1	1	1	1	1	1
	Coll	3	3	3	2	1	3	3	2.5	2.5	2	1	3	2	2	3	3	3	3	2	3
	Lin	2	2	2	3	2	2	2	2.5	2.5	3	2	2	3	3	2	2	2	2	3	2
R3	Ind	3	1	1	2	3	2	1	1	2	2	1	2	3	1	1	2	1	2	1	1
	Coll	1	2	2	1	2	1	3	2	3	1	2	1	1	2	2	1	2	1	3	2
	Lin	2	3	3	3	1	3	2	3	1	3	3	3	2	3	3	3	3	3	2	3
R4	Ind	3	1	3	2	1	2	2	2	2	2	2	2	2	2	2	1	1	2	3	1
	Coll	1.5	2	1	1	3	1	1	1	1	1	1	1	1	1	1	2	2	1	1	2
	Lin	1.5	3	2	3	2	3	3	3	3	3	3	3	3	3	3	3	3	3	2	3
R5	Ind	1	1	1	2	2	2	2	1	1	1	1	1	1	1	2	1	1	1	1	1
	Coll	2	3	2	1	1	1	1	2	3	2	2	3	3	2	1	3	3	3	3	3
	Lin	3	2	3	3	3	3	3	3	2	3	3	2	2	3	3	2	2	2	2	2
R6	Ind	1	1	2	2	1	1	3	1	2	1	1	1	1	1	1	1	1	1	1	1
	Coll	2	2.5	1	1	2	2	1.5	2	1	2	2	2	2	2	2	2	2	2	3	2
	Lin	3	2.5	3	3	3	3	1.5	3	3	3	3	3	3	3	3	3	3	3	2	3
R7	Ind	1	1	2	2	3	1	3	1	1	1	1	1	1	1	1	2	1	2	1	1
	Coll	2	2.5	1	1	1	2	1.5	2	2	2	2	2	2	2	2	1	2	1	3	2
	Lin	3	2.5	3	3	2	3	1.5	3	3	3	3	3	3	3	3	3	3	3	2	3

TABLE A4:10

RESPONSES OF THE MORMONS TO ITEMS FROM THE *time* VALUE-ORIENTATION SERIES

ITEM AND ALTERNATIVES		MEN											WOMEN								
		1	2	3	4	5	6	7	8	9	10	11	1	2	3	4	5	6	7	8	9
T1	Past	3	3	2.5	3	3	3	3	3	3	3	3	3	3	3	2.5	3	3	3	3	2
	Pres	1	1	1	1.5	1	2	1	2	1	1	1	2	2	1	1	1	2	1	2	1
	Fut	2	2	2.5	1.5	2	1	2	1	2	2	2	1	1	2	2.5	2	1	2	1	3
T2	Past	2	1	2	2.5	1	3	3	2	3	3	3	2	2.5	2.5	2	3	2.5	3	1	3
	Pres	3	3	1	2.5	3	1	2	3	2	2	2	3	2.5	2.5	1	2	2.5	2	3	1
	Fut	1	2	3	1	2	2	1	1	1	1	1	1	1	1	3	1	1	1	2	2
T3	Past	3	3	3	3	2	3	3	3	3	3	3	3	3	3	2.5	3	3	3	3	3
	Pres	1	1	1	1	1	2	1	1	1.5	1	1	1	1	1	1	1	2	1	1	1
	Fut	2	2	2	2	3	1	2	2	1.5	2	2	2	2	2	2.5	2	1	2	2	2
T4	Past	2.5	3	1	2	1	2	1	3	3	3	1	2.5	3	3	3	1	3	3	1	3
	Pres	2.5	2	2.5	3	2	1	2	1	2	2	2	2.5	2	2	2	3	1	1	3	2
	Fut	1	1	2.5	1	3	3	3	2	1	1	3	1	1	1	1	2	2	2	2	1
T5	Past	3	1	3	2	2.5	2	1	2	3	3	2	2.5	1	3	3	2	3	2	2.5	2
	Pres	2	2.5	2	3	1	1	3	1	2	2	1	2.5	3	2	2	3	2	3	2.5	3
	Fut	1	2.5	1	1	2.5	3	2	3	1	1	3	1	2	1	1	1	1	1	1	1

BASIC DATA ELICITED FROM THE RESPONDENTS 427

TABLE A4:11
RESPONSES OF THE MORMONS TO ITEMS FROM THE *man-nature* VALUE-ORIENTATION SERIES

ITEM AND ALTERNATIVES		MEN											WOMEN								
		1	2	3	4	5	6	7	8	9	10	11	1	2	3	4	5	6	7	8	9
MN1	Subj	3	1	1	2	1	1	3	1	3	1	2	1.5	2	2	2	2	2	2	2.5	1
	With	2	3	3	3	3	3	1	2.5	2	3	3	3	3	3	3	3	3	3	2.5	3
	Over	1	2	2	1	2	2	2	2.5	1	2	1	1.5	1	1	1	1	1	1	1	2
MN2	Subj	2.5	3	1	2	2	3	2	1	3	3	3	1	1	3	1	2	1	2	3	2
	With	2.5	1	2	1	1	1	1	3	2	3	1	3	2	1	2	1	2	3	1	1
	Over	1	2	3	3	3	2	3	2	1	1	2	2	3	2	3	3	3	1	2	3
MN3	Subj	3	3	3	3	3	3	3	3	3	3	3	3	3	3	3	3	3	3	3	3
	With	2	2	2	1	1	1	2	2	1	2	2	1	1	1	2	1	2	2	2	1
	Over	1	1	1	2	2	2	1	1	2	1	1	2	2	2	1	2	1	1	1	2
MN4	Subj	2	1	1	2.5	2	2	3	1	3	1	3	2.5	3	3	1	3	3	3	2	2
	With	1	2	2	1	1	1	1	3	2	2.5	2	1	2	1	2	1	2	1	1	1
	Over	3	3	3	2.5	3	3	2	2	1	2.5	1	2.5	1	2	3	2	1	2	3	3
MN5	Subj	3	2.5	2	1.5	3	1	3	3	3	3	3	3	3	3	3	1	3	2	3	2
	With	1	2.5	1	3	1.5	2	1	1	1	2	2	2	1	2	1	2	2	3	2	3
	Over	2	1	3	1.5	1.5	3	2	2	2	1	1	1	2	1	2	3	1	1	1	1

TABLE A4:12

Responses of the Mormons to Items from the *activity* Value-Orientation Series

Item and Alternatives		Men											Women								
		1	2	3	4	5	6	7	8	9	10	11	1	2	3	4	5	6	7	8	9
A1	Doing	1	1	2	1	2	1	1	2	1	1	1	1	2	1	2	1	2	1	1	1
	Being	2	2	1	2	1	2	2	1	2	2	2	2	1	2	1	2	1	2	2	2
A2	Doing	1	1	2	1	2	1	1	2	1	2	2	1	2	1	2	2	1	1	1	1
	Being	2	2	1	2	1	2	2	1	2	1	1	2	1	2	1	1	2	2	2	2
A3	Doing	1	1	2	1	1	2	1	1	1	1	1	1	1	1	1	1	1	1	1	1
	Being	2	2	1	2	2	1	2	2	2	2	2	2	2	2	2	2	2	2	2	2
A4	Doing	2	2	2	1	1	2	2	2	1	2	2	2	2	1	1	1	2	2	1.5	1
	Being	1	1	1	2	2	1	1	1	2	1	1	1	1	2	2	2	1	1	1.5	2
A5	Doing	1	2	1	1	2	2	1	1	1	1	2	1	2	1	1	1	1	2	1	1
	Being	2	1	2	2	1	1	2	2	2	2	1	2	1	2	2	2	2	1	2	2
A6	Doing	2	1	1	1	1	1	1	1	1	1	1	1	1	1	1	1	1	1	1	1
	Being	1	2	2	2	2	2	2	2	2	2	2	2	2	2	2	2	2	2	2	2

BASIC DATA ELICITED FROM THE RESPONDENTS 429

TABLE A4:13
RESPONSES OF THE ZUNI TO ITEMS FROM THE *relational* VALUE-ORIENTATION SERIES

Item and Alternatives		Men											Women									
		1	2	3	4	5	6	7	8	9	10	11	1	2	3	4	5	6	7	8	9	10
R1	Ind	1	1	1	1	1	2	2	2	2	3	2	2	2	3	1	1	2	3	2	2	1
	Coll	2	2	2	2	2	1	1	3	3	1	1	3	1	1	3	2	1	1	1	3	3
	Lin	3	3	3	3	3	3	3	1	1	2	3	1	3	2	2	3	3	2	3	1	2
R2	Ind	1	1	1	3	1	2	2	1	3	3	2	2	3	1	3	1	2	2	1	3	3
	Coll	3	3	3	2	2	1	1	3	1	1	1	1	2	3	1	3	1	1	2	1	1
	Lin	2	2	2	1	3	3	3	2	2	2	3	3	1	2	2	2	3	3	3	2	2
R3	Ind	3	3	3	3	3	2	3	3	3	1	2	3	3	3	3	3	1	3	3	2	3
	Coll	1	1	1	2	1	1	2	1	1	2	1	1	1	1	2	1	2	1	2	1	1
	Lin	2	2	2	1	2	3	1	2	2	3	3	2	2	2	1	2	3	2	1	3	2
R4	Ind	3	1	1	1	2	2	2	3	3	2	3	1	3	3	1	2	1	1	3	3	2
	Coll	1	3	2	2	1	1	3	1	1	3	2	2	1	1	2	1	2	2	2	1	3
	Lin	2	2	3	3	3	3	1	2	2	1	1	3	2	2	3	3	3	3	1	2	1
R5	Ind	1	1	1	3	1	3	1	1	3	3	2	1	1	1	3	1	3	3	3	—	1
	Coll	2	2	2	2	2	2	3	2	1	1	1	2	3	3	2	3	1	1	1	—	2
	Lin	3	3	3	1	3	1	2	3	2	2	3	3	2	2	1	2	2	2	2	—	3
R6	Ind	3	1	3	3	3	3	3	3	3	3	1	3	2	2	3	3	2	3	3	2	3
	Coll	1	2	1	2	2	2	2	2	2	2	2	2	3	3	2	1	1	2	2	1	1
	Lin	2	3	2	1	1	1	1	1	1	1	3	1	1	1	1	2	3	1	1	3	2
R7	Ind	3	1	3	1	2	1	1	3	3	1	1	3	3	1	1	2	2	1	1	1	3
	Coll	2	3	1	2	3	2	3	1	2	2	2	2	2	3	3	1	3	3	2	3	1
	Lin	1	2	2	3	1	3	2	2	1	3	3	1	1	2	2	3	1	2	3	2	2

TABLE A4:14
RESPONSES OF THE ZUNI TO ITEMS FROM THE *time* VALUE-ORIENTATION SERIES

Item and Alternatives		Men											Women									
		1	2	3	4	5	6	7	8	9	10	11	1	2	3	4	5	6	7	8	9	10
T1	Past	1	2	2	3	3	3	1	1	3	3	3	2	3	3	3	1	3	2	1	1	2
	Pres	2	1	1	1	1	1	2	2	1	2	2	1	1	2	2	3	2	1	2	2	1
	Fut	3	3	3	2	2	2	3	3	2	1	1	3	2	1	1	2	1	3	3	3	3
T2	Past	3	3	1	1	3	2	3	2	3	2	3	2	3	3	3	2	1	1	2	2	2
	Pres	2	1	2	2	2	3	2	3	2	1	1	1	2	2	1	1	2	3	3	1	1
	Fut	1	2	3	3	1	1	1	1	1	3	2	3	1	1	2	3	3	2	1	3	3
T3	Past	3	1	1	1	1	1	1	1	1	2	3	2	2	1	1	1	1	3	1	2	1
	Pres	1	3	2	2	3	2	3	2	2	1	1	1	1	2	2	2	3	1	2	1	2
	Fut	2	2	3	3	2	3	2	3	3	3	2	3	3	3	3	3	2	2	3	3	3
T4	Past	1	1	1	2	1	1	1	1	1	3	2	1	2	3	2	1	1	1	1	1	1
	Pres	2	2	2	1	2	2	2	2	2	2	1	2	3	1	1	2	2	3	2	2	2
	Fut	3	3	3	3	3	3	3	3	3	1	3	3	1	2	3	3	3	2	3	3	3
T5	Past	1	2	3	3	2	2	3	2	2	1	3	2	1	1	2	3	3	3	2	3	3
	Pres	2	1	1	1	1	1	1	1	3	2	2	3	3	2	1	1	2	1	1	1	1
	Fut	3	3	2	2	3	3	2	3	1	3	1	1	2	3	3	2	1	2	3	2	2

TABLE A4:15
Responses of the Zuni to Items from the *man-nature* Value-Orientation Series

Item and Alternatives		Men											Women									
		1	2	3	4	5	6	7	8	9	10	11	1	2	3	4	5	6	7	8	9	10
MN1	Subj	3	1	3	3	3	2	1	1	3	1	1	3	3	1	3	2	3	2	1	2	1
	With	2	3	2	2	2	3	3	2	1	3	3	1	1	3	2	3	2	1	3	3	2
	Over	1	2	1	1	1	1	2	3	2	2	2	2	2	2	1	1	1	3	2	1	3
MN2	Subj	2	1	2	1	1	1	1	1	2	2	1	2	2	2	1	1	3	2	2	2	1
	With	1	3	1	2	2	2	2	2	1	1	2	1	3	1	2	2	1	3	1	3	2
	Over	3	2	3	3	3	3	3	3	3	3	3	3	1	3	3	3	2	1	3	1	3
MN3	Subj	2	3	3	2	3	3	3	3	3	1	1	3	3	3	3	1	2	2	3	1	3
	With	1	2	2	3	1	2	1	2	1	3	3	1	1	2	2	2	1	3	1	3	1
	Over	3	1	1	1	2	1	2	1	2	2	2	2	2	1	1	3	3	1	2	2	2
MN4	Subj	2	2	2	3	1	1	3	3	2	3	1	3	2	1	2	2	3	2	2	3	2
	With	1	1	1	1	2	2	1	1	1	2	2	2	3	3	1	1	1	1	1	2	1
	Over	3	3	3	2	3	3	2	2	3	1	3	1	1	2	3	3	2	3	3	1	3
MN5	Subj	1	1	1	1	1	1	2	1	3	1	1	3	2	2	3	3	2	1	1	2	1
	With	3	3	2	3	2	2	1	2	2	2	3	2	3	3	1	2	1	2	2	3	3
	Over	2	2	3	2	3	3	3	3	1	3	2	1	1	1	2	1	3	3	3	1	2

BASIC DATA ELICITED FROM THE RESPONDENTS

TABLE A4:16

Responses of the Zuni to Items from the *activity* Value-Orientation Series

Item and Alternatives		Men											Women									
		1	2	3	4	5	6	7	8	9	10	11	1	2	3	4	5	6	7	8	9	10
A1	Doing	2	2	2	2	2	2	1	2	2	2	2	2	2	2	2	2	2	2	2	2	2
	Being	1	1	1	1	1	1	2	1	1	1	1	1	1	1	1	1	1	1	1	1	1
A2	Doing	2	2	2	1	2	2	1	2	2	2	2	2	1	2	2	2	2	2	2	2	2
	Being	1	1	1	2	1	1	2	1	1	1	1	1	2	1	1	1	1	1	1	1	1
A3	Doing	1	2	2	2	2	1	1	1	2	2	2	1	1	1	1	1	1	1	1	1	1
	Being	2	1	1	1	1	2	2	2	1	1	1	2	2	2	2	2	2	2	2	2	2
A4	Doing	2	1	2	1	1	1	1	1	1	2	1	1	1	1	1	1	1	1	1	1	1
	Being	1	2	1	2	2	2	2	2	2	1	2	2	2	2	2	2	2	2	2	2	2
A5	Doing	2	1	1	1	1	1	1	1	1	2	2	1	1	1	1	1	1	1	1	1	1
	Being	1	2	2	2	2	2	2	2	2	1	1	2	2	2	2	2	2	2	2	2	2
A6	Doing	1	1	1	1	1	2	1	1	1	2	1	1	1	1	1	1	2	1	1	1	1
	Being	2	2	2	2	2	1	2	2	2	1	2	2	2	2	2	2	1	2	2	2	2

BASIC DATA ELICITED FROM THE RESPONDENTS 433

TABLE A4:17
RESPONSES OF THE RIMROCK NAVAHO TO ITEMS FROM THE *relational* VALUE-ORIENTATION SERIES

Item and Alternatives		Men												Women									
		1	2	3	4	5	6	7	8	9	10	11	12	1	2	3	4	5	6	7	8	9	10
R1	Ind	2	3	3	2	3	2	2	3	1	3	1	3	3	2	3	3	2	2	3	2	2	1
	Coll	1	1	1	3	2	1	1	1	2	2	3	1	1	1	1	2	1	1	1	1	3	3
	Lin	3	2	2	1	1	3	3	2	3	1	2	2	2	3	2	1	3	3	2	3	1	2
R2	Ind	2	3	2	2	3	3	2	1	2	3	1	2	3	3	2	2	3	3	2	3	3	2.5
	Coll	3	2	1	3	2	2	3	3	3	2	3	3	2	2	3	3	2	1	1	2	2	2.5
	Lin	1	1	3	1	1	1	1	2	1	1	2	1	1	1	1	1	1	2	3	1	1	1
R3	Ind	3	3	1	1	1	3	3	3	3	3	3	1	3	1	1	3	3	1	2	3	3	1
	Coll	1	1	2	2	2	1	1	1	2	1	1	2	2	3	3	2	1	2	1	1	1	2
	Lin	2	2	3	3	3	2	2	2	1	2	2	3	1	2	2	1	2	3	3	2	2	3
R4	Ind	3	1	1	2	2	1	1	3	1	2	1	3	3	3	3	3	3	1	3	3	1	3
	Coll	1	3	3	1	1	2	2	1	3	1	2	1	1	2	1	1	2	2	1	1	3	2
	Lin	2	2	2	3	3	3	3	2	2	3	3	2	2	1	2	2	1	3	2	2	2	1
R5	Ind	1	1	3	3	3	3	3	3	3	3	3	3	3	3	3	3	3	1	3	3	2	1
	Coll	2	2	1	2	1	1	1	1	1	1	1	1	1	1	1	1	1	2	1	1	1	3
	Lin	3	3	2	1	2	2	2	2	2	2	2	2	2	2	2	2	2	3	2	2	3	2
R6	Ind	3	3	3	3	2	1	2	3	3	1	2	2	1	3	1	3	3	1	3	1	2	1
	Coll	1	1	1	1	1	2	3	2	1	3	1	3	3	1	2	1	2	3	1	3	1	2
	Lin	2	2	2	2	3	3	1	1	2	2	3	1	2	2	3	2	1	2	2	2	3	3
R7	Ind	3	3	1	2	1	3	2	2	1	3	3	3	3	3	1	2	2	1	3	1	1	1
	Coll	1	1	2	1	2	2	3	3	3	2	1	1	1	1	2	3	1	3	1	2	2	3
	Lin	2	2	3	3	3	1	1	1	2	1	2	2	2	2	3	1	3	2	2	3	3	2

TABLE A4:18

RESPONSES OF THE RIMROCK NAVAHO TO ITEMS FROM THE *time* VALUE-ORIENTATION SERIES

Item and Alternatives		Men												Women									
		1	2	3	4	5	6	7	8	9	10	11	12	1	2	3	4	5	6	7	8	9	10
T1	Past	1	2	3	2	3	1	3	3	3	3	1	2	1	3	3	2	3	3	3	3	2	3
	Pres	2	1	1	1	1	2	1	1	1	2	3	1	3	2	1	1	1	1	1	1	1	1
	Fut	3	3	2	3	2	3	2	2	2	1	2	3	2	1	2	3	2	2	2	2	3	2
T2	Past	2	1	3	3	3	3	3	1	1	1	3	3	2	2	2	2	3	2	2	3	3	3
	Pres	1	2	2	1	2	2	2	2	3	2	1	2	1	3	3	3	2	3	1	1	2	2
	Fut	3	3	1	2	1	1	1	3	2	3	2	1	3	1	1	1	1	1	3	2	1	1
T3	Past	3	2	3	3	2	3	1	1	3	1	2	3	2	3	2	3	3	3	2	3	3	3
	Pres	2	3	1	2	1	2	3	3	2	2	2	1	3	2	1	1	2	2	1	1	1	2
	Fut	1	1	2	1	3	1	2	2	1	3	2	2	1	1	3	2	1	1	3	2	2	1
T4	Past	1	3	1	3	1	1	1	1	1	1	2	1	3	2	3	1	1	3	3	1	1	1
	Pres	2	2	2	2	2	2	2	2	2	2	1	2	1	1	2	3	3	1	2	2	2	2
	Fut	3	1	3	1	3	3	3	3	3	3	3	3	2	3	1	2	2	2	1	3	3	3
T5	Past	1	1	1	3	1	2	1	1	3	2	3	2	1	2	2	3	2	1	2	2	3	2
	Pres	2	2	2	1	3	1	3	2	1	1	2	1	2	1	1	1	1	3	1	1	1	1
	Fut	3	3	3	2	2	3	2	3	2	3	1	3	3	3	3	2	3	2	3	3	2	3

TABLE A4:19

RESPONSES OF THE RIMROCK NAVAHO TO ITEMS FROM THE *man-nature* VALUE-ORIENTATION SERIES

Item and Alternatives		Men												Women									
		1	2	3	4	5	6	7	8	9	10	11	12	1	2	3	4	5	6	7	8	9	10
MN1	Subj	1	3	1	1	3	1	2	2	2	1	2	3	1	1	2	3	3	2	3	1	2	3
	With	3	2	3	3	1	2	1	1	3	2	3	1	3	3	1	2	2	1	2	2	1	2
	Over	2	1	2	2	2	3	3	3	1	3	1	2	2	2	3	1	1	3	1	3	3	1
MN2	Subj	3	3	3	1	3	2	3	3	3	1	2	2	2	2	3	2	3	2	3	2	1	2
	With	1	1	1	2	1	1	1	1	1	3	1	1	1	1	1	1	1	1	1	1	2	3
	Over	2	2	2	3	2	3	2	2	2	2	3	3	3	3	2	3	2	3	2	3	3	1
MN3	Subj	3	3	3	1	3	3	3	3	3	3	2	2	3	3	3	3	2	2	2	3	1	3
	With	2	2	2	3	1	1	2	1	2	1	3	1	2	2	1	2	1	1	3	1	2	2
	Over	1	1	1	2	2	2	1	2	1	2	1	3	1	1	2	1	3	3	1	2	3	1
MN4	Subj	1	3	2	2	2	2	3	2	3	3	3	3	2	2	3	1	2	2	1	2	1	3
	With	2	1	1	1	1	1	2	1	1	1	1	1	1	1	2	3	3	1	3	1	2	1
	Over	3	2	3	3	3	3	1	3	2	2	2	2	3	3	1	2	1	3	2	3	3	2
MN5	Subj	3	3	3	2	1	1	2	3	3	3	3	3	2	3	3	3	2	2	3	3	2	2
	With	1	2	2	3	2	2	3	2	1	2	2	1	3	2	2	1	3	3	2	1	3	3
	Over	2	1	1	1	3	3	1	1	2	1	1	2	1	1	1	2	1	1	1	2	1	1

TABLE A4:20

Responses of the Rimrock Navaho to Items from the *activity* Value-Orientation Series

Item and Alternatives		Men												Women									
		1	2	3	4	5	6	7	8	9	10	11	12	1	2	3	4	5	6	7	8	9	10
A1	Doing	2	1	2	2	1	2	2	2	2	2	1	1	2	2	2	2	2	2	1	2	2	2
	Being	1	2	1	1	2	1	1	1	1	1	2	2	1	1	1	1	1	1	2	1	1	1
A2	Doing	1	1	2	2	2	2	2	2	2	2	1	2	2	2	1	2	2	1	1	1	2	1
	Being	2	2	1	1	1	1	1	1	1	1	2	1	1	1	2	1	1	2	2	2	1	2
A3	Doing	1	1	1	1	1	1	1	1	1	1	1.5	1	1	1	1	1	1	1	1	1	1	1
	Being	2	2	2	2	2	2	2	2	2	2	1.5	2	2	2	2	2	2	2	2	2	2	2
A4	Doing	1	1	1	1	1	1	1	1	1	1	1	1	1	1	1	1	1	1	1	1	1	1
	Being	2	2	2	2	2	2	2	2	2	2	2	2	2	2	2	2	2	2	2	2	2	2
A5	Doing	1	1	1	1	1	1	1	1	1	1	1.5	1	1	1.5	1	1	1	1	2	1	1	1
	Being	2	2	2	2	2	2	2	2	2	2	1.5	2	2	1.5	2	2	2	2	1	2	2	2
A6	Doing	1	1	1	1	1	1	1	1	1	1	1.5	2	1	1.5	1	1	1	1	1	1	1	1
	Being	2	2	2	2	2	2	2	2	2	2	1.5	1	2	1.5	2	2	2	2	2	2	2	2

TABLE A4:21
AGES OF THE RESPONDENTS FROM THE FIVE RIMROCK COMMUNITIES

	Spanish-Americans	Texans	Mormons	Zuni	Navaho
Males					
1	33	40*	32	47*	50
2	66	50*	67	53*	36
3	52	30*	46	68*	34
4	51	50*	24*	32*	29
5	63	45*	27	73*	—
6	52	35*	25	37*	—
7	58	76	55	29*	52
8	26	42*	33	20*	38*
9	56	48*	25*	58*	25*
10	49	50*	54	39*	38
11	24		—	26*	70*
12	27				45*
Females					
1	36	50*	27	51*	—
2	42	40*	58	28*	25*
3	22	40*	27	20*	43
4	43	40*	27	38*	—
5	24	50*	23	51*	25
6	41	55*	75	70*	22
7	67	70*	21	26*	34
8	34	40*	38	65*	57
9	54	40*	23	26*	60
10	27	30*		53*	40
11	38				

* Age estimated by interviewer.

Index

Acculturation; *see also* Assimilation; Cultural change
 in Atrisco, 256–57
 among Navaho, 323, 324, 326, 327, 330, 336, 339, 360, 361, 362
 in Zuni, 295–96, 300, 307–8, 311, 316, 359
Acoma, 288, 289, 295
"Acquiescent irresponsibility," 199
Activity orientation; *see also under individual communities*
 between-culture differences in, 163, 164, 168, 170
 and conformism, 23–24
 definition of, 15–17
 dimensional analysis of, 135–37, 168, 170
 dominant American, 17, 23–24, 29
 intra-cultural variations in, 144, 147, 150–51, 154, 157
 Japanese, 30
 perceived vs. actual consensus on, 408, 409, 411
 problems in testing, 91
 raw data on, by culture, sex, and item, 420, 424, 428, 432, 436
 schedule items for testing, 77, 80–90
 significance test for, 124n
 by social class, 27–28
 titles and numbers of schedule items for, 140
 within-culture regularities in, 141, 142, 145, 146, 148, 149, 152, 153, 155, 156
Actual consensus; *see* Consensus on values, actual
Adair, John, 310, 310n
Aesthetic behavior sphere; *see* Intellectual-aesthetic behavior sphere
Affective element of evaluative process, 5–6, 8–9
Age
 and Navaho responses, 337, 338
 of research sample, 437
 of Zuni respondents, 287
Agriculture; *see also* Care of Fields item (A4); Help in Misfortune item (R2); Land Inheritance item (R7); Use of Fields item (MN3)
 Mormon, 54, 62, 274
 Navaho, 57, 332
 in Rimrock area generally, 53–54
 Spanish-American, 183, 208–10, 219
 Texan, 54, 64–65, 208–9, 271–72, 274
 Zuni, 51, 54, 55, 56, 288–89, 307
Albert, Ethel, xiii, 339, 339n, 353n
Alienation, 38
American culture; *see* Dominant American culture
Analyses of variance between cultures
 development of technique, 349
 explanation of technique, 135–37
 graphs of, *activity*, 168; *man-nature*, 167; *relational*, 165; *time*, 166
 summary of, by orientation, 169–70
 summary of, overall, 170–71
Analytic constructs vs. empirical generalizations, 99–100, 345
Anomie, 34n
Apache, 180, 181, 245, 289, 296, 301
Apollonian personality, 15, 56, 297, 298
Assimilation
 and education, in Atrisco, 246–47
 in Rimrock area, 70
 and value orientations, 26, 32
Assumed similarity; *see* Consensus on values, perceived
Atkinson, Charles F., 14n
Atrisco, 59–61, 106–11, 140–44, 174–257, 354–55
 activity orientation in, and economic sphere, 144, 206–7, 212–13; and education, 249; and interviewer rapport, 108; male-female differences in, 144, 213; in 1951 vs. 1936, 256–57; vs. other cultures, 163, 164, 168, 170, 353; overall variations in, 144; and parent-child relations, 196–97; perceived vs. actual consensus on, 408, 409, 411; and political sphere, 186; prediction of, 73, 351, 352; raw data on, by sex and item, 420; and recreational sphere, 206–7; regularities in, 141, 142; and religious sphere, 237
 aggressive behavior in, 238–39
 attitudes toward illness in, 235, 239, 242, 243–44, 245
 composition of sample from, 105
 cultural strain in, 199–204, 238, 354–55
 description of, in 1936, 176, 193; in 1951–58, 175
 economic - technological sphere in, 59–60, 206–28; agriculture, 183, 208–10, 219; contractual relations, 107, 211–12, 222; expenditures, 220–21; income, 219–20, 224; land ownership and use, 59–61, 183–84, 185, 187, 213–15, 216; and *patrón* system, 59–60, 183–91, 204, 245; production and consumption patterns, 220–28; property, 197, 199, 200, 201, 215–19; relief, 227–28; stock raising, 59–60, 176, 181–89, 193, 205, 208, 210–15, 216, 219, 222, 246; wage work, 60, 188, 189, 201, 205, 208, 222–23, 225, 240; water supply, 51, 193
 education in, 69–70, 177, 190–91, 193, 226, 246–51
 emigrants from, 192, 198–99, 215, 219, 225–28, 243–44
 family in, 176, 192–202; authority structure of, 181, 182–83; changes in, 61, 73; courtship and marriage in, 195–96, 240–41; and cultural strain, 227, 238; and mate-selection, 194–96, 205, 240, 242; parent-child relations in, 196–97, 198; production and con-

sumption patterns of, 220–27; sibling relations in, 181–84, 195, 197–202, 365; and social control, 192; and social stratification, 204–5
history of, 59–61, 180–91
human nature orientation in, 343
infant mortality in, 245n
intellectual sphere in, 248; *see also* Atrisco, education in
interviewer rapport in, 96, 106–11, 178
man-nature orientation in, and economic sphere, 143–44, 207, 209, 212, 228; in 1951 vs. 1936, 256; vs. other cultures, 162, 164, 167, 169–70, 353; overall variations in, 143–44; perceived vs. actual consensus on, 408, 409, 411; prediction of, 73, 351, 352; raw data on, by sex and item, 419; regularities in, 141, 142; and religion, 144, 238, 244
map of, 50
patrón system in, 59–60, 180–91; and aggression, 238; and economic sphere, 59–60, 183–91, 204, 245; and family structure, 199–200; history of, 180–91; and interviewer rapport, 107; and legitimation of authority, 202–4; and Navaho, 246; and political sphere, 177, 251–56; and religion, 61, 183, 188, 193, 206, 220–23, 232–33, 235–37; and social stratification, 204–5
perceived vs. actual consensus in, 408–15
personality variation in, 302
physiography of, 50–55, 60, 213–14
political sphere in, 69, 177, 185–86, 187–88, 202–4, 206, 251–56
population trends in, 50, 59, 175, 176, 181, 191–93
prediction of value orientations in, 72–73, 76; compared with results, 144, 351, 352
relational orientation in, and economic sphere, 207, 212, 220–22, 224–25, 227, 228; and family structure, 196, 197; historical changes in, 72–73, 256; male-female differences in, 72–73, 142–43, 201; in 1951 vs. 1936, 256; vs. other cultures, 159–60, 164, 165, 169; overall variations in, 142–43, 172–73, 199–204; perceived vs. actual consensus on, 408, 409, 411; and political sphere, 202–4, 256; prediction of, 72–73, 351, 352; raw data on, by sex and item, 417; regularities in, 140–42; and religion, 236, 237; and strains in social organization, 199–204, 238, 354–55
relations of, with Anglo-Americans, 177–78, 192, 199, 245–56; with Homestead, 64, 67, 69, 176, 189–91, 199, 209, 228, 233, 247–48, 249–50, 251–52; with Indians generally, 181, 195, 205, 240; with Navaho, 66, 67, 195, 217, 245–46; with outside world, 68–69, 71, 192, 199, 211–12, 244–56; with Rimrock Mormons, 245; with Zuni, 66, 188, 239, 245
religious - recreational sphere in, 228–44; *activity* orientation, 206–7; and authority structure, 235–36; and building of church, 183, 243; and community intermarriage, 194; dominance of, vs. economic sphere, 206–7, 242–44; *fiesta* in, 61, 228–29, 230–34, 237–38, 242–43, 250; and illness, 235, 242, 243–44; magic and witchcraft in, 239–42; *mayordomos* in, 236–37; *padre* in, 66, 181, 233, 235–37; patron saint in, 234–35; and *patrón* system, 61, 181, 183, 188, 193, 230, 232–33, 235–37; penance in, 230, 235; and Protestantism, 249; and recreation outside Atrisco, 191, 243; recreational aspects of, 61, 191, 206–7, 228–29, 233–34, 243, 244, 246; and special characteristics of Mexican Catholicism, 228–31; and *time* orientation, 73, 144
settlement pattern of, 50, 59, 181, 193
social control in, 192, 244
social organization of (1936), 191–206
social stratification in, 59–60, 204–6, 210, 219–20, 234, 235–36, 240
status of women in, 238, 240
summary of intra-cultural variations in, 142–44
summary of within-culture regularities in, 140–42, 174
time orientation in, changes in, 256, 355; and economic sphere, 207, 217–18, 226, 228, 355; and family structure, 198; vs. other cultures, 161, 164, 166, 169, 353; overall variations in, 143; and parent-child relations, 196–97; perceived vs. actual consensus on, 408, 409, 411; prediction of, 73, 351, 352; raw data on, by sex and item, 418; regularities in, 141, 142; and religion, 73, 143, 233, 237
treatment of transients in, 191–92, 205
use of English language in, 248–49
Atrisco family, 180, 211, 217, 218, 219, 226, 230, 248, 249
Atrisco, Cecelia, 253
Atrisco, Don Juan, 59–61, 176, 180–91, 193, 196, 198, 203, 204, 206, 211, 214, 215, 216, 218, 222, 230, 232, 233, 236, 246, 249, 251–55
Atrisco, Don Manuel, 181, 182, 183, 184
Atrisco, Emilio, 184
Atrisco, Fred, 107, 200, 202, 211, 212, 215, 224, 226, 242, 248
Atrisco, Pablo, 210, 251–54

Baldwin, Alfred L., 402n
Baptists, 260, 269
Barnard, Chester, 202
Barnett, H. G., 45n
Barrida brothers, 195, 200, 213, 224
"Basic personality type," 2
"Basic values," 1–2
  and process, 8–9
  and variation, 4
Bateson, Gregory, 1n, 2, 2n
Behavior, prediction of, from knowledge of value orientations, 96–102
Behavior spheres; *see also* Family; Intellectual-aesthetic behavior sphere; Political behavior sphere; Recreational behavior sphere; *see also* economic-technological behavior sphere *and* religion *under individual communities*

Behavior spheres (*cont.*)
  definition of, 28–29, 342–43
  differential stressing of (by culture), 29–32, 343–44; dominant American, 29–30, 343; Italian-American, 343–44; Japanese, 30; Navaho, 334; Spanish-American, 30, 206–7, 242–44, 343; Zuni, 301
  fusion of, in some societies, 343
  and intra-cultural variation, 104, 121n, 343–44
  and value orientations, 29–32, 100, 206
Being orientation; *see Activity* orientation
Being-in-Becoming orientation; *see Activity* orientation
Belief in Control item (MN4)
  perceived consensus on, 408, 410
  phrasing of, 86–87
  responses to, by all five cultures, 162; complete raw data, 419, 423, 427, 431, 435; Mormon, 148, 149, 150, 162, 272, 410, 427; Mormon vs. Texan, 273, 275; Navaho, 155, 156, 162, 332–33, 435; Spanish-American, 141, 144, 162, 419; Texan, 145, 146, 147, 150, 162, 410, 423; Zuni, 152, 153, 154, 162, 431
  Spanish version of, 374
Bellah, Robert N., 55n
Benedict, Ruth, 1n, 2, 56, 56n, 297, 297n, 298, 301, 305, 306, 310, 310n, 357
Bennett, John W., 298, 298n, 299
Bentley, A. F., 44, 44n
Bertalanffy, Ludwig von, 367
Between-culture differences
  and behavior spheres, 28–30
  and cultural change, 45–46
  number of schedule items needed to test, 102–4
  in perceived vs. actual consensus, 408–15
  and role theory, 34
  statistical definition of, 123
  statistical evidence for, 138, 139, 159–73; shown by analysis of variance, 165–71; shown by graphic method, 159–64
  statistical methods of analyzing, 123–24, 135–37, 349
  summary of, in five cultures, 352–53

Binomial analysis; *see Statistical methods*
Biological directiveness, 6–7
Brew, Joseph O., xiii
British culture
  relational orientation in, 19, 24
  time orientation in, 14–15
Bronfenbrenner, Urie, 402n
Brujeria, 239–42
Bruner, E. M., 339, 339n, 362
Bunzel, Ruth L., 294, 294n, 306, 306n, 310, 310n, 311

Cabot, Hugh, 1n
Calvinism, and Mormonism, 268–69
Cameron, Norman, 40n
Campa, Arthur, 230, 231
Care of Fields item (A4)
  perceived consensus on, 408
  phrasing of, 89
  responses to, by all five cultures, 163; complete raw data, 420, 424, 428, 432, 436; Mormon, 148, 149, 150–51, 163, 428; Mormon vs. Texan, 278; Navaho, 155, 156, 157, 163, 436; Spanish-American, 141, 163, 420; Texan, 145, 146, 147, 150–51, 163, 424; Zuni, 152, 153, 163, 432
  Spanish version of, 376–77
Carr, Anita Osuna, xii, xiv
Cattell, R. B., 392n
Caudill, Mieko, 78n, 363n
Caudill, William, xiii, 78n, 104n, 316n, 363n, 402n
Causal analysis
  in biology, 7
  of cultural change, 42–48
  and value components, 8–9
Ceremonial Innovation item (T4)
  perceived consensus on, 408, 410
  phrasing of, 87
  responses to, by all five cultures, 161; complete raw data, 418, 422, 426, 430, 434; Mormon, 147, 148, 150, 161, 410, 426; Mormon vs. Texan, 270, 271; Navaho, 155, 156, 157, 161, 329, 434; Spanish-American, 141, 143, 161, 418; Texan, 145, 146, 161, 422; Zuni, 152, 153, 154, 161, 359, 430
  Spanish version of, 375
Ceremonialism; *see religion under individual communities*
Chapter (Navaho), 58
Chernoff, Herman, xiv
Child Training item (T1)
  perceived consensus on, 408

phrasing of, 81
  responses to, by all five cultures, 161; complete raw data, 418, 422, 426, 430, 434; Mormon, 147, 148, 149, 161, 426; Mormon vs. Texan, 270; Navaho, 155, 156, 157, 161, 326–27, 434; Spanish-American, 141, 143, 161, 227, 418; Texan, 145, 146, 149, 161, 422; Zuni, 152, 154, 161, 430
  Spanish version of, 369
Chinese culture
  man-nature orientation of, 13
  socialization in, 23
  time orientation of, 14
Chiriguano, 288
Choice of Delegate item (R4)
  perceived consensus on, 408
  phrasing of, 84–85
  responses to, by all five cultures, 159; complete raw data, 417, 421, 425, 429, 433; Mormon, 147, 148, 149, 159, 425; Mormon vs. Texan, 265–66; Navaho, 155, 156, 159, 323, 433; Spanish-American, 140, 141, 143, 159, 201–2, 417; Texan, 144, 145, 146, 149, 159, 421; Zuni, 152, 154, 159, 429
  Spanish version of, 372
  weakness of, 103
Circular reasoning, in study of values, 96–102, 346
Cleveland, Stuart, xiv
Cognitive element of evaluative process, 5–6, 8–9
Collateral orientation; *see Relational* orientation
Common human problems, 10–11
"Configurations," 2, 179, 340
Conformity (conformism), 15
  vs. deviation, 364–65
  and value orientations, 20–24
Consensus on values, 401–15; *see also* perceived vs. actual consensus *under individual communities and individual value orientations*
  actual, amount of, by culture, 411, 415; measure of, 404
  overestimate of, measure of, 405; overall extent of, 409, 414–15
  perceived, conclusions about, 414; definition of terms, 402–6; measure of, 403; method of test-

ing, 402–15; summary of findings on, 406–14
underestimate of, measure of, 405; overall extent of, 409, 414–15
Corona, Jose, 195, 198
Corona, Luis, 188, 193, 195, 198, 217, 219, 226, 233, 251–55
Corona, Rosarita, 195
Coronado, Francisco Vasquez, 296, 300, 309
Cronbach, Lee J., 402
Cronin, Marguerite, xiv
Cross-cultural testing, problems of, 92–94
Cultural change; *see also* Acculturation; Assimilation
  Developmental vs. Causal-Correlational theories of, 42–45
  and evaluative process, 9–10
  summary of, in Atrisco, 256–57
  and variations in value orientations, 41–48, 366–67
Cultural determinism, 3
Culture, vs. social structure, 36–37
Culture-boundness, as methodological problem, 94, 98–99, 108
Culture lag, 42
"Culture themes," 2, 340
Curanderos, 239, 242
Cushing, Frank Hamilton, 56, 56n, 287, 293, 299, 299n, 306, 307, 307n, 308, 312

Defensive responses, controls for, 94–96
Democratic party, 251, 252, 254, 255
Dennis Sheep Company, 178, 187, 188, 189, 192, 210, 214, 215, 218
Descent, rules of, Navaho and Zuni, 58
Developmental theory of cultural change, 42–48
Deviation (deviance), and variation, 34–40, 364–65
Dewey, John, 44, 44n
Diaz, Porfirio, 203
Differentiation, societal, 342–44; *see also* Roles
Dimensional analysis; *see* Analyses of variance between cultures
Dionysian personality, 15
Directiveness
  biological, 6–7
  in evaluative process, 6–10
Doing orientation; *see* Activity orientation
Dominant American culture; *see also* Homestead; Rimrock (Mormon village)
activity orientation of, 17, 23–24
  conformism in, 20–24
  ethnic assimilation in, 25–26, 32, 343–44, 365
  human nature orientation of, 12, 29
  man-nature orientation of, 13, 29
  relational orientation of, 18–19, 23–24
  social-class values in, 26–28
  time orientation of, 14–15, 22–23, 29
  value orientations and behavior spheres in, 29–32, 343–44
Driver, Harold E., 288, 289n
Dry farming, 54, 64
Durkheim, Emile, 17, 33, 34

Economic-technological behavior sphere; *see under* individual communities and cultures; *see also* Agriculture; Electricity; Land ownership and use; Stock raising; Wage work; Water supply
Edmonson, Munro S., 229, 229n, 292, 292n
Education
  in Atrisco, 69–70, 177, 190–91, 193, 226, 246–51
  in Homestead, 190–91, 247–48
  among Navaho, 70, 327, 330
  in Rimrock area, 69–70
  in Zuni, 287–88
Edwards, Allen L., 136n
Eggan, Fred, 289, 289n, 291, 292, 293, 294, 294n, 312, 312n, 313, 314, 314n
Eisenstadt, S. N., 35
El Cerrito, 207
Electricity
  in Atrisco, 61, 175, 224
  in Homestead, 224, 259
  in Rimrock village, 259
  in Zuni, 307
Engels, Mrs., 249–50
Erikson, Erik H., 20, 20n
Ethnic groups
  and behavior-sphere differentiation, 343–44
  variant value orientations of, 25–26, 32
Evaluative process, components of, 5–10
Evil orientation; *see Human nature* orientation
Expectations about Change item (T2)
  perceived consensus on, 408
  phrasing of, 82–83

responses to, by all five cultures, 161; complete raw data, 418, 422, 426, 430, 434; Mormon, 147, 148, 150, 161, 426; Mormon vs. Texan, 270; Navaho, 156, 157, 161, 327–28, 330, 361, 434; Spanish-American, 141, 143, 161, 227, 418; Texan, 145, 146, 150, 161, 422; Zuni, 152, 154, 161, 430
  Spanish version of, 370–71

Facing Conditions item (MN2)
  perceived consensus on, 408
  phrasing of, 83
  responses to, by all five cultures, 162; complete raw data, 419, 423, 427, 431, 435; Mormon, 148, 149, 150, 162, 272, 427; Mormon vs. Texan, 273, 275; Navaho, 155, 156, 162, 332, 435; Spanish-American, 141, 162, 419; Texan, 145, 146, 147, 150, 162, 423; Zuni, 153, 154, 162, 431
  Spanish version of, 371
Factor-analysis technique
  determining average rho for, 385–87
  locating common Mormon-Texas values by, 278–83, 390–400
  vector analysis in, 387–89
Family; *see also* Family Work Relations item (R3); Help in Misfortune item (R2)
  as behavior sphere, 28
  Mormon, 63, 267, 277
  Navaho, 58, 320, 322, 324, 325
  Spanish-American; *see under* Atrisco
  Texan, 65, 260
  and value conflicts, 101
  Zuni, 56, 153, 293, 297, 302–4, 312–14
Family Work Relations item (R3)
  perceived consensus on, 408
  phrasing of, 84
  responses to, by all five cultures, 159; complete raw data, 417, 421, 425, 429, 433; Mormon, 147, 148, 149, 159, 425; Mormon vs. Texan, 265–66; Navaho, 155, 156, 157, 159, 322–23, 361, 433; Spanish-American, 141, 142–43, 159, 201, 212, 417; Texan, 144, 145, 146, 149, 159, 421; Zuni, 151, 152, 153, 159, 429

Family Work Relations item (*cont.*)
  Spanish version of, 372
  validity of, 172–73
Fenneman, Nevin M., 51n, 53
Ferm, Vergilius, 335n, 339n
Fiesta, 16, 30, 61, 206, 228–34, 237–38, 242–43, 250
Folk-culture vs. civilization, 34
Folk-plays, religious, 230–31
Formal vs. informal roles, 40, 41
Freud, Sigmund, 21
Friedman, M., 126
Fromm, Erich, 16, 17, 20
Future orientation; *see Time* orientation

Gemeinschaft vs. *Gesellschaft*, 17, 34
General vs. specific roles, 39–40
General-systems theory, 367
Generalized life situations
  and defensive responses, 95–96
  and prediction of concrete behavior, 96–102
  problems in testing, 79, 92, 93, 104, 345
Geographical environment (Rimrock area), 49–55
Giffin, M. E., 40n
Gilbert, John, xiv, 389n
Gluss, Brian, xiv, 382
Goethals, George, 104n
Good orientation; *see Human nature* orientation
Good-and-Evil orientation; *see Human nature* orientation
Graphic analyses
  of between-culture differences, *activity*, 163, 164; composite, 164; *man-nature*, 162, 164; *relational*, 159–60, 164; *time*, 161, 164
  development of technique, 347–48
  explanation of, 124–30
  limitations of, 348–49
  probability-level approximations in, 384–85
  relationship between S and r in, 380–82
  tied ranks in, 385
  transformation of rank deviation to Cartesian coordinates in, 379–80
  of within-culture regularities, Mormon, 148; Navaho, 156; Spanish-American, 144; Texan, 145; Zuni, 152
Great Man theory of cultural change, 45–46
Grinker, Roy R., 367n
Gross, Neal, 35, 36n

Hallowell, A. Irving, 1n, 5, 5n, 10n, 36n
Halsted, George Bruce, 97n
Hano, 289
Harmony-with-Nature orientation; *see Man-nature* orientation
Harris, Robert, xiv
Harvey, Herbert R., 49n, 55n
Health; *see* Illness, attitudes toward
Hegel, G. W. F., 44
Heider, Fritz, 407
Help in Misfortune item (R2)
  perceived consensus on, 408
  phrasing of, 83–84
  responses to, by all five cultures, 159; complete raw data, 417, 421, 425, 429, 433; Mormon, 147, 148, 149, 159, 425; Mormon vs. Texan, 265–66, 357; Navaho, 155, 156, 159, 321–22, 361, 433; Spanish-American, 140, 141, 142, 159, 417; Texan, 144, 145, 146, 149, 159, 421; Zuni, 152, 154, 159, 429
  Spanish version of, 371–72
Henderson, Laurence J., 97, 97n
Hermano mayor; see Atrisco, family in, sibling relations in
Hermanos Penitentes, 229–30
Hill, W. W., 335n
Historical method, 97 ff.
Hogan (Navaho), 58
Hohokam, 295
Hollenberg, Eleanor, 302, 303, 303n, 304
Homans, George C., xiii
Homestead, 63–65, 111–13, 144–47, 258–83, 355–57
  activity orientation in, 135–37, 276–78; vs. Mormons, 150–51, 275–78; vs. other cultures, 163, 164, 168, 170; overall variations in, 147; perceived vs. actual consensus on, 408, 409, 411; prediction of, 73, 351, 352; raw data on, by sex and item, 424; and recreational sphere, 276–77; regularities in, 145, 146, 258
  aggressive behavior in, 233, 250
  boosterism in, 269
  combined orientations in, vs. Mormons, 278–83
  composition of sample from, 105
  economic - technological sphere in, 64–65; agriculture, 54, 64–65, 208–9, 271–72, 274; community cooperation in, 268; consumption patterns, 260–61; land ownership and use, 64, 215n; property, 64–65; stock raising, 64, 274; wage work, 261; water supply, 51, 54, 260
  education in, 69–70, 190–91, 247–48, 268
  emigrants from, 65
  family in, 65, 260
  history of, 63–65
  interviewer rapport in, 111–13
  loafing pattern in, 73, 276–77
  man-nature orientation in, 271–75; and economic sphere, 147, 271–72, 274, 410; male-female differences in, 275; vs. Mormons, 150, 271–75, 280, 281–83, 356; vs. other cultures, 162, 164, 167, 169–70, 353; overall variations in, 147; perceived vs. actual consensus on, 408–11; prediction of, 73, 351, 352; raw data on, by sex and item, 423; regularities in, 145, 146, 258; and religion, 147, 275
  map of, 50
  perceived vs. actual consensus in, 408–15
  physiography of, 50–55, 111
  political sphere in, 69, 251–52, 254
  population trends in, 50, 64
  prediction of value orientations in, 73, 76; compared with results, 147, 351, 352
  recreational sphere in, 65, 67, 191
  relational orientation in, 264–68; and community organization, 260; and economic sphere, 261, 268; male-female differences in, 265, 266; vs. Mormons, 149, 264–68, 280, 281–83, 356, 357; vs. other cultures, 159–60, 164, 165, 169, 353; overall variations in, 146; perceived vs. actual consensus on, 408, 409, 411; prediction of, 73, 351, 352; raw data on, by sex and item, 421; regularities in, 144–45, 258
  relations of, with Atrisco, 64, 67, 69, 176, 189–91, 199, 209, 228, 233, 247–

48, 249–50, 251–52; with Navaho, 66; with outside world, 68–69, 71, 260; with Rimrock Mormons, 67; with Zuni, 66
religion in, 65, 147, 260, 269, 274–75
settlement pattern of, 50, 51, 64, 260
social organization of, 260–61
social stratification in, 65, 112, 260–61
socialization in, 302–4
summary of intra-cultural variations in, 146–47, 282–83
summary of within-culture regularities in, 144–46, 258
time orientation in, 269–71; vs. Mormons, 149–50, 268–71, 280–83, 357; vs. other cultures, 161, 164, 166, 169, 353; overall variations in, 146; perceived vs. actual consensus on, 408, 409, 411; prediction of, 73, 351, 352; raw data on, by sex and item, 422; regularities in, 144–46, 258; and religion, 269, 271
Hook, Lee Harmon, xiv
Hooke, Robert, 97, 97n
Hopi, 288, 289, 290, 295, 312, 313
Hotelling, Harold, 390, 390n
Housework item (A5)
perceived consensus on, 408
phrasing of, 90
responses to, by all five cultures, 163; complete raw data, 420, 424, 428, 432, 436; Mormon, 148, 149, 150–51, 163, 428; Mormon vs. Texan, 278; Navaho, 155, 156, 157, 163, 436; Spanish-American, 141, 144, 163, 213, 420; Texan, 145, 146, 150–51, 163, 424; Zuni, 152, 153, 163, 432
Spanish version of, 378
Human nature orientation
definition of, 11–12
dominant American, 12, 29
Irish-American, 365
Italian-American, 365–66
Mormon, 269n
Navaho, 334–35
Spanish-American, 343
Human Relations Area File, 93, 346, 414
Hunt, J. McV., 2n

Illness, attitudes toward; *see also* Length of Life item (MN5)
Navaho, 329, 333, 362–63

Spanish-American, 235, 239, 242, 243–44, 245
Zuni, 308, 313
Implicit vs. explicit roles, 40
Individualism vs. individuality, 23–24
Individualistic orientation; *see* Relational orientation
"Informational economy," 301
Institutions, 28–29; *see* Behavior spheres
Integration, cultural
and directiveness, 8–9
and variations in value orientations, 37–38, 43, 44
of Zuni, 293–94, 298, 313–14
Intellectual-aesthetic behavior sphere, 28; *see also* Education
schedule items concerning, 82, 85, 86–87, 89
Inter-cultural variation; *see* Between-culture differences
Intermarriage among Rimrock communities, 67–68
Interviewing techniques, 106–20
Intra-cultural variation
and behavior spheres, 30–32, 121n, 173, 343–44
and cultural change, 45–46
and cultural determinism, 3
definition of, in statistical analysis, 121n
Mormon, 149–51, 282–83
Navaho, 155–58
number of schedule items needed to test, 103–4, 121
and role theory, 34–40
sample size needed to test, 106, 121
Spanish-American, 142–44
Texan, 146–47, 282–83
Zuni, 155–58, 296–315, 357–60
Intra-item patterning
definition of, 122–23
statistical test for, 130–32
Irish-American culture
human nature orientation in, 365
relational orientation in, 365
Irrigation farming, 54–55; *see also* Agriculture
Italian-Americans
as deviants or variants, 365
human nature orientation of, 365–66
and recreational sphere, 344
relational orientation of, 365–66

Jack Mormonism, 74, 264
Japanese culture
use of value-orientation schedule in, 78n, 93–94
value orientations in, 13, 30

Jefe politico
definition of, 177
Don Juan Atrisco as, 185, 251–55
Luis Corona as, 251–55
Don Daniel Lucero as, 202, 256
Job Choice item (A1, A2)
ambiguity of, 91
perceived consensus on, 408
phrasing of, 80
responses to, by all five cultures, 163; complete raw data, 420, 424, 428, 432, 436; Mormon, 148, 149, 150–51, 163, 428; Mormon vs. Texan, 277, 278; Navaho, 155, 156, 157, 163, 436; Spanish-American, 141, 163, 420; Texan, 145, 146, 150–51, 163, 424; Zuni, 152, 153, 154, 163, 432
Spanish version of, 368
Johnson, Adelaide, 40n

Kahl, Joseph A., xiii, 1n
Kaplan, Bert, 302, 302n
Kardiner, Abram, 2
Kendall, Maurice G., xii, 126, 131n, 133, 347, 349n, 385, 385n
Kendall's *S*, table of values for, 126
Kinship; *see* Family
Kitt, Alice, 34, 39
Kluckhohn, Clyde, x, xi, 1n, 2, 2n, 3n, 4, 5, 6, 13, 16, 19, 36n, 55n, 57n, 58, 58n, 71, 72, 75, 105, 117, 179, 179n, 239n, 319, 339, 339n, 352, 360, 361, 362, 363
Kluckhohn, Florence, viii, ix, x, xi, xii, 1n, 30n, 32n, 40n, 41n, 55n, 72, 93n, 94n, 101, 101n, 106, 175, 316n, 319, 353n, 354, 363n
Kluckhohn, Richard, xiii, 104n
Kroeber, Alfred L., 1n, 3n, 5n, 37n, 288, 288n, 293, 293n, 299, 299n, 309, 310n, 312, 314, 358, 364

Laguna, 289
Land ownership and use
Mormon, 62–63, 262–63, 267
Navaho, 57, 325
Spanish-American, 59–61, 183–84, 185, 187, 213–15, 216

Land ownership and use (*cont.*)
  Texan, 63–64, 215n
  Zuni, 55–56, 312
Land Inheritance item (R7)
  perceived consensus on, 408
  phrasing of, 88–89
  responses to, by all five cultures, 160; complete raw data, 417, 421, 425, 429, 433; Mormon responses to, 147, 148, 160, 425; Mormon vs. Texan, 265–66; Navaho, 155, 156, 160, 324, 361, 433; Spanish-American, 141, 143, 160, 212, 417; Texan, 144, 145, 146, 149, 160, 421; Zuni, 152, 153, 160, 429
  Spanish version of, 376
Landgraf, John L., 51n
Language
  and circular reasoning, 98
  and education, in Atrisco, 246–47, 248–49
  and interviewer rapport, 107, 108
  problems of, in constructing schedule, 92–94, 110, 115–16, 117–18, 285–86
  Zuni, 289–90, 290–91, 313–14
Lazarsfeld, Paul F., 34n
Leighton, Dorothea, 58n
Lemann, T. B., 127, 127n
Length of Life item (MN5)
  perceived consensus on, 408
  phrasing of, 89
  responses to, by all five cultures, 162; complete raw data, 419, 423, 427, 431, 435; Mormon, 148, 149, 150, 162, 427; Mormon vs. Texan, 273, 275; Navaho, 155, 156, 157, 162, 333, 362, 435; Spanish-American, 141, 162, 419; Texan, 145, 146, 147, 150, 162, 423; Zuni, 152, 154, 162, 431
  Spanish version of, 377
Lenneberg, Eric H., 287n
Leonard, Olin, 194n, 207, 212n, 219n, 224n, 257
Lepley, Ray, 6n
Li An-che, 305, 305n
Lineal orientation; *see Relational* orientation
Linked rank-order types, definition of, 25
Linton, Ralph, 1n, 2, 33n, 40n
Litin, E. M., 40n
Livestock; *see* Stock raising
Livestock Dying item (MN1)
  perceived consensus on, 408

phrasing of, 81–82
responses to, by all five cultures, 162; complete raw data, 419, 423, 427, 431, 435; Mormon, 148, 150, 162, 427; Mormon vs. Texan, 273, 275; Navaho, 156, 162, 331–32, 333, 435; Spanish-American, 141, 143, 162, 212, 419; Texan, 145, 146, 147, 150, 162, 423; Zuni, 152, 154, 162, 431
Spanish version of, 369–70
Livestock Inheritance item (R6)
  perceived consensus on, 408
  phrasing of, 88
  responses to, by all five cultures, 160; complete raw data, 417, 421, 425, 429, 433; Mormon, 147, 148, 149, 160, 425; Mormon vs. Texan, 265–66; Navaho, 155, 156, 160, 324, 361, 433; Spanish-American, 140, 141, 143, 160, 212, 417; Texan, 144, 145, 146, 149, 160, 421; Zuni, 151, 152, 153, 160, 429
  Spanish version of, 375–76
Loomis, C. P., 194n, 207, 212n, 219n, 224n, 257
Lucero family, 180, 181, 199, 220, 226, 245, 248
Lucero, Don Daniel, 188, 189, 199, 211, 213, 215, 217, 218, 224, 235, 248, 254
  value orientations of, 201, 202
Lucero, Doña Amelia, 235

McArthur, Charles, 27, 28n
McBride, George McCutchen, 203n
McClelland, David C., 402n
McEachern, Alexander W., 35, 36n
McNair, Robert, 335, 335n
MacRae, Duncan, Jr., 390n
Madow, William G., 392n
Maes, Ernest, 219n
Male-female differences
  by culture, Mormon, 151, 265–67, 275, 356–57; Navaho, 157, 336–37, 363; Spanish-American, 142–43, 144, 213; Texan, 265–66, 275; Zuni, 154
  in interviewer rapport, 107, 108, 120, 336–37
  raw data for studying, 416–37
  of research sample, 104–5
  by value orientation, *activity*, 144, 213, 336; *man-nature*, 154, 157,

275, 356–57, 363; *relational*, 142–43, 265–67, 336, 356–57; *time*, 157, 336
Man-nature orientation; *see also under individual communities*
  between-culture differences in, 162, 164, 167, 169–70
  Chinese, 13
  definition of, 13
  dimensional analysis of, 167, 169–70
  dominant American, 13, 29
  intra-cultural variations in, 143–44, 147, 150, 154, 157
  Japanese, 13, 30
  perceived vs. actual consensus on, 408–11
  problems in testing, 91, 92, 94, 102
  raw data on, by culture, sex, and item, 419, 423, 427, 431, 435
  schedule items for testing, 77, 81–89
  Spanish-American, 13, 30; *see also under* Atrisco
  titles and numbers of schedule items for, 140
  within-culture regularities in, 141, 142, 145, 146, 147–49, 152, 153, 155, 156
Marshall, Alfred, 97, 97n
Marx, Karl, 44
Mason, Ward S., 35, 36n
Masserman, Jules H., 41, 366n
Massey, William C., 288, 289n
Mastery-over-Nature orientation; *see Man-nature* orientation
Mayordomos, 236–37
Mead, Margaret, 1n
Mechanical vs. organic solidarity, 17, 34
"Melting pot" ideology, 25
Merton, Robert K., 34, 34n, 35, 38, 39
Methodological problems; *see also* Research schedule; Statistical methods
  in controlling for defensive responses, 94–96, 345
  in cross-cultural testing, 92–94, 345
  and culture-boundness, 94, 98–99
  of interviewing, 106–20
  linguistic, 92, 93, 94, 110, 115–16, 117–18, 285–86, 345
  in locating common factors in four orientations combined, 278–83, 385–400

in predicting behavior from responses to general life situations, 96–102, 345
of sampling, 104–6, 344, 347
significance of lack of Zuni consensus as, 285, 357–58
summary of, 77–79, 344–46
in testing single orientations, 91–92, 345
Metzger, Duane, 314
Mexican culture, 21; *see also* Spanish-American culture
authority structure of, 203
religion in, 228–29, 230–31
Mindeleff, Cosmos, 51, 51n
Misperceived difference, measure of, 406
Moore, Barrington, Jr., xiii, 96n, 99
Moral norms and deviance, 38
Morgan, C. D., 27, 95
Mormons; *see* Rimrock (Mormon village)
Morris, Charles, 15, 16n
Mosteller, Frederick, xi, xiii, 349
Murdock, George Peter, 93, 288, 288n, 289
Murray, Henry A., xiii, 1n, 27, 95

National character, 2
Navaho; *see* Rimrock Navaho group
Newcomb, Franc, 334n
Newman, Stanley S., 36n, 285, 290, 290n
Nonordered type, definition of, 25
Nonworking Time item (A6)
perceived consensus on, 408
phrasing of, 90
responses to, by all five cultures, 163; complete raw data, 420, 424, 428, 432, 436; Mormon, 148, 149, 150–51, 163, 428; Mormon vs. Texan, 278; Navaho, 155, 156, 157, 163, 436; Spanish-American, 141, 142, 144, 163, 420; Texan, 145, 146, 150–51, 163, 424; Zuni, 152, 153, 163, 432
Spanish version of, 378

Oasis culture area, 288–89
O'Dea, Thomas F., 259, 259n, 261, 267, 268n, 356
Oliver, Douglas, xiii
Opler, Morris, 1n, 2
"Organization man," 20, 21
Orientations; *see* Value orientations
Orientations vs. alternatives, 11n

Osanai, Iva, 335n
Outfit (Navaho), 58

Parsons, Talcott, xiii, 2n, 6, 6n, 32, 33, 34, 34n, 37n, 38, 97n, 100, 364, 364n, 367
Past orientation; *see* Time orientation
Pastorelas, 231
Patrón system; *see under* Atrisco,
Pattern variables, 34
Patterning
intra-item, 122–23, 130–32
total item, 122, 124–30
total orientation, 123, 132–34
Payute, 96n
Pelzel, John, xiii, 30n
Penitentism, 229–30
Perceived consensus; *see* Consensus on values, perceived
Perceived difference, measure of, 405
Person-perception studies, 402
Personality
and defensive responses, 94–96
and social structure, 33n
and value orientations, 31–32, 39–41, 365–66
Petrullo, Luigi, 402n
Philosophy of Life item (T3)
perceived consensus on, 408
phrasing of, 85–86
responses to, by all five cultures, 161; complete raw data, 418, 422, 426, 430, 434; Mormon, 147, 148, 150, 161, 426; Mormon vs. Texan, 270, 271; Navaho, 156, 157, 161, 328–29, 330, 361, 434; Spanish-American, 141, 143, 161, 227, 418; Texan, 145, 146, 150, 161, 422; Zuni, 152, 153, 154, 161, 359, 430
Spanish version of, 373–74
Pigou, A. C., 97n
Poincaré, Henri, 97
Political behavior sphere, 28; *see also* Choice of Delegate item (R4)
Mormon, 63
Navaho, 58, 69, 323, 324
in Rimrock area, 69–70
Spanish-American; *see* Atrisco, political sphere
Texan, 69, 251–52, 254
Zuni, 56, 69, 292, 298, 300, 314–15
Polygyny, Navaho, 58
Prediction
of behavior, from knowledge of value orientations, 96–102

of value orientations in five cultures, 72–76; compared with results, summary, 350–52
Presbyterians, 260, 269
Present orientation; *see Time* orientation
Process vs. structure, 8
Promethean personality, 16
Psychoanalysis, 2–3, 21
Pueblo culture area, 288–89, 295
Pure rank-order types, definition of, 25

Questionnaire; *see* Research schedule

Railtown, description of, 68–69
Rank-ordering of value orientations; *see also* Intra-cultural variation; Value orientations, variations in
charting of, 127–29, 135–37
and cultural change, 47
importance of, for role theory, 37
prediction of, for five cultures, 72–76, 350–52
statistical tests for, 124–37
symbolization of, 72n, 131–32
types of, 25 ff.
Rapaport, Robert, 330n, 339, 339n, 362
Recreational behavior sphere, 28; *see also* Housework item (A5); Nonworking Time item (A6)
in American culture, 343–44
Mormon, 63, 67, 261, 275–76
Navaho, 246
Spanish-American; *see* Atrisco, religious-recreational sphere
Texan, 65, 67, 191
Zuni, 308
Redfield, Robert, 1n, 2, 2n, 3n, 10n
Reed, Erik K., 289, 289n
Reference group theory, 34–35
Reichard, Gladys, 334n
Relational orientation; *see also under individual communities*
between-culture differences in, 159–60, 164, 165, 169
British, 19
and conformism, 23–24
definition of, 17–19
dimensional analysis of, 165, 169
dominant American, 18–19, 23–24, 29

Relational orientation *(cont.)*
  intra-cultural variations in, 142–43, 146, 149, 153–54, 155, 157
   Irish-American, 365
   Italian-American, 365–66
   Japanese, 30
  perceived vs. actual consensus on, 408–11
  problems in testing, 91, 92
  raw data on, by culture, sex, and item, 417, 421, 425, 429, 433
  schedule items for testing, 77, 80–90
  by social class, 27–28
  Spanish-American, 30; *see also under* Atrisco
  titles and numbers of schedule items for, 140
  types of rank-order patterns of, 24–25
  within-culture regularities in, 140–42, 144, 145, 147, 148, 151–53, 155, 156
Religion; *see under individual communities*; *see also* Ceremonial Innovation item (T4); Facing Conditions item (MN2)
Republican party, 186, 251–55
Research schedule; *see also* Methodological problems
  actual items, 80–90
  administration of, 106–20, 285–88
  arrangement of items in, 77–78
  evaluation of, among Navaho, 338
  limitations of, 346
  number of items needed for, 102–4
  pre-testing of, 102–3, 113, 115–16, 120, 286
  problems of constructing, 77–79, 91–106, 344–46
  responses to (raw data), 416–37
  Spanish-language version of, 368–78
  summary of responses to, in all five cultures, 138–73
  titles and numbers of items of, 140
Residence, rule of
  Navaho, 58
  Zuni, 56
Riesman, David, 21, 21n
Rimrock (area)
  education in, 69–70
  interaction of communities in, 64, 65–68
  maps of, 50, 52
  physiography of, 49–55
  relations of, with outside world, 68–71

Rimrock (Mormon village), 61–63, 111–13, 147–51, 258–83, 355–57
  activity orientation in, 135–37, 275–78; vs. other cultures, 163, 164, 168, 170; overall variations in, 150–51; perceived vs. actual consensus on, 408–11; prediction of, 74, 351, 352; raw data on, by sex and item, 428; and recreational sphere, 275–76; regularities in, 148, 149, 258; and religion, 276; vs. Texans, 150–51, 275–78
  combined orientations in, vs. Texans, 278–83
  composition of sample from, 105
  economic - technological sphere in, agriculture, 54, 62, 274; competition vs. cooperation in, 262–63, 267–68; consumption patterns, 261; families on relief, 261; land ownership and use, 62–63, 262–63, 267; property, 261–62; role of Church in, 62, 261, 262; stock raising, 54, 62, 63, 262–63; wage work, 62–63; water supply, 51, 259
  education in, 267–68
  emigrants from, 264
  family in, 63, 267, 277
  history of, 61–63
  human nature orientation in, 269n
  interviewer rapport in, 111–13
  man-nature orientation in, 272–75; and age, 275; and economic sphere, 274; historical changes in, 74; male-female differences in, 275, 356–57; vs. other cultures, 162, 164, 167, 169–70, 353; overall variations in, 150; perceived vs. actual consensus on, 408–11; prediction of, 74, 351, 352; raw data on, by sex and item, 427; regularities in, 147–49, 258; and religion, 272, 274, 275, 410; and status, 275; vs. Texans, 150, 271–75, 280–83, 356
  map of, 50
  perceived vs. actual consensus in, 408–15
  physiography of, 50–55, 62, 111
  political sphere in, 63
  population of, 50, 62
  prediction of value orientations in, 73–74, 76;

compared with results, 151, 351, 352
  recreational sphere in, 63, 67, 261, 275–76
  relational orientation in, 129, 130–32, 264–68; and economic sphere, 267–68; male-female differences in, 265–67, 356–57; vs. other cultures, 159–60, 164, 165, 169, 353; overall variations in, 149; perceived vs. actual consensus on, 408–11; prediction of, 74, 351, 352; raw data on, by sex and item, 425; regularities in, 147–48, 258; and religion, 410; vs. Texans, 149, 264–68, 280, 281–83, 356, 357
  relations of, with Atrisco, 245; with Homestead, 67, 68; with Navaho, 66, 262–63; with outside world, 68–69, 70–71, 260, 262; with Utah Mormons, 74, 263–64, 357; with Zuni, 66, 67
  religion in, and agriculture, 272; and attitudes toward outsiders, 262; and attitudes toward schedule items, 112; and attitudes toward work, 275–76; and community organization, 63, 267–68; compared with Utah Mormons, 74, 263–64; and economic support, 62, 261, 262; and Jack Mormonism, 74, 264; and missionary work, 61–62, 70, 263; and perceived consensus, 410; and priesthood, 63; and religious scholarship, 263–64; and settlement pattern, 62, 259; and social status, 261; and *time* orientation, 268–69
  settlement pattern of, 50, 61–62, 259
  social organization of, 259–64, 267–68
  social stratification in, 63, 260, 261–62
  socialization in, 302–4
  summary of intra-cultural variations in, 149–51, 282–83
  summary of within-culture regularities in, 147–49, 258
  time orientation in, 268–71; vs. other cultures, 161, 164, 166, 169, 353; overall variations in, 149–50; perceived vs. actual consensus on,

408–11; prediction of, 74, 351, 352; raw data on, by sex and item, 426; regularities in, 147–48, 258; and religion, 74, 268–69, 410; vs. Texans, 149–50, 268–71, 280–83, 357

Rimrock Navaho group, 57–59, 117–20, 155–58, 318–39, 360–63
activity orientation in, 118, 135–37, 328, 334, 363; vs. dominant American, 76; and economic sphere, 334; male-female differences in, 336; and *man-nature* orientation, 333; vs. other cultures, 163, 164, 168, 170, 353; overall variation in, 157; perceived vs. actual consensus on, 157, 335–36, 408, 409, 411; prediction of, 76, 351, 352; raw data on, by sex and item, 436; regularities in, 155, 156
age differences in, 337, 338
attitudes toward illness in, 329, 333, 362–63
composition of sample from, 105
economic - technological sphere in, agriculture, 57, 332; depressed state of, 75, 119–20, 321–22, 325, 339, 360; families on relief, 321; land ownership and use, 57, 325; vs. religious sphere, 334; stock raising, 57, 331–32; wage work, 57, 246, 321, 334, 360; water supply, 51
education in, 70, 327, 330
emigrants from, 360
evaluation of knowledge in, 320, 326, 327–28, 332
family in, 58, 320, 322, 324, 325
history of, 57–59, 180
human nature orientation in, 334–35
interviewer rapport in, 117–20
male-female differences in, 336–37, 339, 362
man-nature orientation in, 13, 118, 331–34, 362–63; and acculturation, 336; and *activity* orientation, 333; and economic sphere, 331–32; and *human nature* orientation, 335; male-female differences in, 157, 336, 363; and medical care, 333; vs. other cultures, 162, 164, 167, 169–70; overall variations in, 157; perceived vs. actual con-

sensus on, 336, 408, 409, 411; prediction of, 75, 351, 352; raw data on, by sex and item, 435; regularities in, 155, 156; and religion, 326; and *time* orientation, 326, 328, 333
perceived vs. actual consensus in, 335–36, 408–15
personality variation in, 302
political sphere in, 58, 69, 323, 324
population of, 50
prediction of value orientations in, 75–76; compared with results, 158, 319, 351, 352
recreational sphere in, 246
relational orientation in, 19, 117–18, 320–25, 361; and acculturation, 336; and economic sphere, 321–22, 325, 360; and family, 322, 324, 325; male-female differences in, 336; vs. other cultures, 159–60, 164, 165, 169, 353; overall variations in, 155–57; perceived vs. actual consensus on, 336, 408, 409, 411; and political sphere, 323, 324; prediction of, 75, 351, 352; raw data on, by sex and item, 433; regularities in, 155, 156
relations of, with Anglo-Americans, 321–22, 324, 325, 326, 327, 334; with Apache, 289; with Atrisco, 66, 67, 195, 217, 245–46; with Homestead, 66, 329; with outside world, 68–69, 71, 337; with Rimrock Mormons, 66, 262–63; with Zuni, 66, 67–68
religion in, 58–59; curing ceremonies in, 58–59, 119–20, 326, 329; vs. economic sphere, 334; holy people in, 332, 333; and *human nature* orientation, 334–35; and language, 118; male-female differences in, 330, 337, 362; witchcraft in, 335
settlement pattern of, 50, 58, 117
socialization in, 365
summary of intra-cultural variations in, 155–57
summary of within-culture regularities in, 155, 318, 337–39
time orientation in, 117–18, 325–31, 361–62; and acculturation, 327, 330,

336; and age of respondent, 326, 327; and education, 327, 330; and intellectual - aesthetic sphere, 157; male-female differences in, 157, 329, 330, 336, 361–62; vs. other cultures, 161, 164, 166, 169; overall variations in, 157; perceived vs. actual consensus on, 336, 408, 409, 411; prediction of, 75, 351, 352; raw data on, by sex and item, 434; regularities in, 155, 156; and religion, 326, 329, 330
Rio Grande Pueblo, 113
Roberts, John M., viii, ix, xi, 29n, 55n, 56n, 74, 93n, 105, 113, 115n, 285, 286n, 287n, 294n, 308n, 313, 314, 314n, 357, 358, 359, 363
Rockefeller Foundation, viii, xiii
Role theory, and value orientations, 32–41, 98
Roles
classification of, 39–41
vs. culture patterns, 33
definitions of, 32–33
Roman Catholic Church; *see* religion *under* Atrisco; Mexican culture; Spanish-American culture; Zuni
Romney, A. Kimball, ix, xi, 74, 75, 117, 314, 319, 320n, 357, 360, 361, 362, 363
Rosen, Bernard C., 35
Rotter, J. B., 339, 339n, 362
Rural-urban dichotomy, 17, 34

St. John, Marion, 55n, 57n, 210n, 211
Sampling problems, 104–6
Sanchez, Carmelita and Guillermo, 235, 240–42
Sapir, Edward, 1, 1n
Scarr, Harry A., xi, xii
Schedule; *see* Research schedule
Schneider, David M., 287n, 313, 314, 314n
Schools in Rimrock area, 69–70; *see also* Education
Scientific method, in study of values, 96–102; *see also* Methodological problems
Selectivity in evaluative process, 6–10
Self-Action, theory of, 44
Sex; *see* Male-female differences
Sheldon, Richard C., 36
Shils, Edward A., 2n, 6, 6n, 32

Sibling relationships
  and *relational* orientation, 18
  in Spanish-American culture, 181–84, 195, 197–202, 365
Simmons, Ossie, 177n
Simpson, Lesley Byrd, 203n
Smith, Joseph, 62
Smith, Watson, 29n, 56n, 115, 287n, 314, 314n
Social stratification
  Mormon, 63, 260, 261–62
  Spanish-American, 59–60, 204–6, 210, 219–22, 234, 235–36, 240
  Texan, 65, 112, 260–61
  and variant value orientations, 26–28
Social structure
  vs. culture, 36–37, 364
  and variation in value orientations, 32–41
Socialization; *see also* Child Training item (T1)
  anticipatory, 34, 39
  in Atrisco, 196–97, 365
  and conformism, 20–21, 23
  in Homestead, 302–4
  of Navaho, 365
  in Rimrock, 302–4, 365
  and role assumption, 40, 365–66
  in Zuni, 298, 302–4
Solomon, Richard, xiv
Sorokin, Pitirim, 42, 44
Southwest culture area, 288
Spanish-American culture; *see also* Atrisco
  activity orientation in, 16, 30
  and Anglo-American hostility, 177–78
  authority structure of, 203–4
  economic vs. religious-recreational spheres in, 206–7, 343
  economy of, 208
  family in, 181
  history of, 176
  man-nature orientation in, 13, 30
  ownership and use of land in, 183–84
  patrón system in, 31, 177
  relational orientation in, 30
  religion in, 229–31, 237–38
  rule of succession in, 181
  schools in, 246–47
  strains in, 237–38
  time orientation in, 14, 30
  values and behavior spheres in, 30, 31
Spearman, Charles E., 385
Spengler, Oswald, 14, 14n, 42, 44
Spiegel, John P., xiii, 32n, 40, 40n, 41, 101, 101n, 363n, 366n, 367n

Spier, Leslie, 36n, 179n
Statistical methods, 121–37, 346–50; *see also* Methodological problems
  and circular reasoning, 97 ff.
  and factorial approach to Texan-Mormon differences, 278–83, 385–400; *see also* Factor-analysis technique
  special symbolism for, 72n, 131–32, 138–39
  for testing between-culture differences, analysis-of-variance technique, 135–37, 349 (*see also* Analyses of variance between cultures);
    graphic technique, 159–64
  for testing within-culture regularities, 124–34; binomial technique, 130–32, 349; graphic technique, 124–30, 347–49, 379–85 (*see also* Graphic analyses); *t*-test technique, 132–34, 349
Stedman, John, xiv
Stevenson, Matilda Coye, 295, 296n
Stock raising; *see also* Help in Misfortune item (R2); Livestock Dying item (MN1); Livestock Inheritance item (R6)
  Mormon, 54, 62, 63, 262–63
  Navaho, 57, 331–32
  in Rimrock area generally, 54–55
  Spanish-American, 59–60, 176, 181–89, 193, 205, 208, 210–15, 216, 219, 222, 246
  Texan, 64, 274
  Zuni, 54, 55, 56, 307, 308
Stouffer, Samuel A., ix, xi, xiii, 35, 35n, 93n, 349
Strain, social
  in Atrisco, 199–204, 237–38, 256–57, 354–55
  and cultural change, 43–45, 354–55
  among Navaho; *see under* Acculturation
  and variation in value orientations, 37–38
  among Zuni; *see under* Acculturation
Strodtbeck, Fred L., ix, xi, xii, xiv, 111, 124n, 259, 276n, 355, 356, 357, 402n
Structural-functional analysis, 8
Structure vs. process, 8
Subjugation - to - Nature orientation; *see Man-nature* orientation
Swadesh, Morris, 289, 289n
Symbolic notation (for value-orientation patterns), 72n, 131–32, 138–39
Szurek, S. A., 40n

Tagiuri, Renato, 402n
Technology, in Rimrock area, 51; *see also* economic - technological sphere *under individual communities*
Testing; *see* Methodological problems; Research schedule
Texans; *see* Homestead
Thematic Apperception Test, 27–28, 95
Thompson, Laura, 1n, 2
Thurstone, L. L., 389n
Time orientation; *see also under individual communities*
  between-culture differences in, 161, 164, 166, 169
  British, 14–15
  Chinese, 14
  and conformism, 22–23
  definition of, 13–15
  dimensional analysis of, 166, 169
  dominant American, 14–15, 22–23, 29
  intra-cultural variations in, 143, 146, 149–50, 154, 157
  Japanese, 30
  perceived vs. actual consensus on, 408–11
  problems in testing, 91, 92
  raw data on, by culture, sex, and item, 418, 422, 426, 430, 434
  schedule items for testing, 77, 81–90
  by social class, 27–28
  Spanish-American, 14, 30; *see also under* Atrisco
  titles and numbers of schedule items for, 140
  within-culture regularities in, 141, 142, 144–46, 147, 148, 151, 152, 155, 156
Tinbergen, N., 6, 7, 7n, 8
Tönnies, Ferdinand, 17, 33, 34
Total item patterning
  definition of, 122
  statistical test for, 124–30
Total orientation patterning
  definition of, 123
  statistical test for, 132–34
Traditional vs. rational-legal societies, 17, 22, 34
Transactional systems, 7–8, 367
Transportation, in Rimrock area, 53
t-test; *see under* Statistical methods

Tukey, John, xiv, 136, 348, 389n
Turner, Ralph, 35

"Unconscious canons of choice," 1-2, 340
"Unconscious system of meanings," 1-2, 340
Underdeveloped countries, 44
Universals, cultural, 1, 3
  and value orientations, 4
Use of Fields item (MN3)
  perceived consensus on, 408
  phrasing of, 85
  responses to, by all five cultures, 162; complete raw data, 419, 423, 427, 431, 435; Mormon, 148, 149, 150, 162, 272, 427; Mormon vs. Texan, 273; Navaho, 155, 156, 157, 162, 332, 333, 362, 435; Spanish-American, 141, 144, 162, 209, 419; Texan, 145, 146, 147, 150, 162, 423; Zuni, 152, 154, 162, 431
  Spanish version of, 373

Value orientations; see also under individual orientations; see also Evaluative process; Within-culture regularities
  and behavior, 78-79, 92-94, 95-96, 100-102, 364
  classification of, 10-20; table of, 12; typographic conventions for, 11n
  and conformism, 20-24
  definition of, 4-10, 341
  difficulties in testing single, 91-92
  directiveness of, 6-10
  dominant vs. variant, 3, 25-28, 32-41, 341-42, 364-65
  implicit vs. explicit, 5
  prediction of, for five cultures, 72-76; compared with results, 350-52
  schedule for testing, 77-120
  statistical methods for analyzing, 121-37, 346-50
Value orientations, variations in; see also Between-culture differences; Intra-cultural variation; Variation, cultural
  and cultural change, 41-48, 366-67
  method of testing; see Methodological problems
  rank-ordering of, 8-9, 25, 342; see also Rank-ordering of value orientations
  required and permitted, 3, 31-32, 342, 344
  and role theory, 32-41
  schedule results in five cultures, 138-73
  theory of, 1-48; assumptions of, 10; origins of, 179-80; place of, in behavioral studies, 363-69; summarized, 340-44
  types of, 24-32
"Values Project," viii, xiii
Variation, biological, 3-4
Variation, cultural, 1-4; see also Value orientations, variations in
  and basic values, 4
  and deviance, 34-40, 199
  importance of value orientations in, 28
  permitted and required, 31-32
Variation, psychological, 4; see also Personality
Vidrio family, 210, 217, 219, 222, 233, 245, 248
Vidrio, Jose, 188
Voegelin, Carl, 96n
Vogt, Evon Z., viii, ix, xiii, 51n, 55n, 64n, 65, 68n, 72, 73, 189n, 208n, 259, 260, 267, 268n, 276, 277, 310, 310n, 356

Wage work; see also Job Choice item (A1, A2); Wage Work item (R5)
  among Mormons, 62-63
  among Navaho, 57, 246, 321, 334, 360
  among Spanish-Americans, 60, 188, 189, 201, 205, 208, 222-23, 225, 240
  among Texans, 261
  among Zuni, 55, 307
Wage Work item (R5)
  perceived consensus on, 408, 410
  phrasing of, 86
  responses to, by all five cultures, 160; complete raw data, 417, 421, 425, 429, 433; Mormon, 147, 148, 149, 160, 410, 425; Mormon vs. Texan, 265-66; Navaho, 155, 156, 157, 160, 323-24, 433; Spanish-American, 140, 141, 143, 160, 201, 417; Texan, 144, 145, 146, 149, 160, 421; Zuni, 152, 153, 160, 429
  Spanish version of, 374
Walapai, 307
Wallace, David L., xiv
Warner, W. Lloyd, 27
Water Allocation item (T5)
  perceived consensus on, 408
  phrasing of, 89-90
  responses to, by all five cultures, 161; complete raw data, 418, 422, 426, 430, 434; Mormon, 147, 148, 150, 161, 426; Mormon vs. Texan, 270; Navaho, 155, 156, 157, 161, 329-30, 434; Spanish-American, 141, 143, 161, 418; Texan, 145, 146, 161, 422; Zuni, 145, 146, 161, 422
  Spanish version of, 377
Water supply; see also Water Allocation item (T5); Well Arrangements item (R1)
  in Atrisco, 51, 193
  in Homestead, 51, 54, 260
  among Navaho, 51
  in Rimrock area, 51, 53-55, 93-94
  in Rimrock village, 51, 259
  in Zuni, 51, 307-8
Ways of Living item (A3)
  perceived consensus on, 408
  phrasing of, 87-88
  responses to, by all five cultures, 163; complete raw data, 420, 424, 428, 432, 436; Mormon, 148, 149, 150-51, 163, 428; Navaho, 155, 156, 157, 163, 436; Spanish-American, 141, 163, 420; Texan, 145, 146, 150-51, 163, 424; Zuni, 152, 163, 432
  Spanish version of, 375
Weber, Max, 14, 17, 22, 33, 34
Well Arrangements item (R1)
  perceived consensus on, 408
  phrasing of, 80-81
  responses to, by all five cultures, 159; complete raw data, 417, 421, 425, 429, 433; Mormon, 125, 147, 148, 149, 159, 425; Mormon vs. Texan, 265-66; Navaho, 125, 155, 156, 159, 320-21, 433; Spanish-American, 125, 141, 142, 159, 201, 417; table of all, 125; Texan, 125, 144, 145, 146, 149, 159, 421; Zuni, 125, 152, 153, 159, 429
  Spanish version of, 368-69
Weltfish, Gene, 301n
Watson, James B., 41, 41n, 42
Whitehead, Alfred North, 98
Whiting, Beatrice, xiii
Whiting, John W. M., xiii, 93n, 303n
Whorf, Benjamin Lee, 5, 5n
Whyte, William F., 365, 365n

Whyte, William H., Jr., 20, 20n
Witchcraft
  Navaho, 335
  Spanish-American, 239–42
  Zuni, 298
Within-culture regularities
  number of schedule items needed to test, 102–4
  statistical definition of, 121n
  statistical evidence for, 138, 140–58; Mormon, 147–49; Navaho, 155–56; Spanish-American, 140–42; Texan, 144–46; Zuni, 151–53
  statistical methods of analyzing, 122–23, 124–34, 347–49
Within-culture variation; see Intra-cultural variation
Woodbury, Max, xiv
Woodbury, Richard B., 294, 295n
Woodward, Dorothy, 230n
"World view," 2
Wyman, Leland C., 335, 335n

Yaqui, 245

Zamorra, Frank, 211, 212, 215, 218, 224
Zimmerman, Carle C., 219n
Zuni, 55–57, 113–16, 151–55, 284–316, 357–60
  activity orientation in, 135–37, 305–6, 359; according to Benedict, 297, 298, 305; vs. other cultures, 163, 164, 168, 170; overall variation in, 154; perceived vs. actual consensus on, 408, 409, 411; prediction of, 74–75, 351, 352; raw data on, by sex and item, 432; regularities in, 152–53
  attitudes toward illness in, 308, 313
  child-training practices in, 302–3
  clans in, 291, 293, 297, 312–13
  community organization of, 293–94, 313
  composition of sample from, 105, 114–15, 286–88
  "contained variation" in, 290, 300–301, 315, 357, 358
  covert culture of, 298
  cultural complexity of, 290–93, 299, 301
  cultural isolation of, 288–90, 300
  defensiveness in, 95
  economic - technological sphere in, 55–56; agriculture, 51, 54, 55, 56, 288–89, 307; American technology in, 307–8; handicrafts, 55, 307; and kinship, 312; land ownership and use, 55–56, 312; stock raising, 54, 55, 56, 307, 308; types of occupation in, 292, 300, 311; and value orientations, 153; wage work, 55, 307; water supply, 51, 307–8
  education in, 288
  emigrants from, 290
  factionalism in, 114
  family in, 56, 153, 293, 297, 302–4, 312–14
  field methods for studying, 285–88
  history of, 55–57, 292, 294–96
  interviewer rapport in, 96, 113–16, 286
  intra-cultural variation in, 296–315, 357–60; hypotheses concerning, 300–301; in personality, 301–4; sources of, 299–300; in value orientations, 153–54, 304–15
  kinship terminology in, 313–14
  language, 289–91
  lineage group in, 312
  man-nature orientation in, 306–8, 359; according to Benedict, 297, 298; according to Bunzel, 306; male-female differences in, 154; vs. other cultures, 162, 164, 167, 169–70; overall variation in, 154; perceived vs. actual consensus on, 408, 409, 411; prediction of, 74–75, 351, 352; raw data on, by sex and item, 431; regularities in, 152–53; and religion, 306; and technology, 307–8, 359
  map of, 50
  perceived vs. actual consensus in, 408–15
  physiography of, 50–55
  political sphere in, 56, 69, 292, 298, 300, 314–15
  population trends in, 50, 295, 296, 299
  prediction of value orientations in, 74–75, 76; compared with results, 154–55, 351, 352
  recreational sphere in, 308
  relational orientation in, according to Benedict, 297, 298, 358; and economic sphere, 153, 311; and family, 153; and kinship structure, 312 ff.; Lineality vs. Collaterality in, 312–15, 358; vs. Navaho, 75, 154; vs. other cultures, 159–60, 164, 165, 169, 353; overall variation in, 153–54; perceived vs. actual consensus on, 408, 409, 411; and political sphere, 314–15; prediction of, 74–75, 351, 352; raw data on, by sex and item, 429; regularities in, 151–53
  relations of, with Anglo-Americans, 200, 306, 307–8; with Atrisco, 66, 188, 239, 245, 309; with Homestead, 66; with Navaho, 66, 67–68, 301; with other Indian cultures, 288–90, 301, 307; with outside world, 68–69, 71, 288, 290, 292, 301, 309; with Rimrock Mormons, 66, 67
  religion in, and agriculture, 56; ceremonies in, 56, 66, 310; and child-training, 303; and Christianity, 292, 309; cults in, 291–92; decline in ceremonialism in, 56, 301, 311; and economic sphere, 301; and interviewer rapport, 116; and kinship, 297, 312–13; links of, to other structures, 293, 299–300; pattern elaboration of, 301; *pekwin* in, 56, 291, 311, 314; and political structure, 314–15; secrecy concerning, 95, 113–14, 116
  residential groups in, 291, 293
  settlement pattern of, 50, 55, 295
  socialization in, 298, 302–4
  time orientation in, 309–11, 358–59; according to Adair and Vogt, 310; according to Benedict, 297, 298, 310; according to Kroeber, 309–10; and economic sphere, 311; vs. other cultures, 75, 154, 161, 164, 166, 169; overall variation in, 154; perceived vs. actual consensus on, 408, 409, 411; prediction of, 74–75, 351, 352; raw data on, by sex and item, 430; regularities in, 152–53; and religion, 154, 309, 310–11
  witchcraft in, 298
  within-culture regularities in, summary of 151–53, 284
Zuni trading store, 218, 222–23